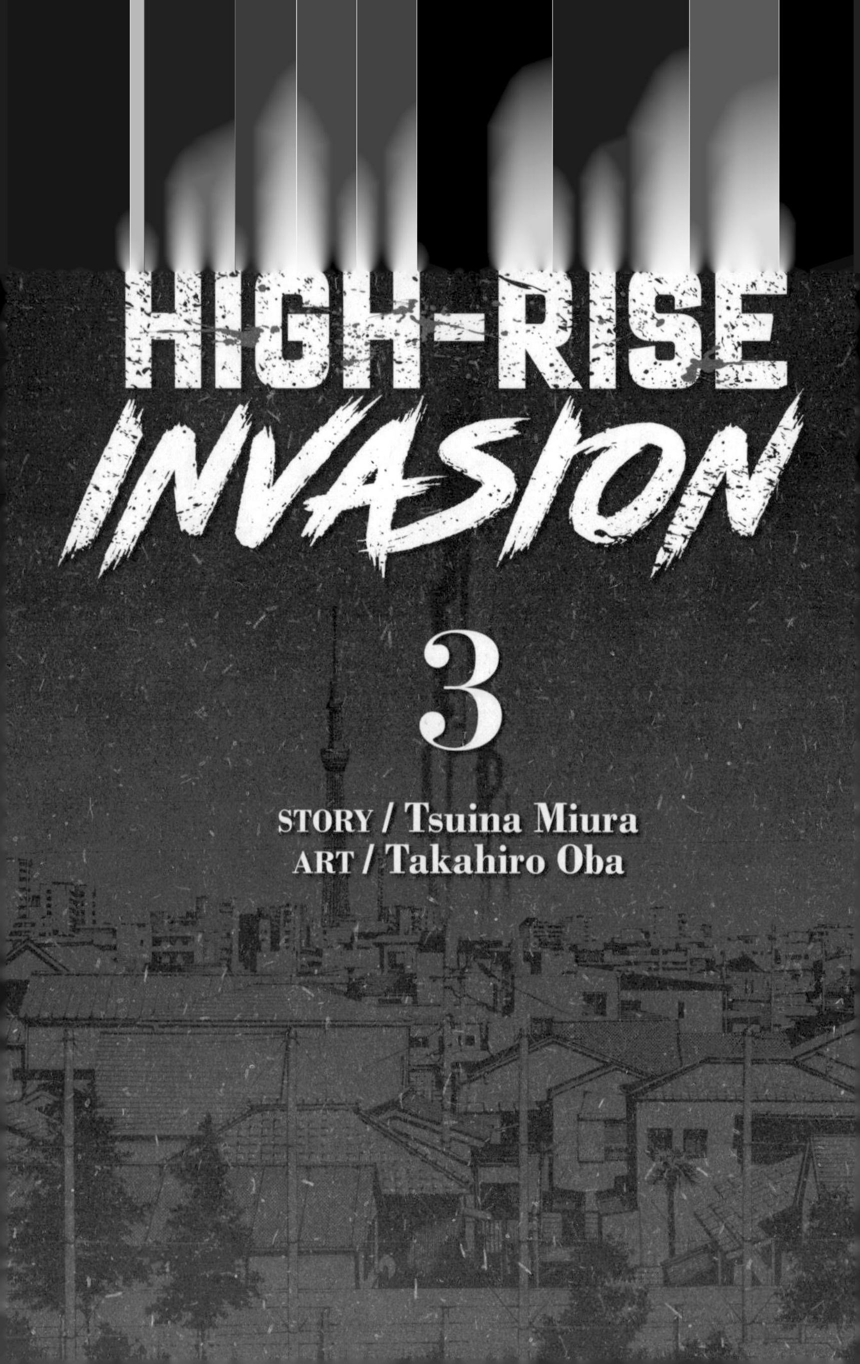
HIGH-RISE
INVASION
3
STORY / Tsuina Miura
ART / Takahiro Oba

HIGH-RISE INVASION

3

CONTENTS

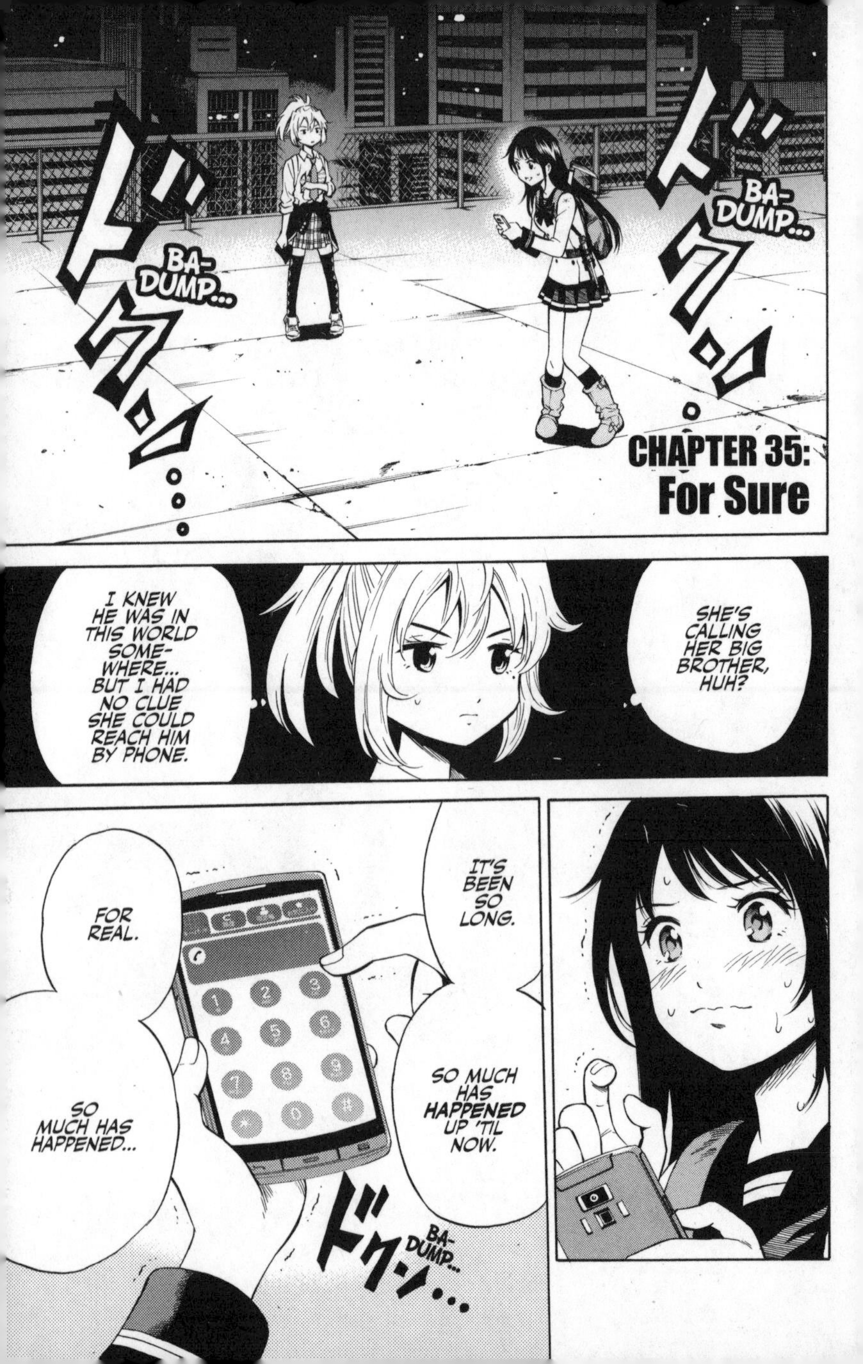
BA-DUMP...
BA-DUMP...
CHAPTER 35: For Sure
SHE'S CALLING HER BIG BROTHER, HUH?
I KNEW HE WAS IN THIS WORLD SOME-WHERE... BUT I HAD NO CLUE SHE COULD REACH HIM BY PHONE.
IT'S BEEN SO LONG.
SO MUCH HAS HAPPENED UP 'TIL NOW.
FOR REAL.
SO MUCH HAS HAPPENED...
BA-DUMP...

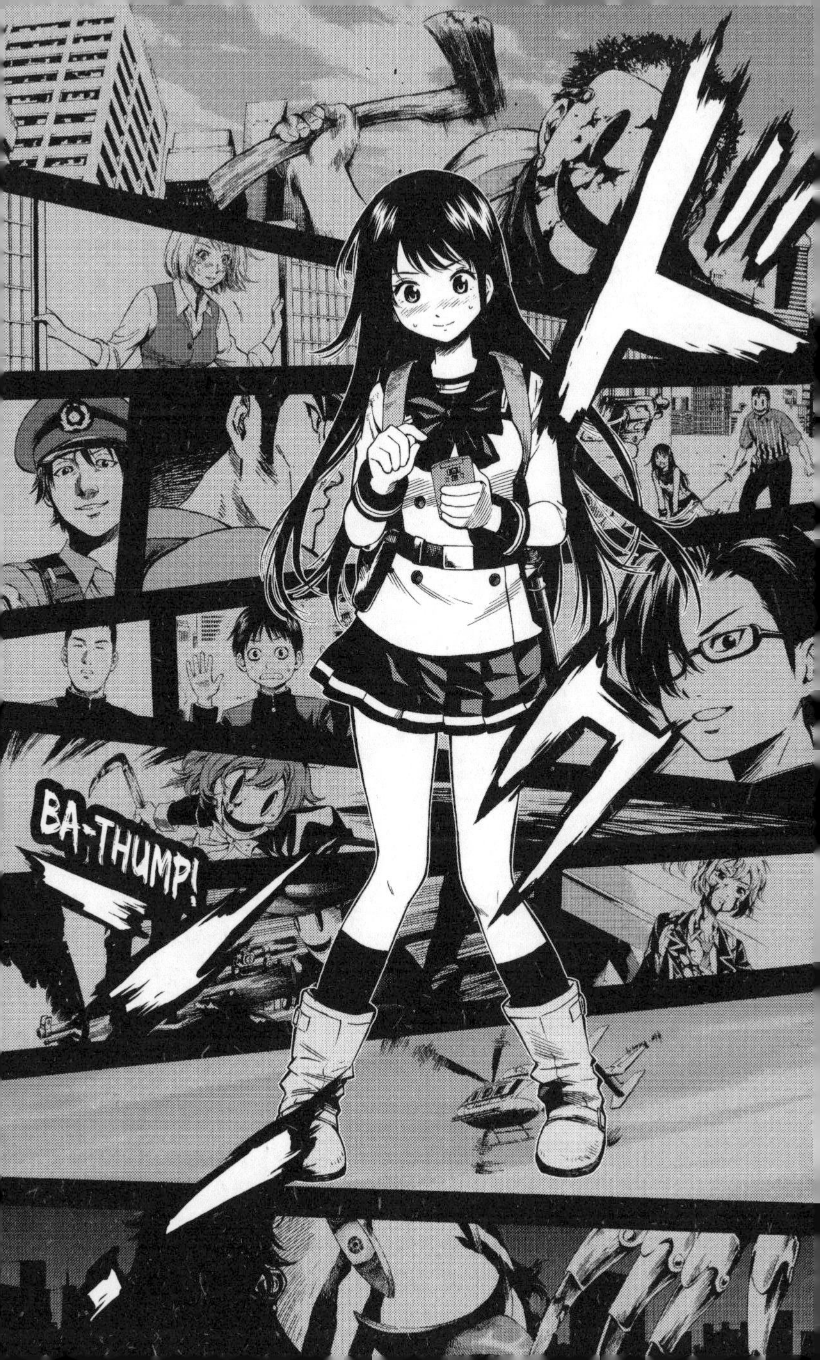
BA-THUMP!

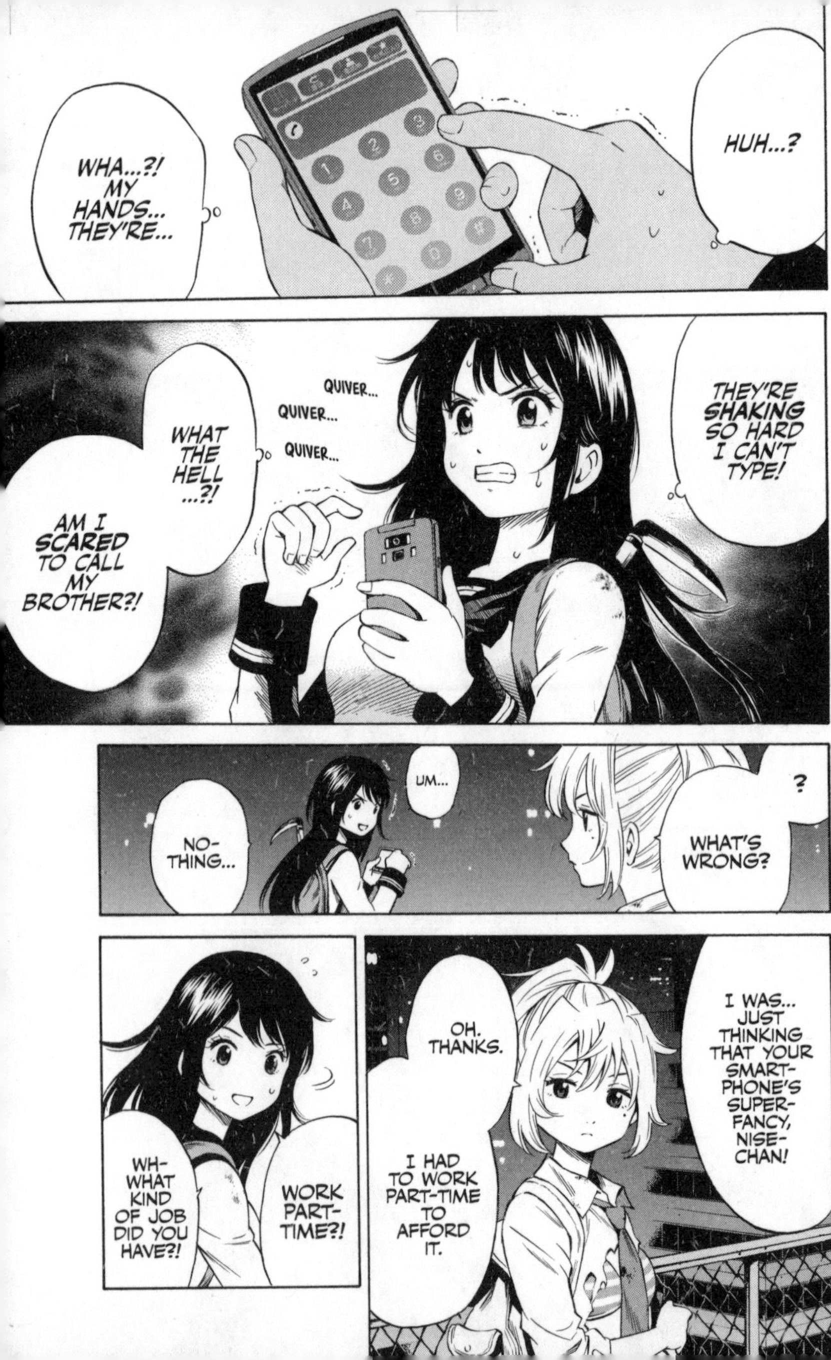
HUH...?
WHA...?! MY HANDS... THEY'RE...
THEY'RE SHAKING SO HARD I CAN'T TYPE!
QUIVER... QUIVER... QUIVER...
WHAT THE HELL ...?!
AM I SCARED TO CALL MY BROTHER?!
?
WHAT'S WRONG?
UM...
NO-THING...
I WAS... JUST THINKING THAT YOUR SMART-PHONE'S SUPER-FANCY, NISE-CHAN!
OH. THANKS.
I HAD TO WORK PART-TIME TO AFFORD IT.
WORK PART-TIME?!
WH-WHAT KIND OF JOB DID YOU HAVE?!

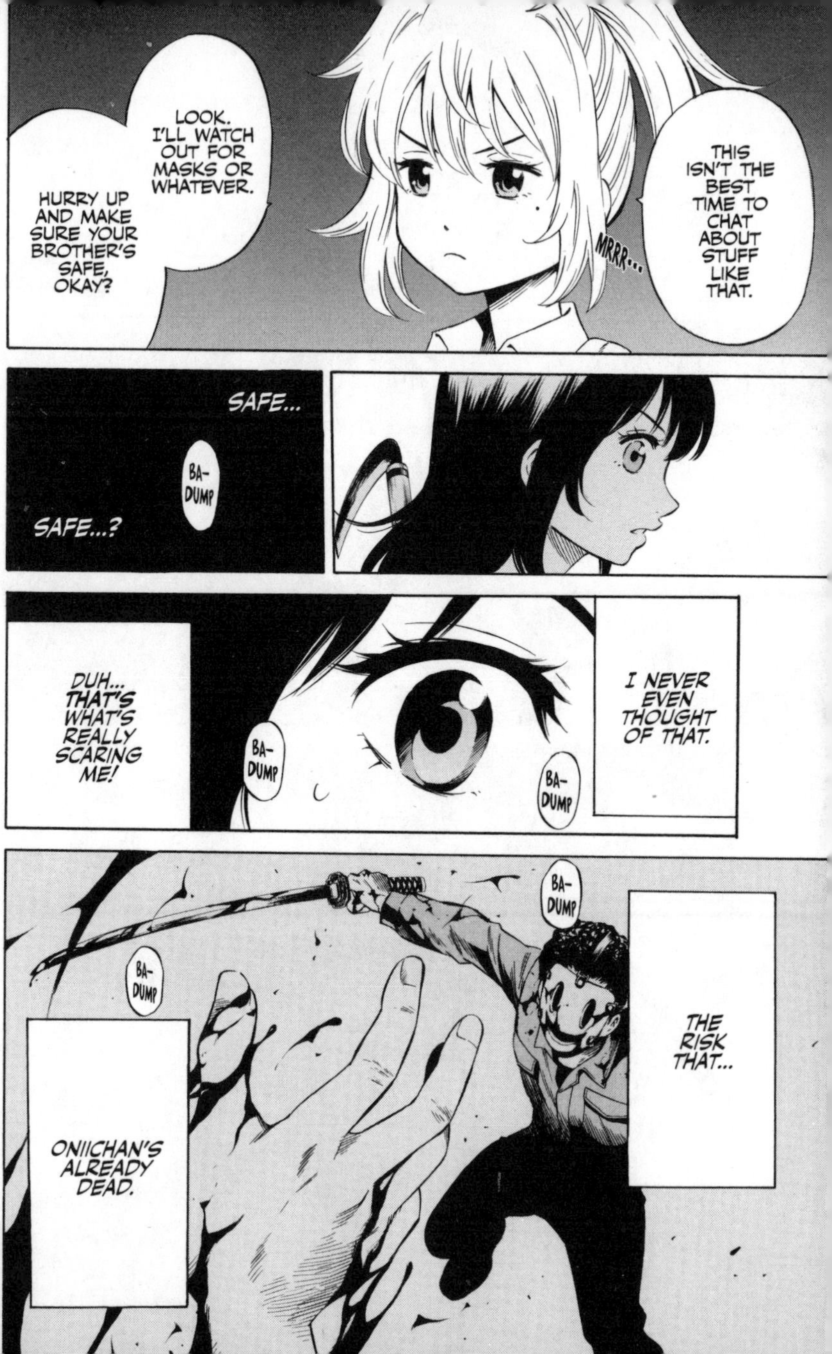
THIS ISN'T THE BEST TIME TO CHAT ABOUT STUFF LIKE THAT.
MRRR...
LOOK. I'LL WATCH OUT FOR MASKS OR WHATEVER.
HURRY UP AND MAKE SURE YOUR BROTHER'S SAFE, OKAY?
SAFE...
BA-DUMP
SAFE...?
I NEVER EVEN THOUGHT OF THAT.
BA-DUMP
BA-DUMP
DUH... THAT'S WHAT'S REALLY SCARING ME!
BA-DUMP
THE RISK THAT...
BA-DUMP
ONIICHAN'S ALREADY DEAD.

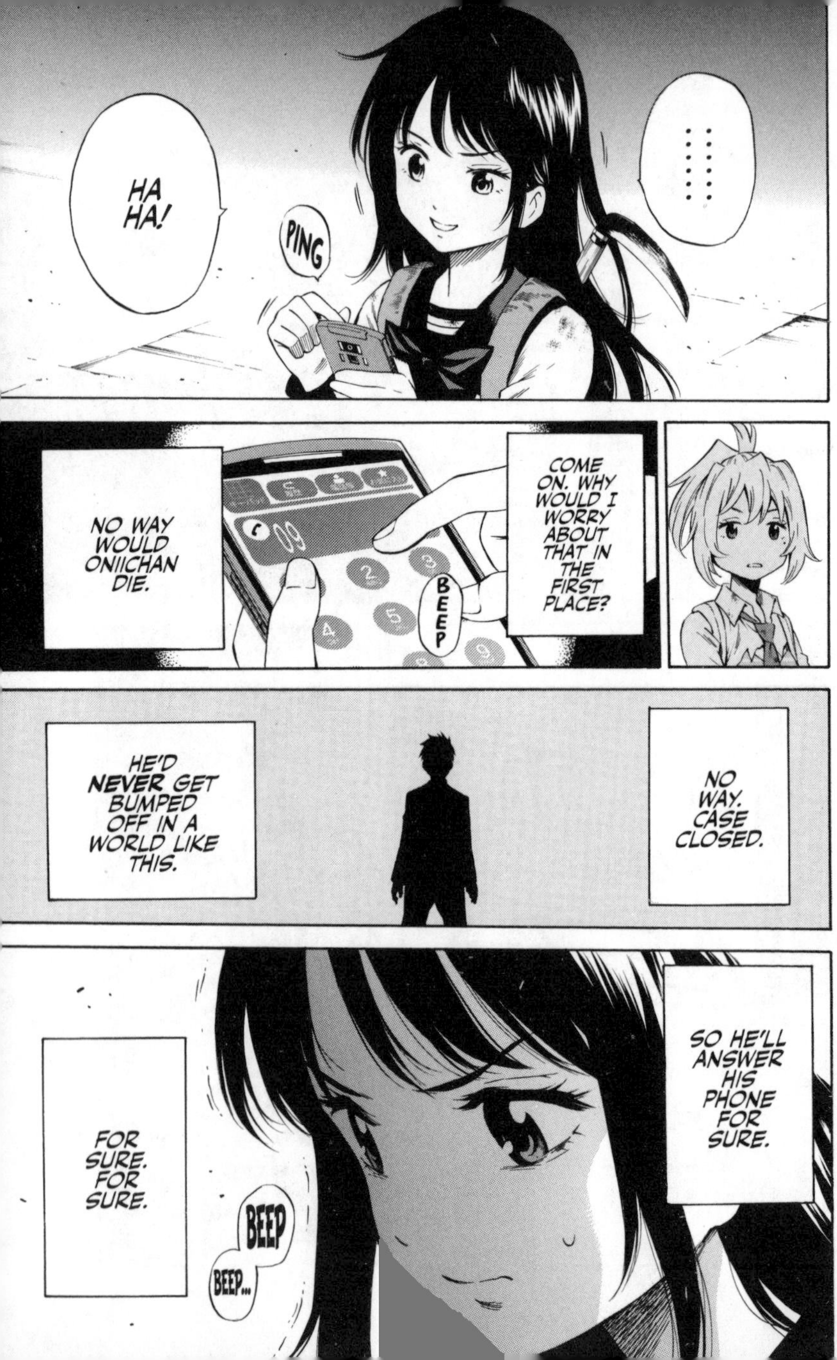
......
HA HA!
PING
COME ON. WHY WOULD I WORRY ABOUT THAT IN THE FIRST PLACE?
BEEP
NO WAY WOULD ONIICHAN DIE.
NO WAY. CASE CLOSED.
HE'D **NEVER** GET BUMPED OFF IN A WORLD LIKE THIS.
SO HE'LL ANSWER HIS PHONE FOR SURE.
FOR SURE. FOR SURE.
BEEP
BEEP...

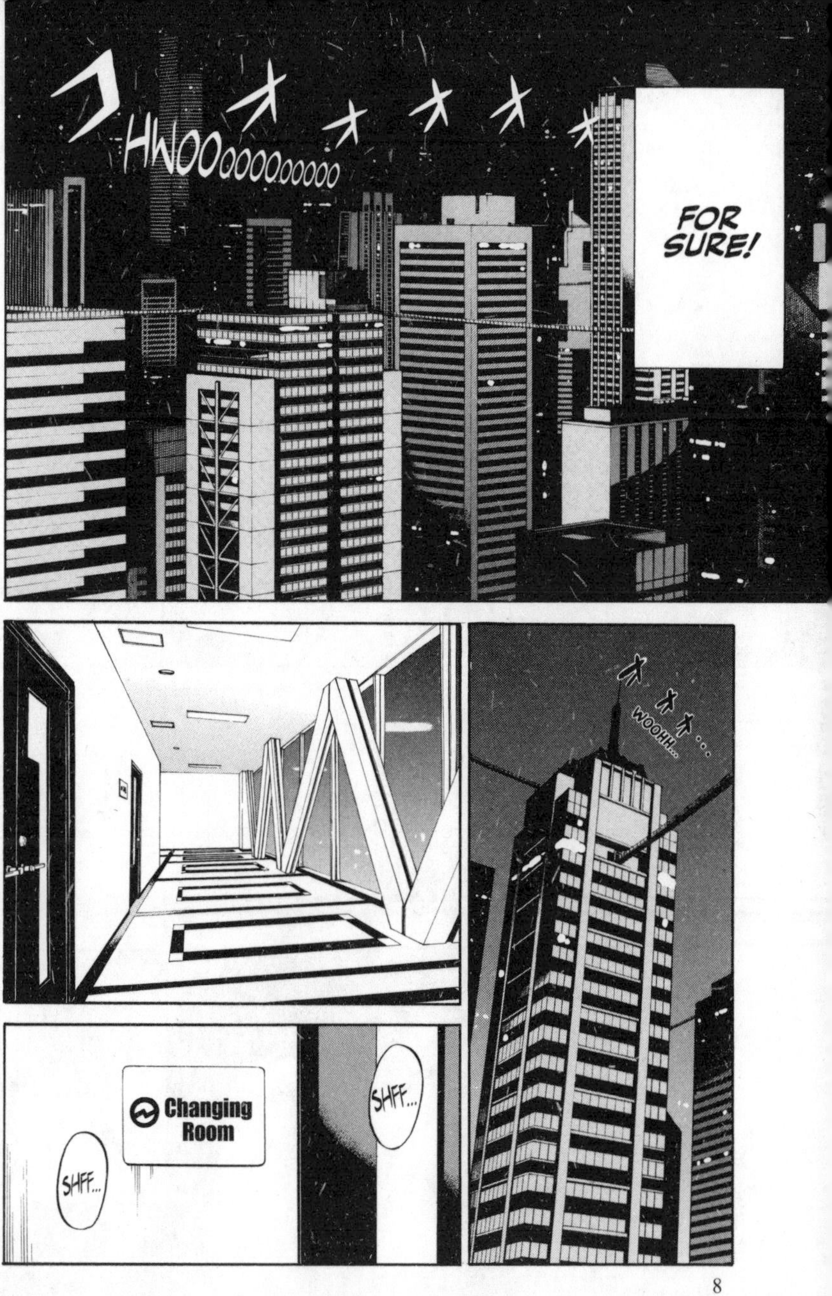
HWOOOOOOOOOOO
FOR SURE!
WOOHH...
SHFF...
Changing Room
SHFF...

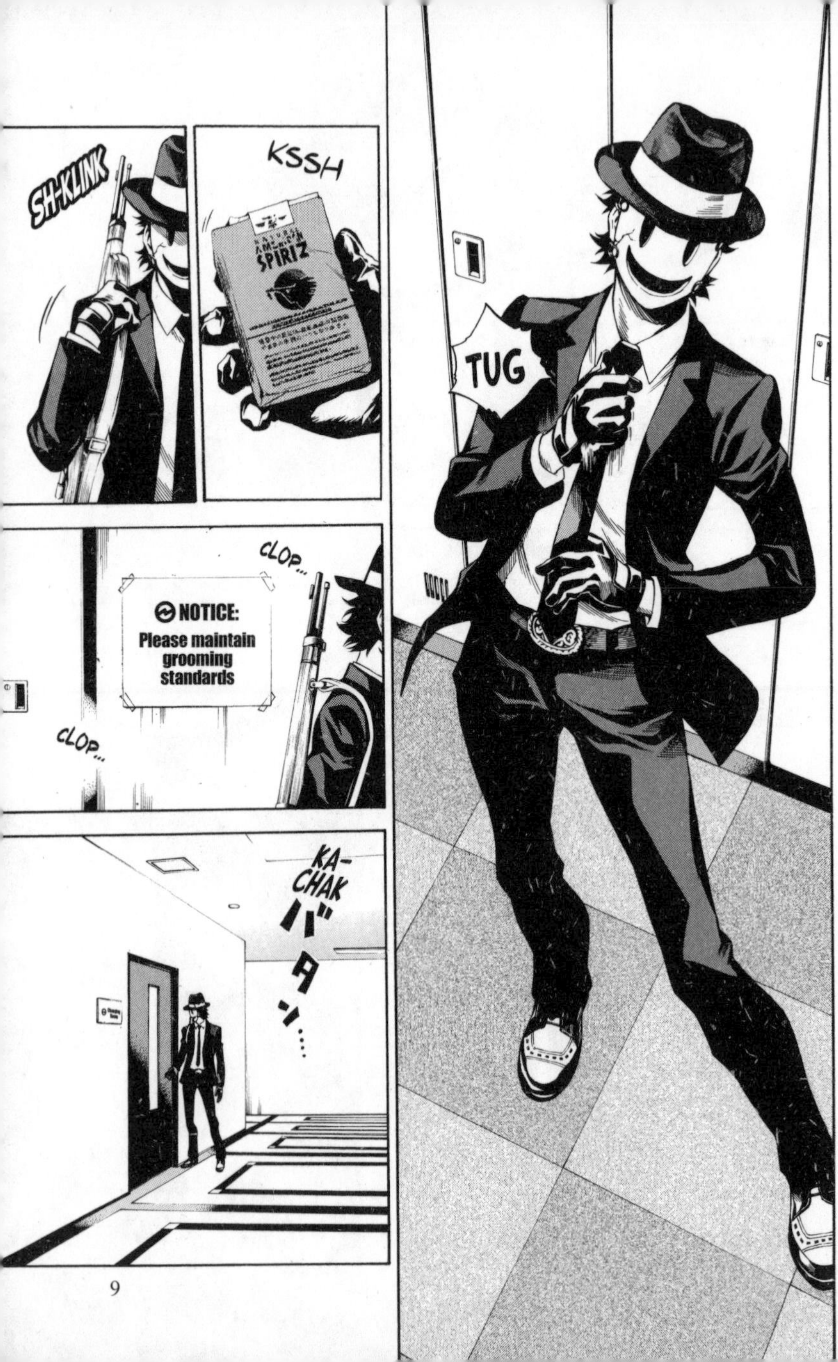
TUG
KSSH
SPIRIZ
SH-KLINK
CLOP...
NOTICE:
Please maintain grooming standards
CLOP...
KA-CHAK
バタン…

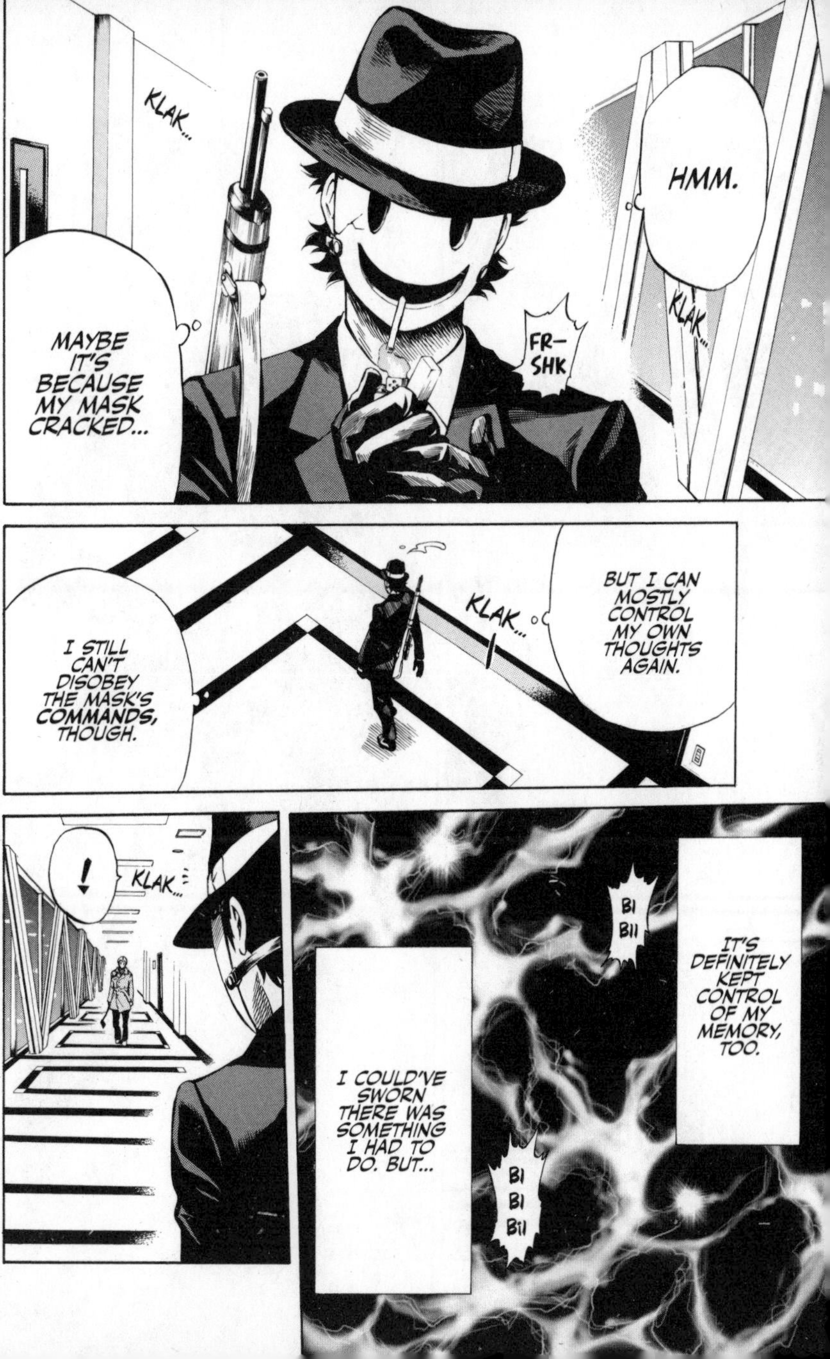
HMM.
KLAK...
FR-SHK
KLAK...
MAYBE IT'S BECAUSE MY MASK CRACKED...
BUT I CAN MOSTLY CONTROL MY OWN THOUGHTS AGAIN.
KLAK...
I STILL CAN'T DISOBEY THE MASK'S COMMANDS, THOUGH.
IT'S DEFINITELY KEPT CONTROL OF MY MEMORY, TOO.
BI BII
I COULD'VE SWORN THERE WAS SOMETHING I HAD TO DO. BUT...
BI BI BII
!
KLAK...

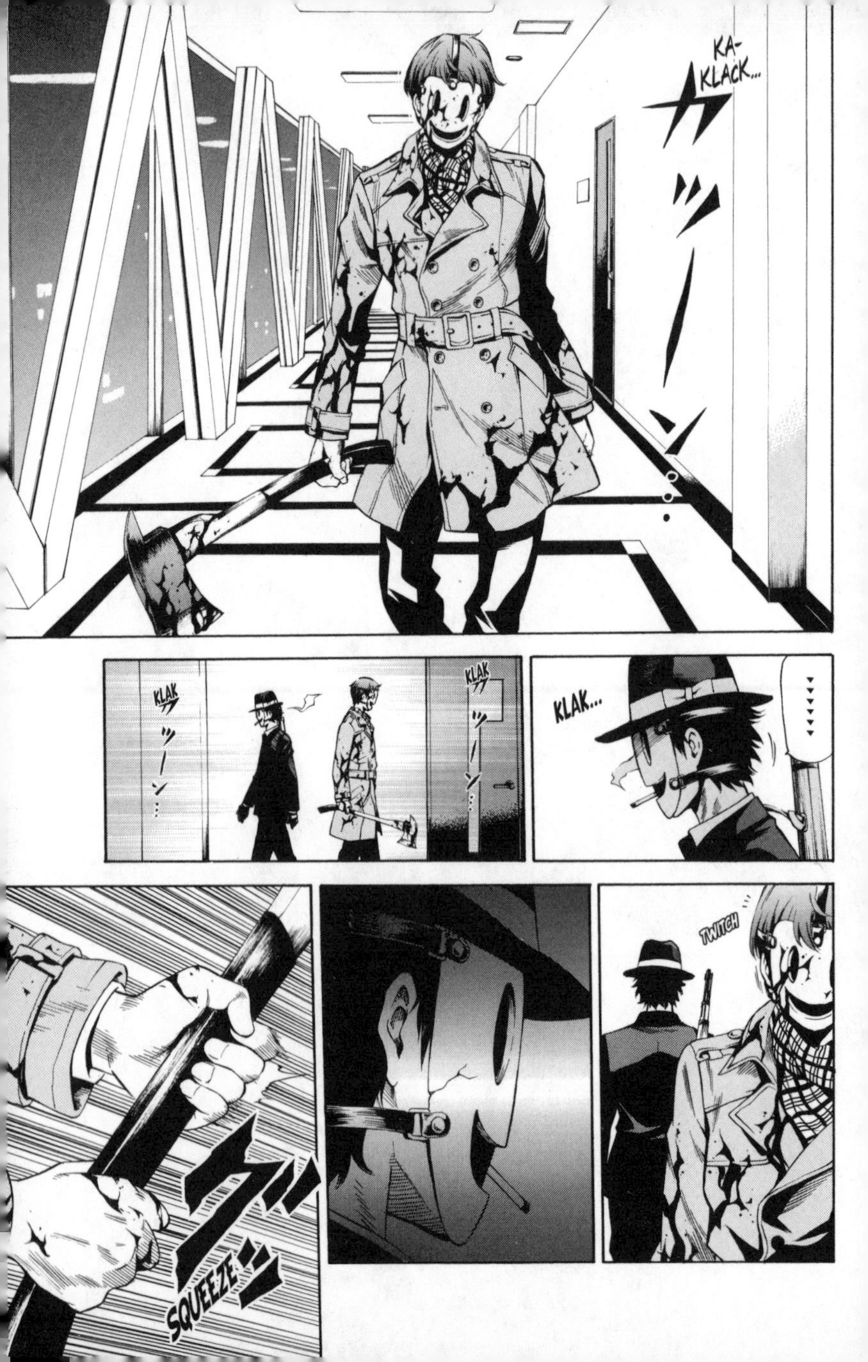
KA-KLACK...
KLAK...
▾▾▾▾▾▾
KLAK
KLAK
TWITCH
SQUEEZE

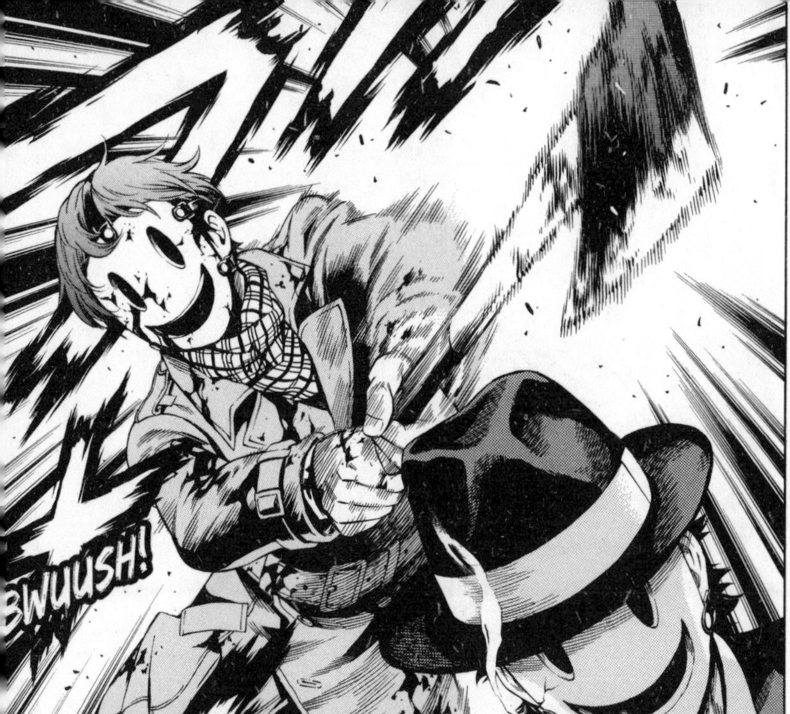
BWUUSH!

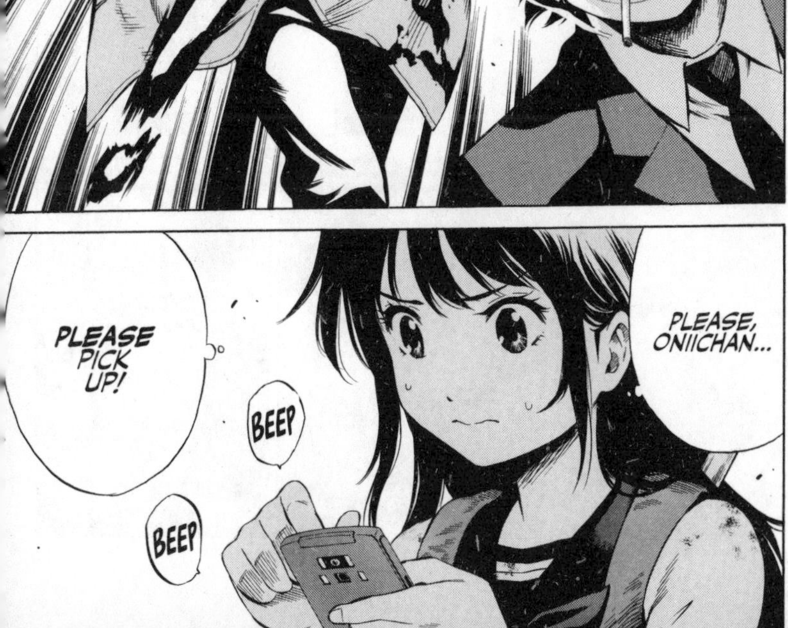
PLEASE, ONIICHAN...
BEEP
PLEASE PICK UP!
BEEP

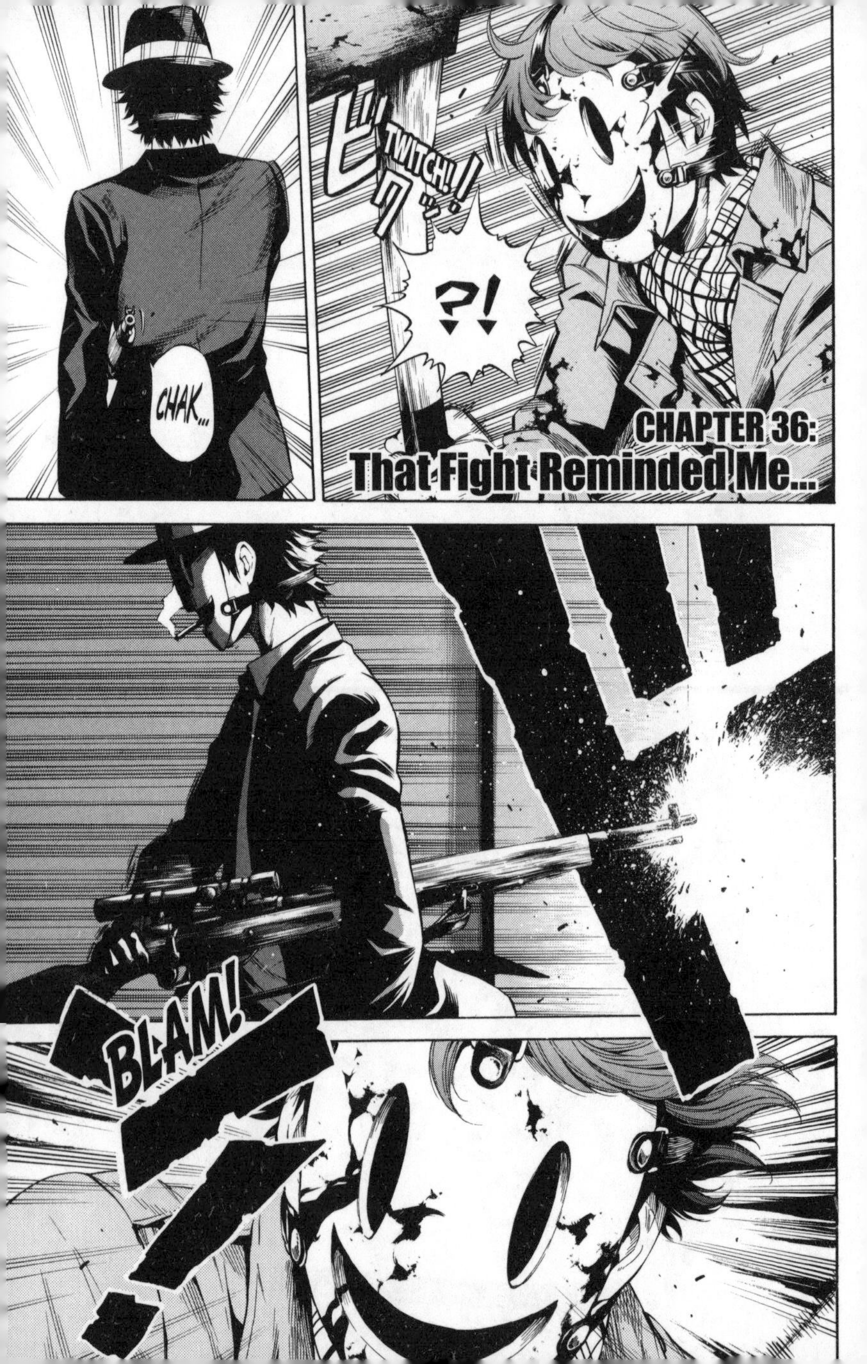

ビクッ
TWITCH!!
?!
CHAPTER 36:
That Fight Reminded Me...
CHAK...
BLAM!

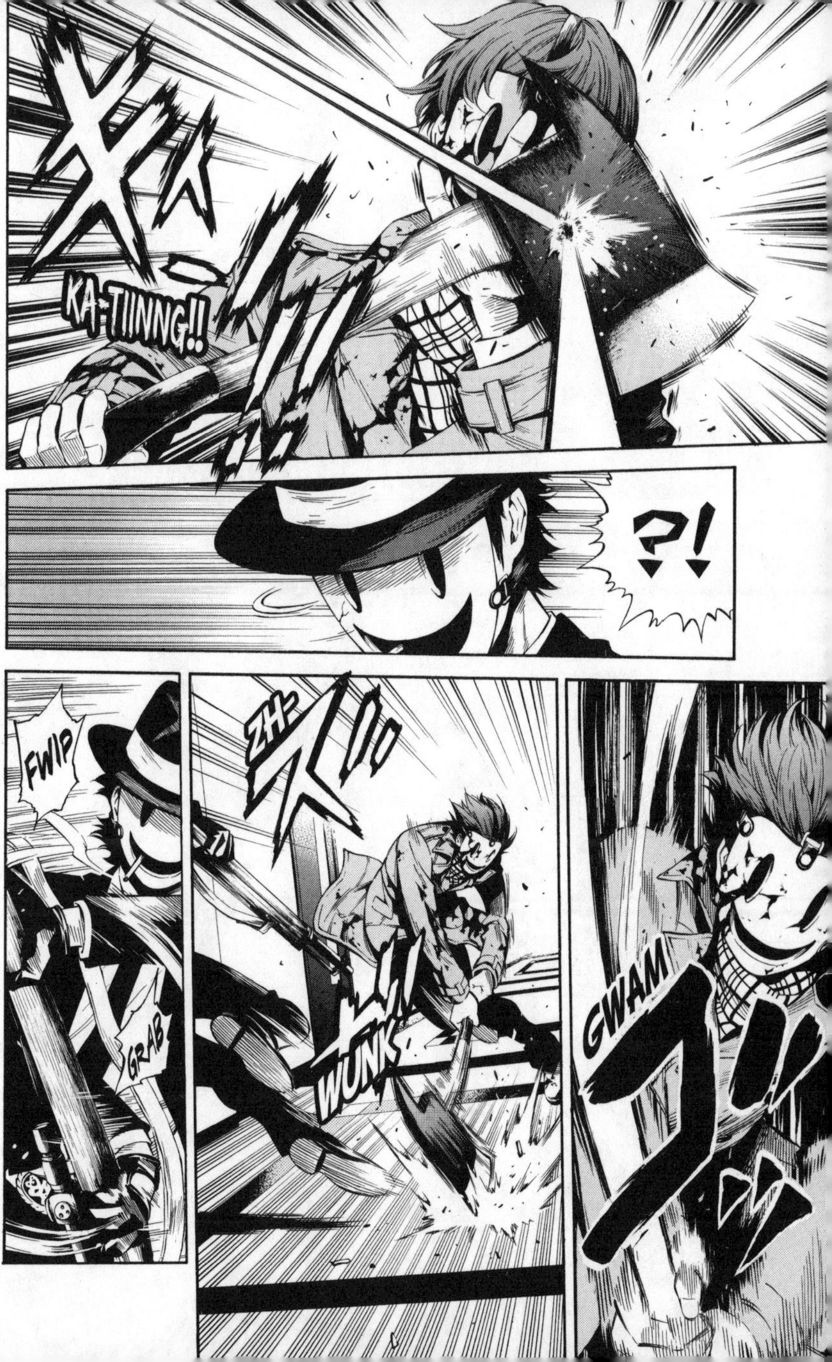
KA-TIINNG!!
?!
GWAM
ZH-
WUNK
FWIP
GRAB

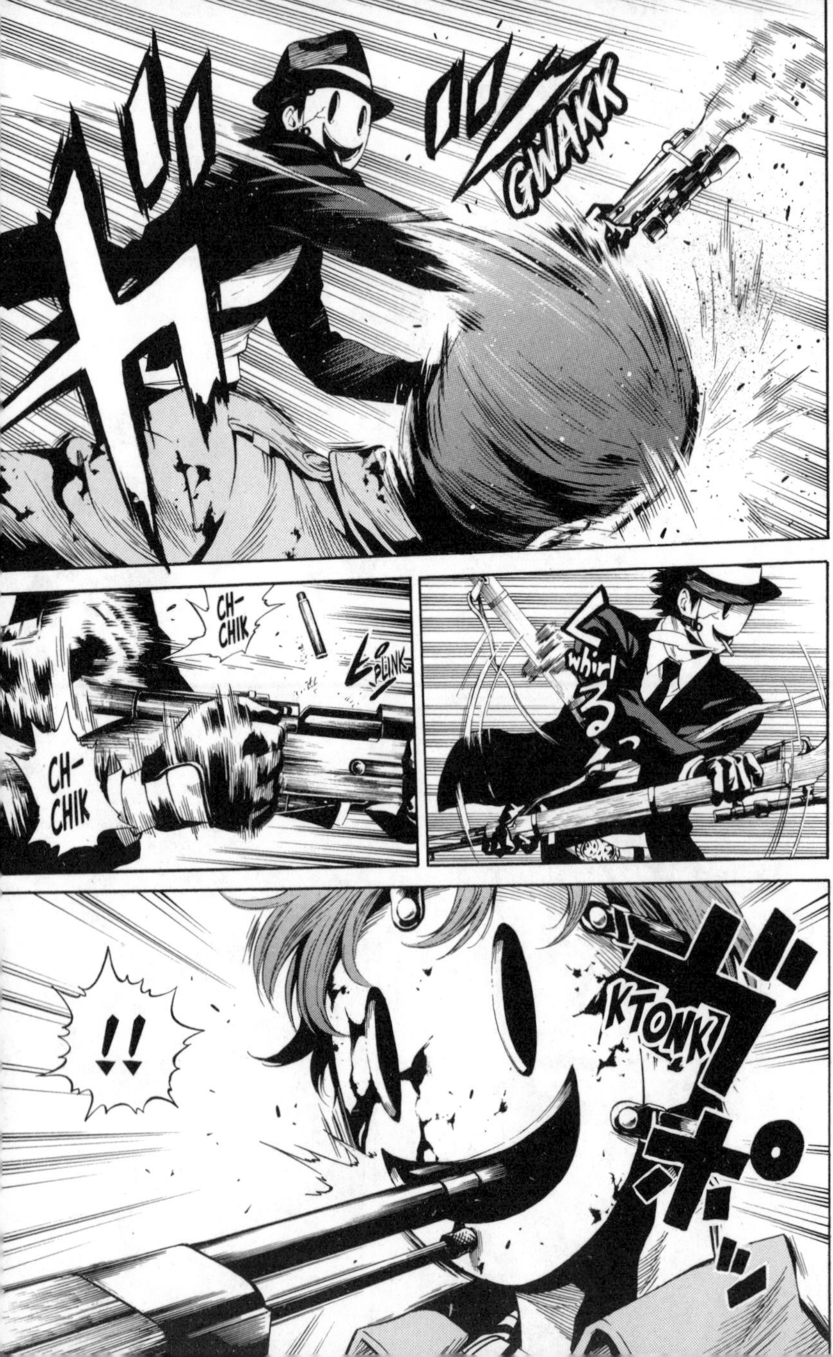
GWAKK
whirl
CH-CHIK
PLINK
CH-CHIK
KTONK
!!

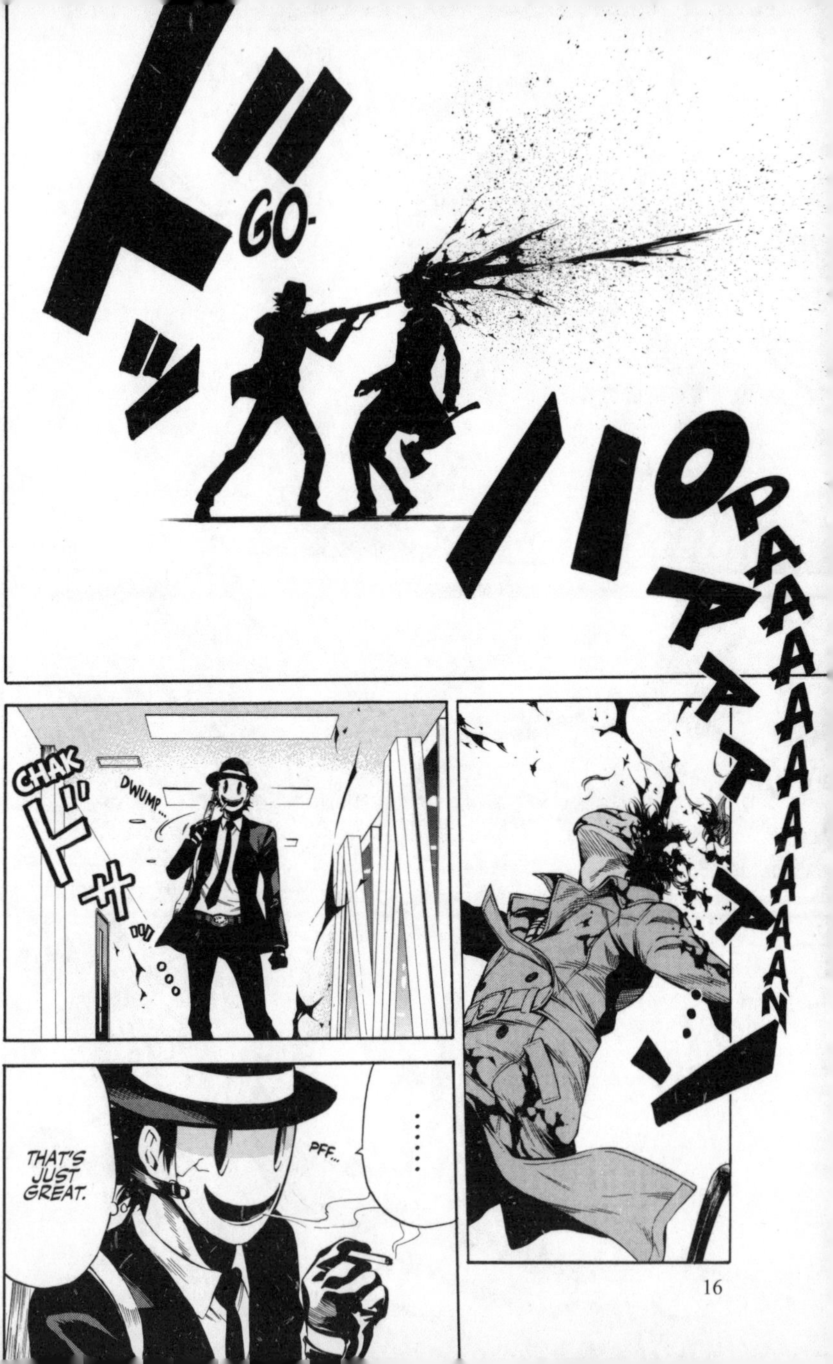
GO-
PAAAAAAAAAAAAN
CHAK
DWUMP...
......
PFF...
THAT'S JUST GREAT.

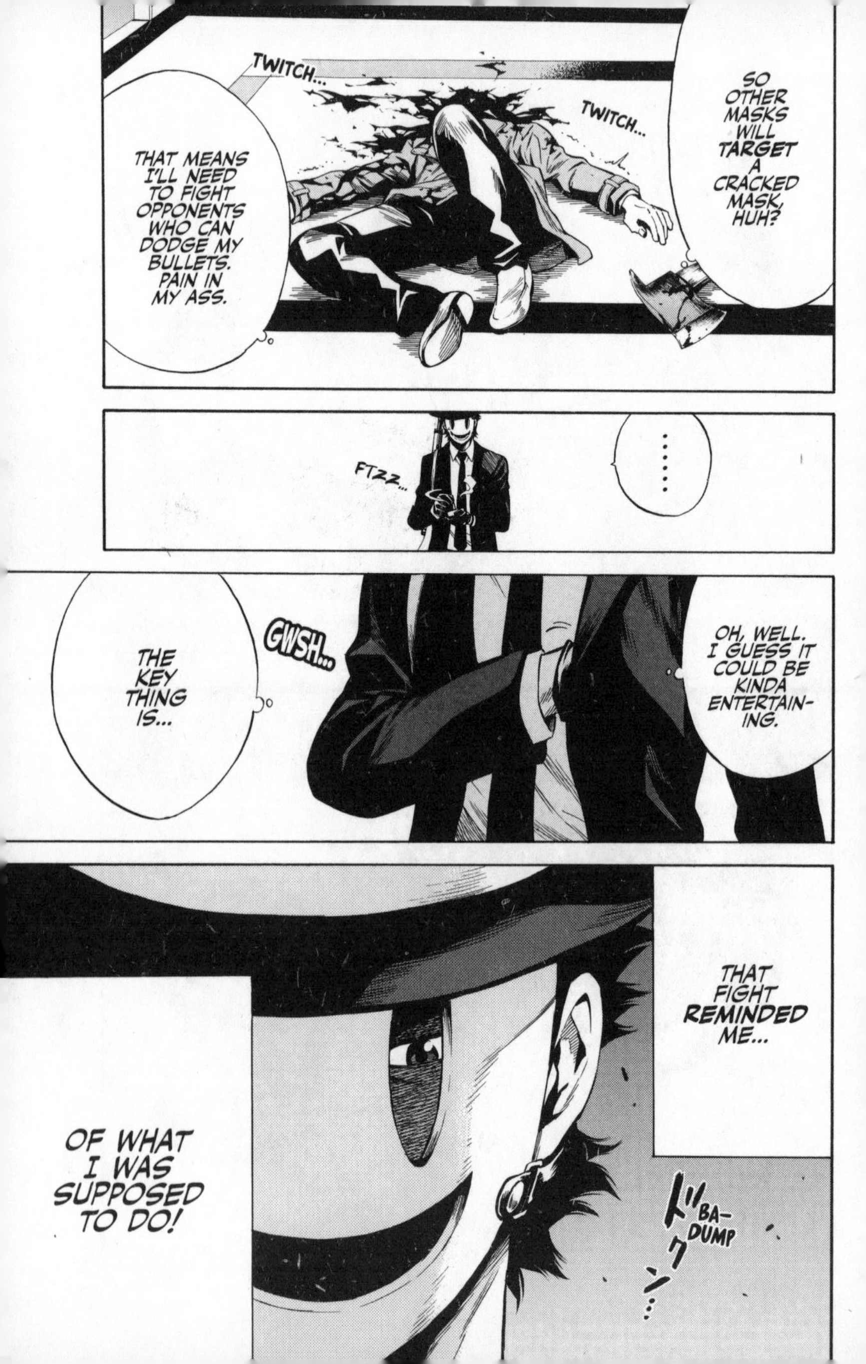
SO OTHER MASKS WILL TARGET A CRACKED MASK, HUH?
TWITCH...
TWITCH...
THAT MEANS I'LL NEED TO FIGHT OPPONENTS WHO CAN DODGE MY BULLETS. PAIN IN MY ASS.
......
FTZZ...
OH, WELL. I GUESS IT COULD BE KINDA ENTERTAIN-ING.
GWSH...
THE KEY THING IS...
THAT FIGHT REMINDED ME...
BA-DUMP
OF WHAT I WAS SUPPOSED TO DO!

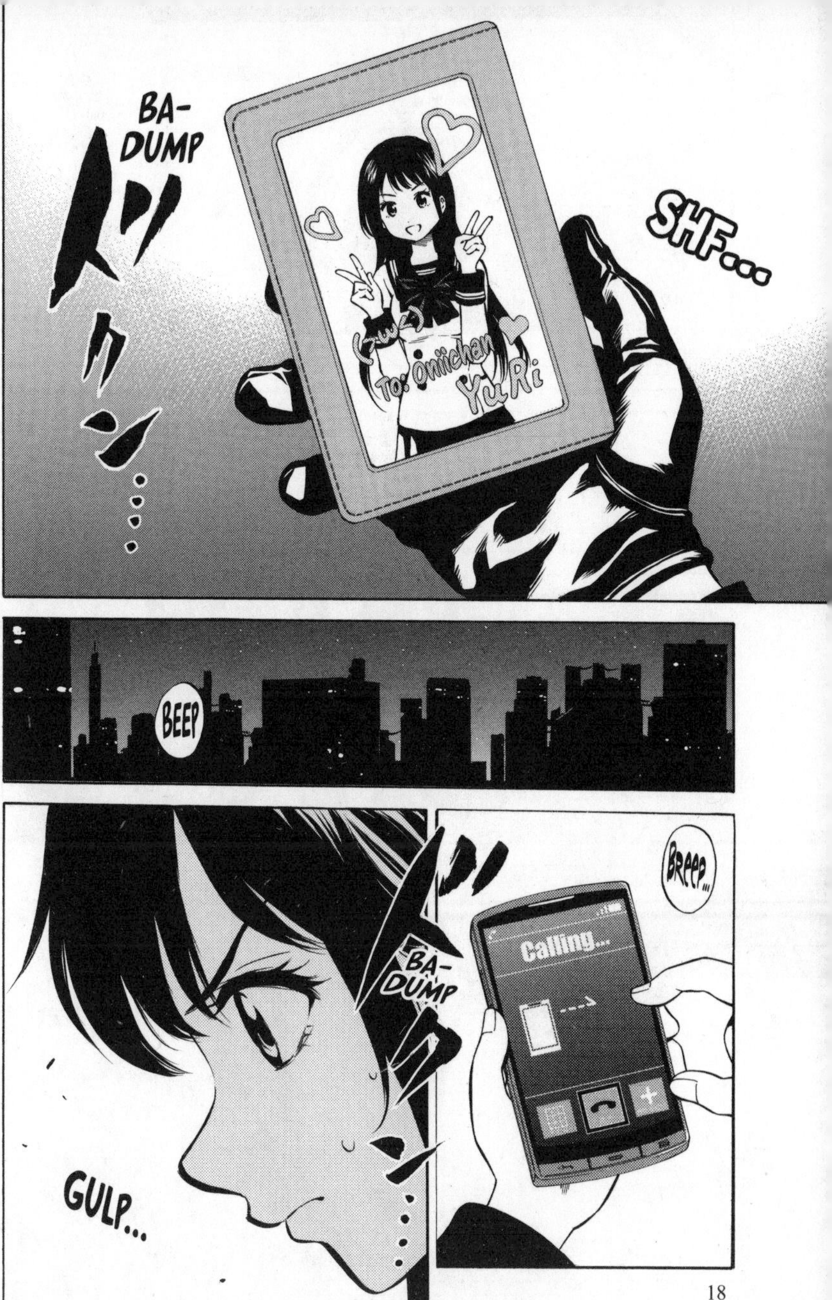
SHF...
To: Oniichan
Yuri
BA-DUMP
BEEP
Breep...
Calling...
BA-DUMP
GULP...

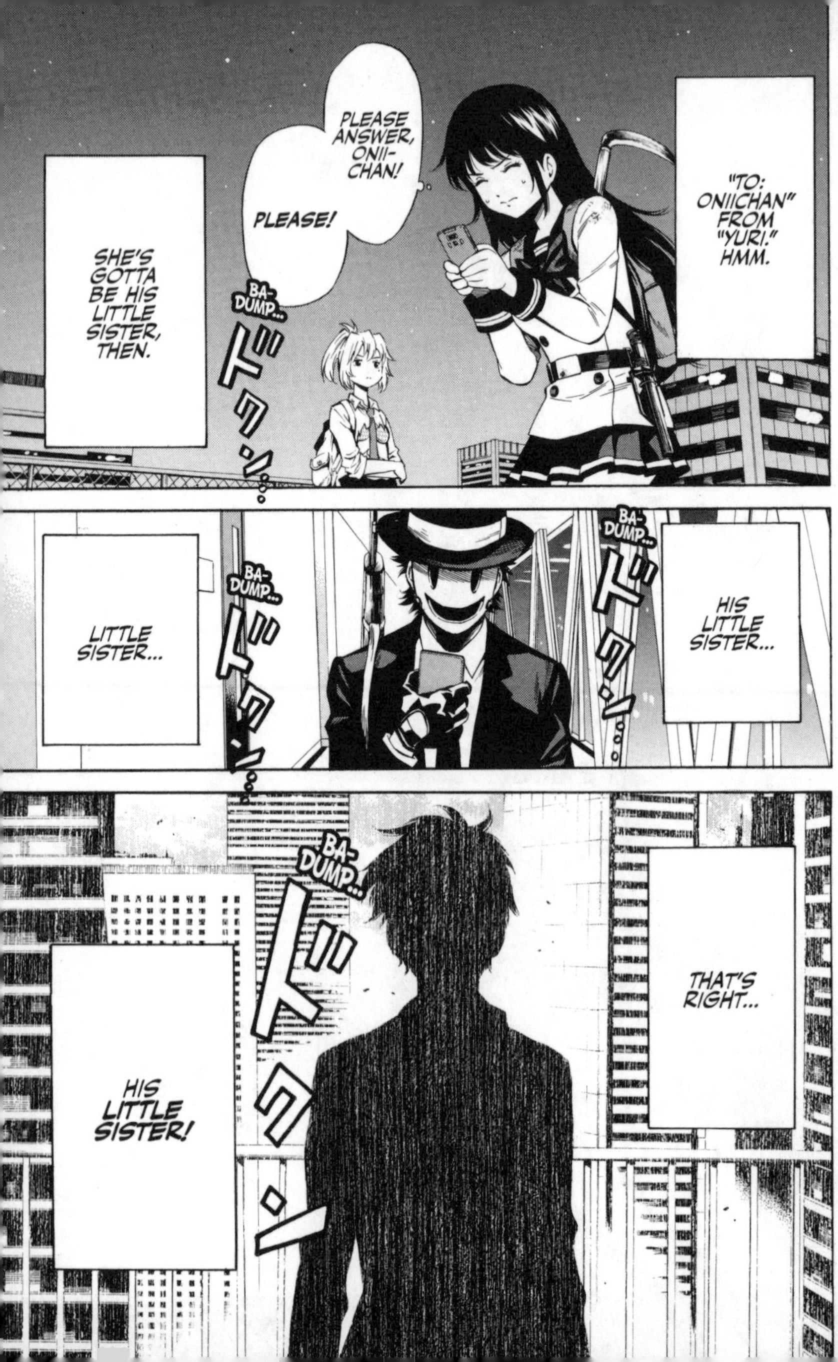
"TO: ONIICHAN" FROM "YURI." HMM.
PLEASE ANSWER, ONII-CHAN!
PLEASE!
BA-DUMP...
ドクン
SHE'S GOTTA BE HIS LITTLE SISTER, THEN.
BA-DUMP...
ドクン
HIS LITTLE SISTER...
BA-DUMP...
ドクン
LITTLE SISTER...
THAT'S RIGHT...
BA-DUMP...
ドクン
HIS LITTLE SISTER!

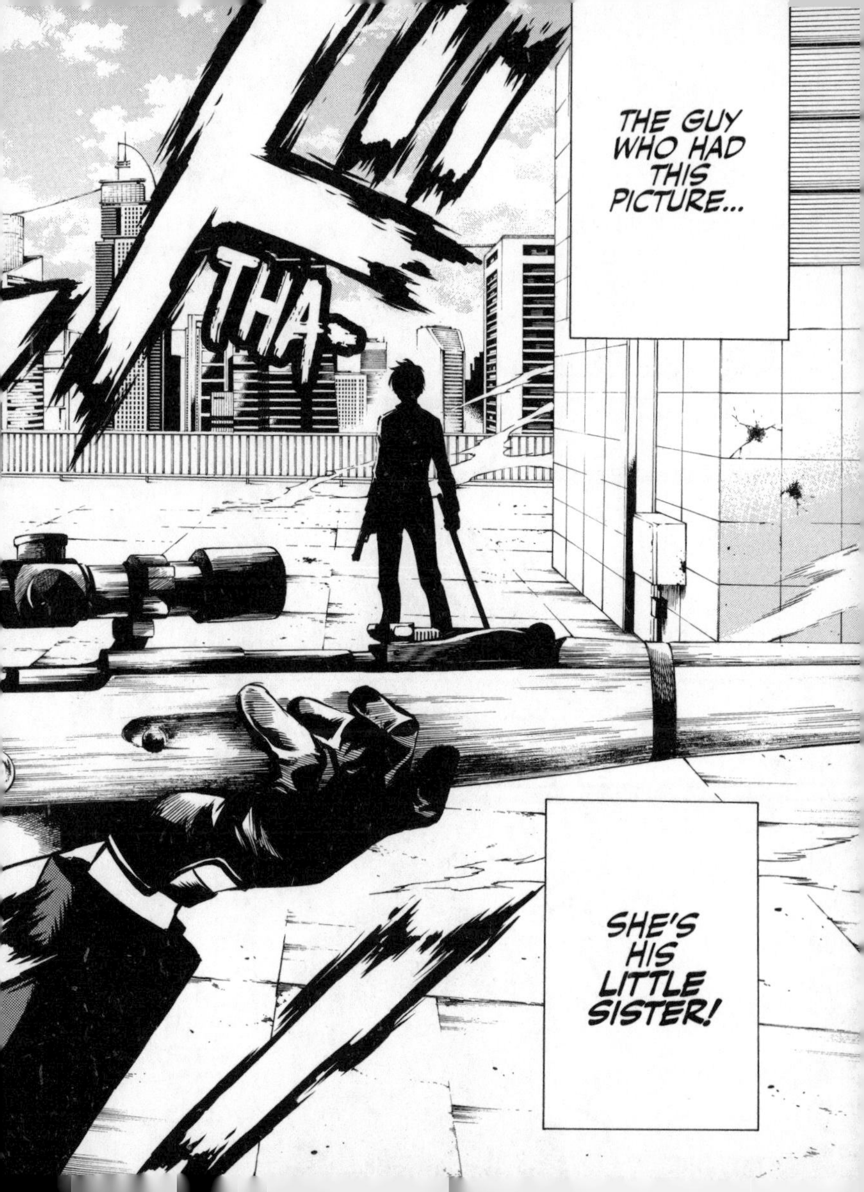
THE GUY WHO HAD THIS PICTURE...
THA
SHE'S HIS LITTLE SISTER!

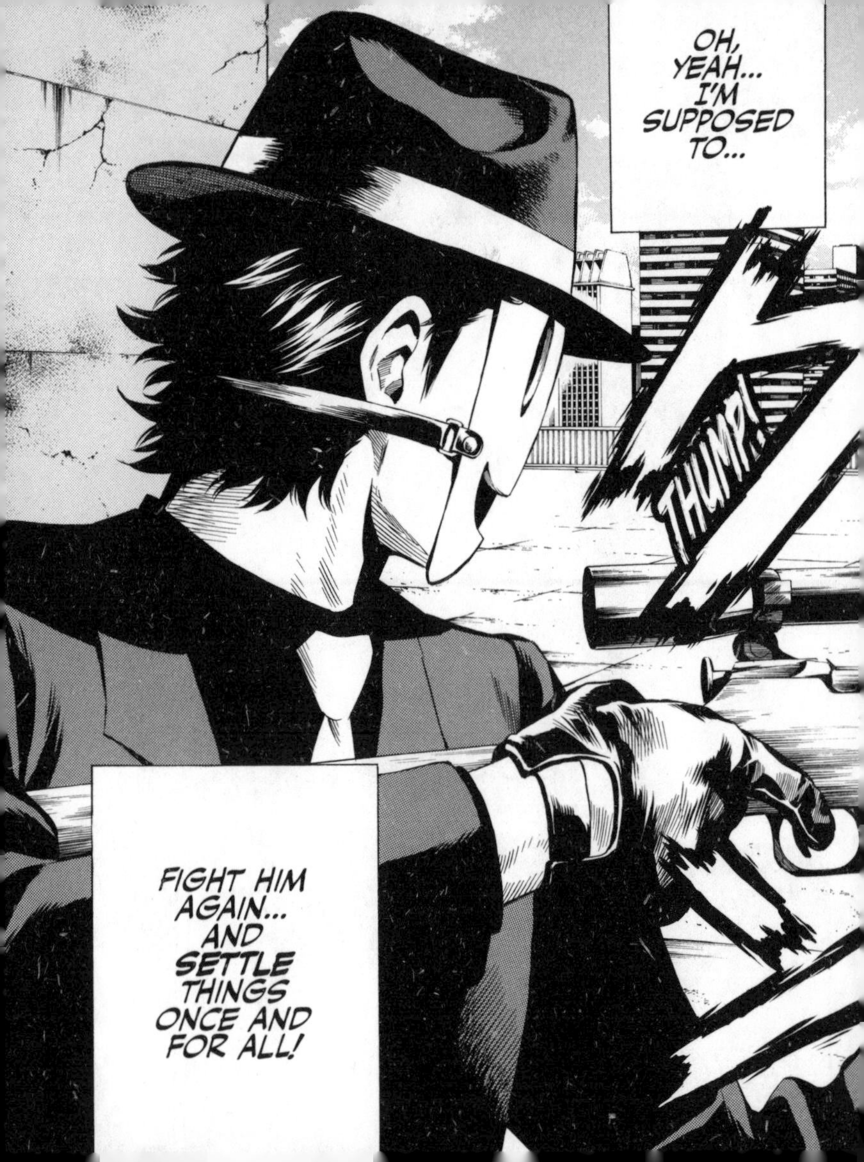
OH, YEAH... I'M SUPPOSED TO...
THUMP!
FIGHT HIM AGAIN... AND SETTLE THINGS ONCE AND FOR ALL!

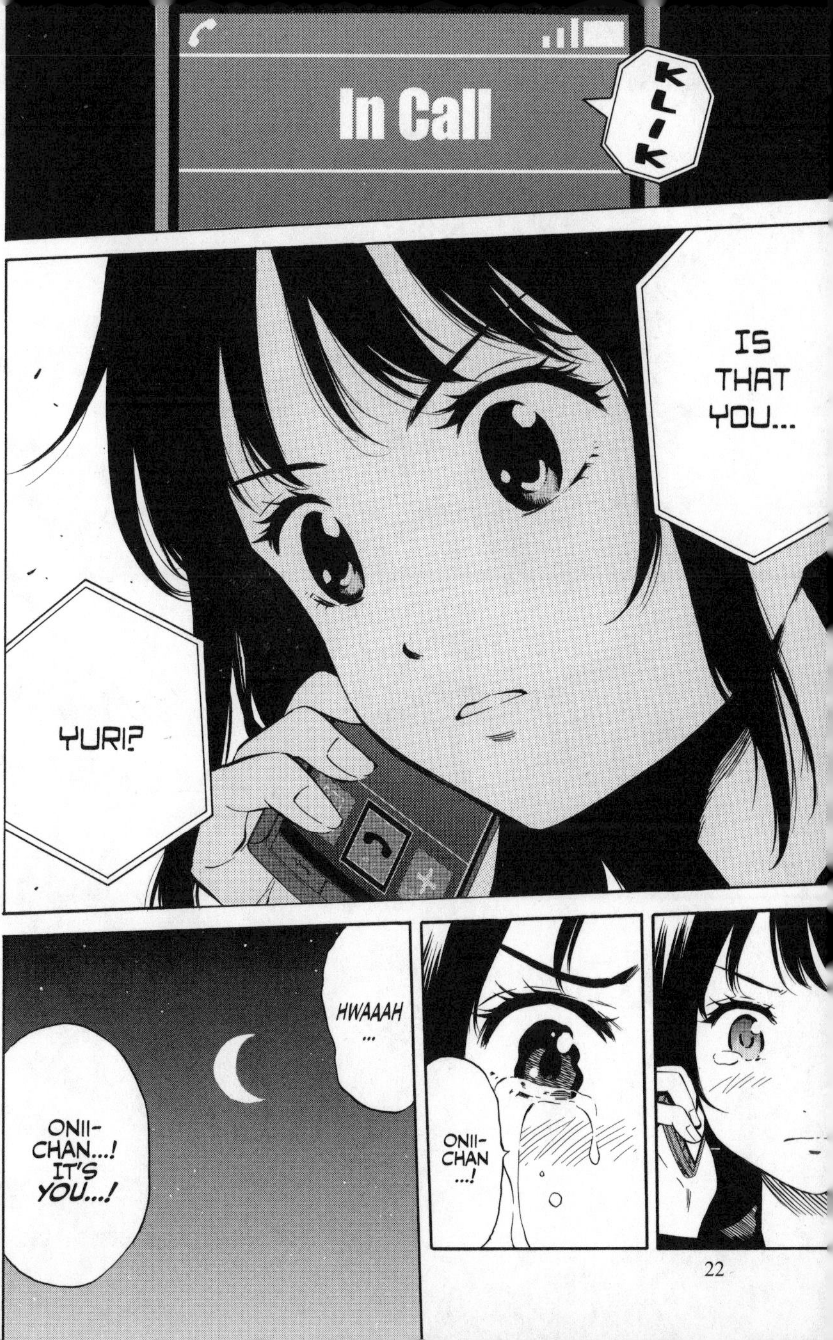
In Call
KLIK
IS THAT YOU...
YURI?
ONII-CHAN...!
HWAAAH...
ONII-CHAN...! IT'S YOU...!

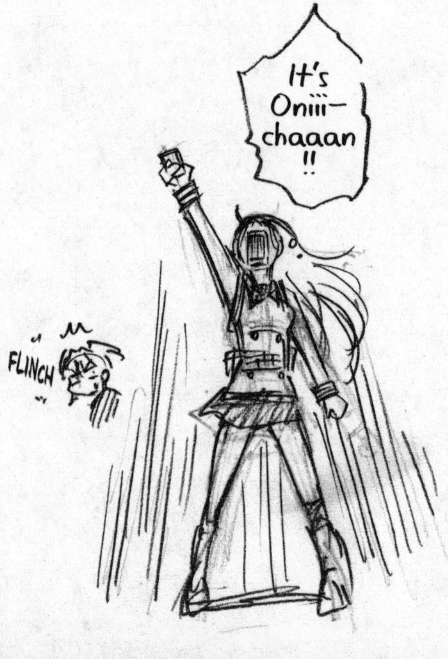
It's Oniii-chaaan !!
FLINCH

HIGH-RISE INVASION

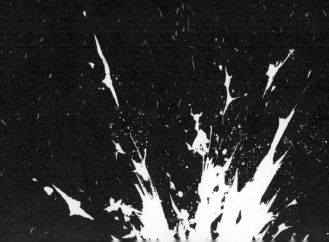

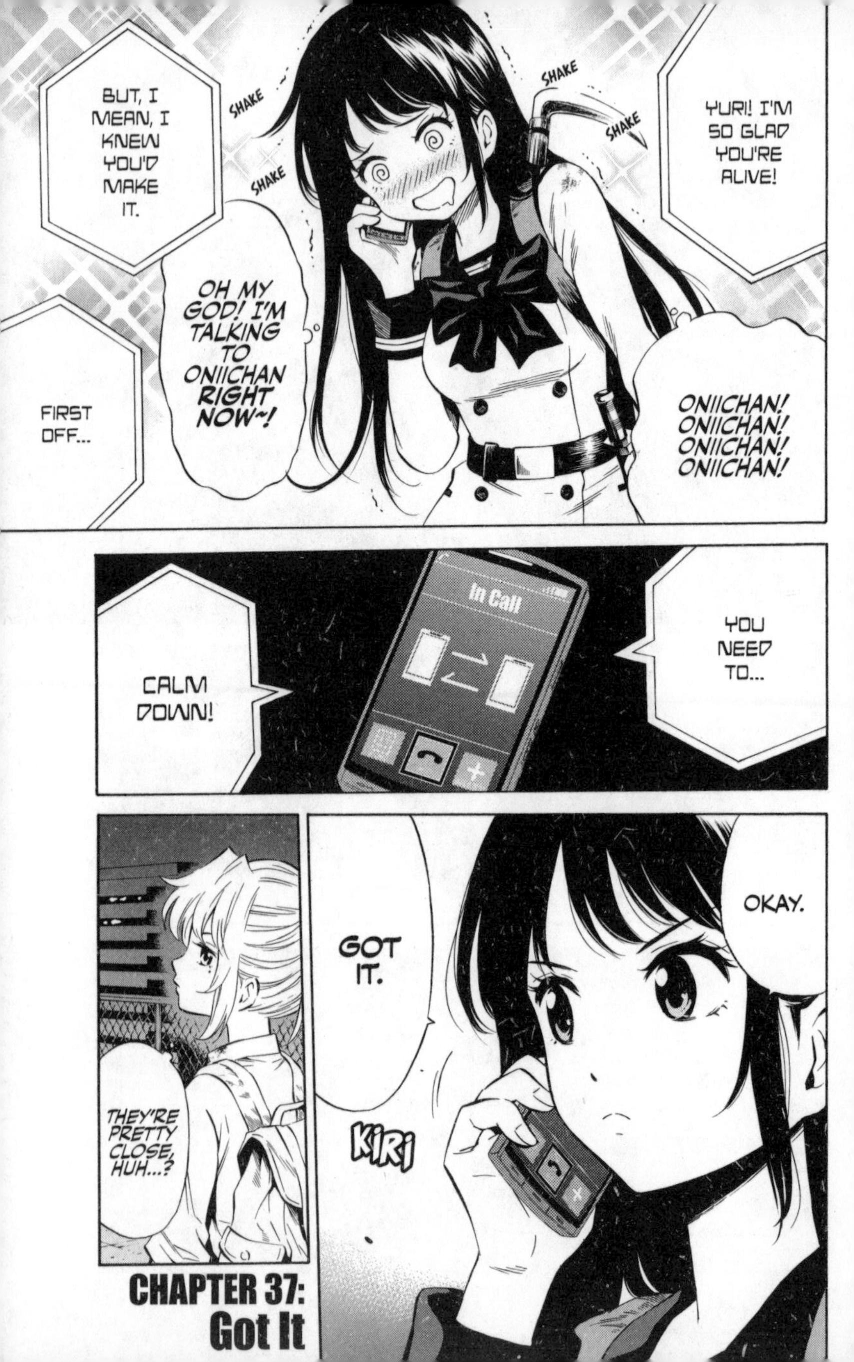
YURI! I'M SO GLAD YOU'RE ALIVE!
SHAKE
SHAKE
ONIICHAN! ONIICHAN! ONIICHAN! ONIICHAN!
OH MY GOD! I'M TALKING TO ONIICHAN RIGHT NOW~!
BUT, I MEAN, I KNEW YOU'D MAKE IT.
SHAKE
SHAKE
FIRST OFF...
YOU NEED TO...
In Call
CALM DOWN!
OKAY.
GOT IT.
KIRI
THEY'RE PRETTY CLOSE, HUH...?

CHAPTER 37: Got It

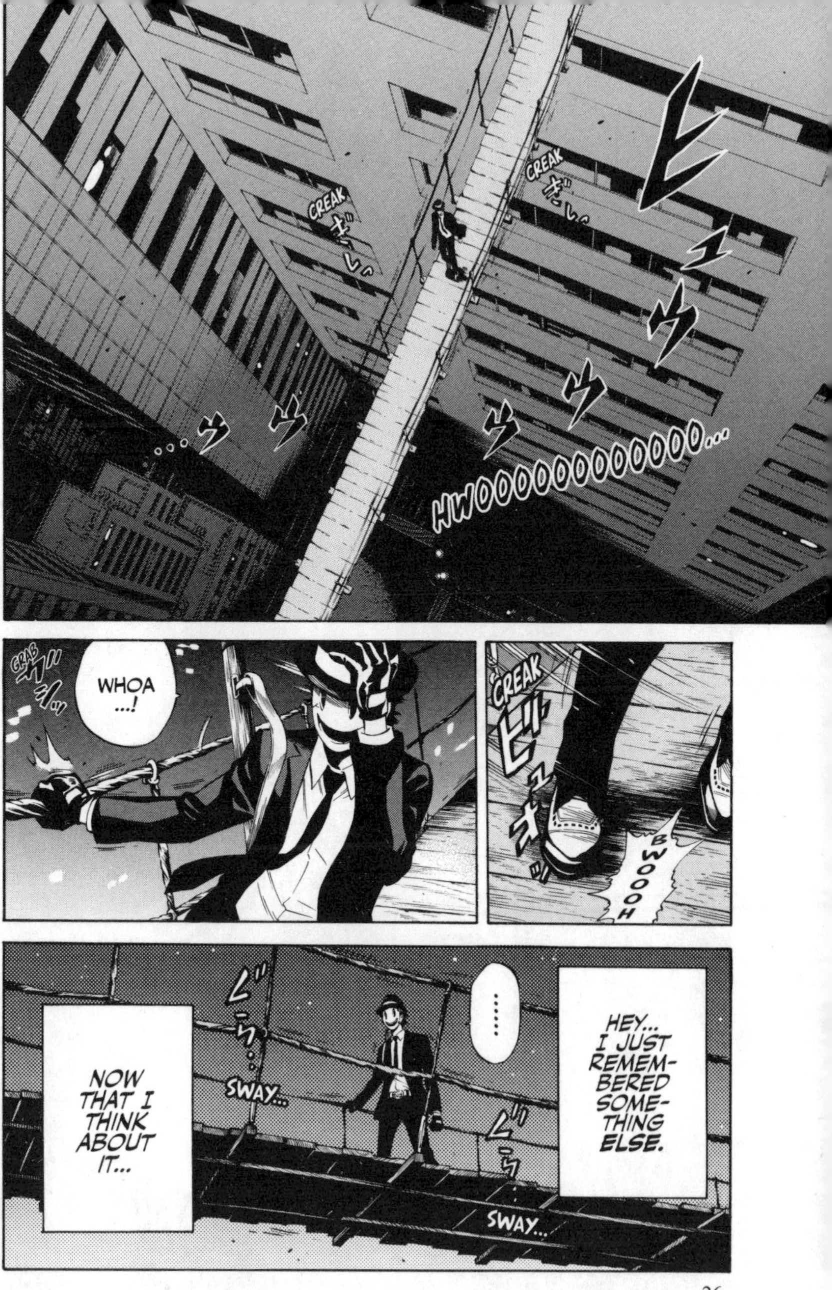
CREAK
CREAK
HWOOOOOOOOOOO...
CREAK
BWOOOH
GRAB
WHOA ...!
HEY... I JUST REMEMBERED SOMETHING ELSE.
......
SWAY...
SWAY...
NOW THAT I THINK ABOUT IT...

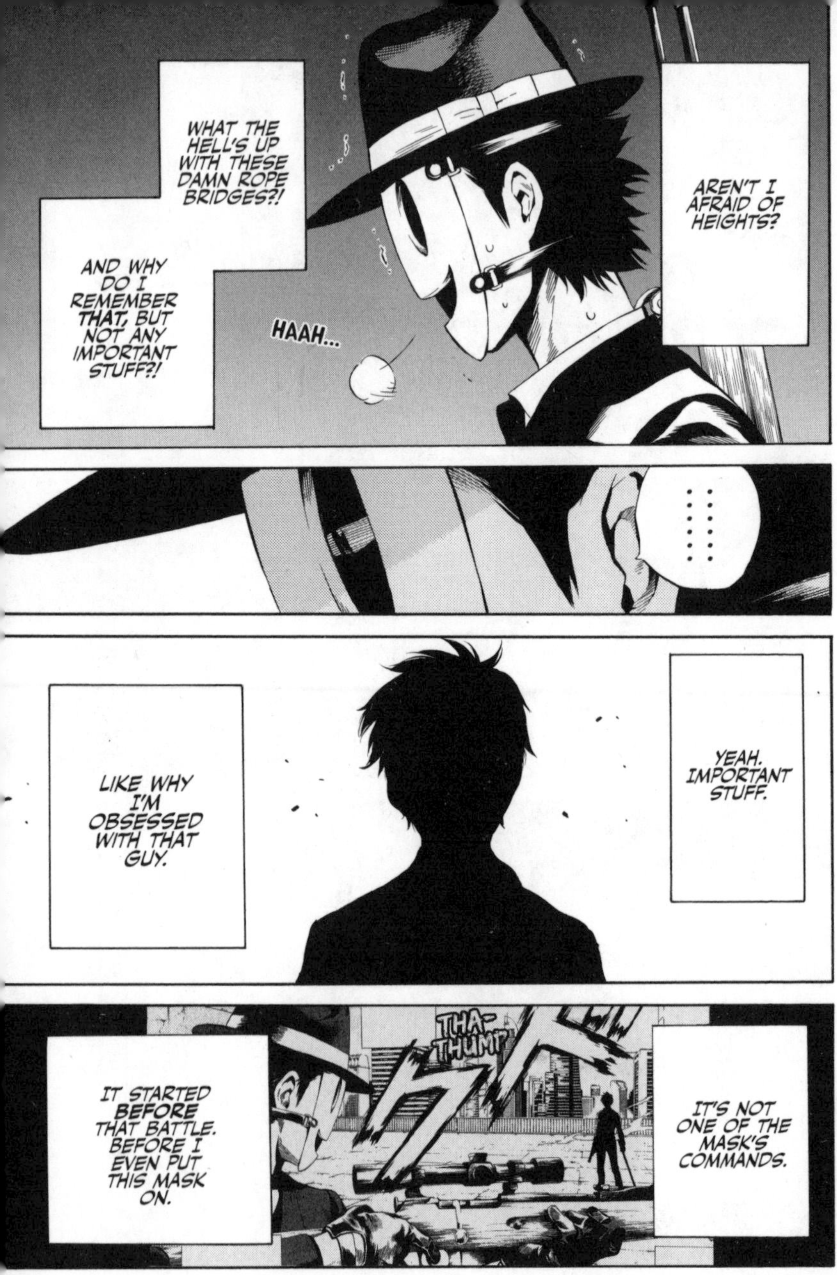

AREN'T I AFRAID OF HEIGHTS?
WHAT THE HELL'S UP WITH THESE DAMN ROPE BRIDGES?!
HAAH...
AND WHY DO I REMEMBER THAT, BUT NOT ANY IMPORTANT STUFF?!
YEAH. IMPORTANT STUFF.
LIKE WHY I'M OBSESSED WITH THAT GUY.
IT'S NOT ONE OF THE MASK'S COMMANDS.
THA-THUMP
IT STARTED BEFORE THAT BATTLE. BEFORE I EVEN PUT THIS MASK ON.

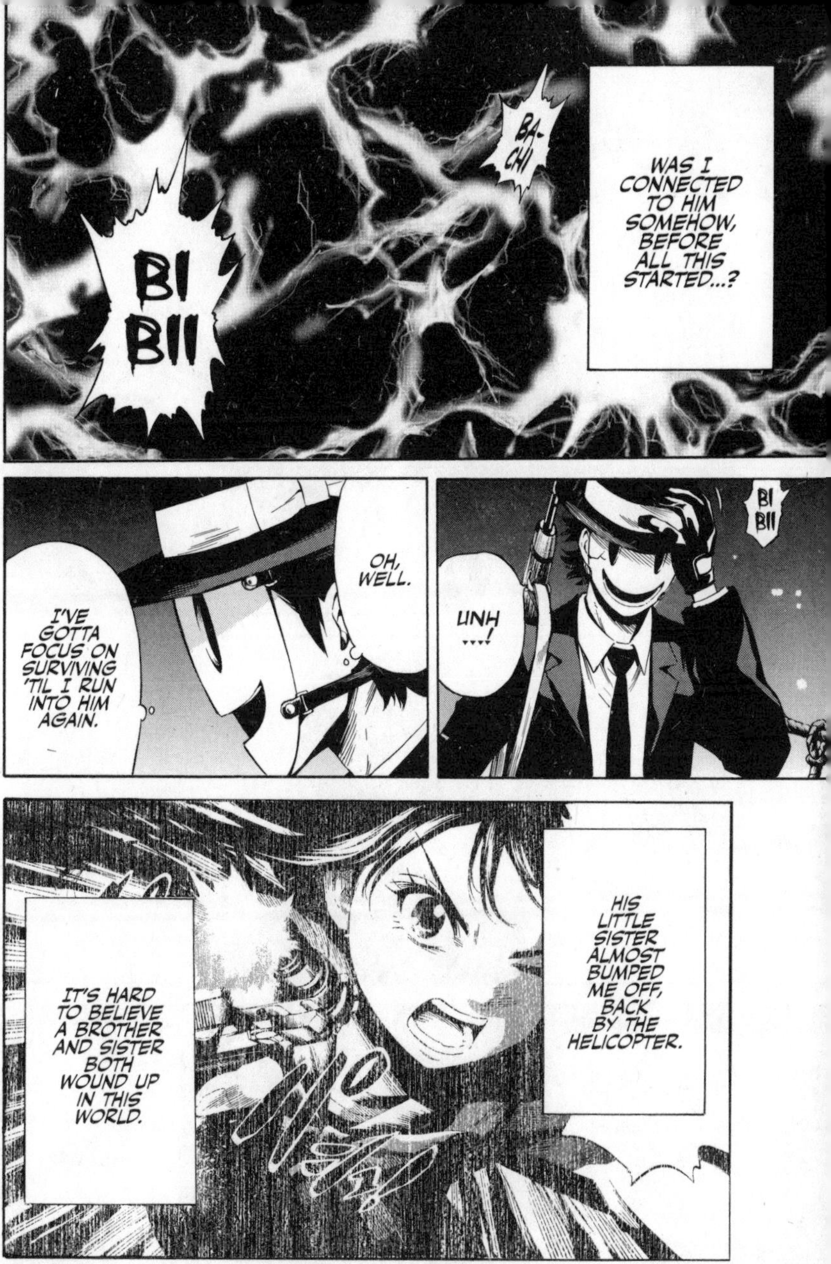
WAS I CONNECTED TO HIM SOMEHOW, BEFORE ALL THIS STARTED...?
BA-CHI
BI BII
BI BII
UNH...!
OH, WELL.
I'VE GOTTA FOCUS ON SURVIVING 'TIL I RUN INTO HIM AGAIN.
HIS LITTLE SISTER ALMOST BUMPED ME OFF, BACK BY THE HELICOPTER.
IT'S HARD TO BELIEVE A BROTHER AND SISTER BOTH WOUND UP IN THIS WORLD.

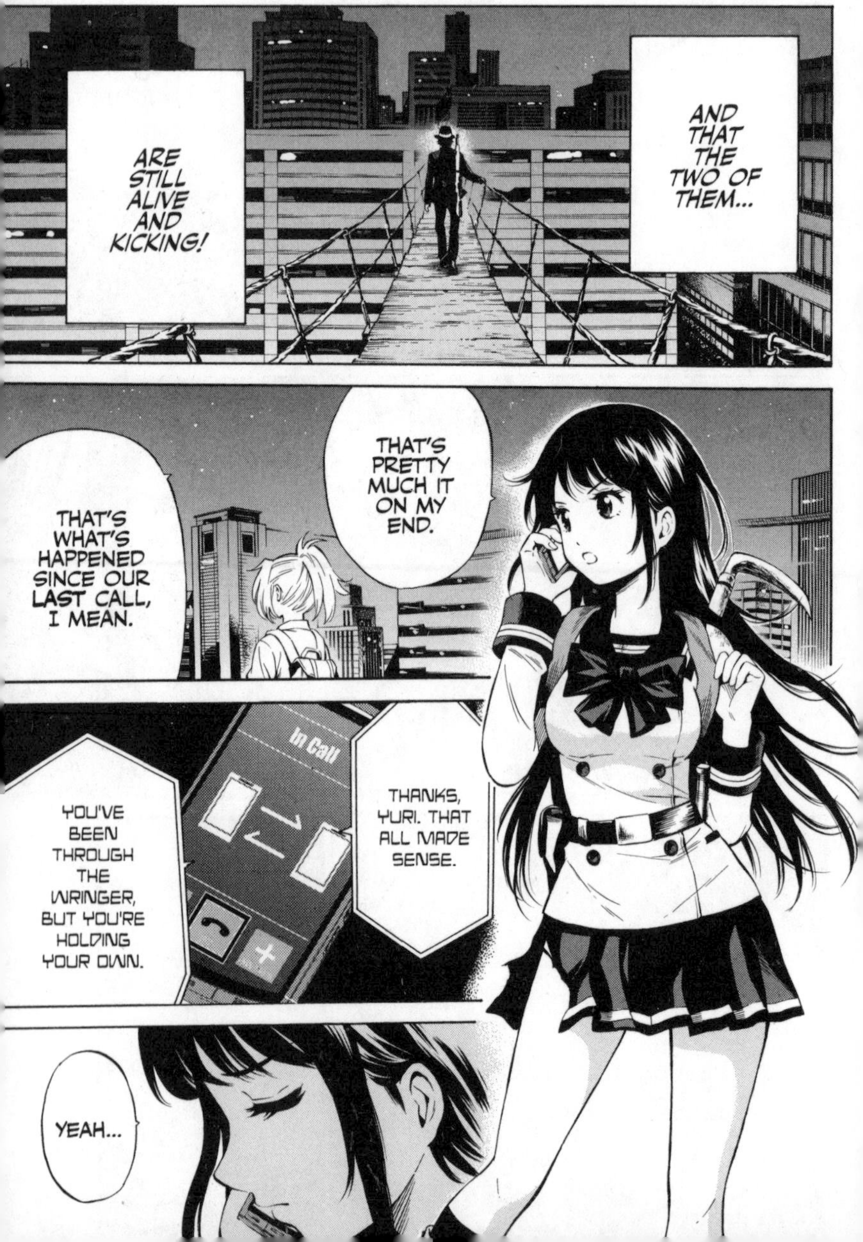
AND THAT THE TWO OF THEM...
ARE STILL ALIVE AND KICKING!
THAT'S PRETTY MUCH IT ON MY END.
THAT'S WHAT'S HAPPENED SINCE OUR LAST CALL, I MEAN.
In Call
THANKS, YURI. THAT ALL MADE SENSE.
YOU'VE BEEN THROUGH THE WRINGER, BUT YOU'RE HOLDING YOUR OWN.
YEAH...

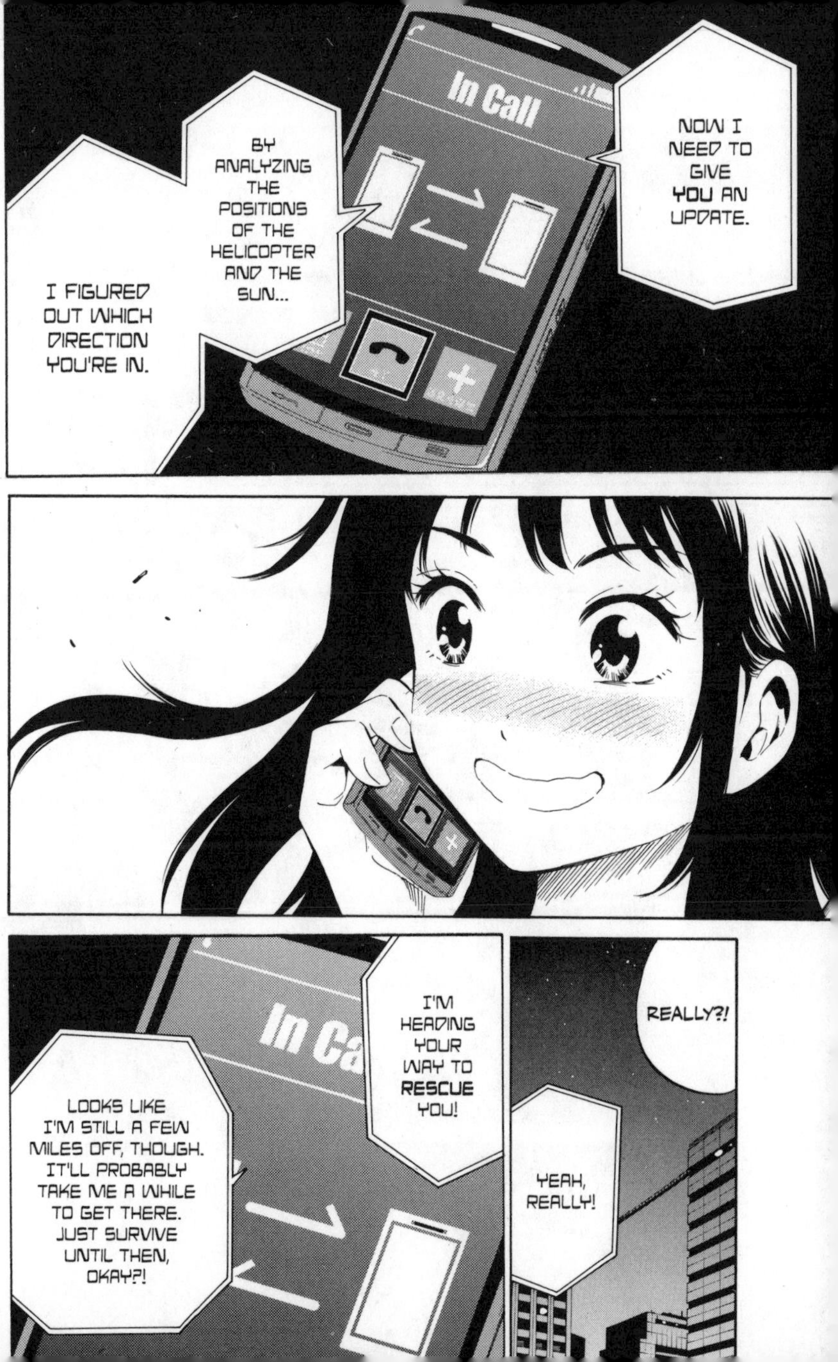
NOW I NEED TO GIVE YOU AN UPDATE.
In Call
BY ANALYZING THE POSITIONS OF THE HELICOPTER AND THE SUN...
I FIGURED OUT WHICH DIRECTION YOU'RE IN.
REALLY?!
YEAH, REALLY!
I'M HEADING YOUR WAY TO RESCUE YOU!
In Ca
LOOKS LIKE I'M STILL A FEW MILES OFF, THOUGH. IT'LL PROBABLY TAKE ME A WHILE TO GET THERE. JUST SURVIVE UNTIL THEN, OKAY?!

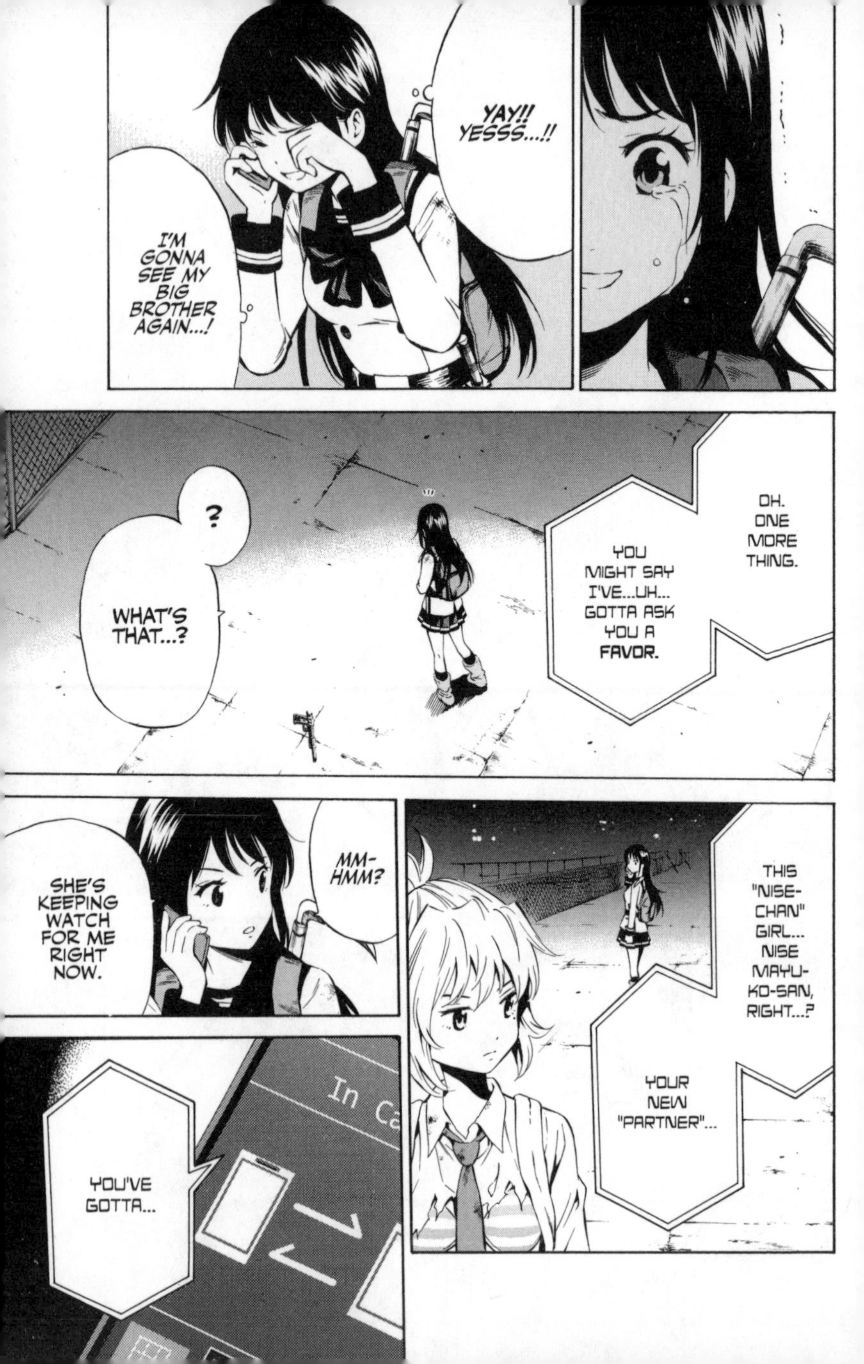
YAY!! YESSS...!!
I'M GONNA SEE MY BIG BROTHER AGAIN...!
OH. ONE MORE THING.
YOU MIGHT SAY I'VE...UH... GOTTA ASK YOU A FAVOR.
?
WHAT'S THAT...?
THIS "NISE-CHAN" GIRL... NISE MAYU-KO-SAN, RIGHT...?
YOUR NEW "PARTNER"...
MM-HMM?
SHE'S KEEPING WATCH FOR ME RIGHT NOW.
YOU'VE GOTTA...

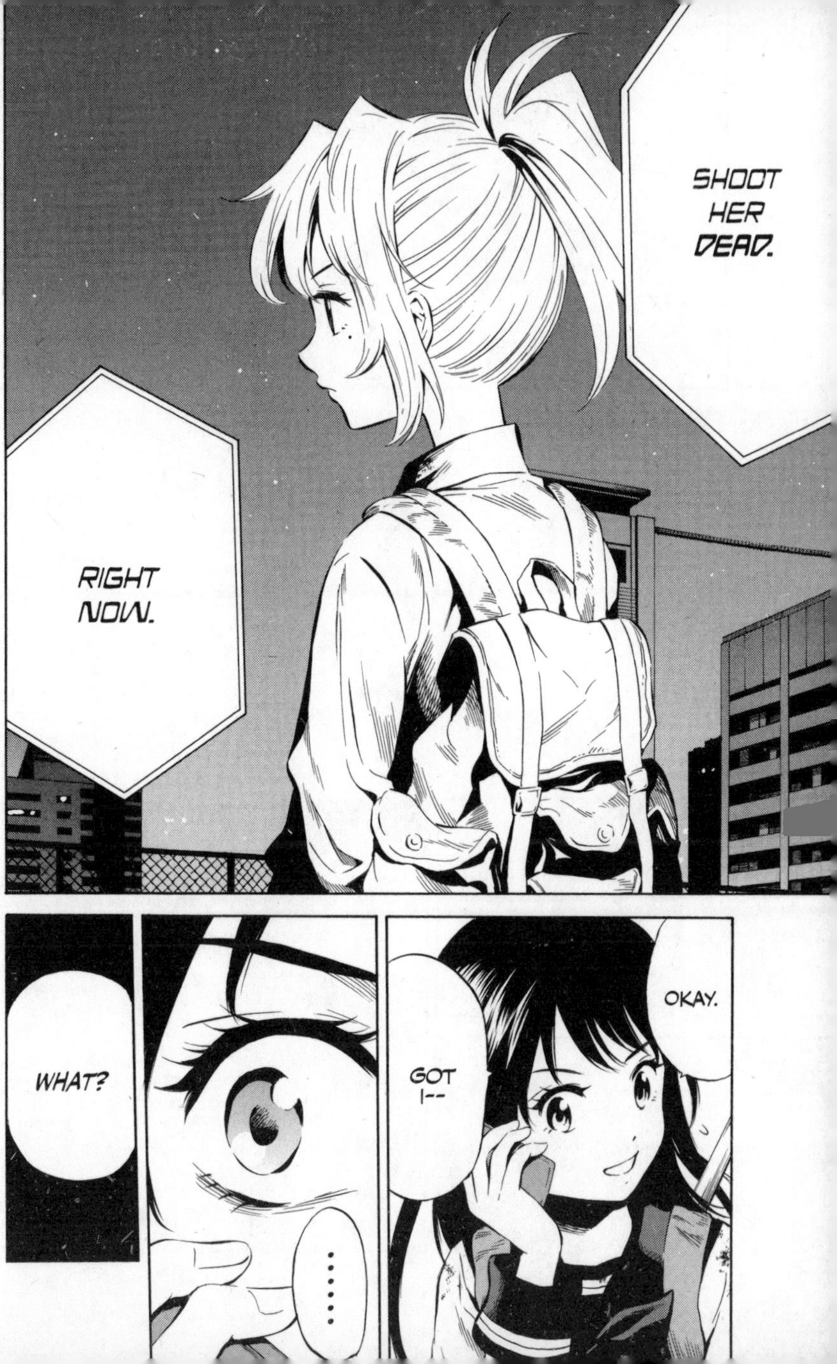
SHOOT HER DEAD.
RIGHT NOW.
OKAY.
GOT I--
......
WHAT?

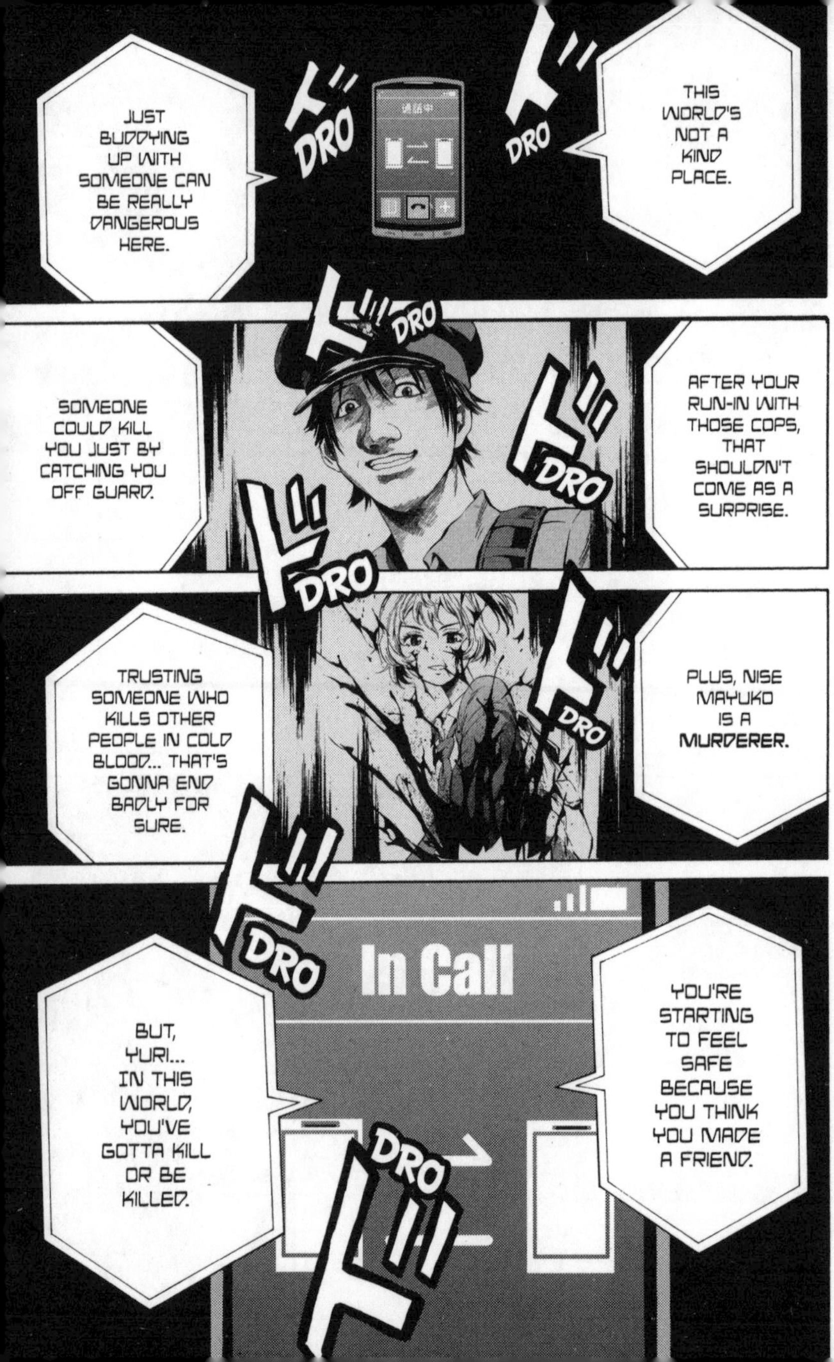

THIS WORLD'S NOT A KIND PLACE.
ド DRO
通話中
ド DRO
JUST BUDDYING UP WITH SOMEONE CAN BE REALLY DANGEROUS HERE.
ド DRO
AFTER YOUR RUN-IN WITH THOSE COPS, THAT SHOULDN'T COME AS A SURPRISE.
ド DRO
SOMEONE COULD KILL YOU JUST BY CATCHING YOU OFF GUARD.
ド DRO
PLUS, NISE MAYUKO IS A **MURDERER.**
ド DRO
TRUSTING SOMEONE WHO KILLS OTHER PEOPLE IN COLD BLOOD... THAT'S GONNA END BADLY FOR SURE.
ド DRO
In Call
YOU'RE STARTING TO FEEL SAFE BECAUSE YOU THINK YOU MADE A FRIEND.
ド DRO
BUT, YURI... IN THIS WORLD, YOU'VE GOTTA KILL OR BE KILLED.

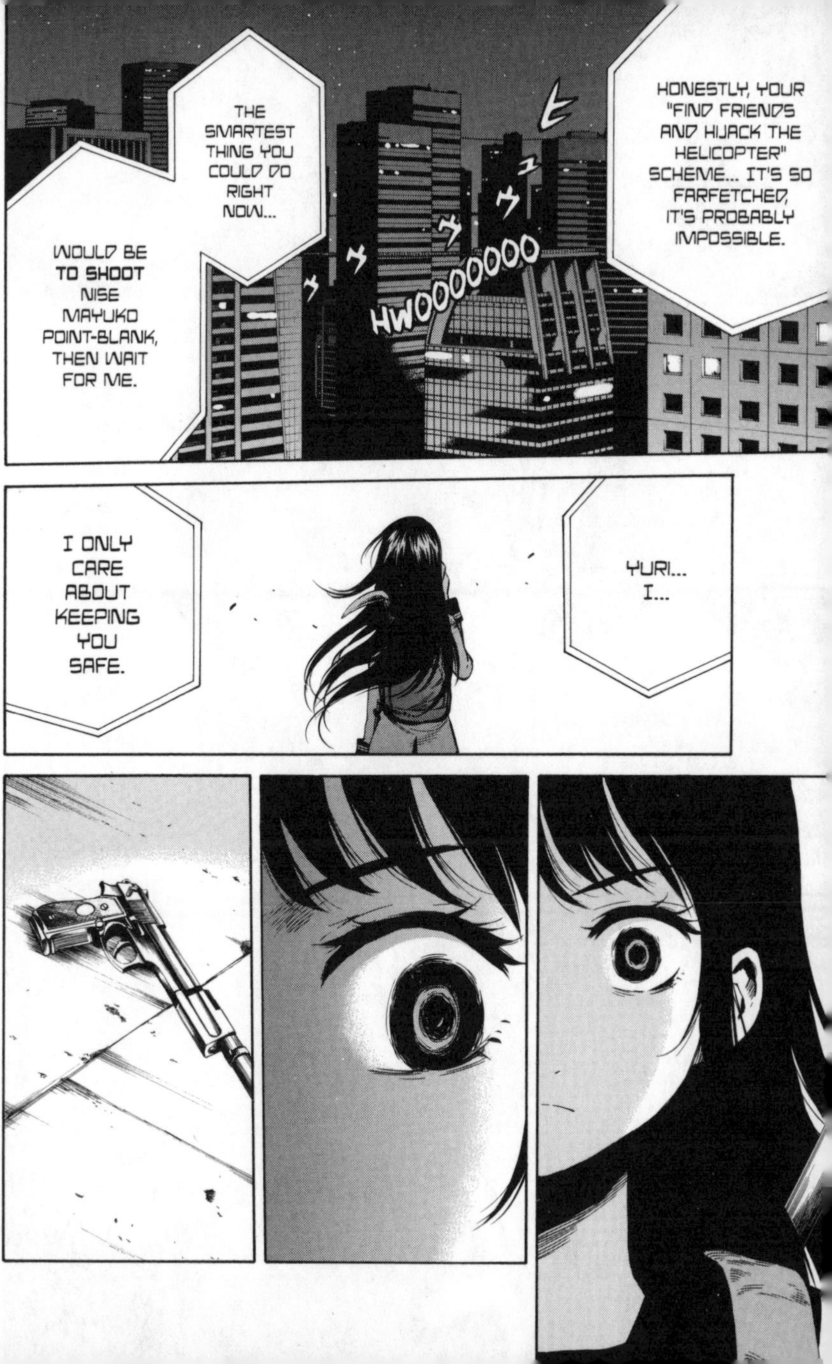
HONESTLY, YOUR "FIND FRIENDS AND HIJACK THE HELICOPTER" SCHEME... IT'S SO FARFETCHED, IT'S PROBABLY IMPOSSIBLE.
HWOOOOOOO
THE SMARTEST THING YOU COULD DO RIGHT NOW...
WOULD BE TO SHOOT NISE MAYUKO POINT-BLANK, THEN WAIT FOR ME.
YURI... I...
I ONLY CARE ABOUT KEEPING YOU SAFE.

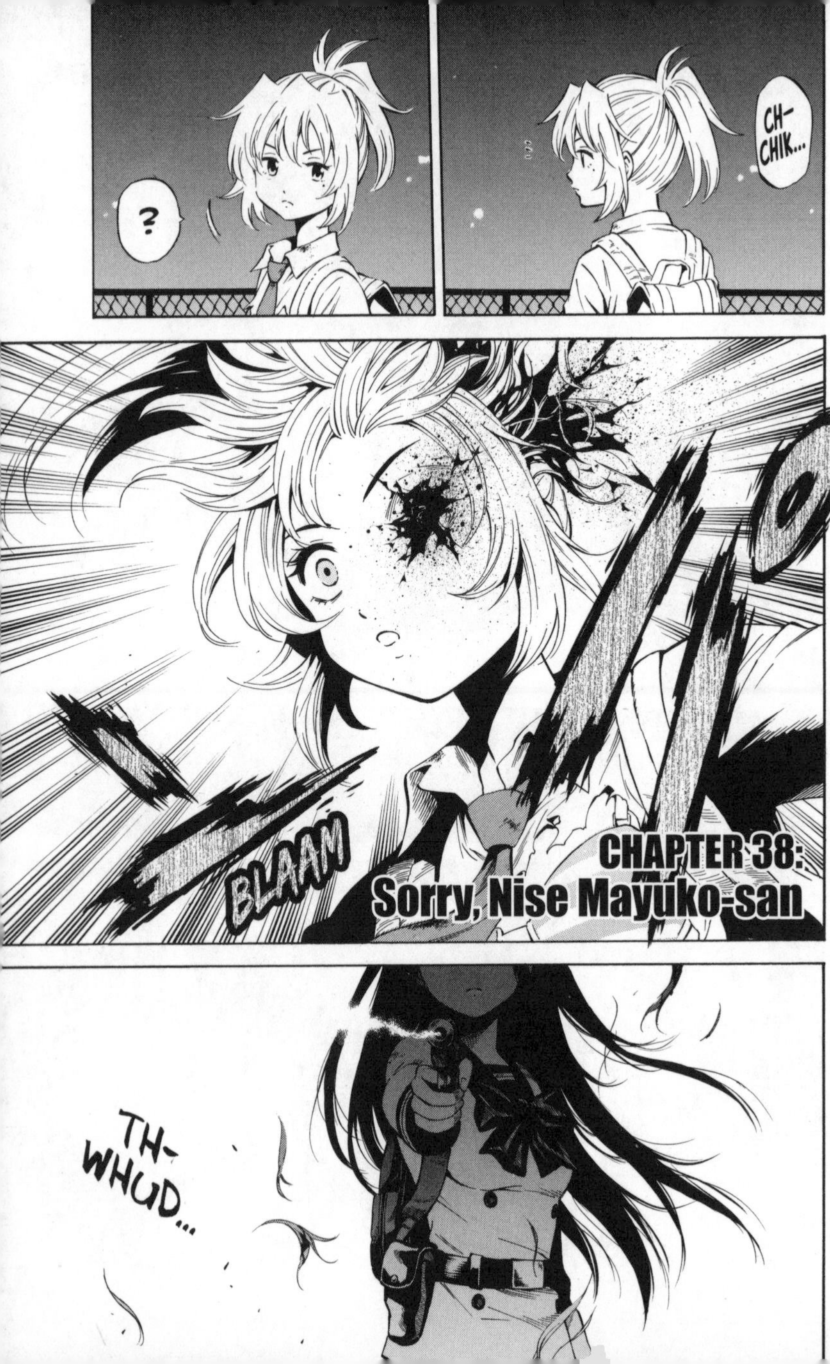
CH-
CHIK...
?
BLAAM
TH-
WHUD...

CHAPTER 38: Sorry, Nise Mayuko-san

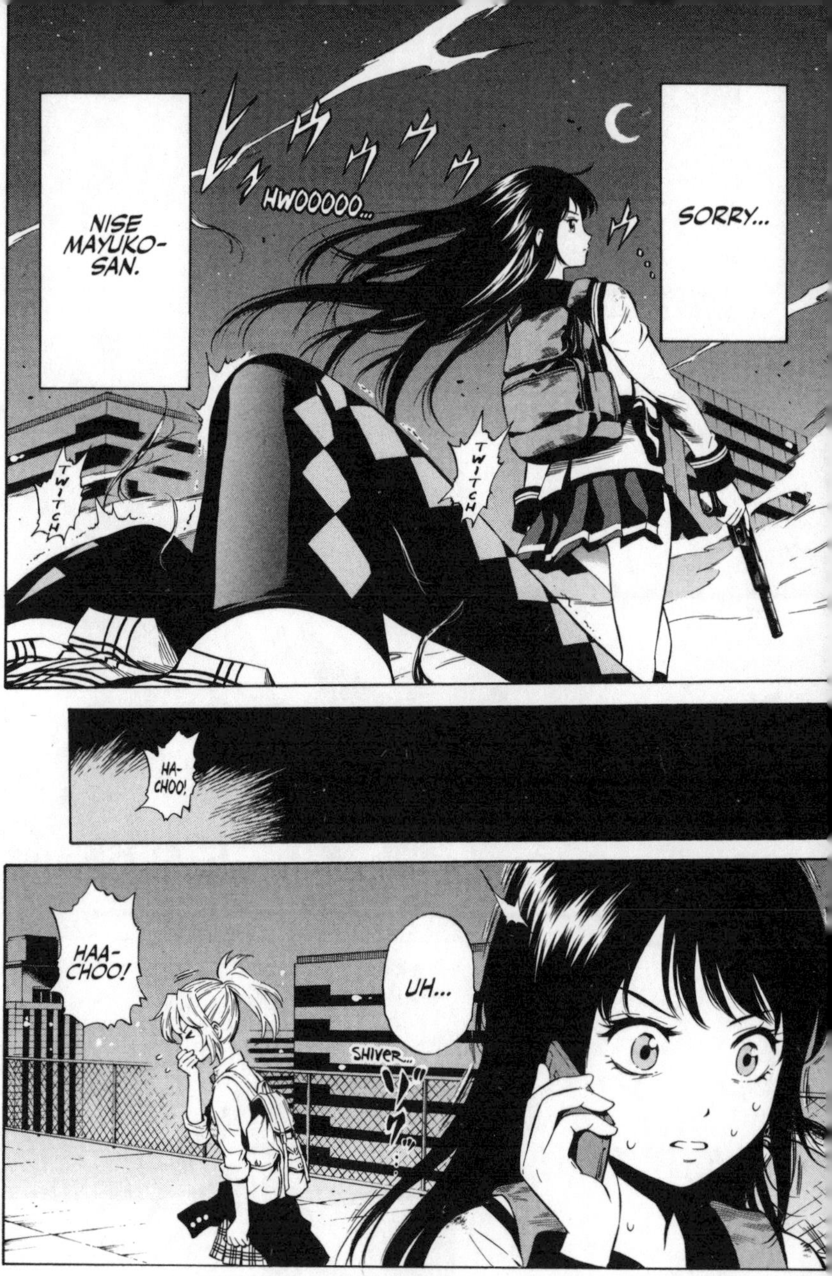
SORRY...
HWOOOOO...
TWITCH
TWITCH
NISE MAYUKO-SAN.
HA-CHOO!
UH...
SHIVER...
HAA-CHOO!

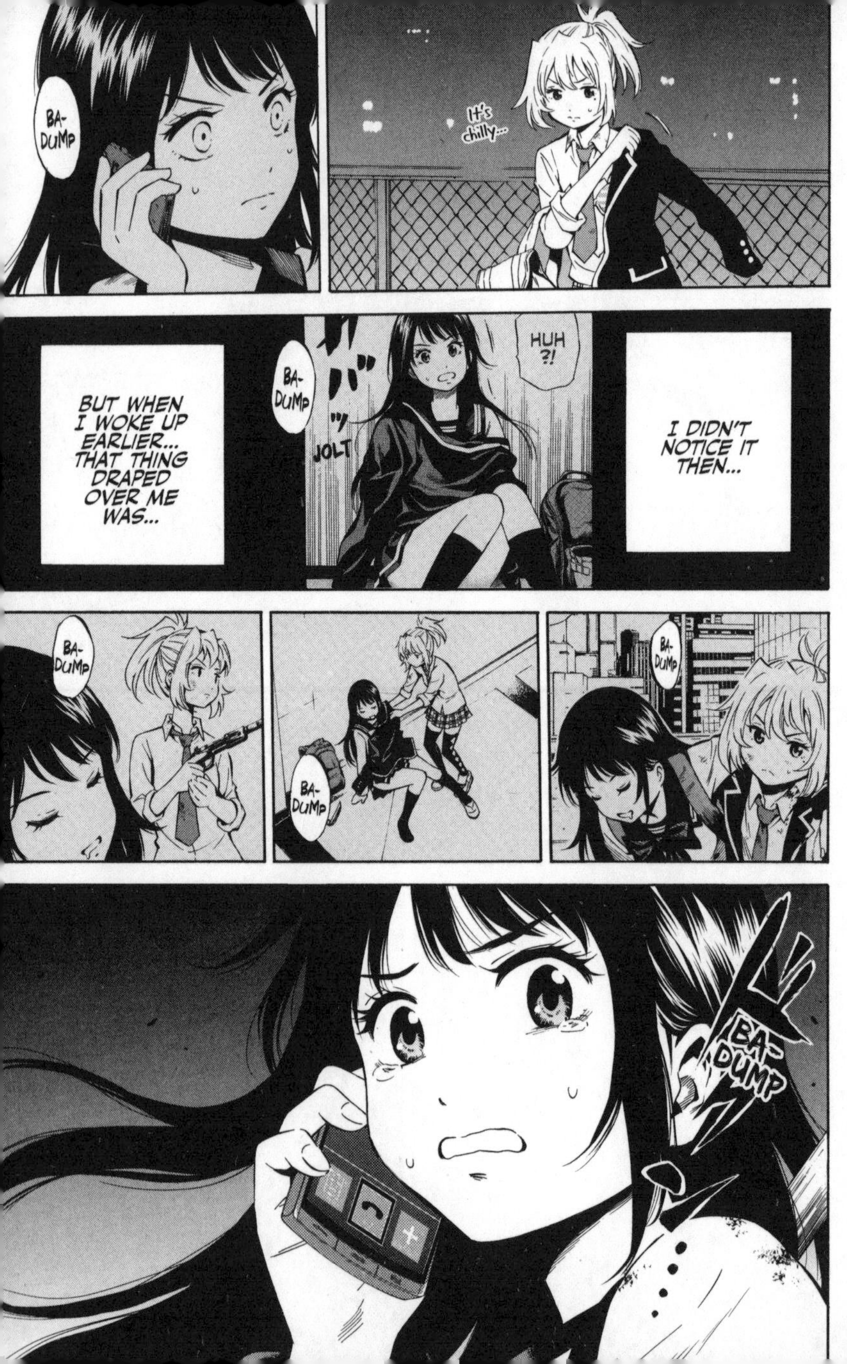
It's chilly...
BA-DUMP
I DIDN'T NOTICE IT THEN...
HUH?!
BA-DUMP
JOLT
BUT WHEN I WOKE UP EARLIER... THAT THING DRAPED OVER ME WAS...
BA-DUMP
BA-DUMP
BA-DUMP
BA-DUMP

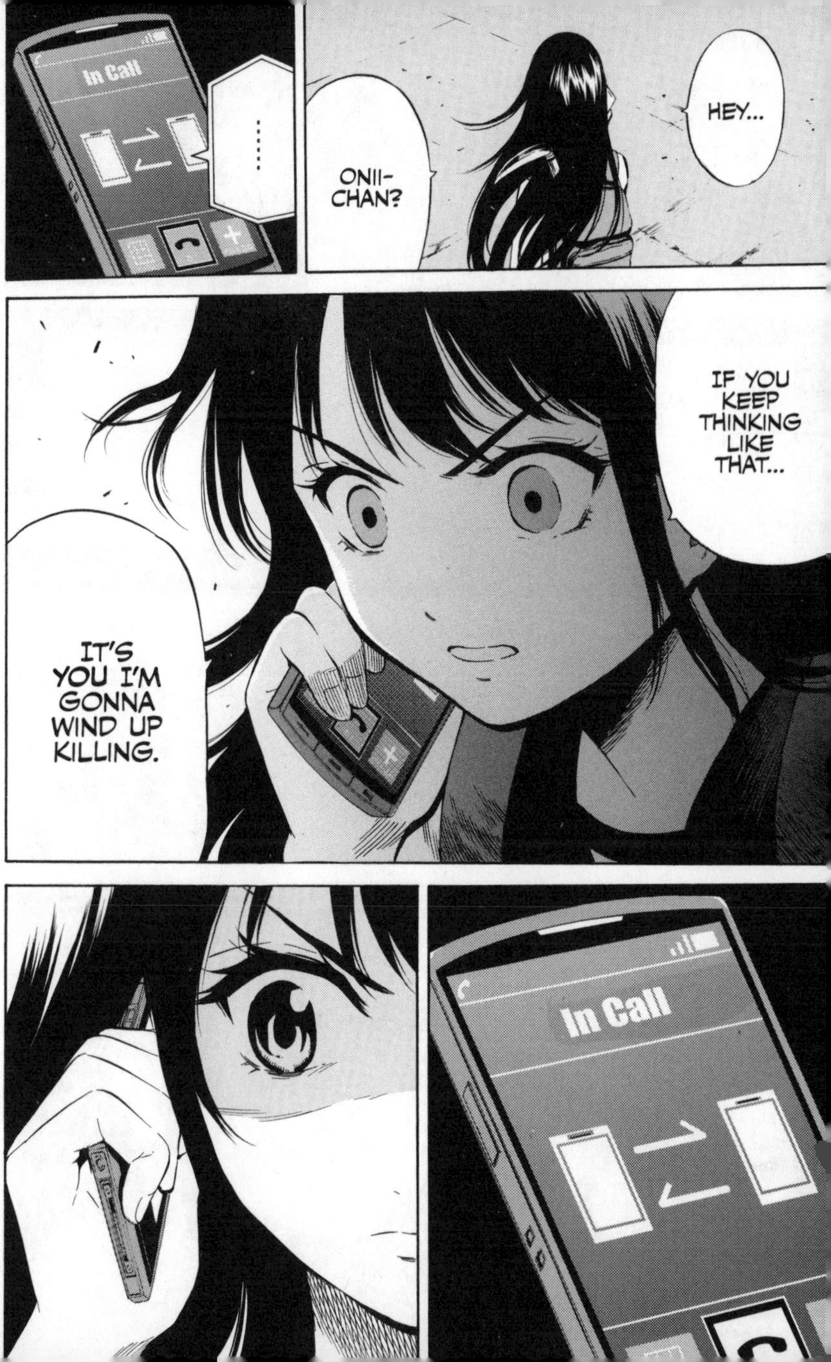
HEY...
ONII-CHAN?
In Call
......
IF YOU KEEP THINKING LIKE THAT...
IT'S YOU I'M GONNA WIND UP KILLING.
In Call

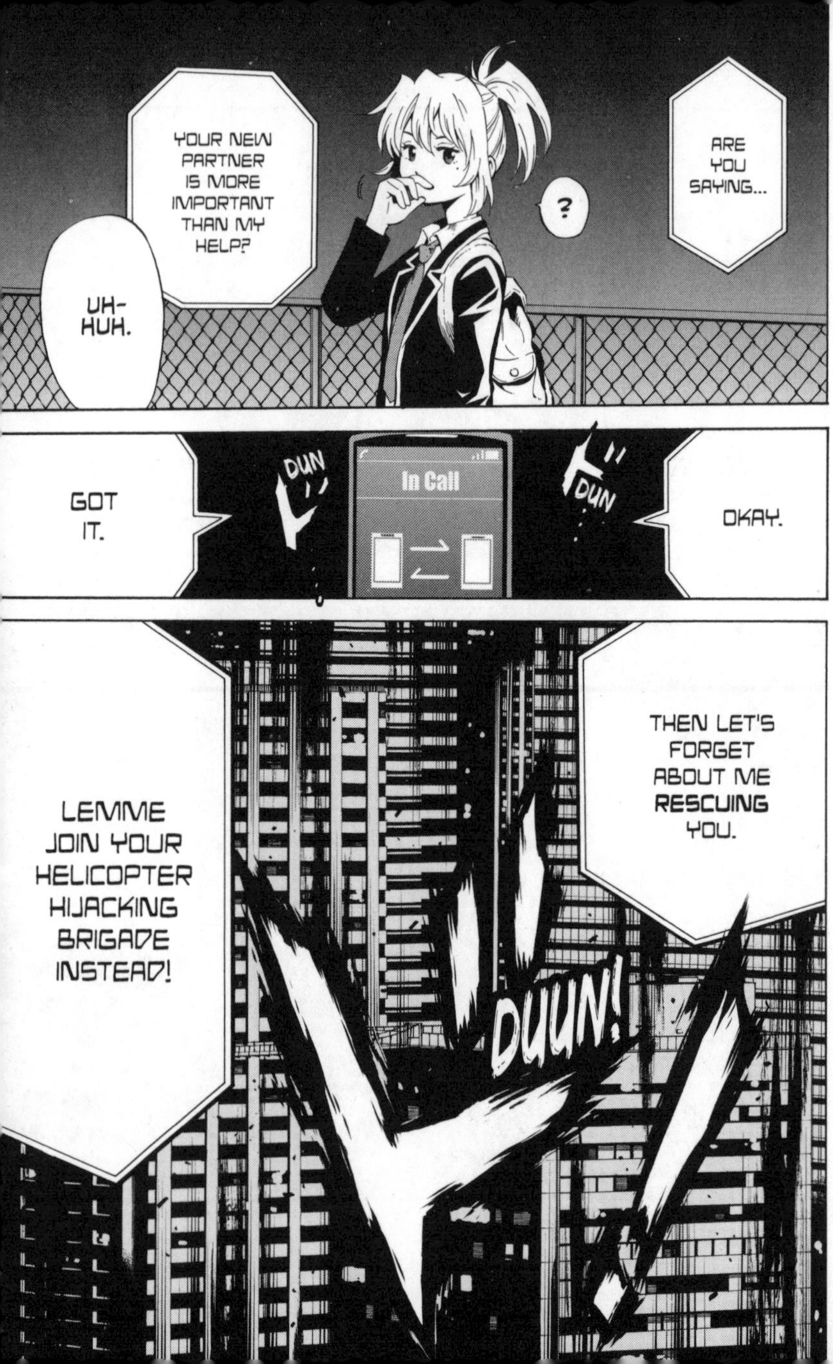
ARE YOU SAYING...
?
YOUR NEW PARTNER IS MORE IMPORTANT THAN MY HELP?
UH-HUH.
OKAY.
DUN
In Call
DUN
GOT IT.
THEN LET'S FORGET ABOUT ME RESCUING YOU.
DUUN!
LEMME JOIN YOUR HELICOPTER HIJACKING BRIGADE INSTEAD!

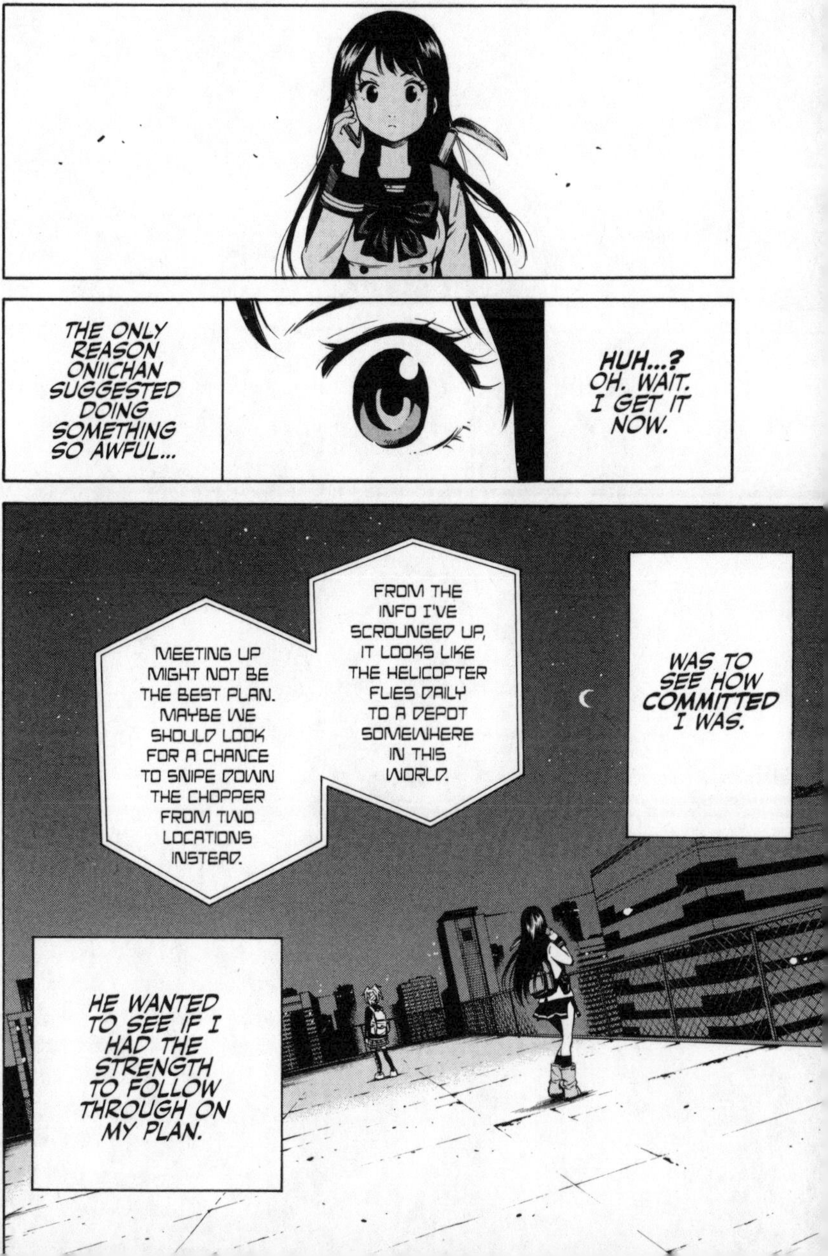
HUH...? OH. WAIT. I GET IT NOW.
THE ONLY REASON ONIICHAN SUGGESTED DOING SOMETHING SO AWFUL...
WAS TO SEE HOW COMMITTED I WAS.
FROM THE INFO I'VE SCROUNGED UP, IT LOOKS LIKE THE HELICOPTER FLIES DAILY TO A DEPOT SOMEWHERE IN THIS WORLD.
MEETING UP MIGHT NOT BE THE BEST PLAN. MAYBE WE SHOULD LOOK FOR A CHANCE TO SNIPE DOWN THE CHOPPER FROM TWO LOCATIONS INSTEAD.
HE WANTED TO SEE IF I HAD THE STRENGTH TO FOLLOW THROUGH ON MY PLAN.

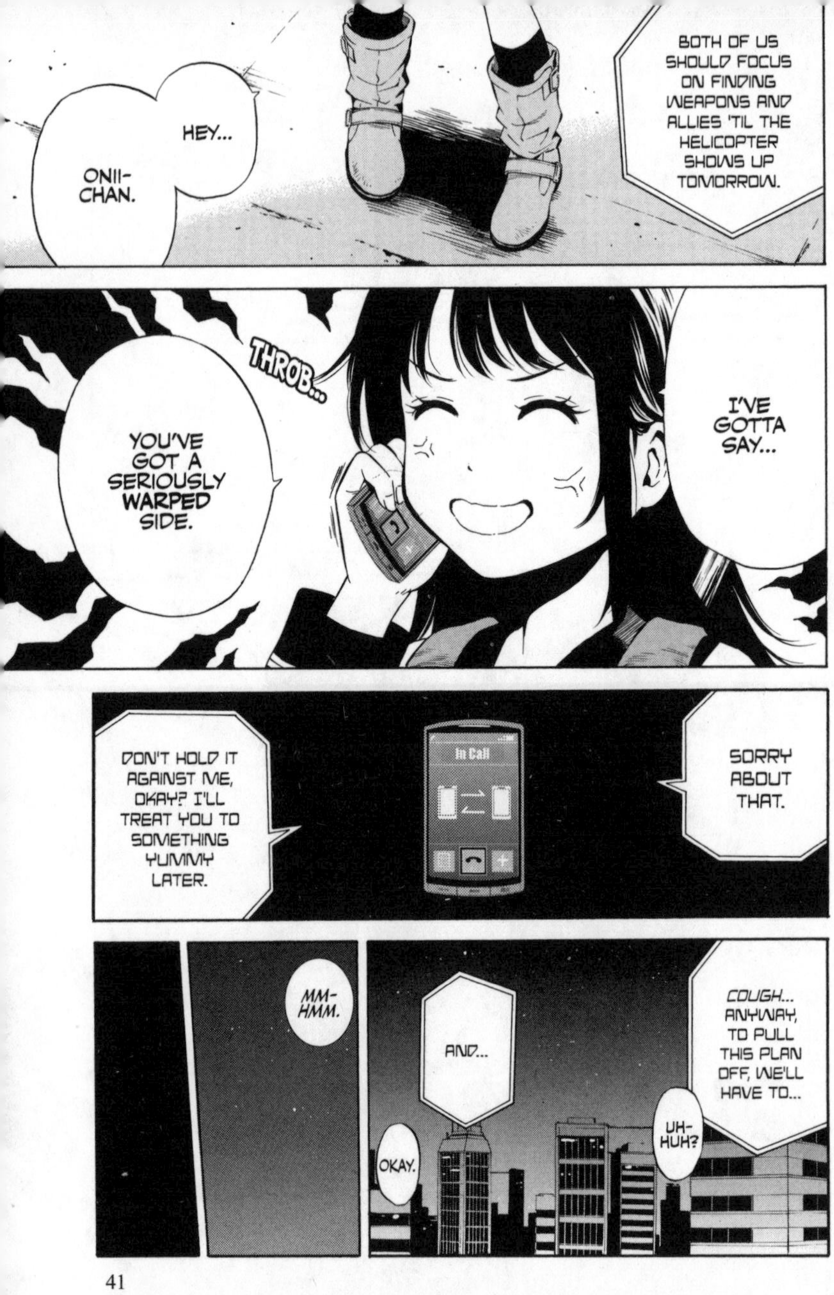
BOTH OF US SHOULD FOCUS ON FINDING WEAPONS AND ALLIES 'TIL THE HELICOPTER SHOWS UP TOMORROW.
HEY... ONII-CHAN.
I'VE GOTTA SAY...
THROB...
YOU'VE GOT A SERIOUSLY WARPED SIDE.
SORRY ABOUT THAT.
In Call
DON'T HOLD IT AGAINST ME, OKAY? I'LL TREAT YOU TO SOMETHING YUMMY LATER.
COUGH... ANYWAY, TO PULL THIS PLAN OFF, WE'LL HAVE TO...
UH-HUH?
AND...
OKAY.
MM-HMM.

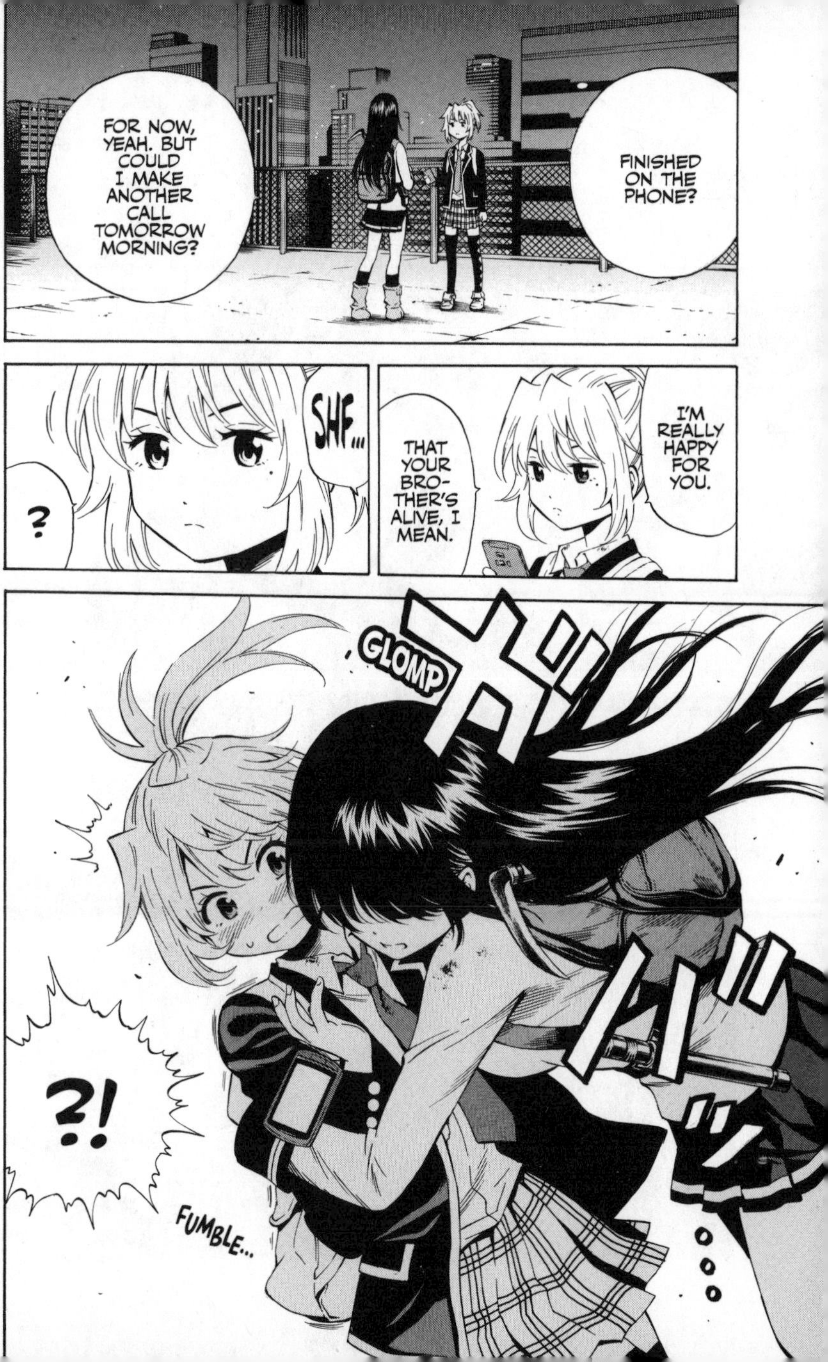
FINISHED ON THE PHONE?
FOR NOW, YEAH. BUT COULD I MAKE ANOTHER CALL TOMORROW MORNING?
I'M REALLY HAPPY FOR YOU.
THAT YOUR BRO-THER'S ALIVE, I MEAN.
SHF...
?
GLOMP
?!
FUMBLE...

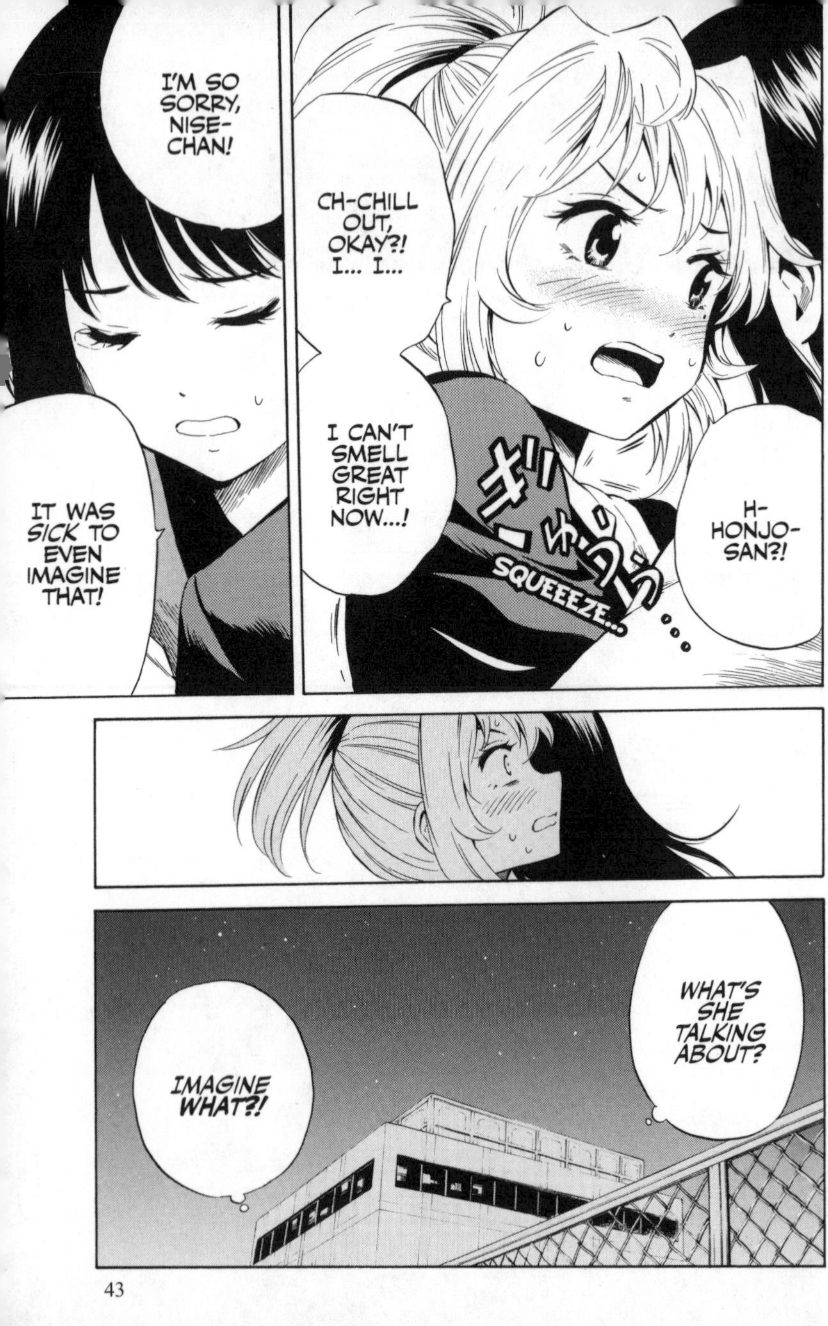
H-HONJO-SAN?!
ぎゅうう
SQUEEEZE...
CH-CHILL OUT, OKAY?! I... I...
I CAN'T SMELL GREAT RIGHT NOW...!
I'M SO SORRY, NISE-CHAN!
IT WAS *SICK* TO EVEN IMAGINE THAT!
WHAT'S SHE TALKING ABOUT?
IMAGINE WHAT?!

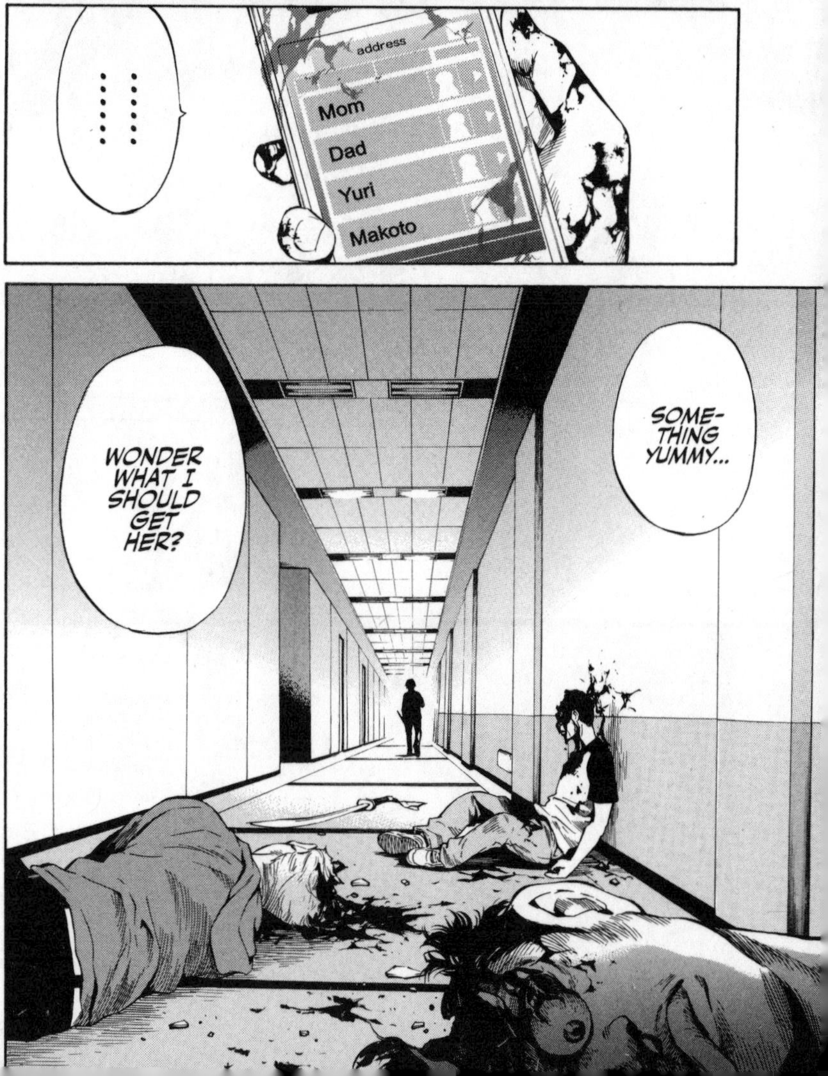
......
address
Mom
Dad
Yuri
Makoto
SOME-THING YUMMY...
WONDER WHAT I SHOULD GET HER?

HIGH-RISE INVASION

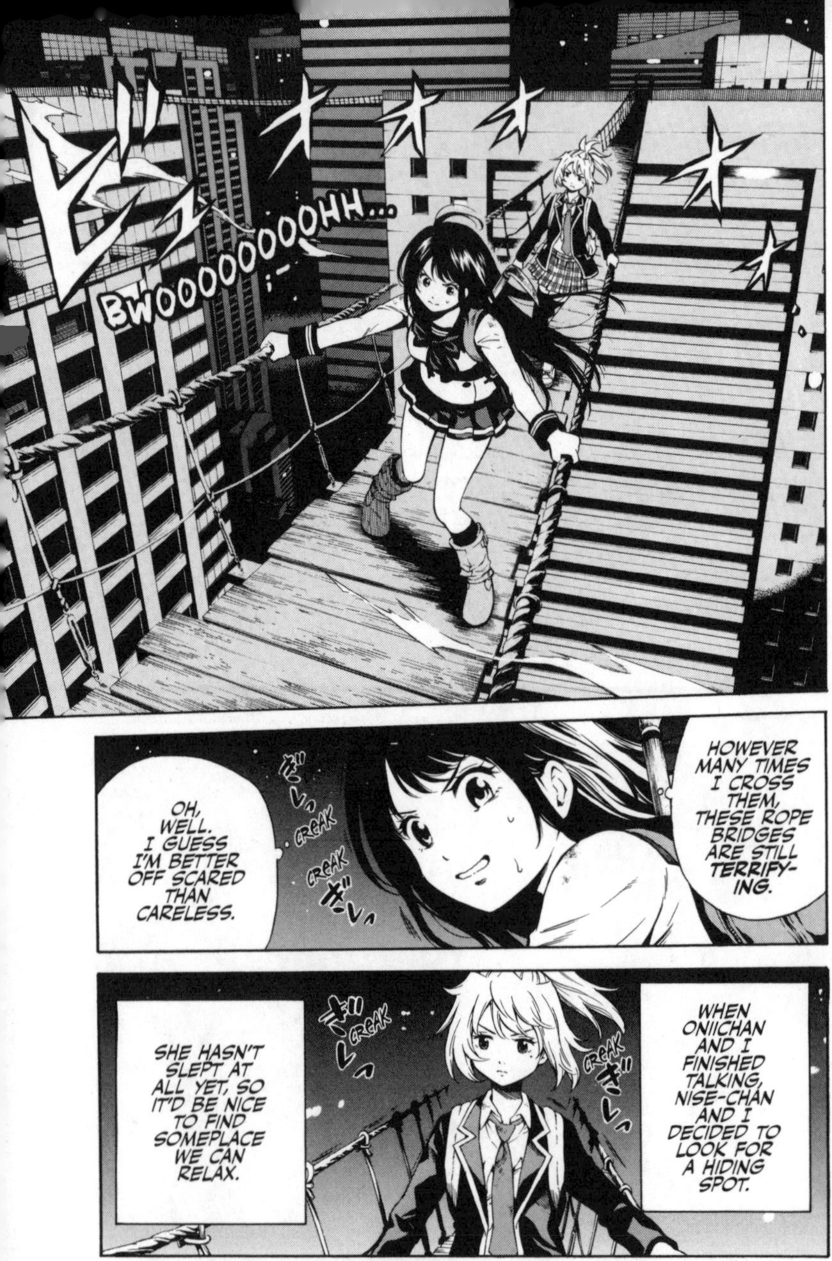
BWOOOOOOOOOHH...
HOWEVER MANY TIMES I CROSS THEM, THESE ROPE BRIDGES ARE STILL TERRIFYING.
CREAK
CREAK
OH, WELL. I GUESS I'M BETTER OFF SCARED THAN CARELESS.
WHEN ONIICHAN AND I FINISHED TALKING, NISE-CHAN AND I DECIDED TO LOOK FOR A HIDING SPOT.
CREAK
CREAK
SHE HASN'T SLEPT AT ALL YET, SO IT'D BE NICE TO FIND SOMEPLACE WE CAN RELAX.

CHAPTER 39: A Lame Name

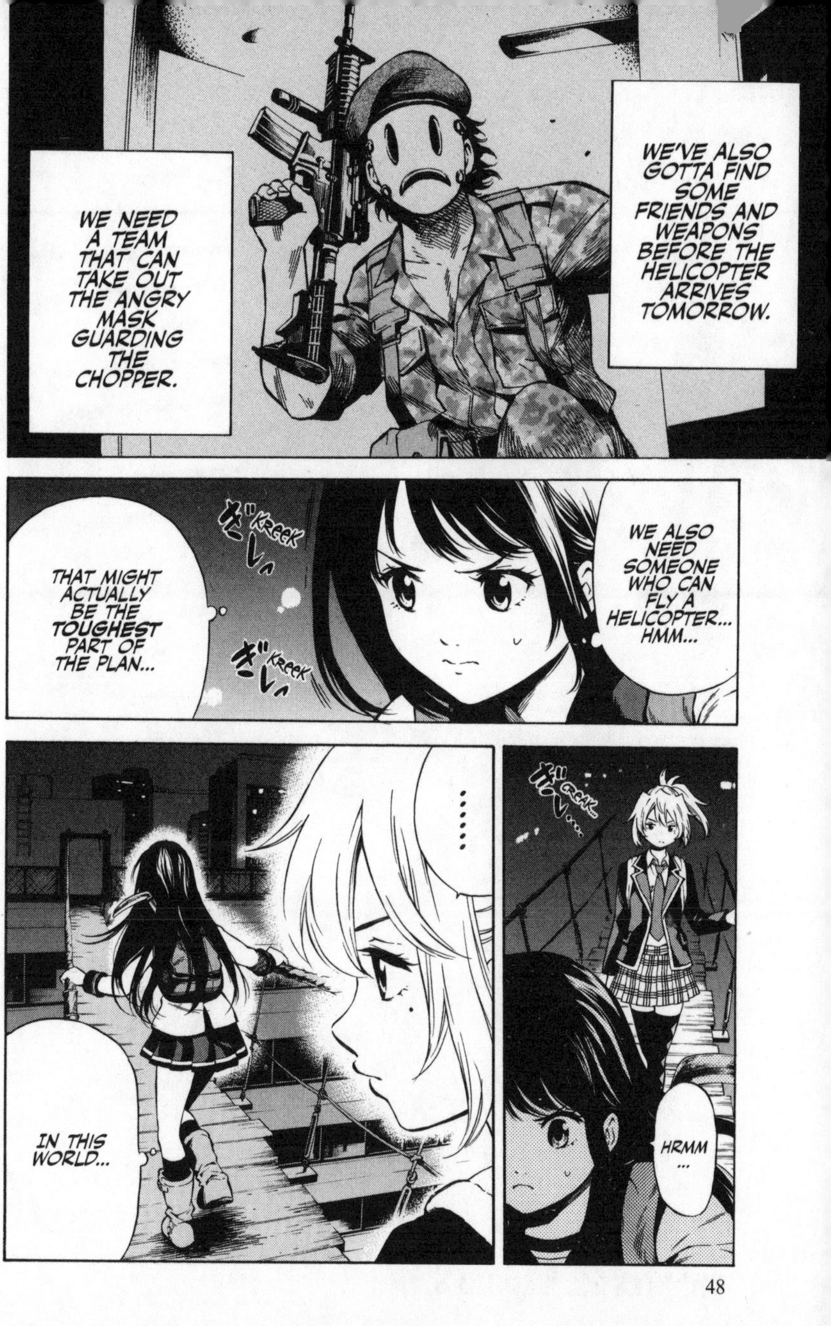
WE'VE ALSO GOTTA FIND SOME FRIENDS AND WEAPONS BEFORE THE HELICOPTER ARRIVES TOMORROW.
WE NEED A TEAM THAT CAN TAKE OUT THE ANGRY MASK GUARDING THE CHOPPER.
WE ALSO NEED SOMEONE WHO CAN FLY A HELICOPTER... HMM...
ぎし KREEK
ぎし KREEK
THAT MIGHT ACTUALLY BE THE TOUGHEST PART OF THE PLAN...
ぎし CREAK...
HRMM ...
......
IN THIS WORLD...

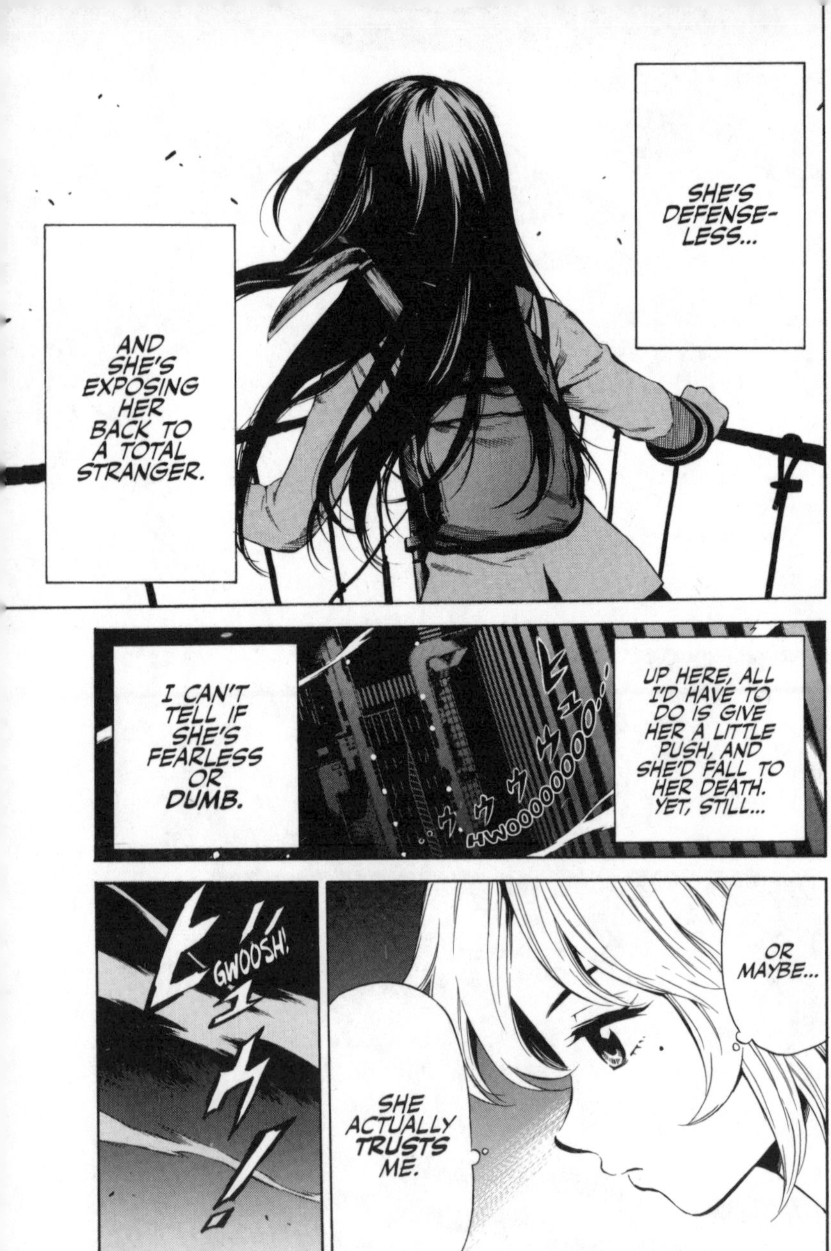
SHE'S DEFENSE-LESS...
AND SHE'S EXPOSING HER BACK TO A TOTAL STRANGER.
UP HERE, ALL I'D HAVE TO DO IS GIVE HER A LITTLE PUSH, AND SHE'D FALL TO HER DEATH. YET, STILL...
HWOOOOOOOO
I CAN'T TELL IF SHE'S FEARLESS OR DUMB.
OR MAYBE...
SHE ACTUALLY TRUSTS ME.
GWOOSH!

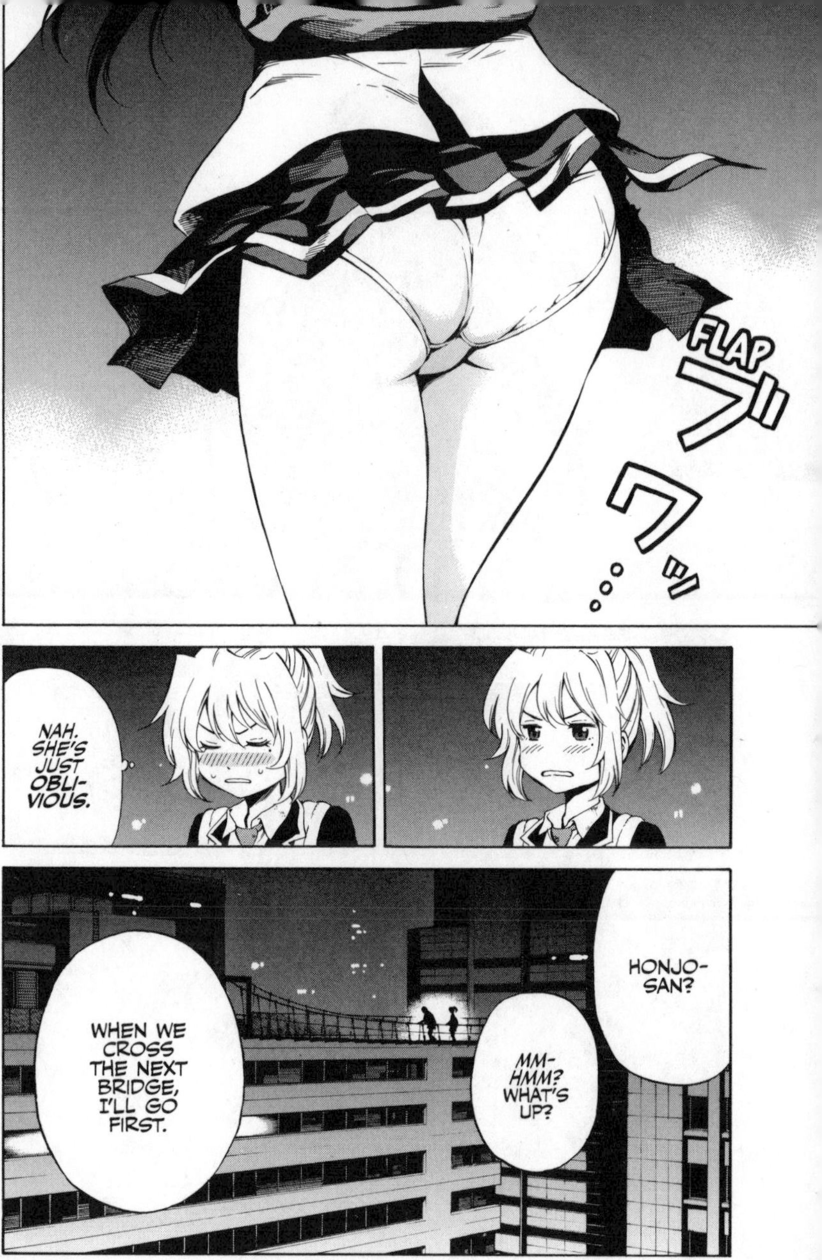
FLAP
ブワッ
NAH. SHE'S JUST OBLI-VIOUS.
HONJO-SAN?
MM-HMM? WHAT'S UP?
WHEN WE CROSS THE NEXT BRIDGE, I'LL GO FIRST.

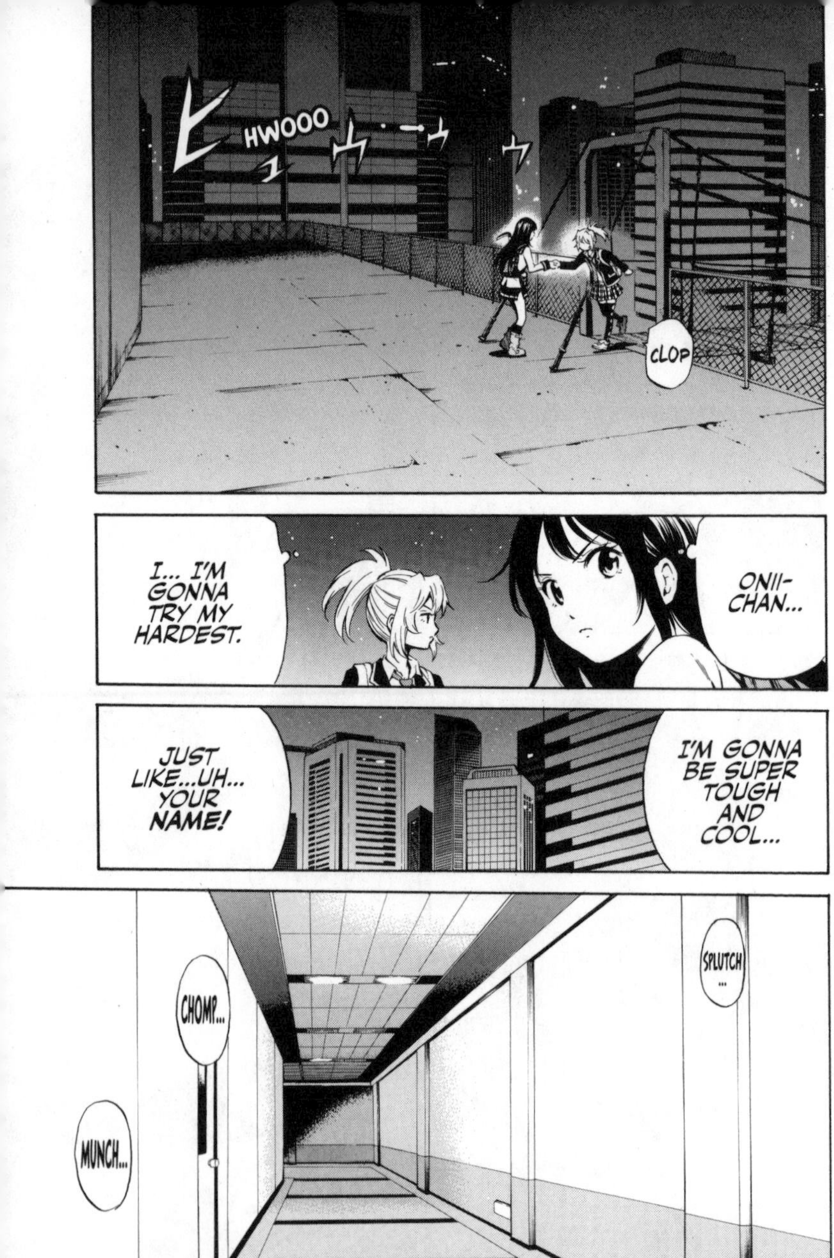
HWOOO
CLOP
ONII-CHAN...
I... I'M GONNA TRY MY HARDEST.
I'M GONNA BE SUPER TOUGH AND COOL...
JUST LIKE...UH... YOUR NAME!
SPLUTCH...
CHOMP...
MUNCH...

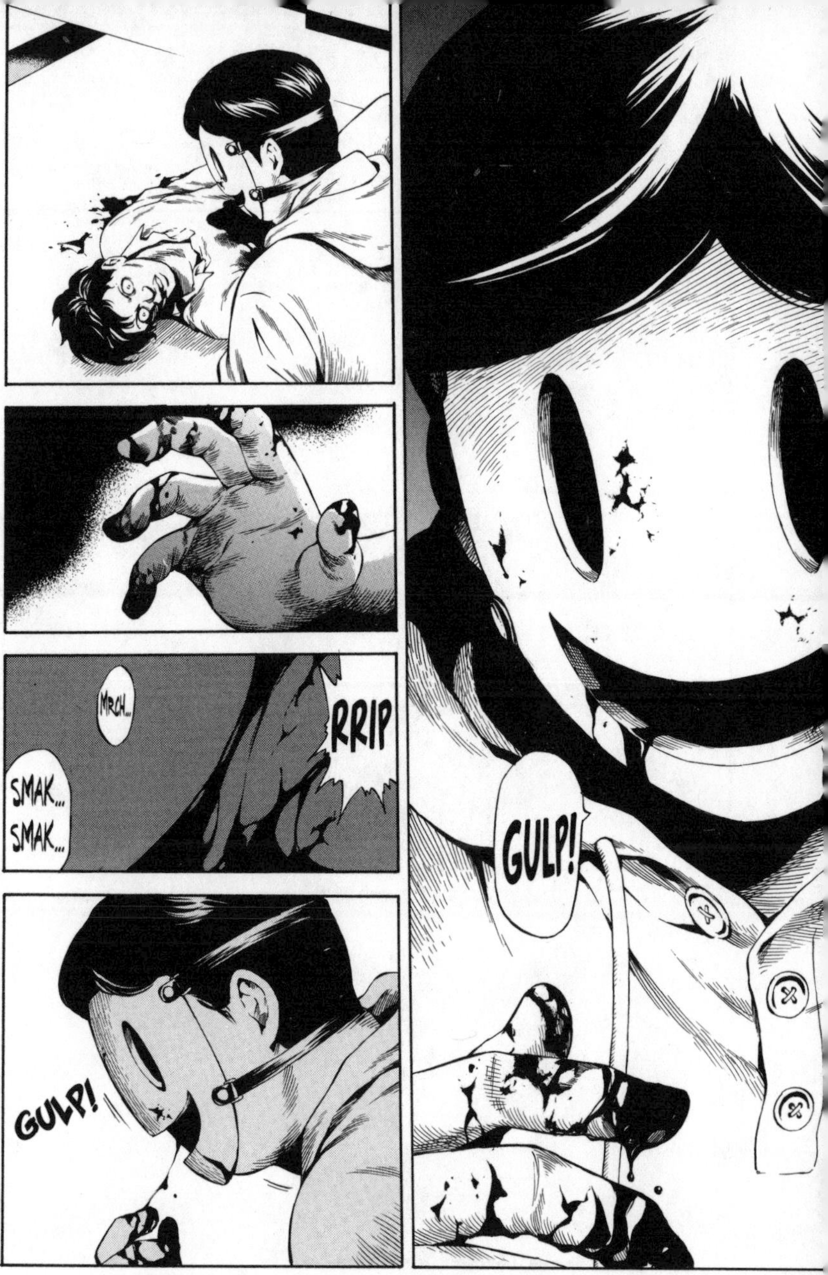
GULP!
MRCH...
RRIP
SMAK... SMAK...
GULP!

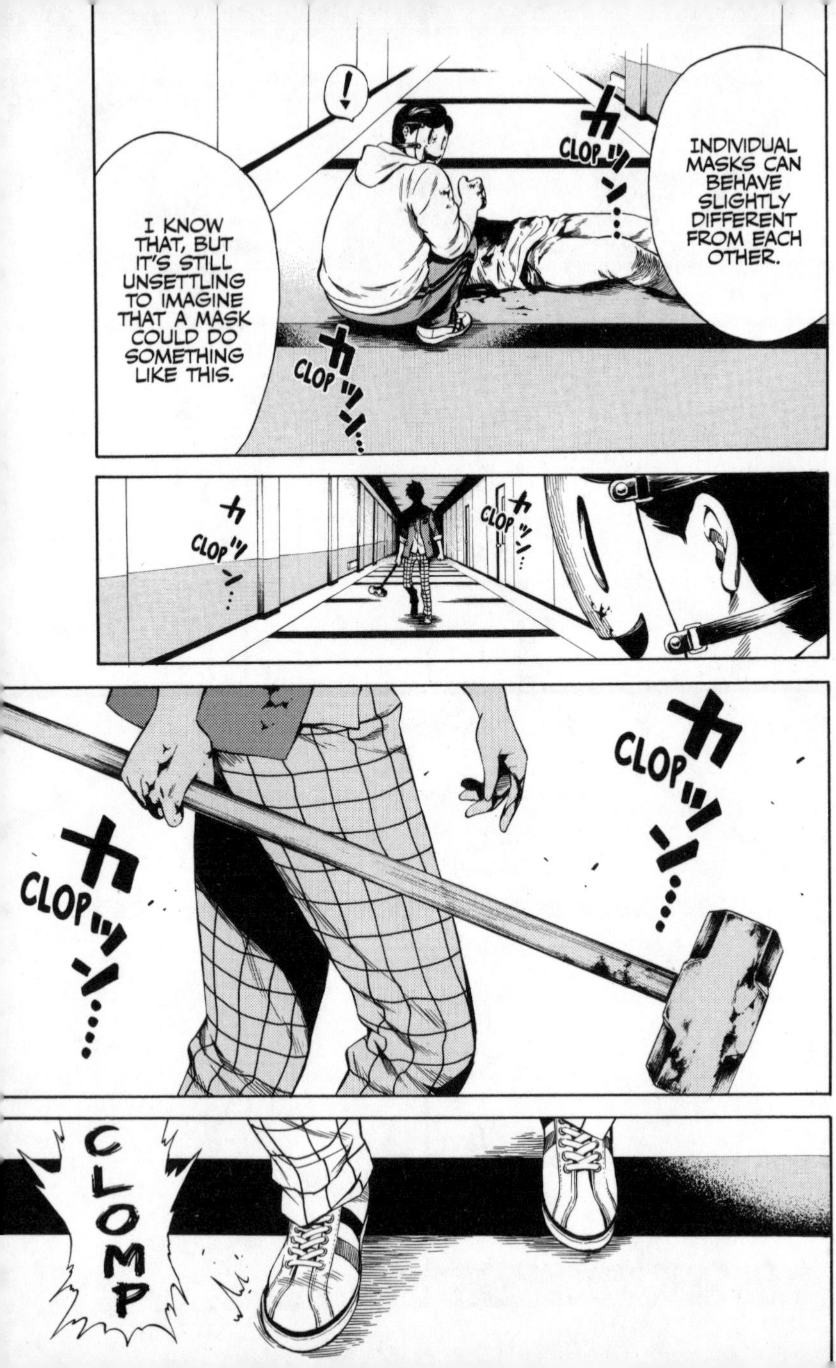
INDIVIDUAL MASKS CAN BEHAVE SLIGHTLY DIFFERENT FROM EACH OTHER.
CLOP
!
I KNOW THAT, BUT IT'S STILL UNSETTLING TO IMAGINE THAT A MASK COULD DO SOMETHING LIKE THIS.
CLOP
CLOP
CLOP
CLOP
CLOP
CLOMP

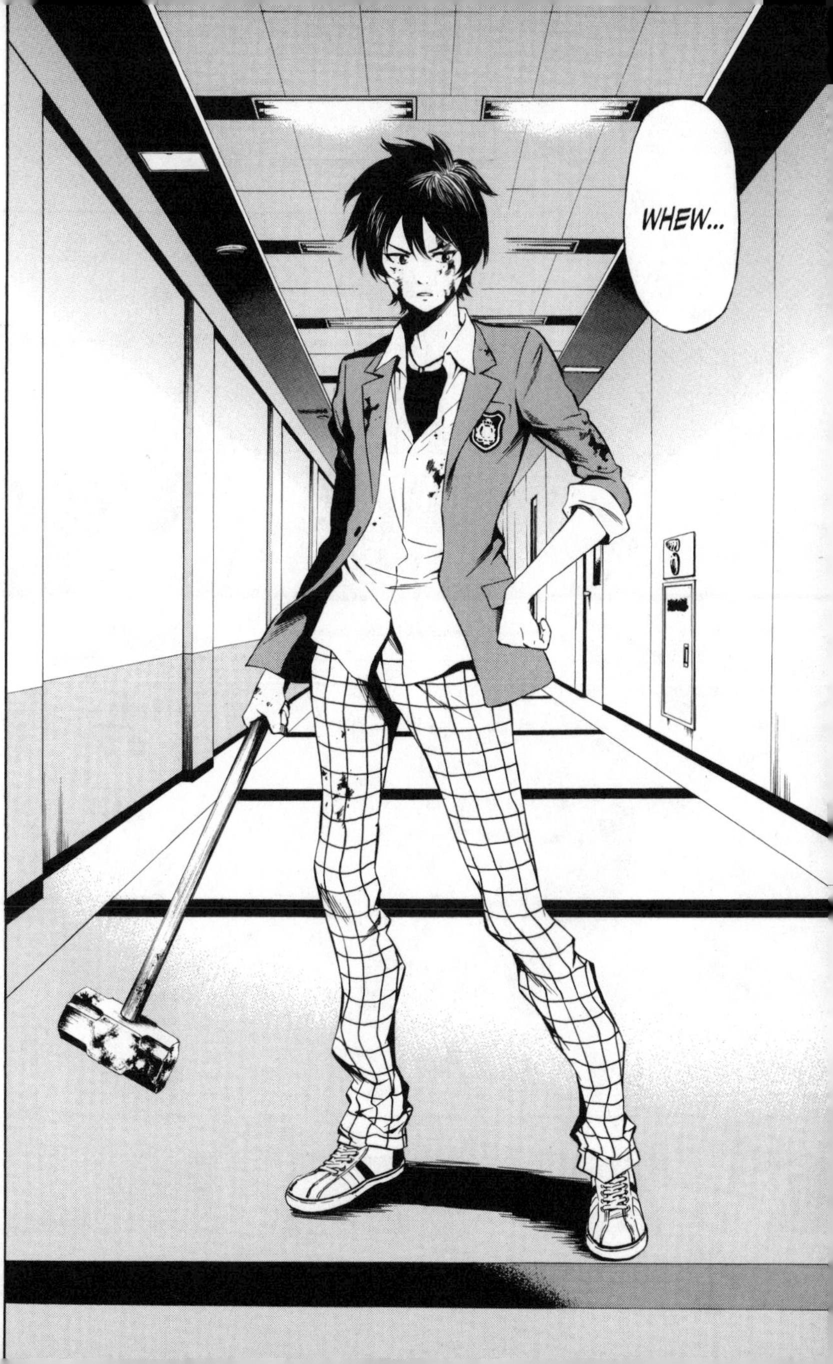
WHEW...

HAAAH...
ARE YOU ABLE TO TALK?
I JUST WANNA MAKE SURE.
SHF...
......
SIGH...

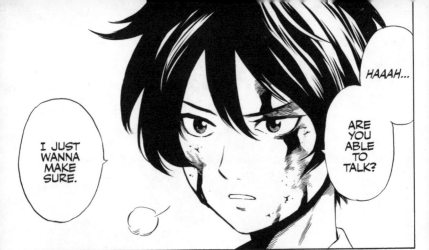

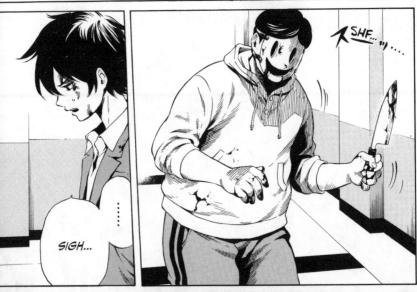

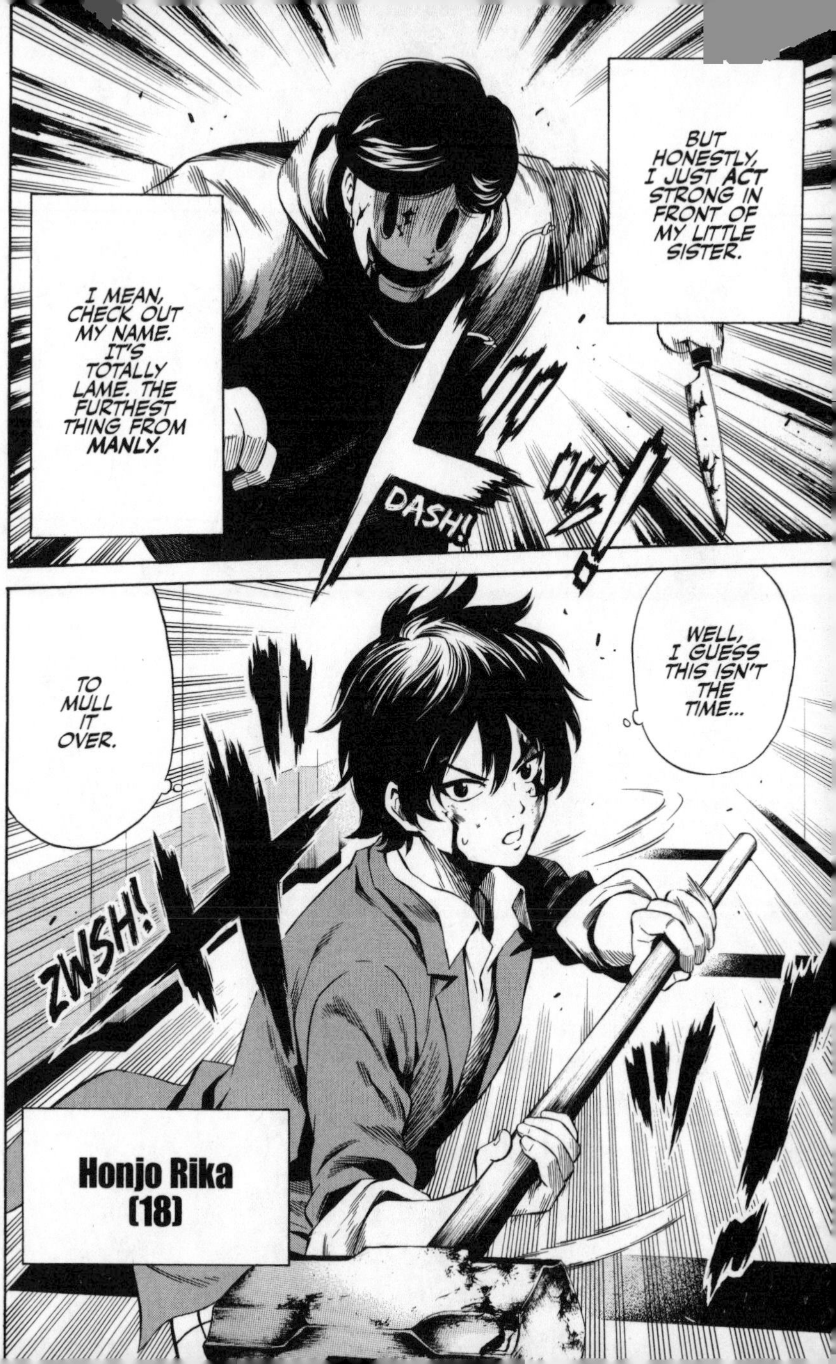
BUT HONESTLY, I JUST ACT STRONG IN FRONT OF MY LITTLE SISTER.
I MEAN, CHECK OUT MY NAME. IT'S TOTALLY LAME. THE FURTHEST THING FROM MANLY.
DASH!
WELL, I GUESS THIS ISN'T THE TIME...
TO MULL IT OVER.
ZWSH!
Honjo Rika (18)

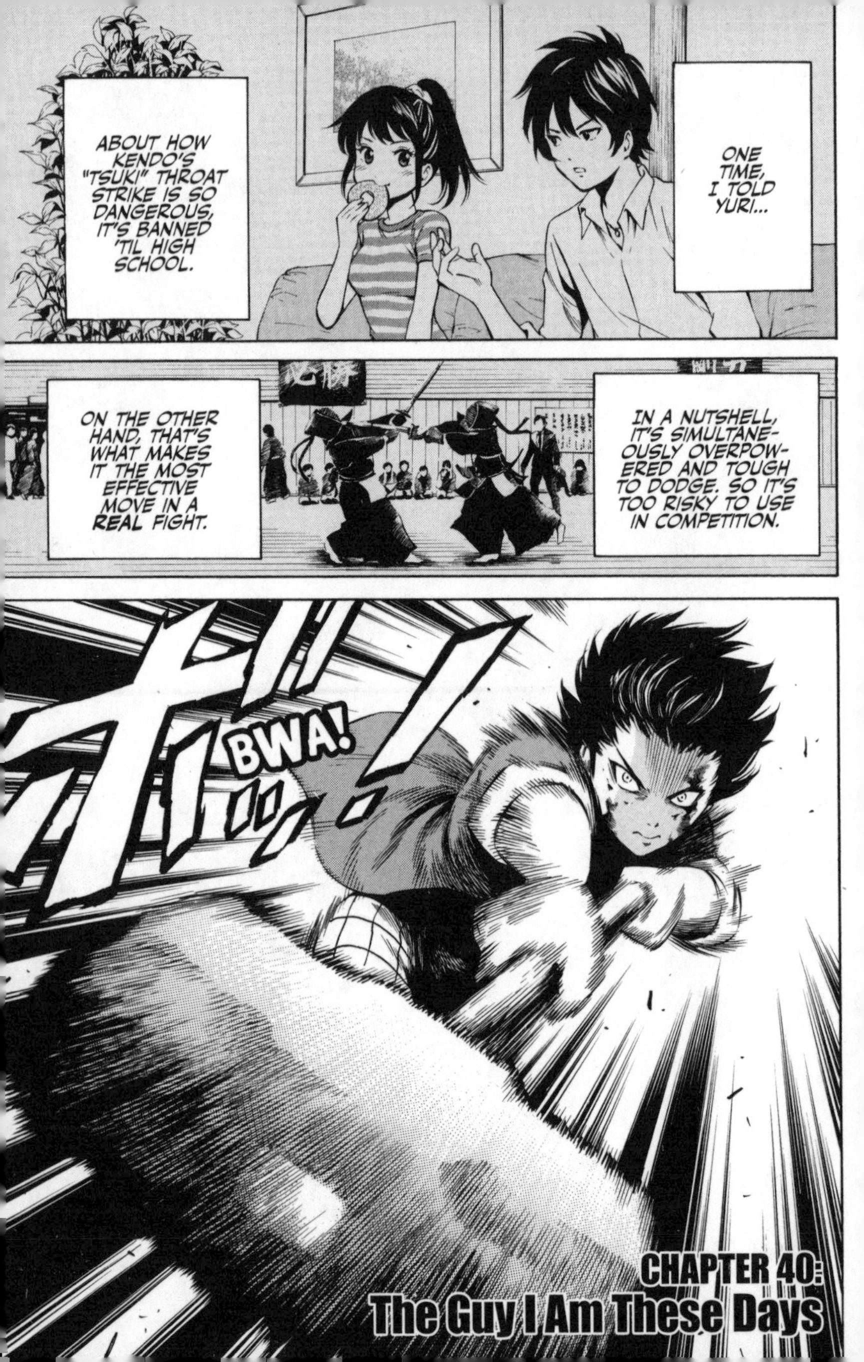
ONE TIME, I TOLD YURI...
ABOUT HOW KENDO'S "TSUKI" THROAT STRIKE IS SO DANGEROUS, IT'S BANNED 'TIL HIGH SCHOOL.
IN A NUTSHELL, IT'S SIMULTANE-OUSLY OVERPOW-ERED AND TOUGH TO DODGE. SO IT'S TOO RISKY TO USE IN COMPETITION.
ON THE OTHER HAND, THAT'S WHAT MAKES IT THE MOST EFFECTIVE MOVE IN A REAL FIGHT.
BWA!
CHAPTER 40:
The Guy I Am These Days

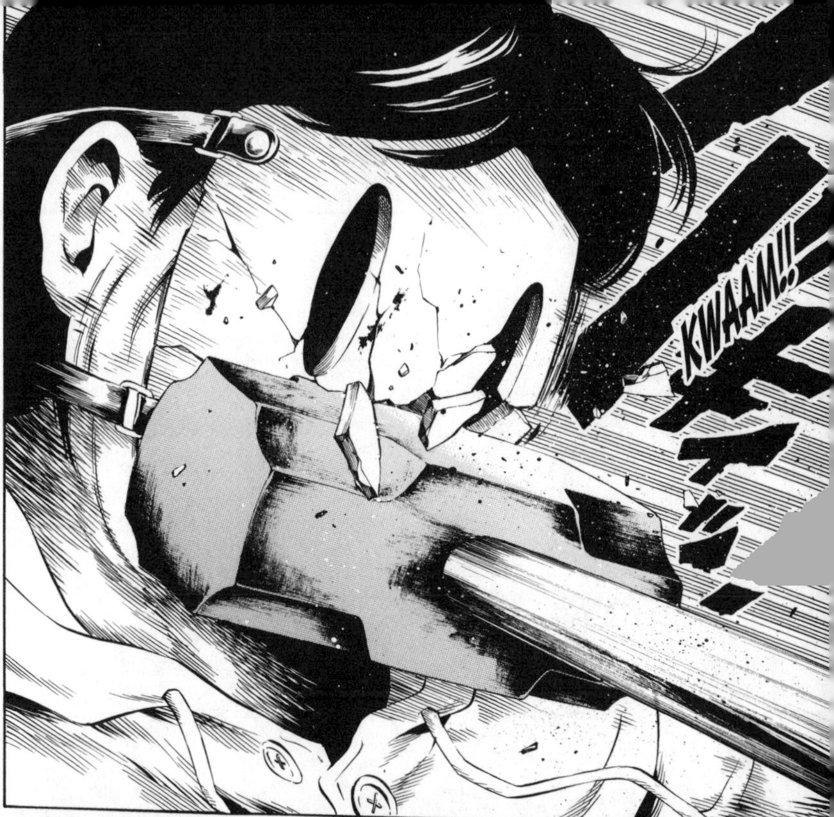
KWAAM!!

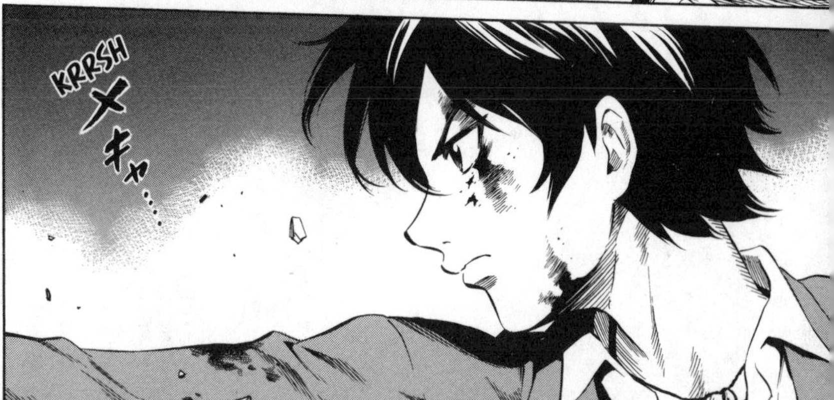
KRRSH
メキャ.....

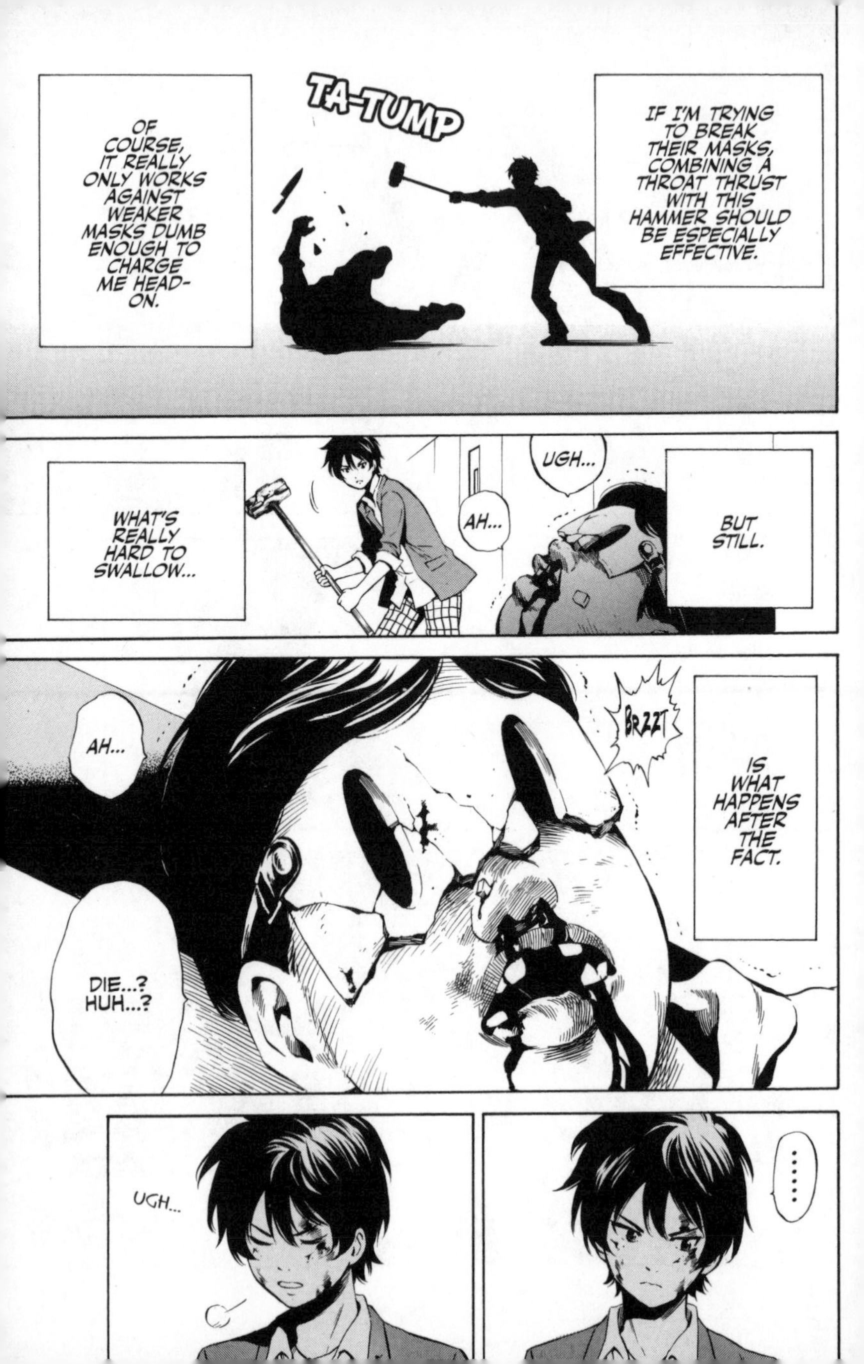
IF I'M TRYING TO BREAK THEIR MASKS, COMBINING A THROAT THRUST WITH THIS HAMMER SHOULD BE ESPECIALLY EFFECTIVE.
TA-TUMP
OF COURSE, IT REALLY ONLY WORKS AGAINST WEAKER MASKS DUMB ENOUGH TO CHARGE ME HEAD-ON.
BUT STILL.
UGH...
AH...
WHAT'S REALLY HARD TO SWALLOW...
BRZZT
IS WHAT HAPPENS AFTER THE FACT.
AH...
DIE...? HUH...?
......
UGH...

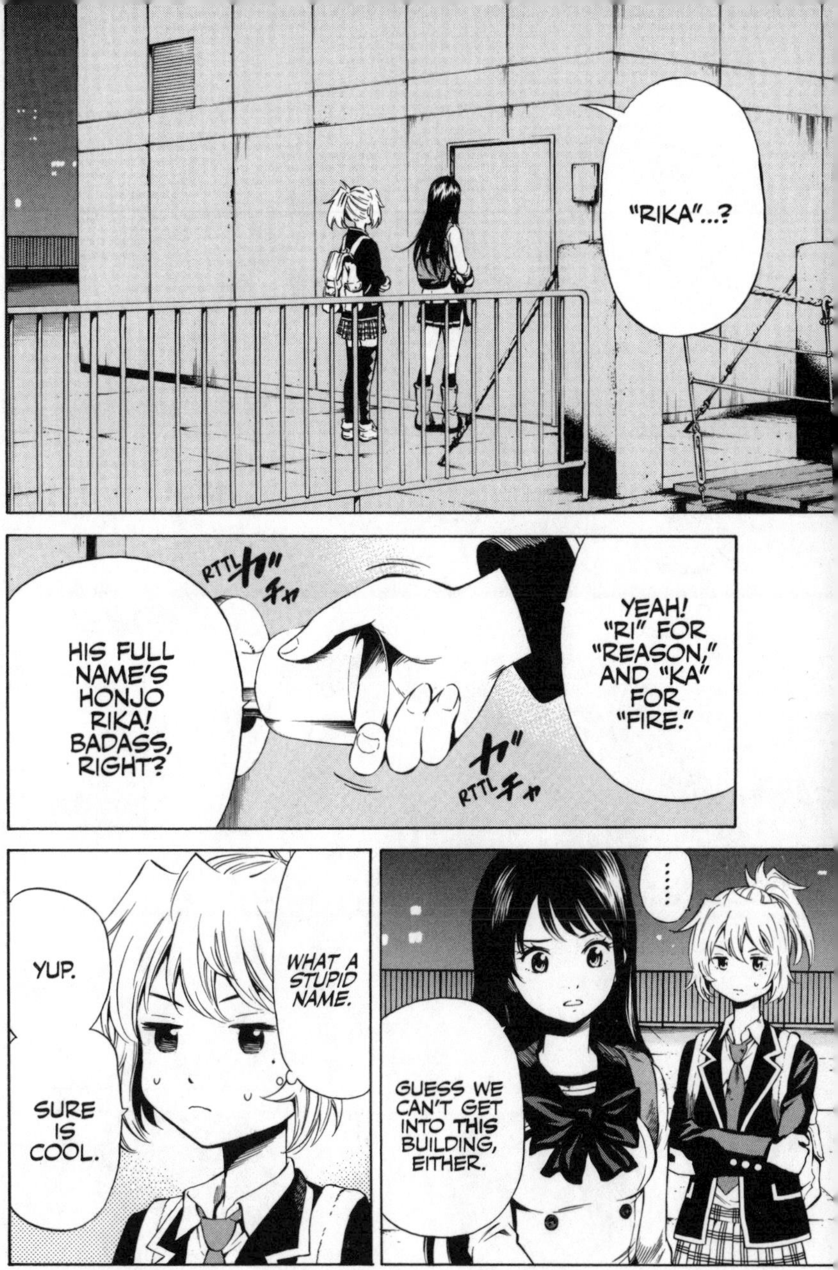
"RIKA"...?
YEAH! "RI" FOR "REASON," AND "KA" FOR "FIRE."
RTTL ガチャ
HIS FULL NAME'S HONJO RIKA! BADASS, RIGHT?
RTTL ガチャ
......
GUESS WE CAN'T GET INTO THIS BUILDING, EITHER.
WHAT A STUPID NAME.
YUP.
SURE IS COOL.

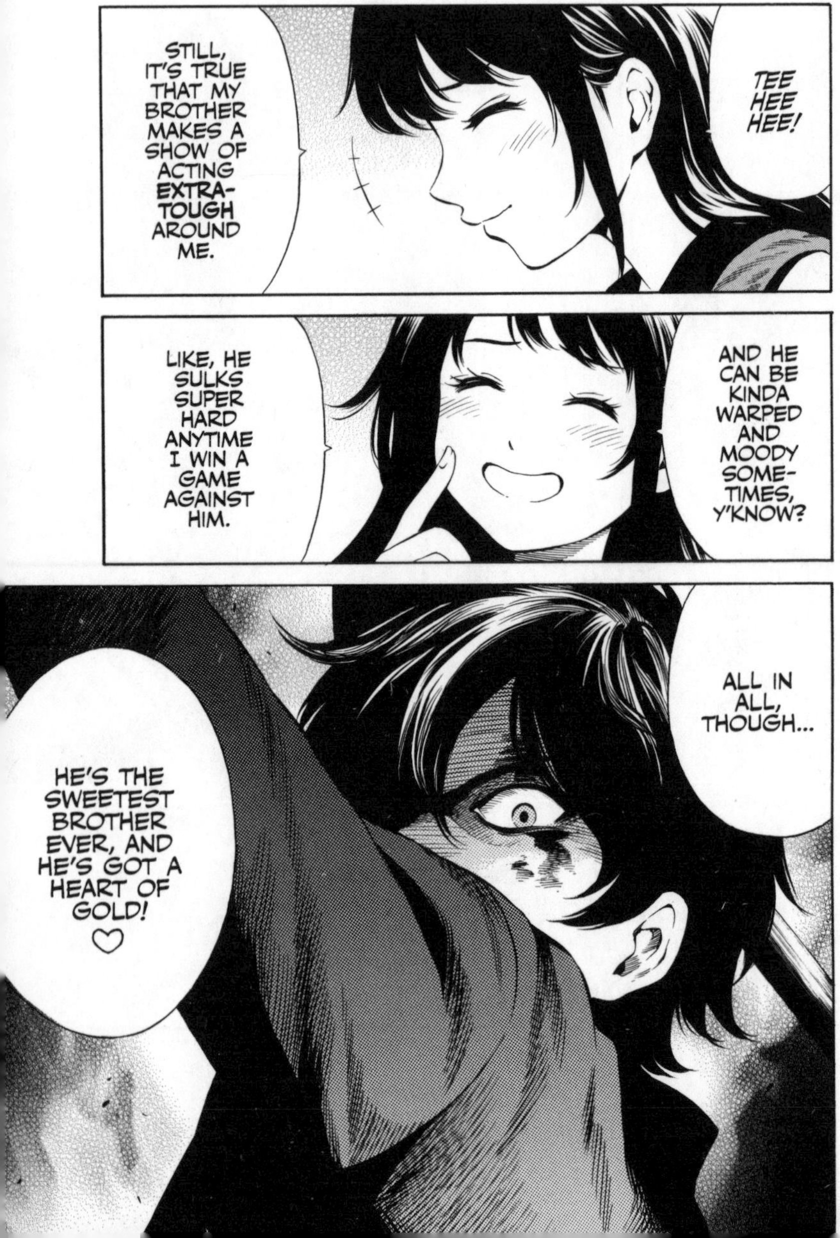
TEE HEE HEE!
STILL, IT'S TRUE THAT MY BROTHER MAKES A SHOW OF ACTING **EXTRA-TOUGH** AROUND ME.
AND HE CAN BE KINDA WARPED AND MOODY SOME-TIMES, Y'KNOW?
LIKE, HE SULKS SUPER HARD ANYTIME I WIN A GAME AGAINST HIM.
ALL IN ALL, THOUGH...
HE'S THE SWEETEST BROTHER EVER, AND HE'S GOT A HEART OF GOLD! ♡

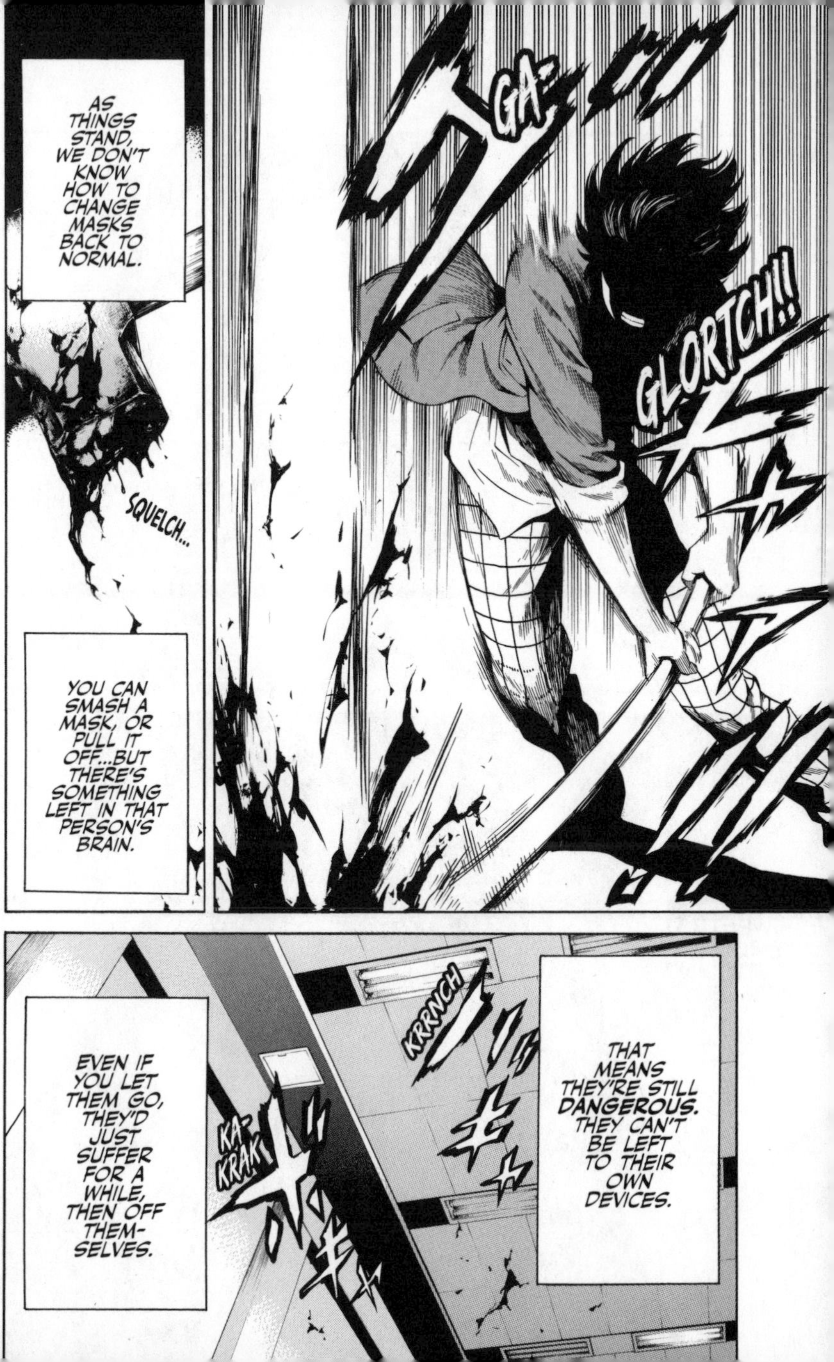
GA-
GLORTCH!!
AS THINGS STAND, WE DON'T KNOW HOW TO CHANGE MASKS BACK TO NORMAL.
SQUELCH...
YOU CAN SMASH A MASK, OR PULL IT OFF...BUT THERE'S SOMETHING LEFT IN THAT PERSON'S BRAIN.
THAT MEANS THEY'RE STILL **DANGEROUS.** THEY CAN'T BE LEFT TO THEIR OWN DEVICES.
KRRNCH
KA-KRAK
EVEN IF YOU LET THEM GO, THEY'D JUST SUFFER FOR A WHILE, THEN OFF THEM-SELVES.

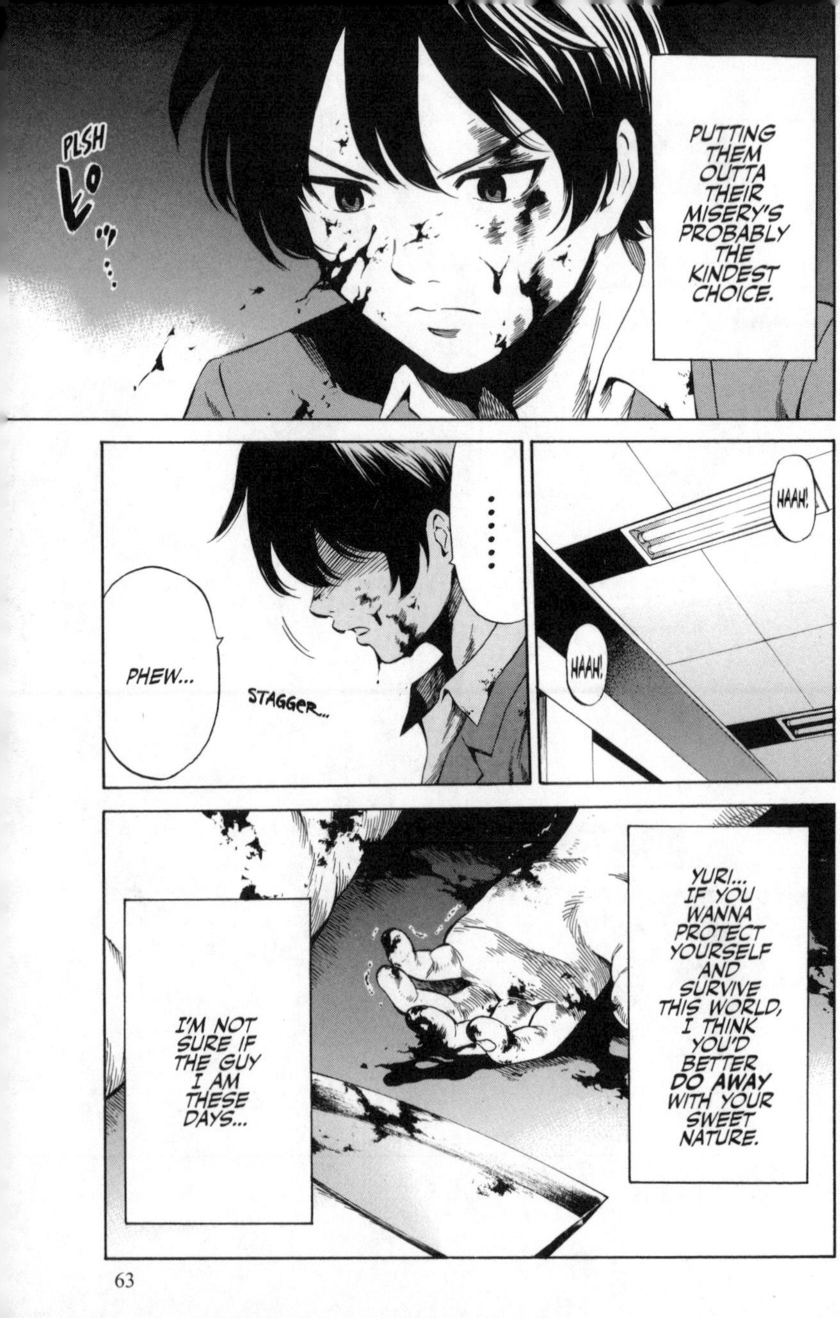
PUTTING THEM OUTTA THEIR MISERY'S PROBABLY THE KINDEST CHOICE.
PLSH
HAAH!
HAAH!
......
PHEW...
STAGGER...
YURI... IF YOU WANNA PROTECT YOURSELF AND SURVIVE THIS WORLD, I THINK YOU'D BETTER DO AWAY WITH YOUR SWEET NATURE.
I'M NOT SURE IF THE GUY I AM THESE DAYS...

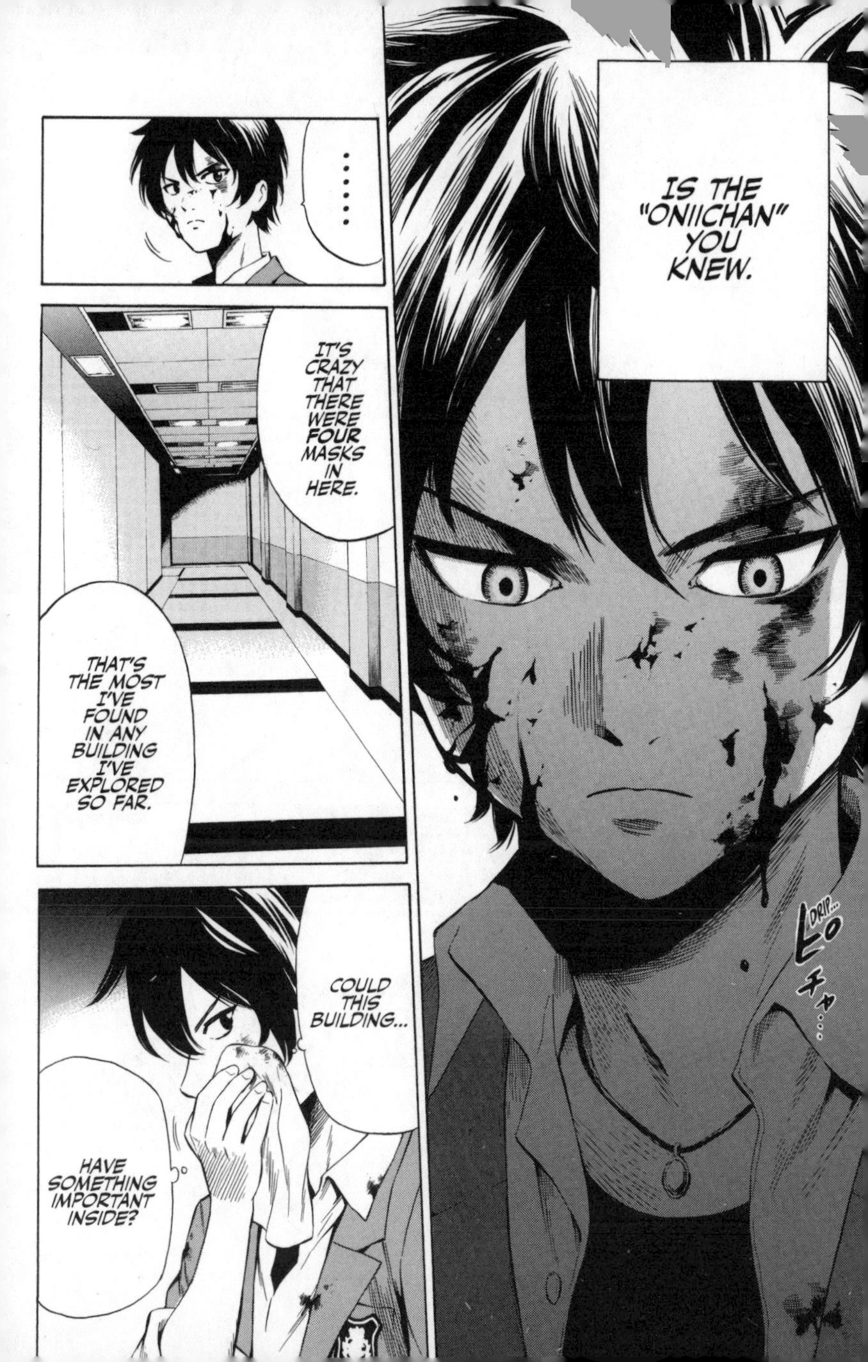
IS THE "ONIICHAN" YOU KNEW.
DRIP...
ピチャ…
......
IT'S CRAZY THAT THERE WERE FOUR MASKS IN HERE.
THAT'S THE MOST I'VE FOUND IN ANY BUILDING I'VE EXPLORED SO FAR.
COULD THIS BUILDING...
HAVE SOMETHING IMPORTANT INSIDE?

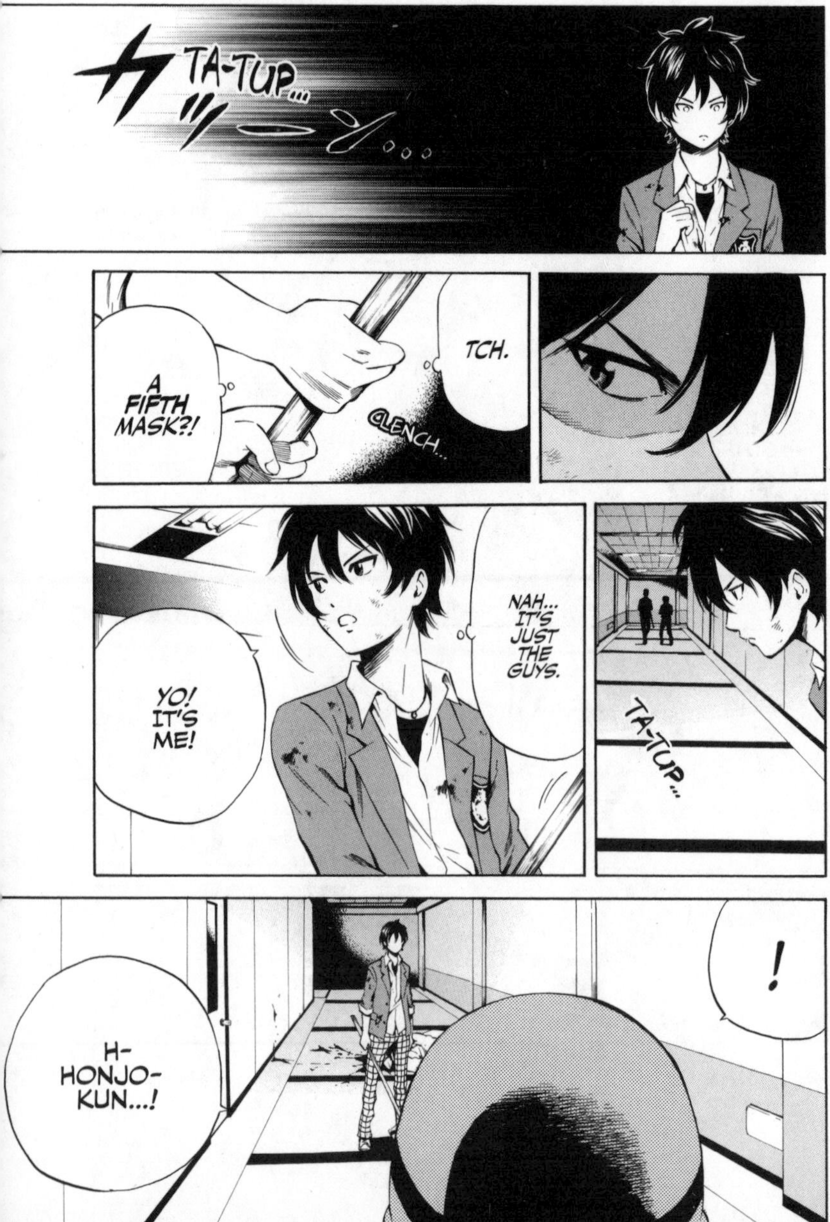
TA-TUP...
TCH.
A FIFTH MASK?!
CLENCH...
TA-TUP...
NAH... IT'S JUST THE GUYS.
YO! IT'S ME!
!
H-HONJO-KUN...!

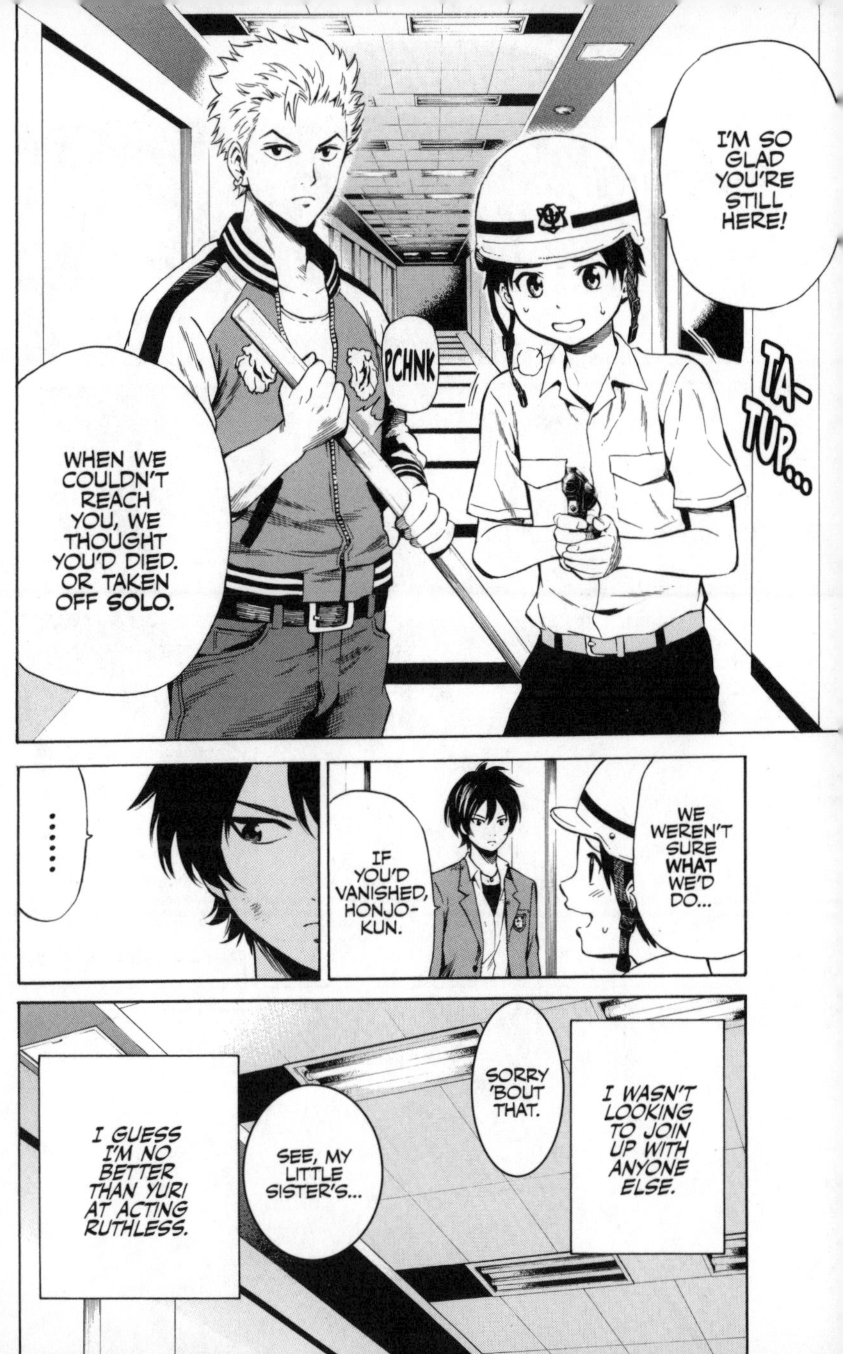
I'M SO GLAD YOU'RE STILL HERE!
TA-TUP...
PCHNK
WHEN WE COULDN'T REACH YOU, WE THOUGHT YOU'D DIED. OR TAKEN OFF SOLO.
WE WEREN'T SURE WHAT WE'D DO...
IF YOU'D VANISHED, HONJO-KUN.
......
I WASN'T LOOKING TO JOIN UP WITH ANYONE ELSE.
SORRY 'BOUT THAT.
SEE, MY LITTLE SISTER'S...
I GUESS I'M NO BETTER THAN YURI AT ACTING RUTHLESS.

HIGH-RISE INVASION

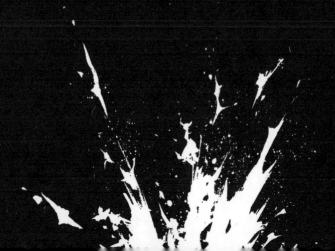

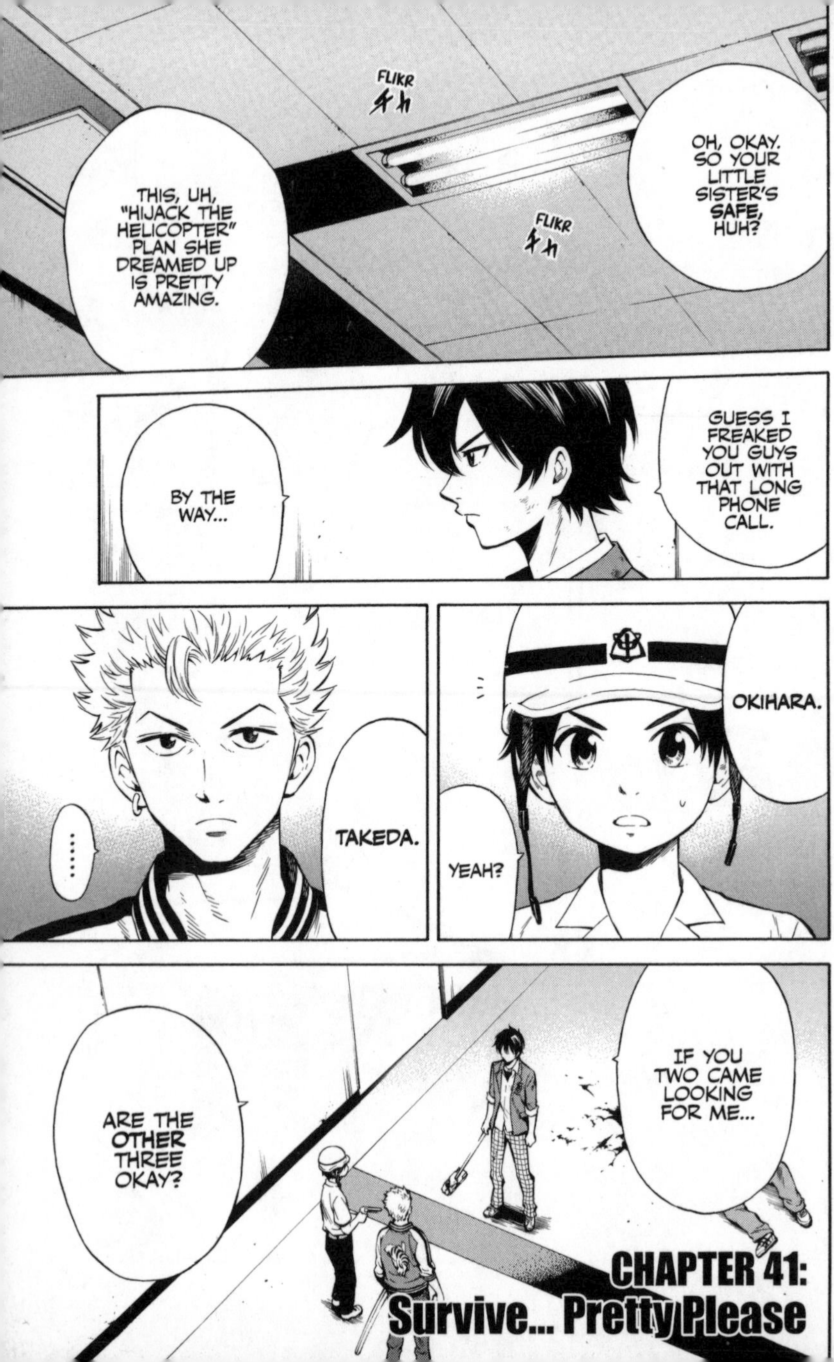
OH, OKAY. SO YOUR LITTLE SISTER'S SAFE, HUH?
FLIKR
FLIKR
THIS, UH, "HIJACK THE HELICOPTER" PLAN SHE DREAMED UP IS PRETTY AMAZING.
GUESS I FREAKED YOU GUYS OUT WITH THAT LONG PHONE CALL.
BY THE WAY...
OKIHARA.
YEAH?
TAKEDA.
......
IF YOU TWO CAME LOOKING FOR ME...
ARE THE OTHER THREE OKAY?
CHAPTER 41:
Survive... Pretty Please

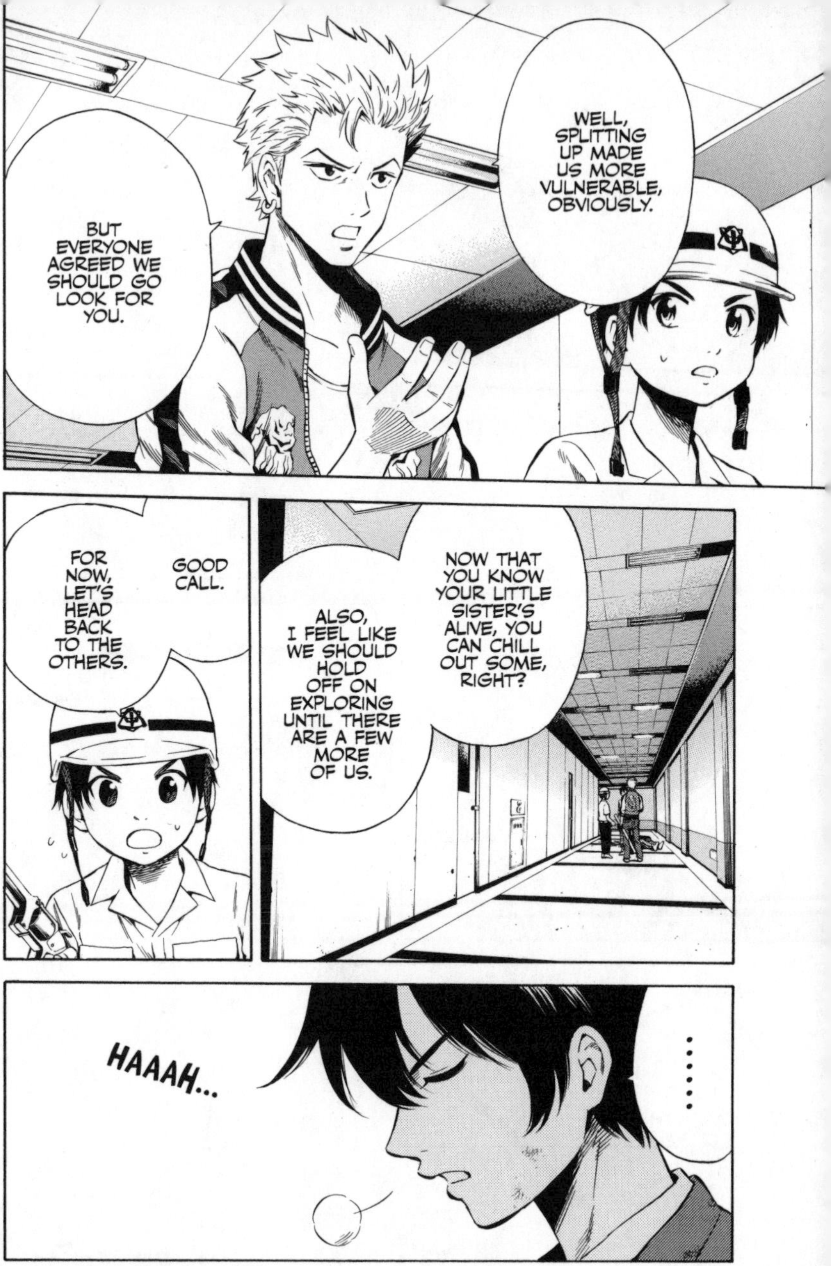
WELL, SPLITTING UP MADE US MORE VULNERABLE, OBVIOUSLY.
BUT EVERYONE AGREED WE SHOULD GO LOOK FOR YOU.
NOW THAT YOU KNOW YOUR LITTLE SISTER'S ALIVE, YOU CAN CHILL OUT SOME, RIGHT?
ALSO, I FEEL LIKE WE SHOULD HOLD OFF ON EXPLORING UNTIL THERE ARE A FEW MORE OF US.
GOOD CALL.
FOR NOW, LET'S HEAD BACK TO THE OTHERS.
......
HAAAH...

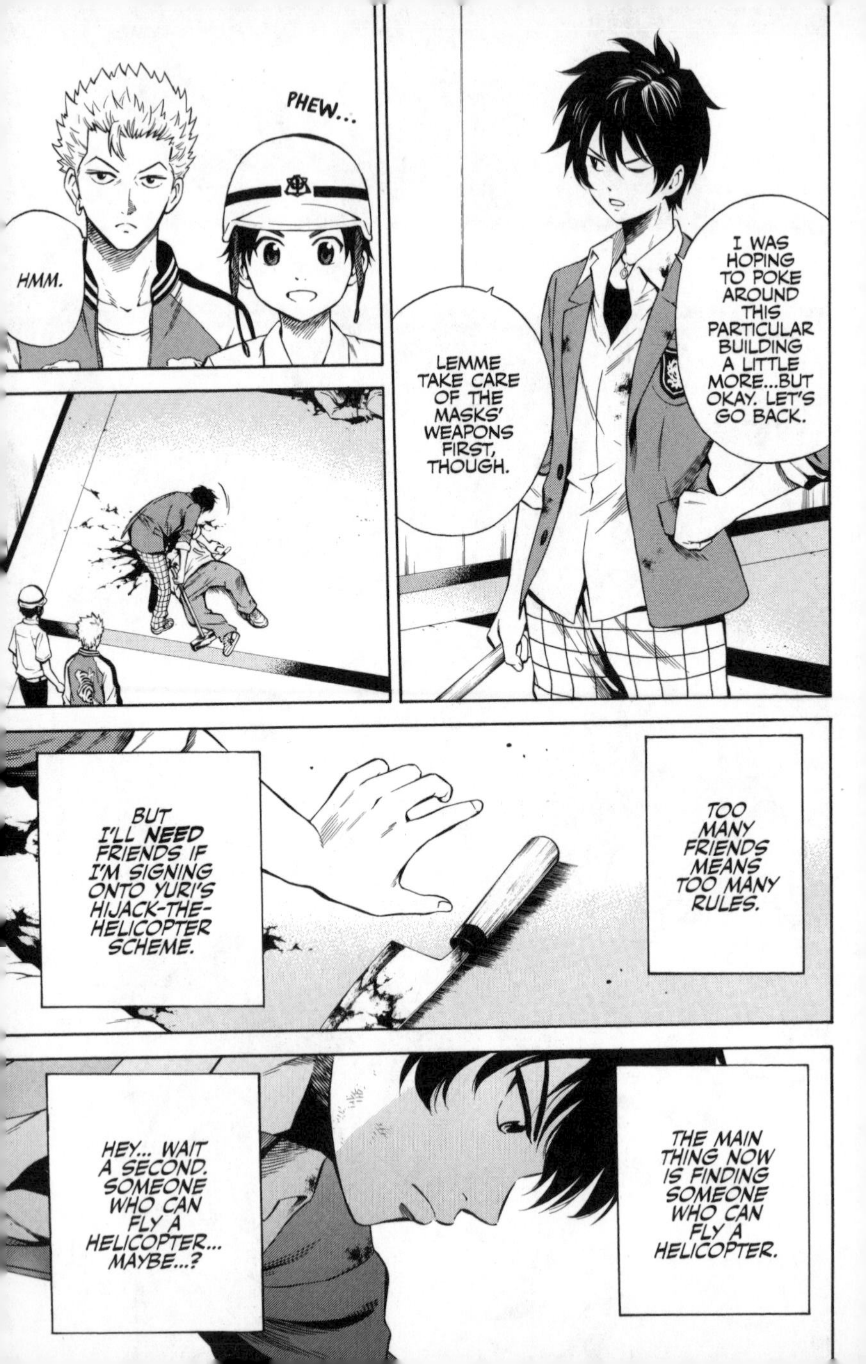
I WAS HOPING TO POKE AROUND THIS PARTICULAR BUILDING A LITTLE MORE...BUT OKAY. LET'S GO BACK.
LEMME TAKE CARE OF THE MASKS' WEAPONS FIRST, THOUGH.
PHEW...
HMM.
TOO MANY FRIENDS MEANS TOO MANY RULES.
BUT I'LL **NEED** FRIENDS IF I'M SIGNING ONTO YURI'S HIJACK-THE-HELICOPTER SCHEME.
THE MAIN THING NOW IS FINDING SOMEONE WHO CAN FLY A HELICOPTER.
HEY... WAIT A SECOND. SOMEONE WHO CAN FLY A HELICOPTER... MAYBE...?

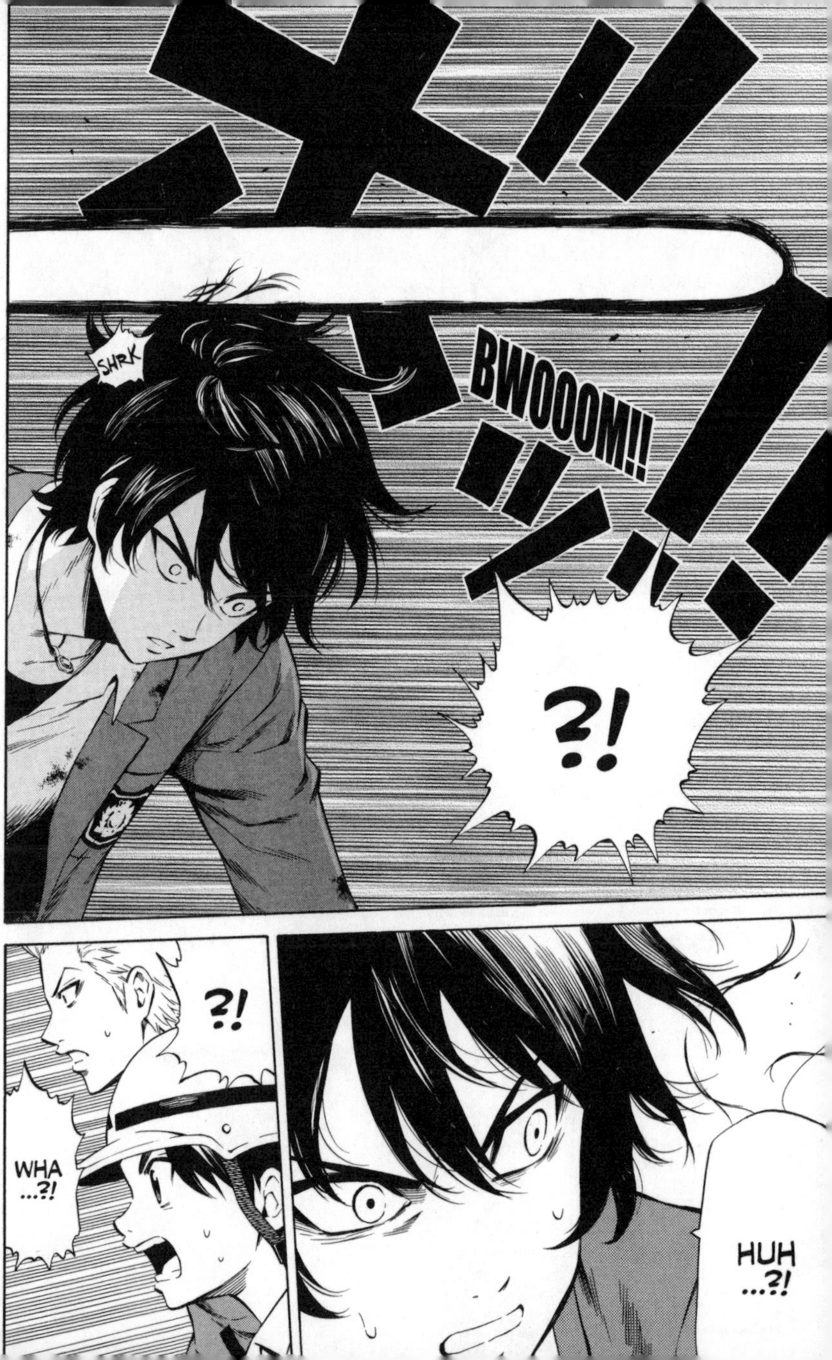
BWOOOM!!
SHRK
?!
HUH ...?!
?!
WHA ...?!

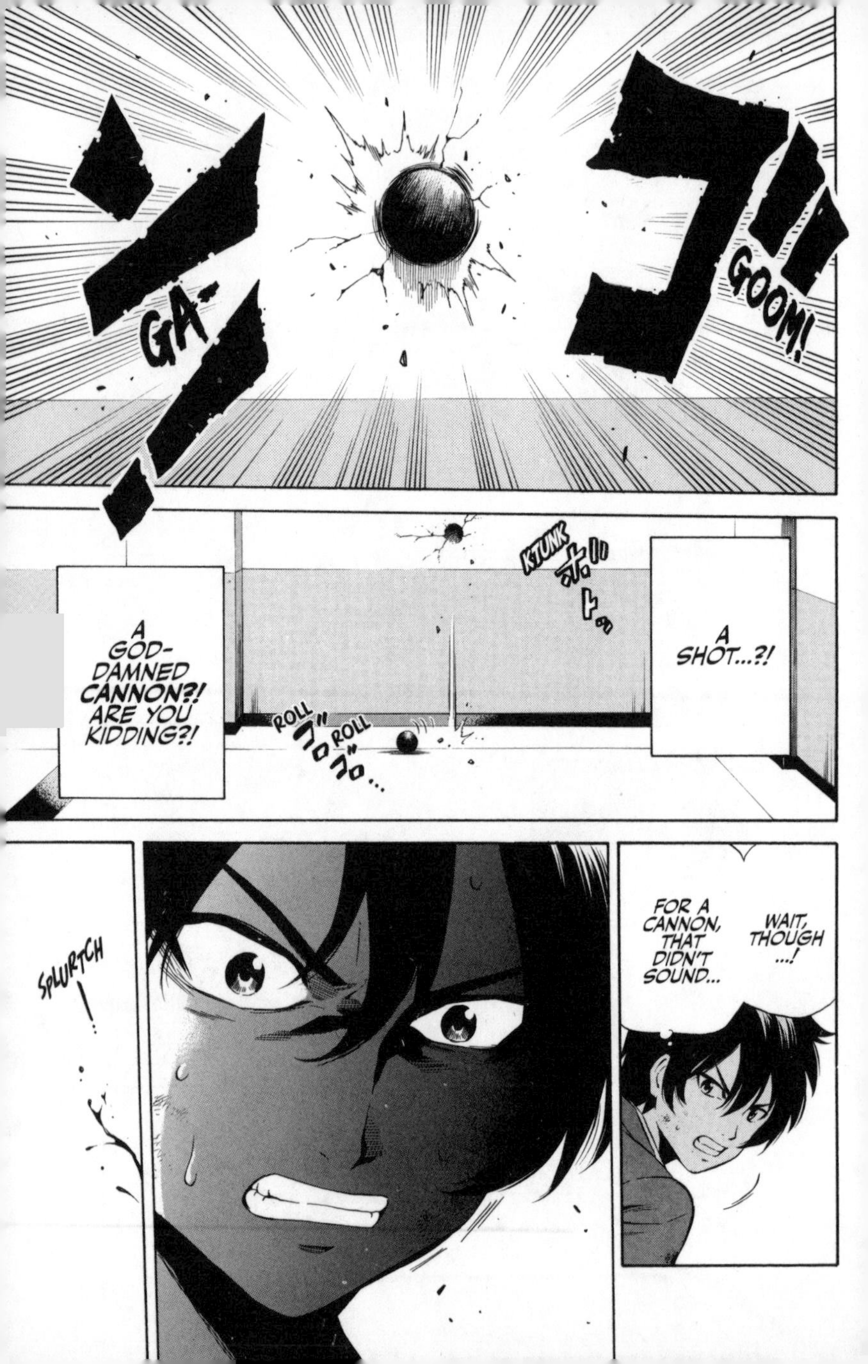
GOOM!
GA-
A SHOT...?!
KTUNK
ROLL ROLL...
A GOD-DAMNED CANNON?! ARE YOU KIDDING?!
WAIT, THOUGH...!
FOR A CANNON, THAT DIDN'T SOUND...
SPLURTCH

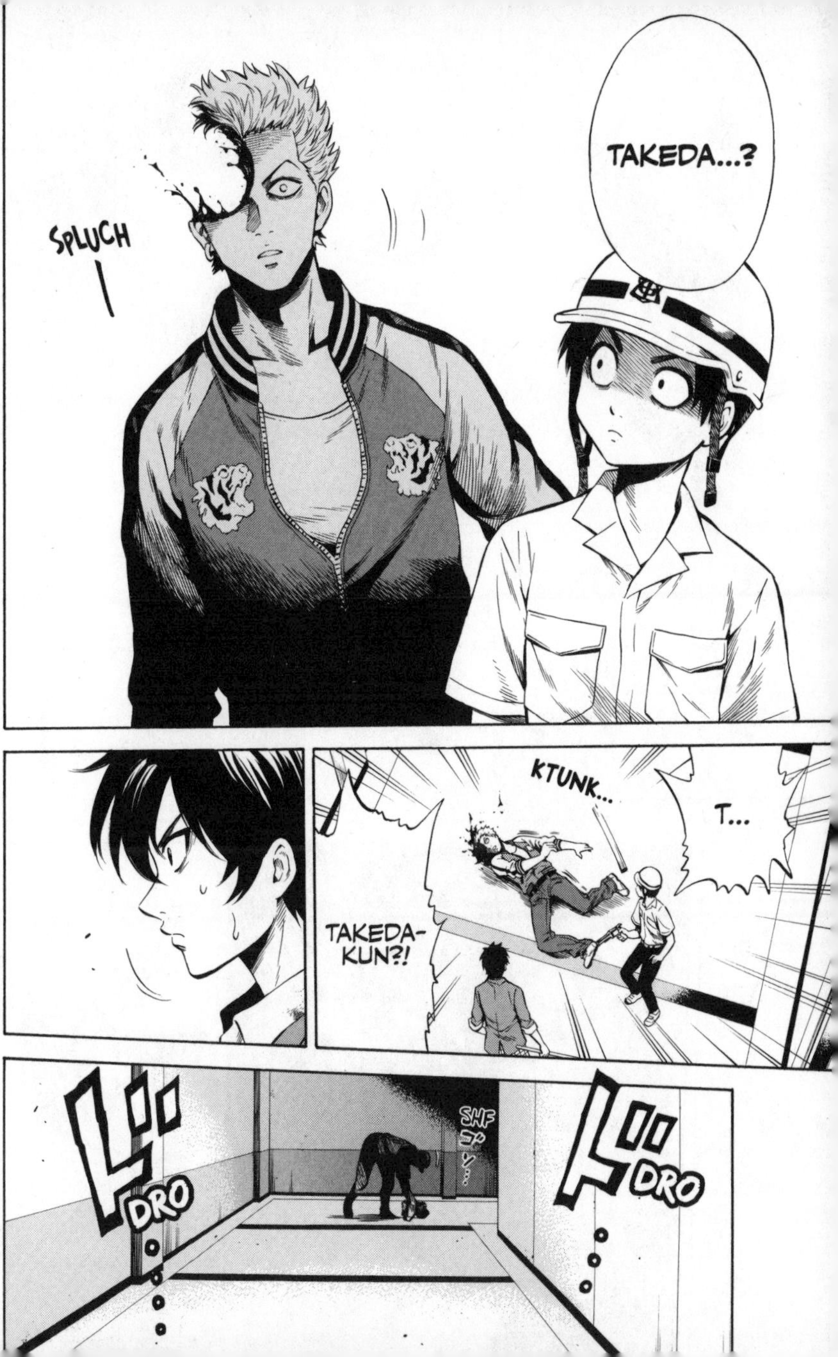
TAKEDA...?
SPLUCH
T...
KTUNK...
TAKEDA-KUN?!
DRO
SHF
ゴソ…
DRO

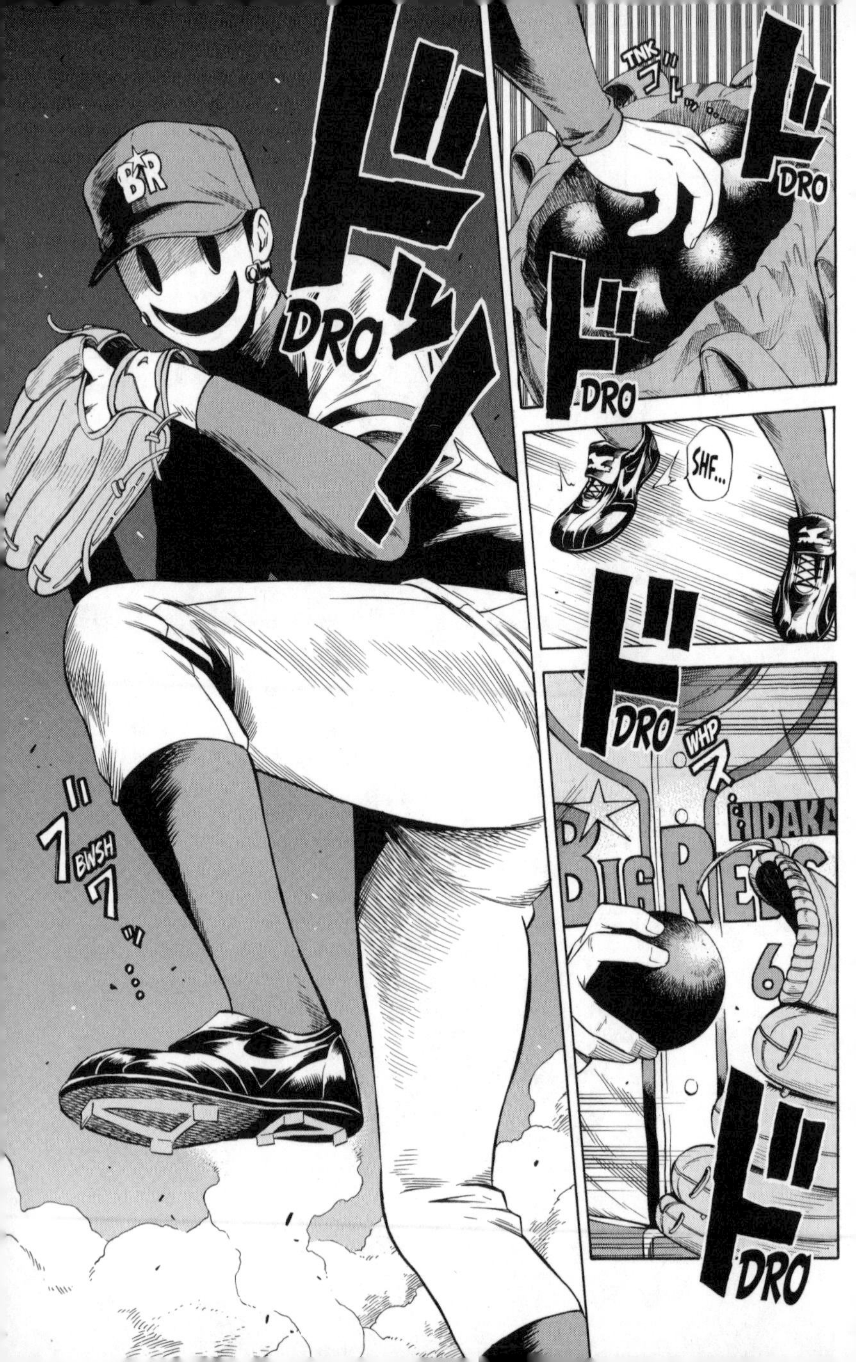
TNK
DRO
DRO
SHF...
DRO
WHP
DRO
DRO
BWSH

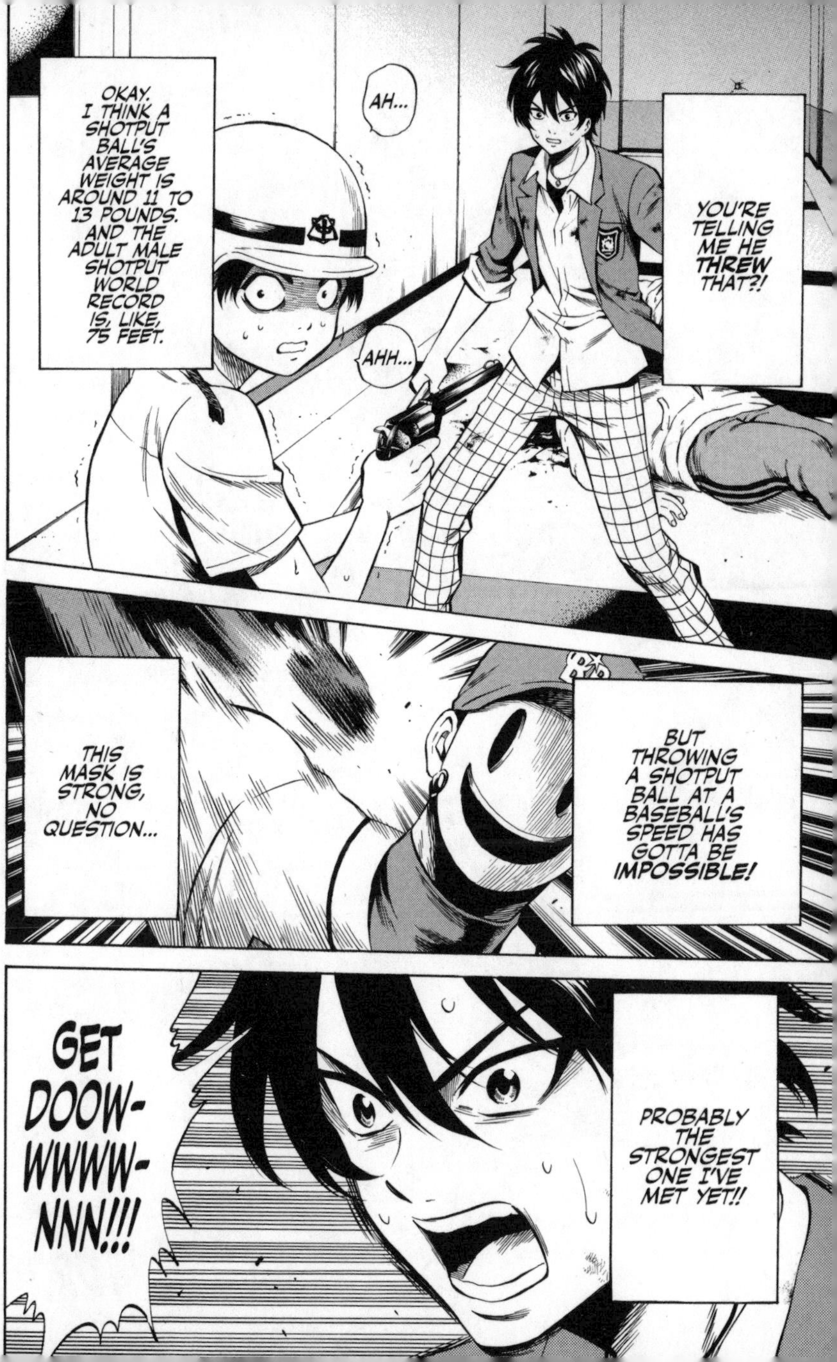

YOU'RE TELLING ME HE THREW THAT?!
AH...
OKAY. I THINK A SHOTPUT BALL'S AVERAGE WEIGHT IS AROUND 11 TO 13 POUNDS. AND THE ADULT MALE SHOTPUT WORLD RECORD IS, LIKE, 75 FEET.
AHH...
THIS MASK IS STRONG, NO QUESTION...
BUT THROWING A SHOTPUT BALL AT A BASEBALL'S SPEED HAS GOTTA BE IMPOSSIBLE!
PROBABLY THE STRONGEST ONE I'VE MET YET!!
GET DOOW-WWWW-NNN!!!

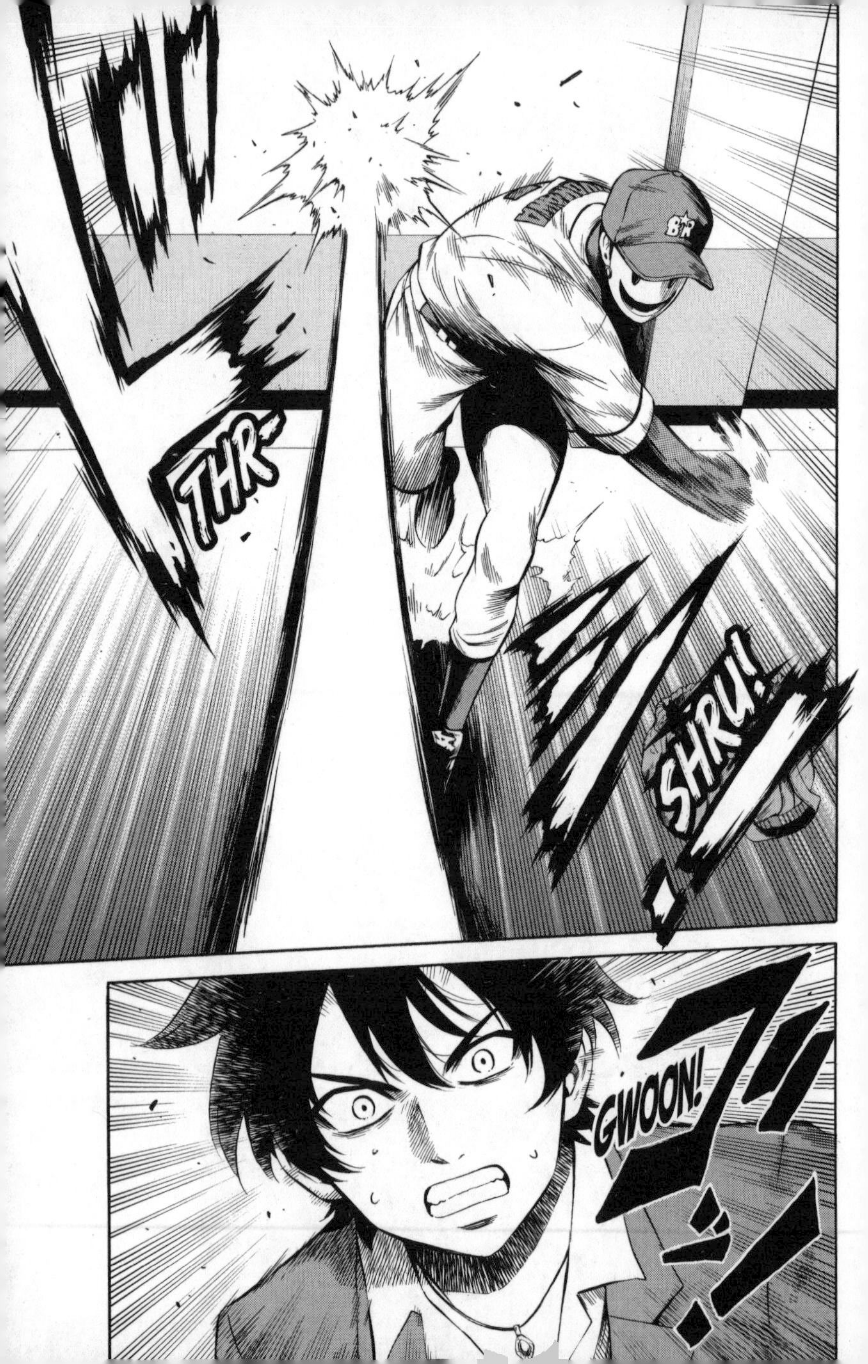
THR-
SHRU!
GWOON!

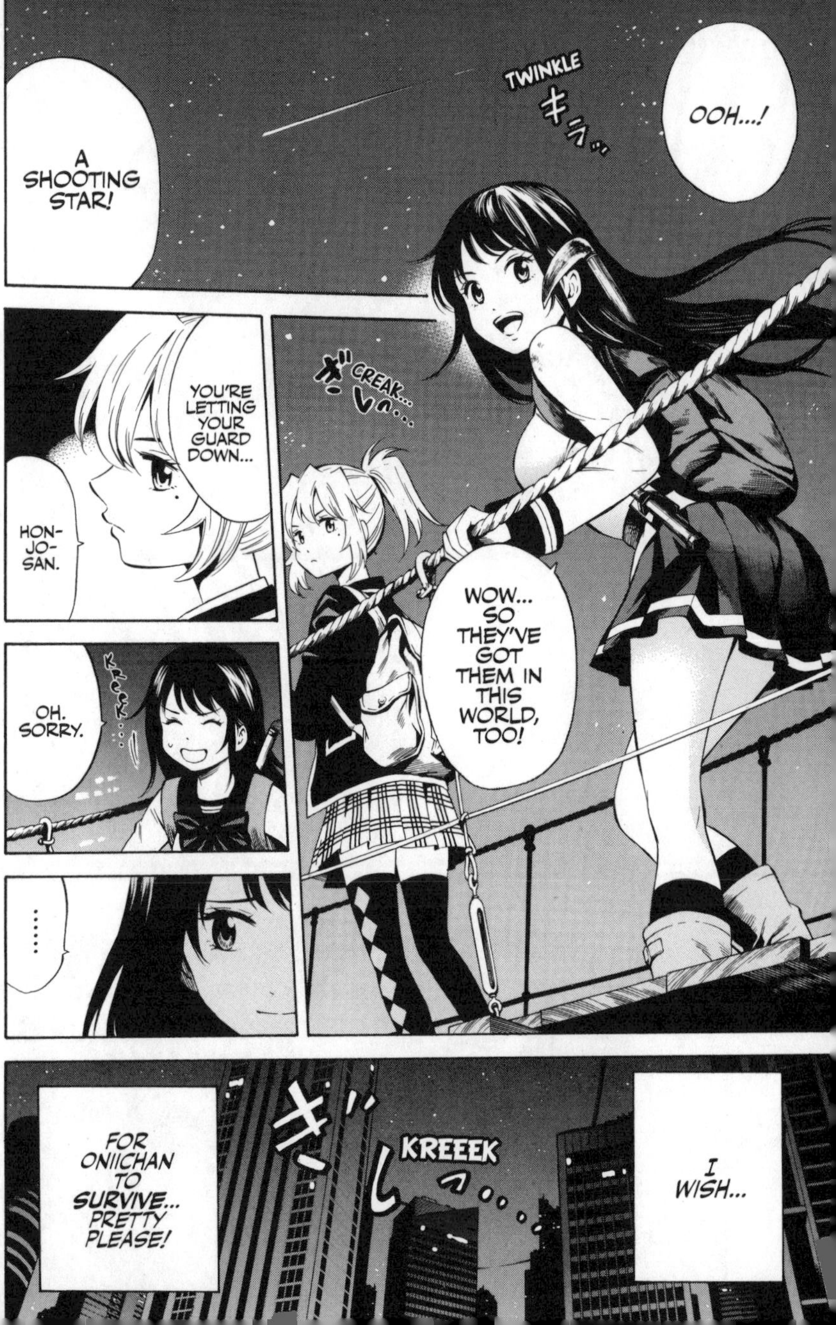
OOH...!
TWINKLE
A SHOOTING STAR!
CREAK...
WOW... SO THEY'VE GOT THEM IN THIS WORLD, TOO!
YOU'RE LETTING YOUR GUARD DOWN...
HON-JO-SAN.
OH. SORRY.
KREEK...
......
I WISH...
KREEEK
FOR ONIICHAN TO SURVIVE... PRETTY PLEASE!

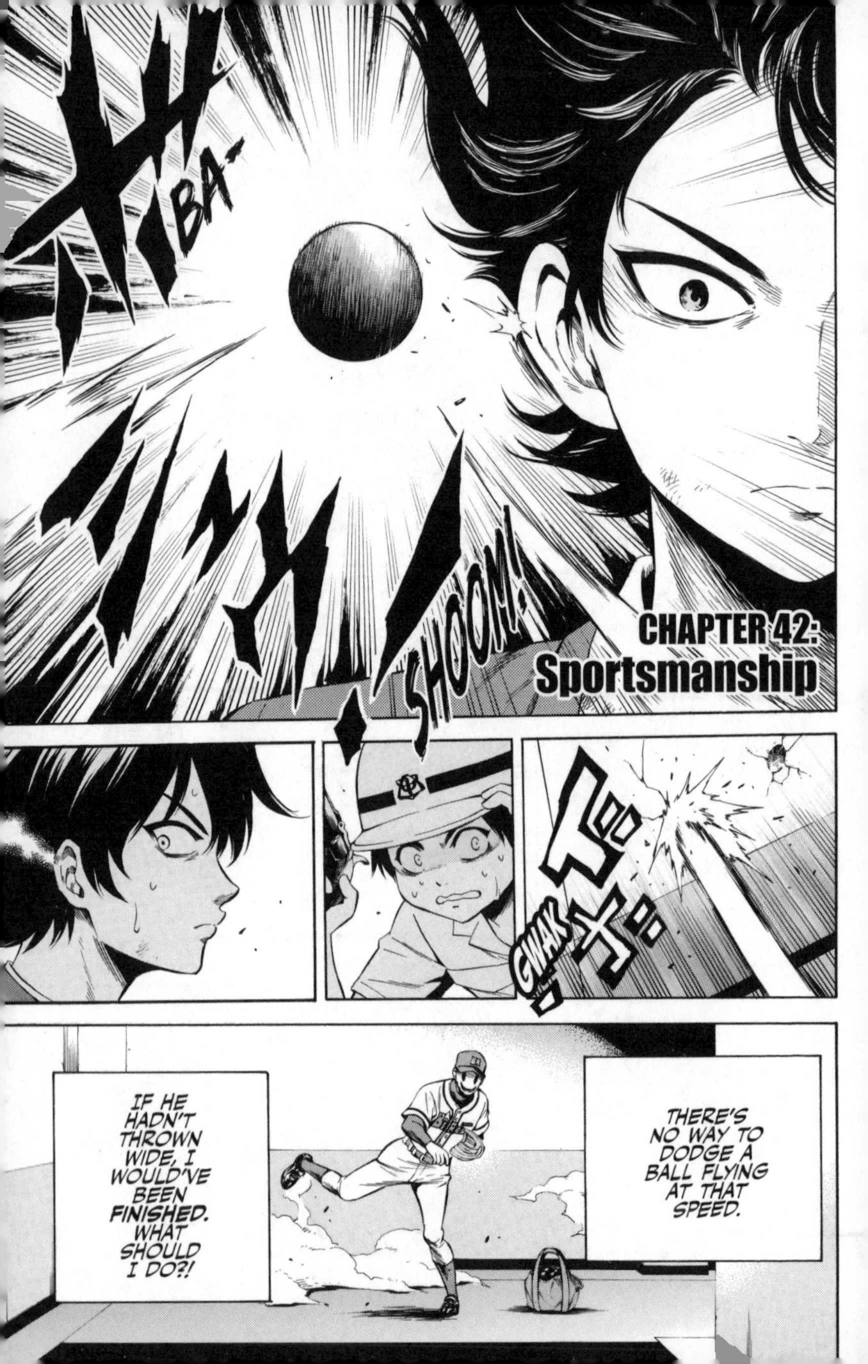
BA-
SHOOM!
CHAPTER 42: Sportsmanship
GWAK
THERE'S NO WAY TO DODGE A BALL FLYING AT THAT SPEED.
IF HE HADN'T THROWN WIDE, I WOULD'VE BEEN FINISHED. WHAT SHOULD I DO?!

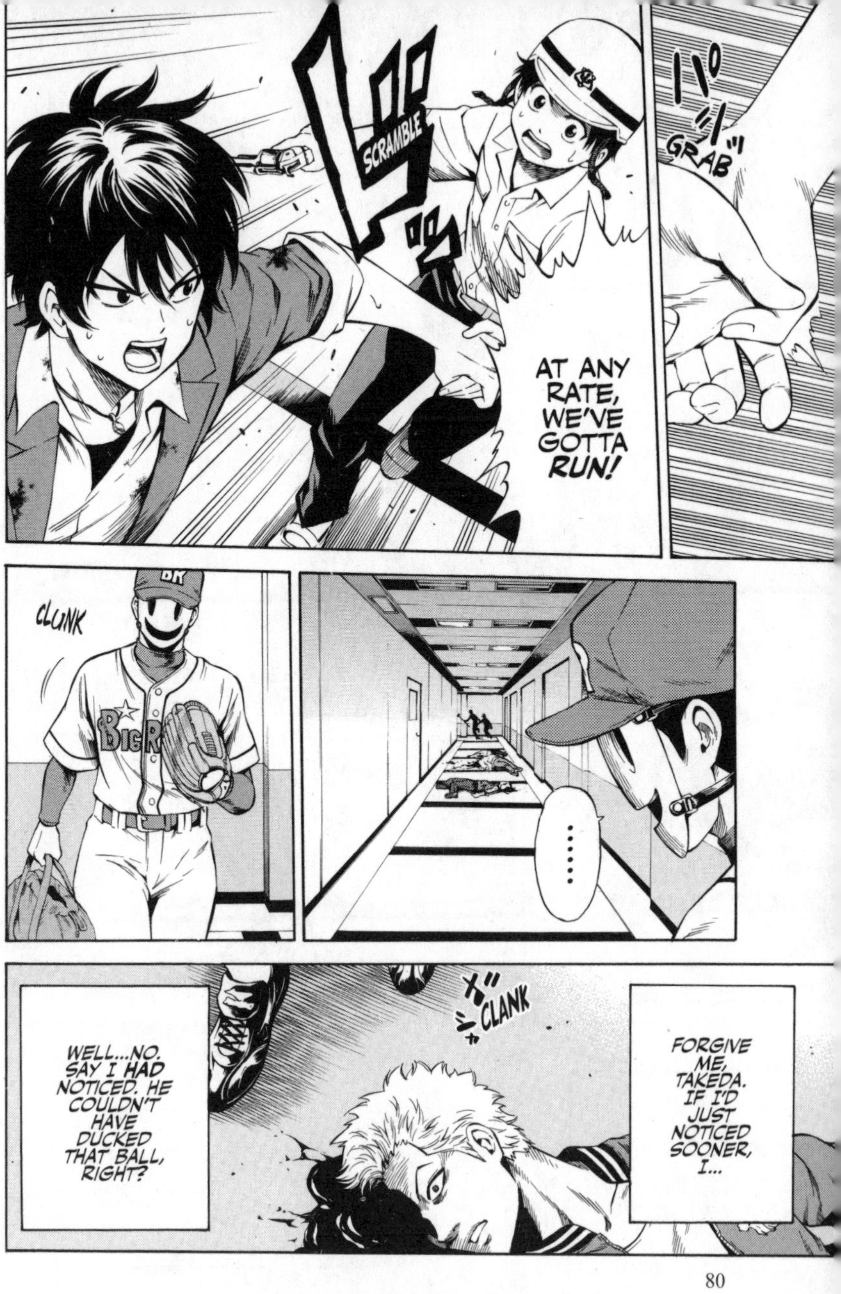
GRAB
SCRAMBLE
AT ANY RATE, WE'VE GOTTA RUN!
......
CLUNK
FORGIVE ME, TAKEDA. IF I'D JUST NOTICED SOONER, I...
CLANK
WELL...NO. SAY I HAD NOTICED. HE COULDN'T HAVE DUCKED THAT BALL, RIGHT?

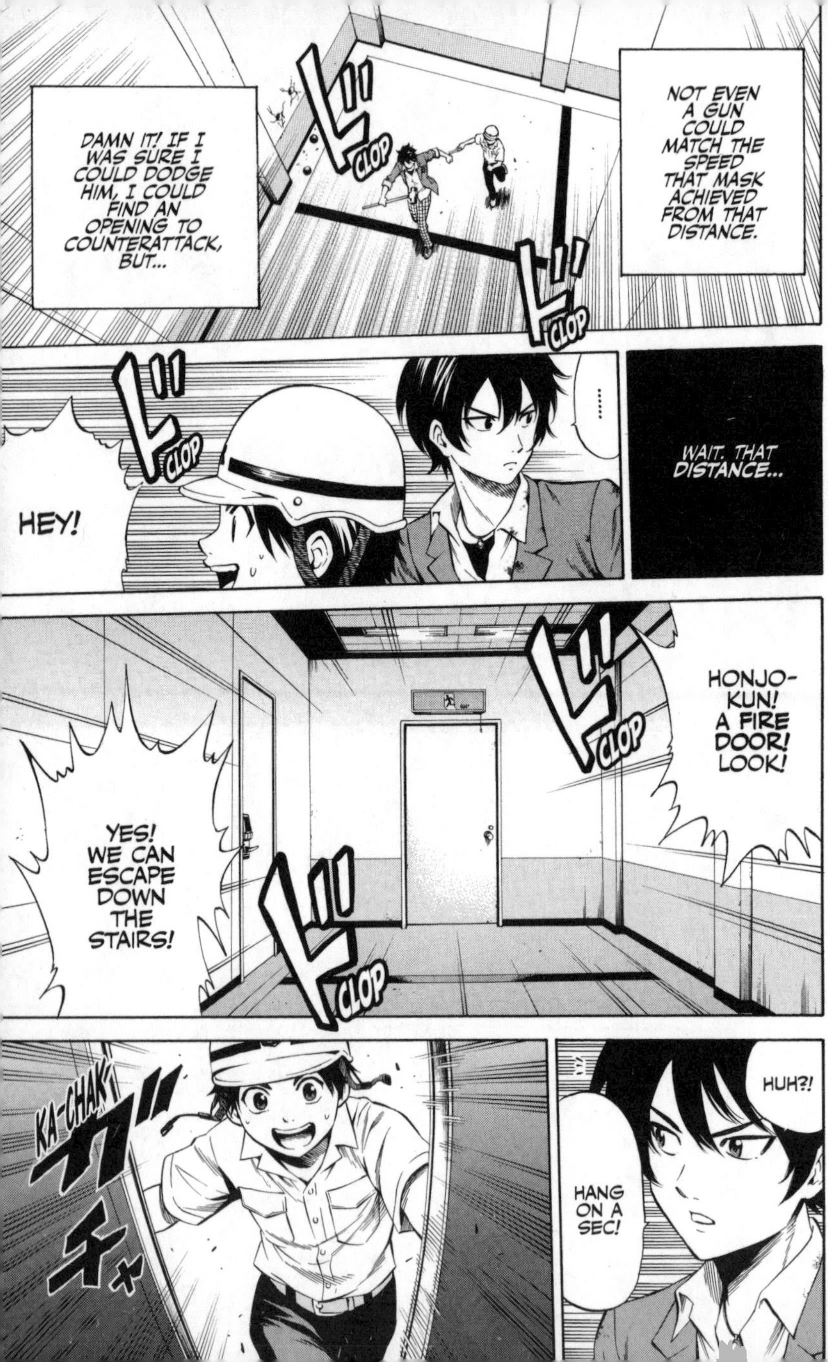
NOT EVEN A GUN COULD MATCH THE SPEED THAT MASK ACHIEVED FROM THAT DISTANCE.
CLOP
CLOP
DAMN IT! IF I WAS SURE I COULD DODGE HIM, I COULD FIND AN OPENING TO COUNTERATTACK, BUT...
WAIT. THAT DISTANCE...
......
CLOP
HEY!
HONJO-KUN! A FIRE DOOR! LOOK!
CLOP
CLOP
YES! WE CAN ESCAPE DOWN THE STAIRS!
HUH?!
HANG ON A SEC!
KA-CHAK

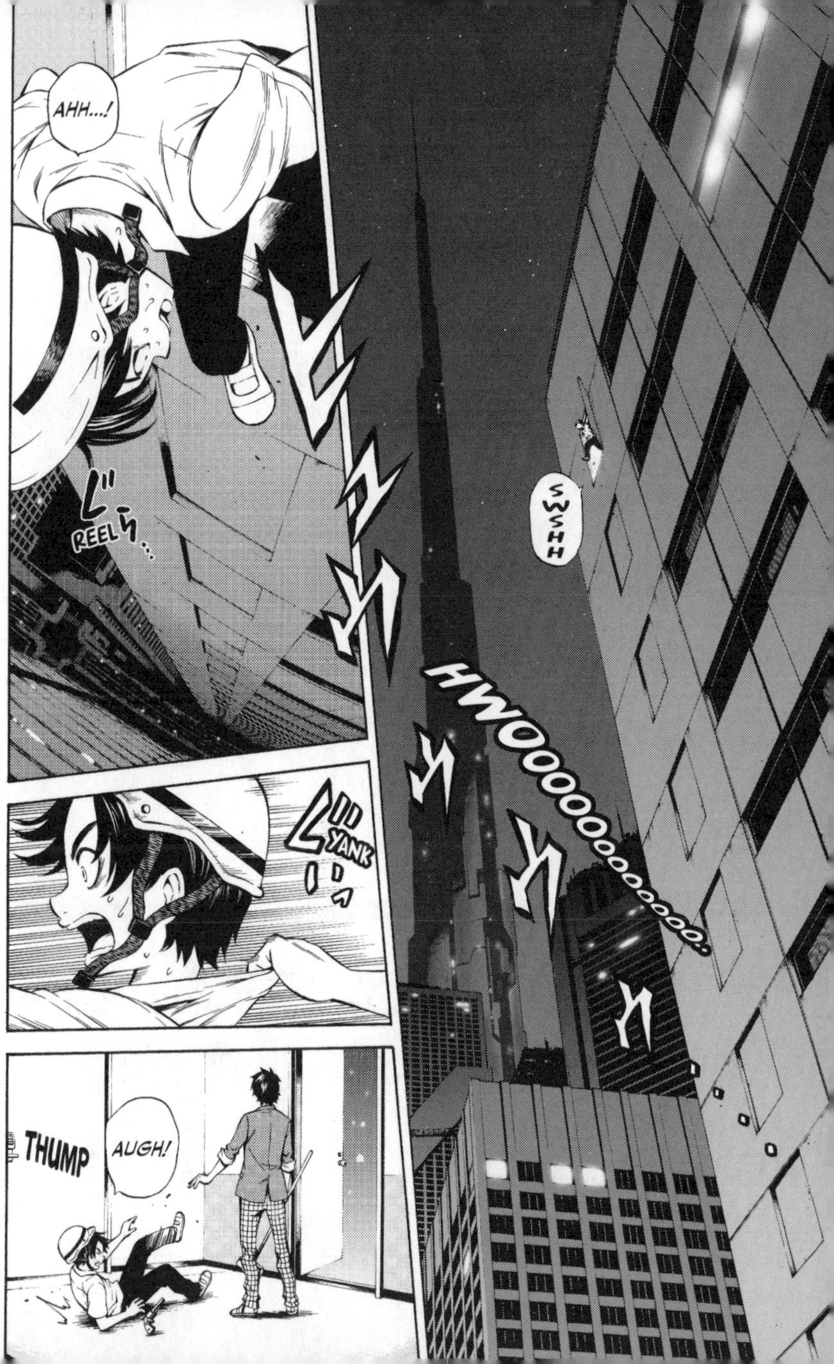

SWSHH
HWOOOOOOOOOOOOO...
AHH...!
REEL...
YANK
AUGH!
THUMP

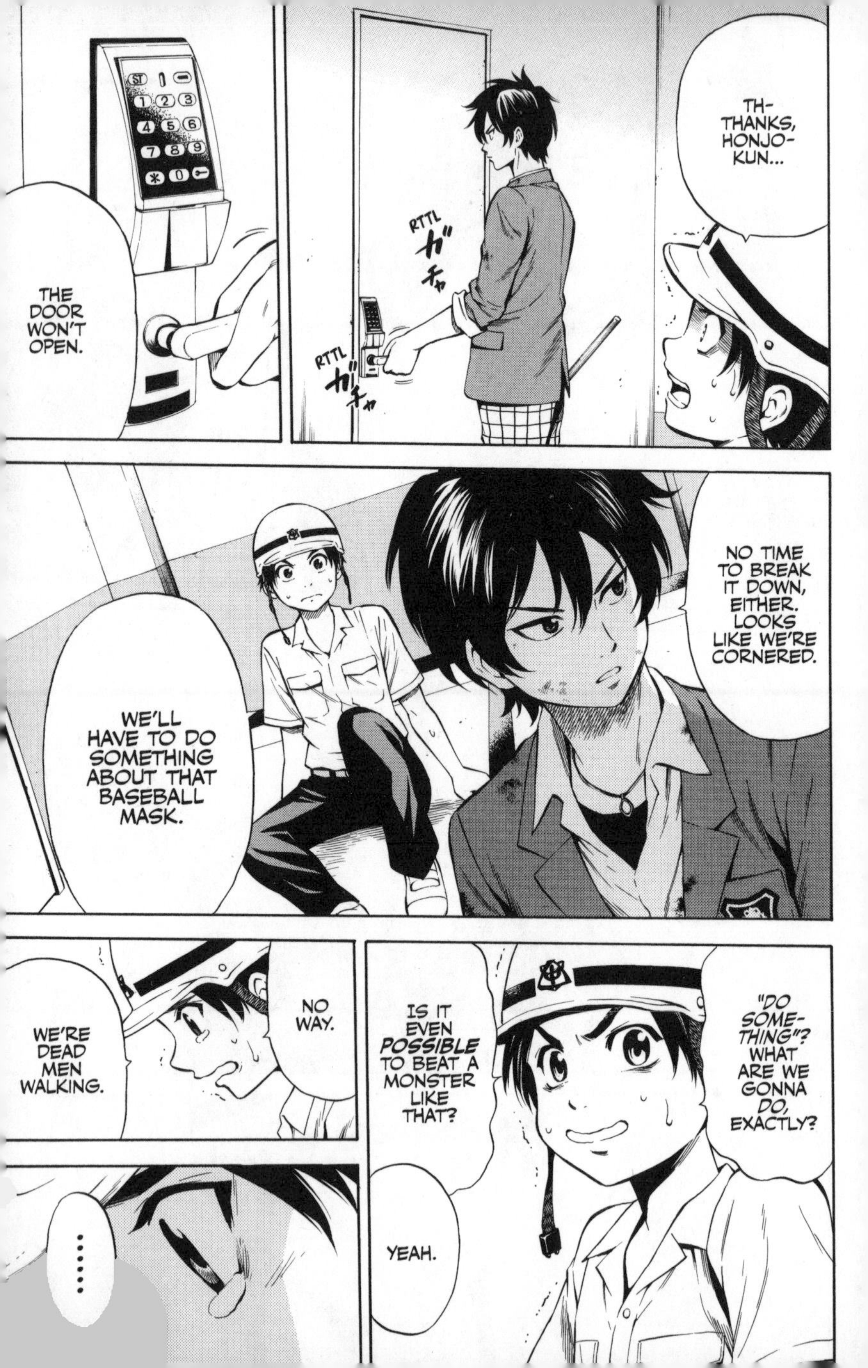

TH- THANKS, HONJO-KUN...
RTTL
ガチャ
RTTL
ガチャ
THE DOOR WON'T OPEN.
NO TIME TO BREAK IT DOWN, EITHER. LOOKS LIKE WE'RE CORNERED.
WE'LL HAVE TO DO SOMETHING ABOUT THAT BASEBALL MASK.
"DO SOME-THING"? WHAT ARE WE GONNA *DO*, EXACTLY?
IS IT EVEN *POSSIBLE* TO BEAT A MONSTER LIKE THAT?
YEAH.
NO WAY.
WE'RE DEAD MEN WALKING.
......

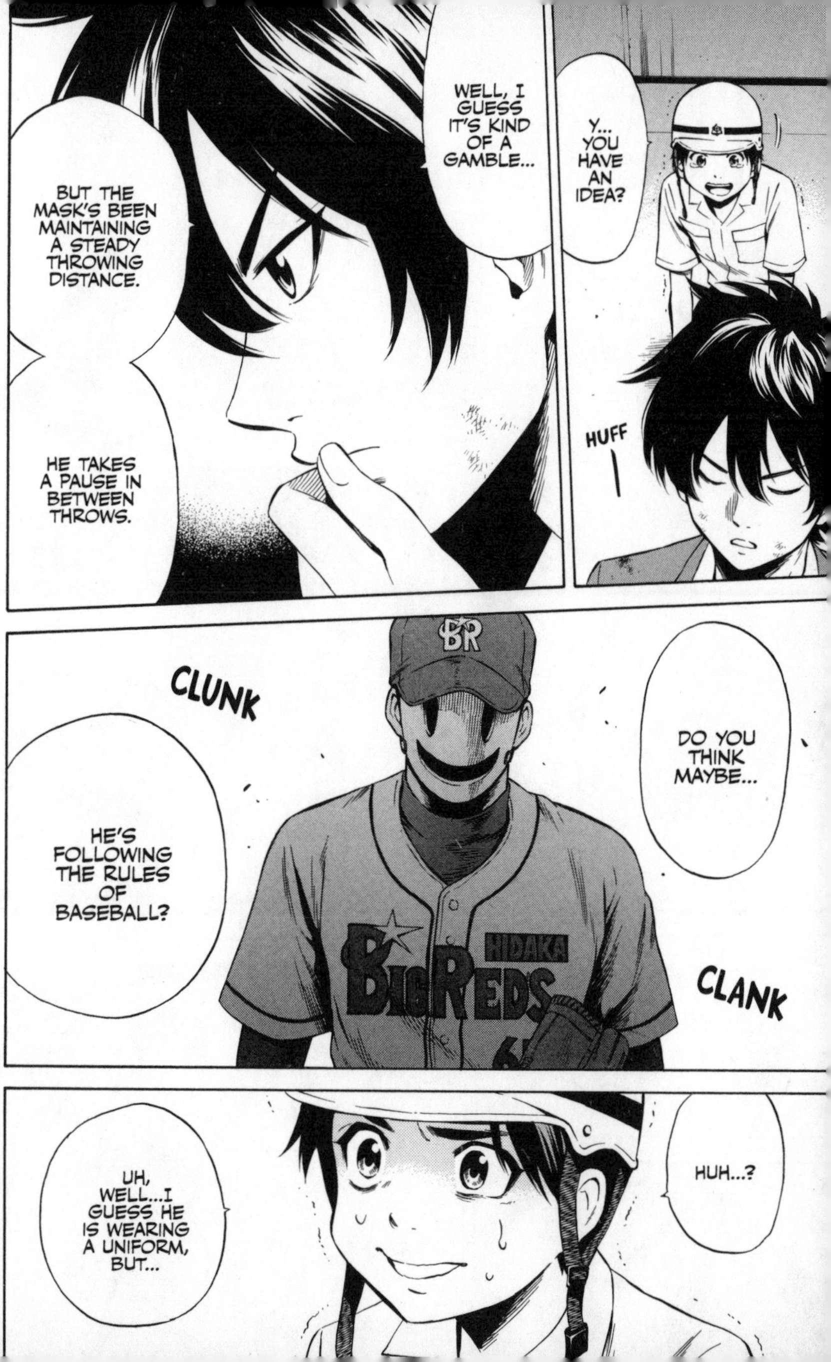
Y... YOU HAVE AN IDEA?
HUFF
WELL, I GUESS IT'S KIND OF A GAMBLE...
BUT THE MASK'S BEEN MAINTAINING A STEADY THROWING DISTANCE.
HE TAKES A PAUSE IN BETWEEN THROWS.
DO YOU THINK MAYBE...
CLUNK
HE'S FOLLOWING THE RULES OF BASEBALL?
CLANK
BR
HIDAKA BIGREDS
HUH...?
UH, WELL...I GUESS HE IS WEARING A UNIFORM, BUT...

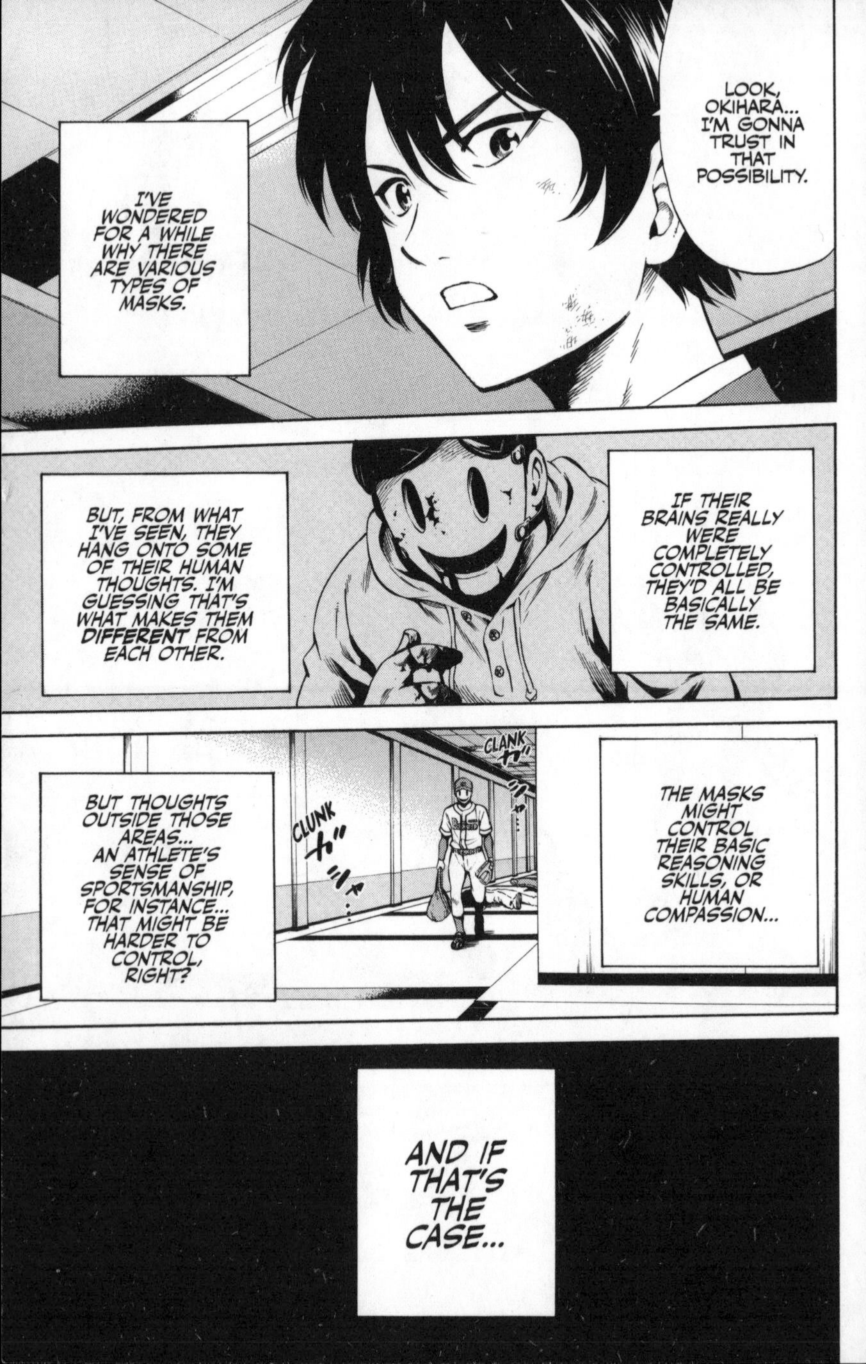
LOOK, OKIHARA... I'M GONNA TRUST IN THAT POSSIBILITY.
I'VE WONDERED FOR A WHILE WHY THERE ARE VARIOUS TYPES OF MASKS.
IF THEIR BRAINS REALLY WERE COMPLETELY CONTROLLED, THEY'D ALL BE BASICALLY THE SAME.
BUT, FROM WHAT I'VE SEEN, THEY HANG ONTO SOME OF THEIR HUMAN THOUGHTS. I'M GUESSING THAT'S WHAT MAKES THEM **DIFFERENT** FROM EACH OTHER.
THE MASKS MIGHT CONTROL THEIR BASIC REASONING SKILLS, OR HUMAN COMPASSION...
CLANK
CLUNK
BUT THOUGHTS OUTSIDE THOSE AREAS... AN ATHLETE'S SENSE OF SPORTSMANSHIP, FOR INSTANCE... THAT MIGHT BE HARDER TO CONTROL, RIGHT?
AND IF THAT'S THE CASE...

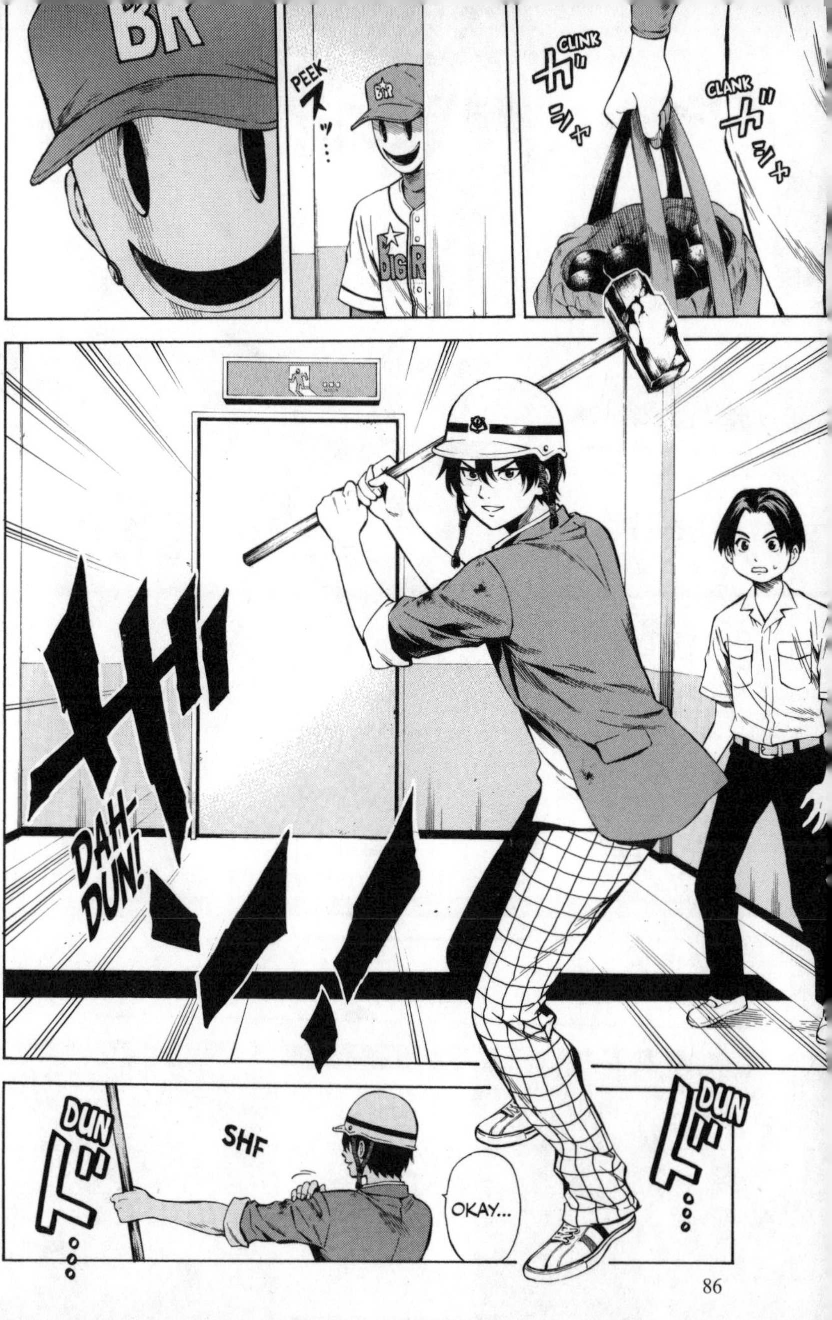
CLINK
CLANK
PEEK
DAH-DUN!
DUN
OKAY...
SHF
DUN

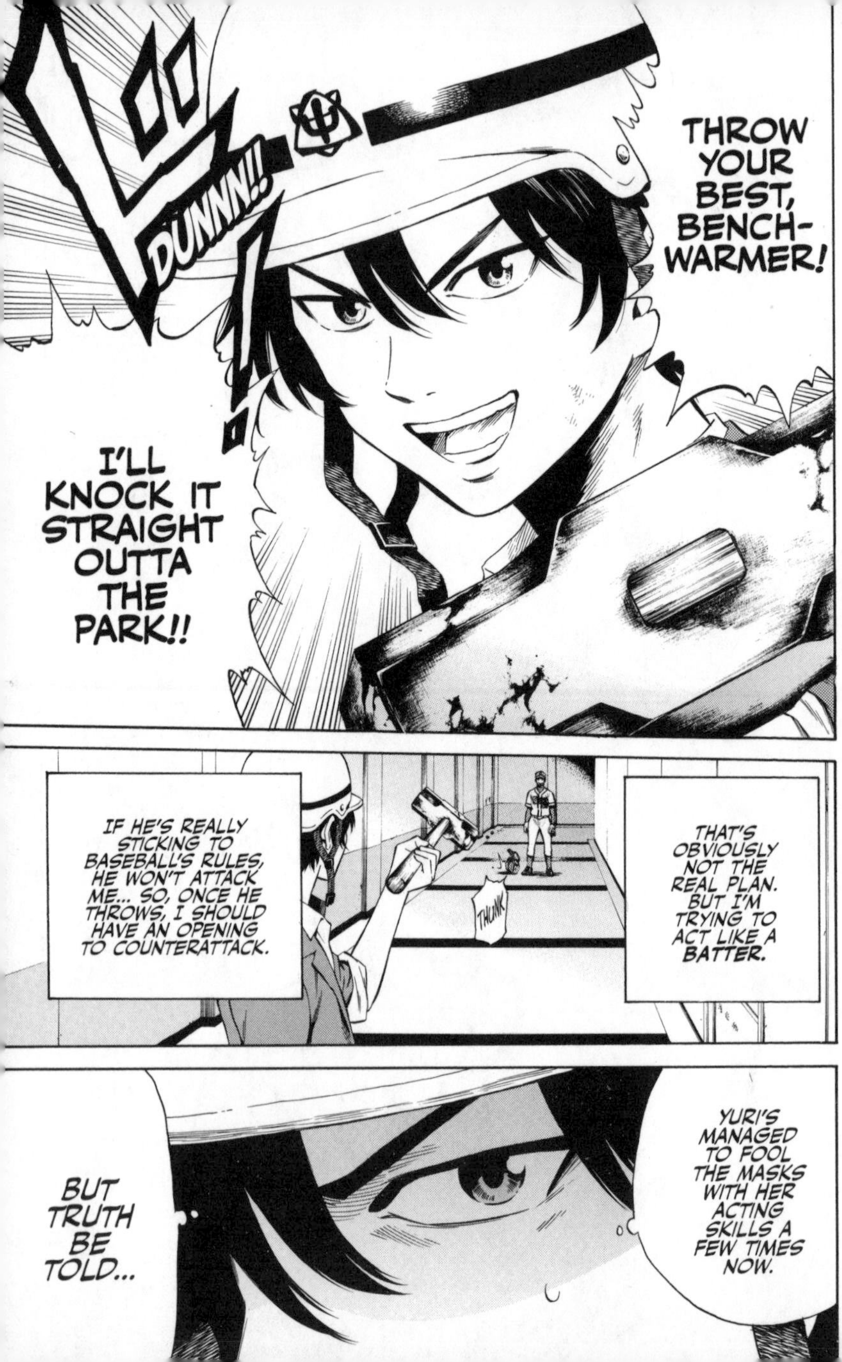
THROW YOUR BEST, BENCH-WARMER!
DUNNN!!
I'LL KNOCK IT STRAIGHT OUTTA THE PARK!!
THAT'S OBVIOUSLY NOT THE REAL PLAN. BUT I'M TRYING TO ACT LIKE A BATTER.
THUNK
IF HE'S REALLY STICKING TO BASEBALL'S RULES, HE WON'T ATTACK ME... SO, ONCE HE THROWS, I SHOULD HAVE AN OPENING TO COUNTERATTACK.
YURI'S MANAGED TO FOOL THE MASKS WITH HER ACTING SKILLS A FEW TIMES NOW.
BUT TRUTH BE TOLD...

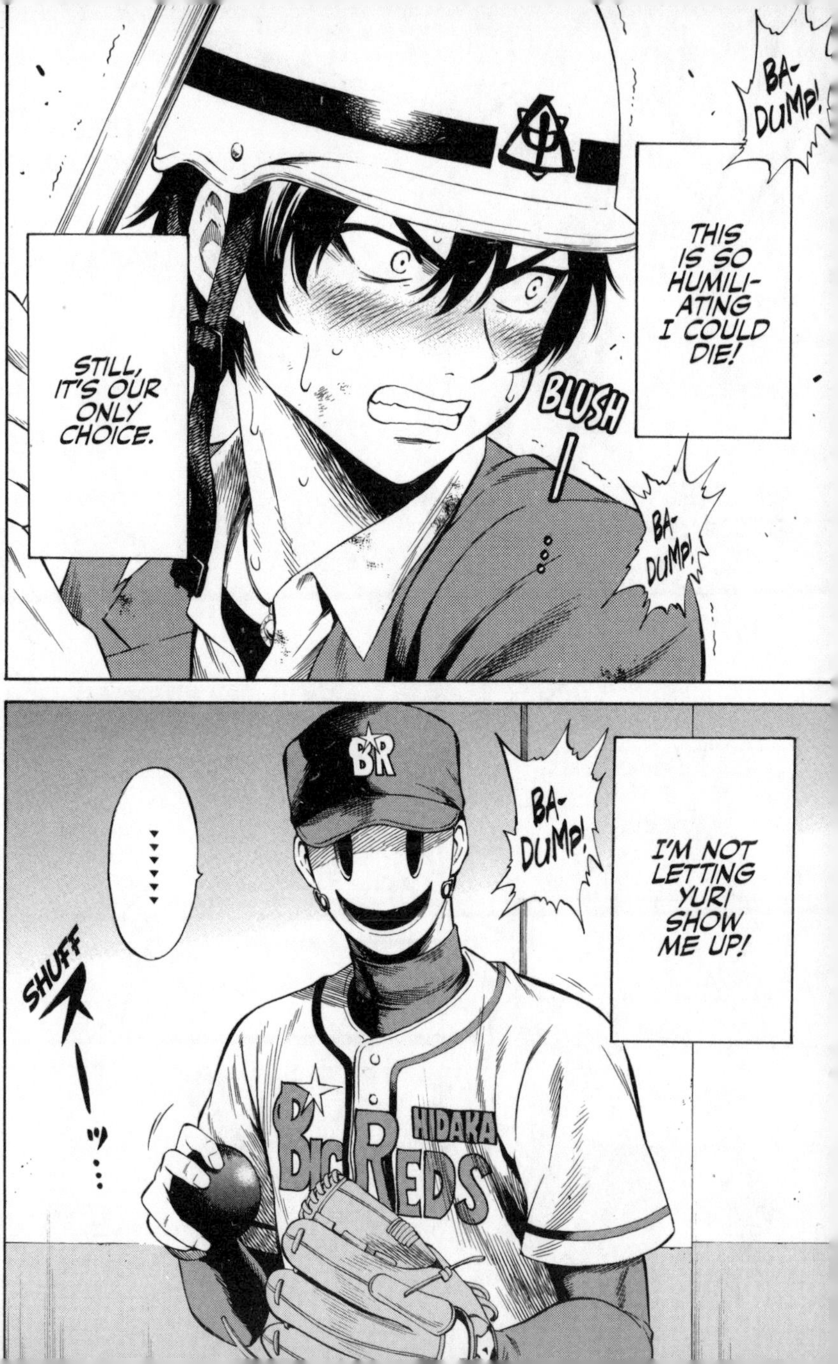
BA-DUMP!
THIS IS SO HUMILIATING I COULD DIE!
BLUSH
BA-DUMP!
STILL, IT'S OUR ONLY CHOICE.
BA-DUMP!
I'M NOT LETTING YURI SHOW ME UP!
BR
HIDAKA
BIG REDS
SHUFF

HIGH-RISE INVASION

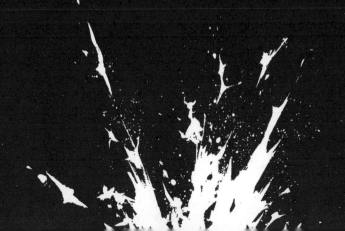

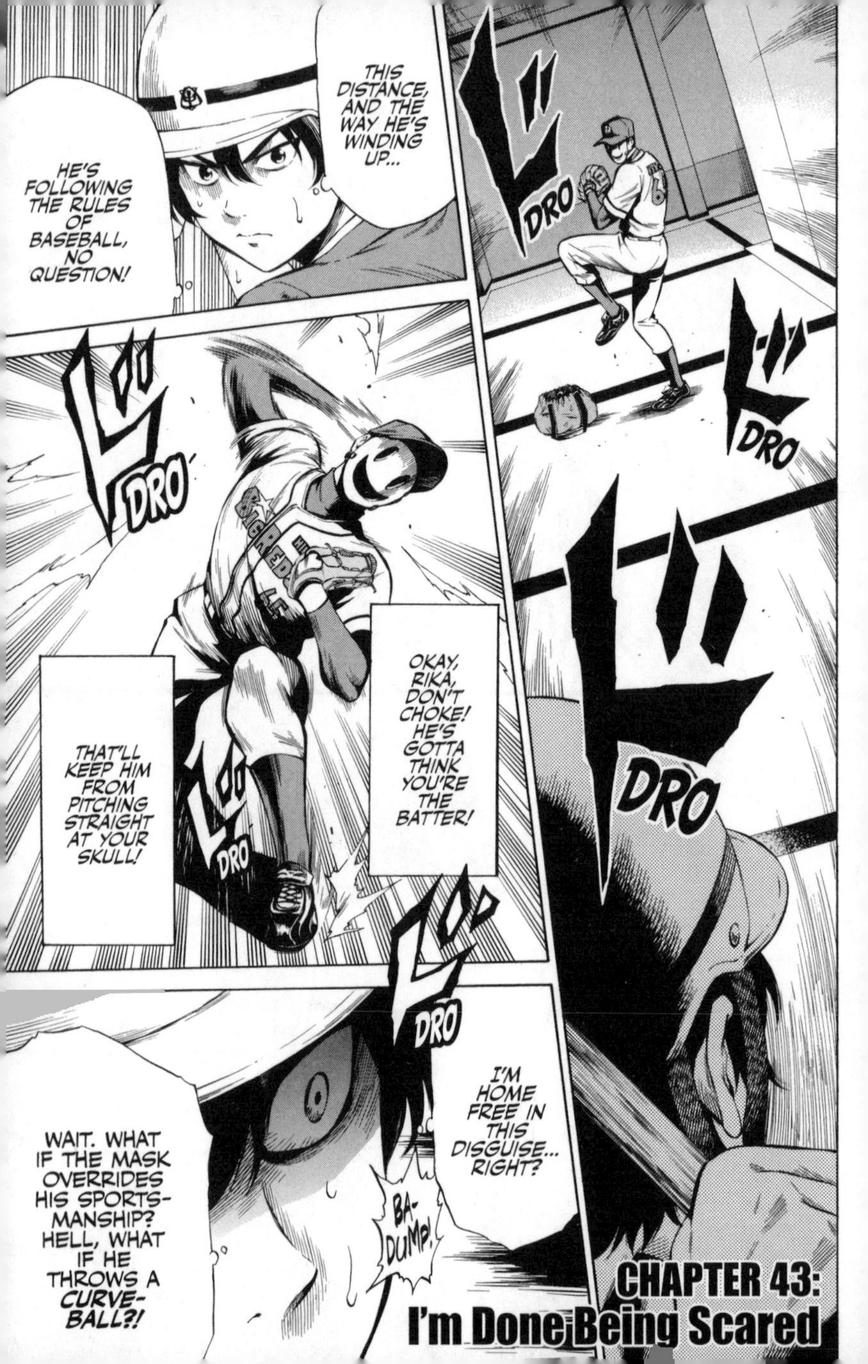
DRO
DRO
THIS DISTANCE, AND THE WAY HE'S WINDING UP...
HE'S FOLLOWING THE RULES OF BASEBALL, NO QUESTION!
DRO
DRO
OKAY, RIKA, DON'T CHOKE! HE'S GOTTA THINK YOU'RE THE BATTER!
THAT'LL KEEP HIM FROM PITCHING STRAIGHT AT YOUR SKULL!
DRO
DRO
I'M HOME FREE IN THIS DISGUISE... RIGHT?
BA-DUMP!
WAIT. WHAT IF THE MASK OVERRIDES HIS SPORTS-MANSHIP? HELL, WHAT IF HE THROWS A *CURVE-BALL*?!

CHAPTER 43: I'm Done Being Scared

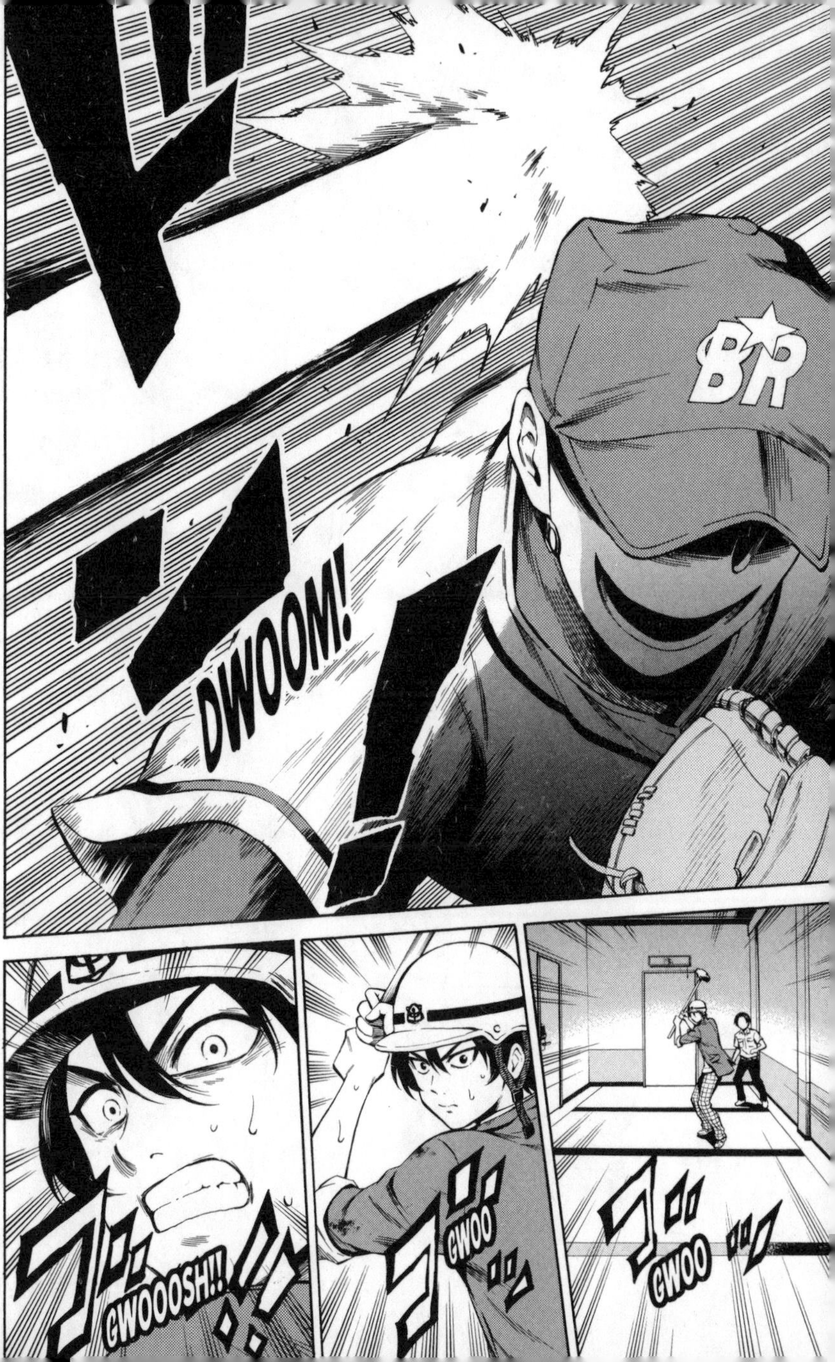
DWOOM!
GWOO
GWOO
GWOOOSH!!

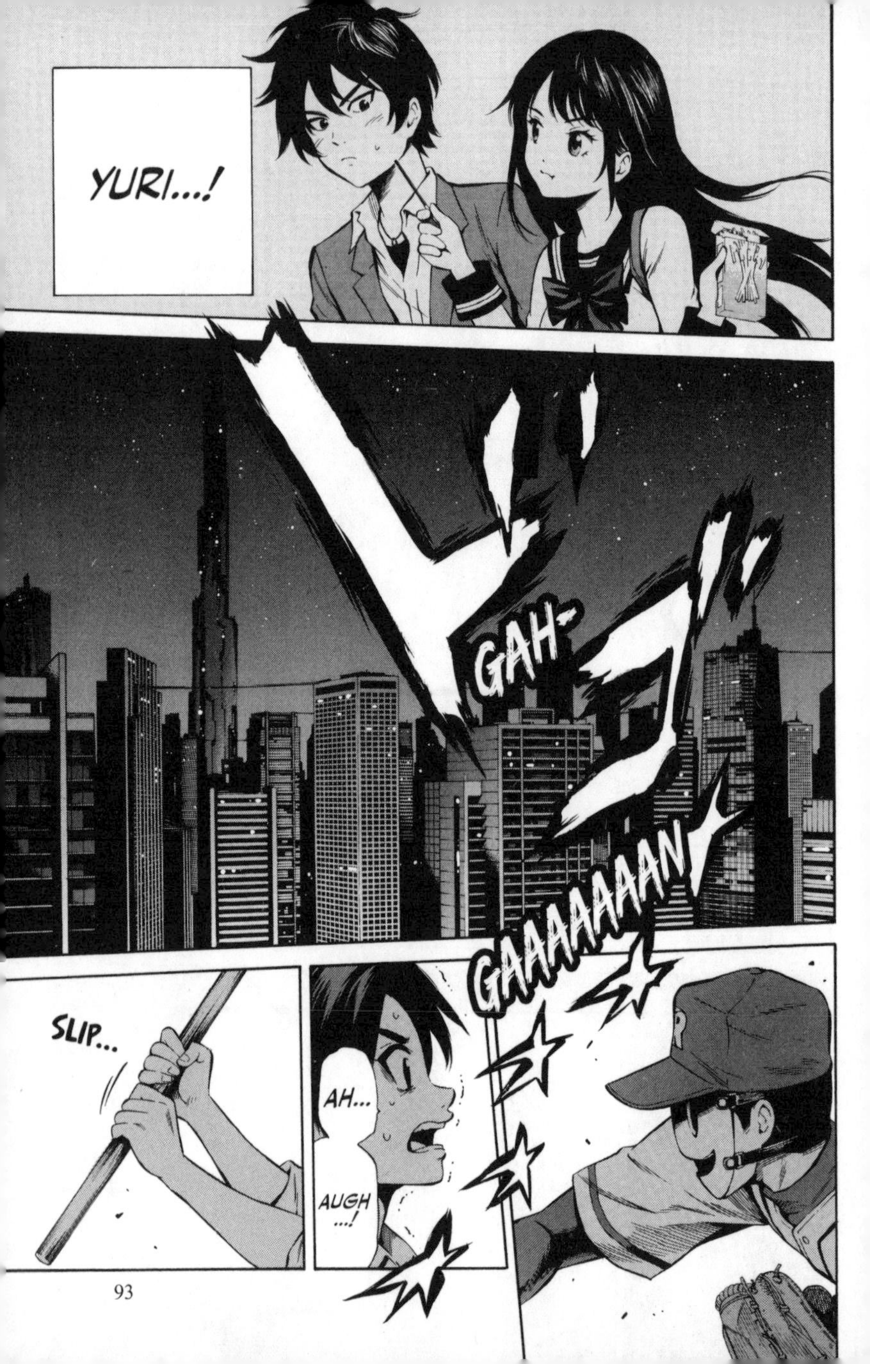
YURI...!
GAH-
GAAAAAAAN
AH...
AUGH ...!
SLIP...

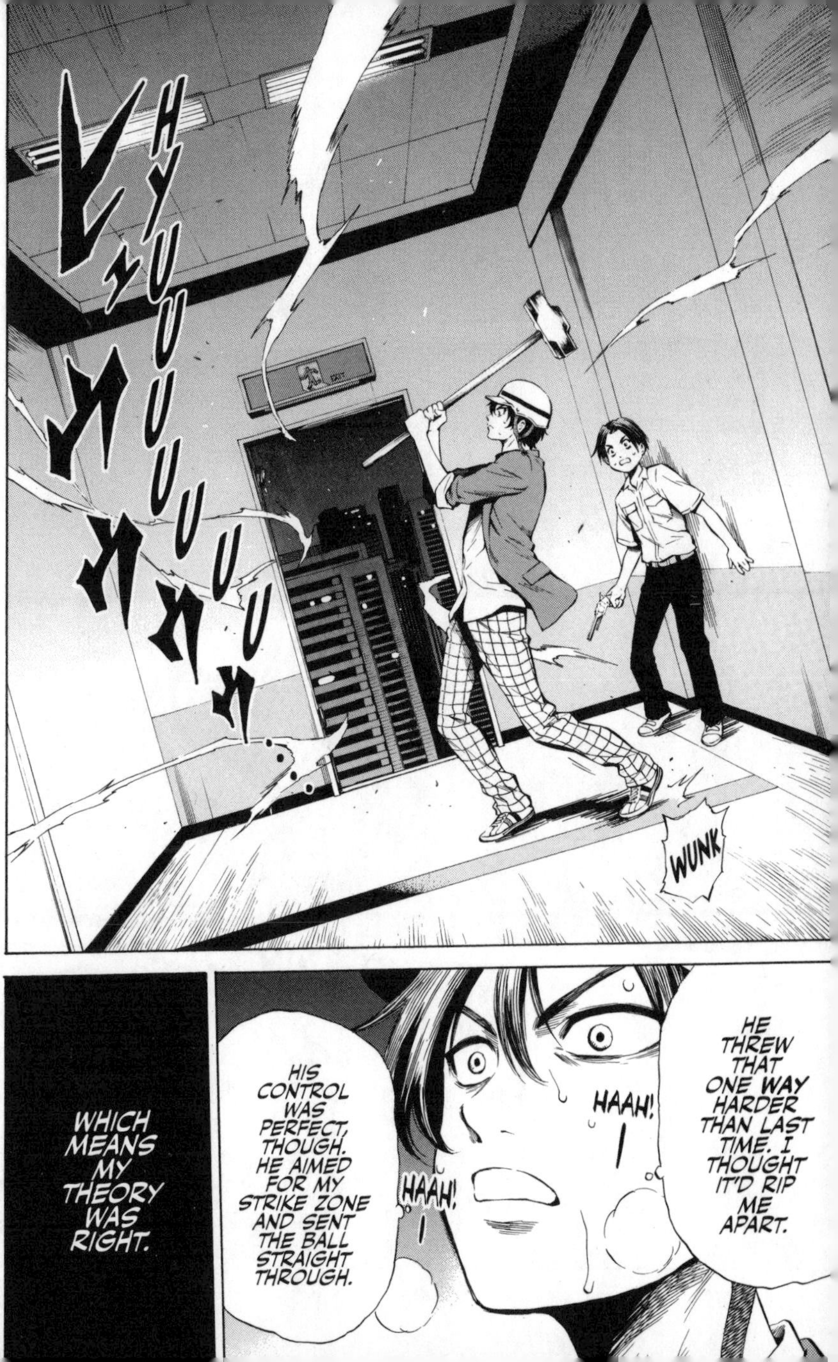

HYUUUUUUU
WUNK
HE THREW THAT ONE WAY HARDER THAN LAST TIME. I THOUGHT IT'D RIP ME APART.
HAAH!
HAAH!
HIS CONTROL WAS PERFECT, THOUGH. HE AIMED FOR MY STRIKE ZONE AND SENT THE BALL STRAIGHT THROUGH.
WHICH MEANS MY THEORY WAS RIGHT.

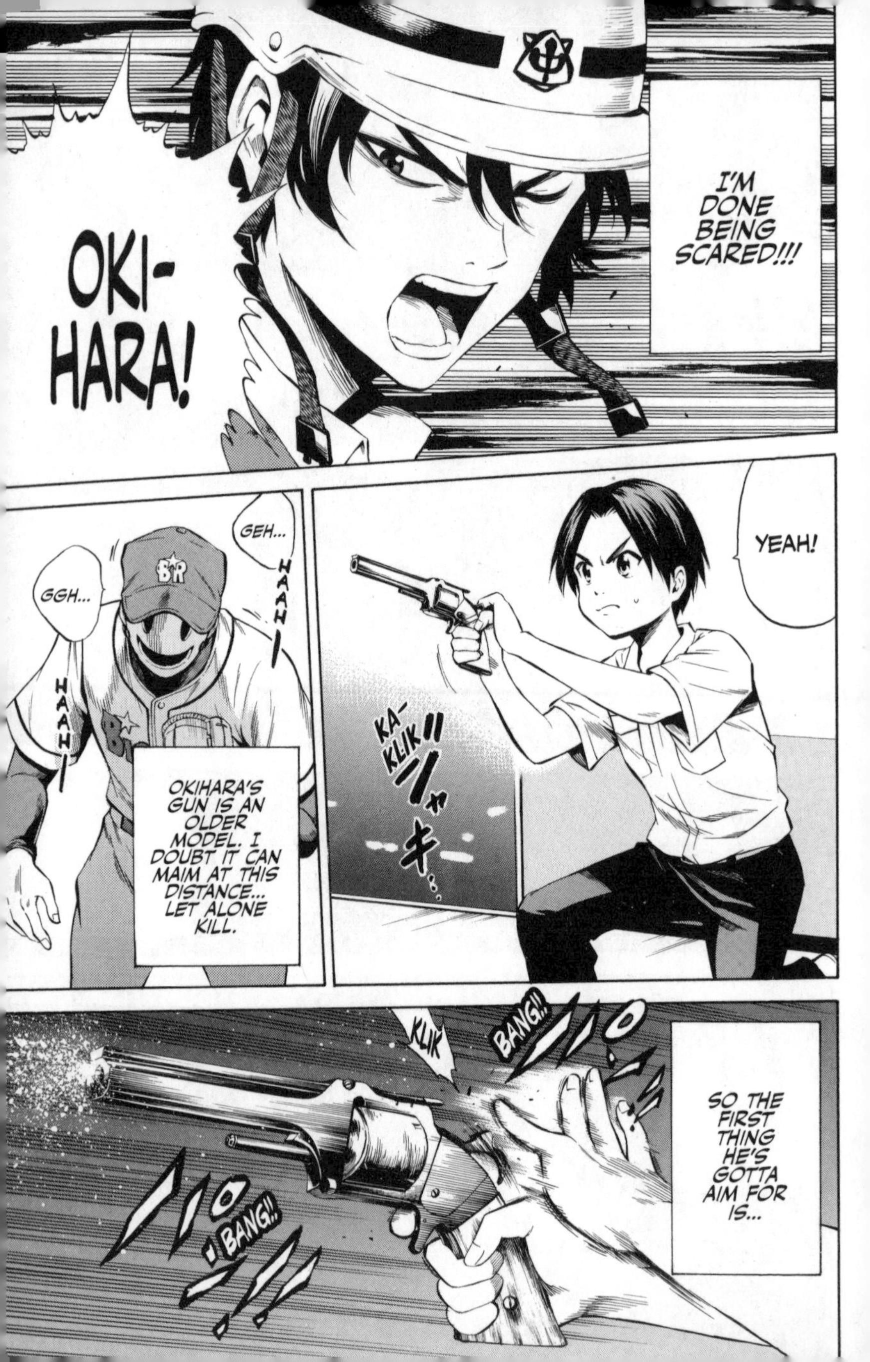
I'M DONE BEING SCARED!!!
OKI-HARA!
YEAH!
KA-KLIK
GEH...
HAAAH
GGH...
HAAAH
OKIHARA'S GUN IS AN OLDER MODEL. I DOUBT IT CAN MAIM AT THIS DISTANCE... LET ALONE KILL.
SO THE FIRST THING HE'S GOTTA AIM FOR IS...
BANG!!
KLIK
BANG!!

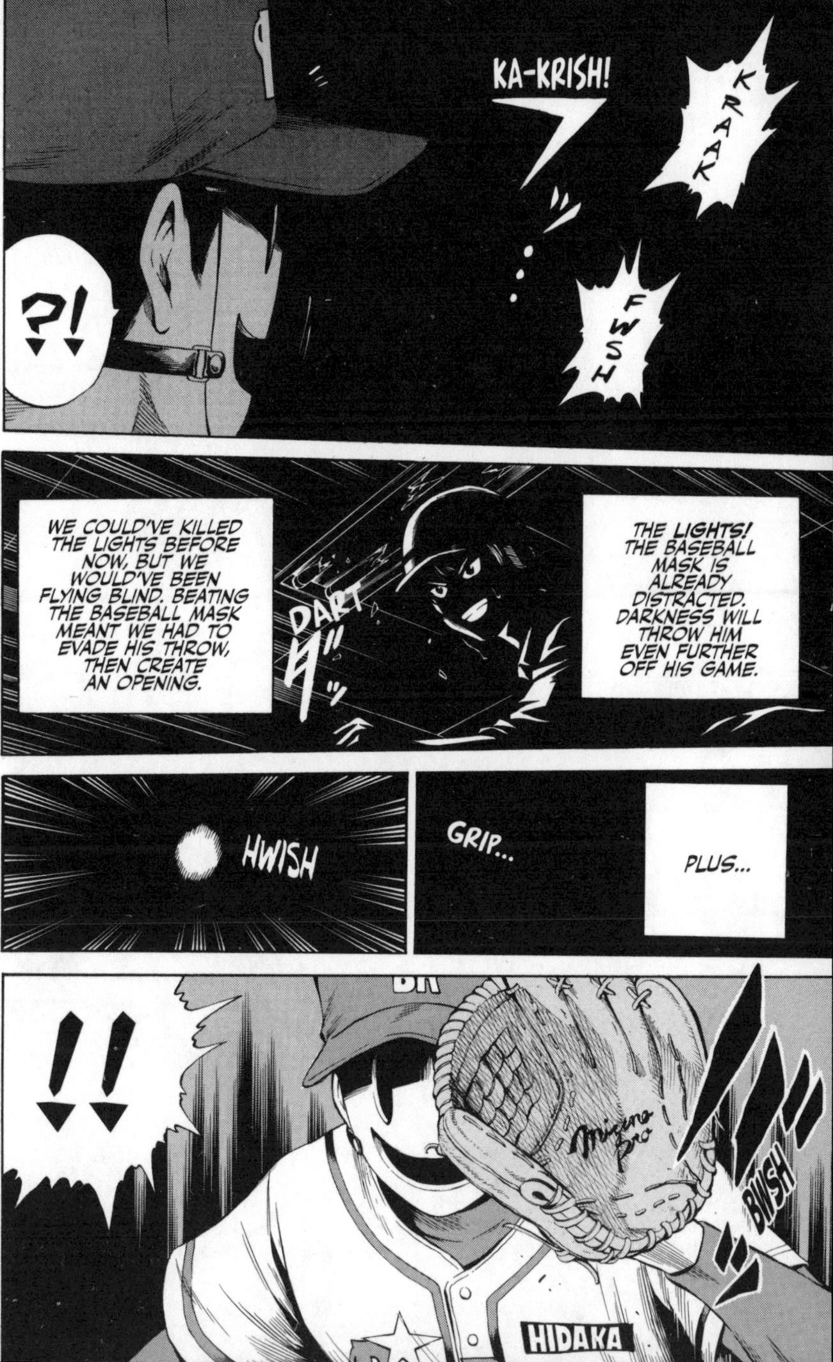
KRAAK
KA-KRISH!
FWSH
?!
THE LIGHTS! THE BASEBALL MASK IS ALREADY DISTRACTED. DARKNESS WILL THROW HIM EVEN FURTHER OFF HIS GAME.
DART
WE COULD'VE KILLED THE LIGHTS BEFORE NOW, BUT WE WOULD'VE BEEN FLYING BLIND. BEATING THE BASEBALL MASK MEANT WE HAD TO EVADE HIS THROW, THEN CREATE AN OPENING.
PLUS...
GRIP...
HWISH
BWISH
!!
HIDAKA

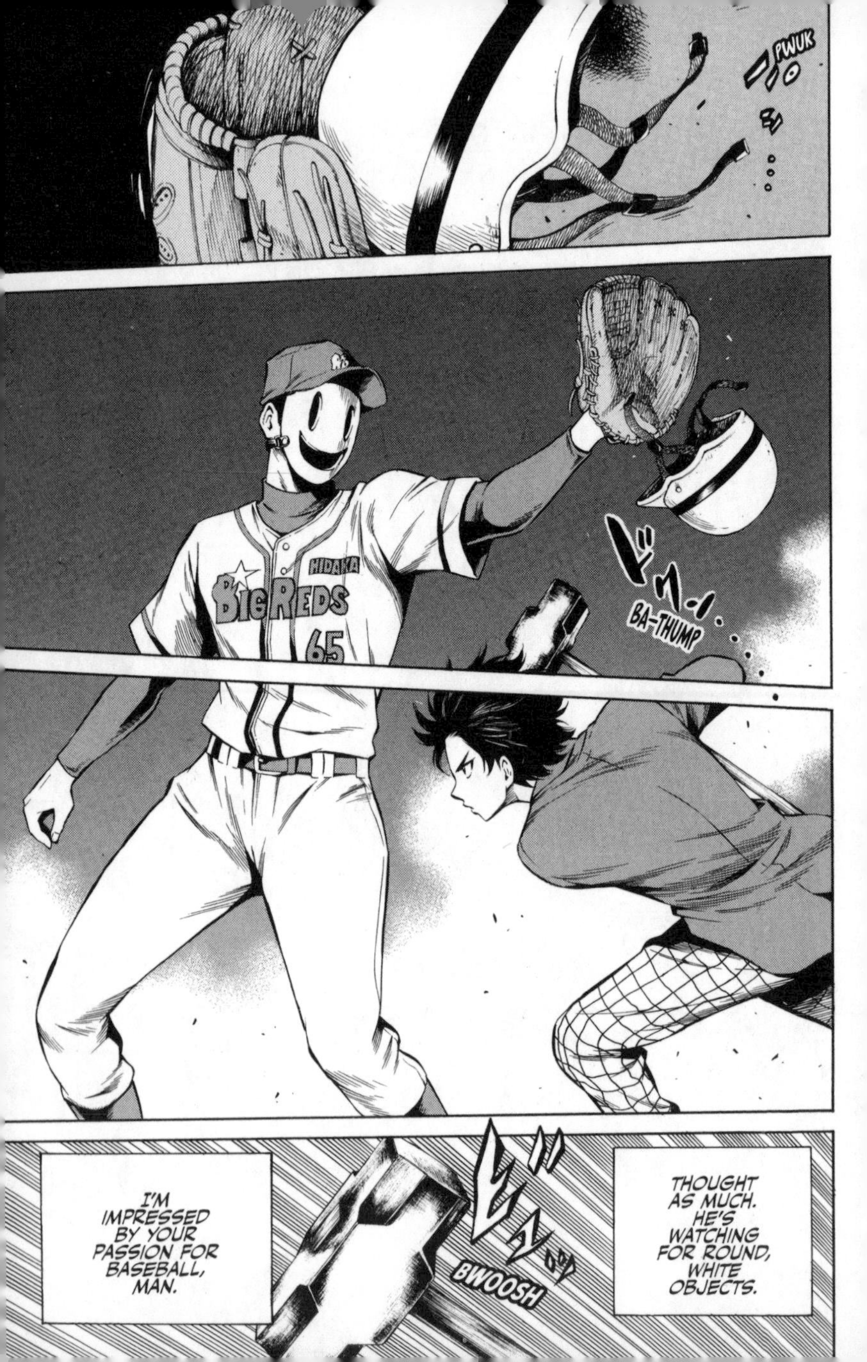
PWUK
BA-THUMP
THOUGHT AS MUCH. HE'S WATCHING FOR ROUND, WHITE OBJECTS.
BWOOSH
I'M IMPRESSED BY YOUR PASSION FOR BASEBALL, MAN.

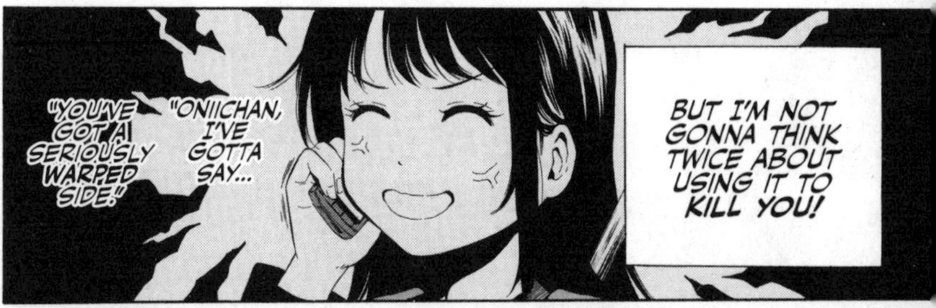
BUT I'M NOT GONNA THINK TWICE ABOUT USING IT TO KILL YOU!
"ONIICHAN, I'VE GOTTA SAY...
"YOU'VE GOT A SERIOUSLY WARPED SIDE."

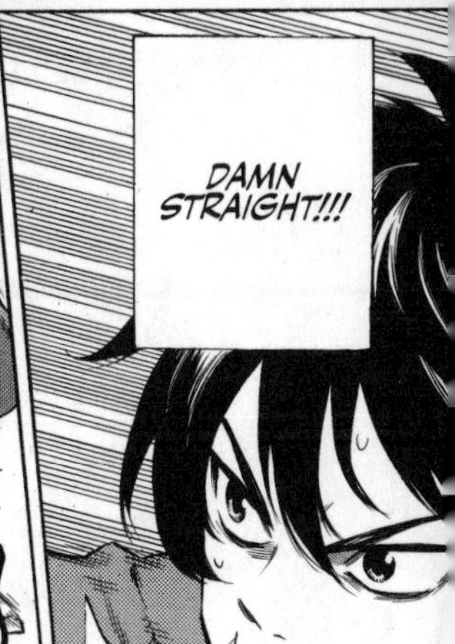
DAMN STRAIGHT!!!
RAAUGH!!
BWAA

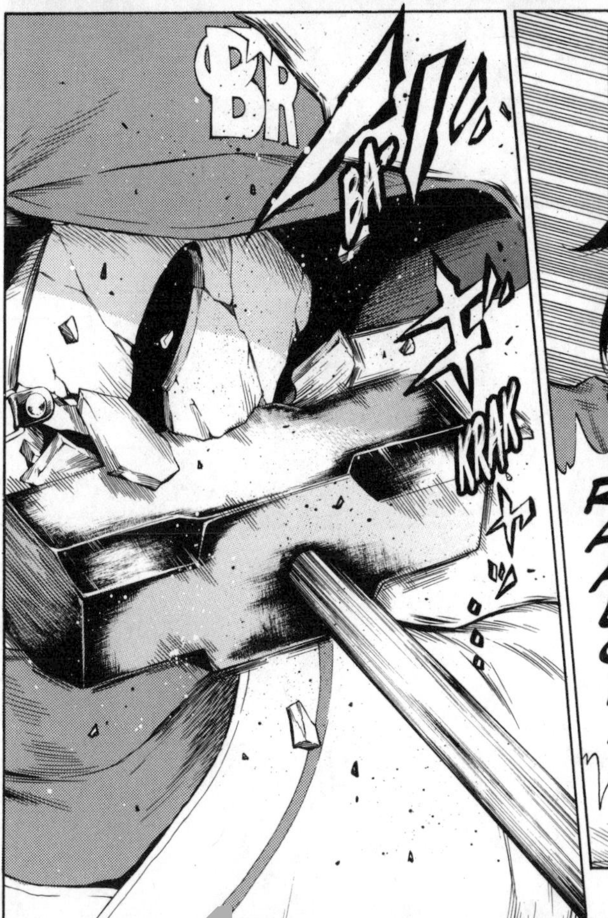
KRAK

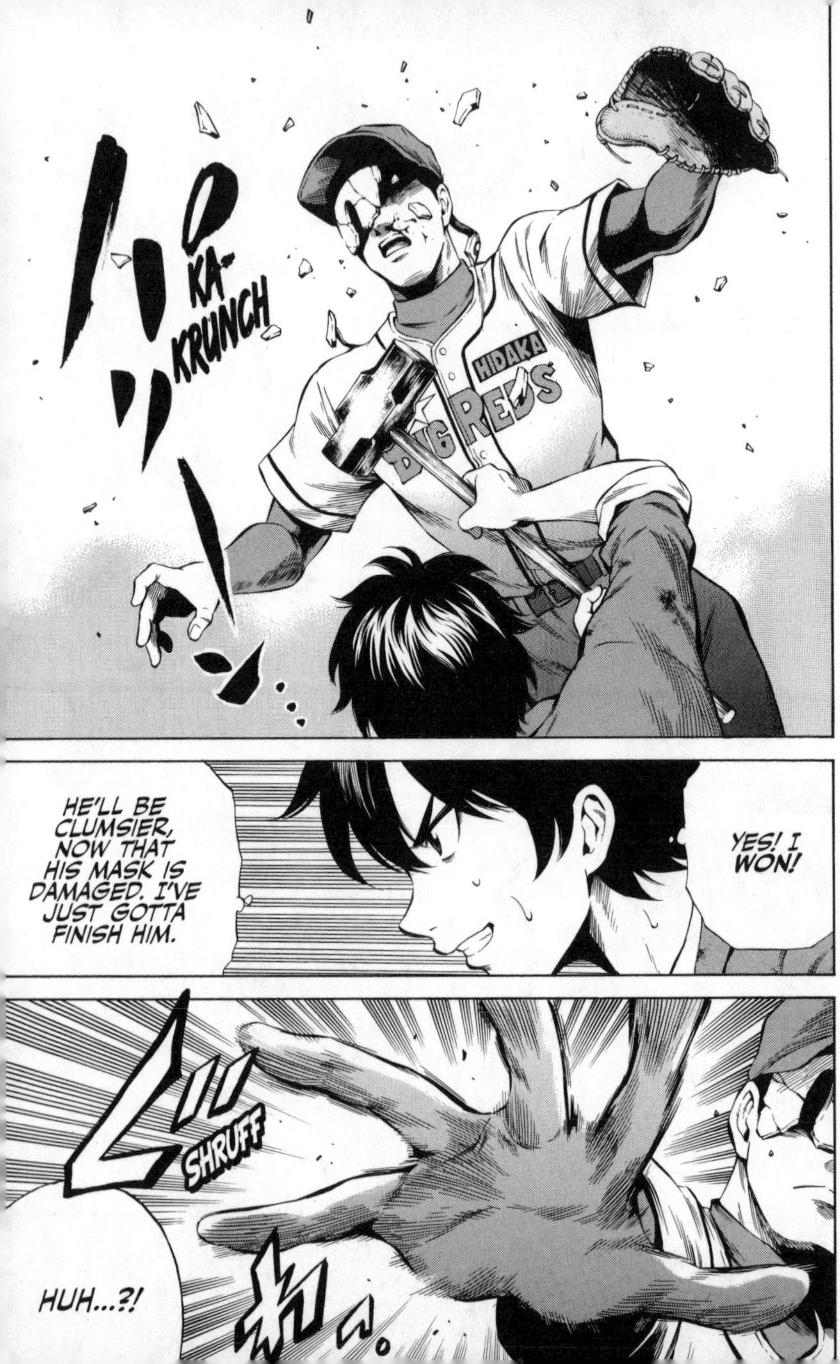
KA-KRUNCH
HIDAKA
BIG REDS
YES! I WON!
HE'LL BE CLUMSIER, NOW THAT HIS MASK IS DAMAGED. I'VE JUST GOTTA FINISH HIM.
SHRUFF
HUH...?!

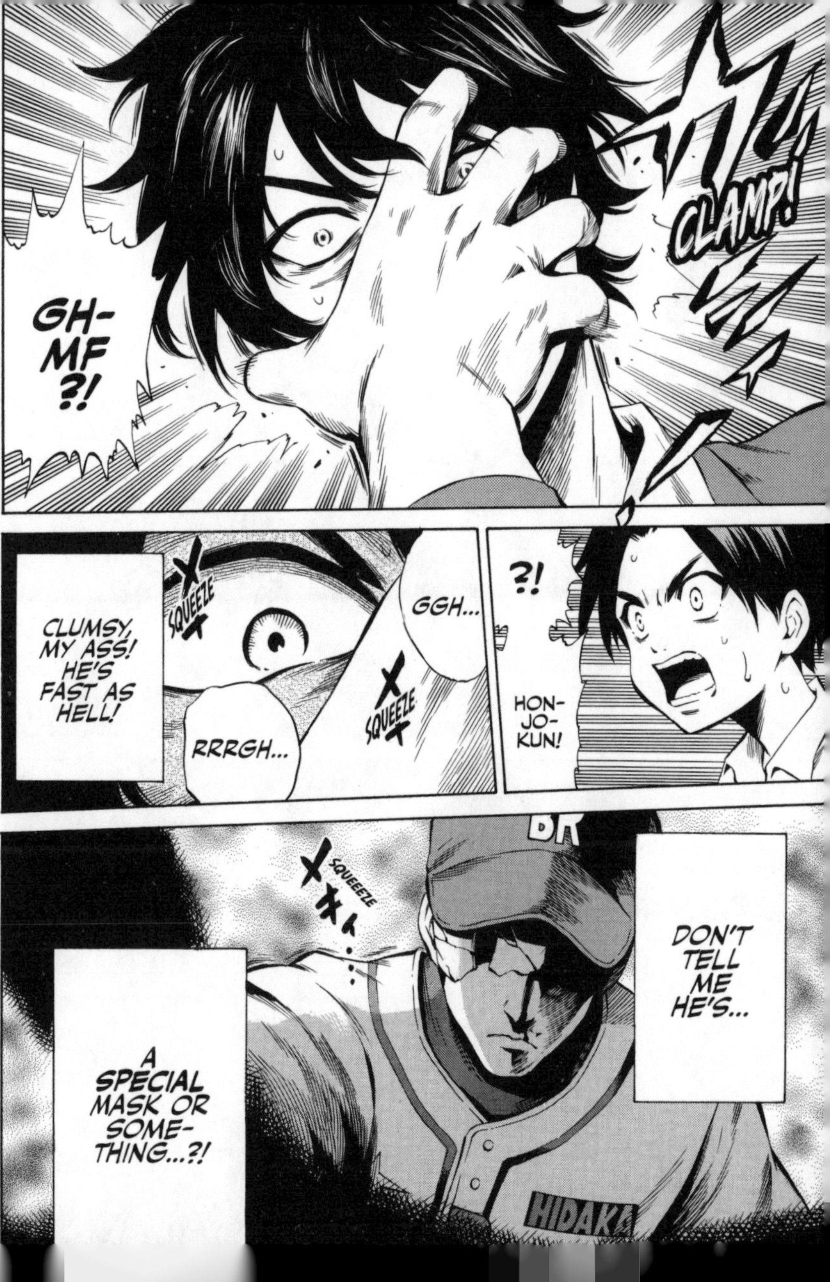
CLAMP!
GH-MF?!
?!
HON-JO-KUN!
GGH...
SQUEEZE
CLUMSY, MY ASS! HE'S FAST AS HELL!
SQUEEZE
RRRGH...
BR
DON'T TELL ME HE'S...
SQUEEEZE
A SPECIAL MASK OR SOME-THING...?!
HIDAKA

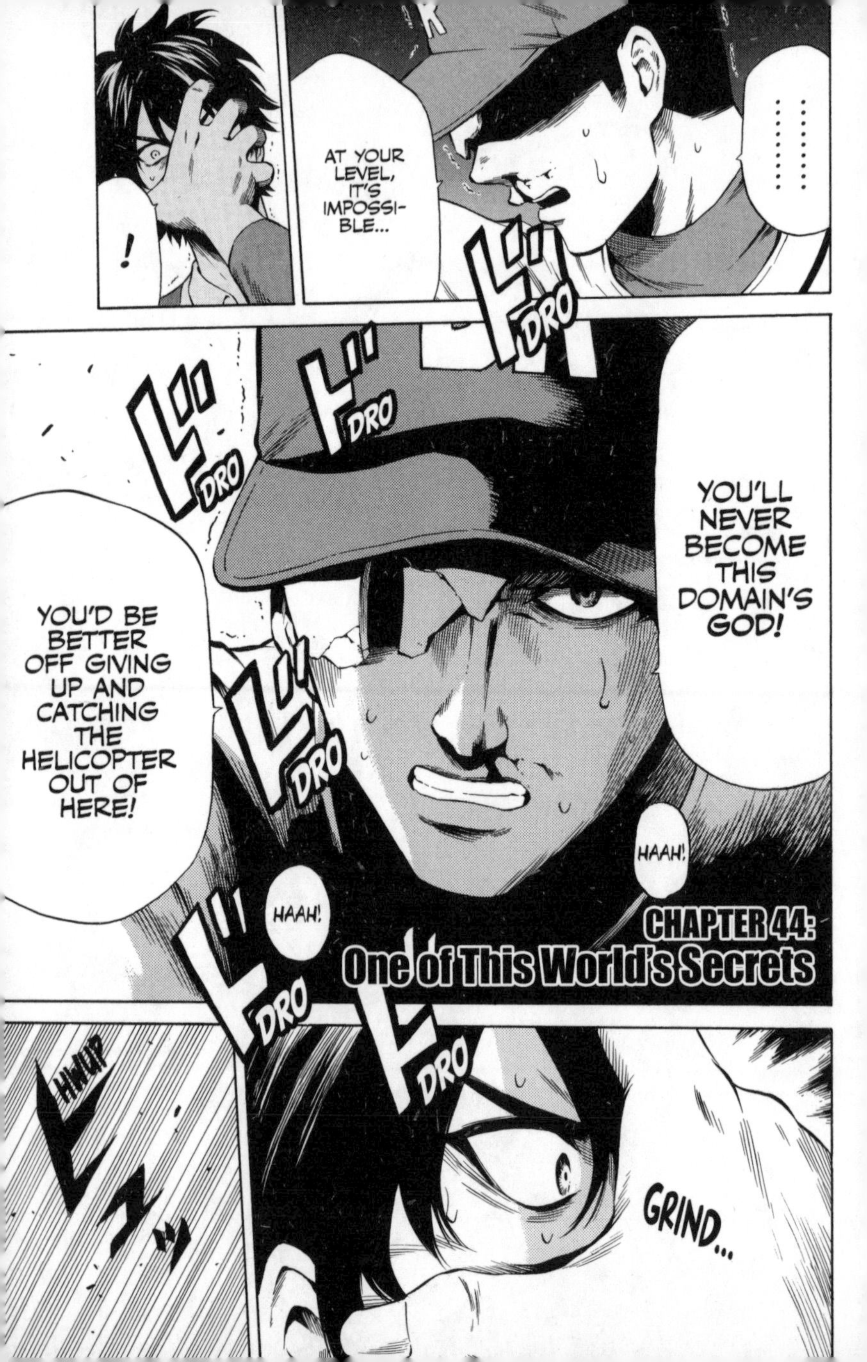
......
AT YOUR LEVEL, IT'S IMPOSSIBLE...
DRO
!
YOU'LL NEVER BECOME THIS DOMAIN'S GOD!
DRO
DRO
DRO
YOU'D BE BETTER OFF GIVING UP AND CATCHING THE HELICOPTER OUT OF HERE!
DRO
HAAH!
HAAH!
CHAPTER 44:
One of This World's Secrets
DRO
DRO
GRIND...
HWUP

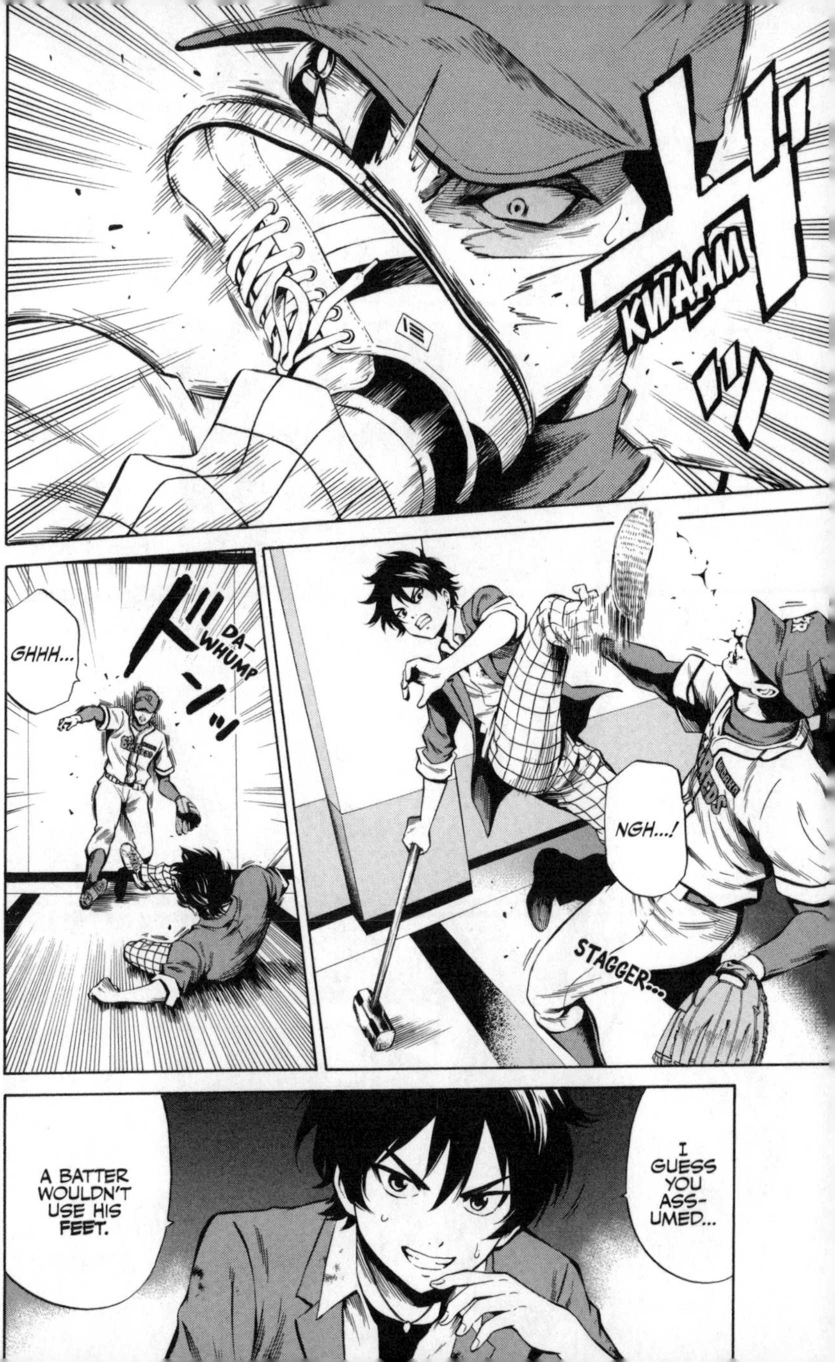
KWAAM
NGH...!
STAGGER...
GHHH...
DA-WHUMP
I GUESS YOU ASS-UMED...
A BATTER WOULDN'T USE HIS FEET.

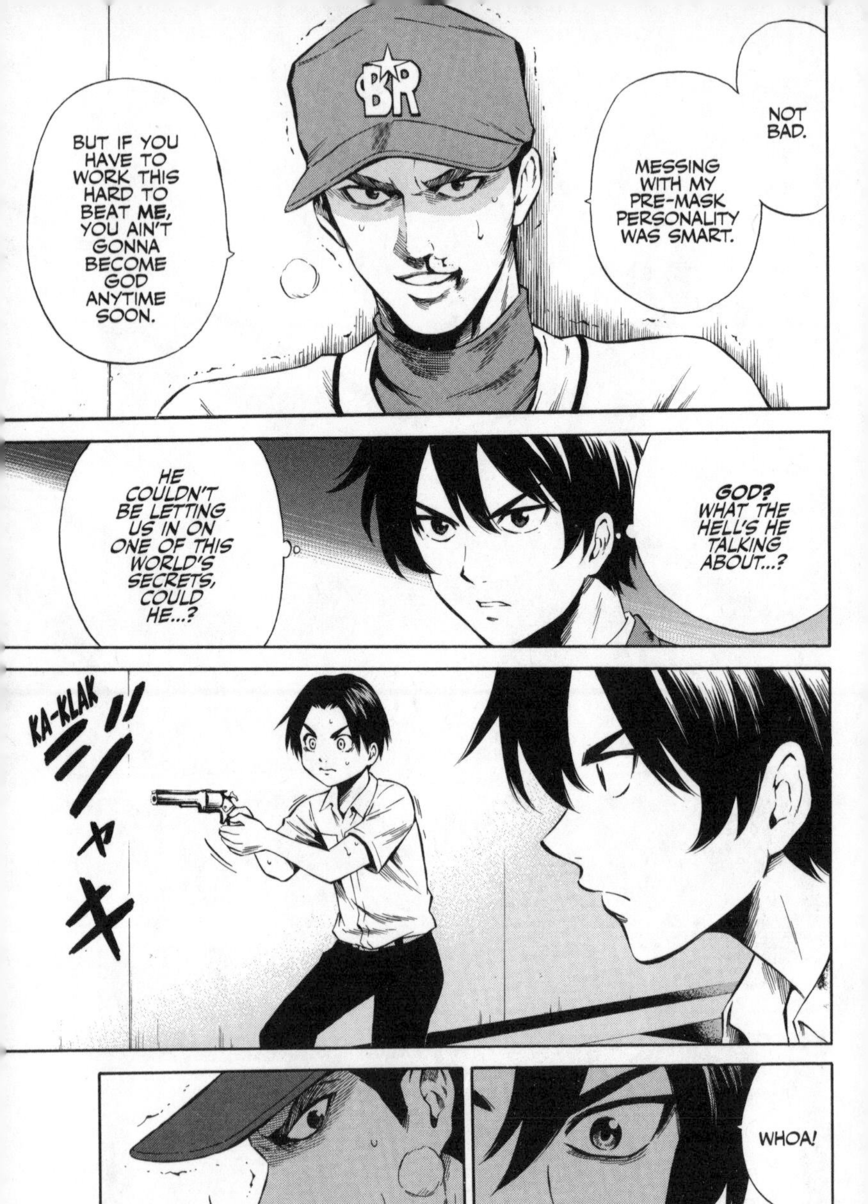
NOT BAD.
MESSING WITH MY PRE-MASK PERSONALITY WAS SMART.
BUT IF YOU HAVE TO WORK THIS HARD TO BEAT ME, YOU AIN'T GONNA BECOME GOD ANYTIME SOON.
GOD? WHAT THE HELL'S HE TALKING ABOUT...?
HE COULDN'T BE LETTING US IN ON ONE OF THIS WORLD'S SECRETS, COULD HE...?
KA-KLAK
ジャキ
WHOA!

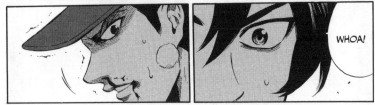

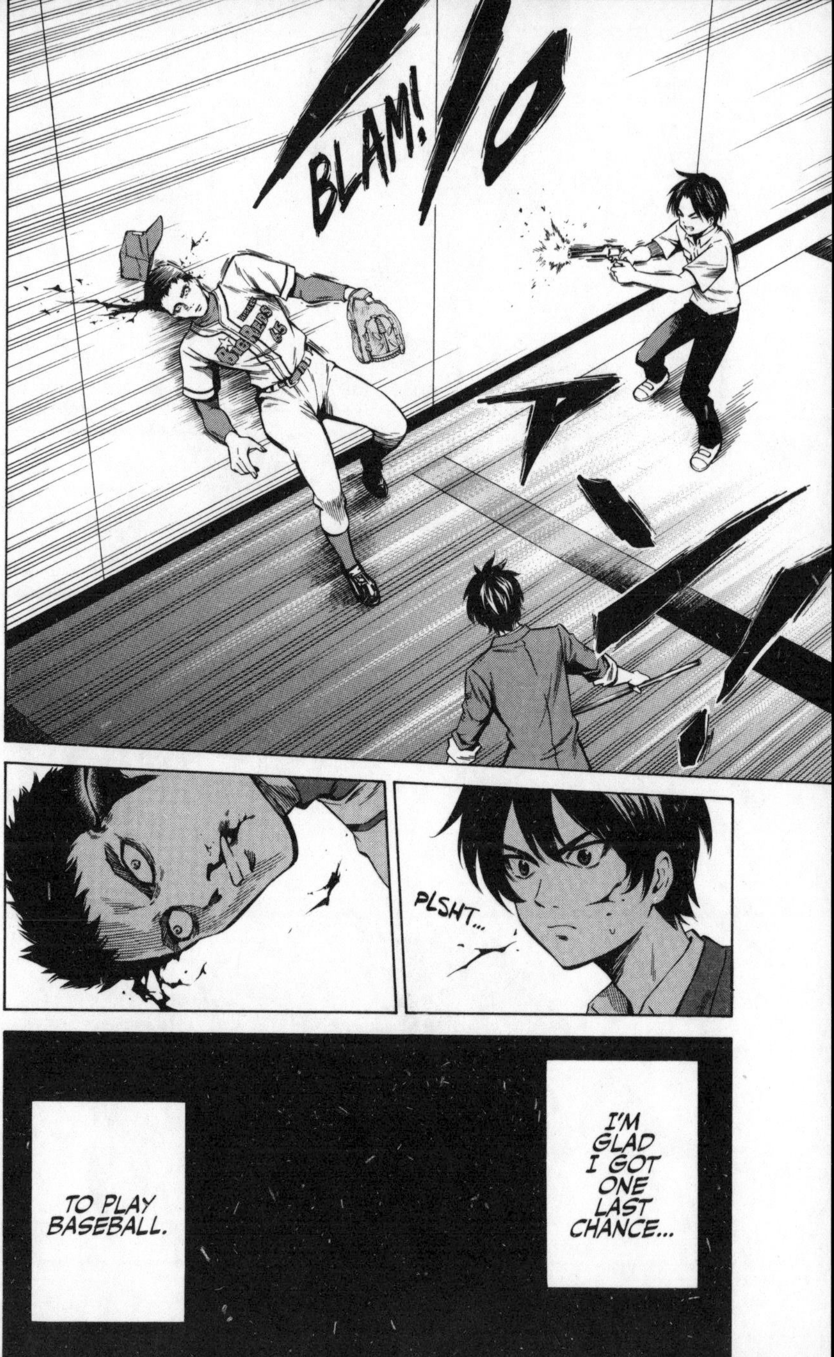
BLAM!
PLSHT...
I'M GLAD I GOT ONE LAST CHANCE...
TO PLAY BASEBALL.

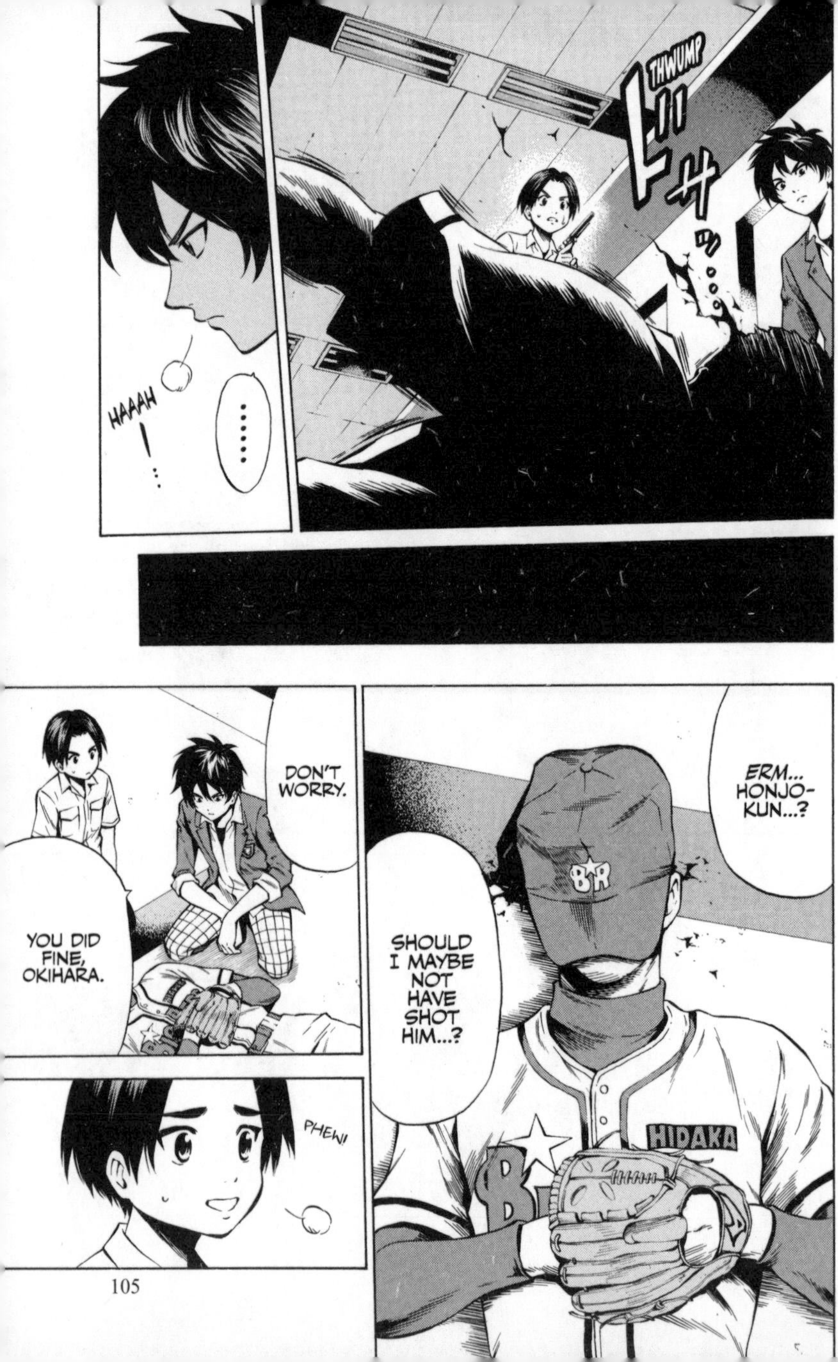
THWUMP
HAAAH
......
ERM... HONJO-KUN...?
SHOULD I MAYBE NOT HAVE SHOT HIM...?
DON'T WORRY.
YOU DID FINE, OKIHARA.
PHEW!

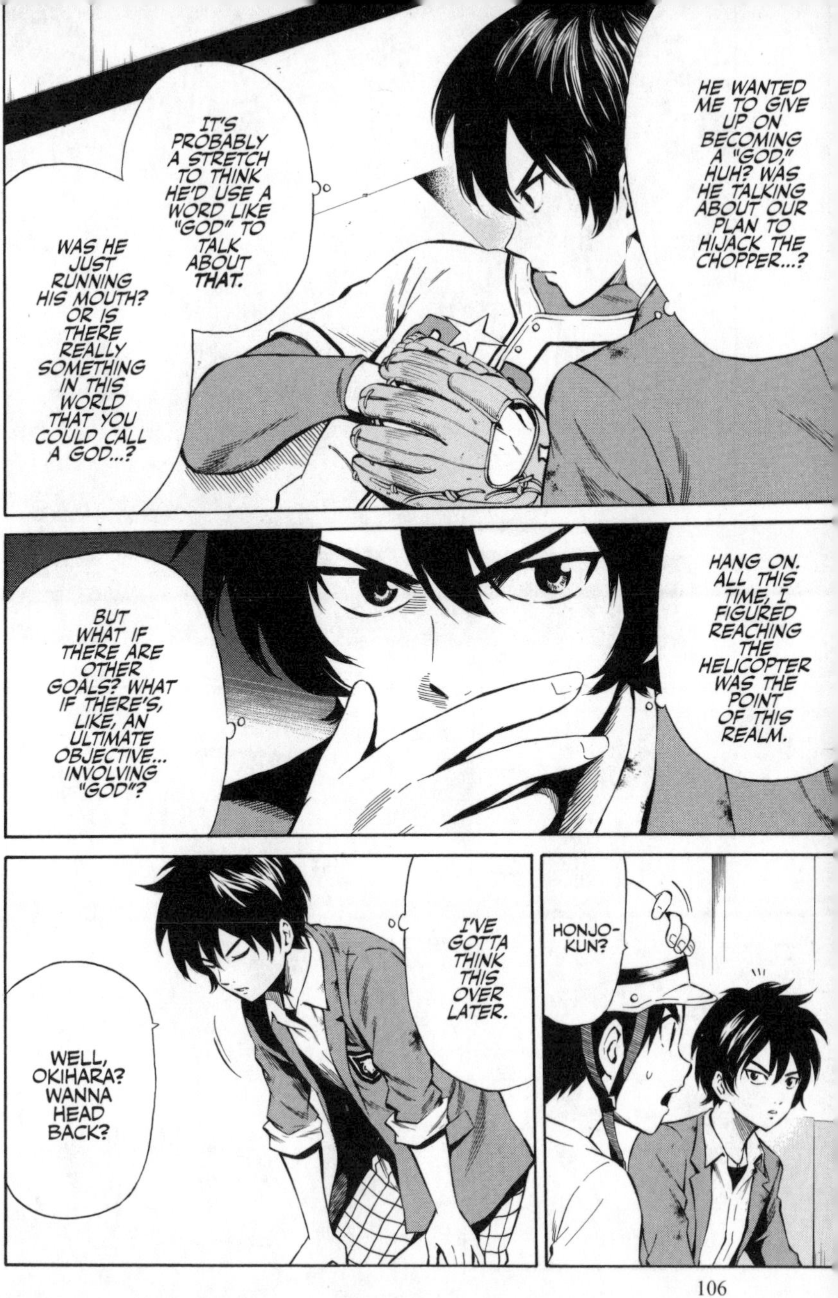
HE WANTED ME TO GIVE UP ON BECOMING A "GOD," HUH? WAS HE TALKING ABOUT OUR PLAN TO HIJACK THE CHOPPER...?
IT'S PROBABLY A STRETCH TO THINK HE'D USE A WORD LIKE "GOD" TO TALK ABOUT THAT.
WAS HE JUST RUNNING HIS MOUTH? OR IS THERE REALLY SOMETHING IN THIS WORLD THAT YOU COULD CALL A GOD...?
HANG ON. ALL THIS TIME, I FIGURED REACHING THE HELICOPTER WAS THE POINT OF THIS REALM.
BUT WHAT IF THERE ARE OTHER GOALS? WHAT IF THERE'S, LIKE, AN ULTIMATE OBJECTIVE... INVOLVING "GOD"?
HONJO-KUN?
I'VE GOTTA THINK THIS OVER LATER.
WELL, OKIHARA? WANNA HEAD BACK?

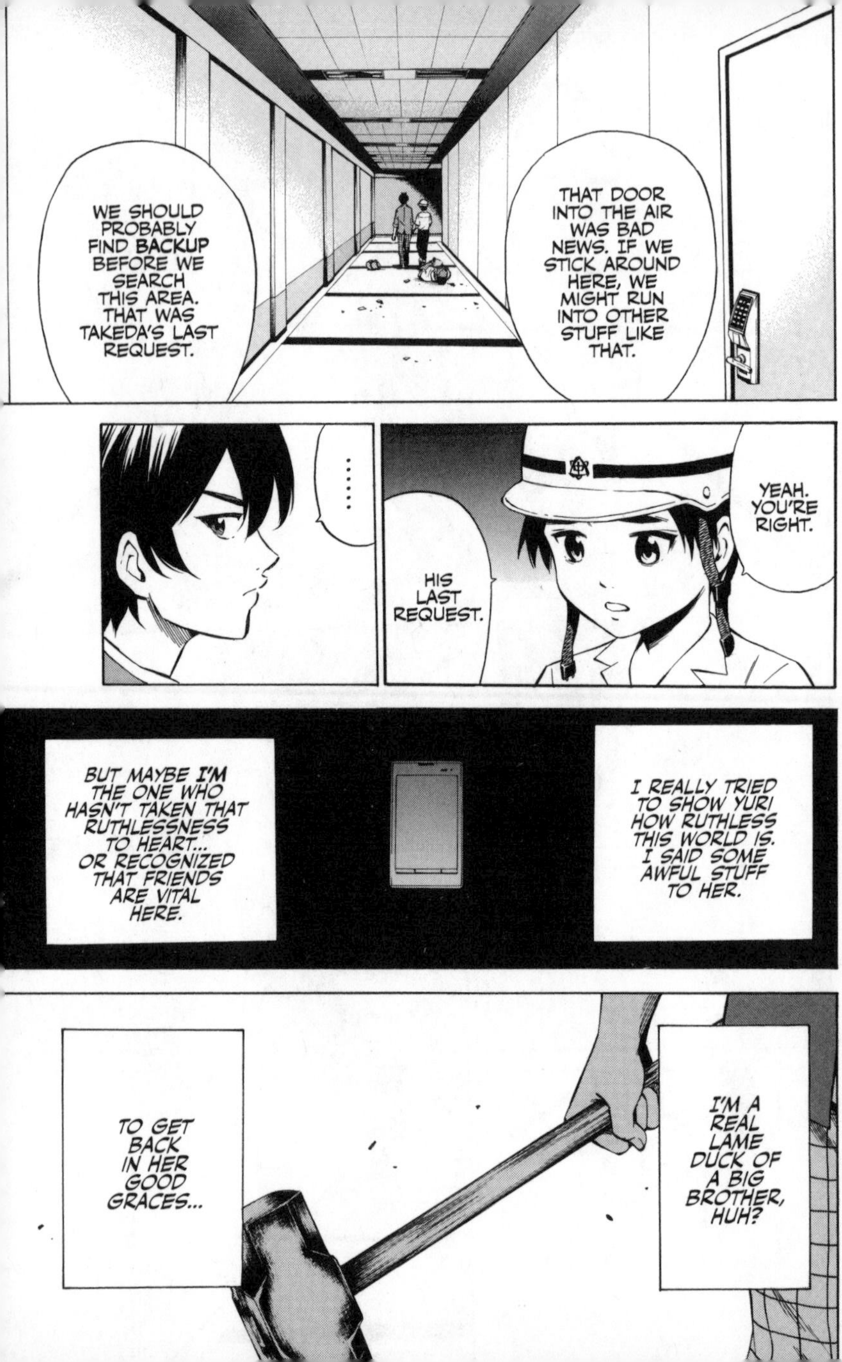
THAT DOOR INTO THE AIR WAS BAD NEWS. IF WE STICK AROUND HERE, WE MIGHT RUN INTO OTHER STUFF LIKE THAT.
WE SHOULD PROBABLY FIND **BACKUP** BEFORE WE SEARCH THIS AREA. THAT WAS TAKEDA'S LAST REQUEST.
YEAH. YOU'RE RIGHT.
HIS LAST REQUEST.
......
I REALLY TRIED TO SHOW YURI HOW RUTHLESS THIS WORLD IS. I SAID SOME AWFUL STUFF TO HER.
BUT MAYBE *I'M* THE ONE WHO HASN'T TAKEN THAT RUTHLESSNESS TO HEART... OR RECOGNIZED THAT FRIENDS ARE VITAL HERE.
I'M A REAL LAME DUCK OF A BIG BROTHER, HUH?
TO GET BACK IN HER GOOD GRACES...

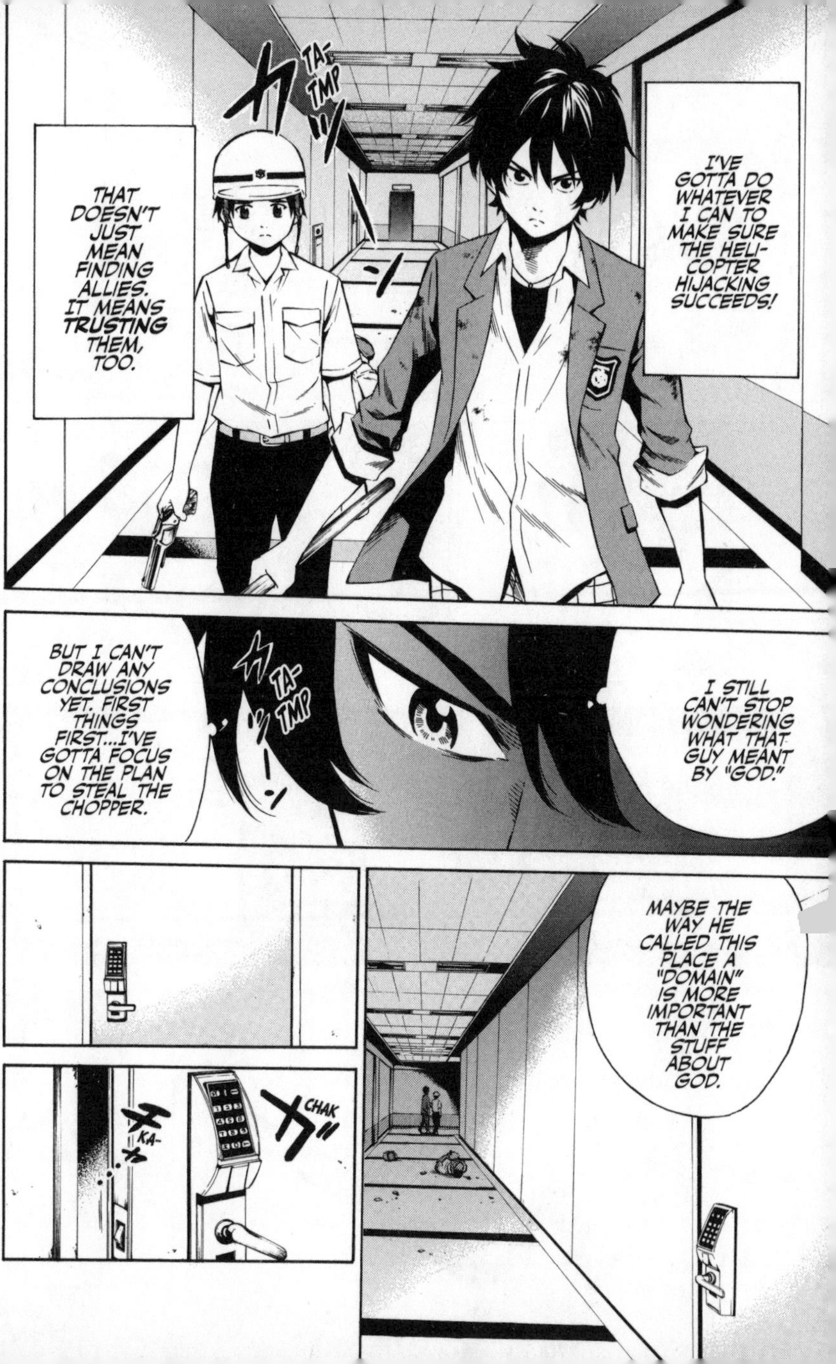
I'VE GOTTA DO WHATEVER I CAN TO MAKE SURE THE HELI-COPTER HIJACKING SUCCEEDS!
TA-TMP
THAT DOESN'T JUST MEAN FINDING ALLIES. IT MEANS **TRUSTING** THEM, TOO.
I STILL CAN'T STOP WONDERING WHAT THAT GUY MEANT BY "GOD."
TA-TMP
BUT I CAN'T DRAW ANY CONCLUSIONS YET. FIRST THINGS FIRST...I'VE GOTTA FOCUS ON THE PLAN TO STEAL THE CHOPPER.
MAYBE THE WAY HE CALLED THIS PLACE A "DOMAIN" IS MORE IMPORTANT THAN THE STUFF ABOUT GOD.
CHAK
KA-

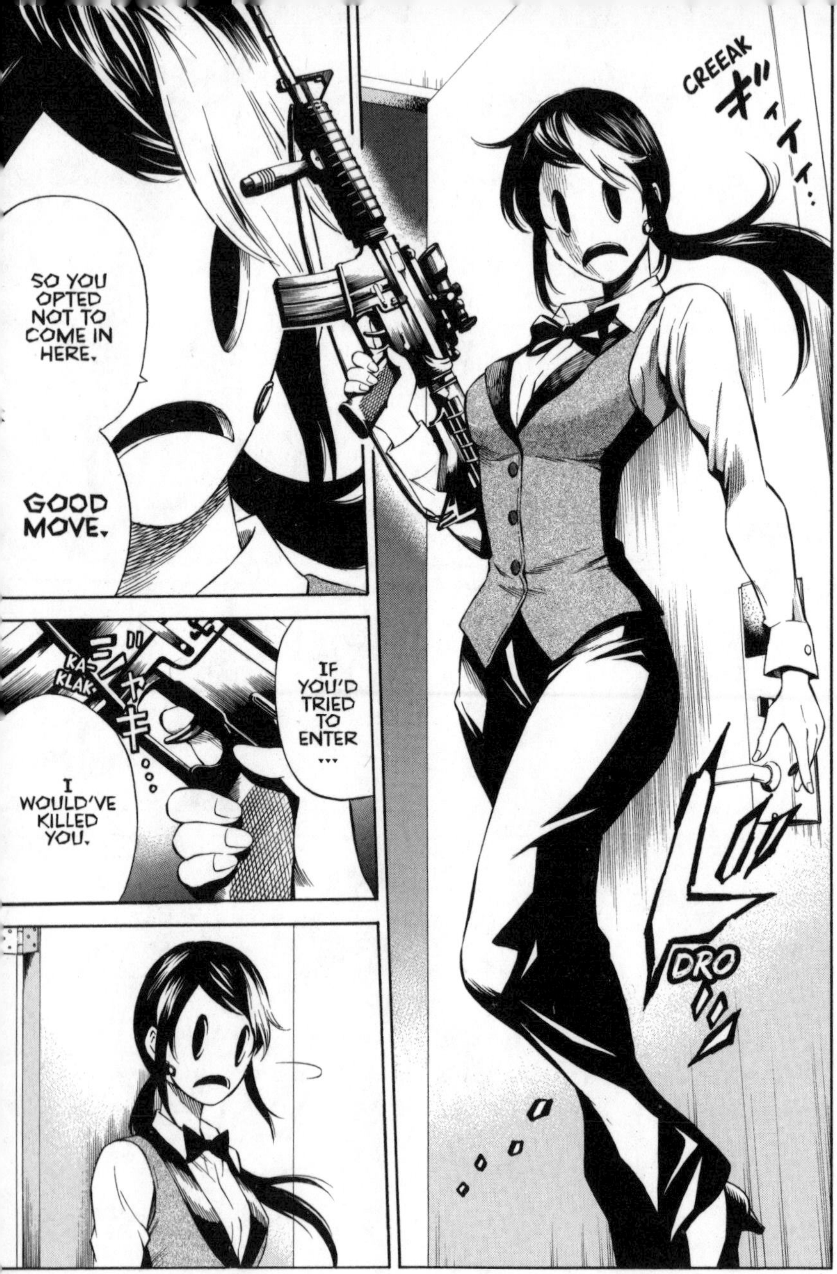
CREEAK
ギィィィ..
DRO
SO YOU OPTED NOT TO COME IN HERE.
GOOD MOVE.
KA-KLAK.
ジャキ
IF YOU'D TRIED TO ENTER...
I WOULD'VE KILLED YOU.

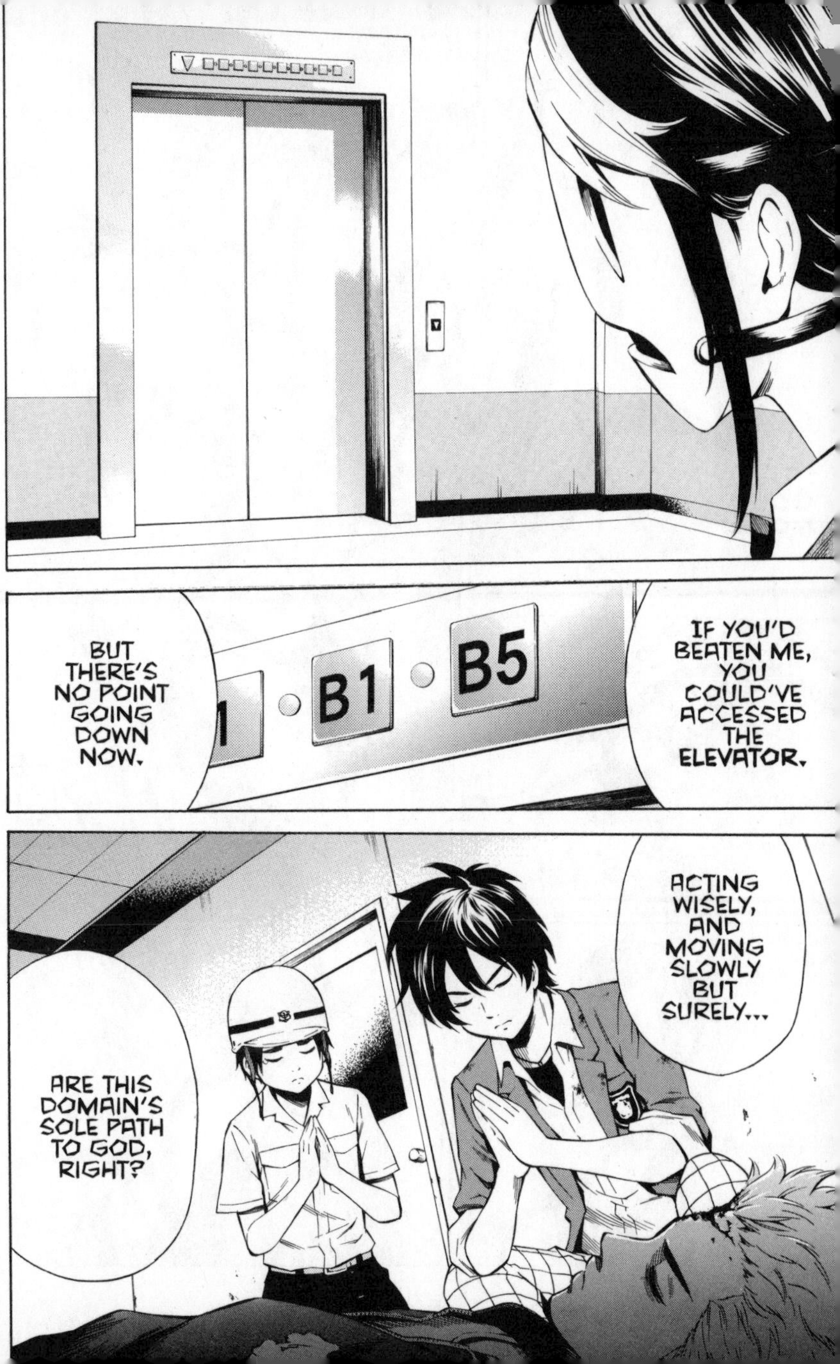
IF YOU'D BEATEN ME, YOU COULD'VE ACCESSED THE ELEVATOR.
B5
B1
BUT THERE'S NO POINT GOING DOWN NOW.
ACTING WISELY, AND MOVING SLOWLY BUT SURELY...
ARE THIS DOMAIN'S SOLE PATH TO GOD, RIGHT?

Takeda...

HIGH-RISE INVASION

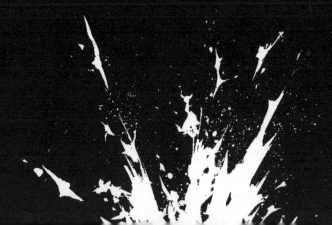

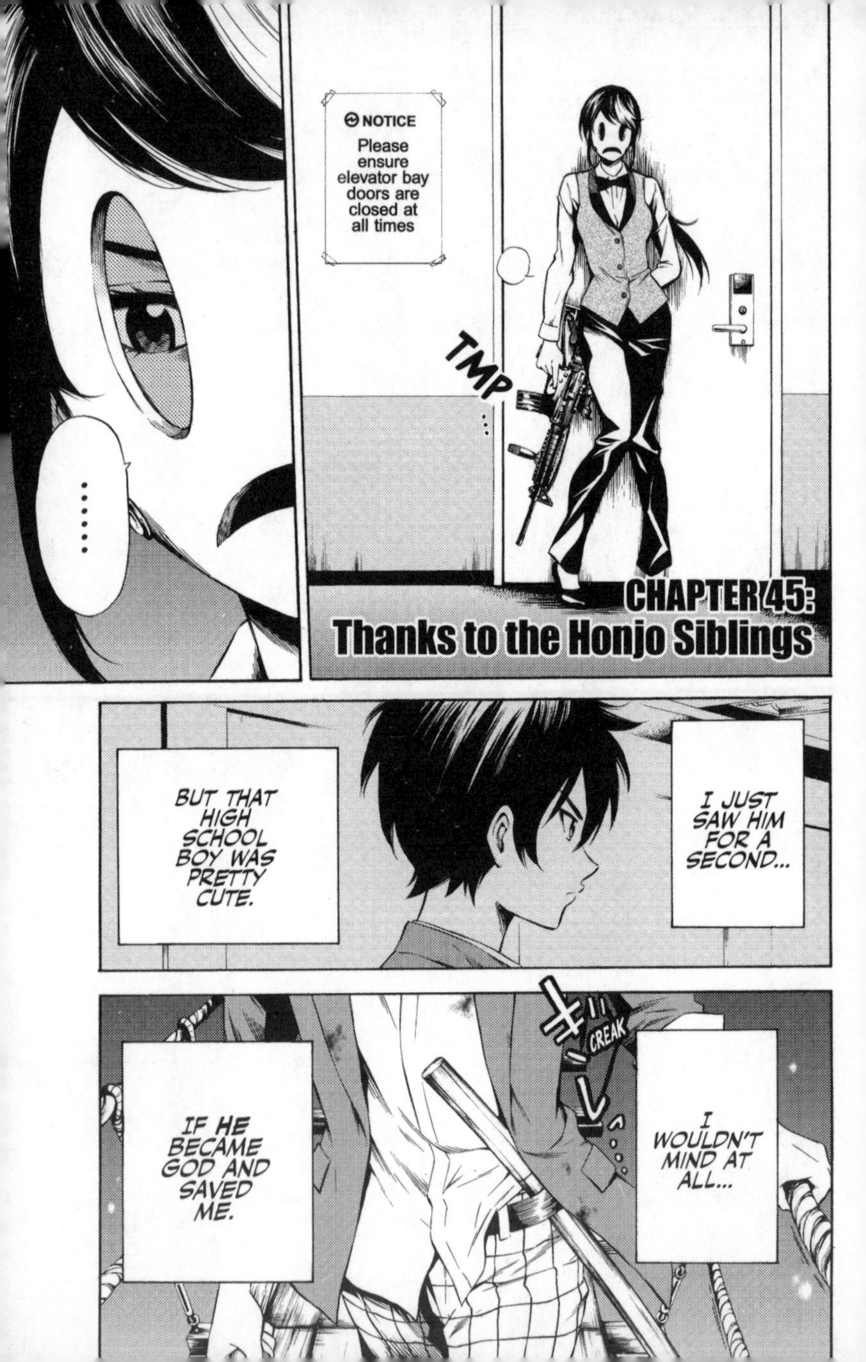
NOTICE
Please ensure elevator bay doors are closed at all times
TMP
...
CHAPTER 45:
Thanks to the Honjo Siblings
......
I JUST SAW HIM FOR A SECOND...
BUT THAT HIGH SCHOOL BOY WAS PRETTY CUTE.
CREAK
I WOULDN'T MIND AT ALL...
IF HE BECAME GOD AND SAVED ME.

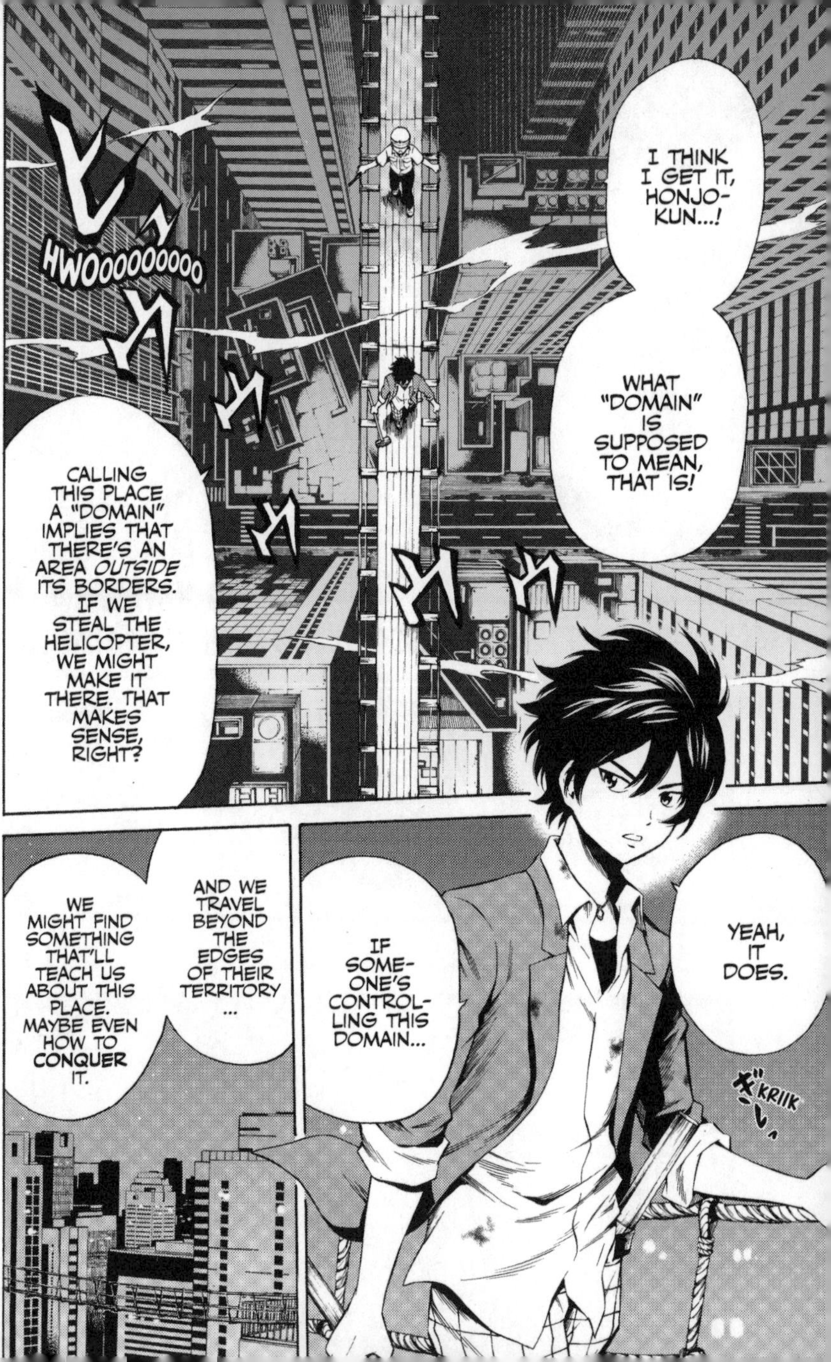
I THINK I GET IT, HONJO-KUN...!
WHAT "DOMAIN" IS SUPPOSED TO MEAN, THAT IS!
HWOOOOOOOO
CALLING THIS PLACE A "DOMAIN" IMPLIES THAT THERE'S AN AREA *OUTSIDE* ITS BORDERS. IF WE STEAL THE HELICOPTER, WE MIGHT MAKE IT THERE. THAT MAKES SENSE, RIGHT?
YEAH, IT DOES.
IF SOMEONE'S CONTROLLING THIS DOMAIN...
KRIIK
AND WE TRAVEL BEYOND THE EDGES OF THEIR TERRITORY ...
WE MIGHT FIND SOMETHING THAT'LL TEACH US ABOUT THIS PLACE. MAYBE EVEN HOW TO **CONQUER** IT.

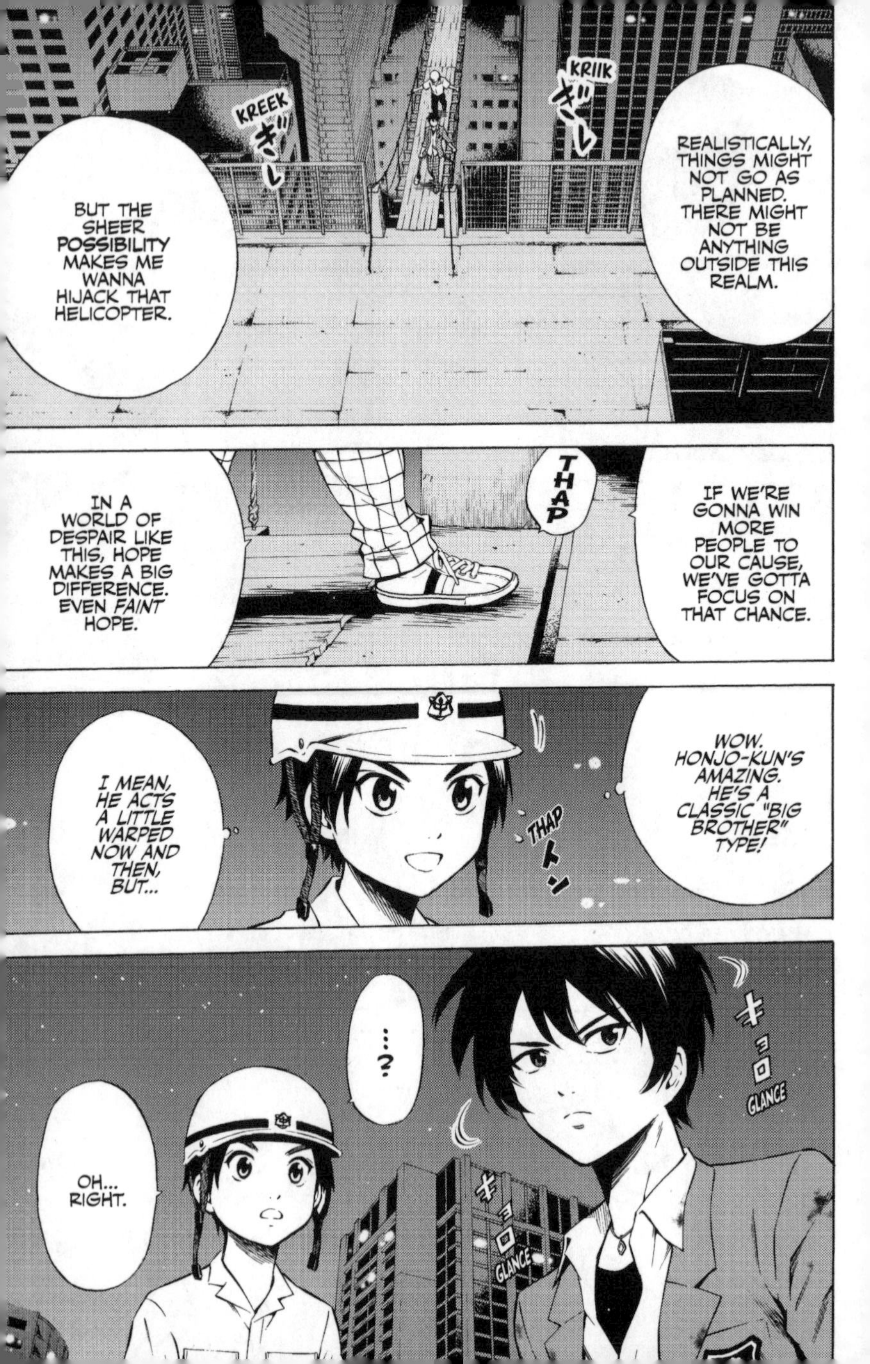
REALISTICALLY, THINGS MIGHT NOT GO AS PLANNED. THERE MIGHT NOT BE ANYTHING OUTSIDE THIS REALM.
KRIIK
KREEK
BUT THE SHEER POSSIBILITY MAKES ME WANNA HIJACK THAT HELICOPTER.
IF WE'RE GONNA WIN MORE PEOPLE TO OUR CAUSE, WE'VE GOTTA FOCUS ON THAT CHANCE.
THAP
IN A WORLD OF DESPAIR LIKE THIS, HOPE MAKES A BIG DIFFERENCE. EVEN *FAINT* HOPE.
WOW. HONJO-KUN'S AMAZING. HE'S A CLASSIC "BIG BROTHER" TYPE!
THAP
I MEAN, HE ACTS A LITTLE WARPED NOW AND THEN, BUT...
GLANCE
...?
GLANCE
OH... RIGHT.

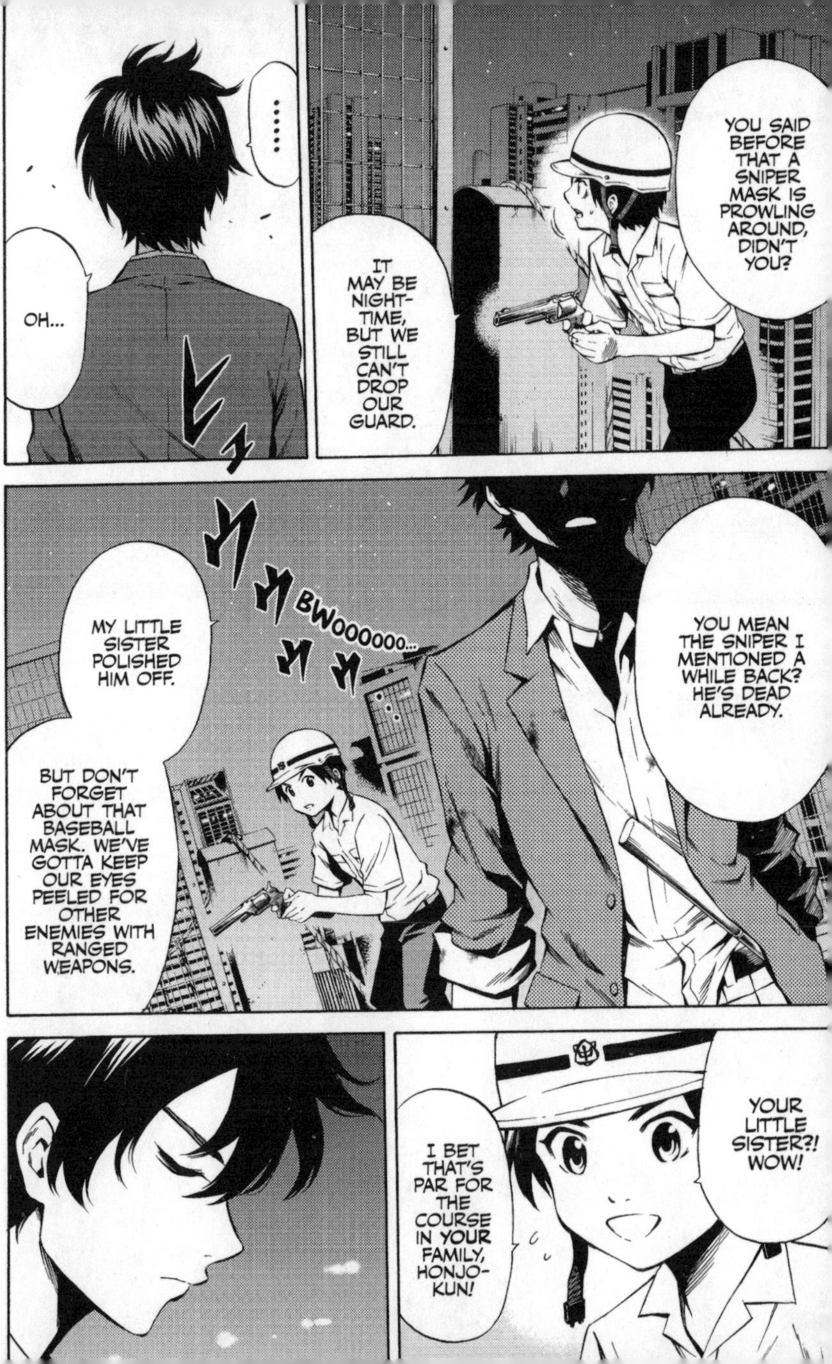
YOU SAID BEFORE THAT A SNIPER MASK IS PROWLING AROUND, DIDN'T YOU?
IT MAY BE NIGHT-TIME, BUT WE STILL CAN'T DROP OUR GUARD.
......
OH...
YOU MEAN THE SNIPER I MENTIONED A WHILE BACK? HE'S DEAD ALREADY.
MY LITTLE SISTER POLISHED HIM OFF.
BWOOOOOOO...
BUT DON'T FORGET ABOUT THAT BASEBALL MASK. WE'VE GOTTA KEEP OUR EYES PEELED FOR OTHER ENEMIES WITH RANGED WEAPONS.
YOUR LITTLE SISTER?! WOW!
I BET THAT'S PAR FOR THE COURSE IN YOUR FAMILY, HONJO-KUN!

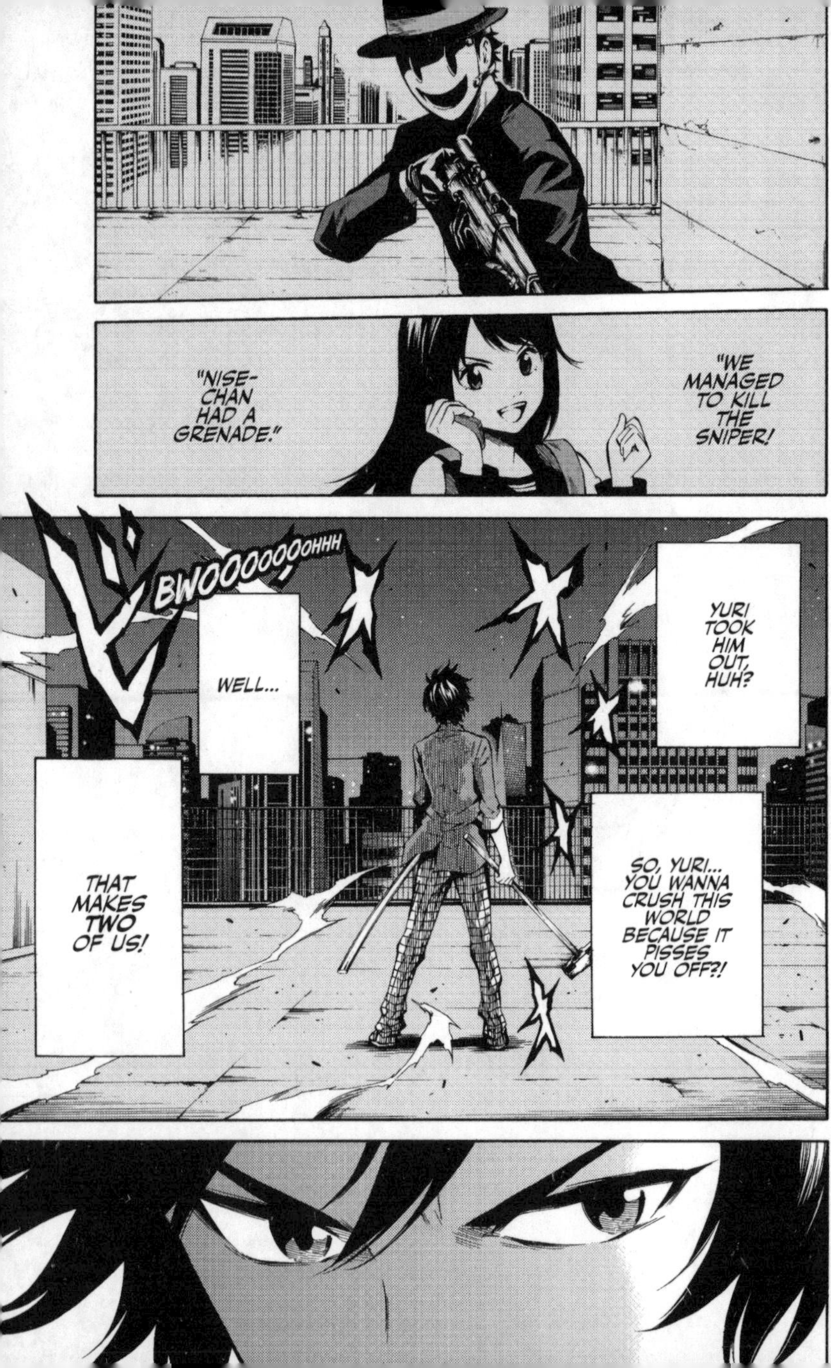
"WE MANAGED TO KILL THE SNIPER!
"NISE-CHAN HAD A GRENADE."
YURI TOOK HIM OUT, HUH?
BWOOOOOOOHHH
WELL...
SO, YURI... YOU WANNA CRUSH THIS WORLD BECAUSE IT PISSES YOU OFF?!
THAT MAKES TWO OF US!

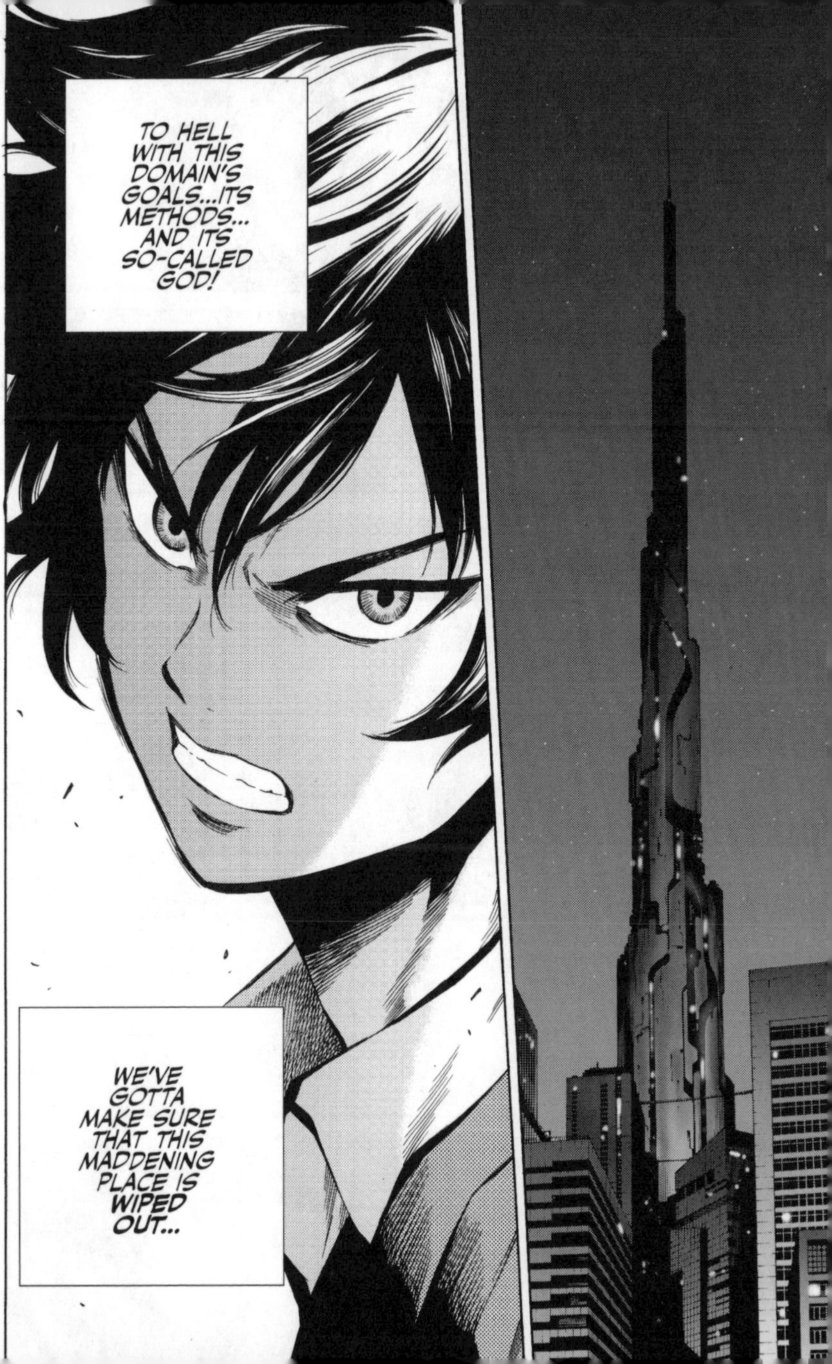
TO HELL WITH THIS DOMAIN'S GOALS...ITS METHODS... AND ITS SO-CALLED GOD!
WE'VE GOTTA MAKE SURE THAT THIS MADDENING PLACE IS WIPED OUT...

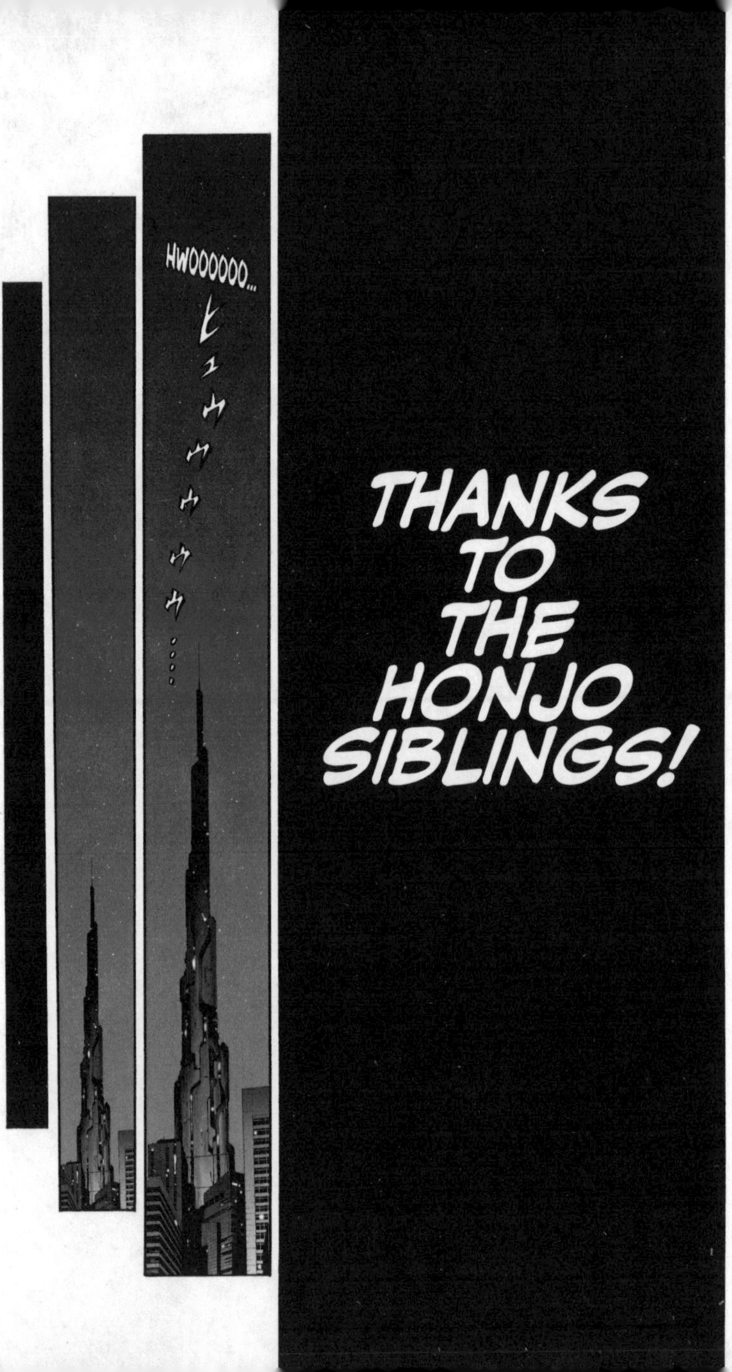
THANKS TO THE HONJO SIBLINGS!
HWOOOOOO...

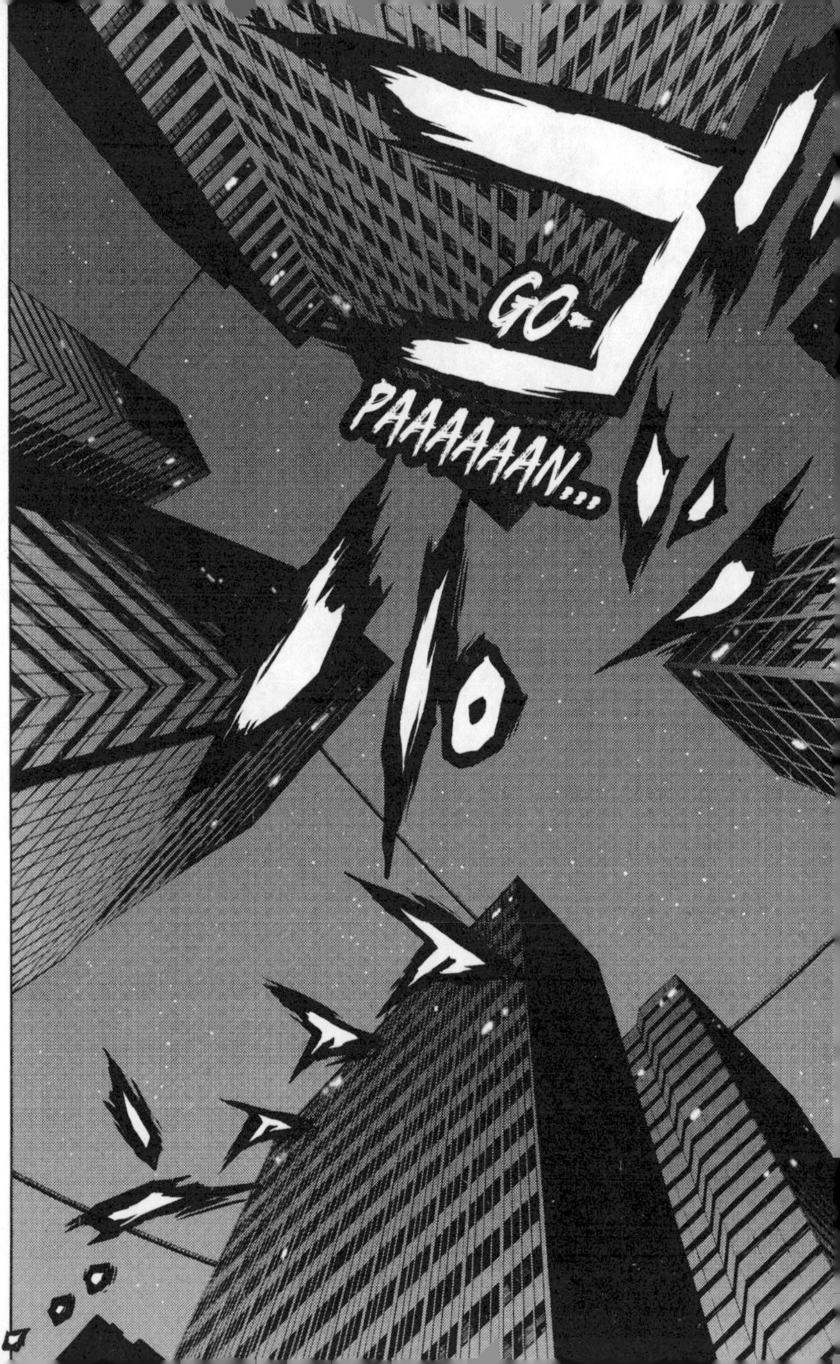
GO-
PAAAAAAN...

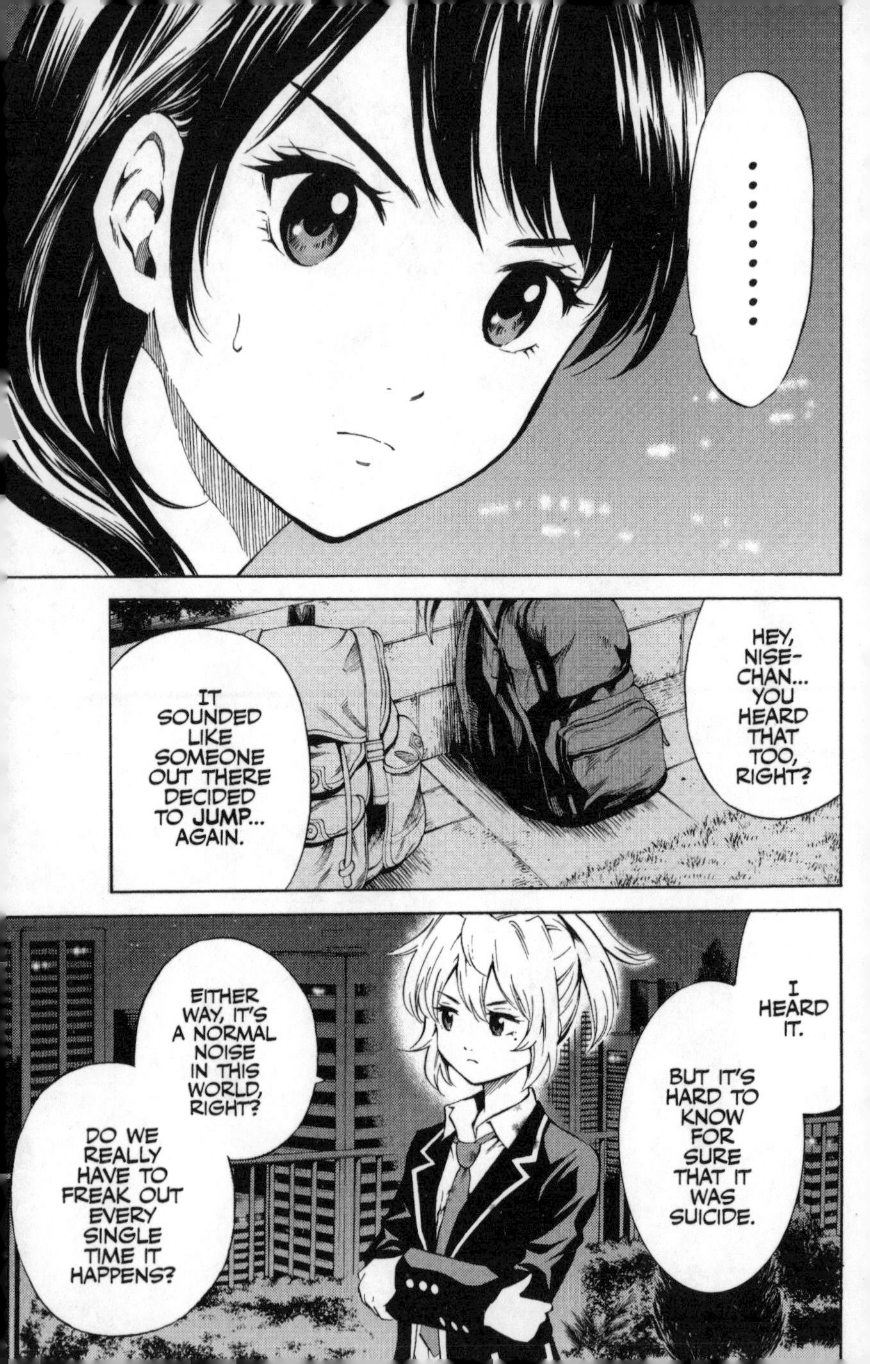
....
HEY, NISE-CHAN... YOU HEARD THAT TOO, RIGHT?
IT SOUNDED LIKE SOMEONE OUT THERE DECIDED TO JUMP... AGAIN.
I HEARD IT.
BUT IT'S HARD TO KNOW FOR SURE THAT IT WAS SUICIDE.
EITHER WAY, IT'S A NORMAL NOISE IN THIS WORLD, RIGHT?
DO WE REALLY HAVE TO FREAK OUT EVERY SINGLE TIME IT HAPPENS?

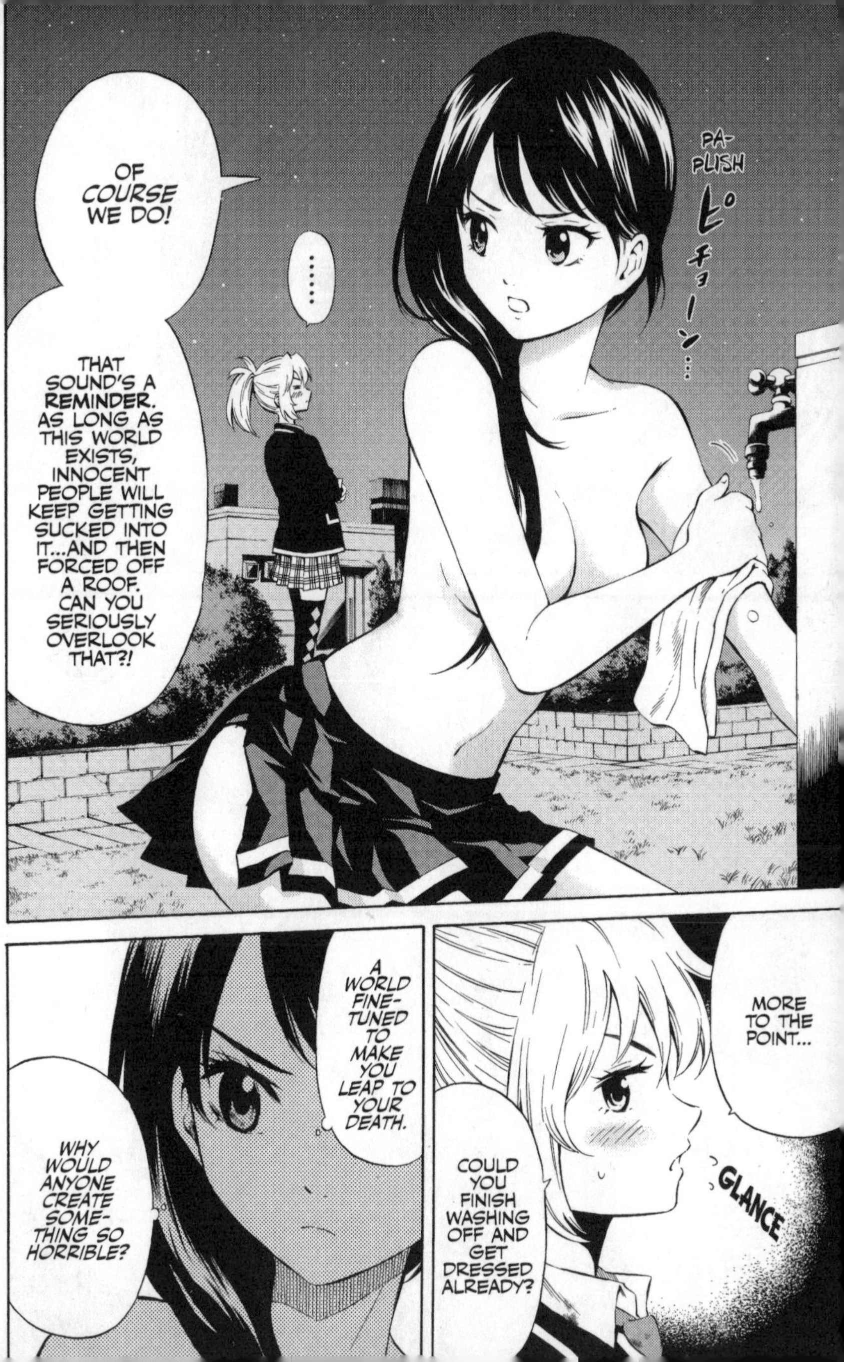
PA-PLISH
ピチョーン…
……
OF COURSE WE DO!
THAT SOUND'S A REMINDER. AS LONG AS THIS WORLD EXISTS, INNOCENT PEOPLE WILL KEEP GETTING SUCKED INTO IT...AND THEN FORCED OFF A ROOF. CAN YOU SERIOUSLY OVERLOOK THAT?!
MORE TO THE POINT...
GLANCE
COULD YOU FINISH WASHING OFF AND GET DRESSED ALREADY?
A WORLD FINE-TUNED TO MAKE YOU LEAP TO YOUR DEATH.
WHY WOULD ANYONE CREATE SOME-THING SO HORRIBLE?

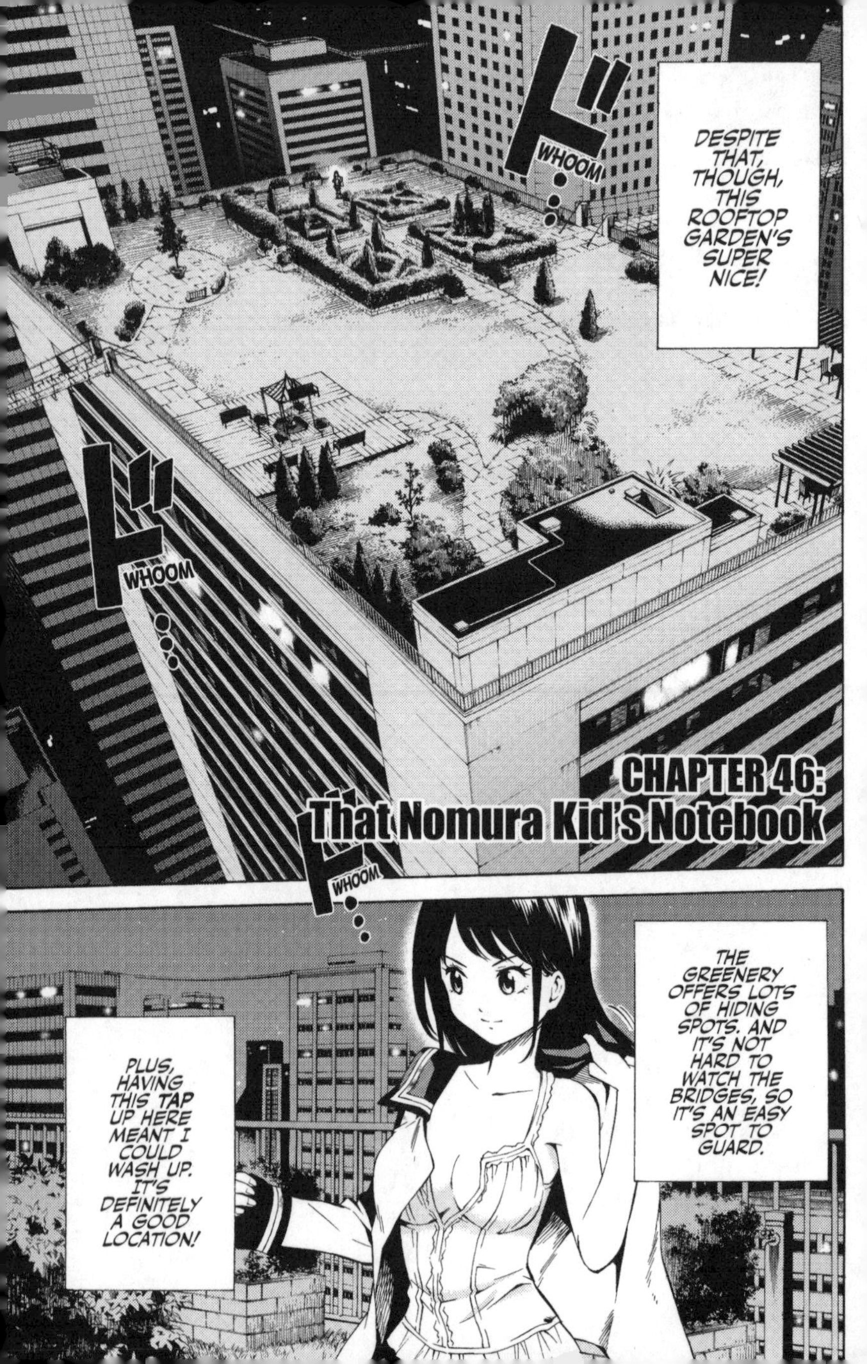
ド WHOOM...
DESPITE THAT, THOUGH, THIS ROOFTOP GARDEN'S SUPER NICE!
ド WHOOM...
CHAPTER 46: That Nomura Kid's Notebook
ド WHOOM...
THE GREENERY OFFERS LOTS OF HIDING SPOTS. AND IT'S NOT HARD TO WATCH THE BRIDGES, SO IT'S AN EASY SPOT TO GUARD.
PLUS, HAVING THIS TAP UP HERE MEANT I COULD WASH UP. IT'S DEFINITELY A GOOD LOCATION!

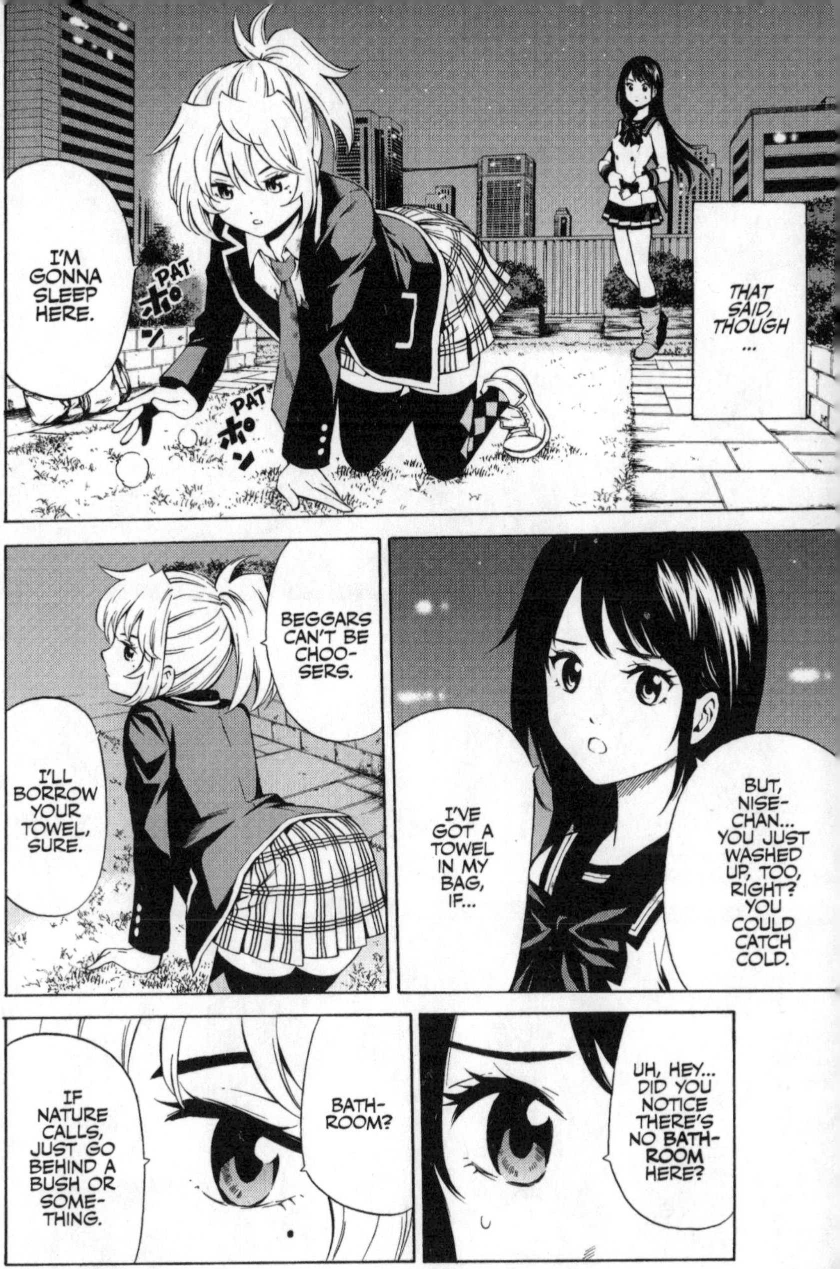
THAT SAID, THOUGH...
I'M GONNA SLEEP HERE.
PAT ポン
PAT ポン
BUT, NISE-CHAN... YOU JUST WASHED UP, TOO, RIGHT? YOU COULD CATCH COLD.
I'VE GOT A TOWEL IN MY BAG, IF...
BEGGARS CAN'T BE CHOOSERS.
I'LL BORROW YOUR TOWEL, SURE.
UH, HEY... DID YOU NOTICE THERE'S NO BATHROOM HERE?
BATHROOM?
IF NATURE CALLS, JUST GO BEHIND A BUSH OR SOMETHING.

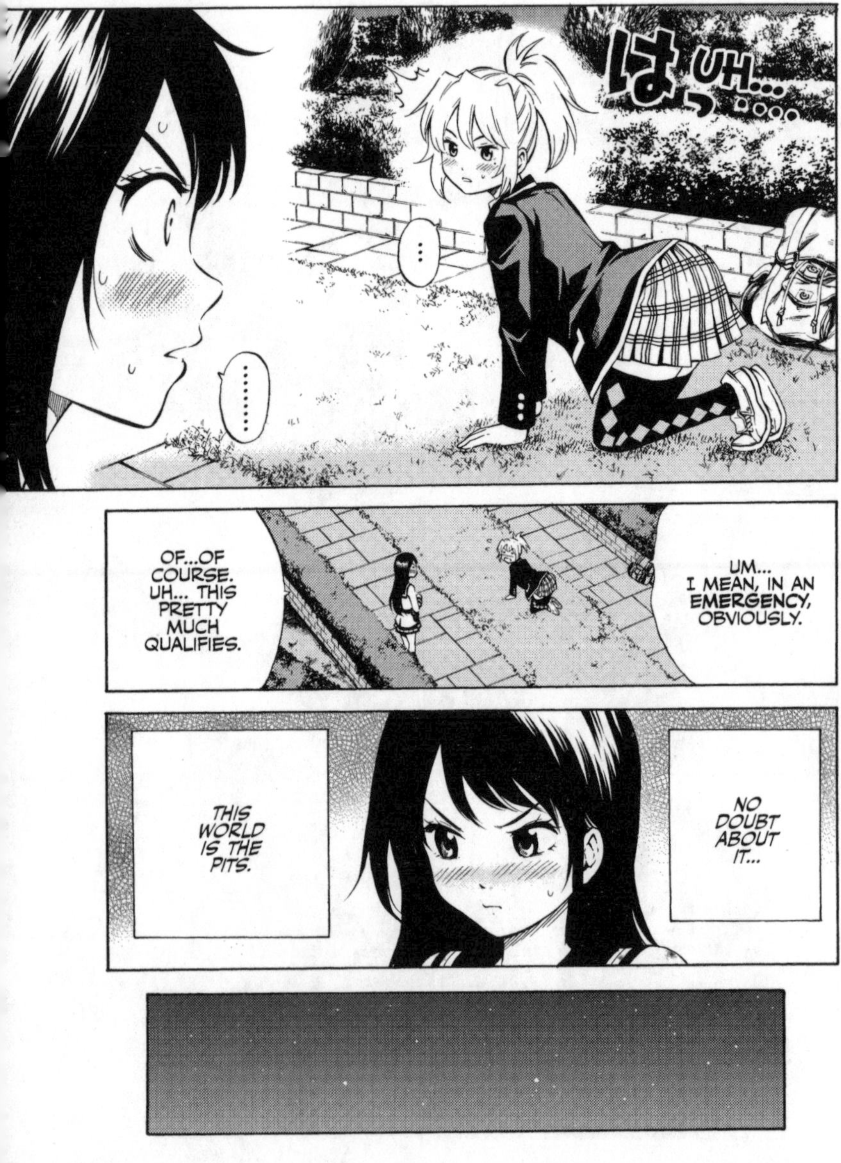
はっ UH...
....
...
....
UM... I MEAN, IN AN EMERGENCY, OBVIOUSLY.
OF...OF COURSE. UH... THIS PRETTY MUCH QUALIFIES.
NO DOUBT ABOUT IT...
THIS WORLD IS THE PITS.

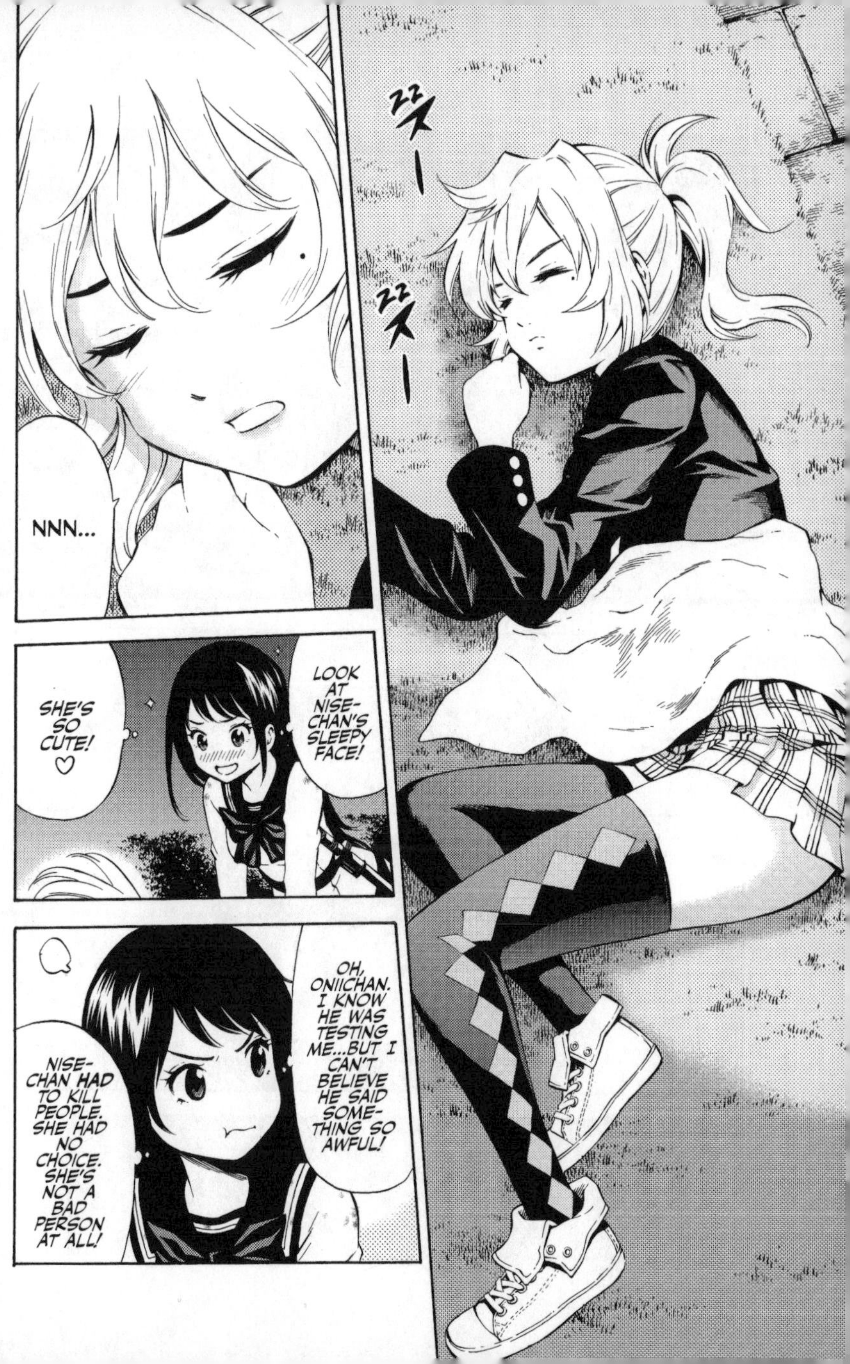
ZZ スー
ZZ スー
NNN...
LOOK AT NISE-CHAN'S SLEEPY FACE!
SHE'S SO CUTE! ♡
OH, ONIICHAN. I KNOW HE WAS TESTING ME...BUT I CAN'T BELIEVE HE SAID SOME-THING SO AWFUL!
NISE-CHAN HAD TO KILL PEOPLE. SHE HAD NO CHOICE. SHE'S NOT A BAD PERSON AT ALL!

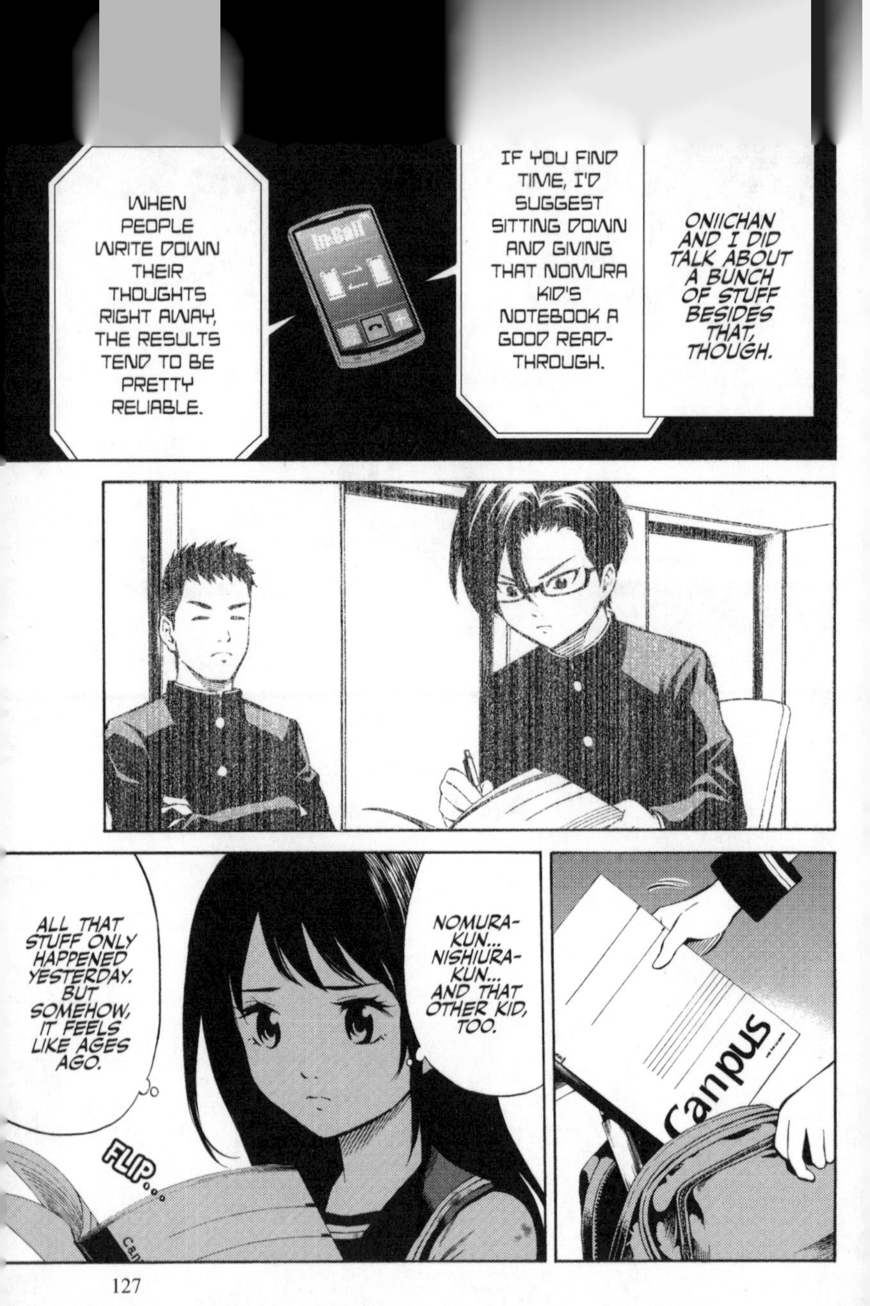
ONIICHAN AND I DID TALK ABOUT A BUNCH OF STUFF BESIDES THAT, THOUGH.
IF YOU FIND TIME, I'D SUGGEST SITTING DOWN AND GIVING THAT NOMURA KID'S NOTEBOOK A GOOD READ-THROUGH.
WHEN PEOPLE WRITE DOWN THEIR THOUGHTS RIGHT AWAY, THE RESULTS TEND TO BE PRETTY RELIABLE.
Canpus
NOMURA-KUN... NISHIURA-KUN... AND THAT OTHER KID, TOO.
ALL THAT STUFF ONLY HAPPENED YESTERDAY. BUT SOMEHOW, IT FEELS LIKE AGES AGO.
FLIP...

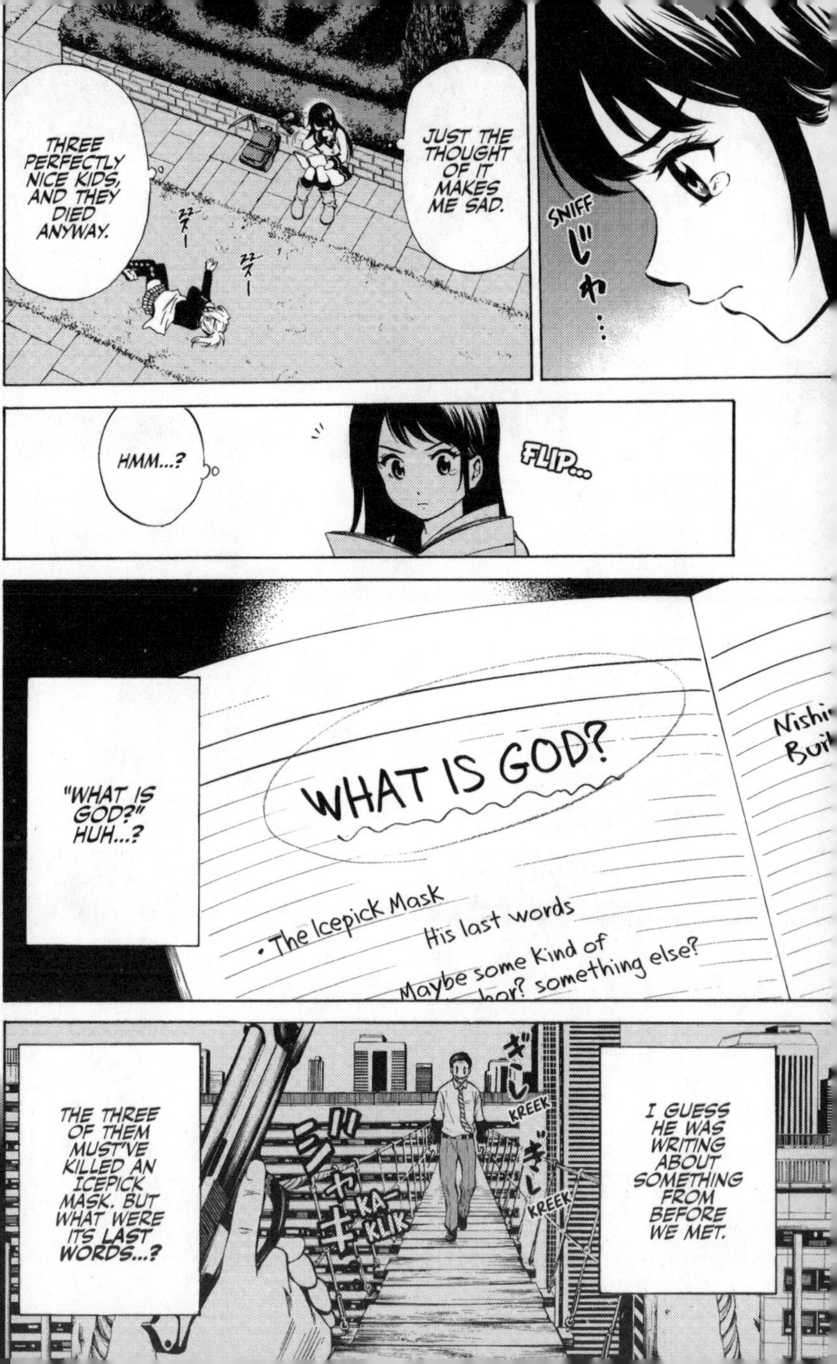
SNIFF
じゃ…
JUST THE THOUGHT OF IT MAKES ME SAD.
THREE PERFECTLY NICE KIDS, AND THEY DIED ANYWAY.
HMM...?
FLIP...
"WHAT IS GOD?" HUH...?
WHAT IS GOD?
• The Icepick Mask
His last words
Maybe some kind of
something else?
I GUESS HE WAS WRITING ABOUT SOMETHING FROM BEFORE WE MET.
KREEK
KREEK
KA-KLIK
THE THREE OF THEM MUST'VE KILLED AN ICEPICK MASK. BUT WHAT WERE ITS LAST WORDS...?

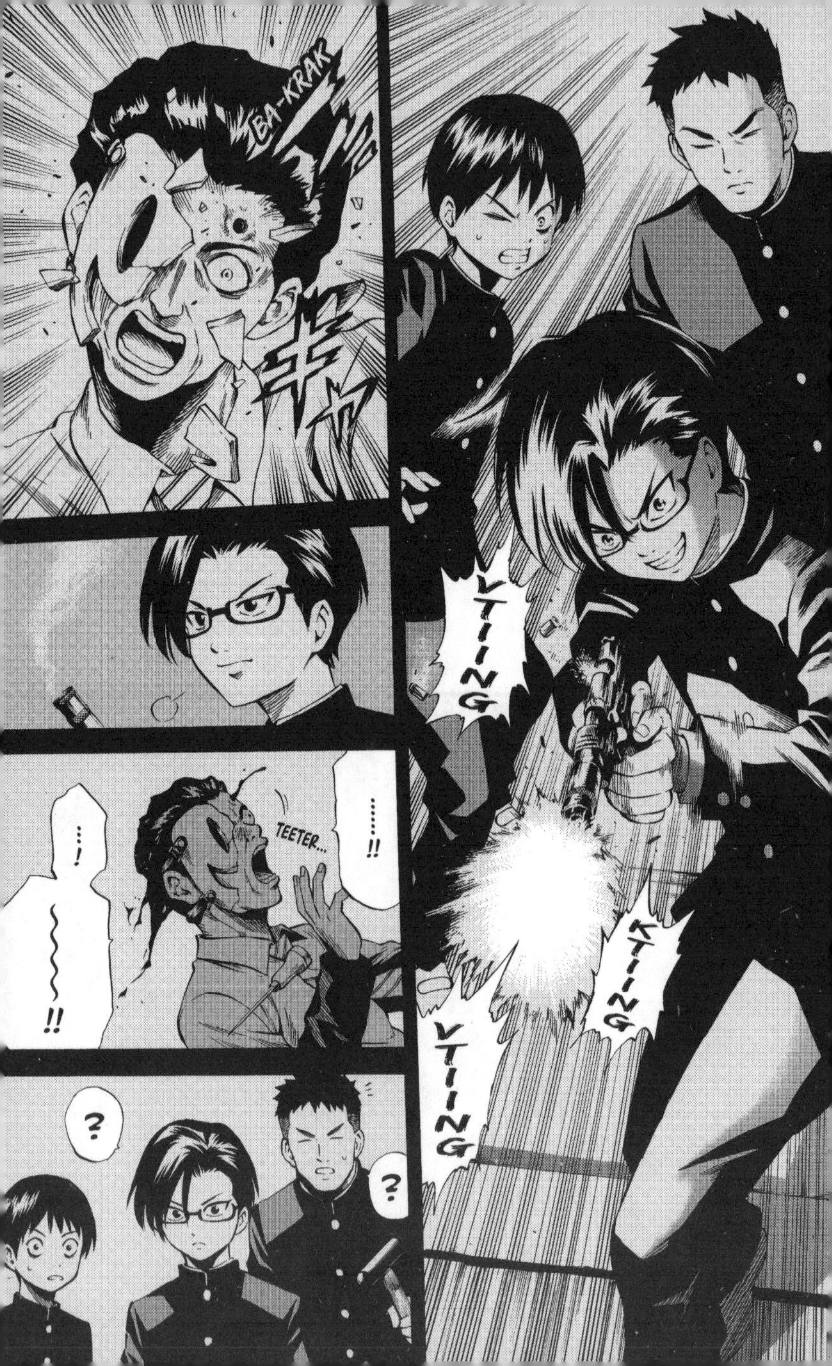
VTIING
KTIING
VTIING
BA-KRAK
......!!
TEETER...
...!
~~~~~!!
?
?
~~~~~

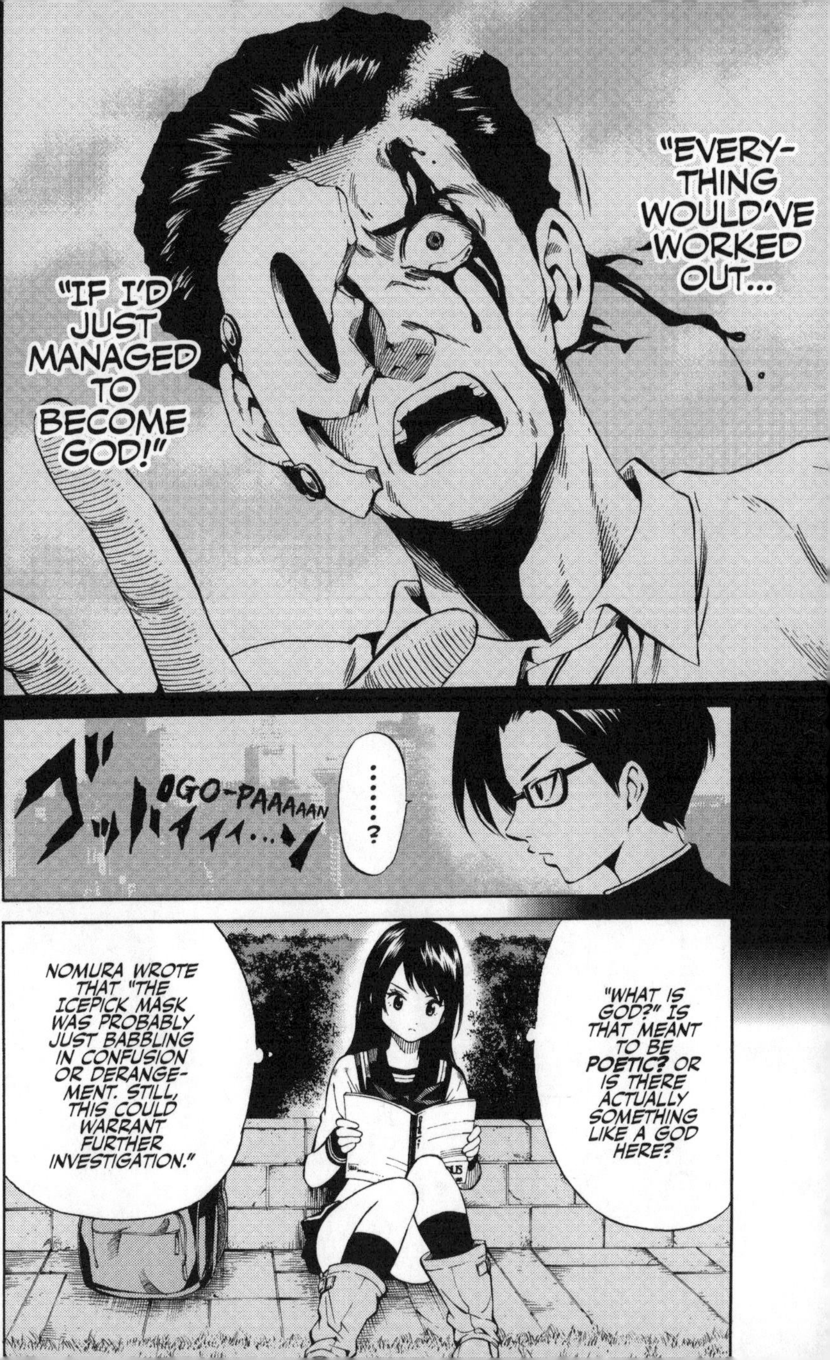
"EVERY-THING WOULD'VE WORKED OUT...
"IF I'D JUST MANAGED TO BECOME GOD!"
......?
GO-PAAAAAN
"WHAT IS GOD?" IS THAT MEANT TO BE POETIC? OR IS THERE ACTUALLY SOMETHING LIKE A GOD HERE?
NOMURA WROTE THAT "THE ICEPICK MASK WAS PROBABLY JUST BABBLING IN CONFUSION OR DERANGE-MENT. STILL, THIS COULD WARRANT FURTHER INVESTIGATION."

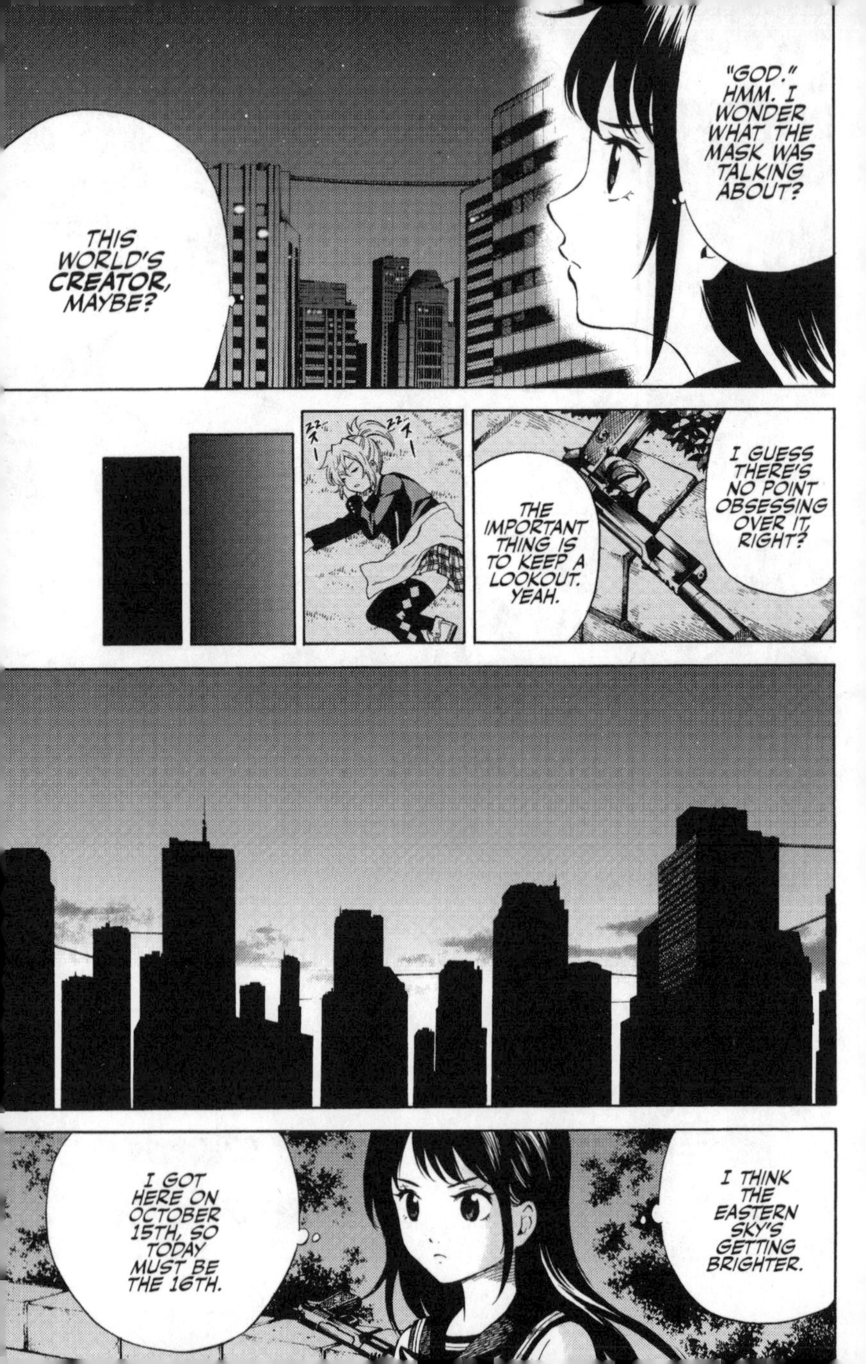
"GOD." HMM. I WONDER WHAT THE MASK WAS TALKING ABOUT?
THIS WORLD'S CREATOR, MAYBE?
I GUESS THERE'S NO POINT OBSESSING OVER IT, RIGHT?
THE IMPORTANT THING IS TO KEEP A LOOKOUT. YEAH.
I THINK THE EASTERN SKY'S GETTING BRIGHTER.
I GOT HERE ON OCTOBER 15TH, SO TODAY MUST BE THE 16TH.

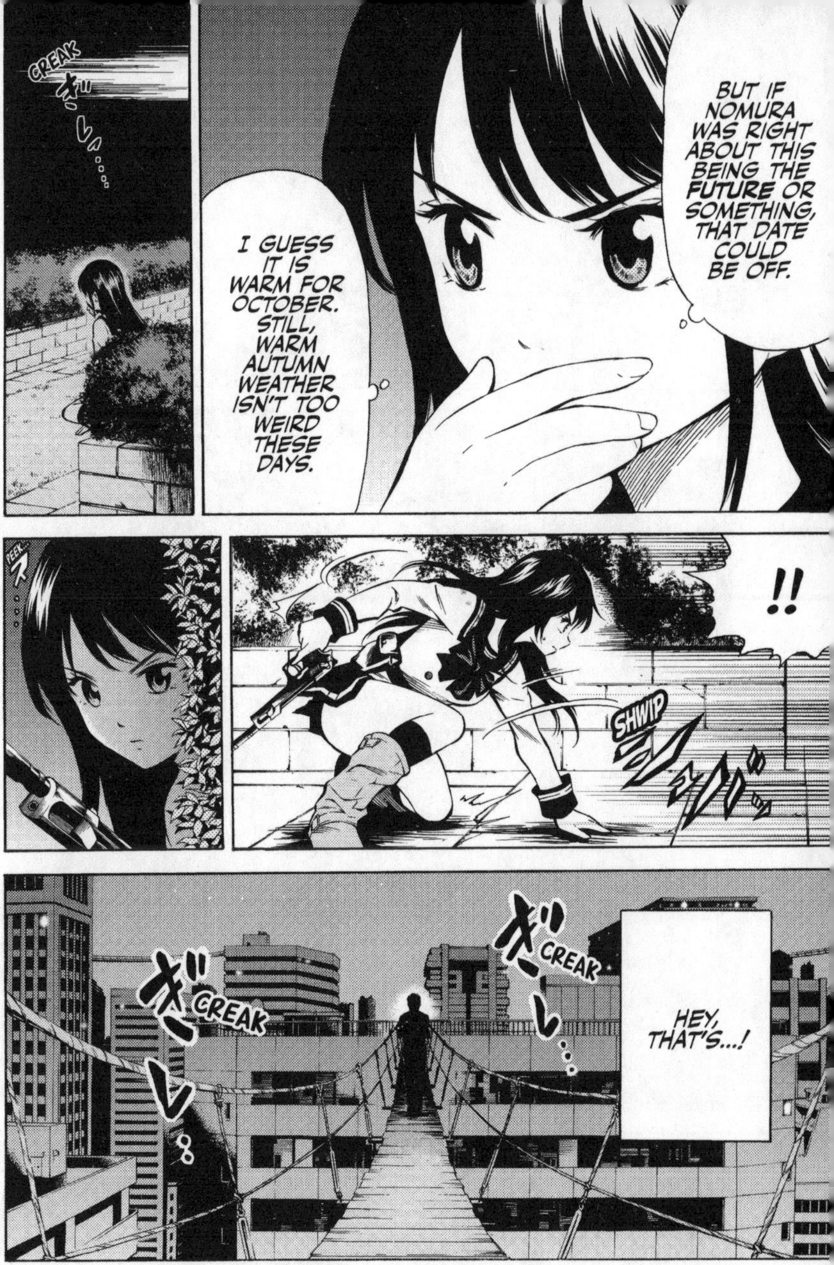

BUT IF NOMURA WAS RIGHT ABOUT THIS BEING THE **FUTURE** OR SOMETHING, THAT DATE COULD BE OFF.
I GUESS IT IS WARM FOR OCTOBER. STILL, WARM AUTUMN WEATHER ISN'T TOO WEIRD THESE DAYS.
CREAK
!!
SHWIP
PEEK
HEY, THAT'S...!
CREAK
CREAK

HIGH-RISE INVASION

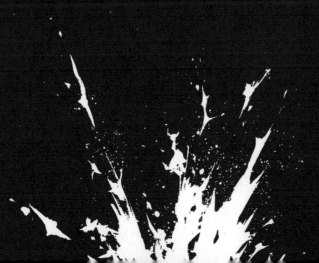

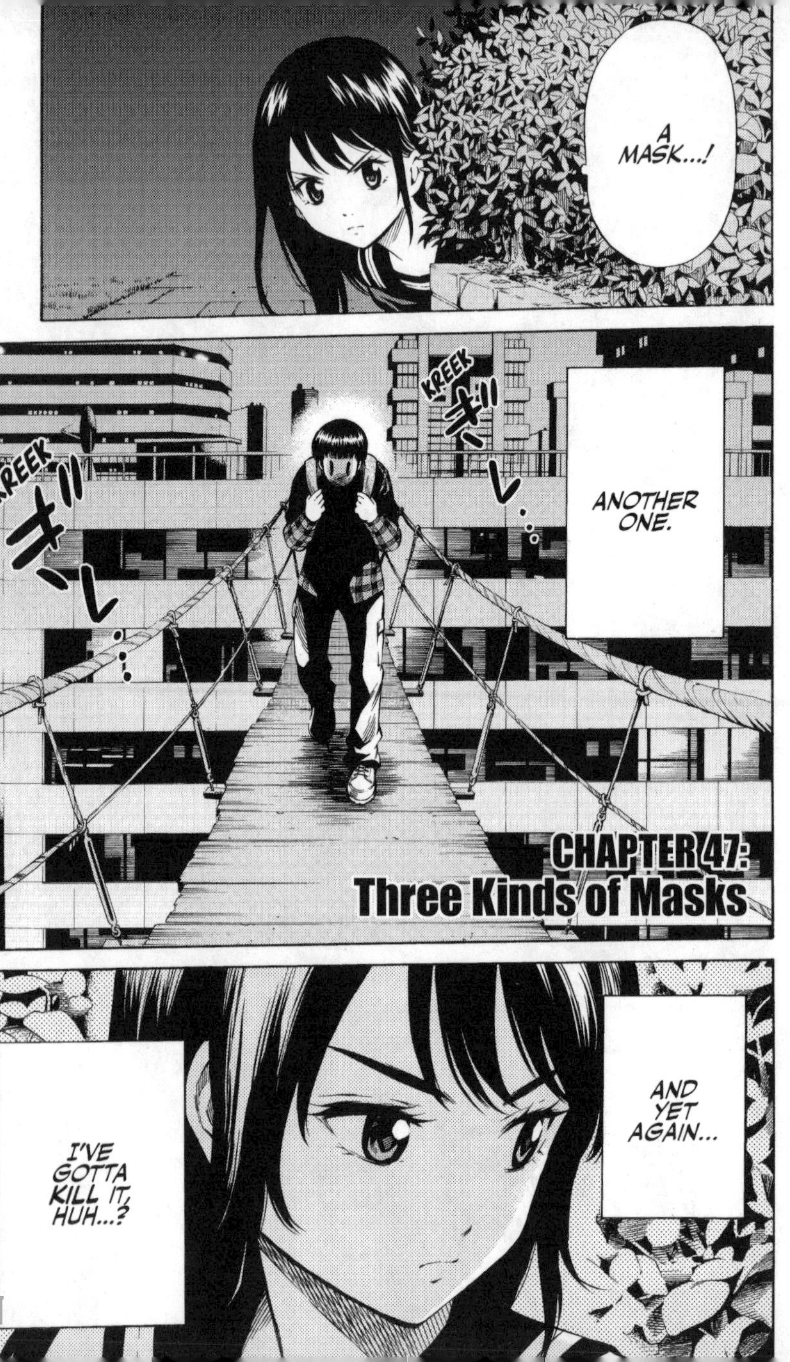
A MASK...!
ANOTHER ONE.
KREEK
KREEK
CHAPTER 47:
Three Kinds of Masks
AND YET AGAIN...
I'VE GOTTA KILL IT, HUH...?

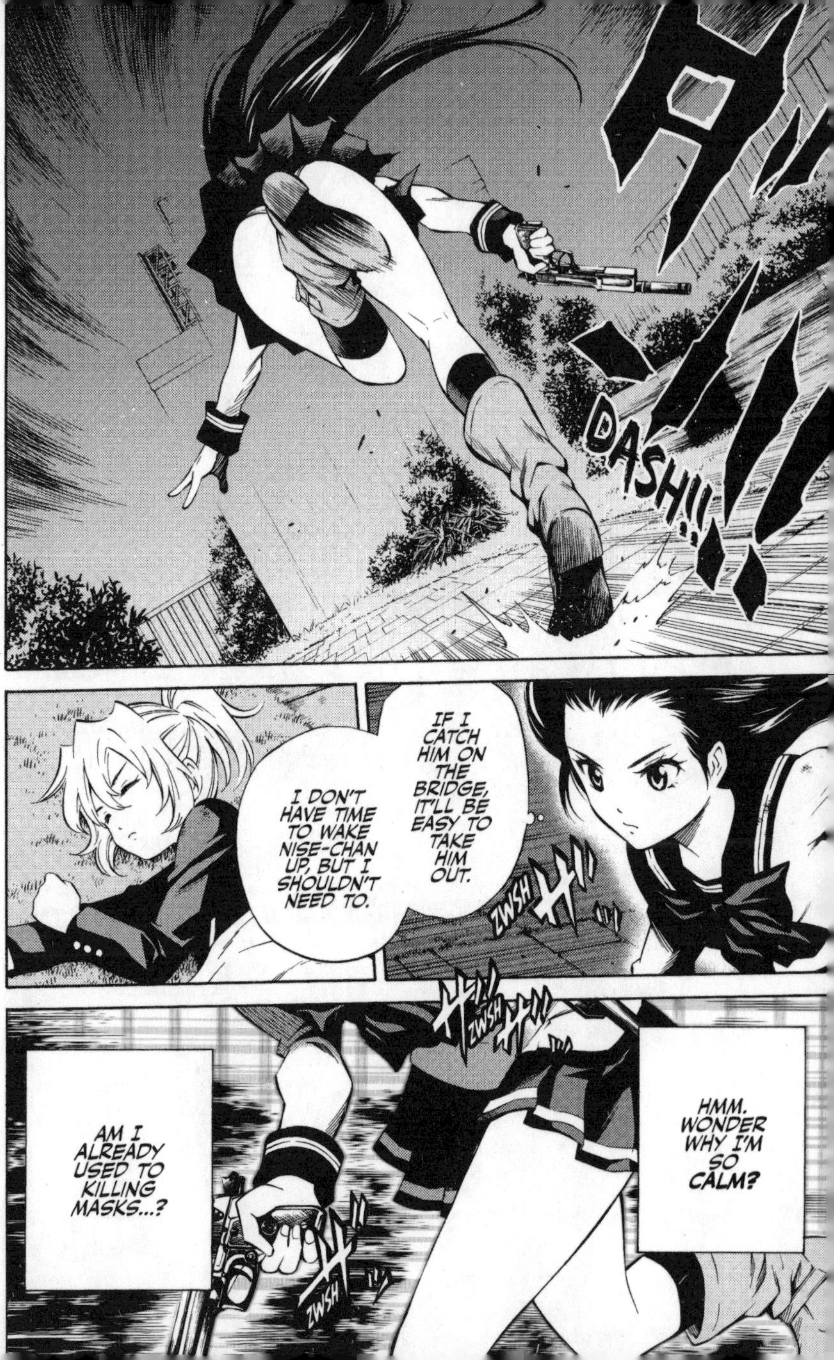
DASH!!
ZWSH
IF I CATCH HIM ON THE BRIDGE, IT'LL BE EASY TO TAKE HIM OUT.
I DON'T HAVE TIME TO WAKE NISE-CHAN UP, BUT I SHOULDN'T NEED TO.
ZWSH
HMM. WONDER WHY I'M SO CALM?
AM I ALREADY USED TO KILLING MASKS...?
ZWSH

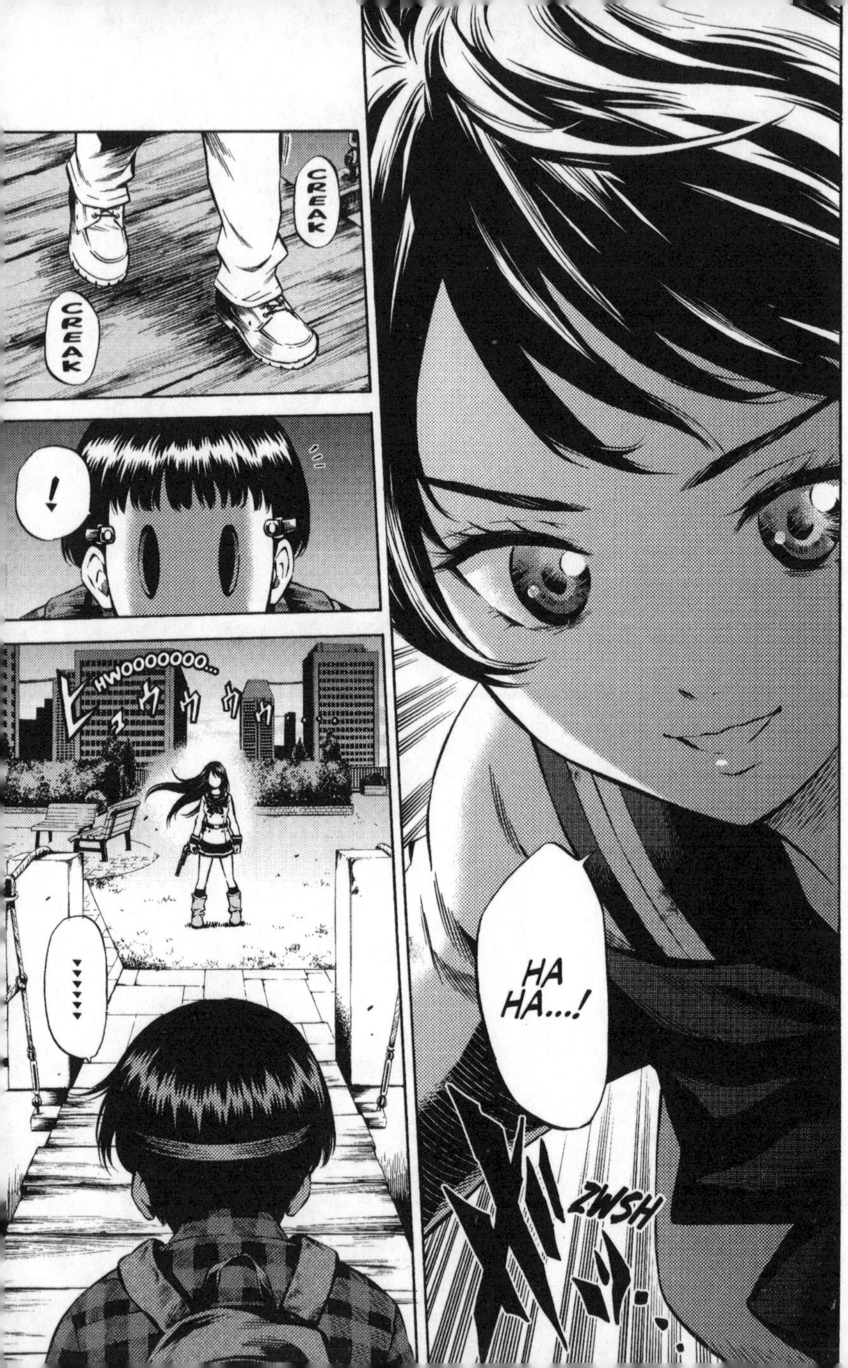
HA HA...!
ZWSH
CREAK
CREAK
!
HWOOOOOOO...
......

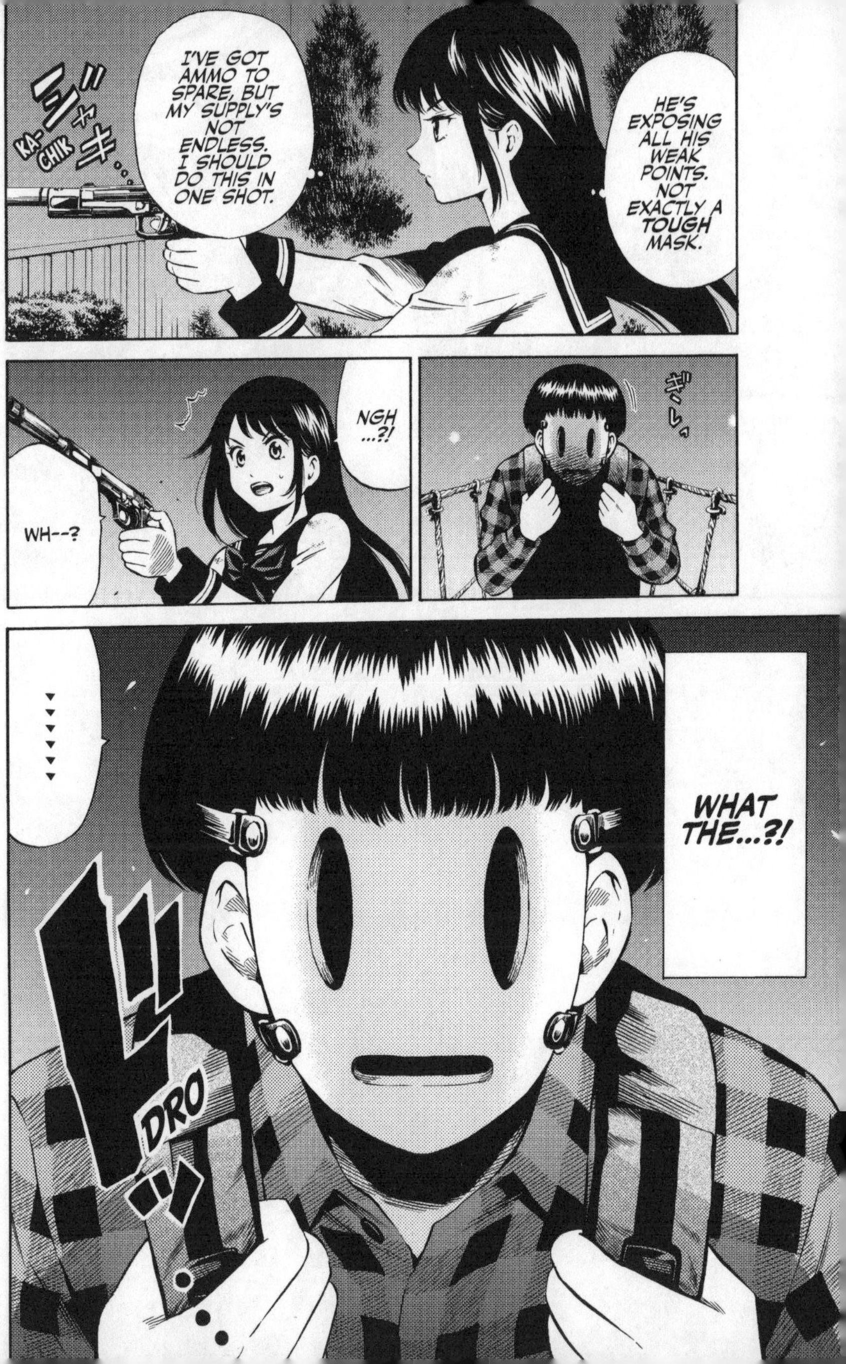
HE'S EXPOSING ALL HIS WEAK POINTS. NOT EXACTLY A TOUGH MASK.
I'VE GOT AMMO TO SPARE, BUT MY SUPPLY'S NOT ENDLESS. I SHOULD DO THIS IN ONE SHOT.
KA-CHIK
NGH ...?!
WH--?
WHAT THE...?!
DRO

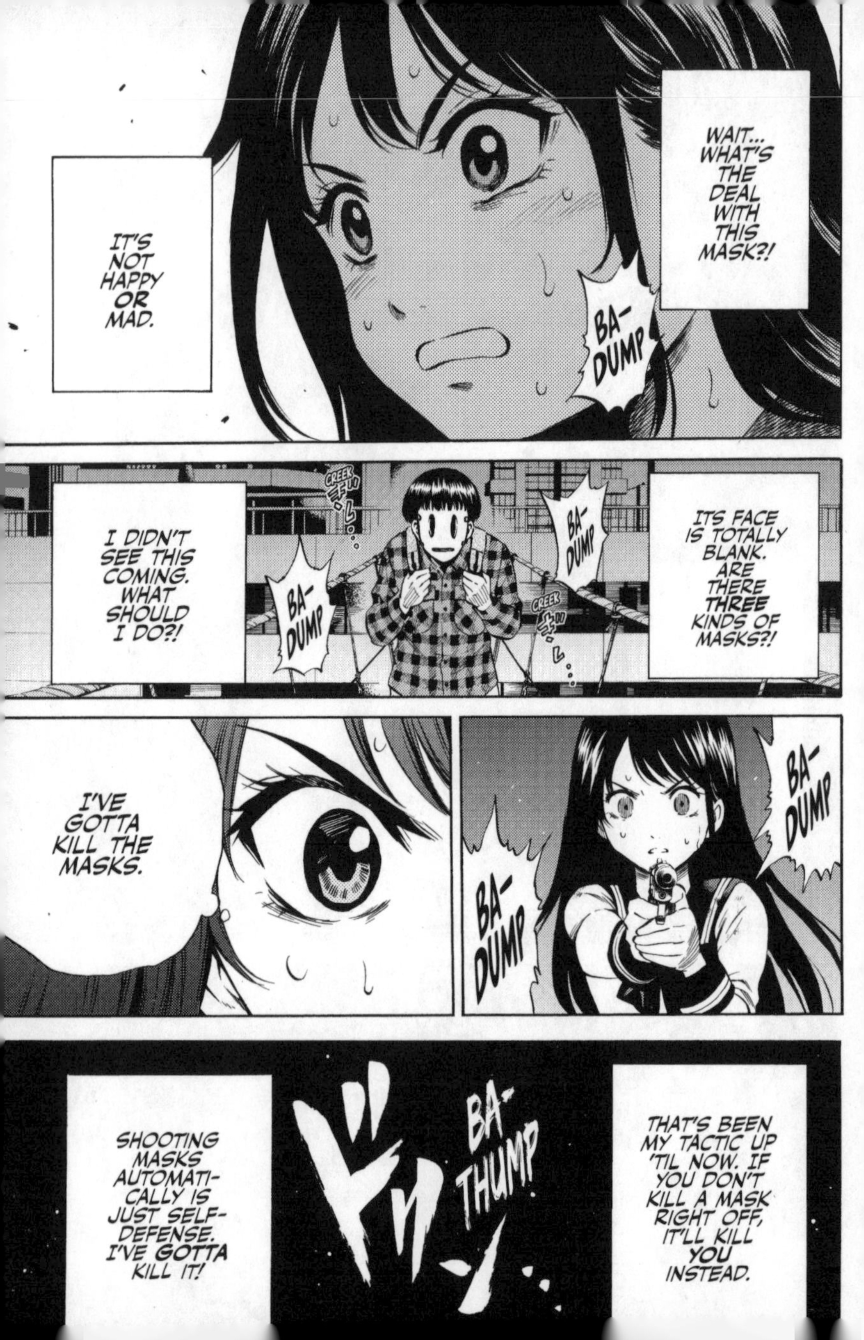
WAIT... WHAT'S THE DEAL WITH THIS MASK?!
BA-DUMP
IT'S NOT HAPPY OR MAD.
ITS FACE IS TOTALLY BLANK. ARE THERE THREE KINDS OF MASKS?!
BA-DUMP
CREEK
BA-DUMP
CREEK
I DIDN'T SEE THIS COMING. WHAT SHOULD I DO?!
BA-DUMP
BA-DUMP
I'VE GOTTA KILL THE MASKS.
THAT'S BEEN MY TACTIC UP 'TIL NOW. IF YOU DON'T KILL A MASK RIGHT OFF, IT'LL KILL YOU INSTEAD.
BA-THUMP
SHOOTING MASKS AUTOMATI-CALLY IS JUST SELF-DEFENSE. I'VE GOTTA KILL IT!

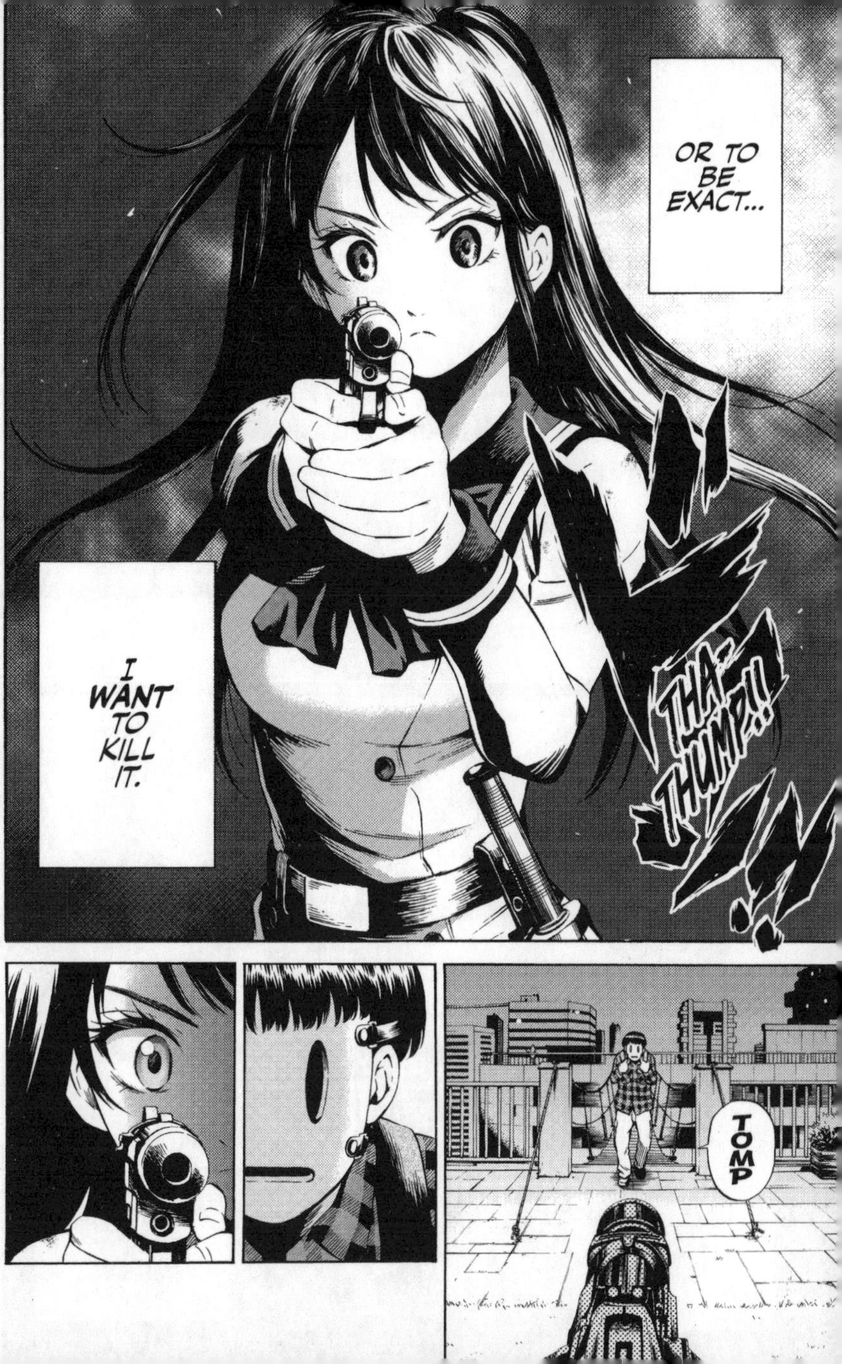
OR TO BE EXACT...
I WANT TO KILL IT.
THA-THUMP!!
TOMP

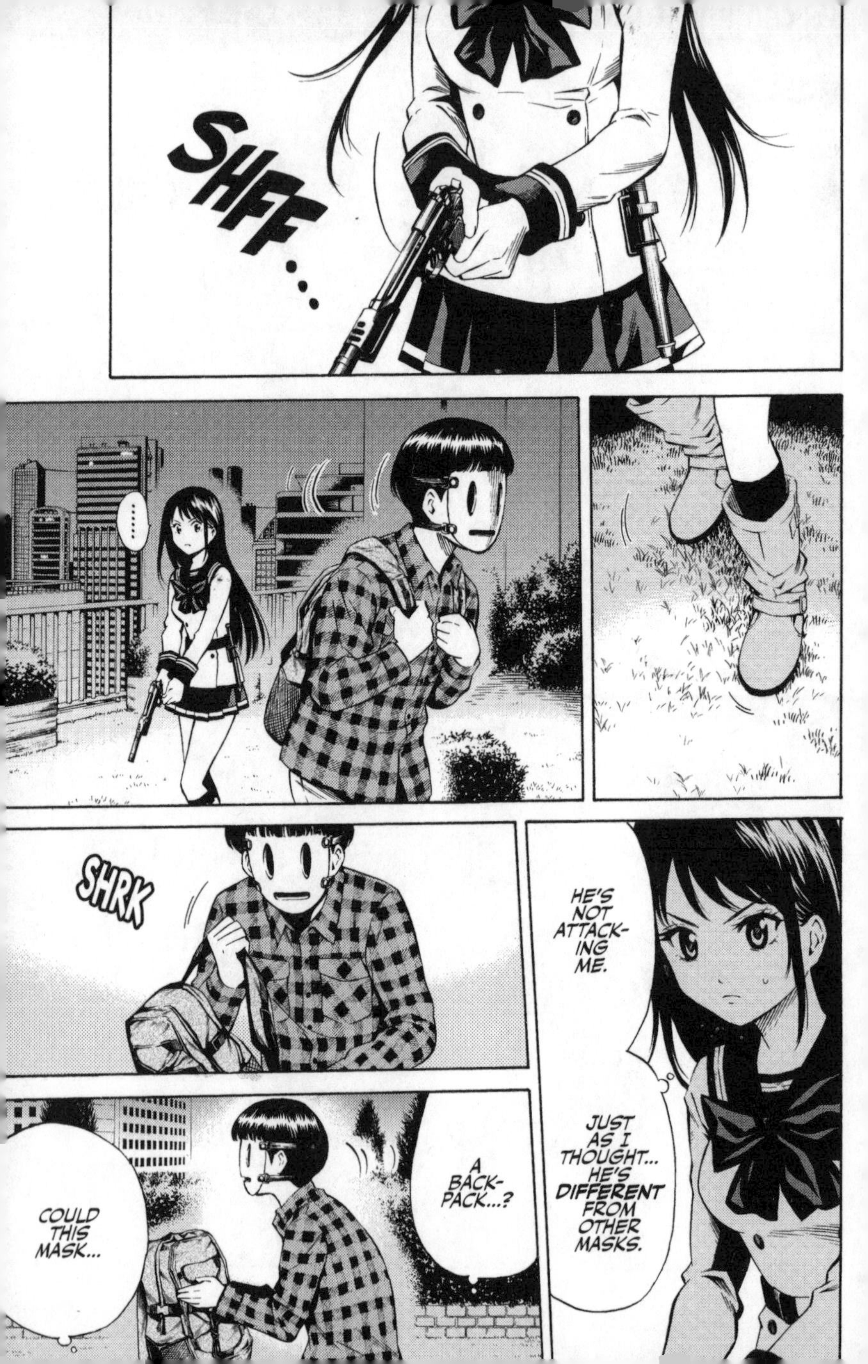
SHFF...
......
HE'S NOT ATTACKING ME.
JUST AS I THOUGHT... HE'S DIFFERENT FROM OTHER MASKS.
SHRK
A BACKPACK...?
COULD THIS MASK...

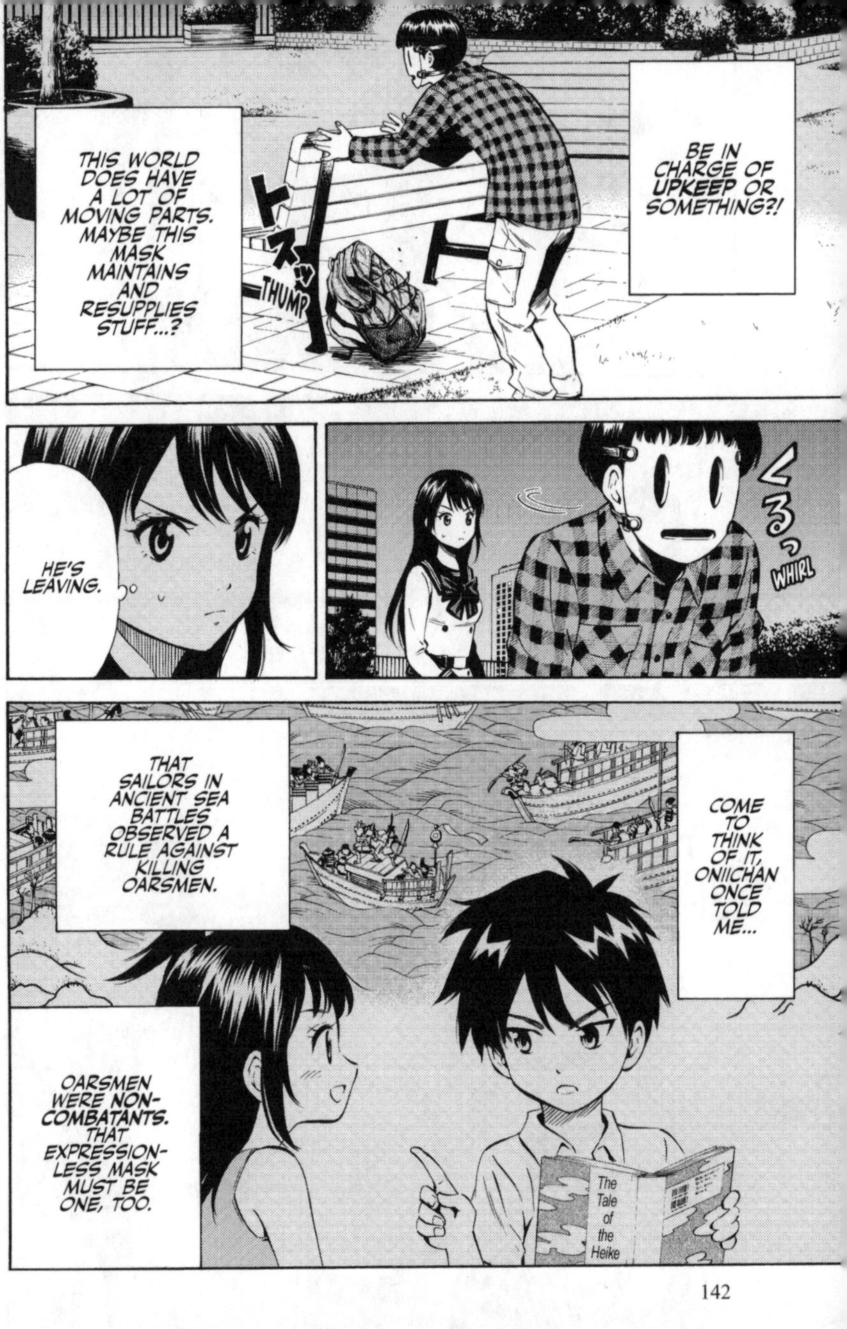
BE IN CHARGE OF UPKEEP OR SOMETHING?!
THIS WORLD DOES HAVE A LOT OF MOVING PARTS. MAYBE THIS MASK MAINTAINS AND RESUPPLIES STUFF...?
トスッ
THUMP
くるっ
WHIRL
HE'S LEAVING.
COME TO THINK OF IT, ONIICHAN ONCE TOLD ME...
THAT SAILORS IN ANCIENT SEA BATTLES OBSERVED A RULE AGAINST KILLING OARSMEN.
OARSMEN WERE NON-COMBATANTS. THAT EXPRESSION-LESS MASK MUST BE ONE, TOO.
The Tale of the Heike

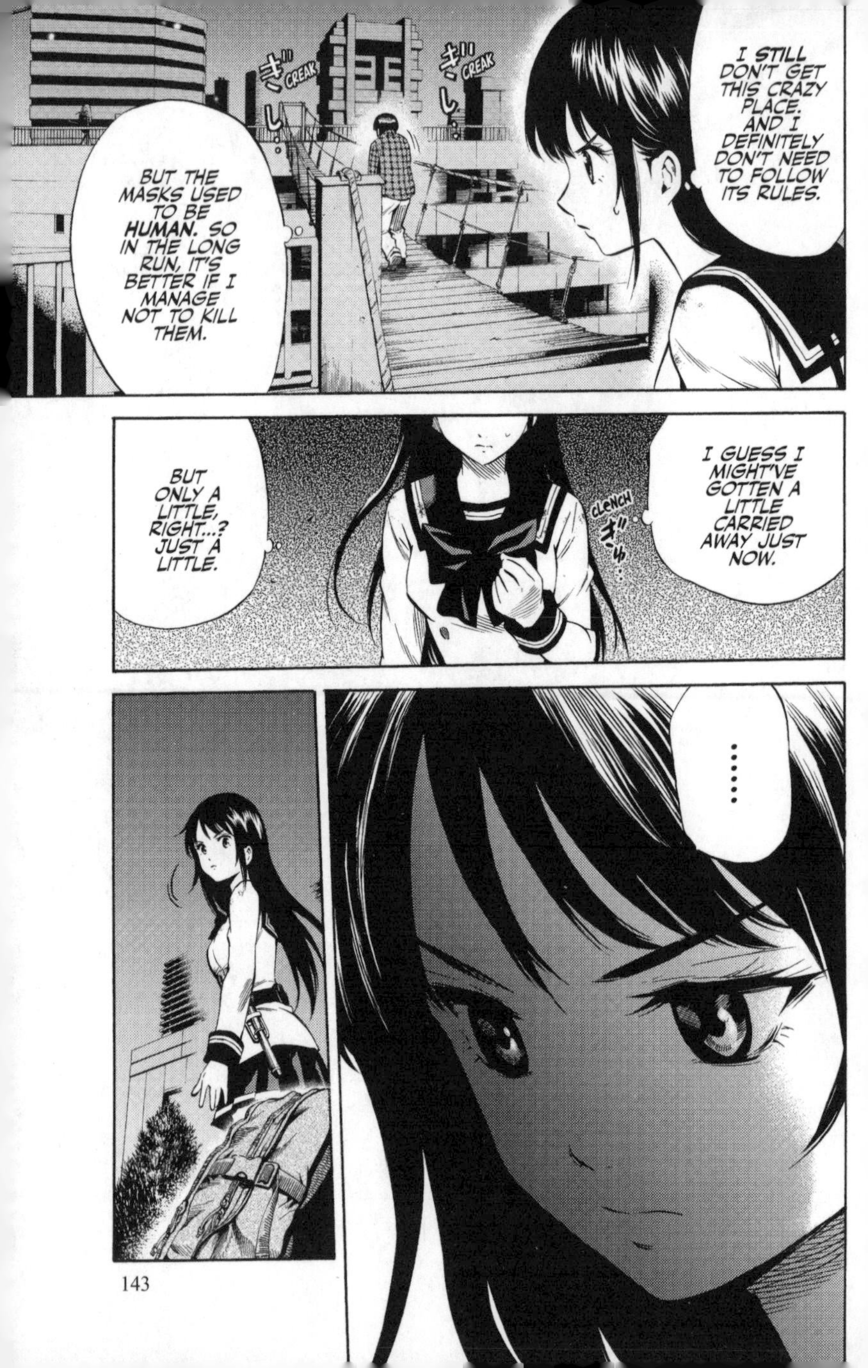
I STILL DON'T GET THIS CRAZY PLACE. AND I DEFINITELY DON'T NEED TO FOLLOW ITS RULES.
きし CREAK
きし CREAK
BUT THE MASKS USED TO BE HUMAN. SO IN THE LONG RUN, IT'S BETTER IF I MANAGE NOT TO KILL THEM.
I GUESS I MIGHT'VE GOTTEN A LITTLE CARRIED AWAY JUST NOW.
ぎゅ… CLENCH
BUT ONLY A LITTLE, RIGHT...? JUST A LITTLE.
......

ANYWAY, I AM CURIOUS ABOUT WHAT'S INSIDE HIS BAG.

I CAN'T HELP BUT HAVE A BAD FEELING ABOUT IT.

BA—DUMP

·····

DOZE

YAWN.

!!

LURCH

?!

144

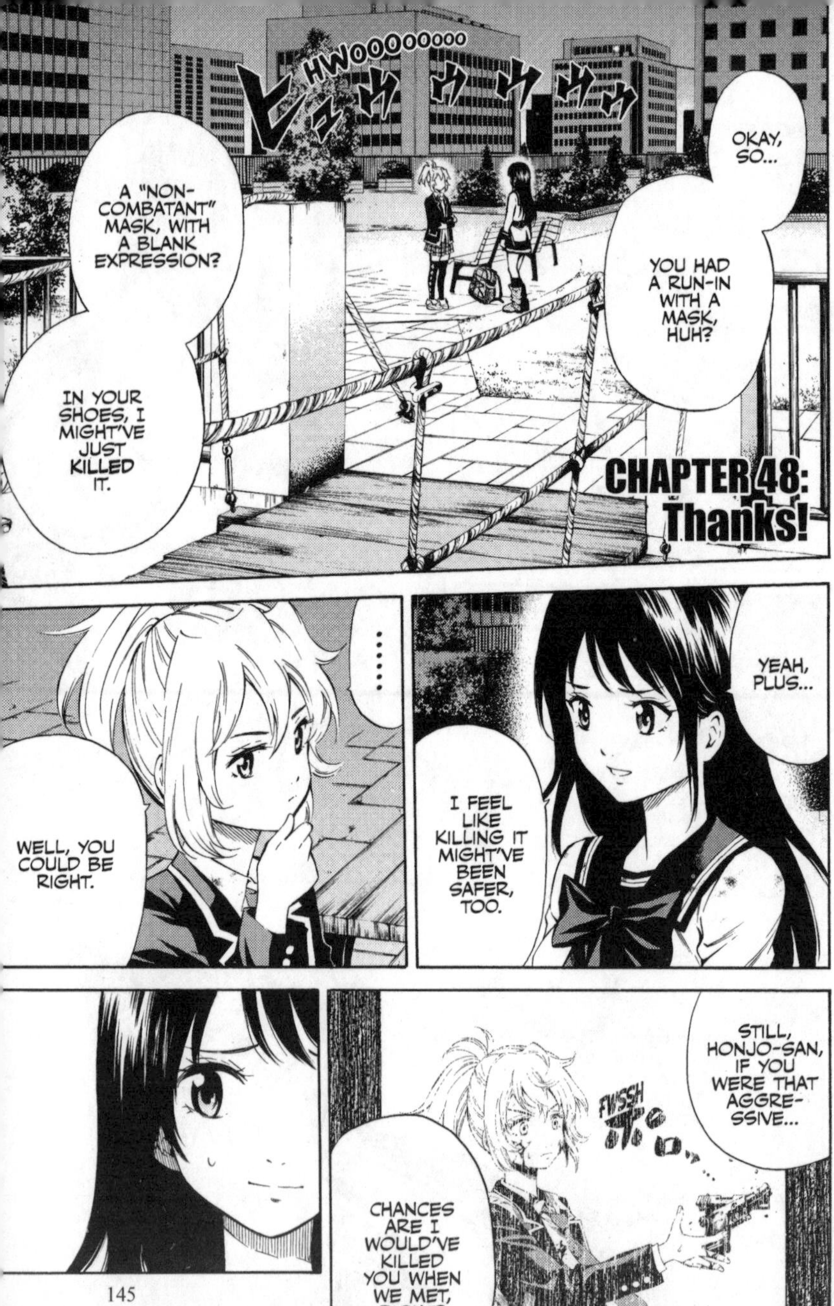
HWOOOOOOOO
OKAY, SO...
YOU HAD A RUN-IN WITH A MASK, HUH?
A "NON-COMBATANT" MASK, WITH A BLANK EXPRESSION?
IN YOUR SHOES, I MIGHT'VE JUST KILLED IT.
CHAPTER 48: Thanks!
YEAH, PLUS...
I FEEL LIKE KILLING IT MIGHT'VE BEEN SAFER, TOO.
......
WELL, YOU COULD BE RIGHT.
STILL, HONJO-SAN, IF YOU WERE THAT AGGRE-SSIVE...
FWSSH
CHANCES ARE I WOULD'VE KILLED YOU WHEN WE MET, RIGHT?

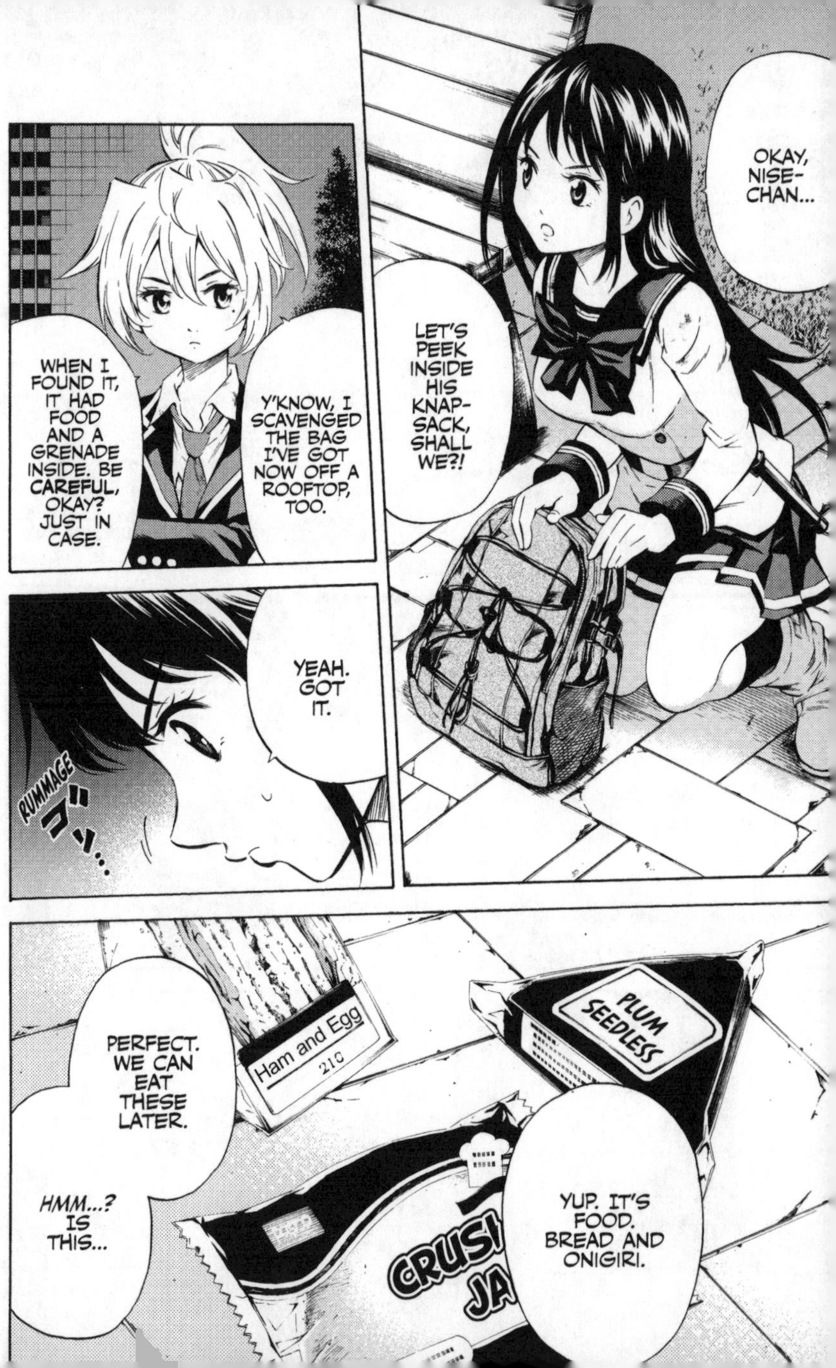
OKAY, NISE-CHAN...
LET'S PEEK INSIDE HIS KNAPSACK, SHALL WE?!
Y'KNOW, I SCAVENGED THE BAG I'VE GOT NOW OFF A ROOFTOP, TOO.
WHEN I FOUND IT, IT HAD FOOD AND A GRENADE INSIDE. BE CAREFUL, OKAY? JUST IN CASE.
YEAH. GOT IT.
RUMMAGE
PLUM SEEDLESS
Ham and Egg
210
PERFECT. WE CAN EAT THESE LATER.
YUP. IT'S FOOD. BREAD AND ONIGIRI.
HMM...? IS THIS...

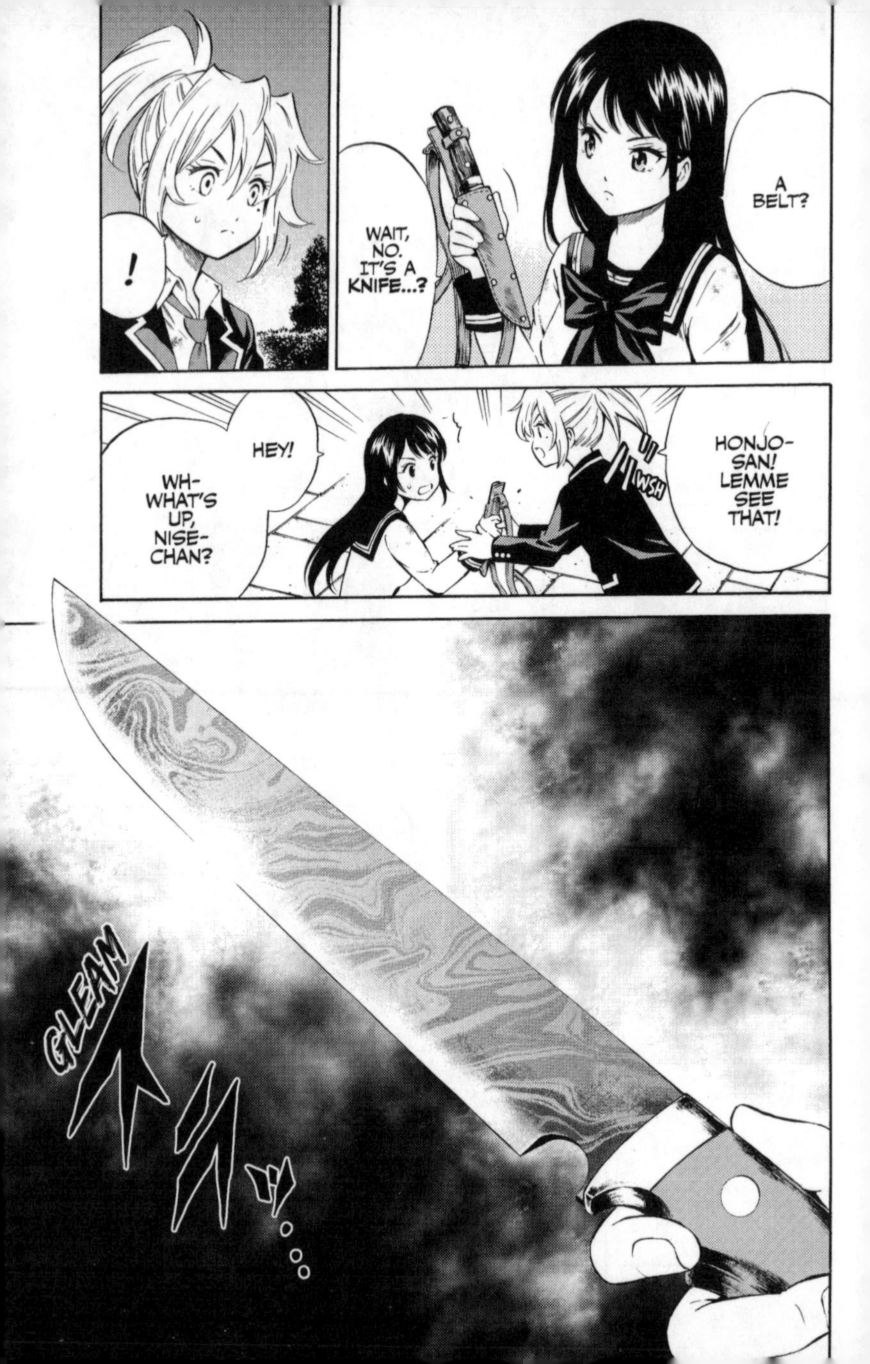
A BELT?
WAIT, NO. IT'S A KNIFE...?
!
HONJO-SAN! LEMME SEE THAT!
WSH
HEY!
WH- WHAT'S UP, NISE-CHAN?
GLEAM

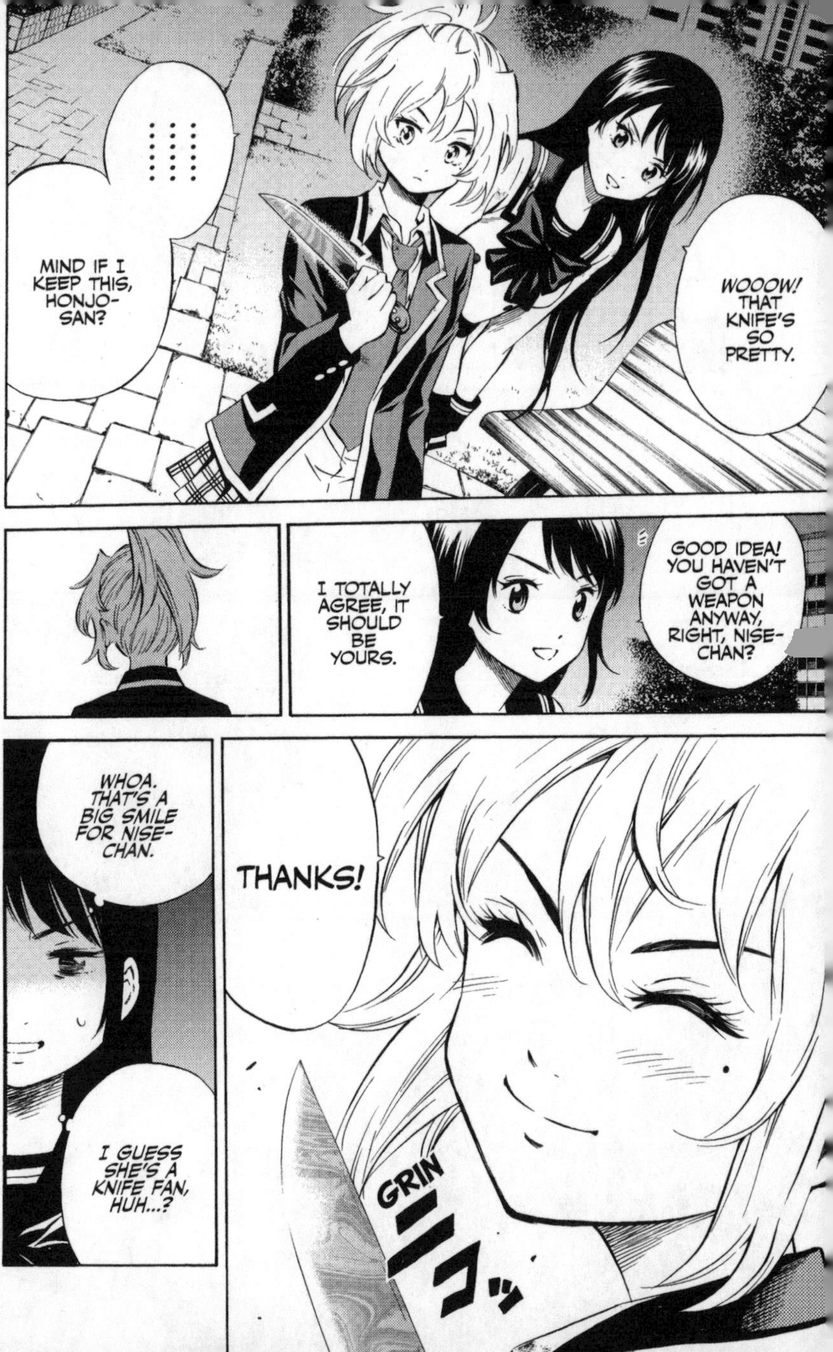
WOOOW! THAT KNIFE'S SO PRETTY.
......
MIND IF I KEEP THIS, HONJO-SAN?
GOOD IDEA! YOU HAVEN'T GOT A WEAPON ANYWAY, RIGHT, NISE-CHAN?
I TOTALLY AGREE, IT SHOULD BE YOURS.
THANKS!
GRIN
WHOA. THAT'S A BIG SMILE FOR NISE-CHAN.
I GUESS SHE'S A KNIFE FAN, HUH...?

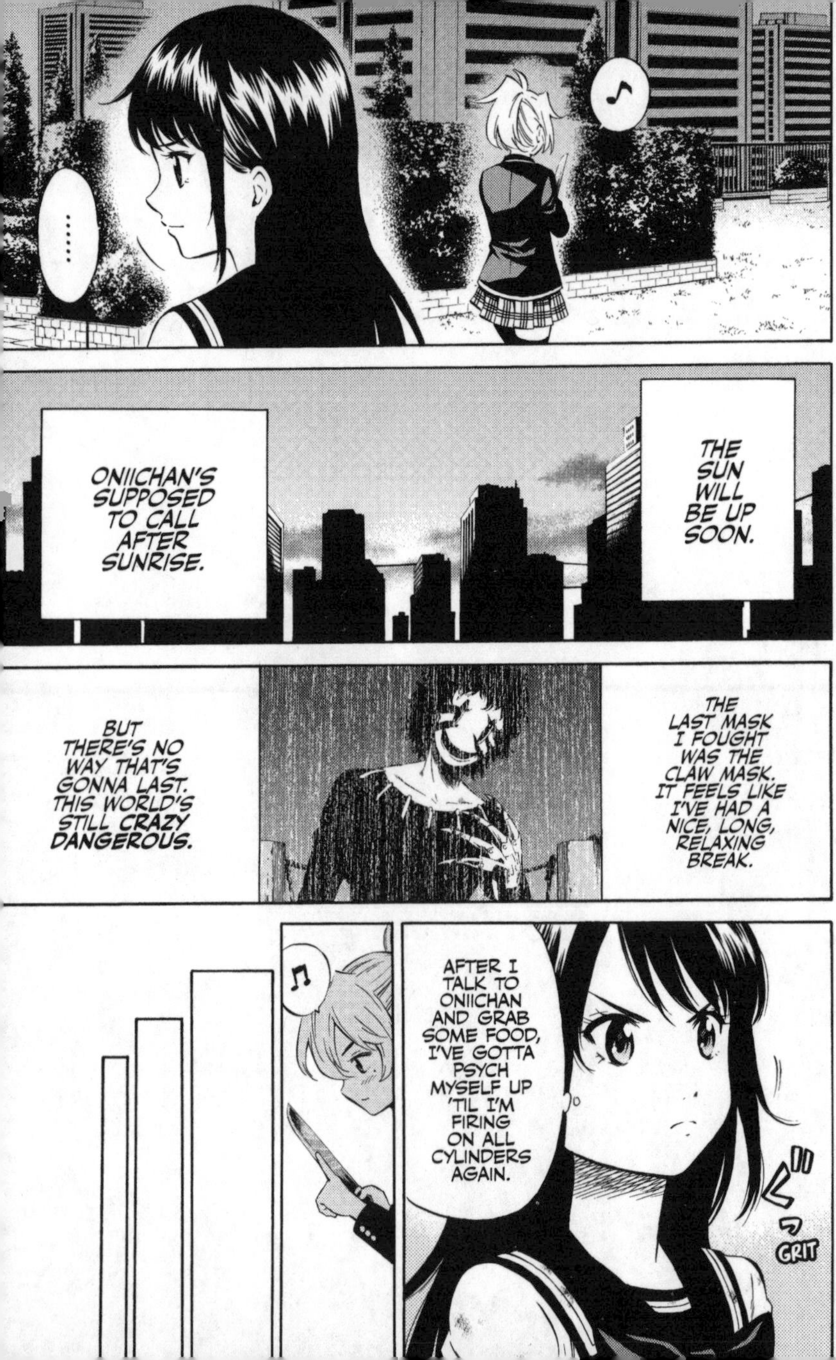
♪
......
THE SUN WILL BE UP SOON.
ONIICHAN'S SUPPOSED TO CALL AFTER SUNRISE.
THE LAST MASK I FOUGHT WAS THE CLAW MASK. IT FEELS LIKE I'VE HAD A NICE, LONG, RELAXING BREAK.
BUT THERE'S NO WAY THAT'S GONNA LAST. THIS WORLD'S STILL CRAZY DANGEROUS.
AFTER I TALK TO ONIICHAN AND GRAB SOME FOOD, I'VE GOTTA PSYCH MYSELF UP 'TIL I'M FIRING ON ALL CYLINDERS AGAIN.
GRIT
♫

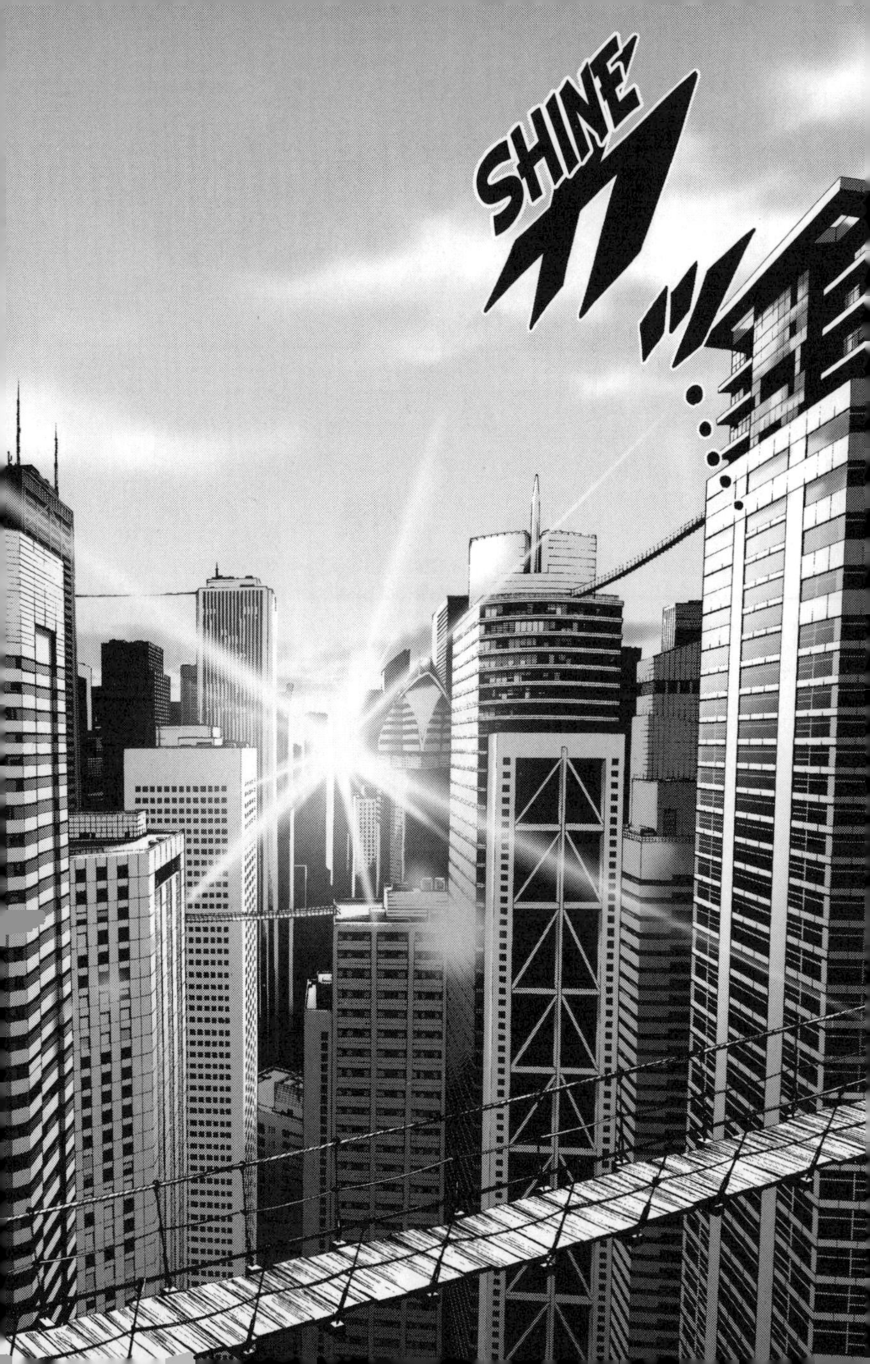
SHINE

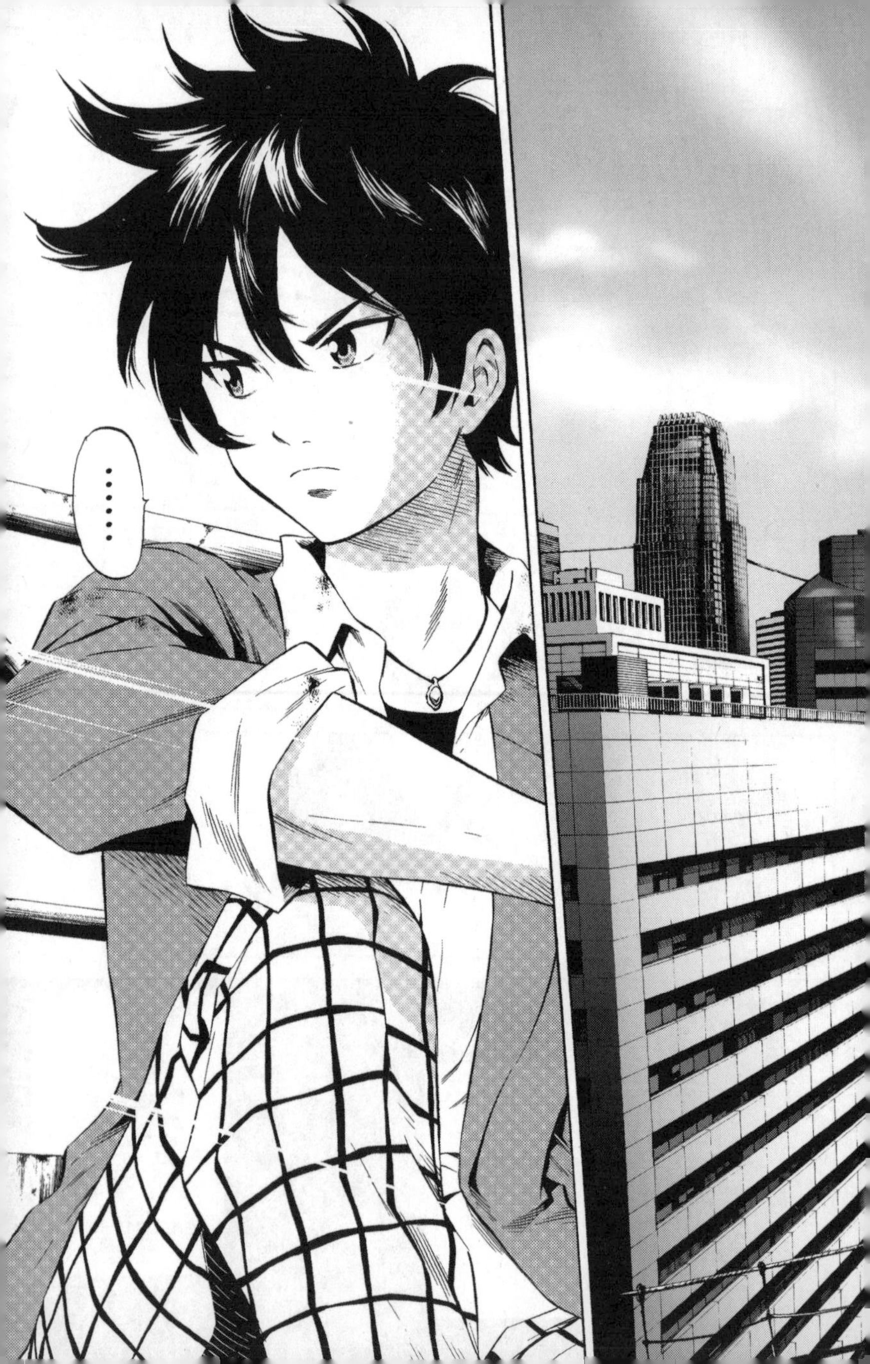

......

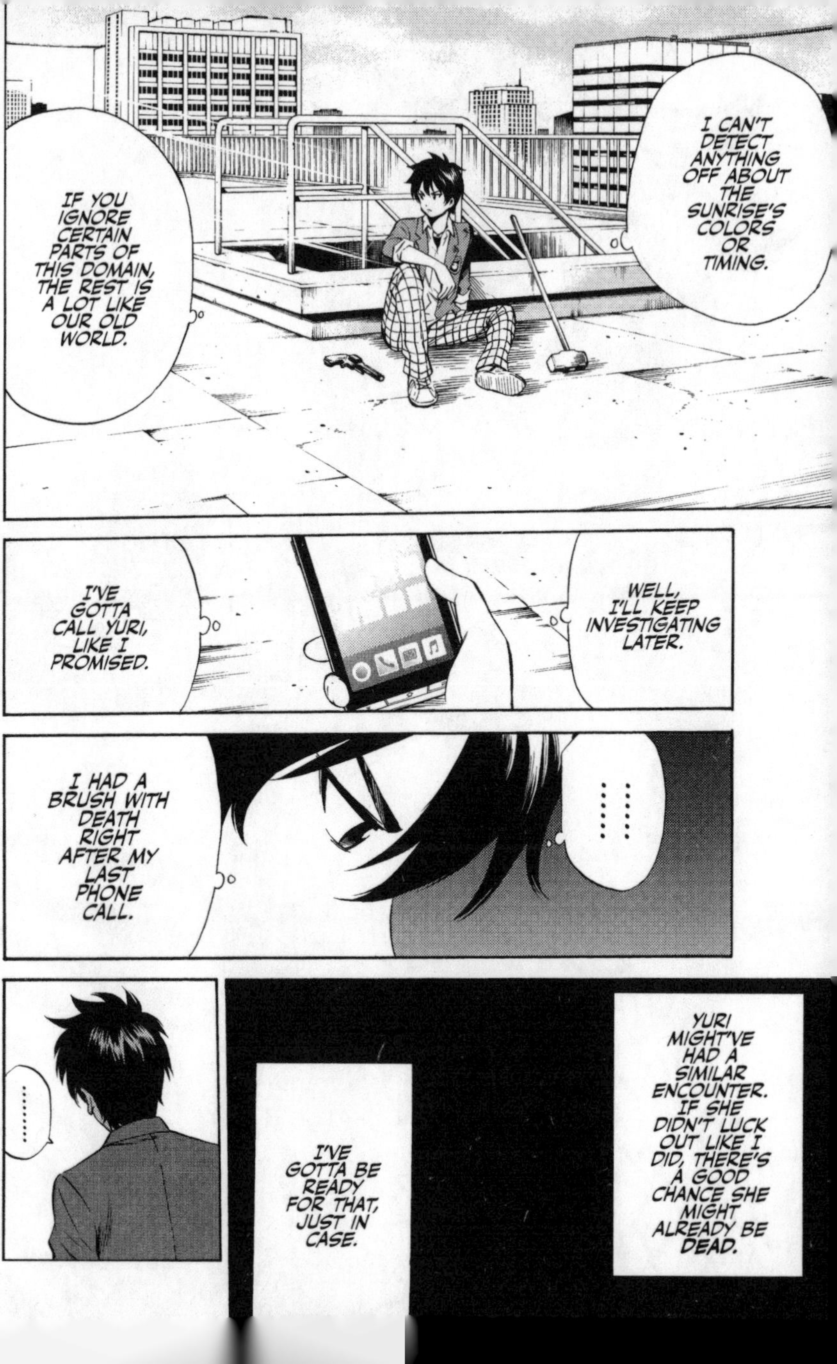
I CAN'T DETECT ANYTHING OFF ABOUT THE SUNRISE'S COLORS OR TIMING.
IF YOU IGNORE CERTAIN PARTS OF THIS DOMAIN, THE REST IS A LOT LIKE OUR OLD WORLD.
WELL, I'LL KEEP INVESTIGATING LATER.
I'VE GOTTA CALL YURI, LIKE I PROMISED.
......
I HAD A BRUSH WITH DEATH RIGHT AFTER MY LAST PHONE CALL.
YURI MIGHT'VE HAD A SIMILAR ENCOUNTER. IF SHE DIDN'T LUCK OUT LIKE I DID, THERE'S A GOOD CHANCE SHE MIGHT ALREADY BE DEAD.
I'VE GOTTA BE READY FOR THAT, JUST IN CASE.
......

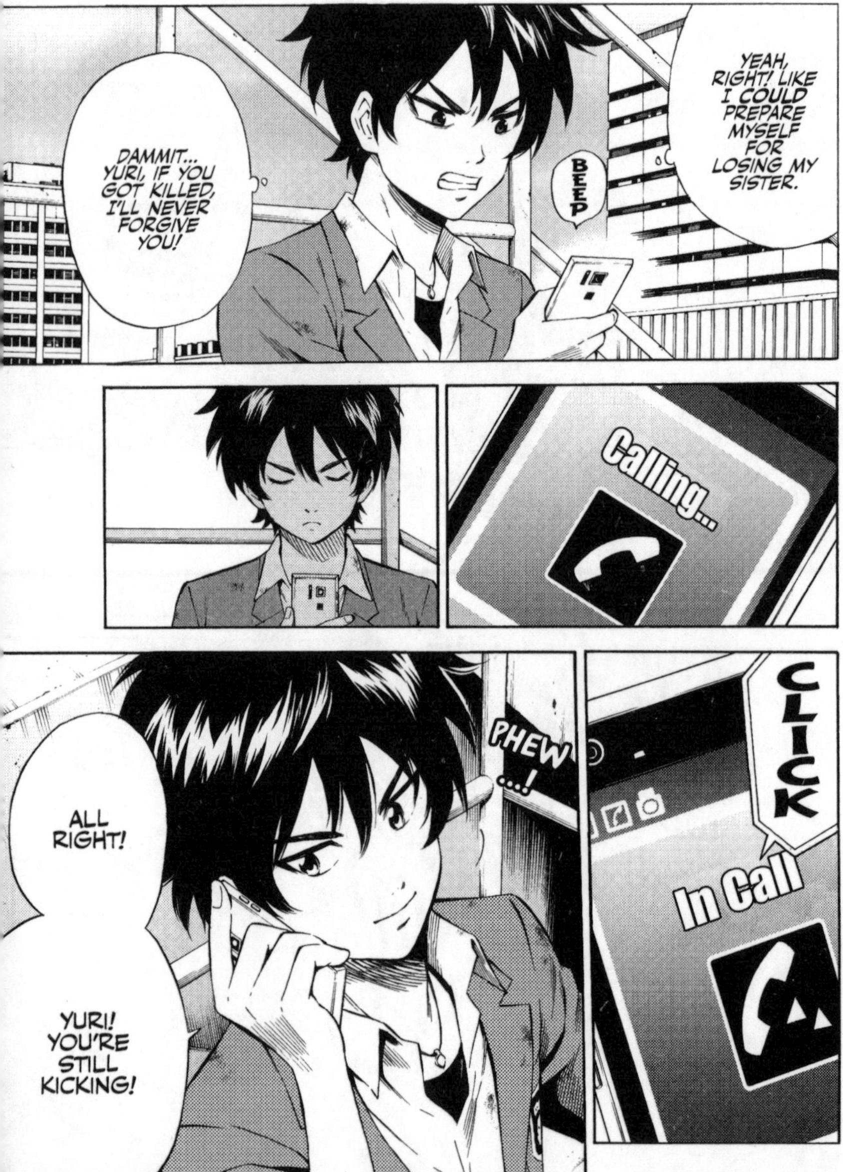
YEAH, RIGHT! LIKE I COULD PREPARE MYSELF FOR LOSING MY SISTER.
BEEP
DAMMIT... YURI, IF YOU GOT KILLED, I'LL NEVER FORGIVE YOU!
Calling...
CLICK
In Call
PHEW...!
ALL RIGHT!
YURI! YOU'RE STILL KICKING!

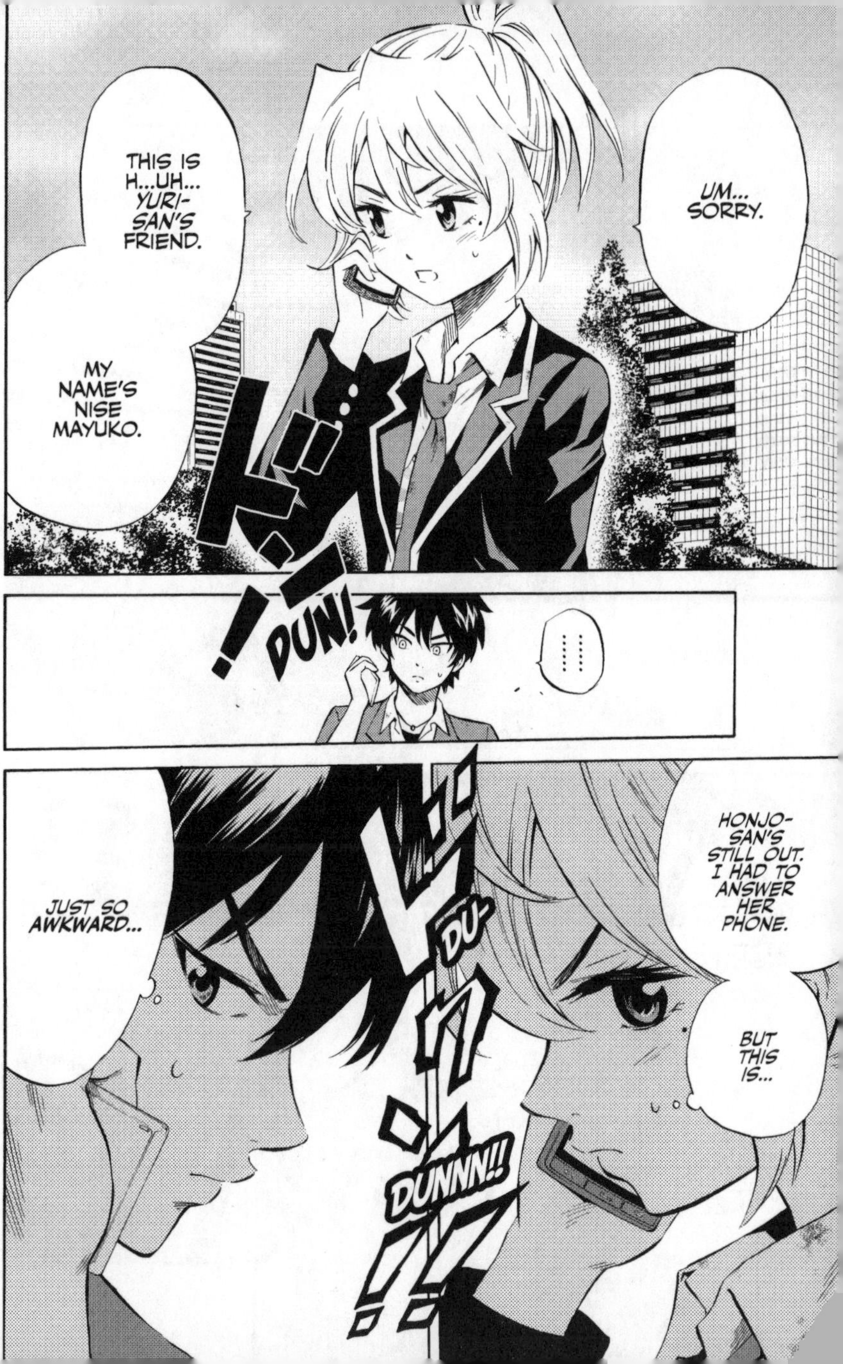
UM... SORRY.
THIS IS H...UH... YURI-SAN'S FRIEND.
MY NAME'S NISE MAYUKO.
DUN!
......
HONJO-SAN'S STILL OUT. I HAD TO ANSWER HER PHONE.
BUT THIS IS...
DU-DUNNN!!
JUST SO AWKWARD...

HIGH-RISE INVASION

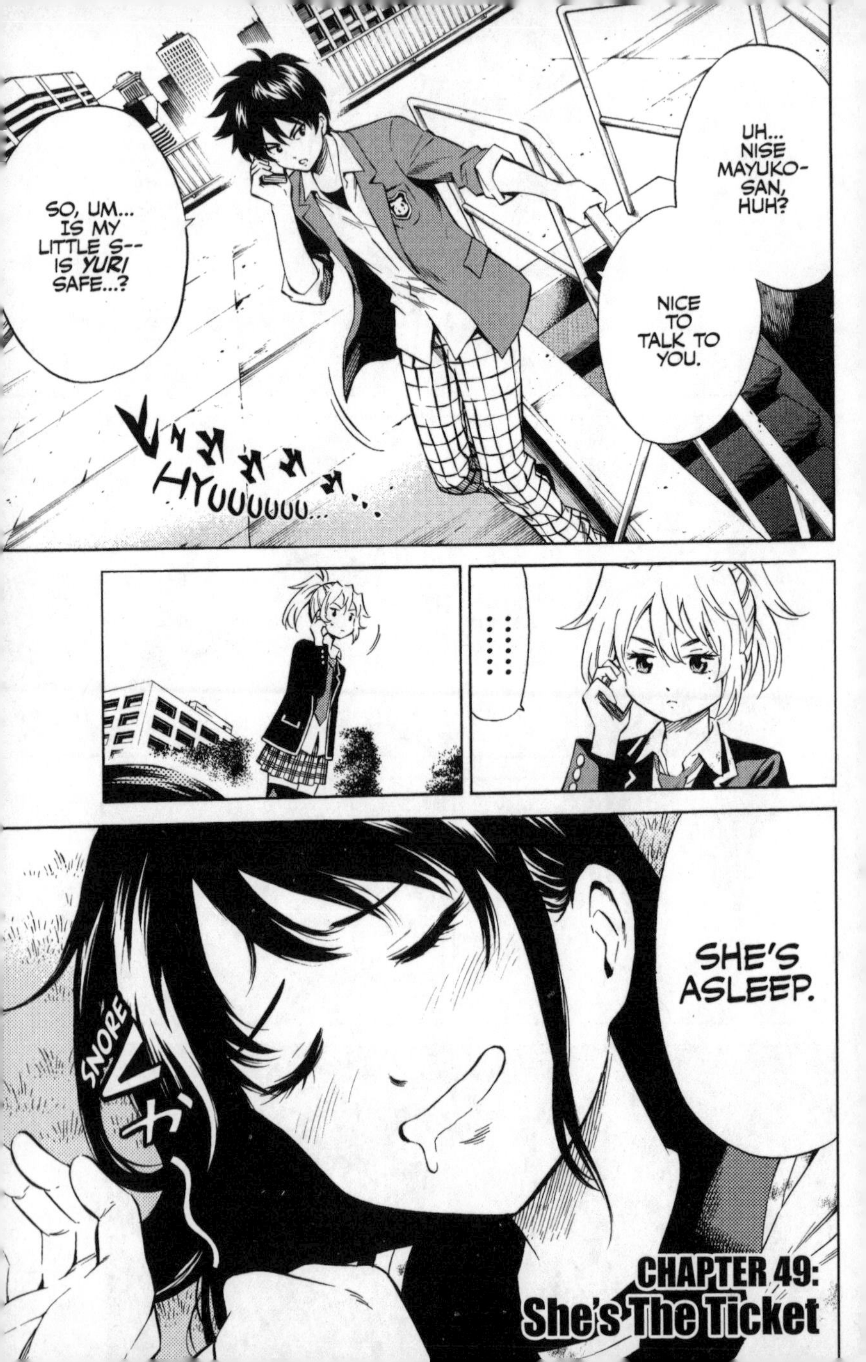
UH... NISE MAYUKO-SAN, HUH?
NICE TO TALK TO YOU.
SO, UM... IS MY LITTLE S-- IS YURI SAFE...?
HYUUUUUU...
......
SHE'S ASLEEP.
SNORE
CHAPTER 49:
She's The Ticket

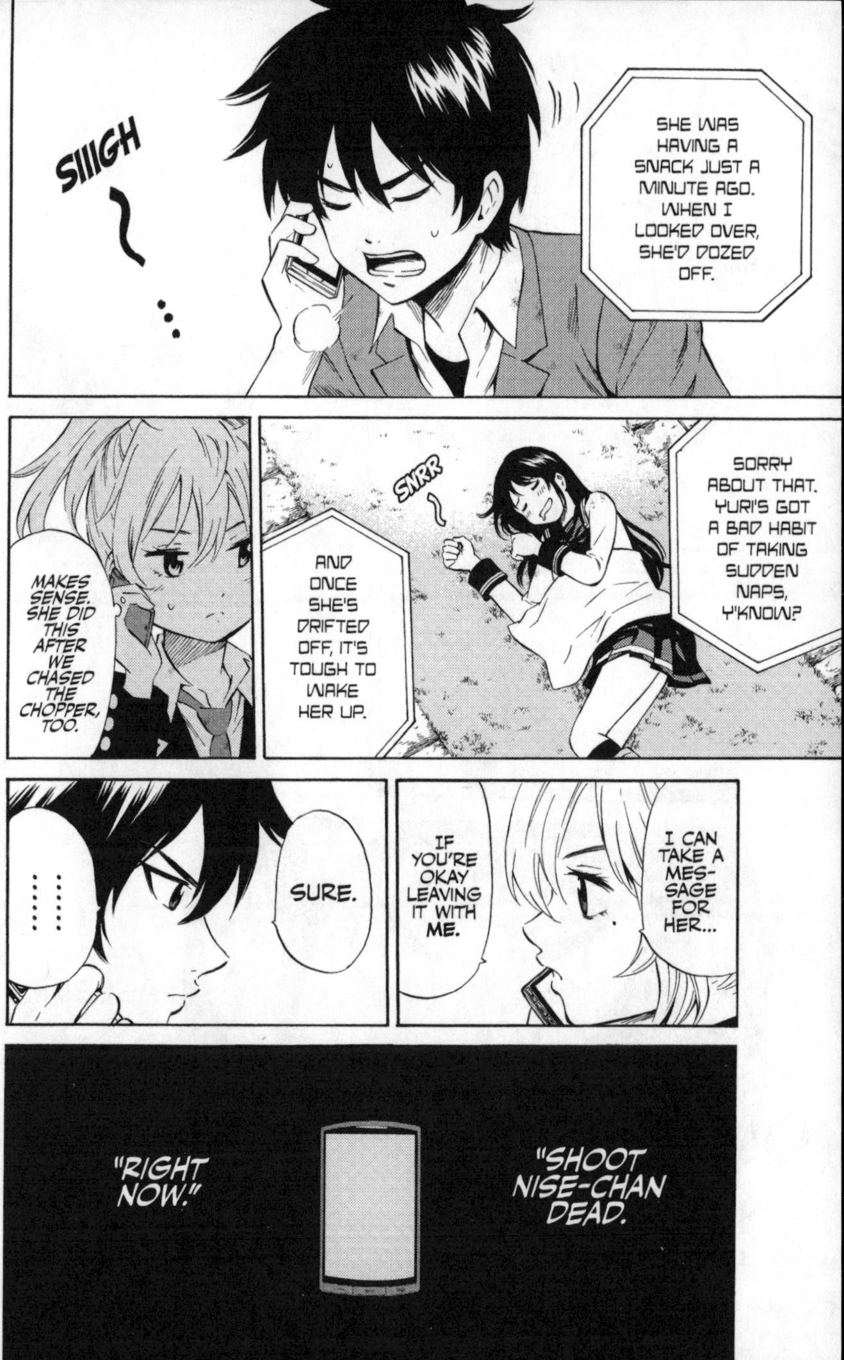
SHE WAS HAVING A SNACK JUST A MINUTE AGO. WHEN I LOOKED OVER, SHE'D DOZED OFF.
SIIIGH
...
SORRY ABOUT THAT. YURI'S GOT A BAD HABIT OF TAKING SUDDEN NAPS, Y'KNOW?
SNRR
AND ONCE SHE'S DRIFTED OFF, IT'S TOUGH TO WAKE HER UP.
MAKES SENSE. SHE DID THIS AFTER WE CHASED THE CHOPPER, TOO.
I CAN TAKE A MES-SAGE FOR HER...
IF YOU'RE OKAY LEAVING IT WITH ME.
SURE.
......
"SHOOT NISE-CHAN DEAD.
"RIGHT NOW."

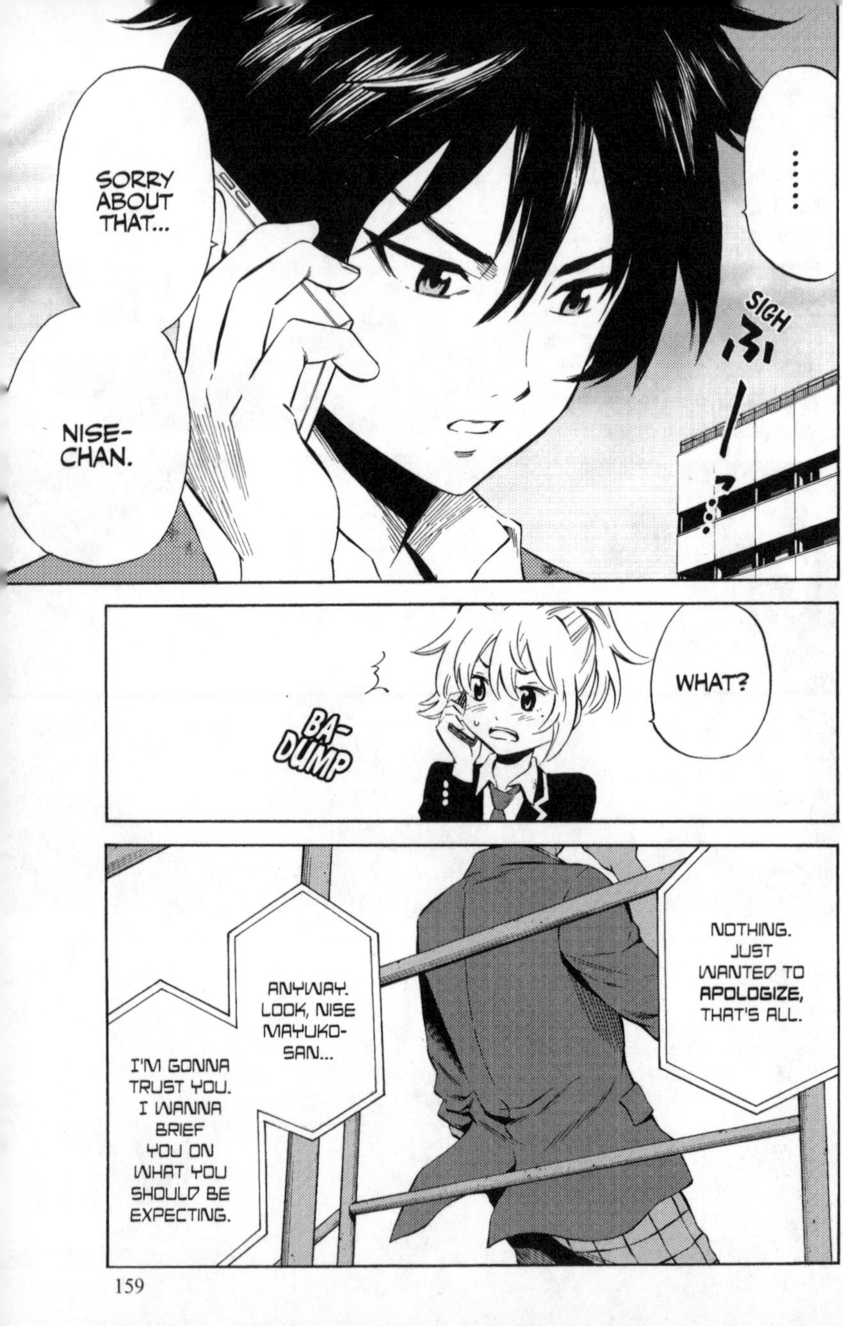
......
SIGH
ふー…
SORRY ABOUT THAT... NISE-CHAN.
WHAT?
BA-DUMP
NOTHING. JUST WANTED TO APOLOGIZE, THAT'S ALL.
ANYWAY. LOOK, NISE MAYUKO-SAN...
I'M GONNA TRUST YOU. I WANNA BRIEF YOU ON WHAT YOU SHOULD BE EXPECTING.

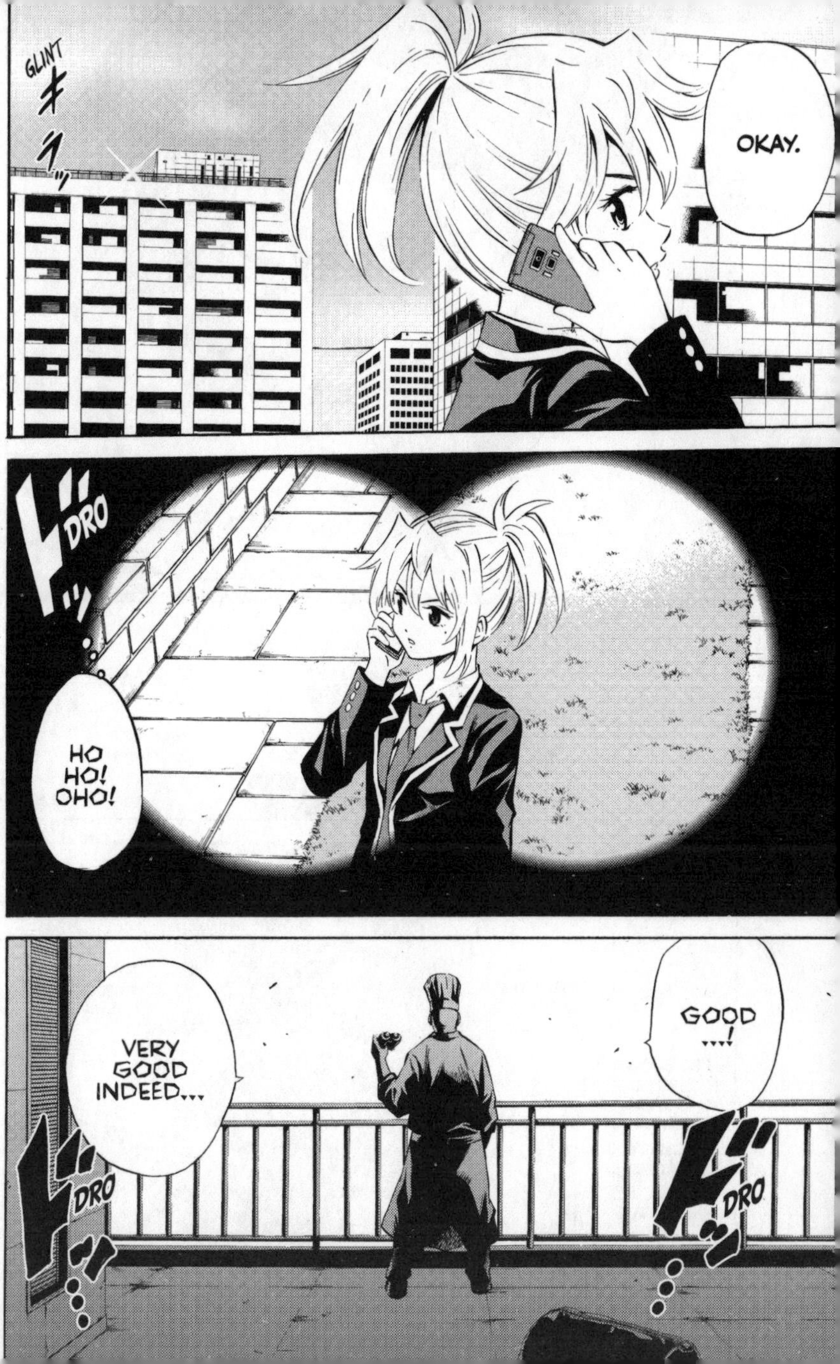
OKAY.
GLINT
DRO
HO HO! OHO!
GOOD ...!
DRO
VERY GOOD INDEED...
DRO

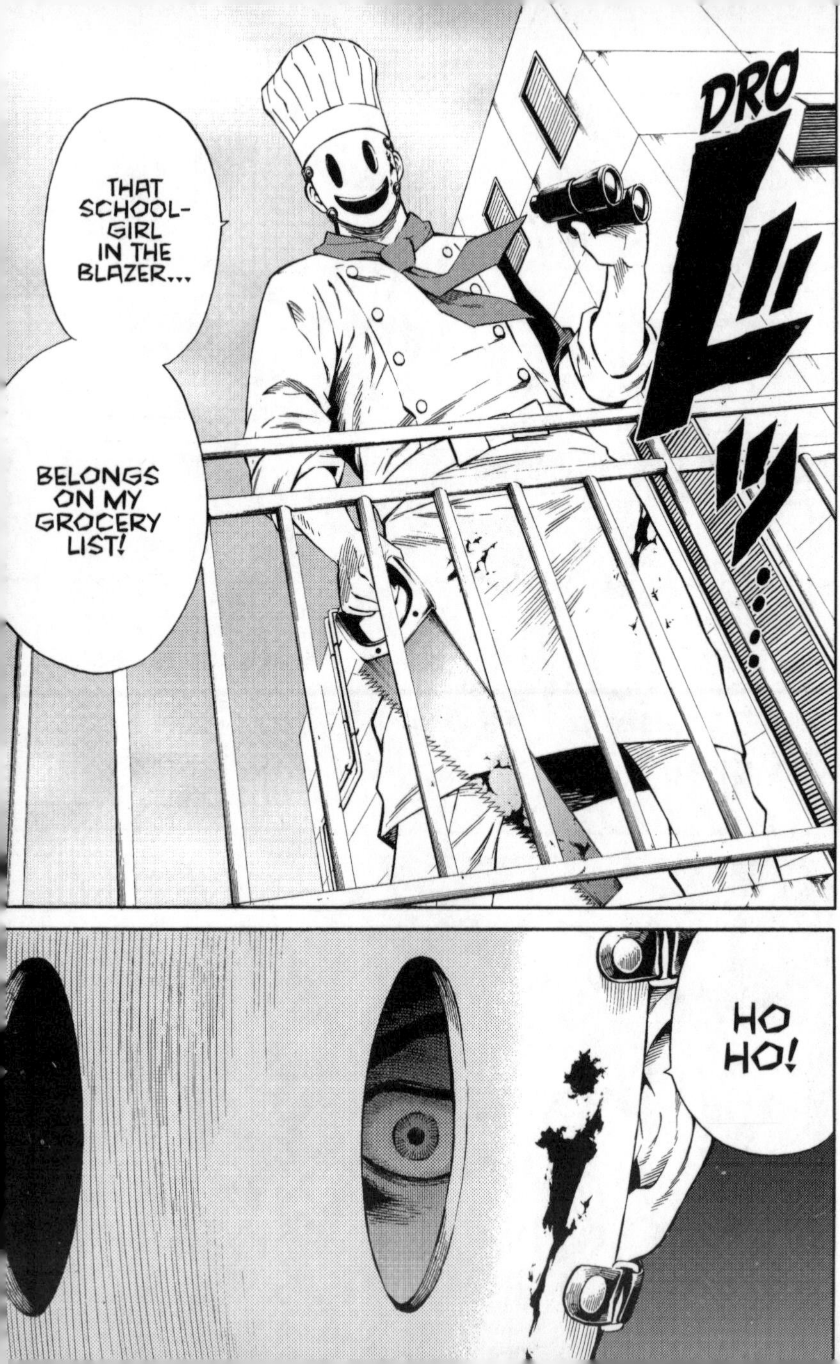
DRO
THAT SCHOOL-GIRL IN THE BLAZER...
BELONGS ON MY GROCERY LIST!
HO HO!

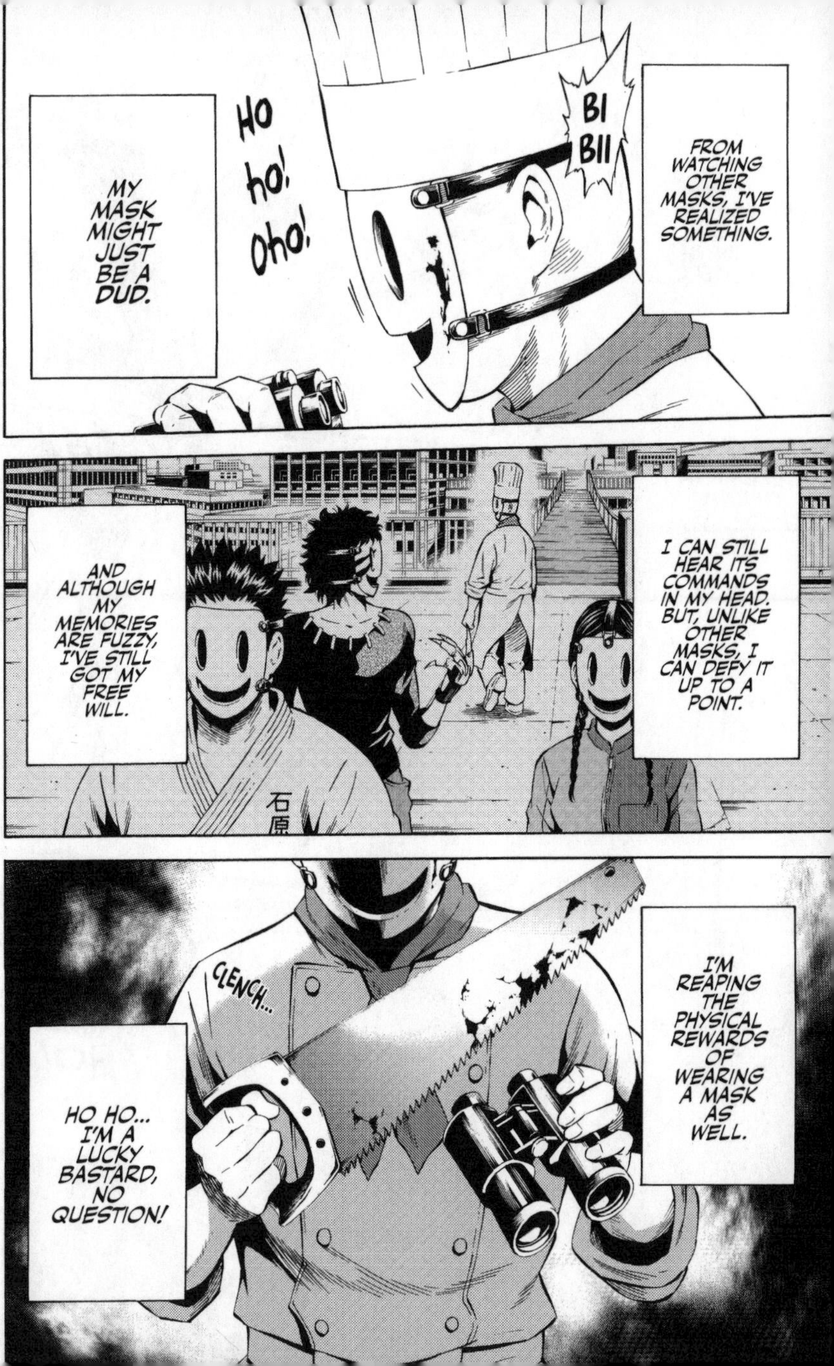

FROM WATCHING OTHER MASKS, I'VE REALIZED SOMETHING.
BI BII
HO ho! Oho!
MY MASK MIGHT JUST BE A DUD.
I CAN STILL HEAR ITS COMMANDS IN MY HEAD. BUT, UNLIKE OTHER MASKS, I CAN DEFY IT UP TO A POINT.
AND ALTHOUGH MY MEMORIES ARE FUZZY, I'VE STILL GOT MY FREE WILL.
石原
I'M REAPING THE PHYSICAL REWARDS OF WEARING A MASK AS WELL.
CLENCH...
HO HO... I'M A LUCKY BASTARD, NO QUESTION!

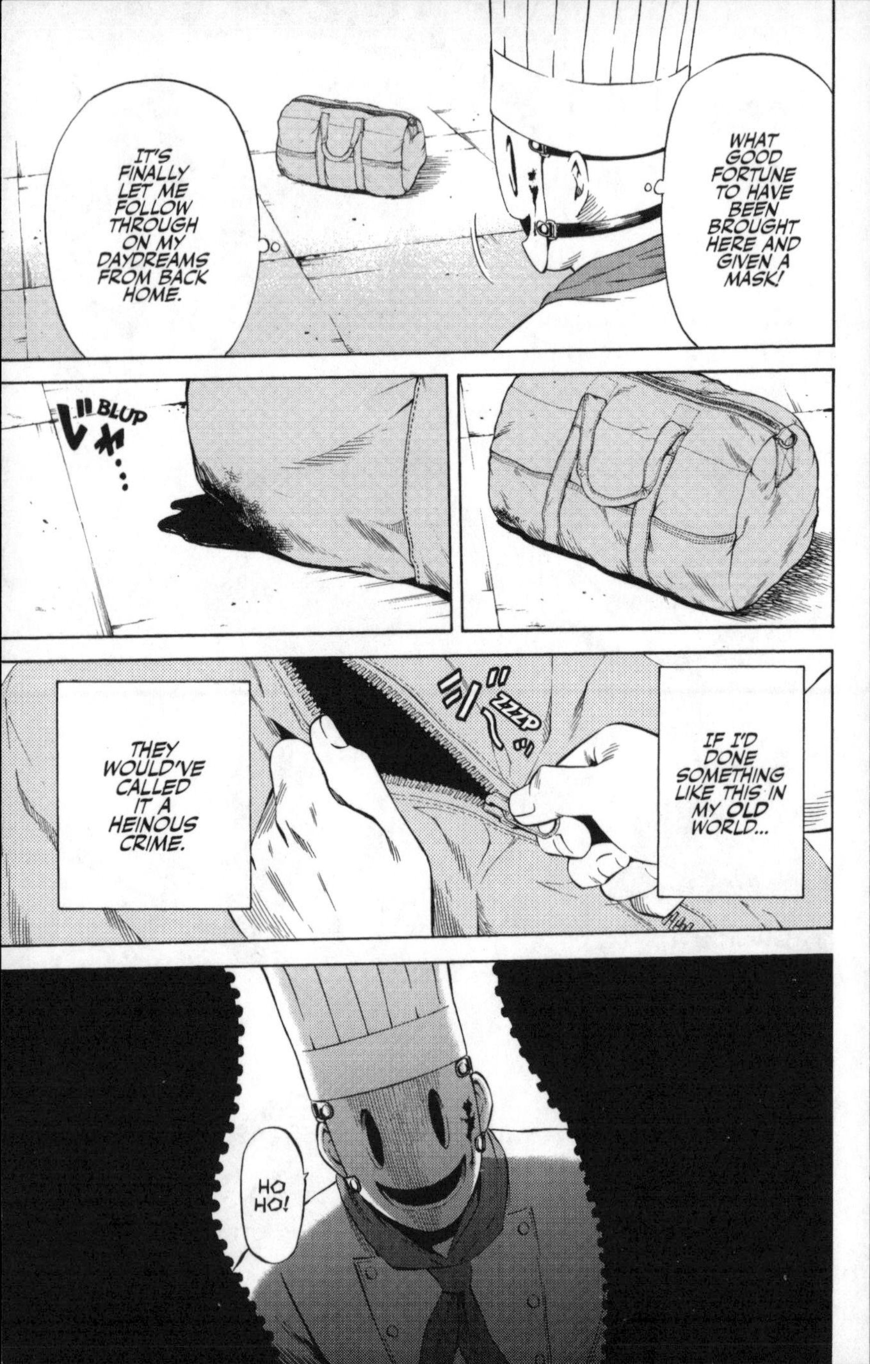
WHAT GOOD FORTUNE TO HAVE BEEN BROUGHT HERE AND GIVEN A MASK!
IT'S FINALLY LET ME FOLLOW THROUGH ON MY DAYDREAMS FROM BACK HOME.
BLUP
ZZZP
IF I'D DONE SOMETHING LIKE THIS IN MY OLD WORLD...
THEY WOULD'VE CALLED IT A HEINOUS CRIME.
HO HO!

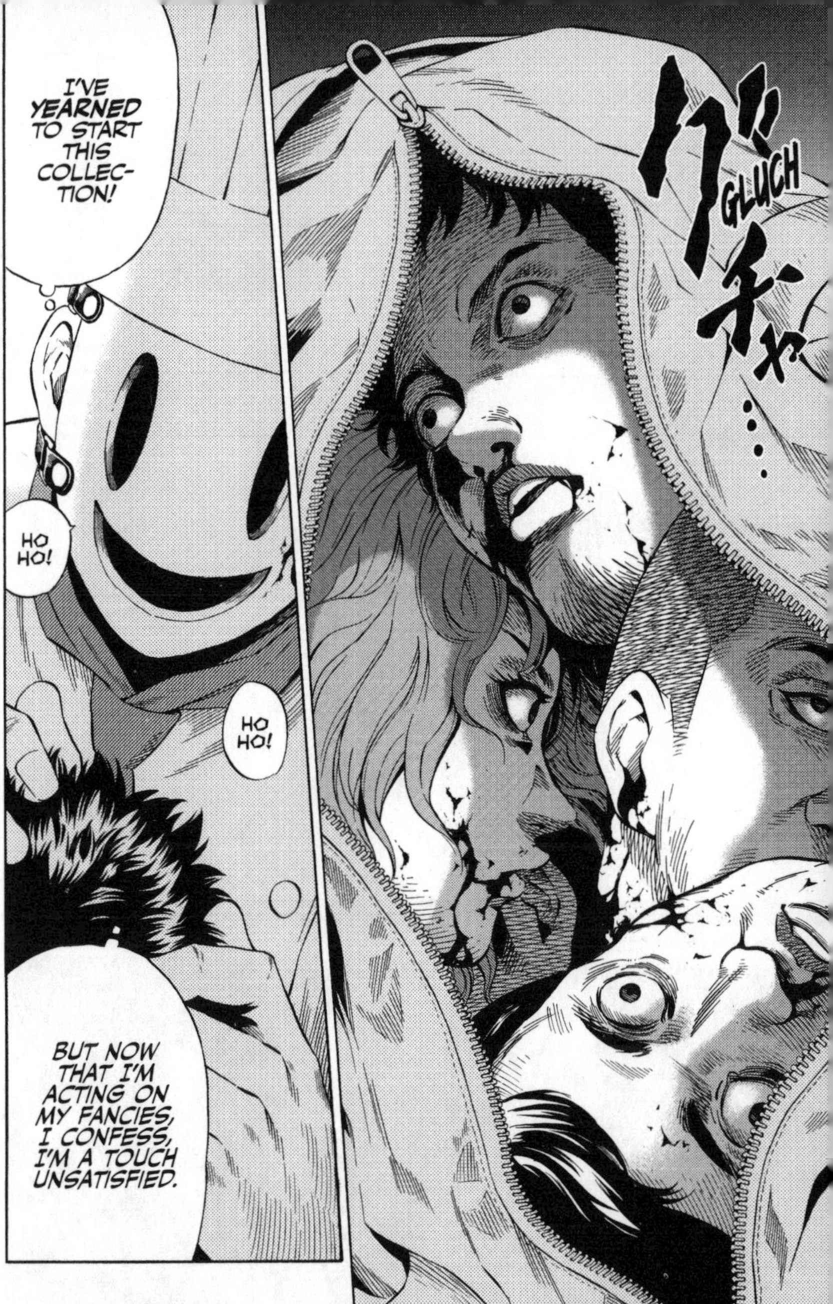
GLUCH
I'VE YEARNED TO START THIS COLLECTION!
HO HO!
HO HO!
BUT NOW THAT I'M ACTING ON MY FANCIES, I CONFESS, I'M A TOUCH UNSATISFIED.

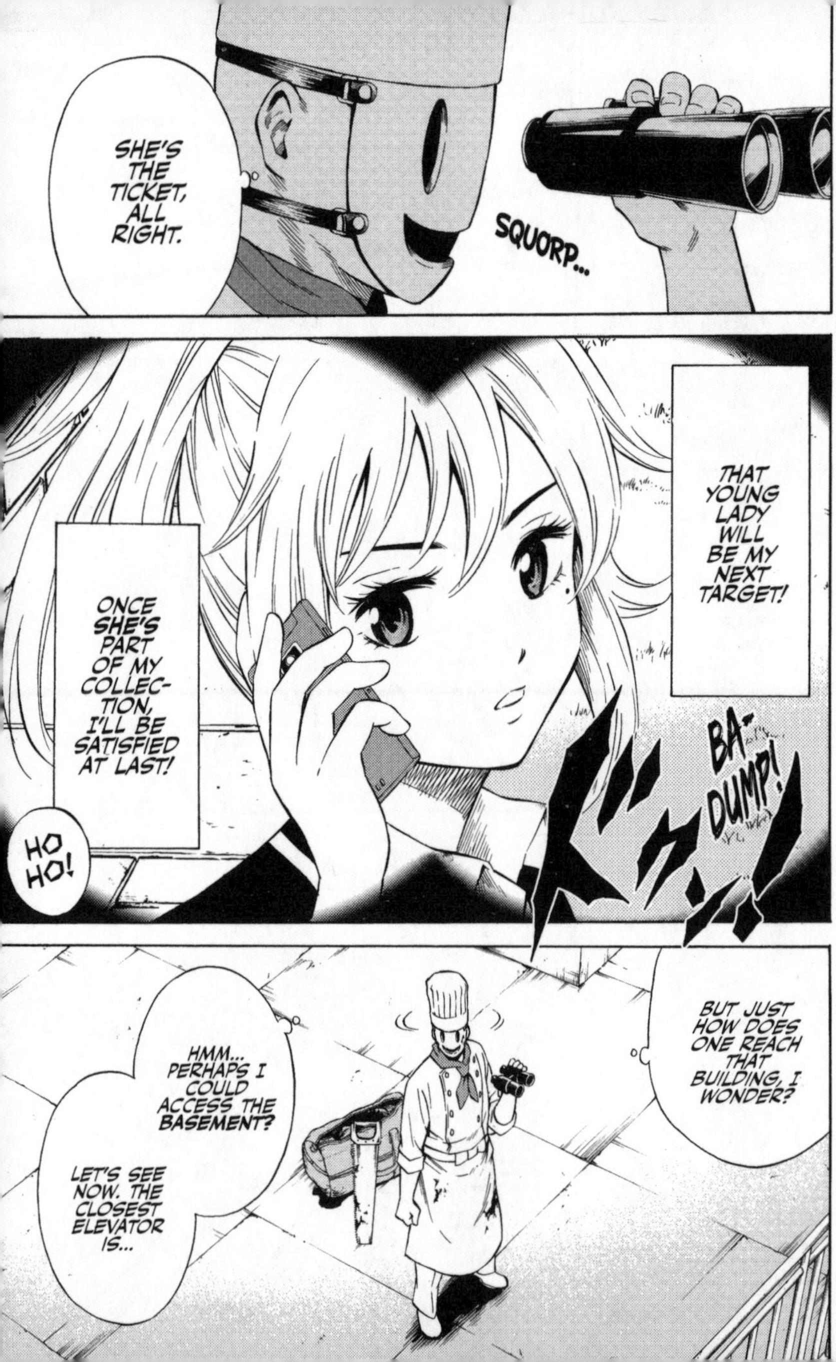
SQUORP...
SHE'S THE TICKET, ALL RIGHT.
THAT YOUNG LADY WILL BE MY NEXT TARGET!
BA-DUMP!
ONCE SHE'S PART OF MY COLLECTION, I'LL BE SATISFIED AT LAST!
HO HO!
BUT JUST HOW DOES ONE REACH THAT BUILDING, I WONDER?
HMM... PERHAPS I COULD ACCESS THE BASEMENT?
LET'S SEE NOW. THE CLOSEST ELEVATOR IS...

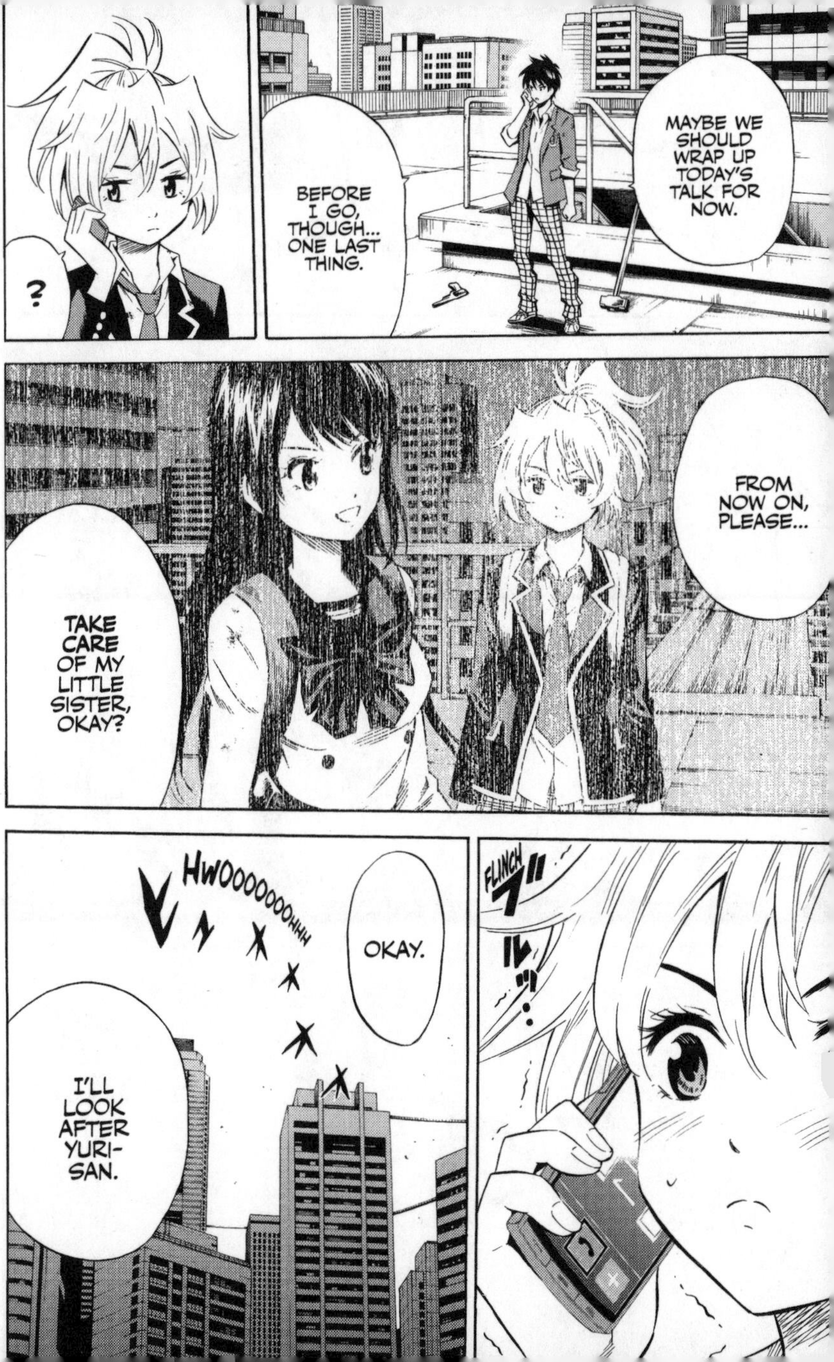
MAYBE WE SHOULD WRAP UP TODAY'S TALK FOR NOW.
BEFORE I GO, THOUGH... ONE LAST THING.
?
FROM NOW ON, PLEASE...
TAKE CARE OF MY LITTLE SISTER, OKAY?
FLINCH
OKAY.
HWOOOOOOOOHHH
I'LL LOOK AFTER YURI-SAN.

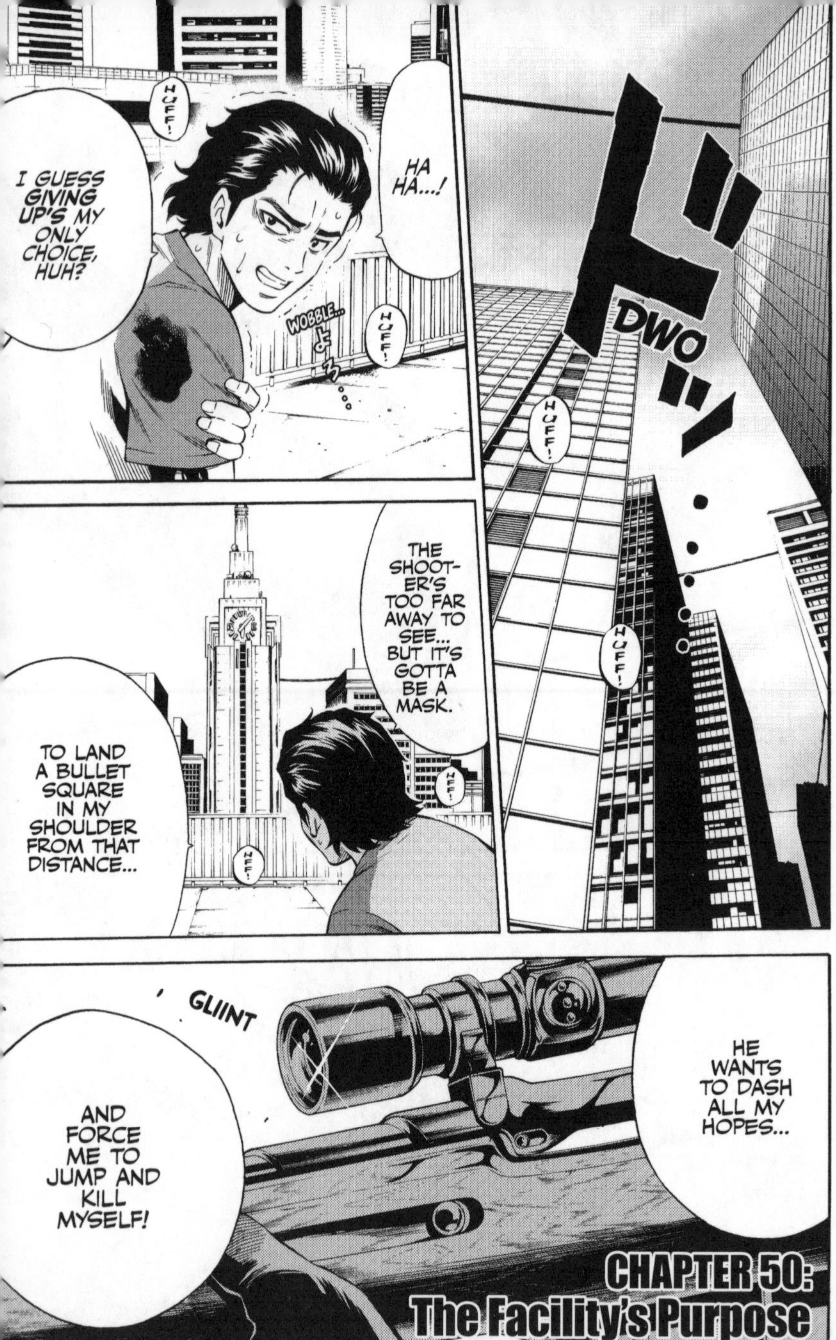
ド
DWO
ッ
HUFF!
HUFF!
HA HA...!
HUFF!
WOBBLE...
よろ
HUFF!
I GUESS GIVING UP'S MY ONLY CHOICE, HUH?
THE SHOOTER'S TOO FAR AWAY TO SEE... BUT IT'S GOTTA BE A MASK.
HFF!
HFF!
TO LAND A BULLET SQUARE IN MY SHOULDER FROM THAT DISTANCE...
HE WANTS TO DASH ALL MY HOPES...
GLIINT
AND FORCE ME TO JUMP AND KILL MYSELF!
CHAPTER 50:
The Facility's Purpose

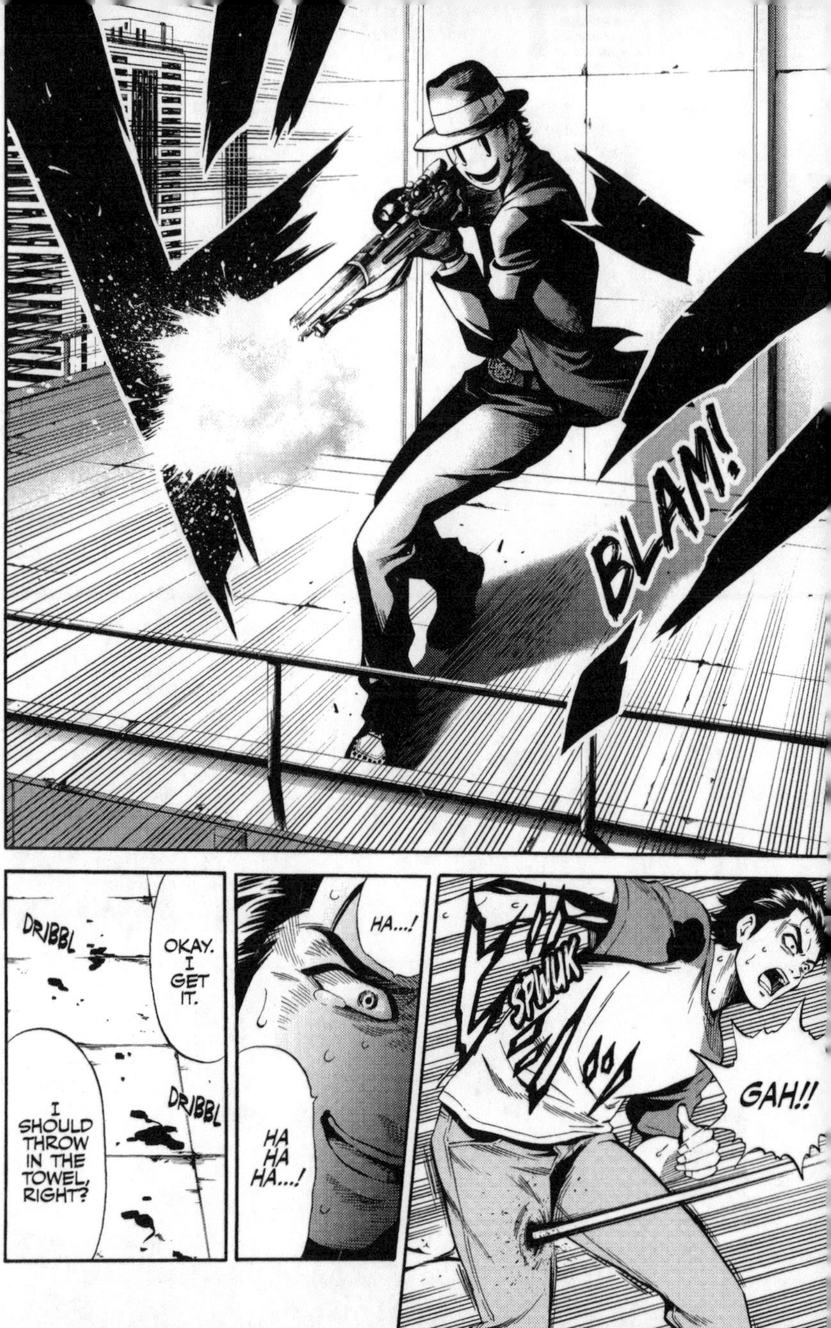
BLAM!
SPWUK
GAH!!
HA...!
HA HA HA...!
DRIBBL
OKAY. I GET IT.
DRIBBL
I SHOULD THROW IN THE TOWEL, RIGHT?

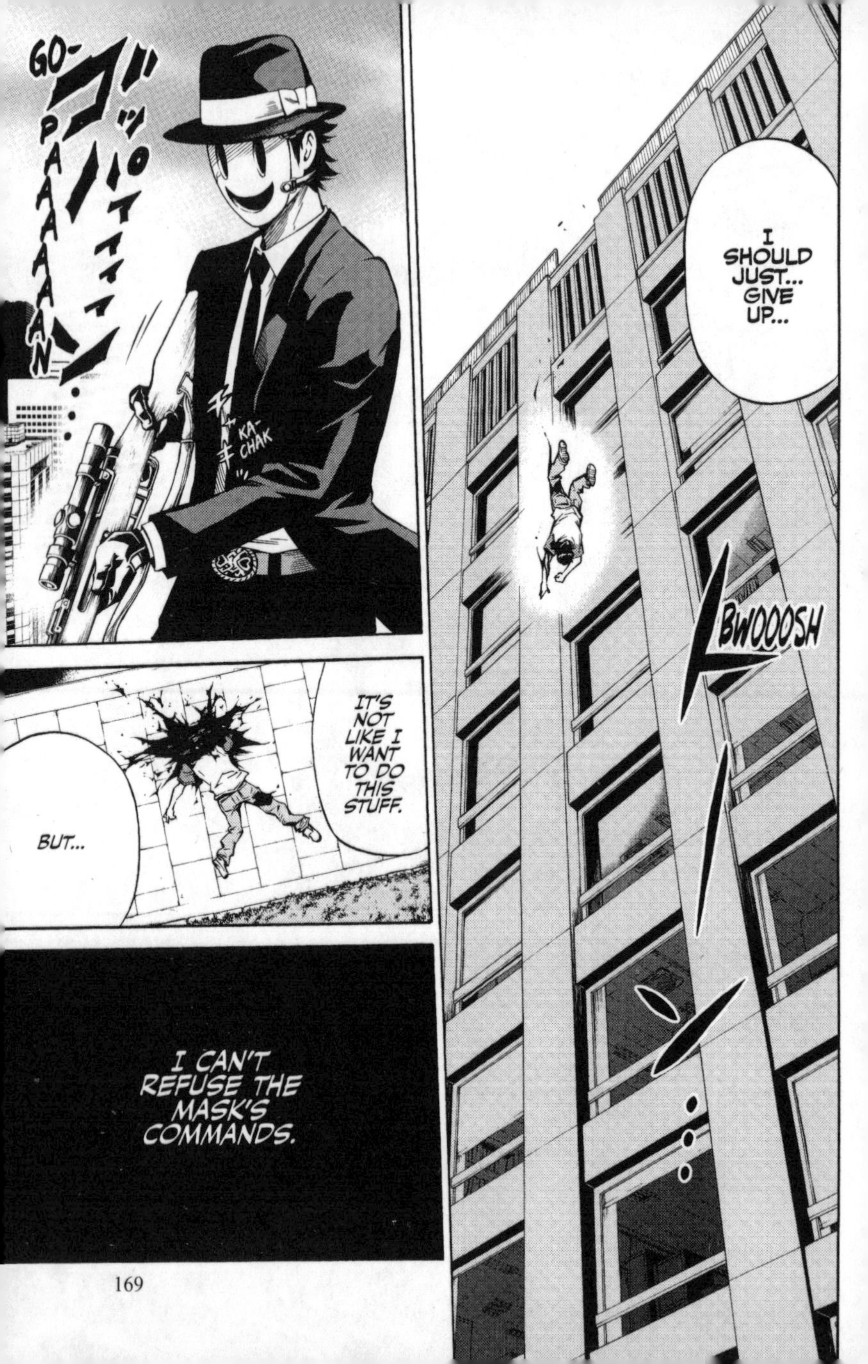
I SHOULD JUST... GIVE UP...
BWOOOSH
GO-PAAAAAAN...
KA-CHAK
IT'S NOT LIKE I WANT TO DO THIS STUFF.
BUT...
I CAN'T REFUSE THE MASK'S COMMANDS.

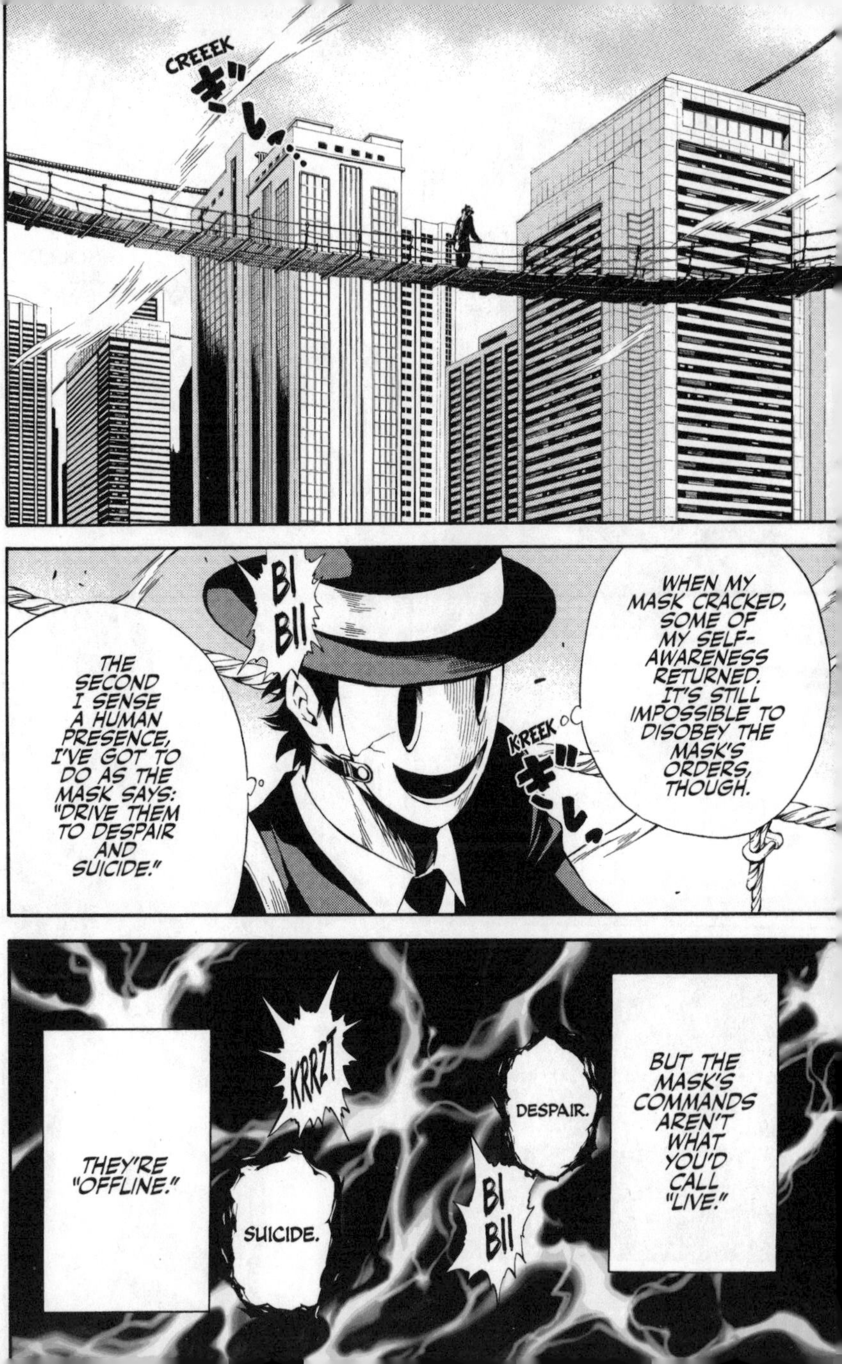
CREEEK
WHEN MY MASK CRACKED, SOME OF MY SELF-AWARENESS RETURNED. IT'S STILL IMPOSSIBLE TO DISOBEY THE MASK'S ORDERS, THOUGH.
K-REEK
BI BII
THE SECOND I SENSE A HUMAN PRESENCE, I'VE GOT TO DO AS THE MASK SAYS: "DRIVE THEM TO DESPAIR AND SUICIDE."
BUT THE MASK'S COMMANDS AREN'T WHAT YOU'D CALL "LIVE."
DESPAIR.
KRRZT
BI BII
SUICIDE.
THEY'RE "OFFLINE."

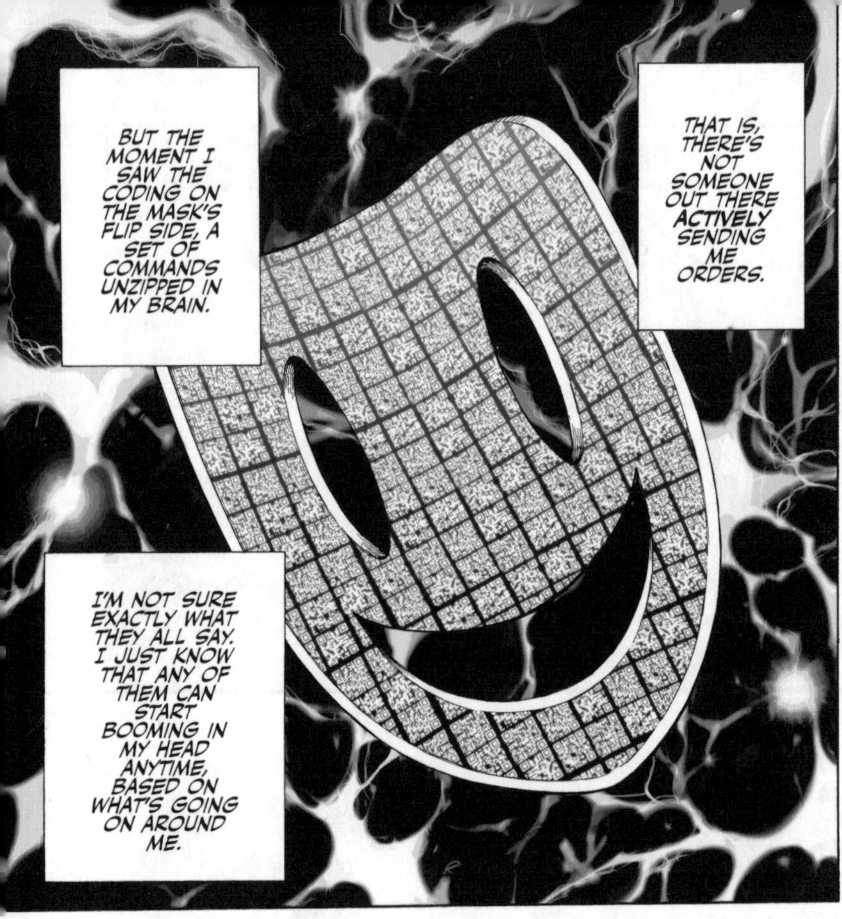
THAT IS, THERE'S NOT SOMEONE OUT THERE ACTIVELY SENDING ME ORDERS.
BUT THE MOMENT I SAW THE CODING ON THE MASK'S FLIP SIDE, A SET OF COMMANDS UNZIPPED IN MY BRAIN.
I'M NOT SURE EXACTLY WHAT THEY ALL SAY. I JUST KNOW THAT ANY OF THEM CAN START BOOMING IN MY HEAD ANYTIME, BASED ON WHAT'S GOING ON AROUND ME.

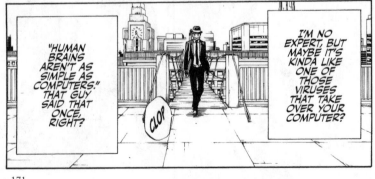

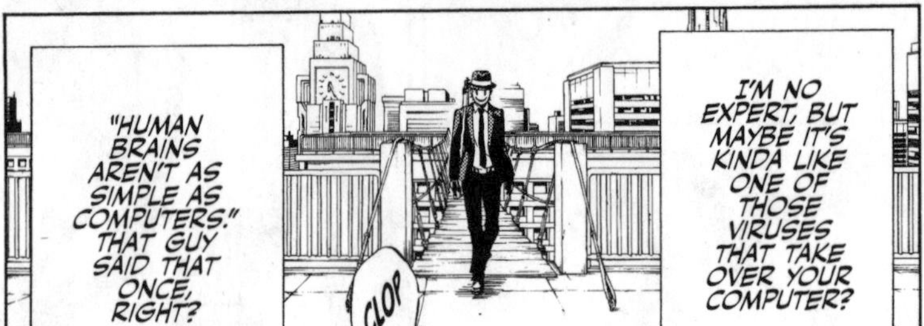
I'M NO EXPERT, BUT MAYBE IT'S KINDA LIKE ONE OF THOSE VIRUSES THAT TAKE OVER YOUR COMPUTER?
CLOP
"HUMAN BRAINS AREN'T AS SIMPLE AS COMPUTERS." THAT GUY SAID THAT ONCE, RIGHT?

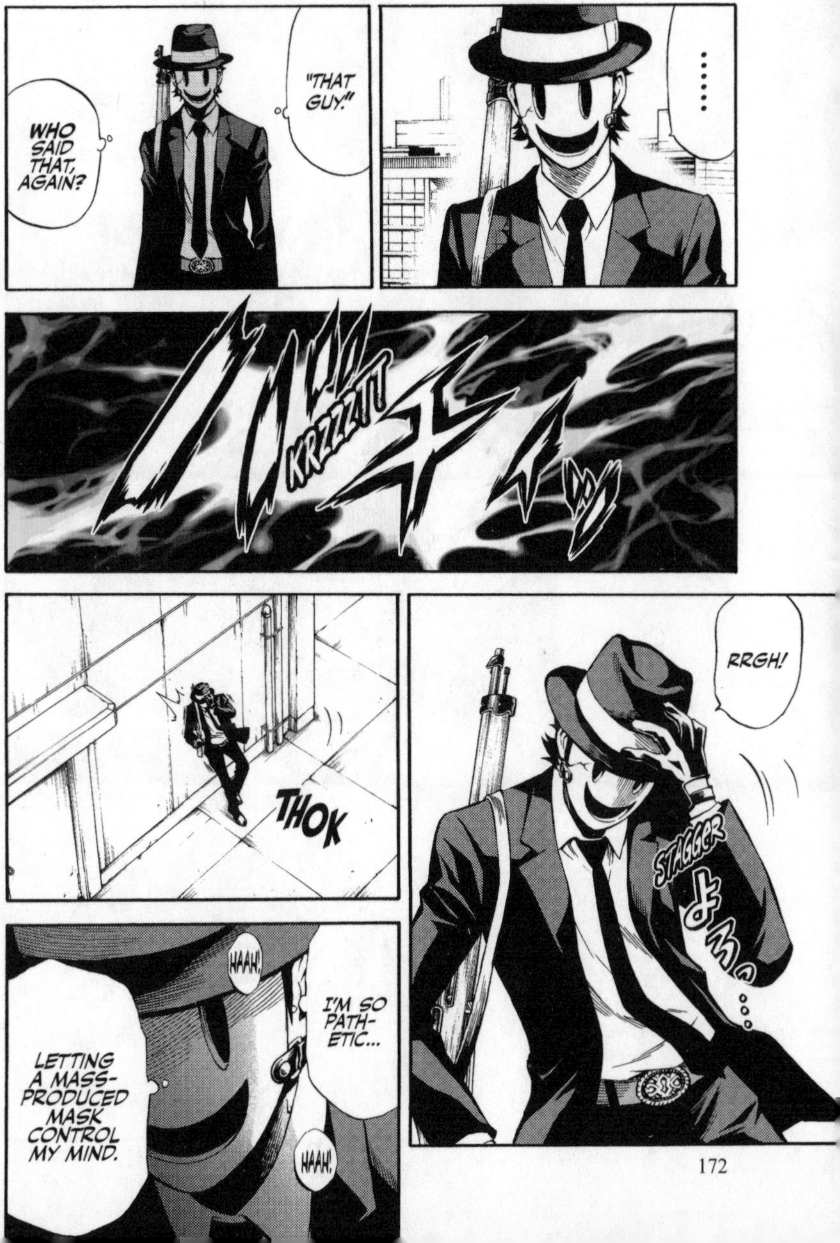
……
"THAT GUY."
WHO SAID THAT, AGAIN?
KRZZZTT
RRGH!
STAGGER
THOK
HAAH!
I'M SO PATHETIC...
LETTING A MASS-PRODUCED MASK CONTROL MY MIND.
HAAH!

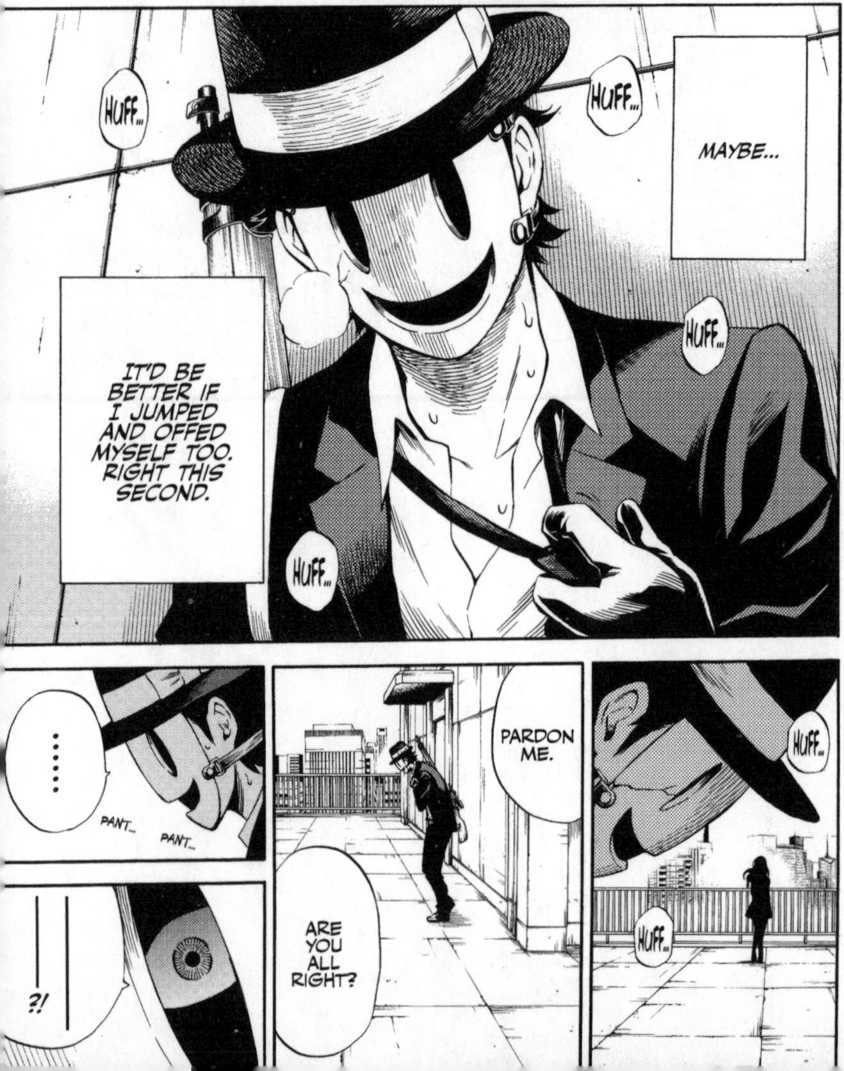
MAYBE...
HUFF...
HUFF...
HUFF...
IT'D BE BETTER IF I JUMPED AND OFFED MYSELF TOO. RIGHT THIS SECOND.
HUFF...
HUFF...
HUFF...
PARDON ME.
ARE YOU ALL RIGHT?
......
PANT... PANT...
?!

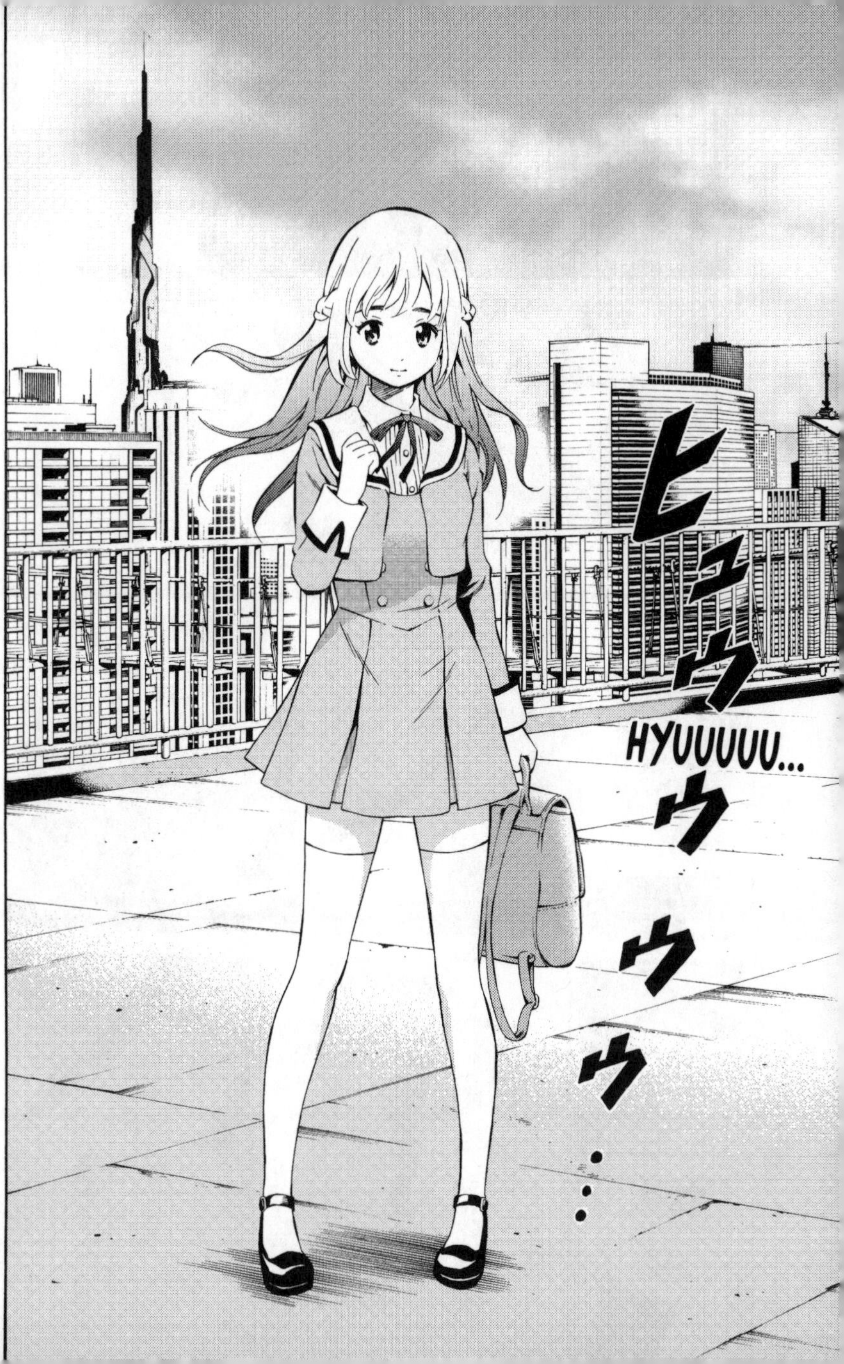
ヒュウ
HYUUUUU...
ウウウ...

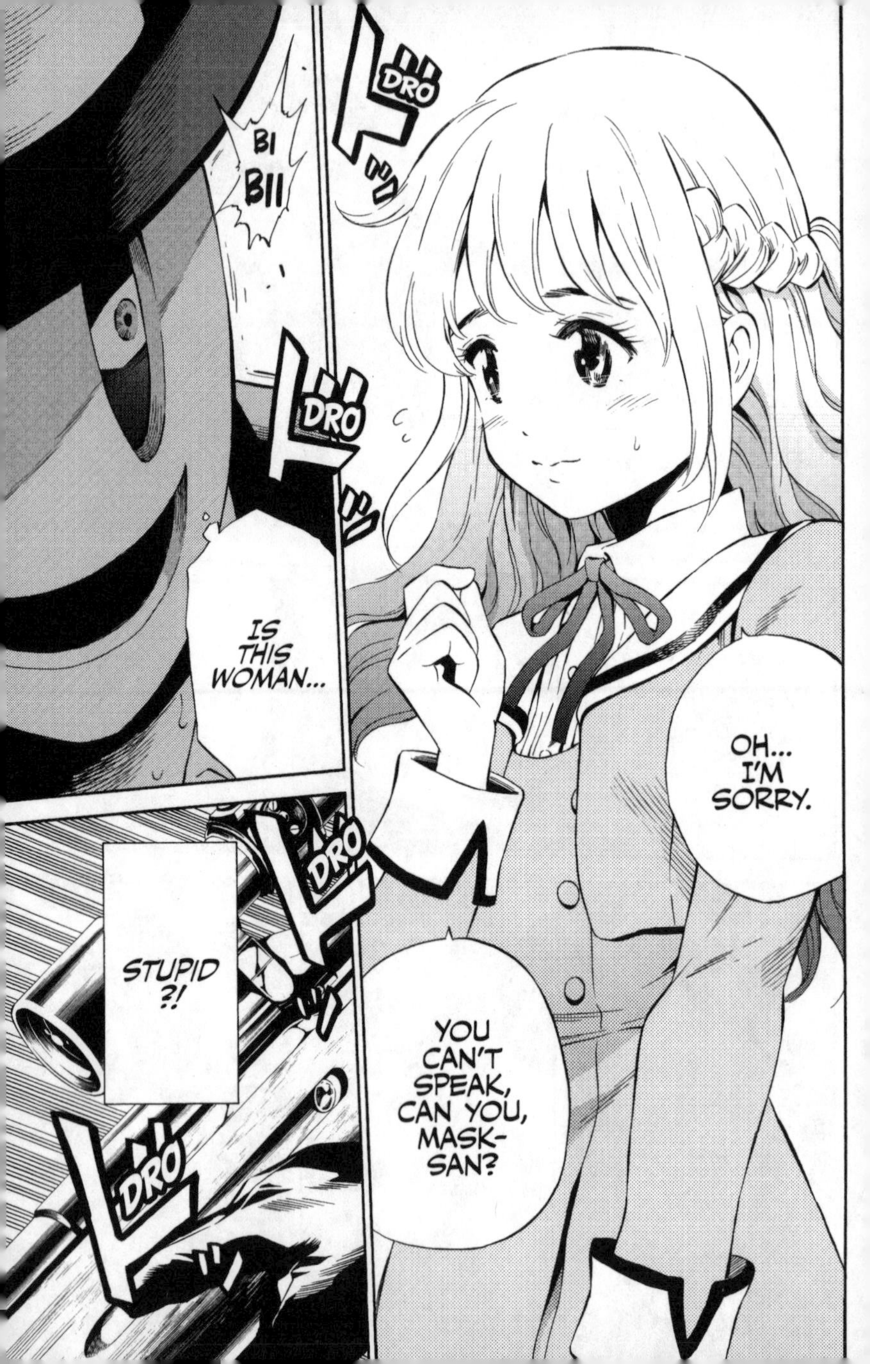
OH... I'M SORRY.
YOU CAN'T SPEAK, CAN YOU, MASK-SAN?
DRO
BI BII
DRO
IS THIS WOMAN...
DRO
STUPID ?!
DRO

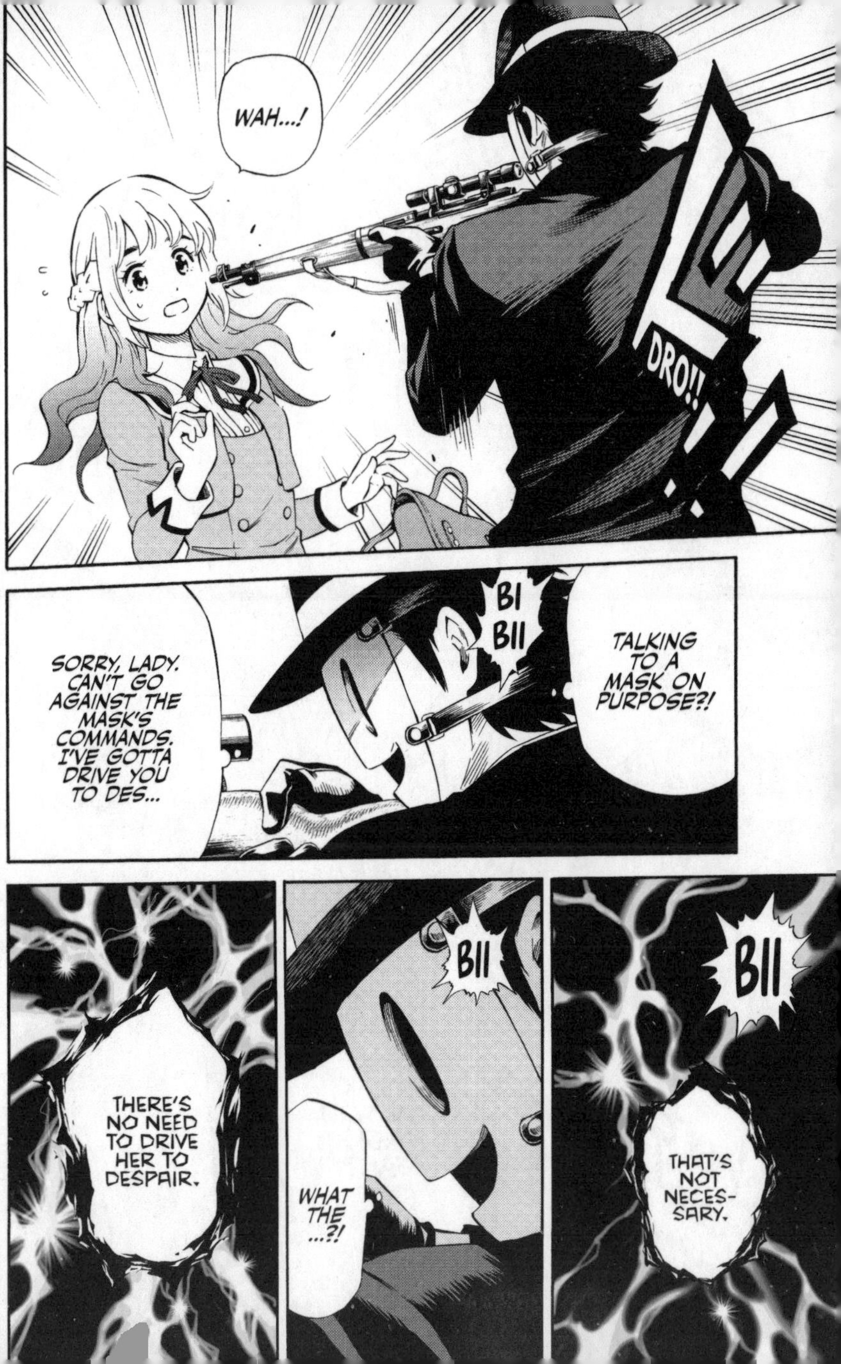
WAH...!
DRO!!
TALKING TO A MASK ON PURPOSE?!
BI BII
SORRY, LADY. CAN'T GO AGAINST THE MASK'S COMMANDS. I'VE GOTTA DRIVE YOU TO DES...
BII
THAT'S NOT NECES-SARY.
BII
WHAT THE ...?!
THERE'S NO NEED TO DRIVE HER TO DESPAIR.

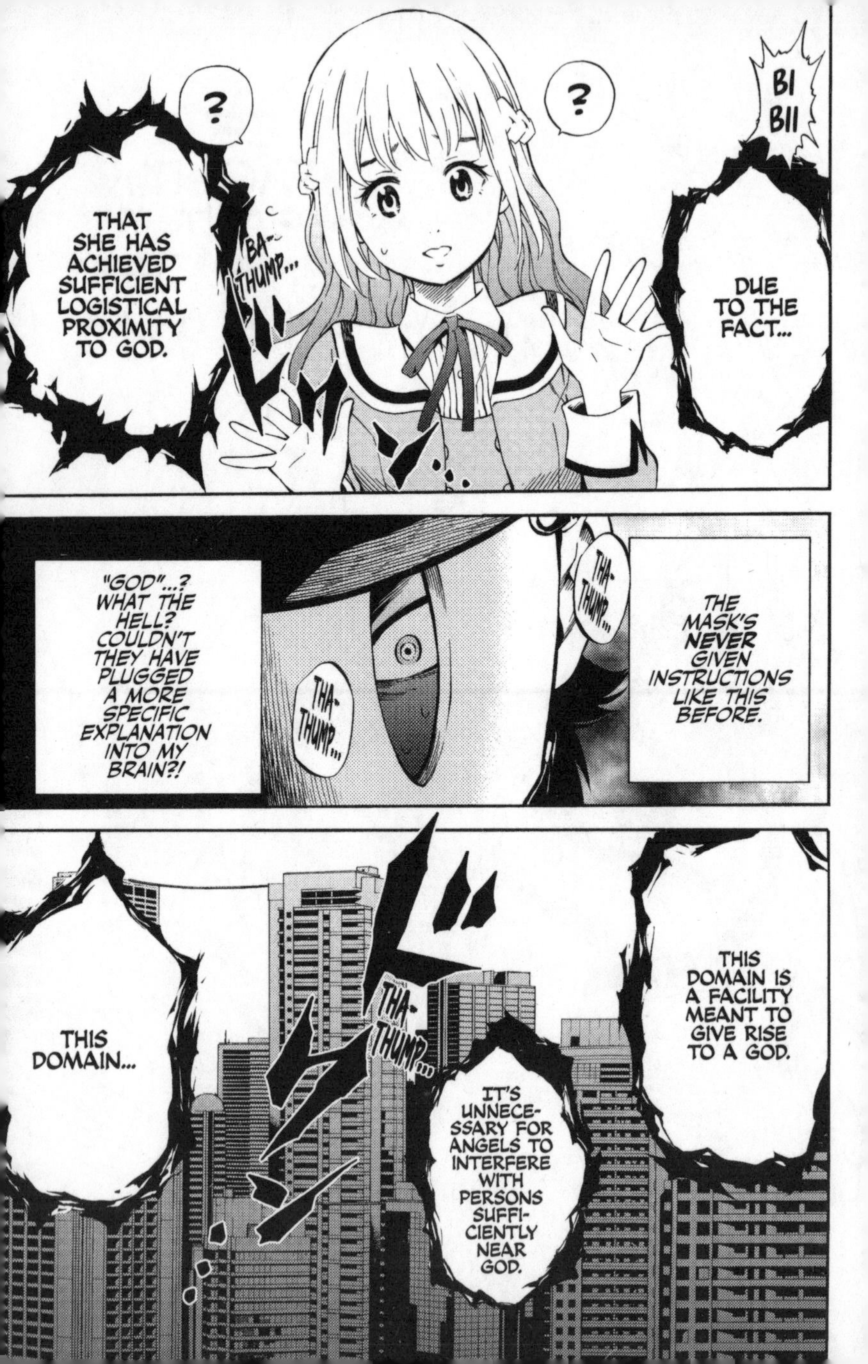
BI BII
DUE TO THE FACT...
?
?
BA-THUMP...
THAT SHE HAS ACHIEVED SUFFICIENT LOGISTICAL PROXIMITY TO GOD.
THE MASK'S NEVER GIVEN INSTRUCTIONS LIKE THIS BEFORE.
THA-THUMP...
THA-THUMP...
"GOD"...? WHAT THE HELL? COULDN'T THEY HAVE PLUGGED A MORE SPECIFIC EXPLANATION INTO MY BRAIN?!
THIS DOMAIN IS A FACILITY MEANT TO GIVE RISE TO A GOD.
IT'S UNNECESSARY FOR ANGELS TO INTERFERE WITH PERSONS SUFFICIENTLY NEAR GOD.
THA-THUMP...
THIS DOMAIN...

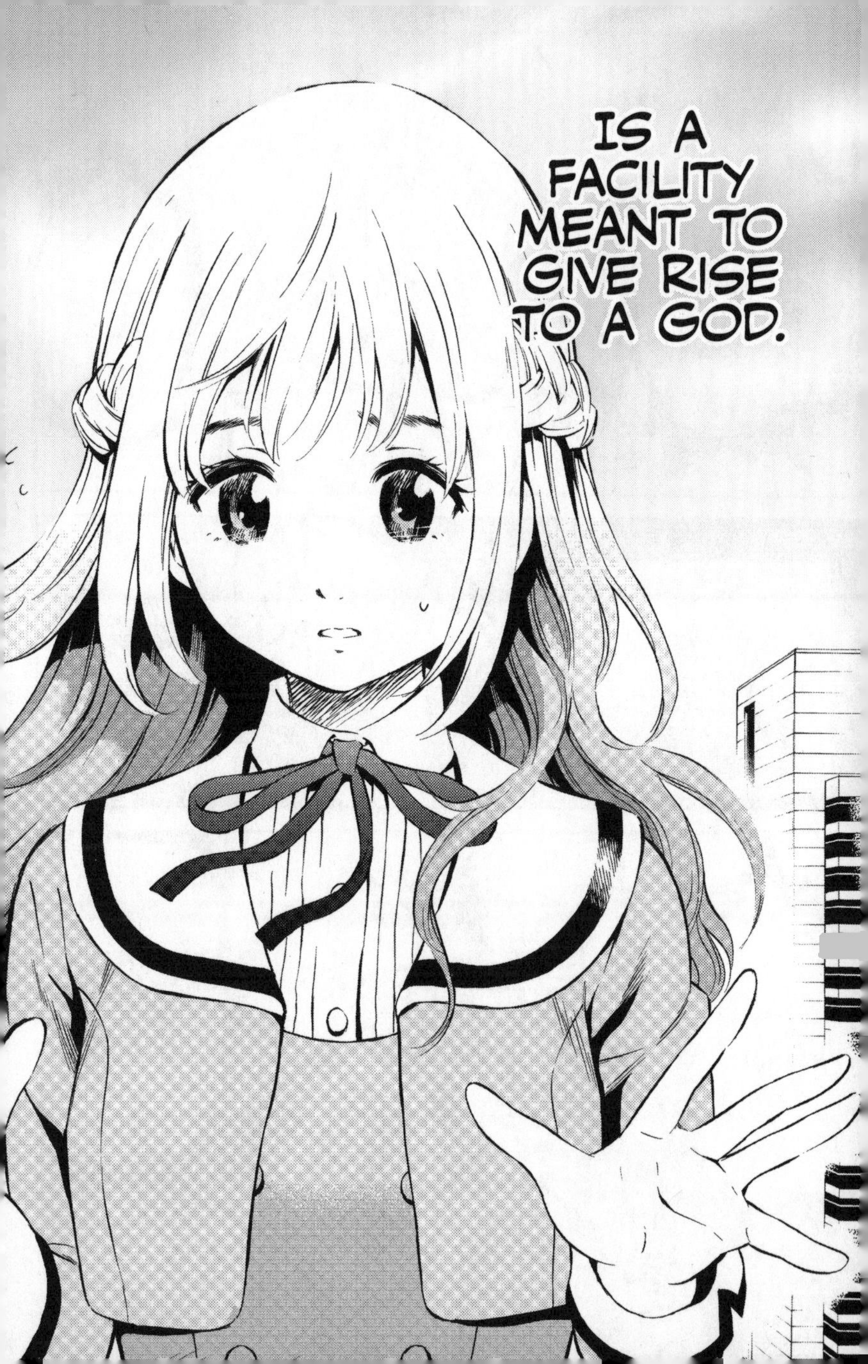
IS A FACILITY MEANT TO GIVE RISE TO A GOD.

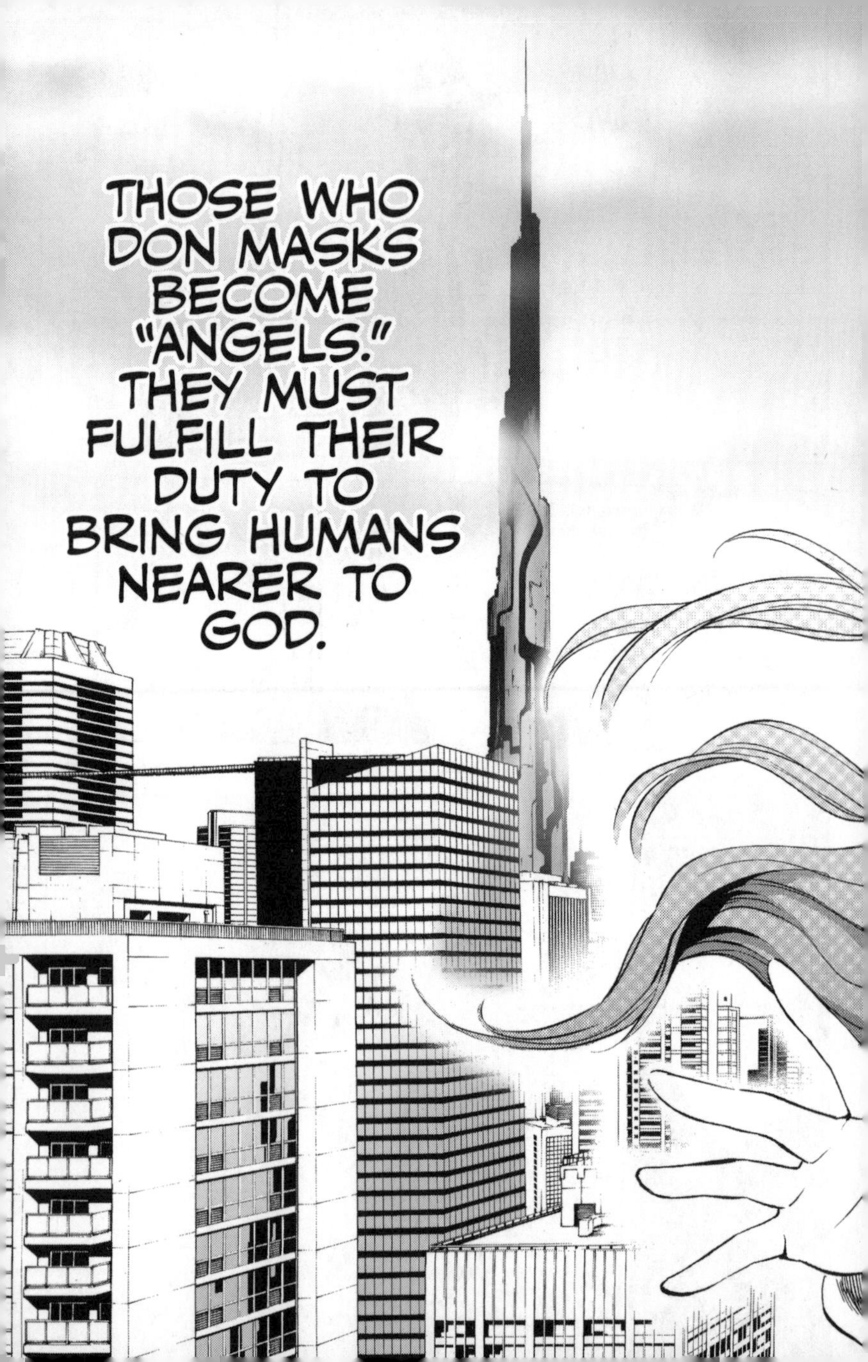
THOSE WHO DON MASKS BECOME "ANGELS." THEY MUST FULFILL THEIR DUTY TO BRING HUMANS NEARER TO GOD.

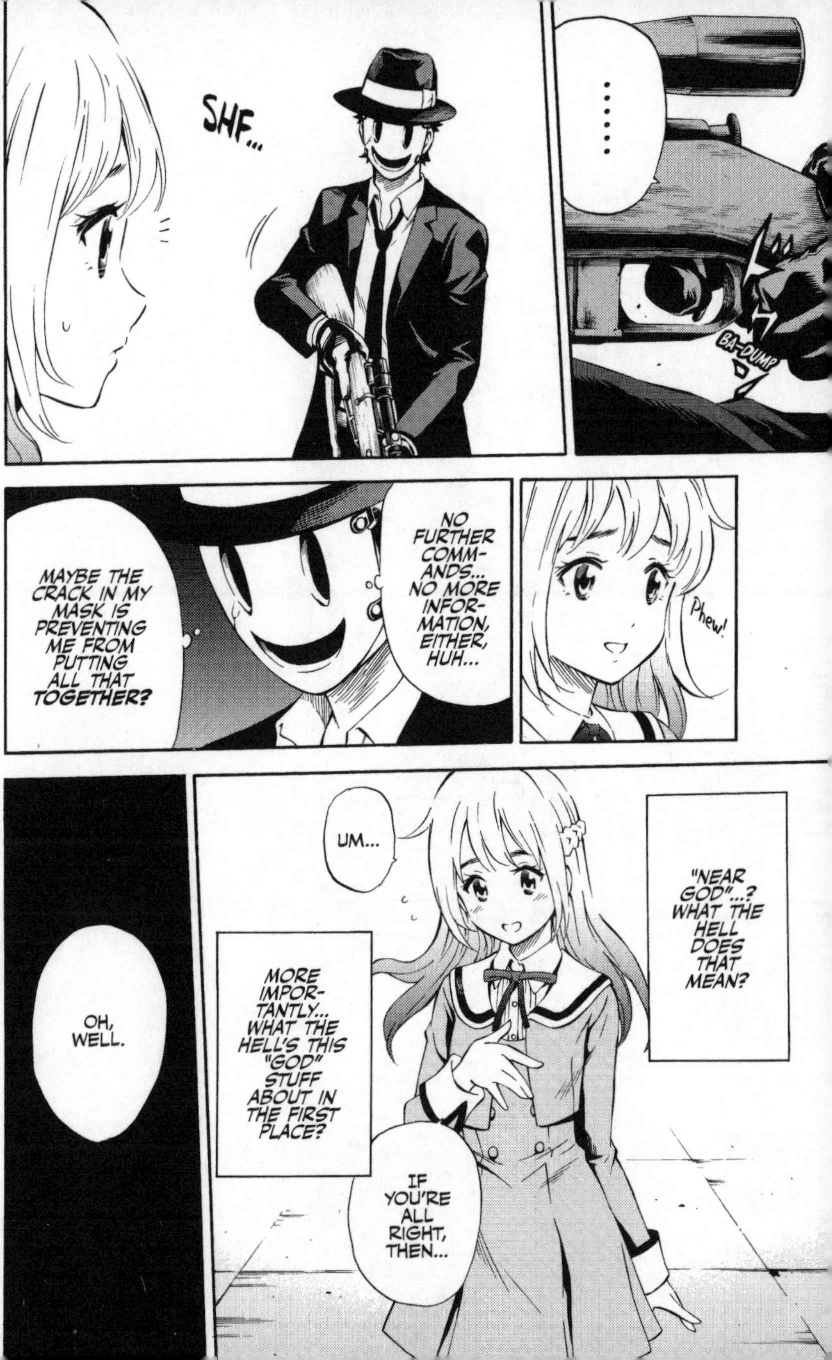
......
BA-DUMP
SHF...
Phew!
NO FURTHER COMMANDS... NO MORE INFORMATION, EITHER, HUH...
MAYBE THE CRACK IN MY MASK IS PREVENTING ME FROM PUTTING ALL THAT TOGETHER?
"NEAR GOD"...? WHAT THE HELL DOES THAT MEAN?
UM...
MORE IMPORTANTLY... WHAT THE HELL'S THIS "GOD" STUFF ABOUT IN THE FIRST PLACE?
IF YOU'RE ALL RIGHT, THEN...
OH, WELL.

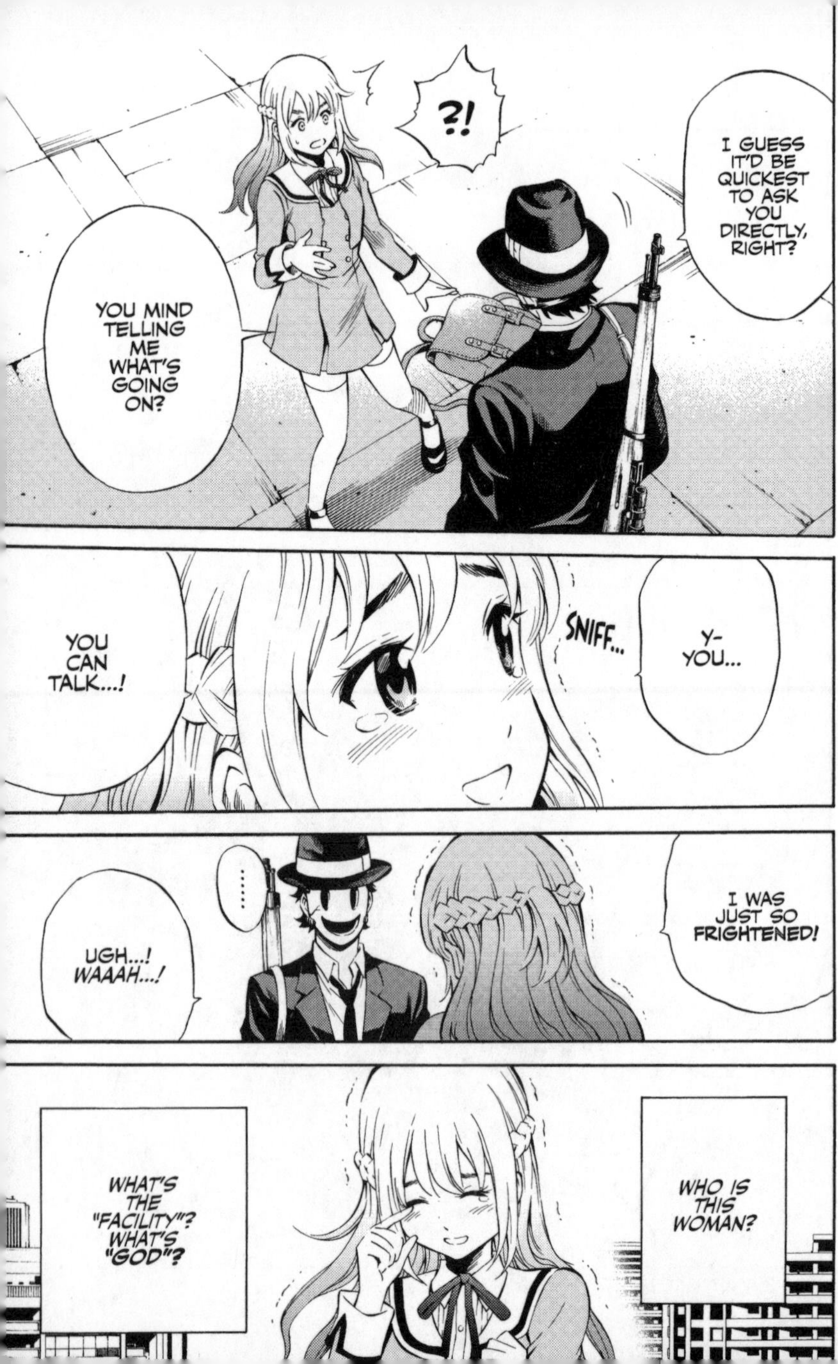
I GUESS IT'D BE QUICKEST TO ASK YOU DIRECTLY, RIGHT?
?!
YOU MIND TELLING ME WHAT'S GOING ON?
Y- YOU...
SNIFF...
YOU CAN TALK...!
I WAS JUST SO FRIGHTENED!
......
UGH...! WAAAH...!
WHO IS THIS WOMAN?
WHAT'S THE "FACILITY"? WHAT'S "GOD"?

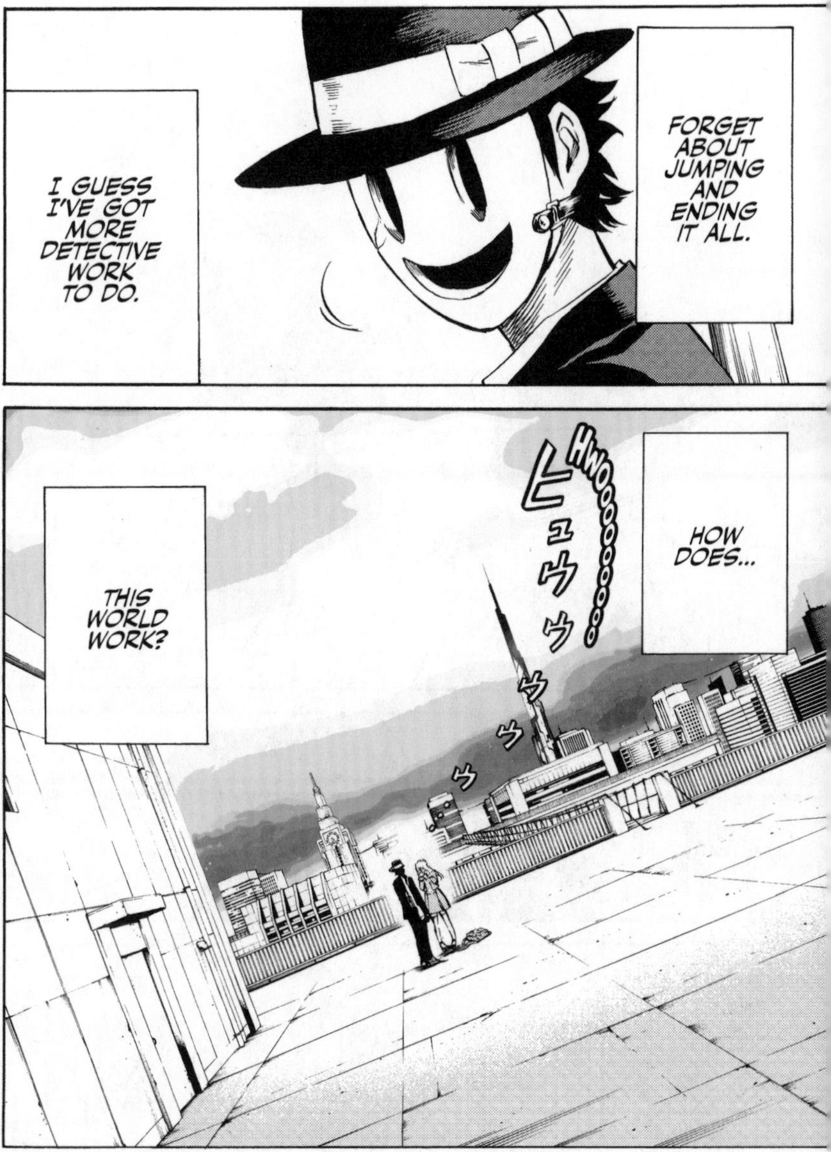
FORGET ABOUT JUMPING AND ENDING IT ALL.
I GUESS I'VE GOT MORE DETECTIVE WORK TO DO.
HOW DOES...
HWOOOOOOOOOOO
ヒュウウウウウウ
THIS WORLD WORK?

HIGH-RISE INVASION

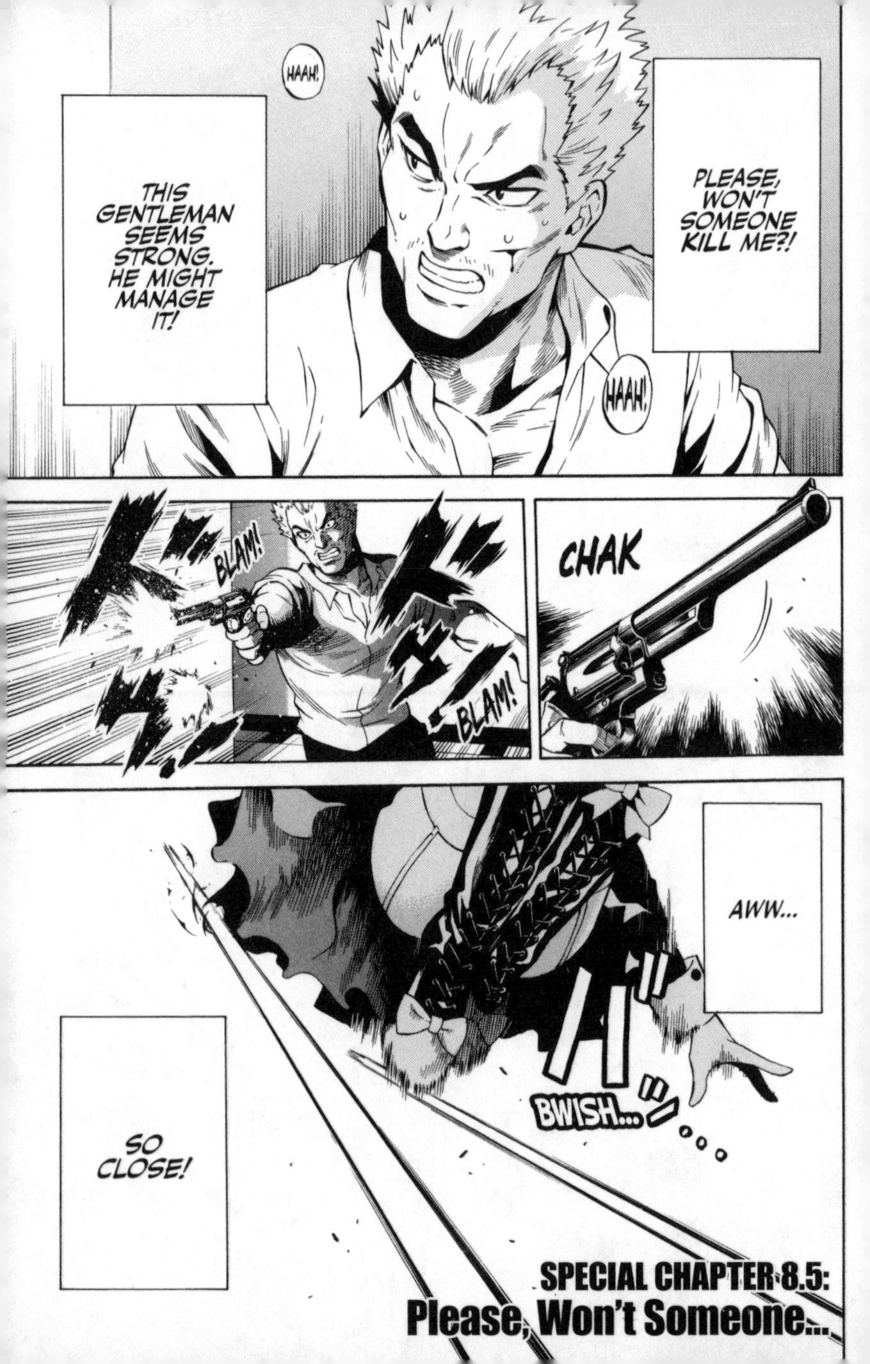
PLEASE, WON'T SOMEONE KILL ME?!
HAAH!
THIS GENTLEMAN SEEMS STRONG. HE MIGHT MANAGE IT!
HAAH!
CHAK
BLAM!
BLAM!
AWW...
BWISH...
SO CLOSE!

SPECIAL CHAPTER 8.5: Please, Won't Someone...

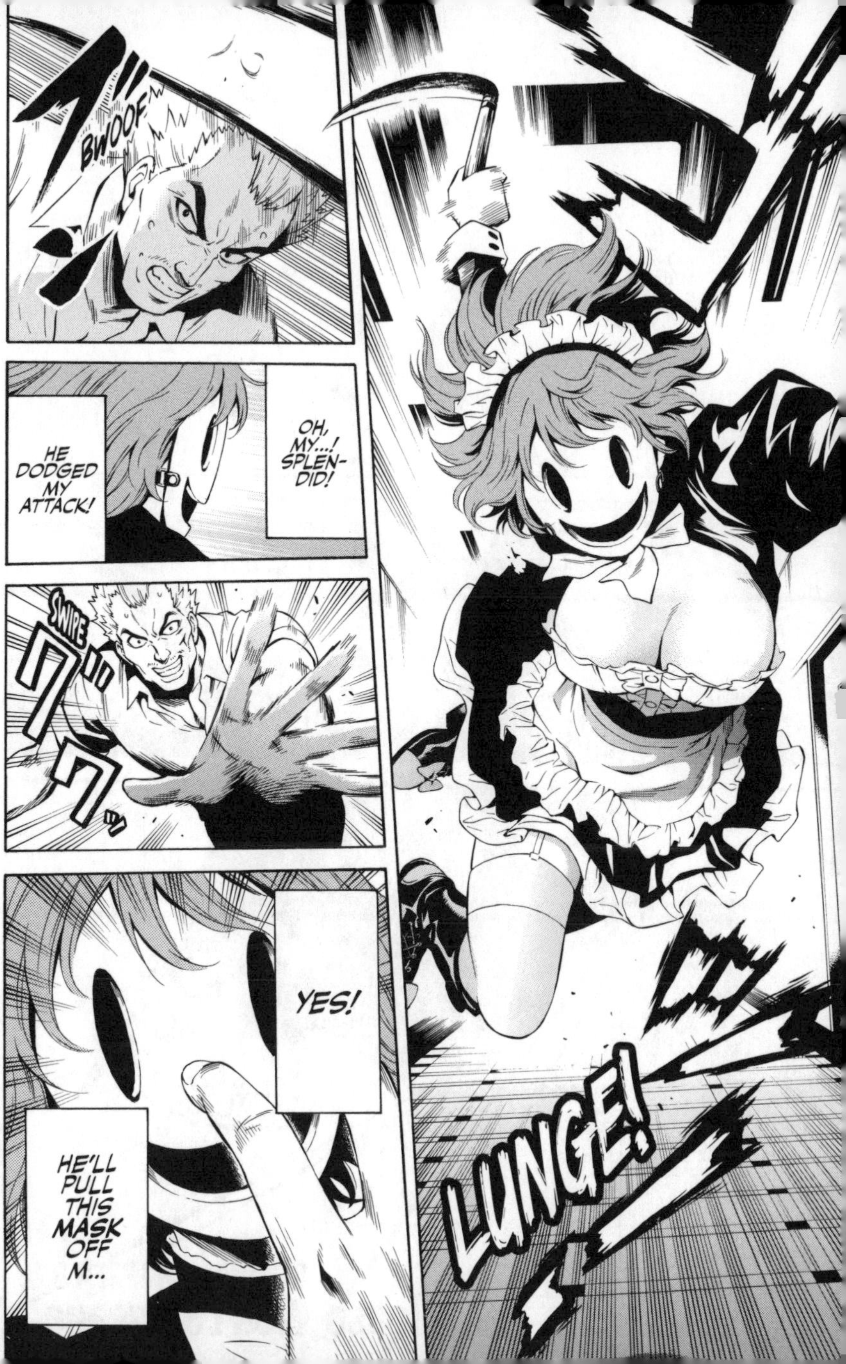
LUNGE!
BWOOF
OH, MY...! SPLEN-DID!
HE DODGED MY ATTACK!
SWIPE
YES!
HE'LL PULL THIS MASK OFF M...

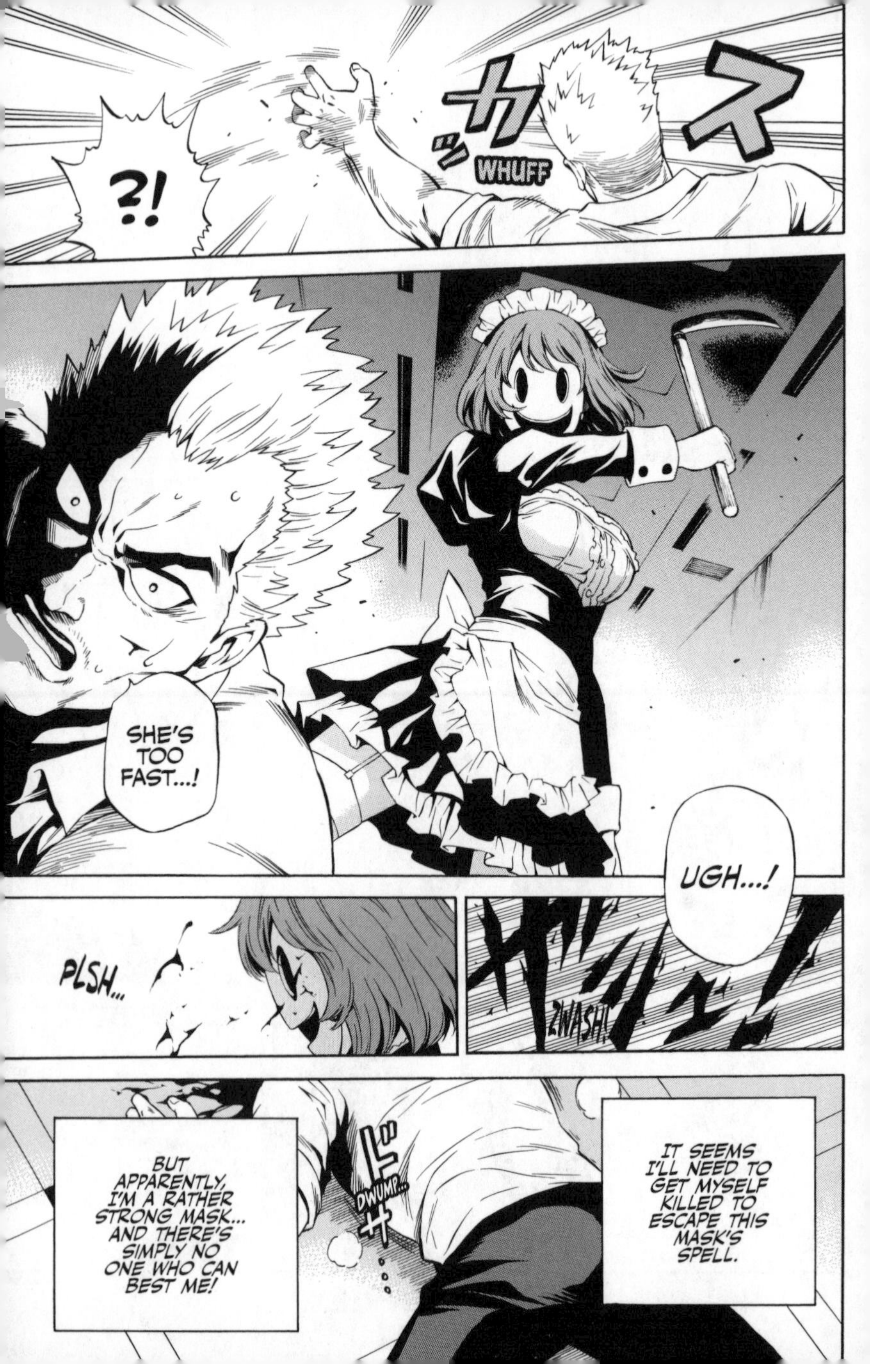
WHUFF
?!
SHE'S TOO FAST...!
UGH...!
ZWASH!
PLSH...
IT SEEMS I'LL NEED TO GET MYSELF KILLED TO ESCAPE THIS MASK'S SPELL.
DWUMP...
BUT APPARENTLY, I'M A RATHER STRONG MASK... AND THERE'S SIMPLY NO ONE WHO CAN BEST ME!

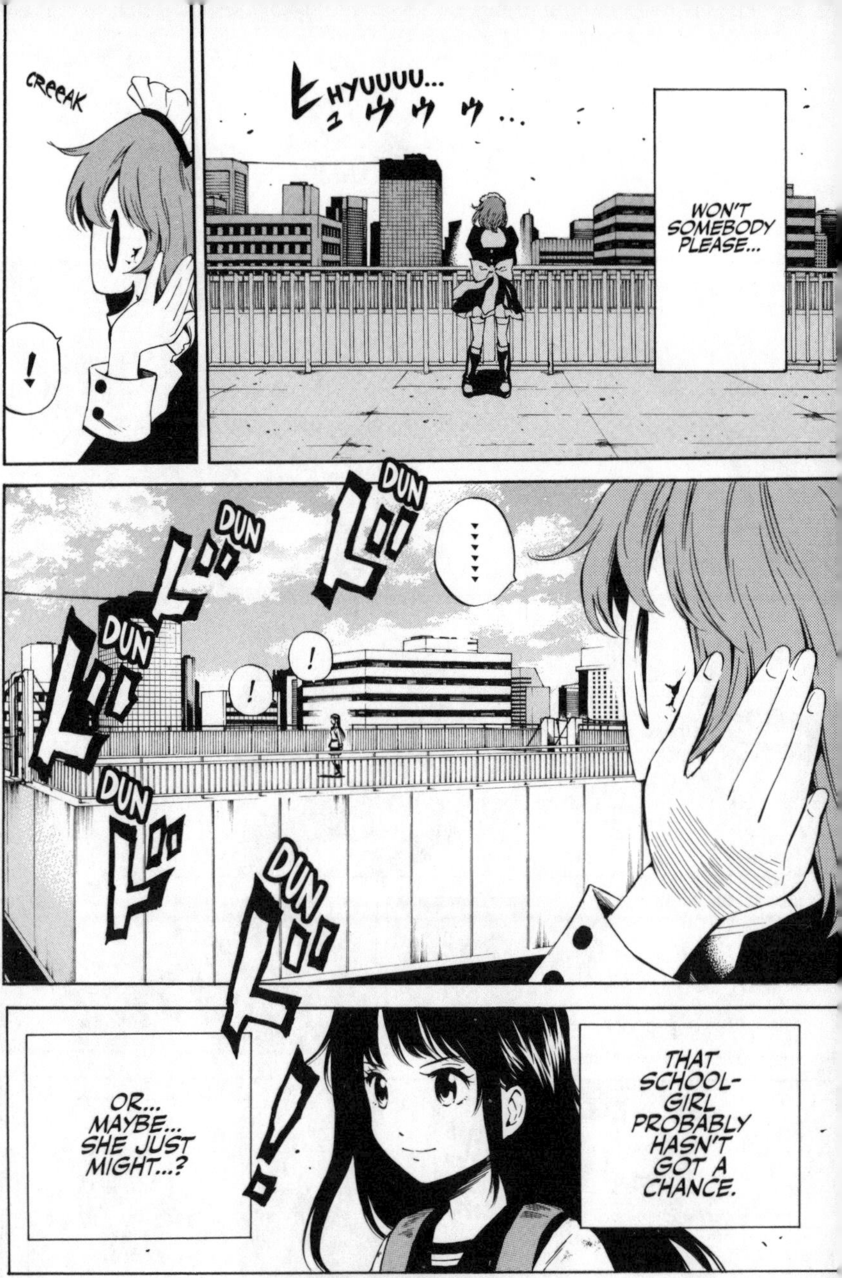
HYUUUU...
WON'T SOMEBODY PLEASE...
CREEAK
!
DUN
DUN
DUN
DUN
DUN
......
!
!
THAT SCHOOL-GIRL PROBABLY HASN'T GOT A CHANCE.
OR... MAYBE... SHE JUST MIGHT...?

SPECIAL CHAPTER:
The End

HIGH-RISE INVASION

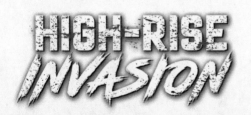

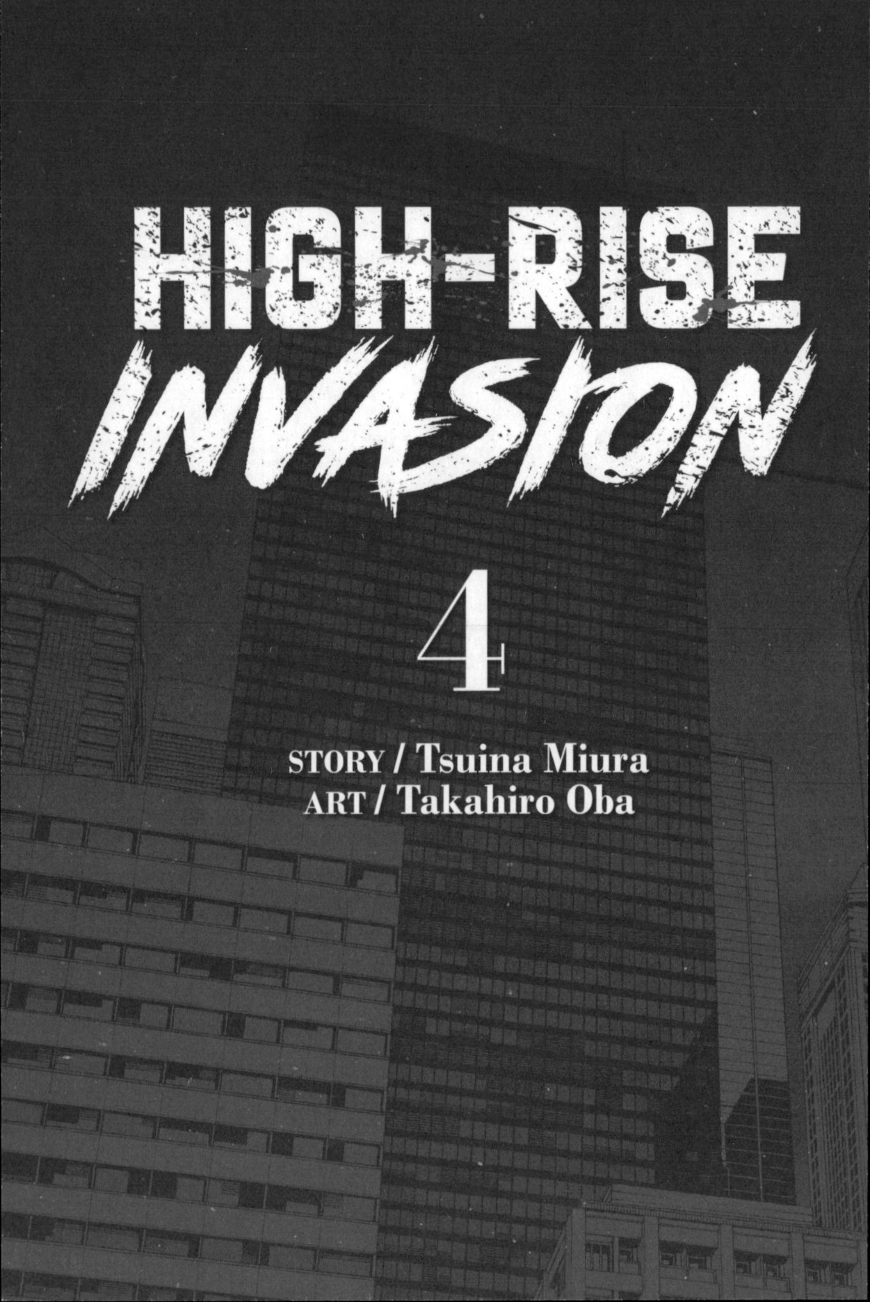
HIGH-RISE INVASION
4
STORY / Tsuina Miura
ART / Takahiro Oba

HIGH-RISE INVASION

4

CONTENTS

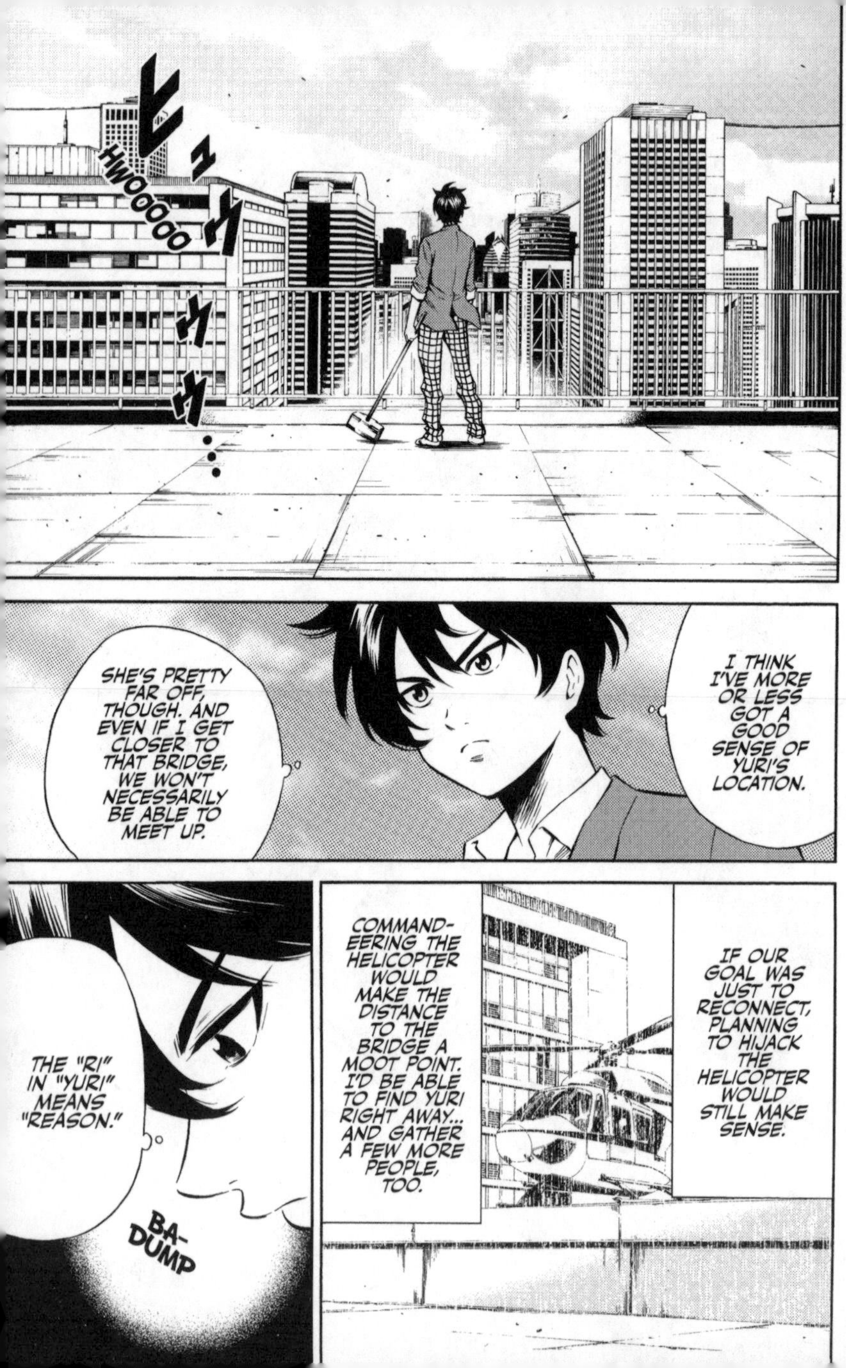
HWOOOOO
I THINK I'VE MORE OR LESS GOT A GOOD SENSE OF YURI'S LOCATION.
SHE'S PRETTY FAR OFF, THOUGH. AND EVEN IF I GET CLOSER TO THAT BRIDGE, WE WON'T NECESSARILY BE ABLE TO MEET UP.
IF OUR GOAL WAS JUST TO RECONNECT, PLANNING TO HIJACK THE HELICOPTER WOULD STILL MAKE SENSE.
COMMANDEERING THE HELICOPTER WOULD MAKE THE DISTANCE TO THE BRIDGE A MOOT POINT. I'D BE ABLE TO FIND YURI RIGHT AWAY... AND GATHER A FEW MORE PEOPLE, TOO.
THE "RI" IN "YURI" MEANS "REASON."
BA-DUMP

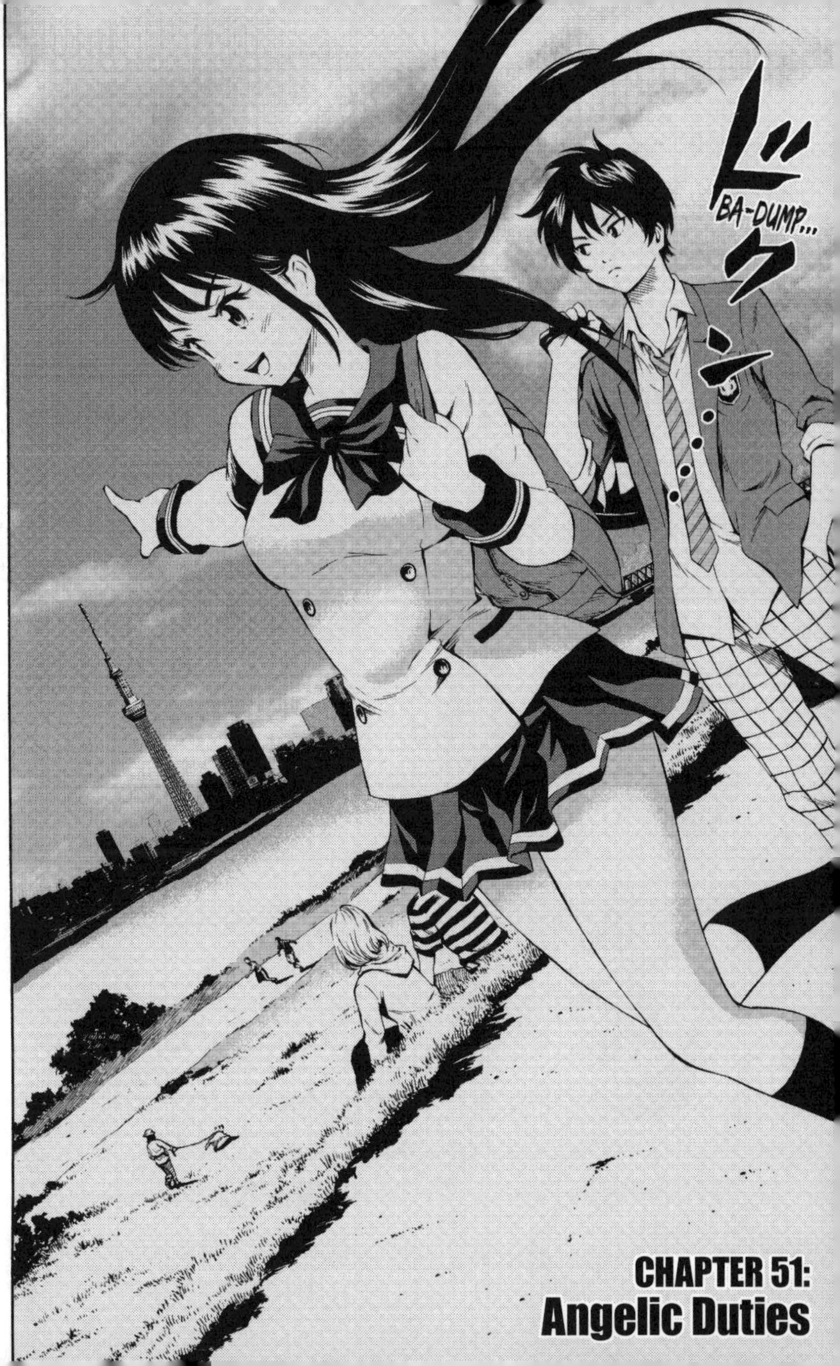
ドクン
BA-DUMP...

CHAPTER 51: Angelic Duties

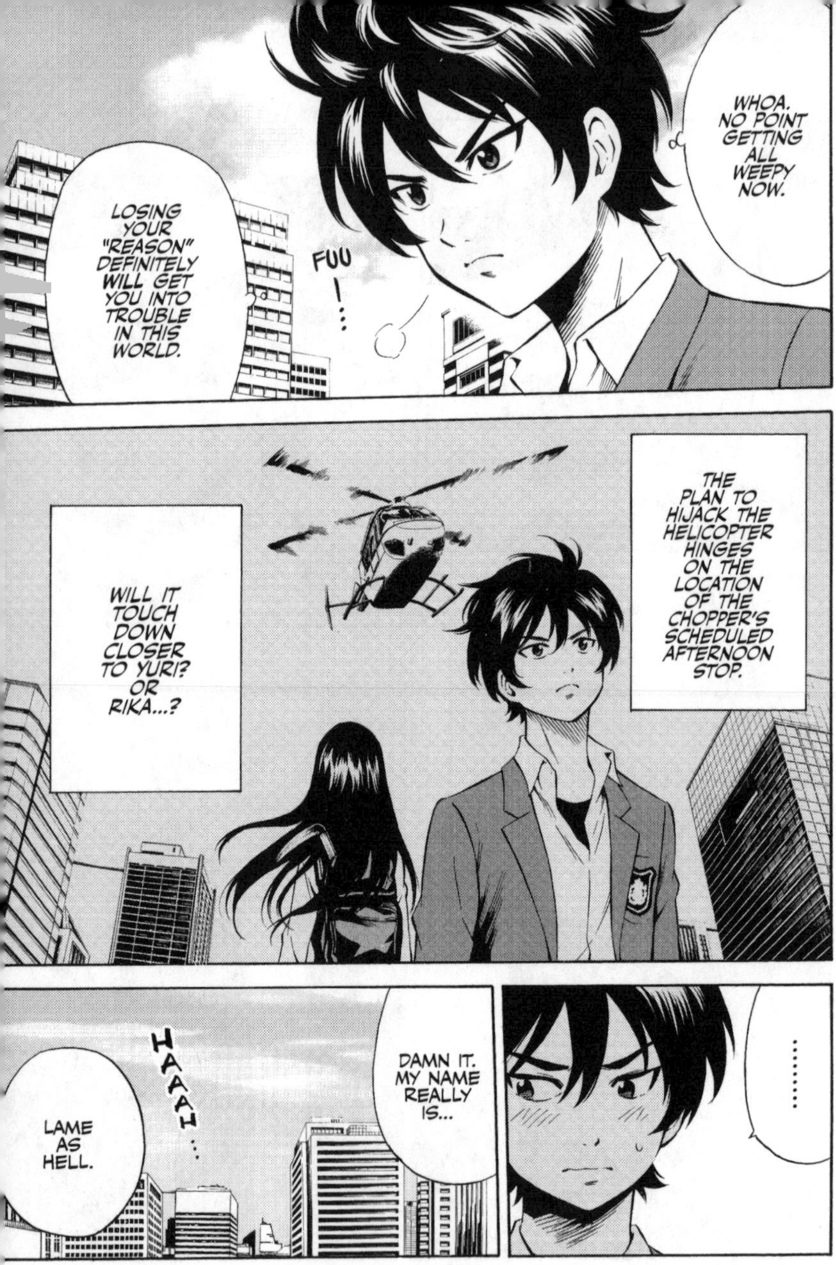

WHOA. NO POINT GETTING ALL WEEPY NOW.
FUU...
LOSING YOUR "REASON" DEFINITELY WILL GET YOU INTO TROUBLE IN THIS WORLD.
THE PLAN TO HIJACK THE HELICOPTER HINGES ON THE LOCATION OF THE CHOPPER'S SCHEDULED AFTERNOON STOP.
WILL IT TOUCH DOWN CLOSER TO YURI? OR RIKA...?
....
DAMN IT. MY NAME REALLY IS...
HAAAH...
LAME AS HELL.

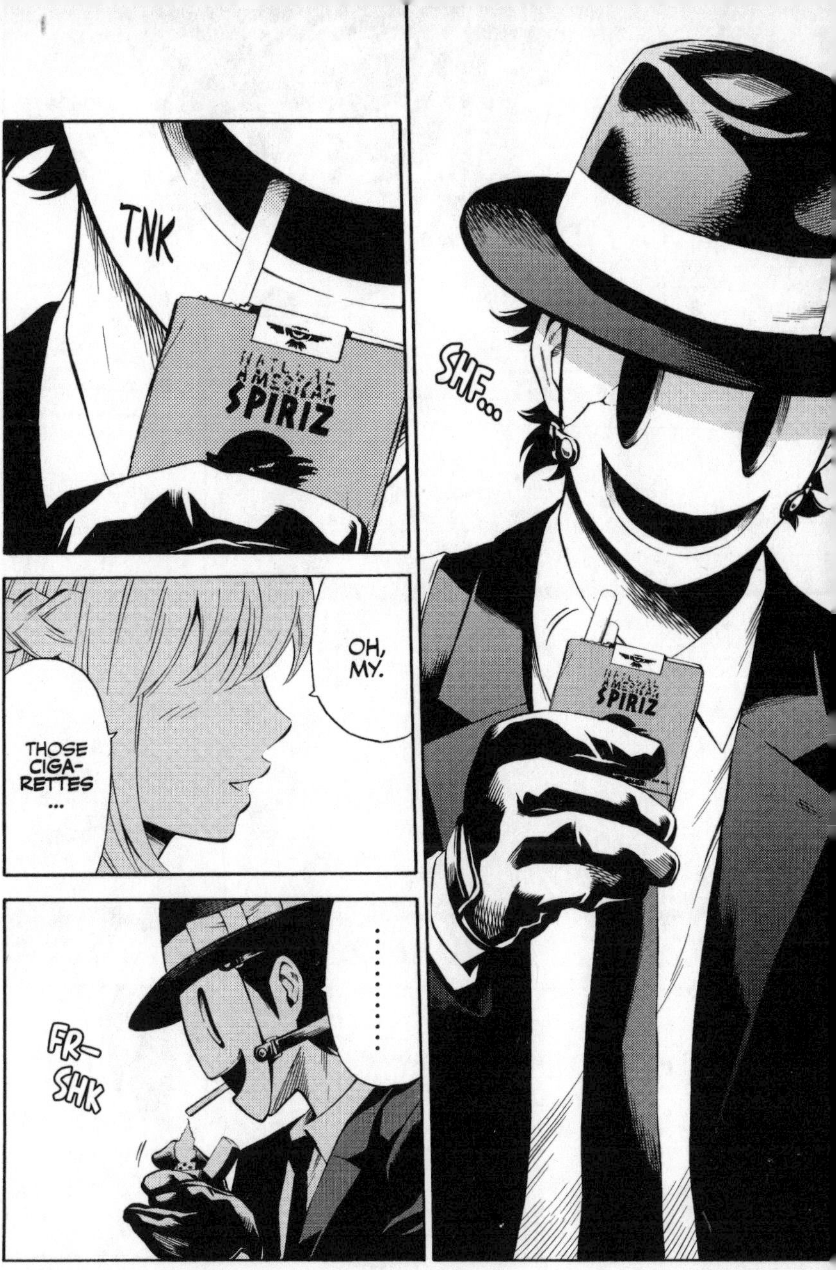
SHF...
SPIRIZ
TNK
SPIRIZ
OH, MY.
THOSE CIGA-RETTES ...
......
FR-SHK

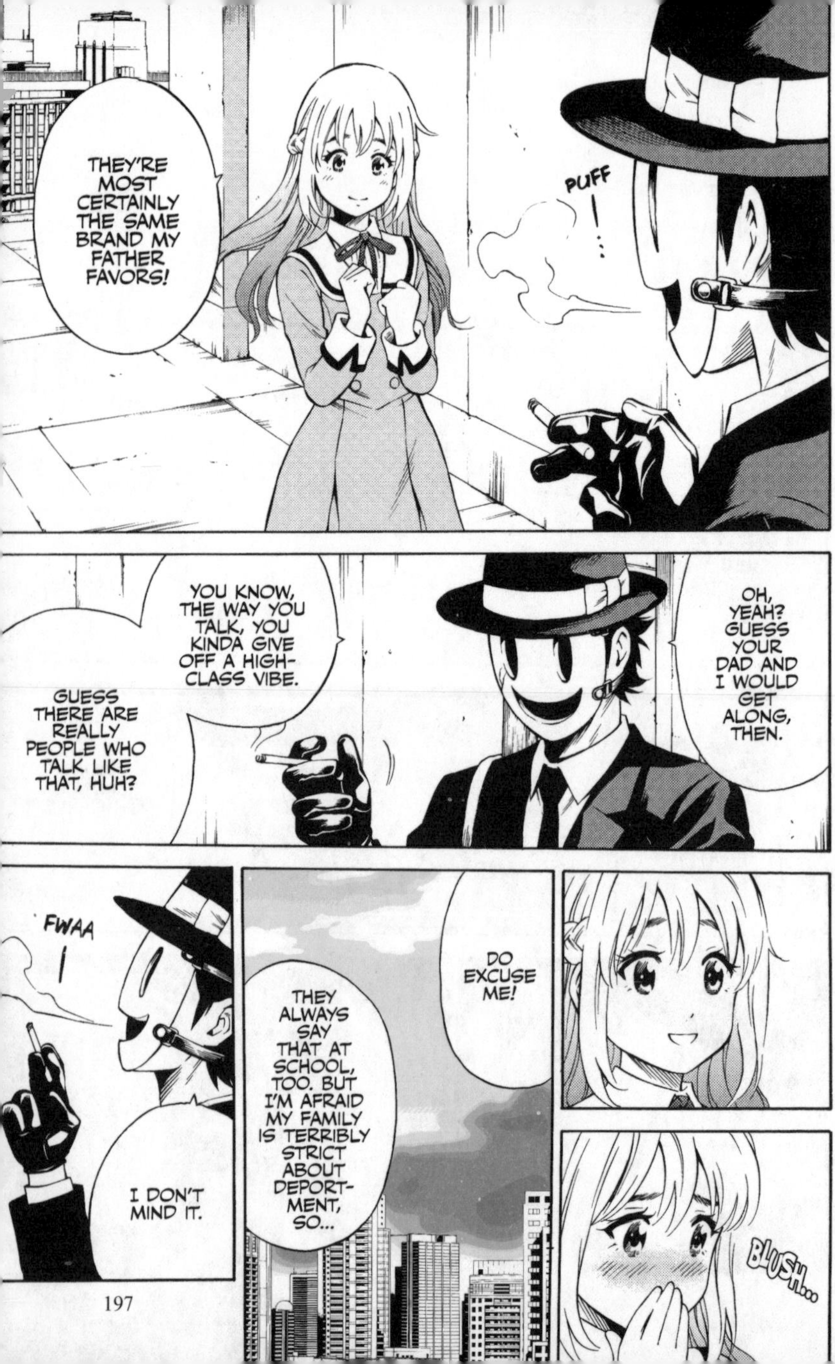
PUFF
THEY'RE MOST CERTAINLY THE SAME BRAND MY FATHER FAVORS!
OH, YEAH? GUESS YOUR DAD AND I WOULD GET ALONG, THEN.
YOU KNOW, THE WAY YOU TALK, YOU KINDA GIVE OFF A HIGH-CLASS VIBE.
GUESS THERE ARE REALLY PEOPLE WHO TALK LIKE THAT, HUH?
DO EXCUSE ME!
THEY ALWAYS SAY THAT AT SCHOOL, TOO. BUT I'M AFRAID MY FAMILY IS TERRIBLY STRICT ABOUT DEPORTMENT, SO...
FWAA
I DON'T MIND IT.
BLUSH...

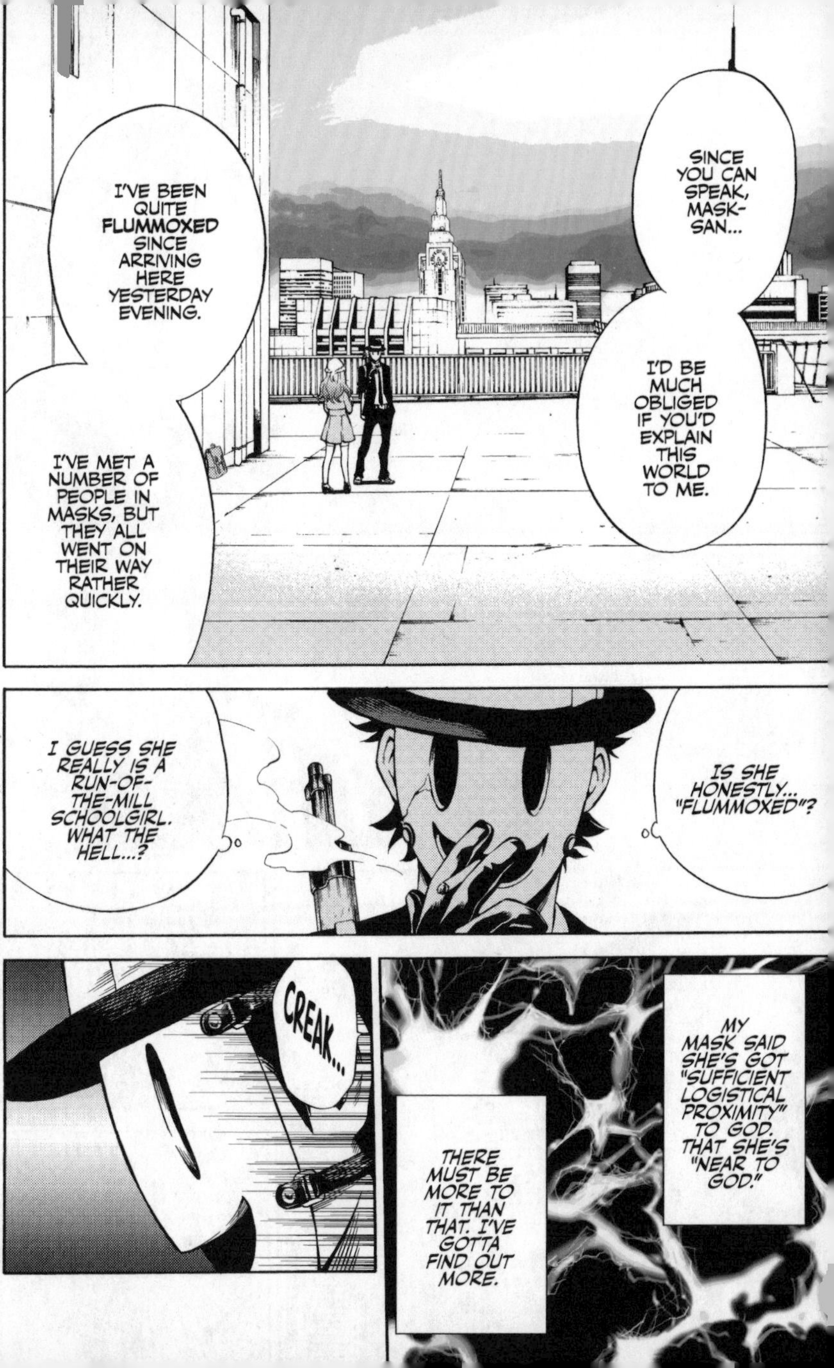
SINCE YOU CAN SPEAK, MASK-SAN...
I'D BE MUCH OBLIGED IF YOU'D EXPLAIN THIS WORLD TO ME.
I'VE BEEN QUITE **FLUMMOXED** SINCE ARRIVING HERE YESTERDAY EVENING.
I'VE MET A NUMBER OF PEOPLE IN MASKS, BUT THEY ALL WENT ON THEIR WAY RATHER QUICKLY.
IS SHE HONESTLY... "FLUMMOXED"?
I GUESS SHE REALLY IS A RUN-OF-THE-MILL SCHOOLGIRL. WHAT THE HELL...?
MY MASK SAID SHE'S GOT "SUFFICIENT LOGISTICAL PROXIMITY" TO GOD. THAT SHE'S "NEAR TO GOD."
THERE MUST BE MORE TO IT THAN THAT. I'VE GOTTA FIND OUT MORE.
CREAK...

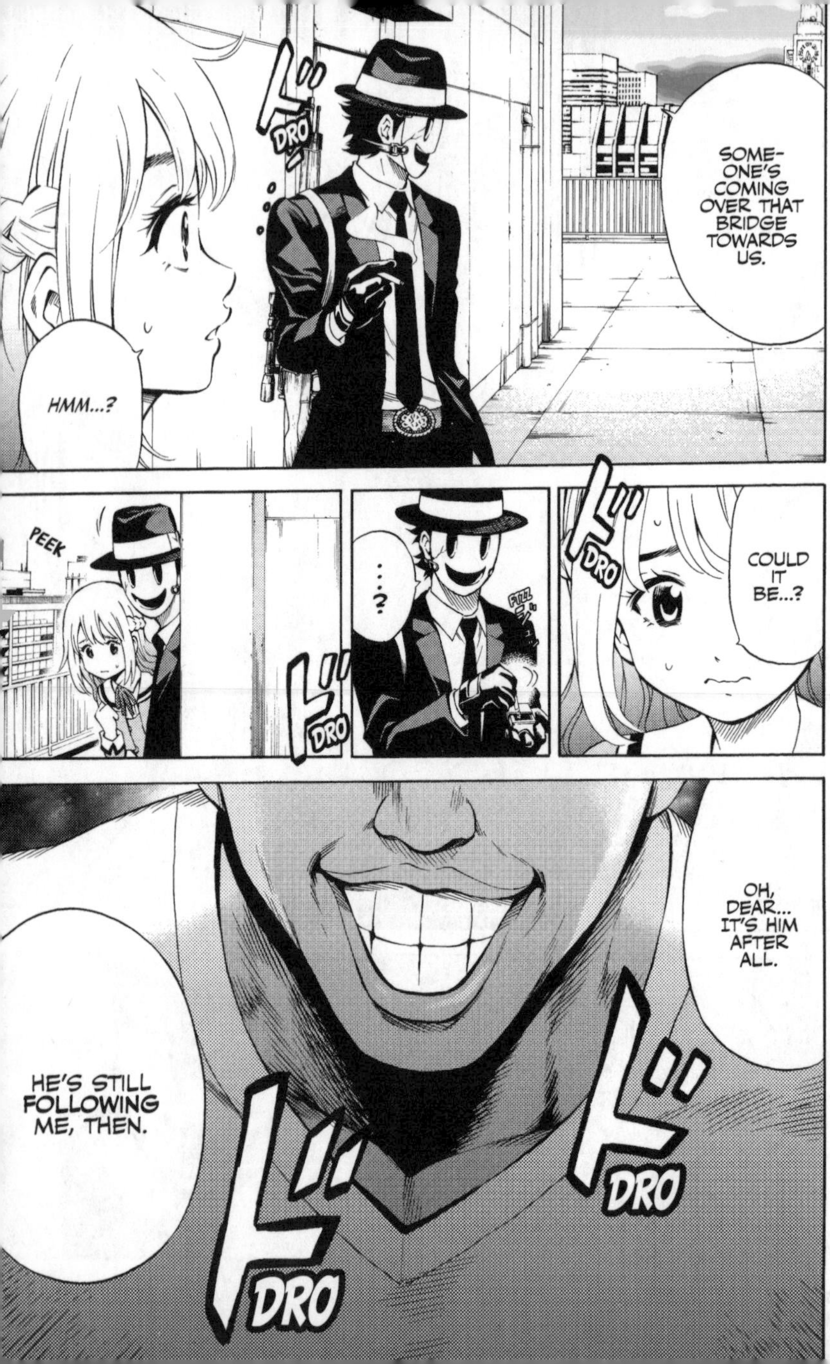
SOME-ONE'S COMING OVER THAT BRIDGE TOWARDS US.
DRO
HMM...?
COULD IT BE...?
DRO
...?
FIZZ
DRO
PEEK
OH, DEAR... IT'S HIM AFTER ALL.
DRO
DRO
HE'S STILL FOLLOWING ME, THEN.

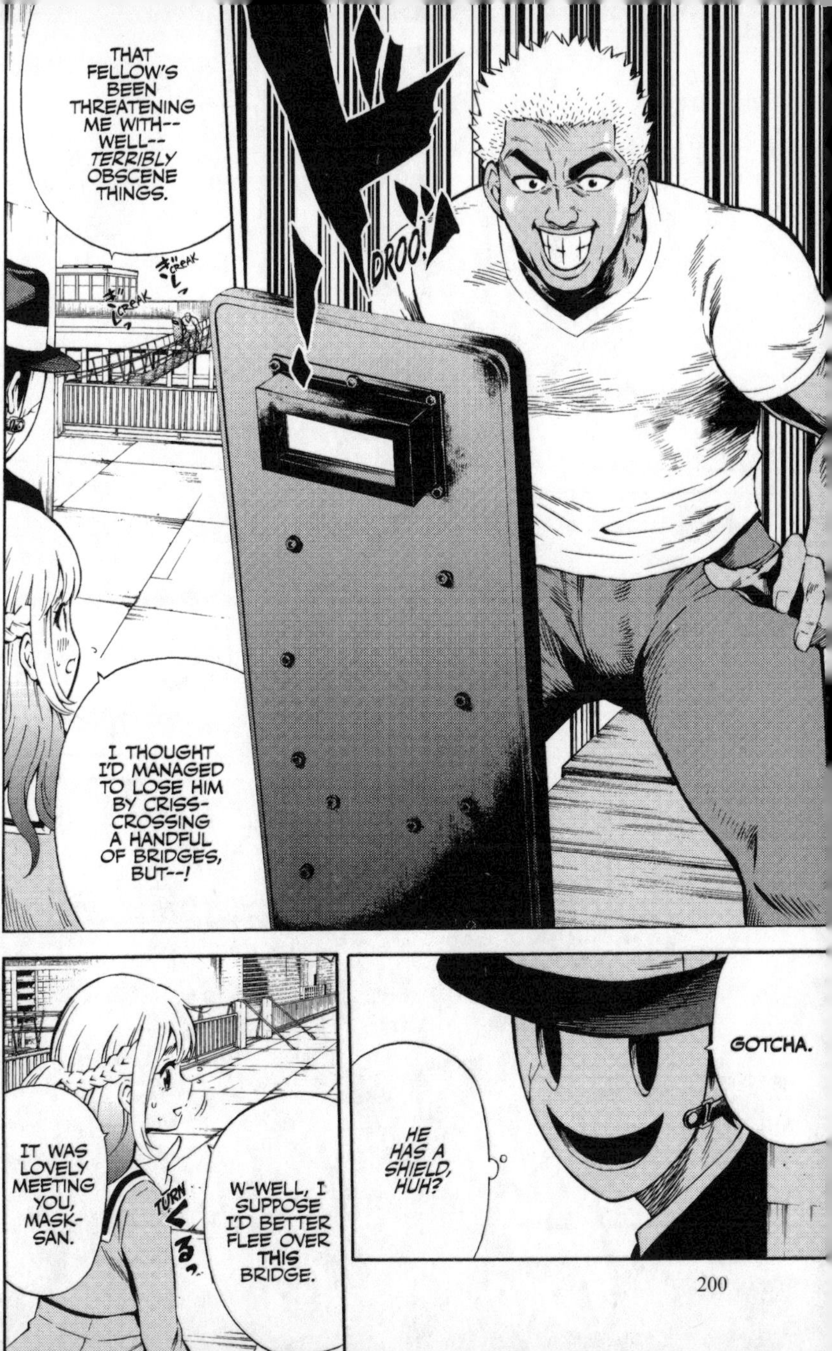
THAT FELLOW'S BEEN THREATENING ME WITH-- WELL-- *TERRIBLY* OBSCENE THINGS.
DROO!
CREAK
CREAK
I THOUGHT I'D MANAGED TO LOSE HIM BY CRISS-CROSSING A HANDFUL OF BRIDGES, BUT--!
GOTCHA.
HE HAS A SHIELD, HUH?
W-WELL, I SUPPOSE I'D BETTER FLEE OVER THIS BRIDGE.
TURN
IT WAS LOVELY MEETING YOU, MASK-SAN.

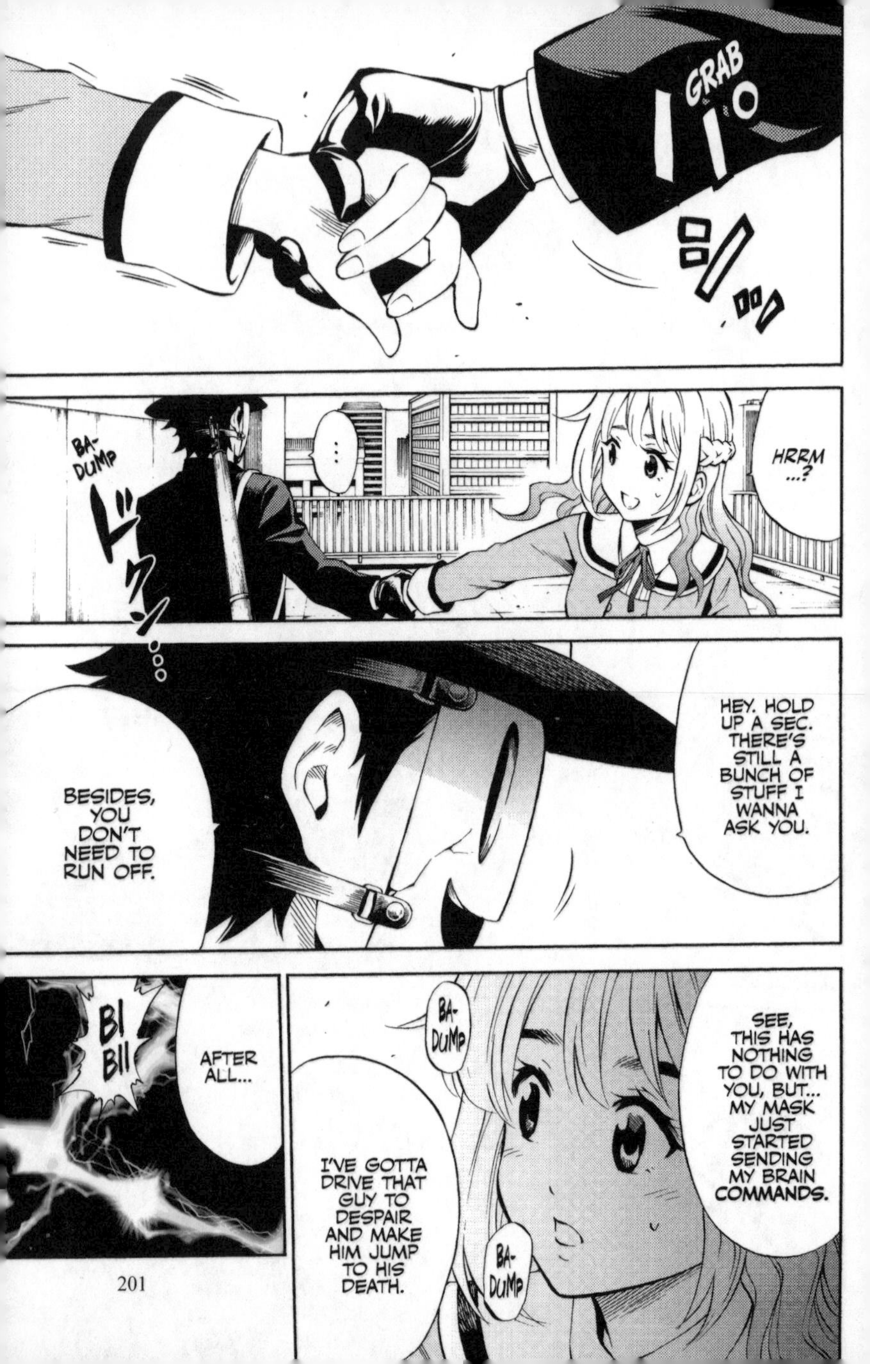
GRAB
HRRM ...?
...
BA-DUMP
HEY. HOLD UP A SEC. THERE'S STILL A BUNCH OF STUFF I WANNA ASK YOU.
BESIDES, YOU DON'T NEED TO RUN OFF.
BA-DUMP
SEE, THIS HAS NOTHING TO DO WITH YOU, BUT... MY MASK JUST STARTED SENDING MY BRAIN COMMANDS.
I'VE GOTTA DRIVE THAT GUY TO DESPAIR AND MAKE HIM JUMP TO HIS DEATH.
BA-DUMP
BI BII
AFTER ALL...

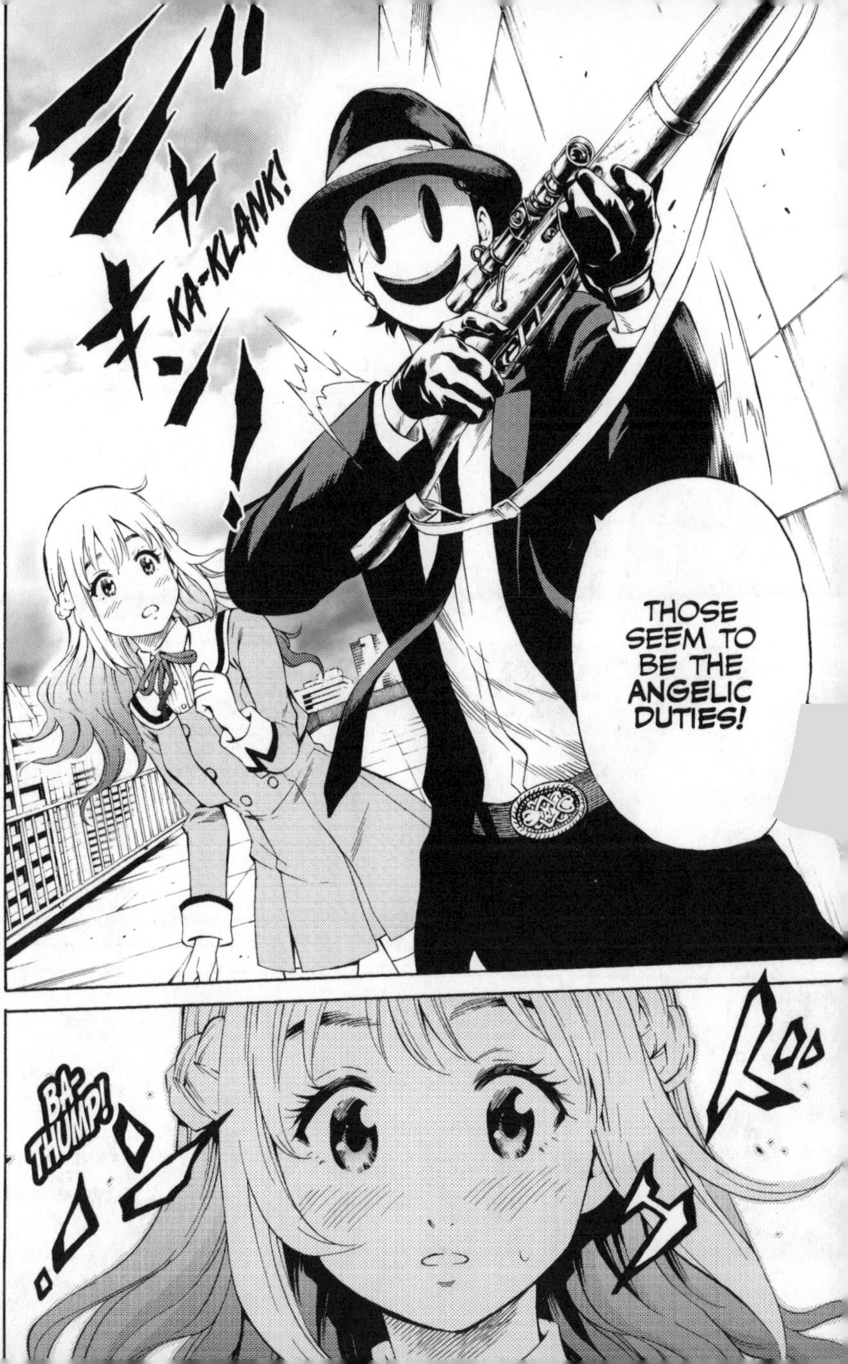
ジャキーン!
KA-KLANK!
THOSE SEEM TO BE THE ANGELIC DUTIES!
BA-THUMP!

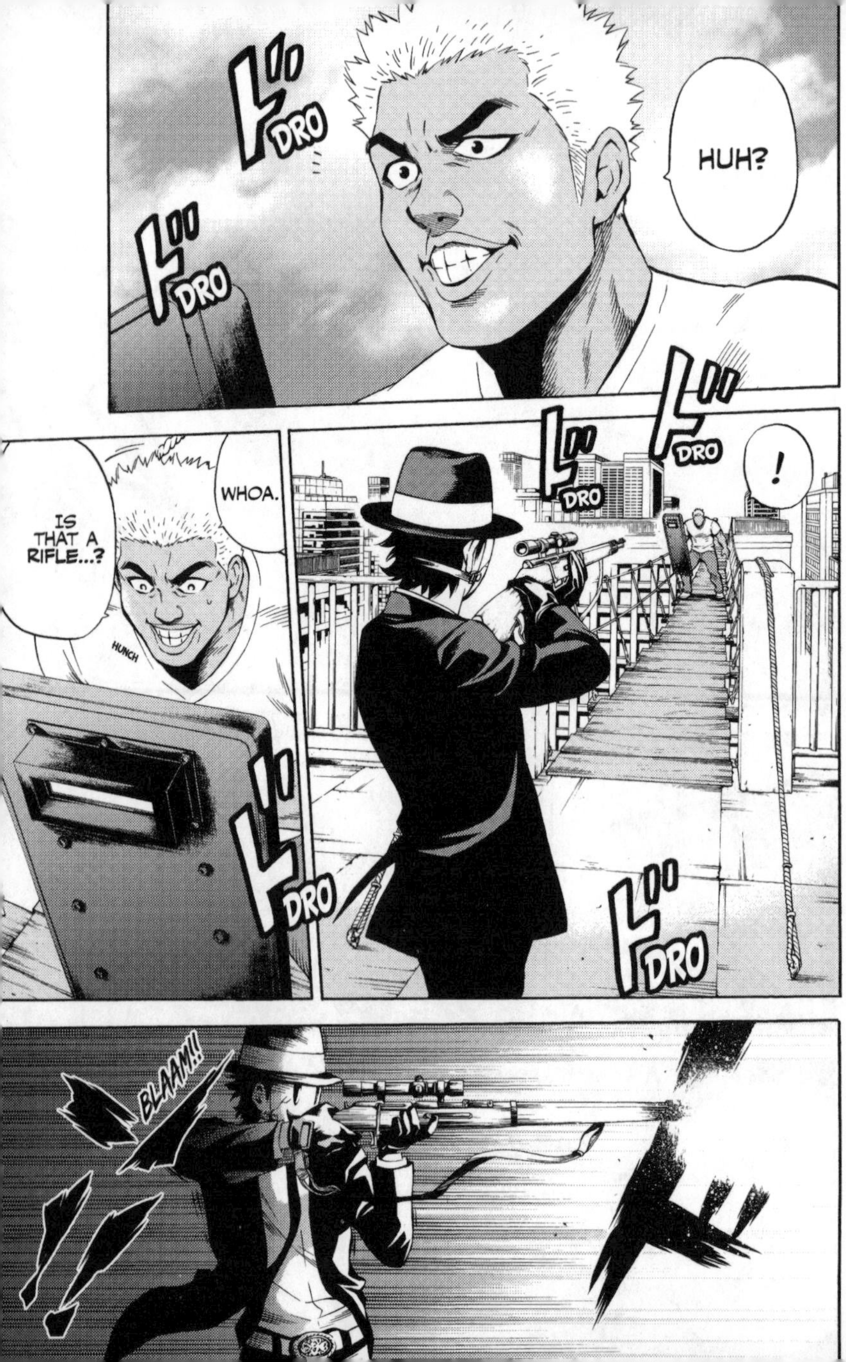
HUH?
DRO
DRO
!
DRO
DRO
DRO
DRO
WHOA.
IS THAT A RIFLE...?
HUNCH
DRO
BLAAM!!

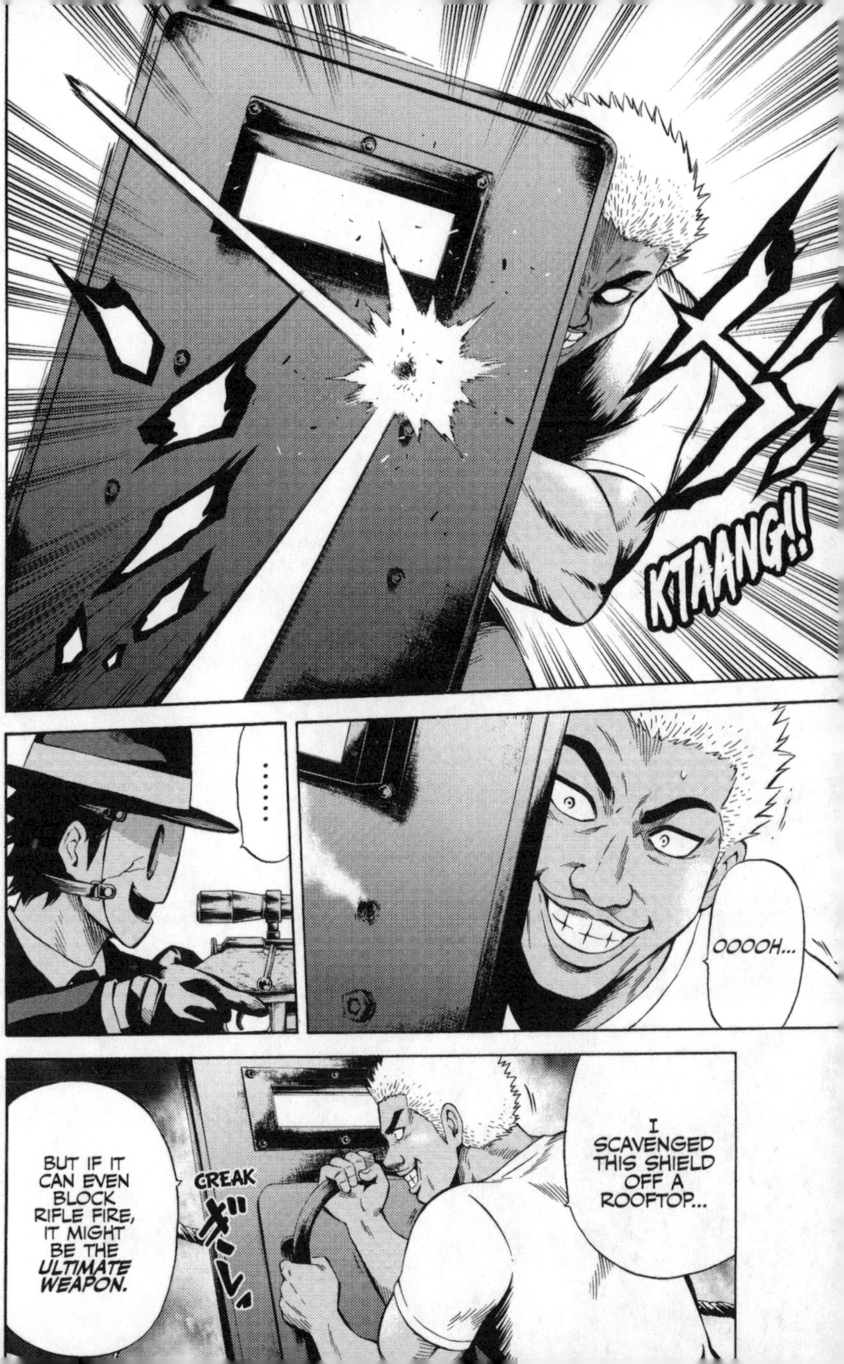
KTAANG!!
OOOOH...
......
I SCAVENGED THIS SHIELD OFF A ROOFTOP...
CREAK
BUT IF IT CAN EVEN BLOCK RIFLE FIRE, IT MIGHT BE THE *ULTIMATE* WEAPON.

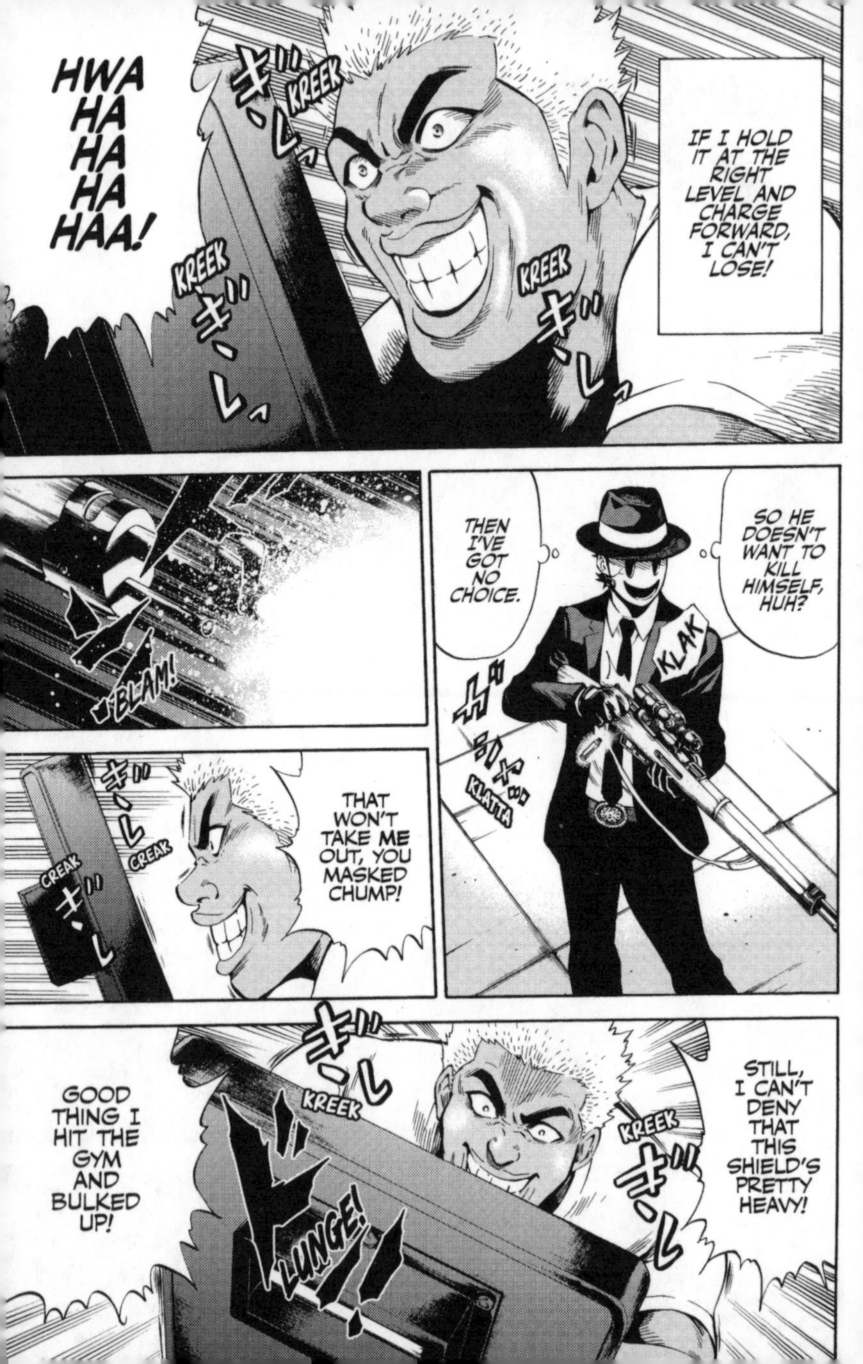
IF I HOLD IT AT THE RIGHT LEVEL AND CHARGE FORWARD, I CAN'T LOSE!
KREEK
KREEK
HWA HA HA HA HA HAA!
KREEK
SO HE DOESN'T WANT TO KILL HIMSELF, HUH?
THEN I'VE GOT NO CHOICE.
KLAK
KLATTA
BLAM!
THAT WON'T TAKE ME OUT, YOU MASKED CHUMP!
CREAK
CREAK
STILL, I CAN'T DENY THAT THIS SHIELD'S PRETTY HEAVY!
KREEK
KREEK
LUNGE!
GOOD THING I HIT THE GYM AND BULKED UP!

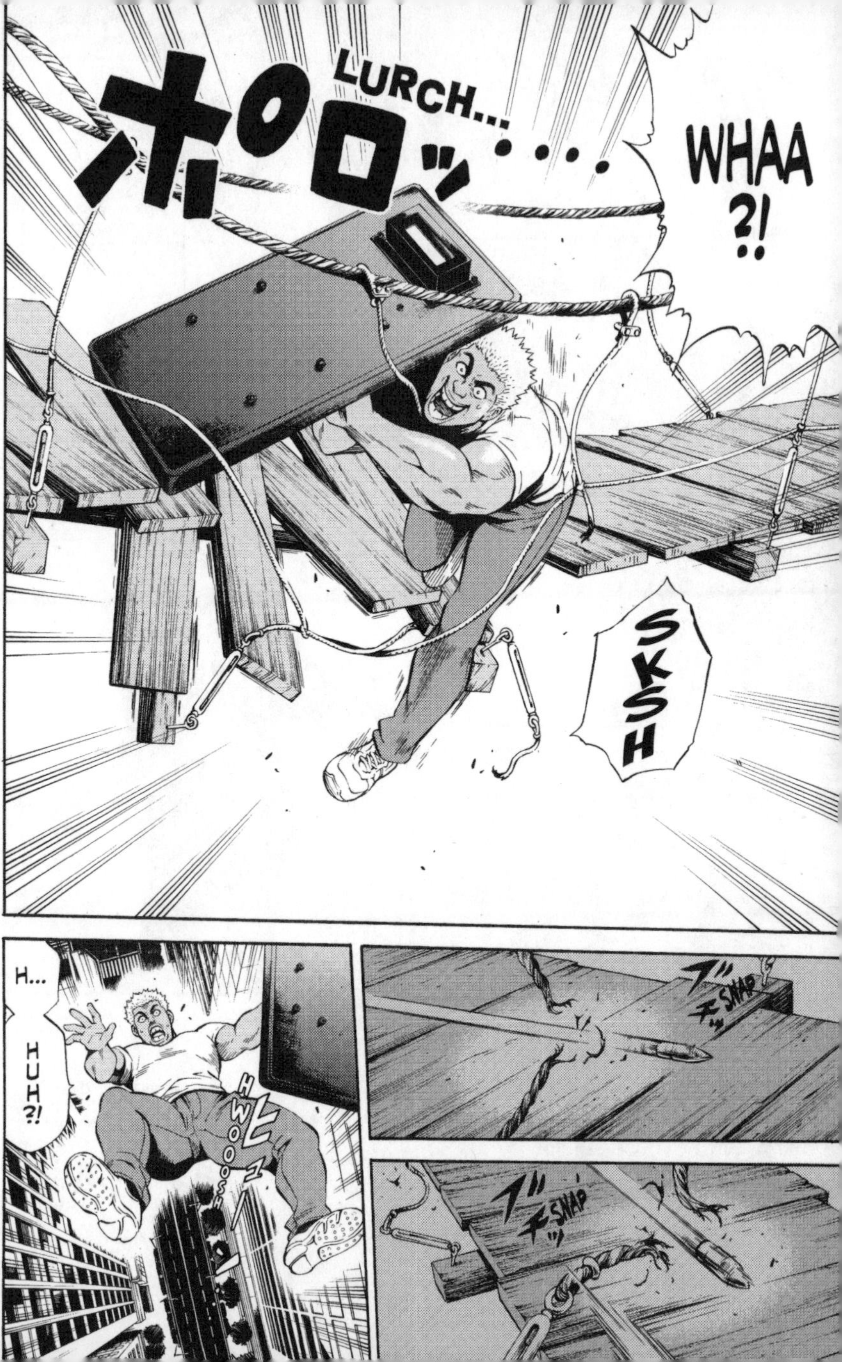
LURCH...
WHAA ?!
SKSH
SNAP
SNAP
H...
HUH ?!
HWOOOOSH

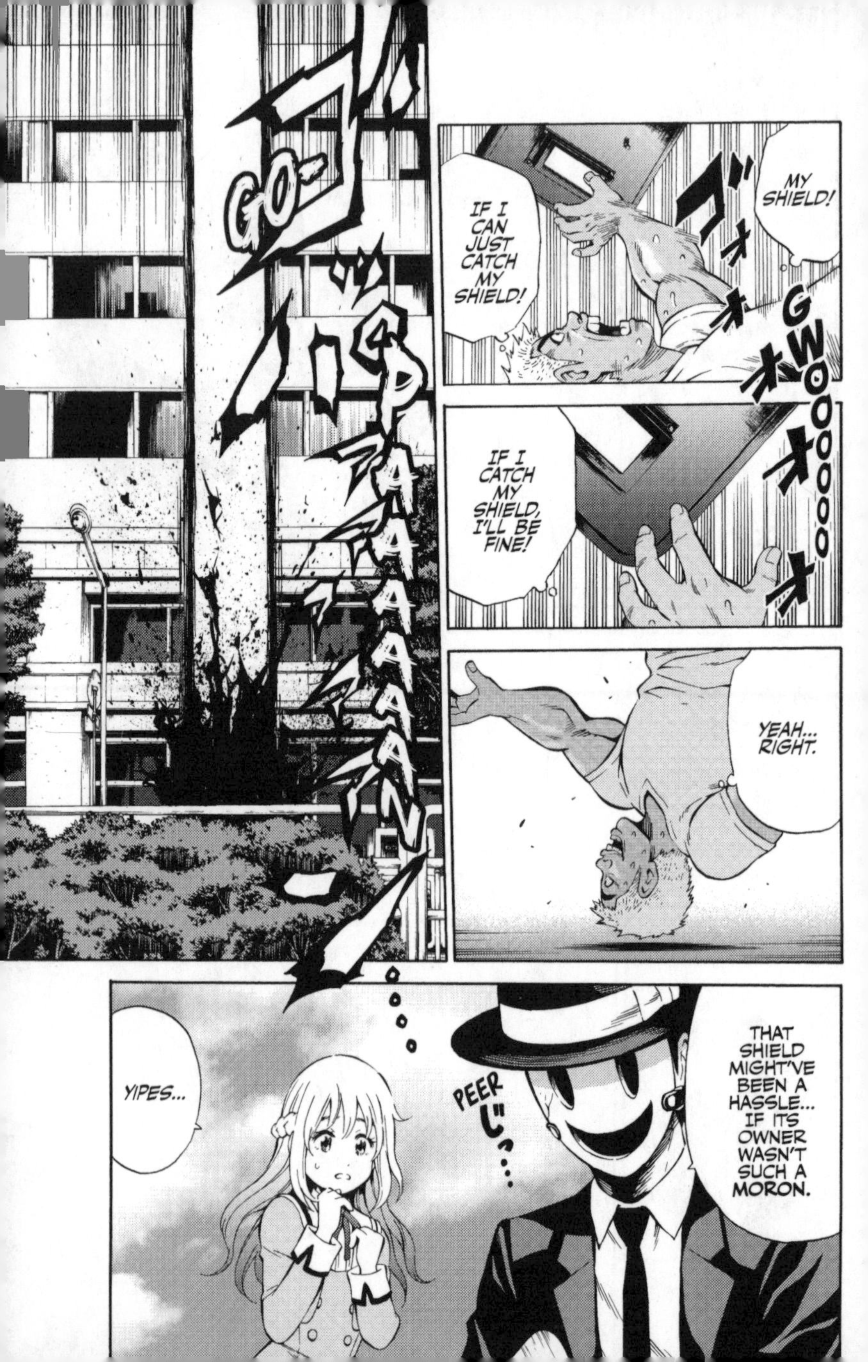
MY SHIELD!
IF I CAN JUST CATCH MY SHIELD!
GWOOOOOO
IF I CATCH MY SHIELD, I'LL BE FINE!
YEAH... RIGHT.
GO-
PAAAAAAN
THAT SHIELD MIGHT'VE BEEN A HASSLE... IF ITS OWNER WASN'T SUCH A MORON.
PEER
YIPES...

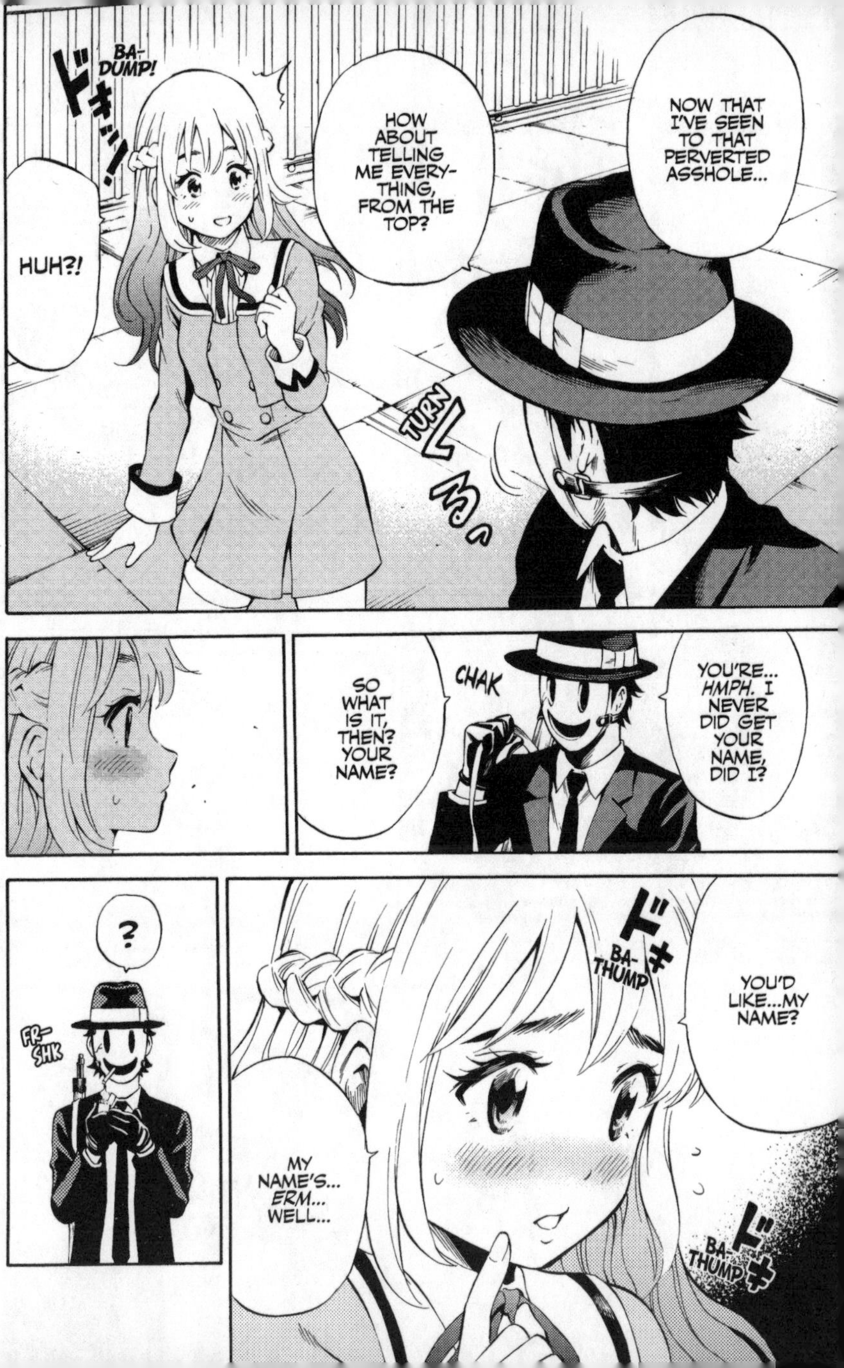
NOW THAT I'VE SEEN TO THAT PERVERTED ASSHOLE...
HOW ABOUT TELLING ME EVERYTHING, FROM THE TOP?
TURN
BA-DUMP!
HUH?!
YOU'RE... *HMPH.* I NEVER DID GET YOUR NAME, DID I?
CHAK
SO WHAT IS IT, THEN? YOUR NAME?
YOU'D LIKE...MY NAME?
BA-THUMP
MY NAME'S... *ERM*... WELL...
BA-THUMP
?
FR-SHK

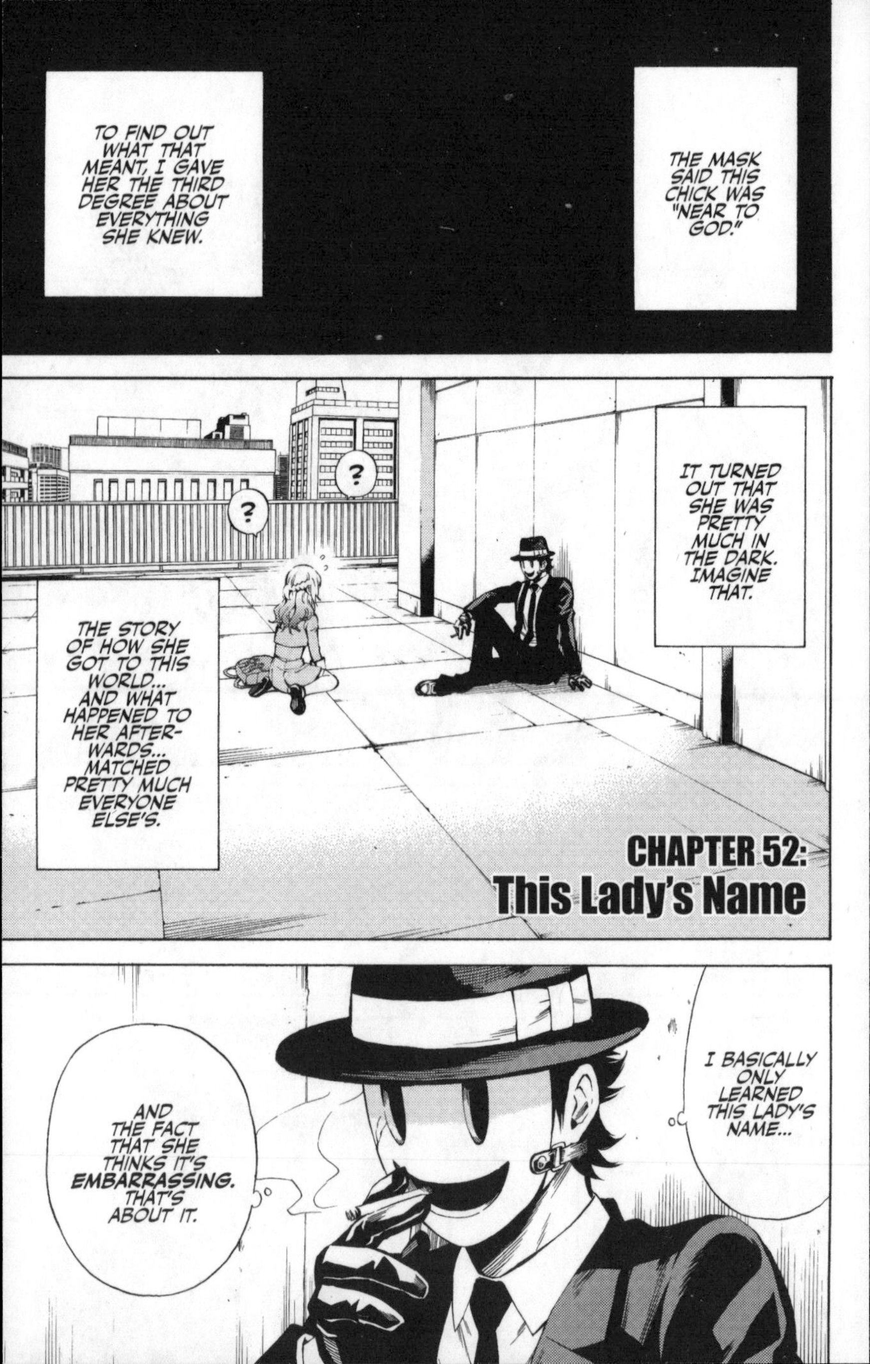
THE MASK SAID THIS CHICK WAS "NEAR TO GOD."
TO FIND OUT WHAT THAT MEANT, I GAVE HER THE THIRD DEGREE ABOUT EVERYTHING SHE KNEW.
IT TURNED OUT THAT SHE WAS PRETTY MUCH IN THE DARK. IMAGINE THAT.
?
?
THE STORY OF HOW SHE GOT TO THIS WORLD... AND WHAT HAPPENED TO HER AFTER-WARDS... MATCHED PRETTY MUCH EVERYONE ELSE'S.
CHAPTER 52:
This Lady's Name
I BASICALLY ONLY LEARNED THIS LADY'S NAME...
AND THE FACT THAT SHE THINKS IT'S EMBARRASSING. THAT'S ABOUT IT.

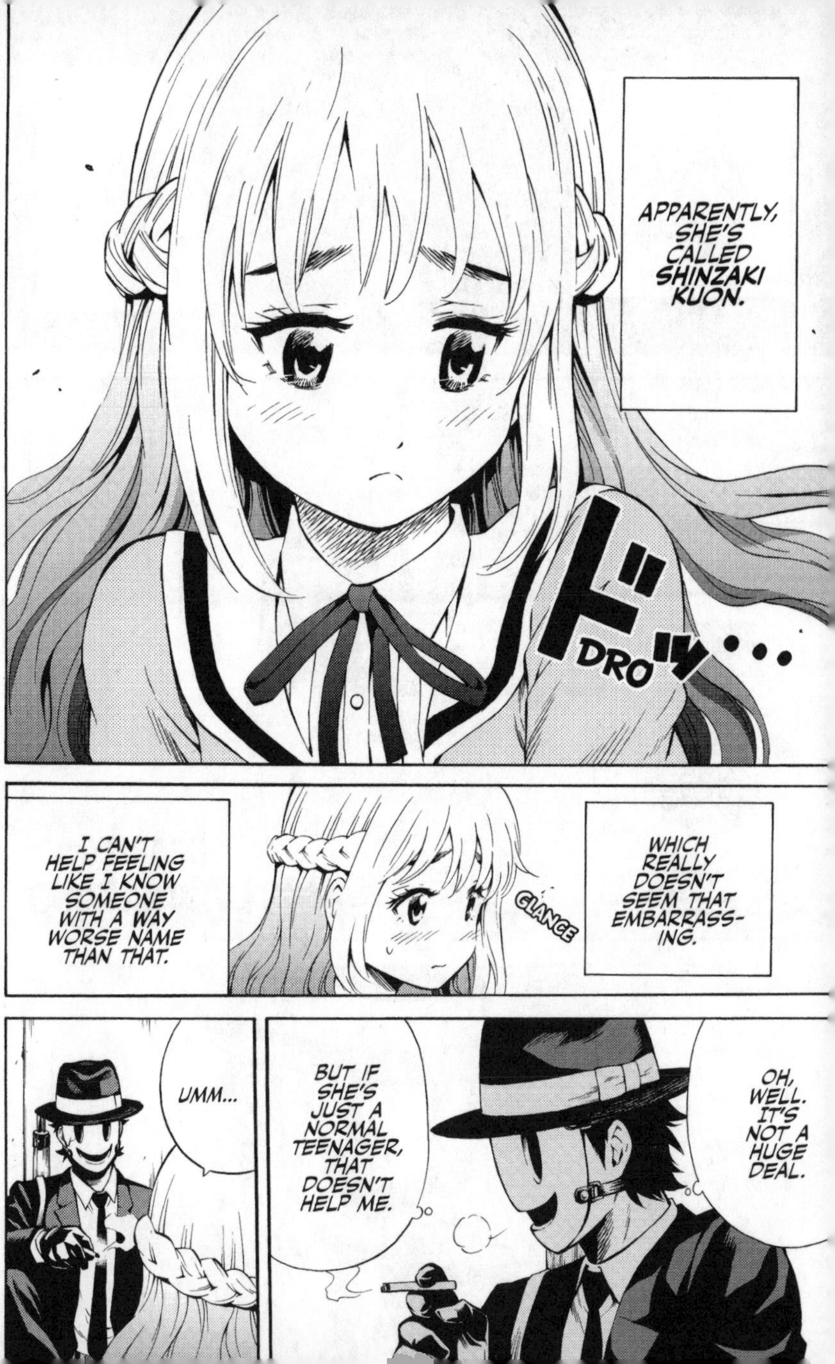
APPARENTLY, SHE'S CALLED SHINZAKI KUON.
DRO...
WHICH REALLY DOESN'T SEEM THAT EMBARRASS-ING.
GLANCE
I CAN'T HELP FEELING LIKE I KNOW SOMEONE WITH A WAY WORSE NAME THAN THAT.
OH, WELL. IT'S NOT A HUGE DEAL.
BUT IF SHE'S JUST A NORMAL TEENAGER, THAT DOESN'T HELP ME.
UMM...

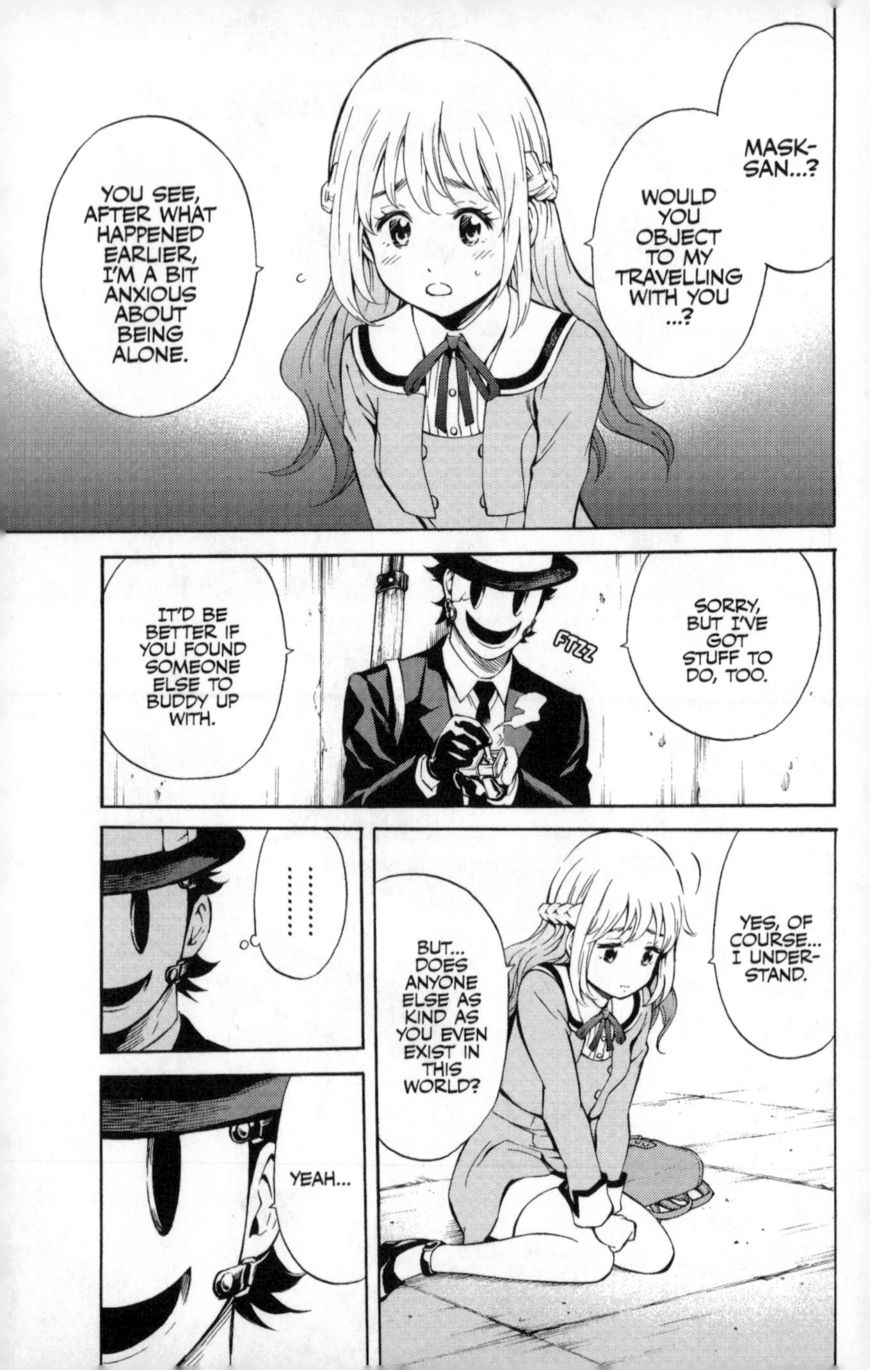
MASK-SAN...?
WOULD YOU OBJECT TO MY TRAVELLING WITH YOU ...?
YOU SEE, AFTER WHAT HAPPENED EARLIER, I'M A BIT ANXIOUS ABOUT BEING ALONE.
SORRY, BUT I'VE GOT STUFF TO DO, TOO.
FTZZ
IT'D BE BETTER IF YOU FOUND SOMEONE ELSE TO BUDDY UP WITH.
YES, OF COURSE... I UNDERSTAND.
BUT... DOES ANYONE ELSE AS KIND AS YOU EVEN EXIST IN THIS WORLD?
......
YEAH...

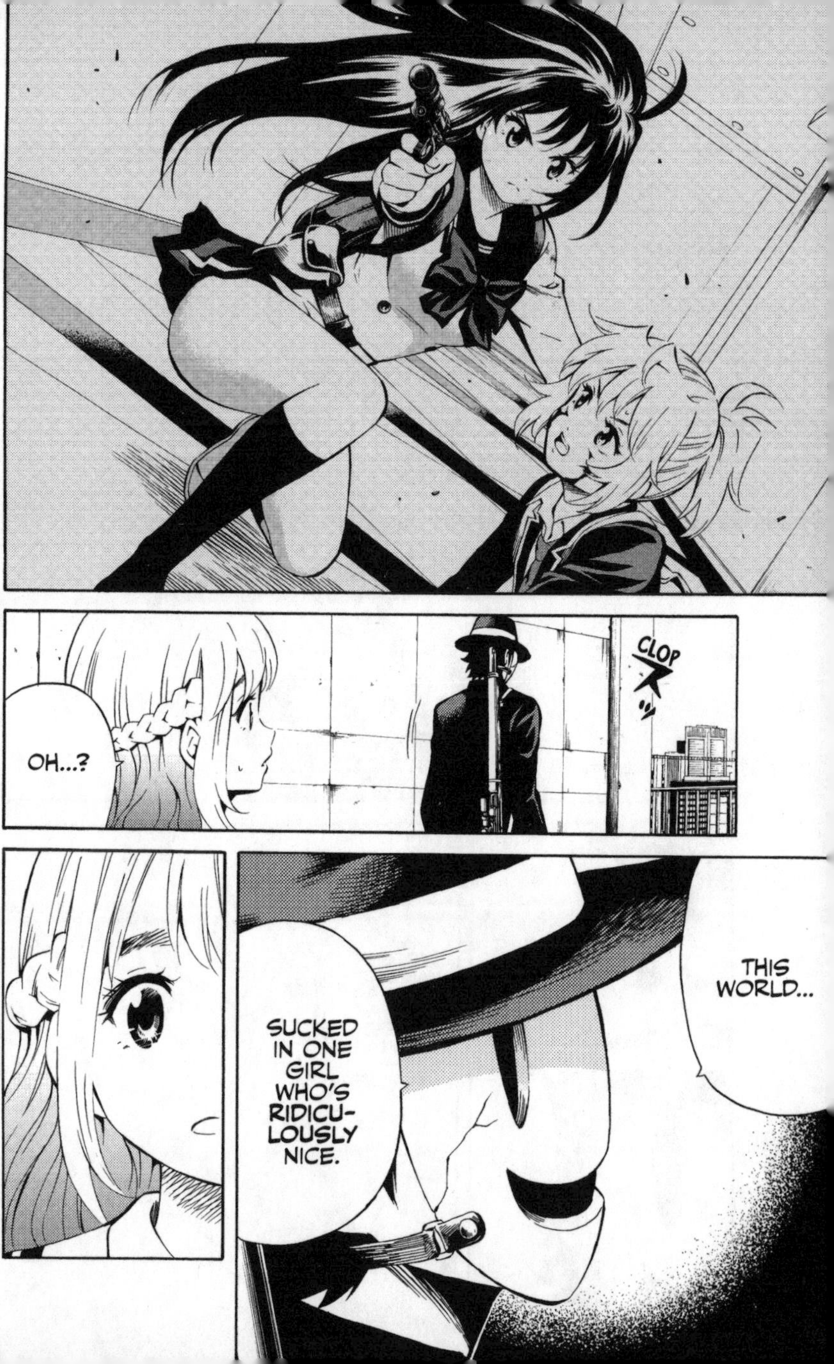
CLOP
OH...?
THIS WORLD...
SUCKED IN ONE GIRL WHO'S RIDICU-LOUSLY NICE.

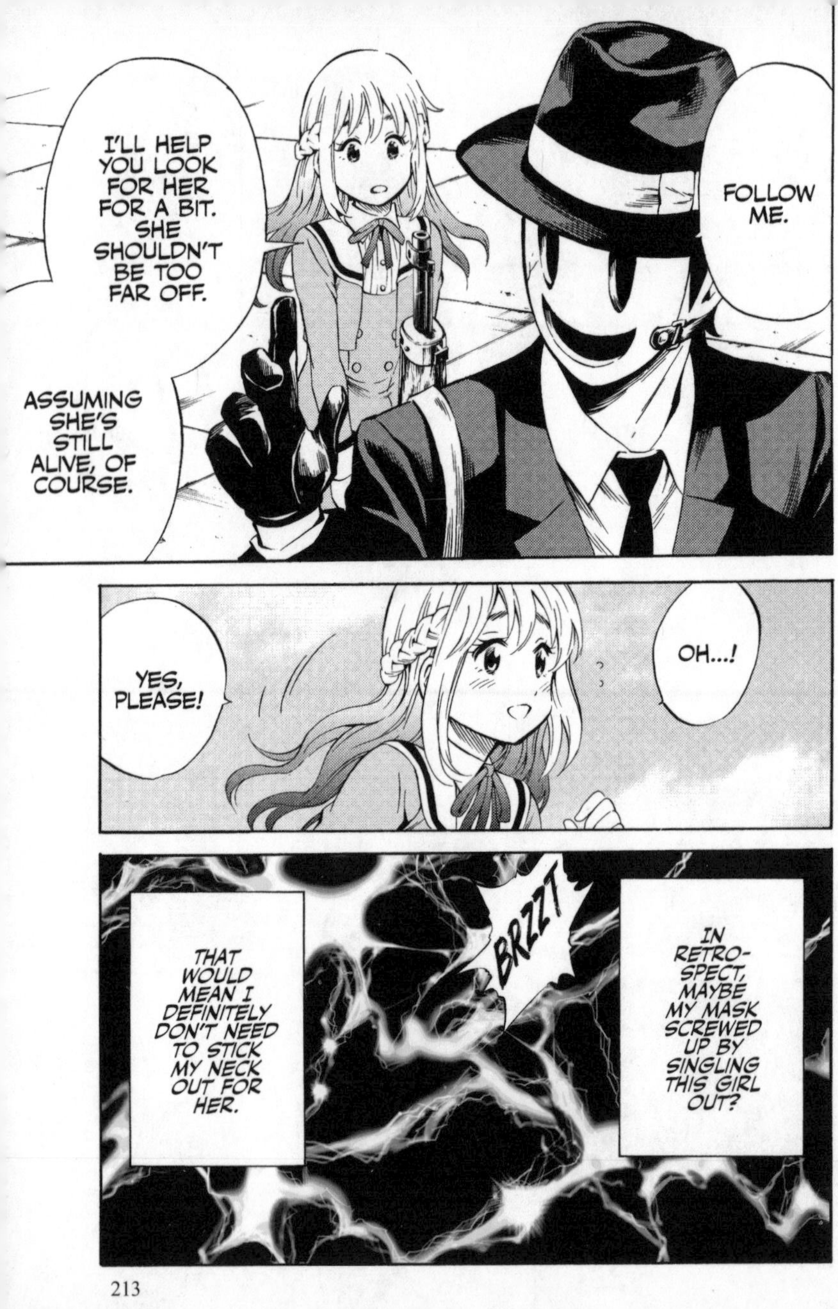
FOLLOW ME.
I'LL HELP YOU LOOK FOR HER FOR A BIT. SHE SHOULDN'T BE TOO FAR OFF.
ASSUMING SHE'S STILL ALIVE, OF COURSE.
OH...!
YES, PLEASE!
IN RETRO-SPECT, MAYBE MY MASK SCREWED UP BY SINGLING THIS GIRL OUT?
BRZZT
THAT WOULD MEAN I DEFINITELY DON'T NEED TO STICK MY NECK OUT FOR HER.

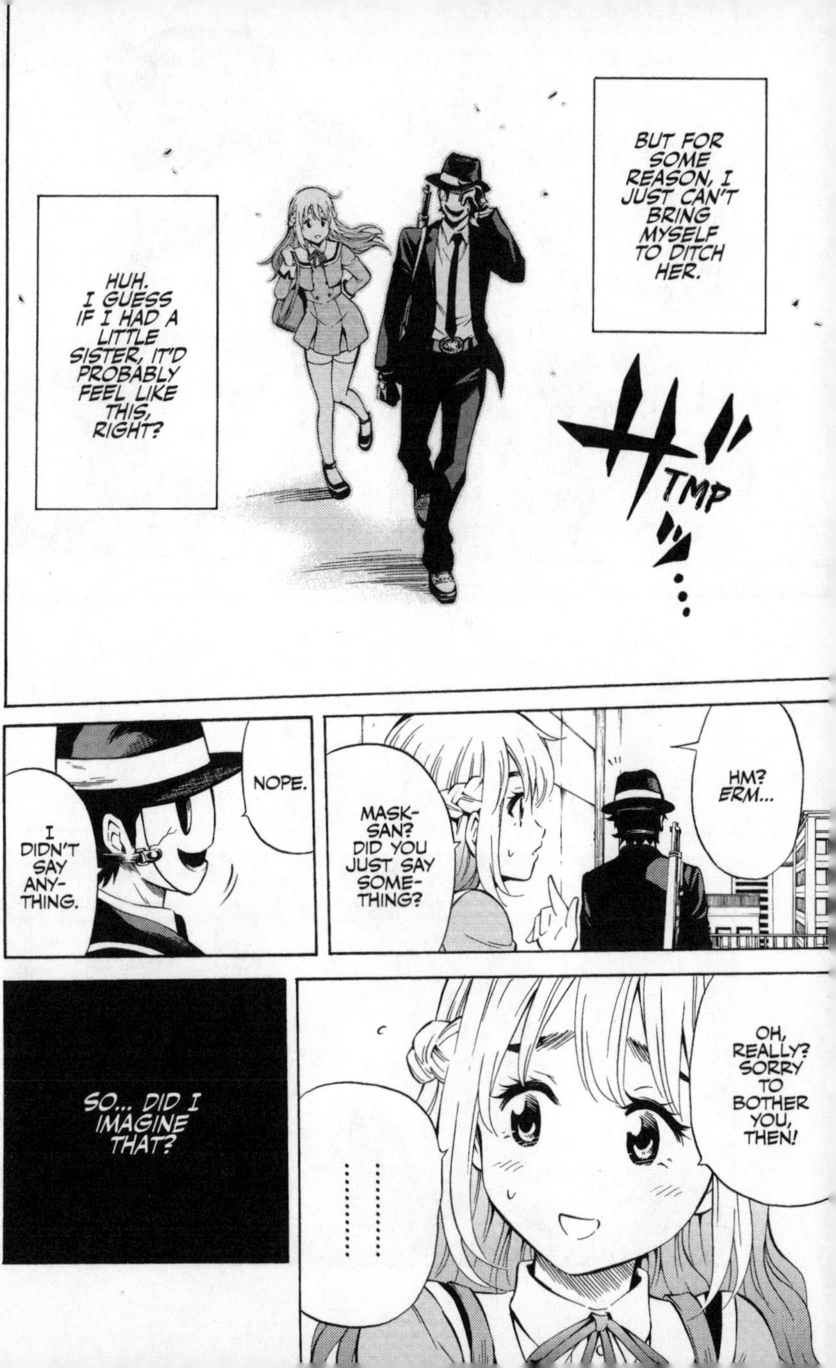
BUT FOR SOME REASON, I JUST CAN'T BRING MYSELF TO DITCH HER.
HUH. I GUESS IF I HAD A LITTLE SISTER, IT'D PROBABLY FEEL LIKE THIS, RIGHT?
TMP
HM? ERM...
MASK-SAN? DID YOU JUST SAY SOME-THING?
NOPE.
I DIDN'T SAY ANY-THING.
OH, REALLY? SORRY TO BOTHER YOU, THEN!
SO... DID I IMAGINE THAT?
......

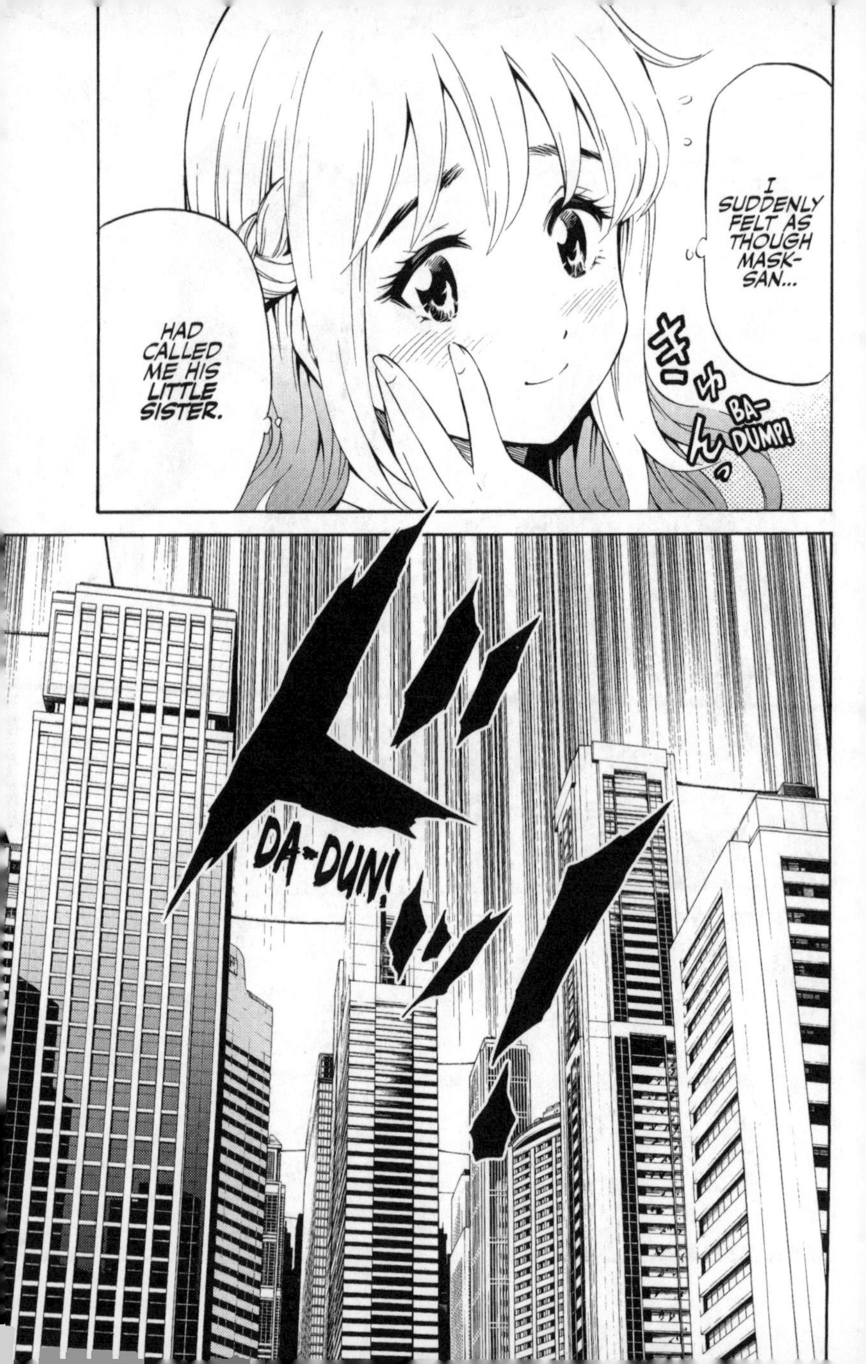
I SUDDENLY FELT AS THOUGH MASK-SAN...
きゅんっ
BA-DUMP!
HAD CALLED ME HIS LITTLE SISTER.
DA-DUN!

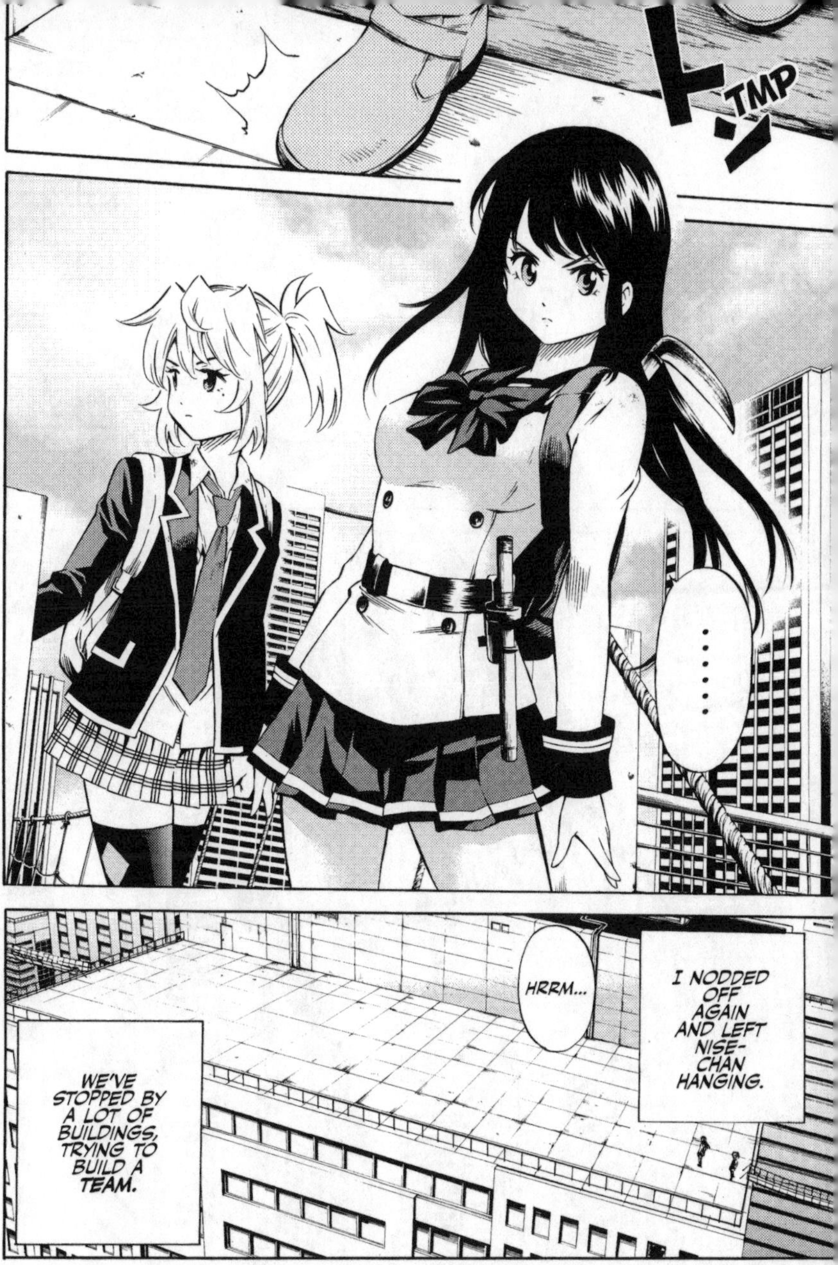
トッ
TMP
......
I NODDED OFF AGAIN AND LEFT NISE-CHAN HANGING.
HRRM...
WE'VE STOPPED BY A LOT OF BUILDINGS, TRYING TO BUILD A TEAM.

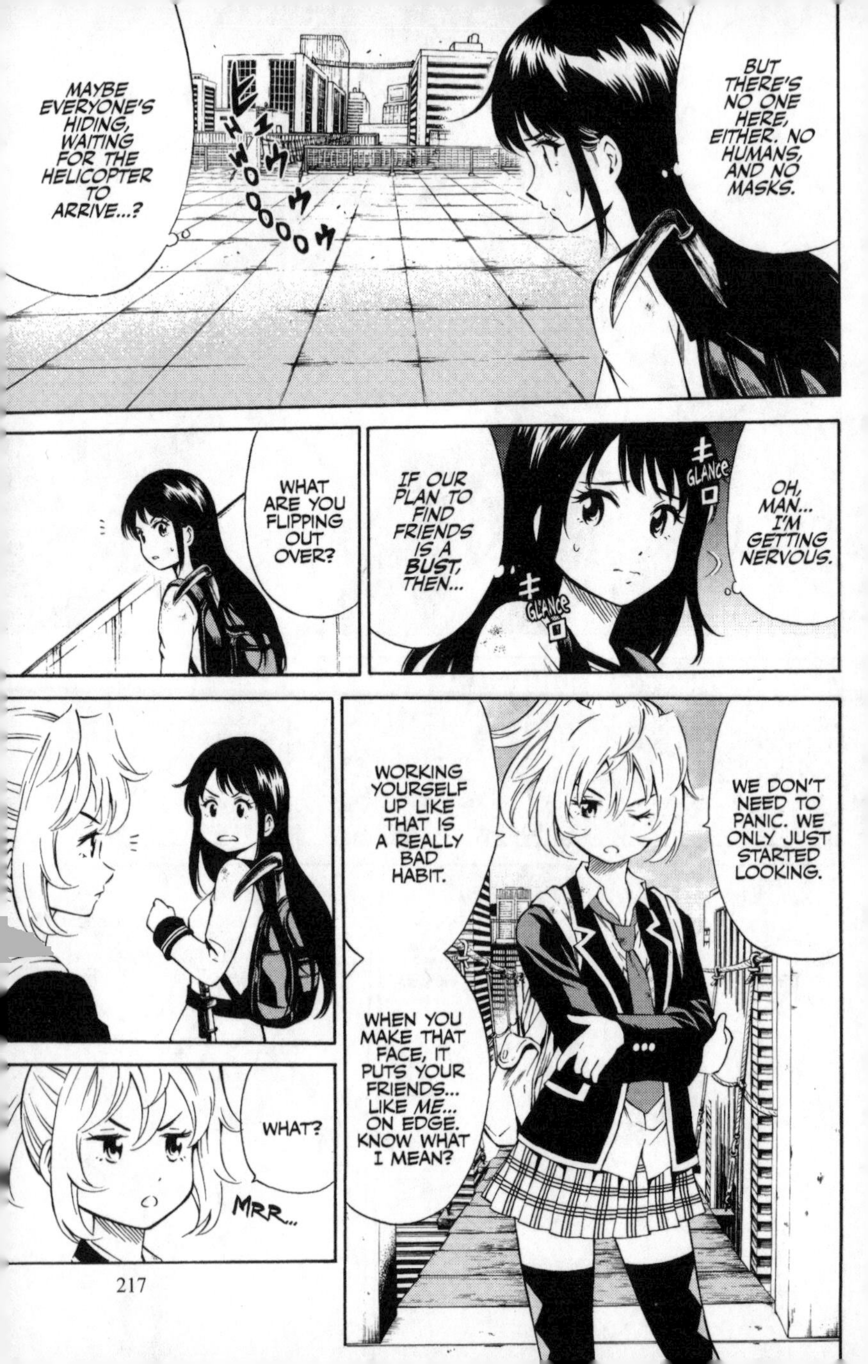
BUT THERE'S NO ONE HERE, EITHER. NO HUMANS, AND NO MASKS.
HWOOOO
MAYBE EVERYONE'S HIDING, WAITING FOR THE HELICOPTER TO ARRIVE...?
OH, MAN... I'M GETTING NERVOUS.
GLANCE
GLANCE
IF OUR PLAN TO FIND FRIENDS IS A *BUST*, THEN...
WHAT ARE YOU FLIPPING OUT OVER?
WE DON'T NEED TO PANIC. WE ONLY JUST STARTED LOOKING.
WORKING YOURSELF UP LIKE THAT IS A REALLY BAD HABIT.
WHEN YOU MAKE THAT FACE, IT PUTS YOUR FRIENDS... LIKE *ME*... ON EDGE. KNOW WHAT I MEAN?
WHAT?
MRR...

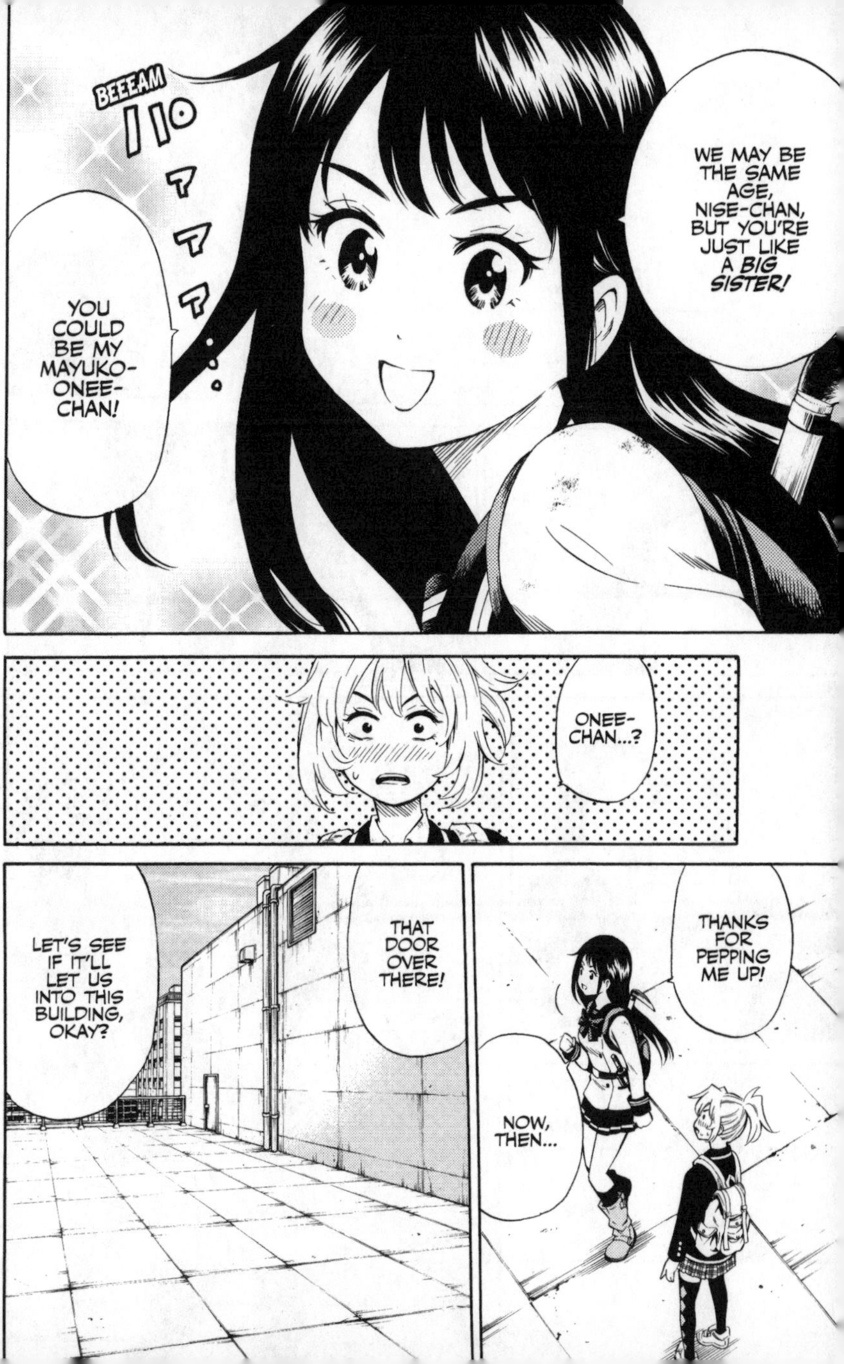
WE MAY BE THE SAME AGE, NISE-CHAN, BUT YOU'RE JUST LIKE A *BIG SISTER!*
BEEEAM
YOU COULD BE MY MAYUKO-ONEE-CHAN!
ONEE-CHAN...?
THANKS FOR PEPPING ME UP!
NOW, THEN...
THAT DOOR OVER THERE!
LET'S SEE IF IT'LL LET US INTO THIS BUILDING, OKAY?

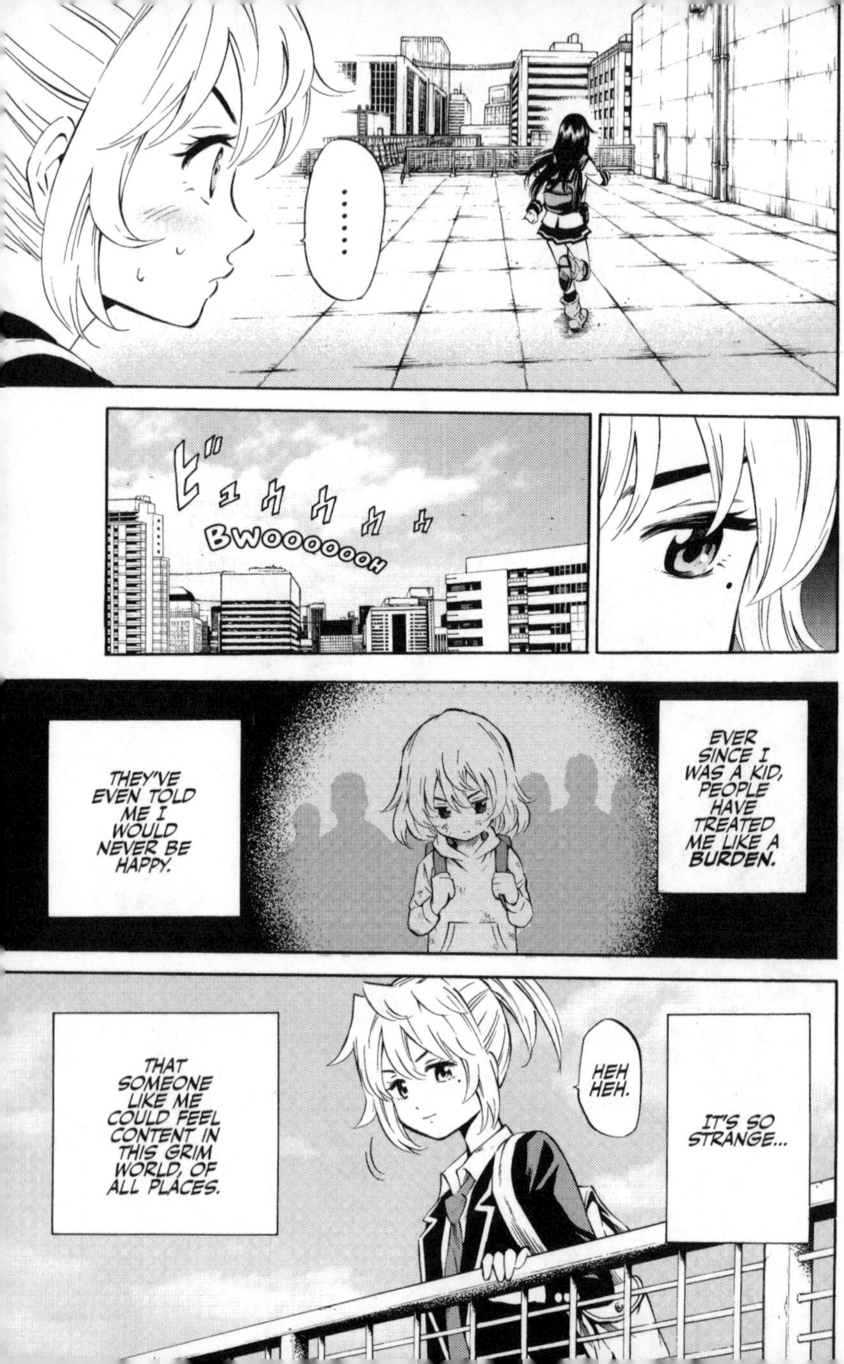
......
ビュゥゥゥゥ
BWOOOOOOOH
EVER SINCE I WAS A KID, PEOPLE HAVE TREATED ME LIKE A BURDEN.
THEY'VE EVEN TOLD ME I WOULD NEVER BE HAPPY.
IT'S SO STRANGE...
HEH HEH.
THAT SOMEONE LIKE ME COULD FEEL CONTENT IN THIS GRIM WORLD, OF ALL PLACES.

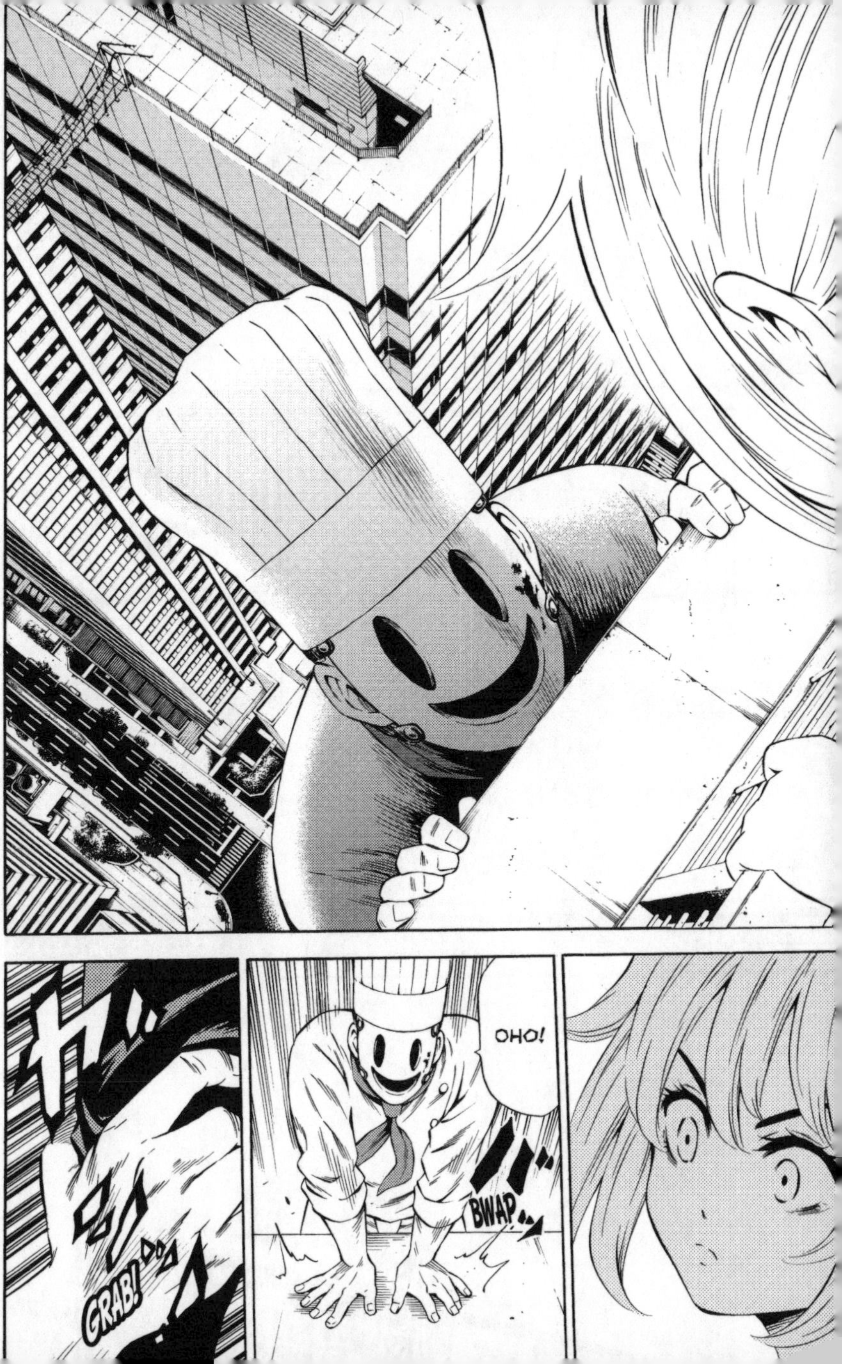
OHO!
BWAP
GRAB!

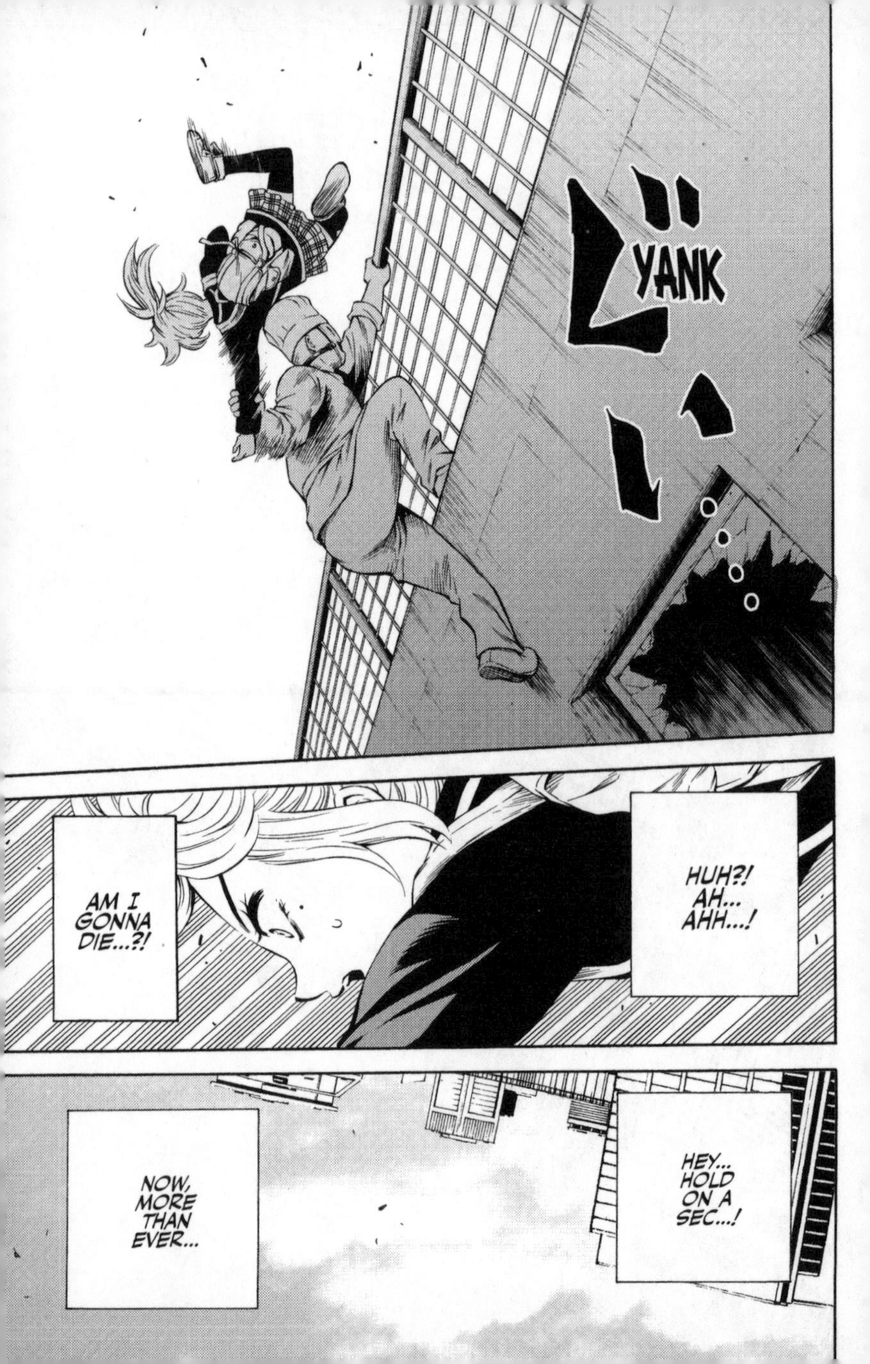
YANK
HUH?! AH... AHH...!
AM I GONNA DIE...?!
HEY... HOLD ON A SEC...!
NOW, MORE THAN EVER...

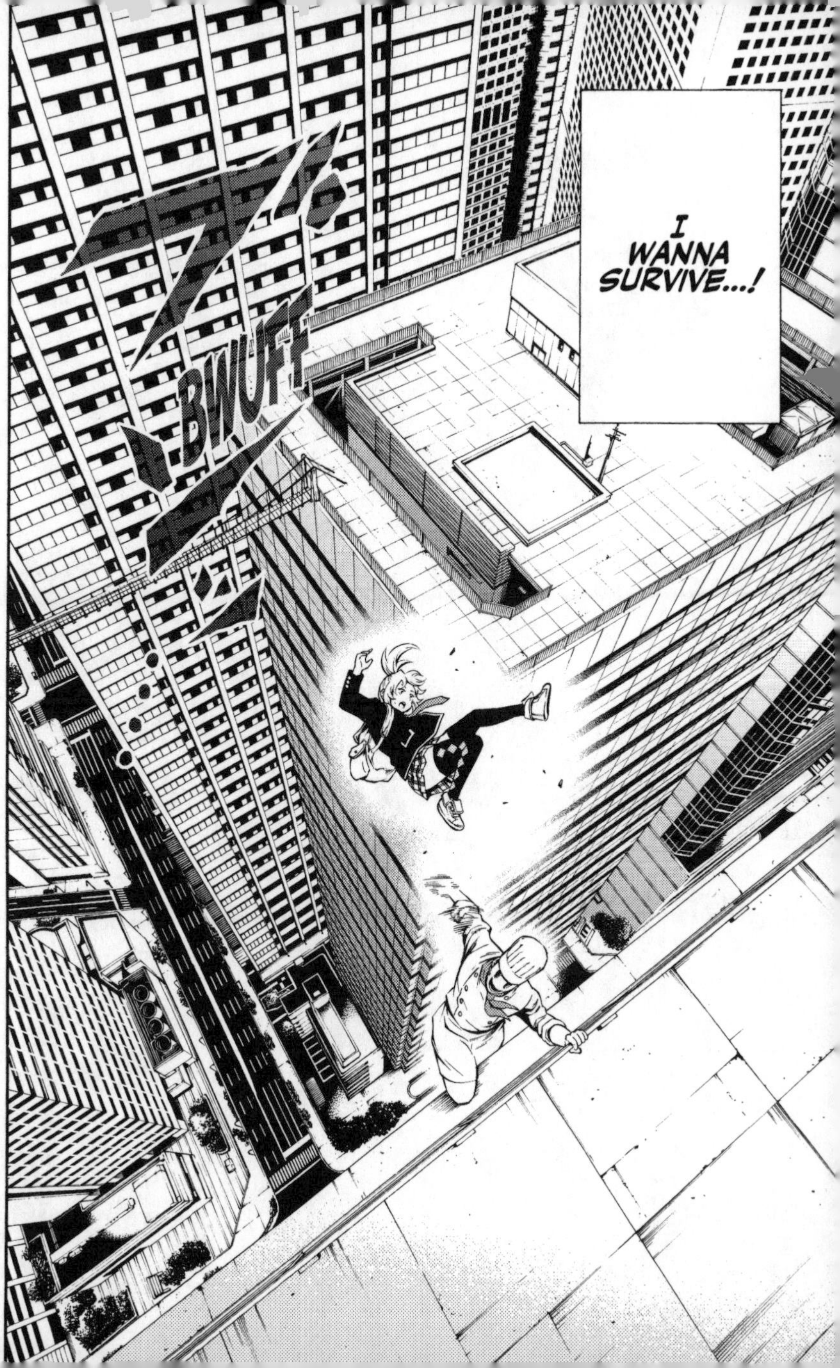
I WANNA SURVIVE...!
BWUFF

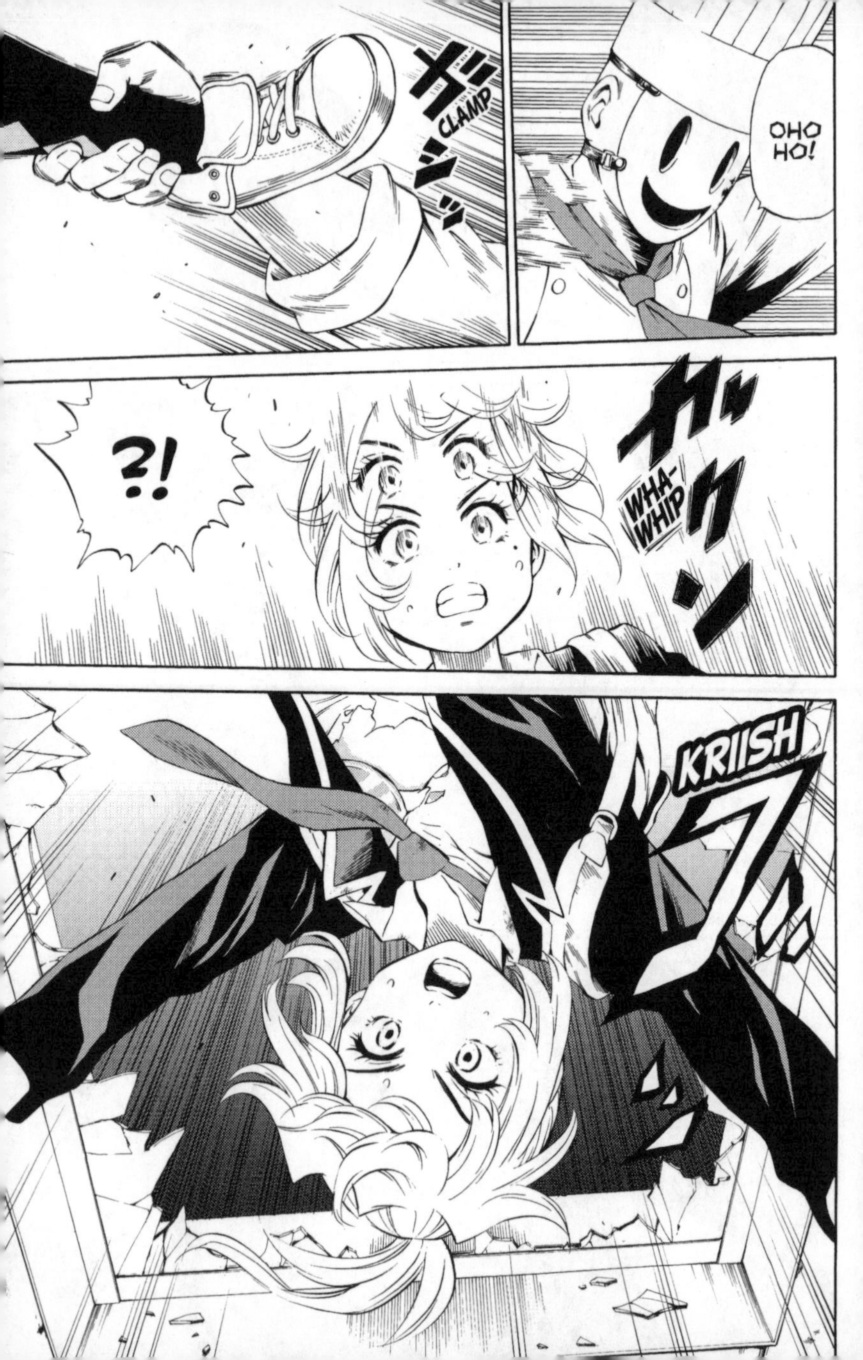
OHO HO!
CLAMP
WHA-WHIP
?!
KRIISH

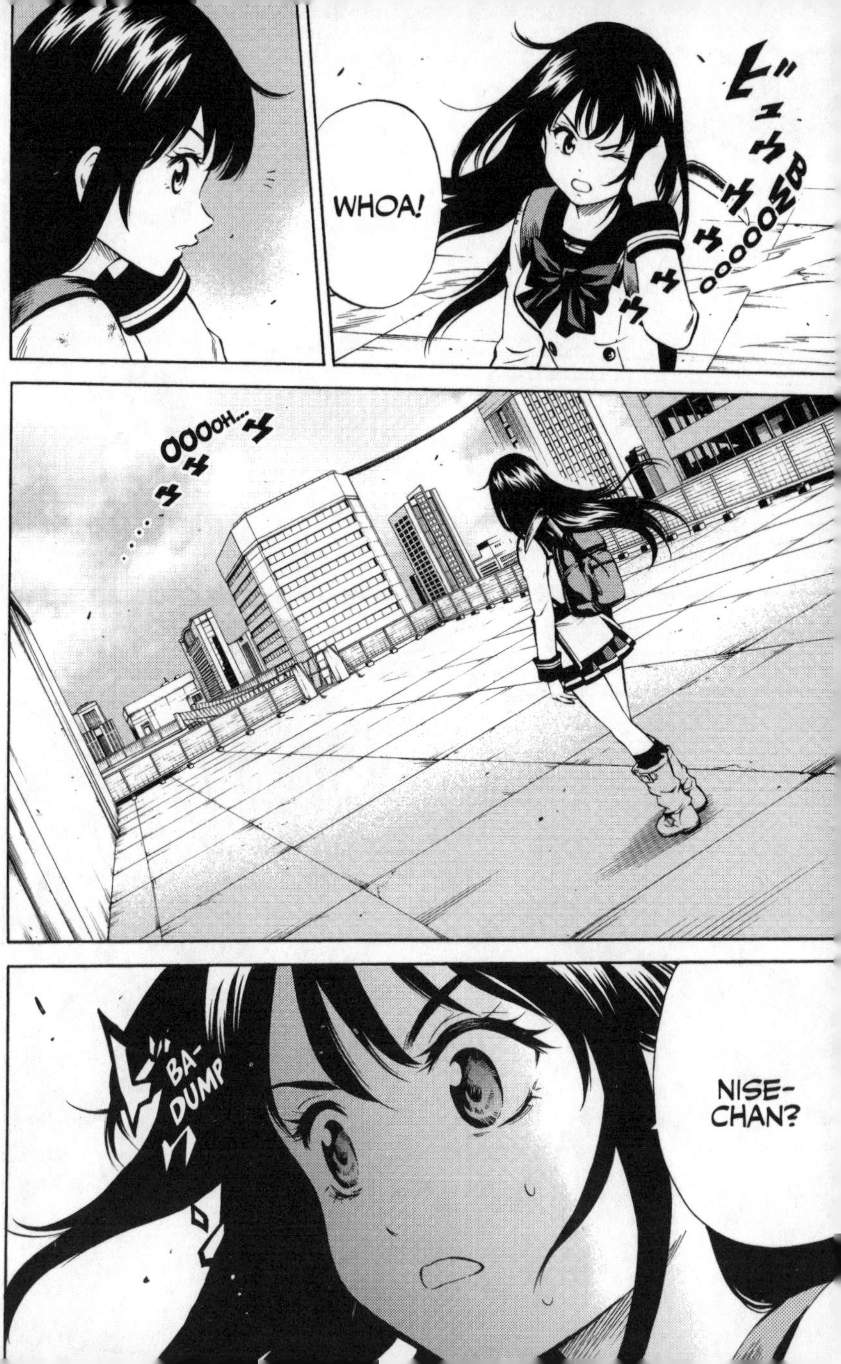
BWOOOOOOO
WHOA!
OOOOH...
NISE-CHAN?
BA-DUMP

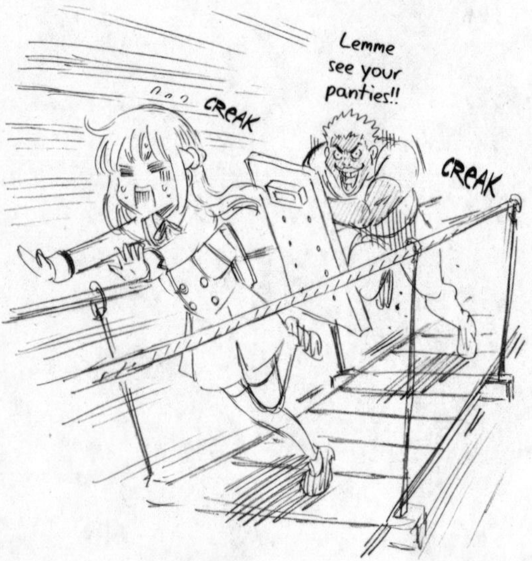
Lemme see your panties!!
CREAK
CREAK

HIGH-RISE INVASION

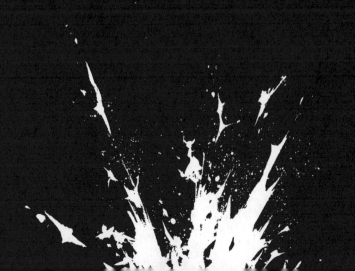

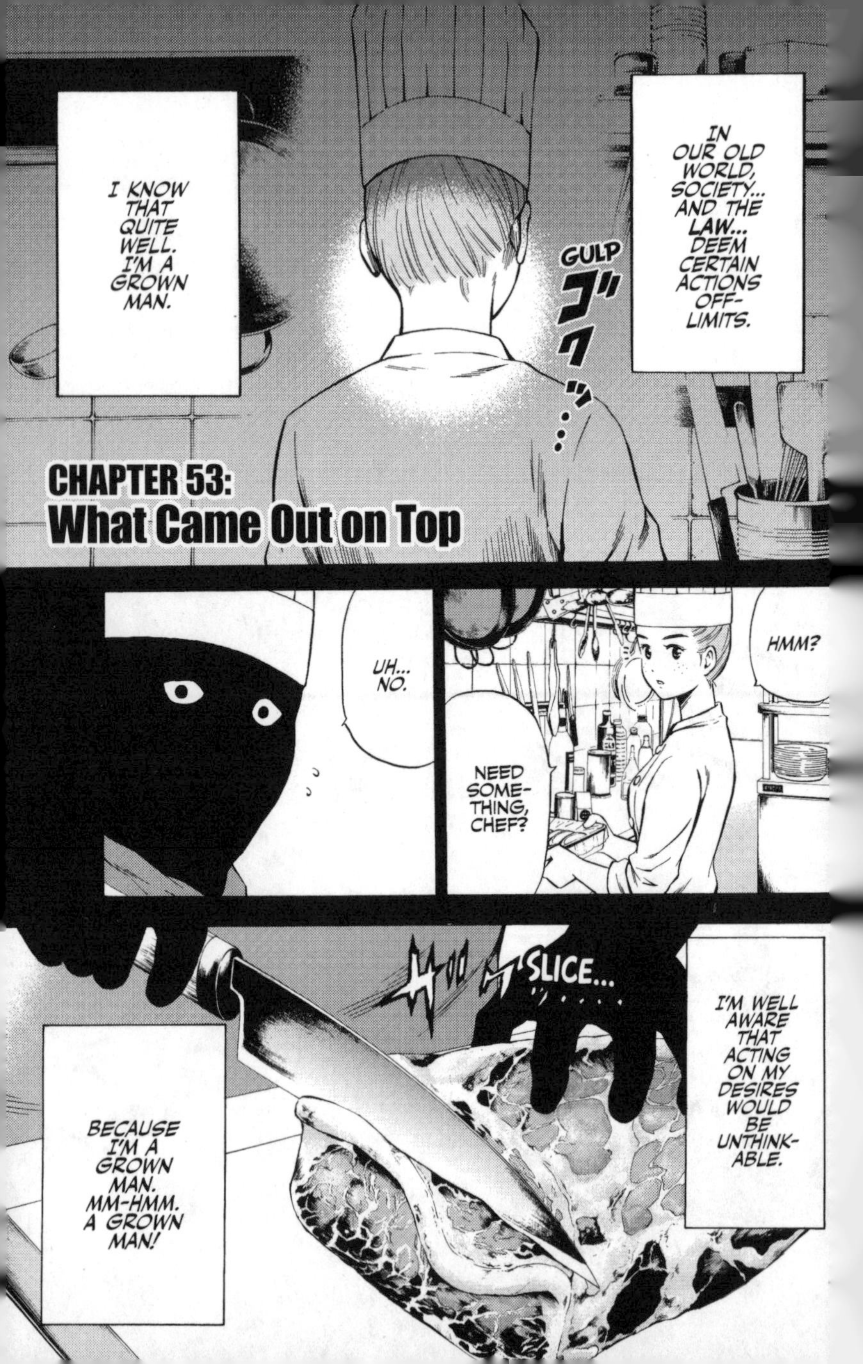
IN OUR OLD WORLD, SOCIETY... AND THE LAW... DEEM CERTAIN ACTIONS OFF-LIMITS.
GULP
I KNOW THAT QUITE WELL. I'M A GROWN MAN.
CHAPTER 53:
What Came Out on Top
HMM?
NEED SOMETHING, CHEF?
UH... NO.
I'M WELL AWARE THAT ACTING ON MY DESIRES WOULD BE UNTHINKABLE.
SLICE...
BECAUSE I'M A GROWN MAN. MM-HMM. A GROWN MAN!

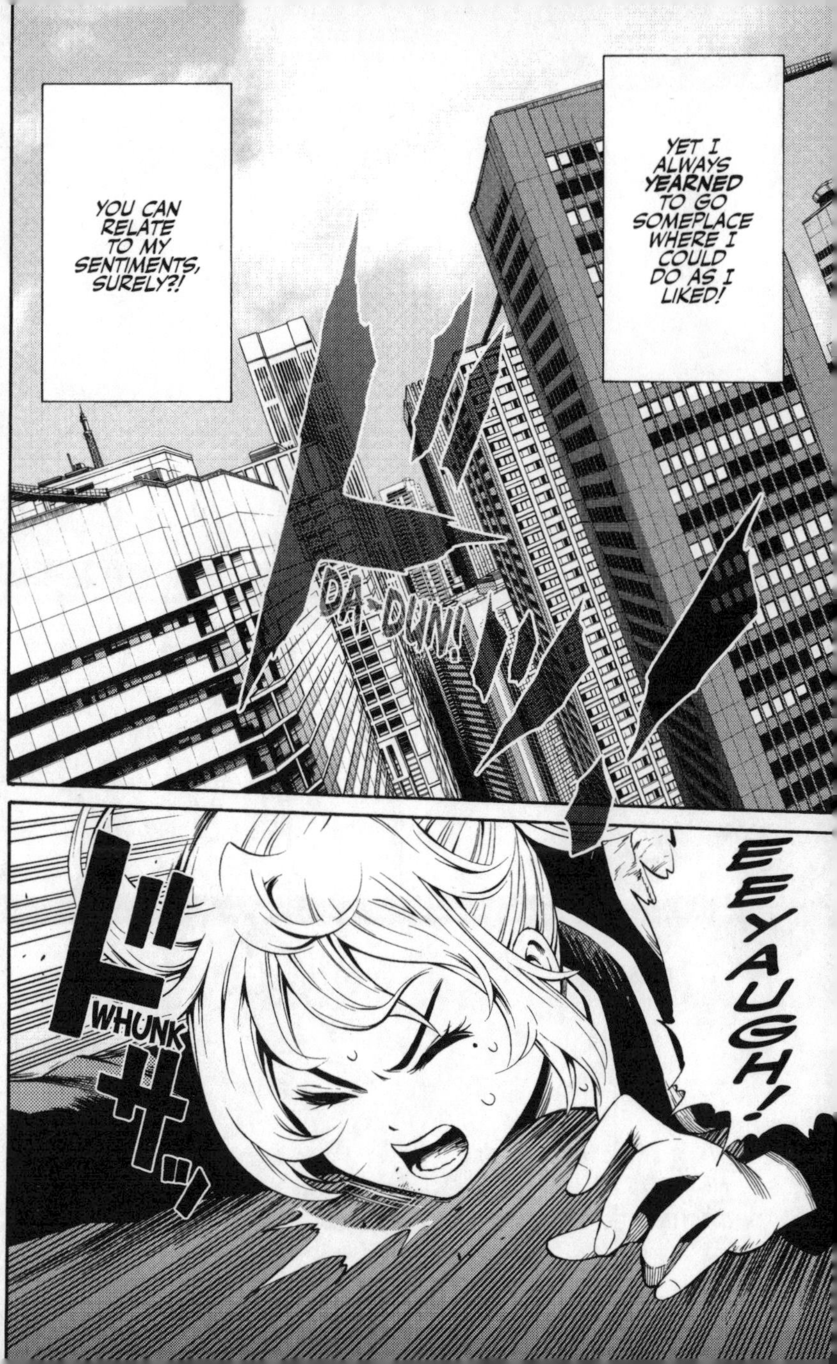
YET I ALWAYS YEARNED TO GO SOMEPLACE WHERE I COULD DO AS I LIKED!
YOU CAN RELATE TO MY SENTIMENTS, SURELY?!
DA-DUN!
EEYAUGH!
WHUNK

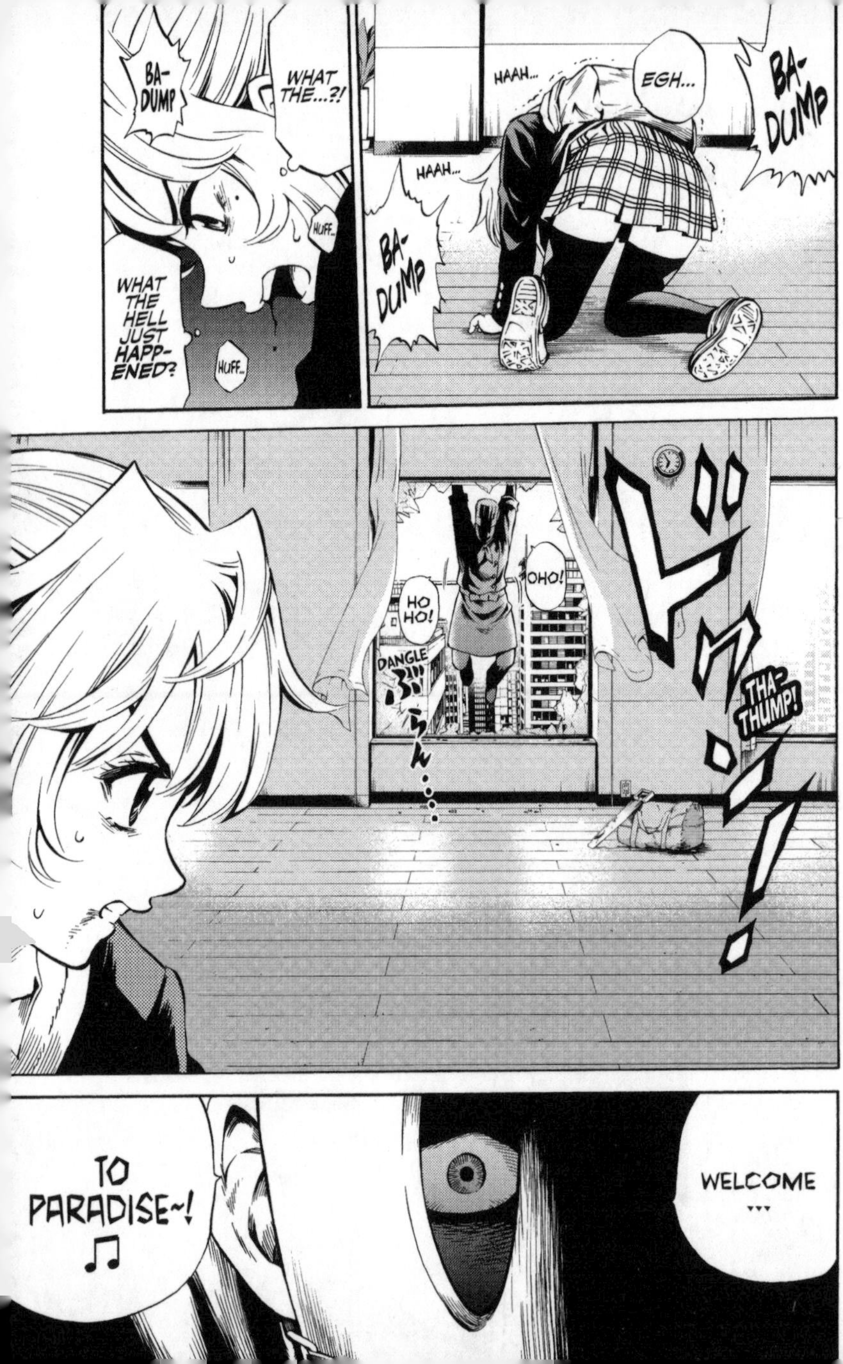
BA-DUMP
EGH...
HAAH...
HAAH...
BA-DUMP
WHAT THE...?!
BA-DUMP
HUFF...
WHAT THE HELL JUST HAPPENED?
HUFF...
THA-THUMP!
OHO!
HO HO!
DANGLE
WELCOME ...
TO PARADISE~! ♫

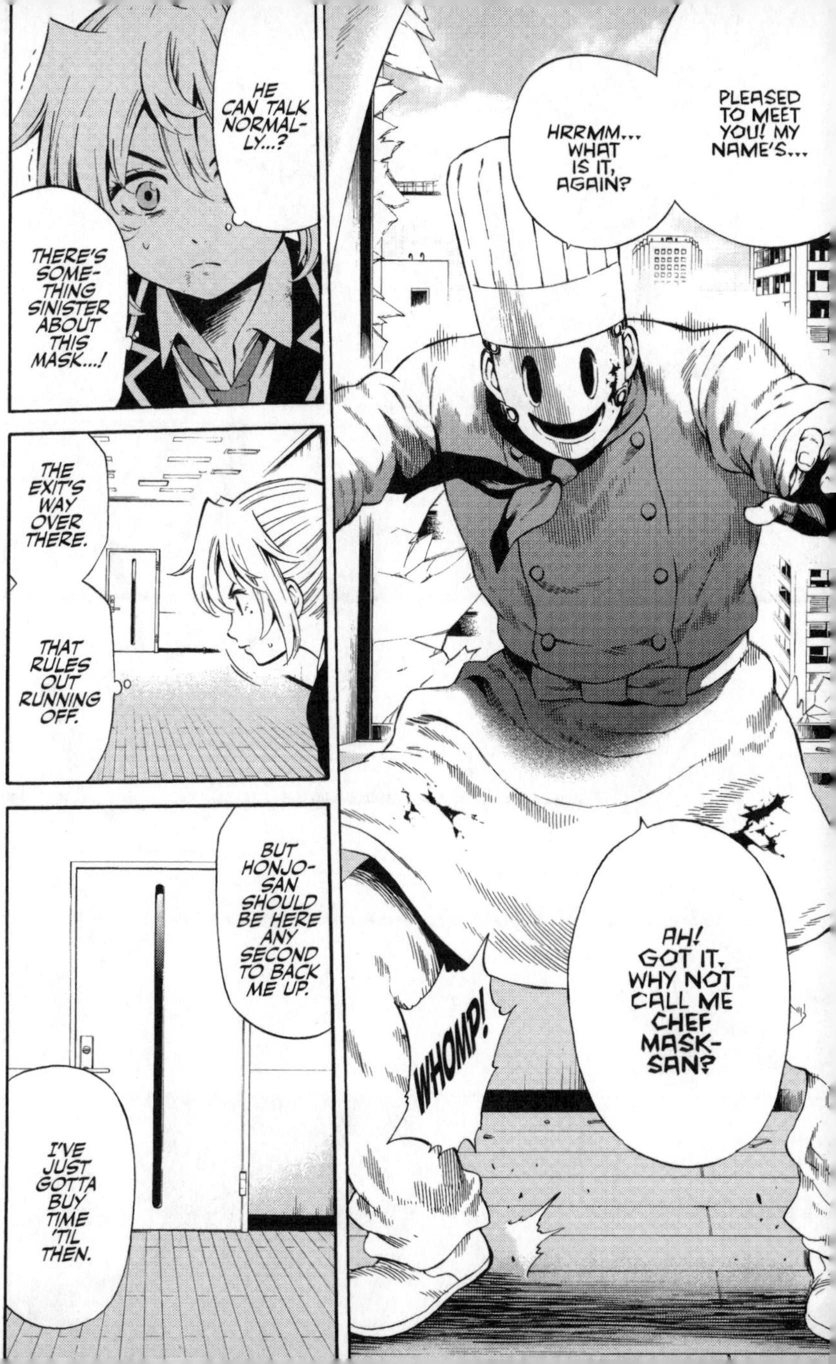
PLEASED TO MEET YOU! MY NAME'S...
HRRMM... WHAT IS IT, AGAIN?
AH! GOT IT. WHY NOT CALL ME CHEF MASK-SAN?
WHOMP!
HE CAN TALK NORMAL-LY...?
THERE'S SOME-THING SINISTER ABOUT THIS MASK...!
THE EXIT'S WAY OVER THERE.
THAT RULES OUT RUNNING OFF.
BUT HONJO-SAN SHOULD BE HERE ANY SECOND TO BACK ME UP.
I'VE JUST GOTTA BUY TIME 'TIL THEN.

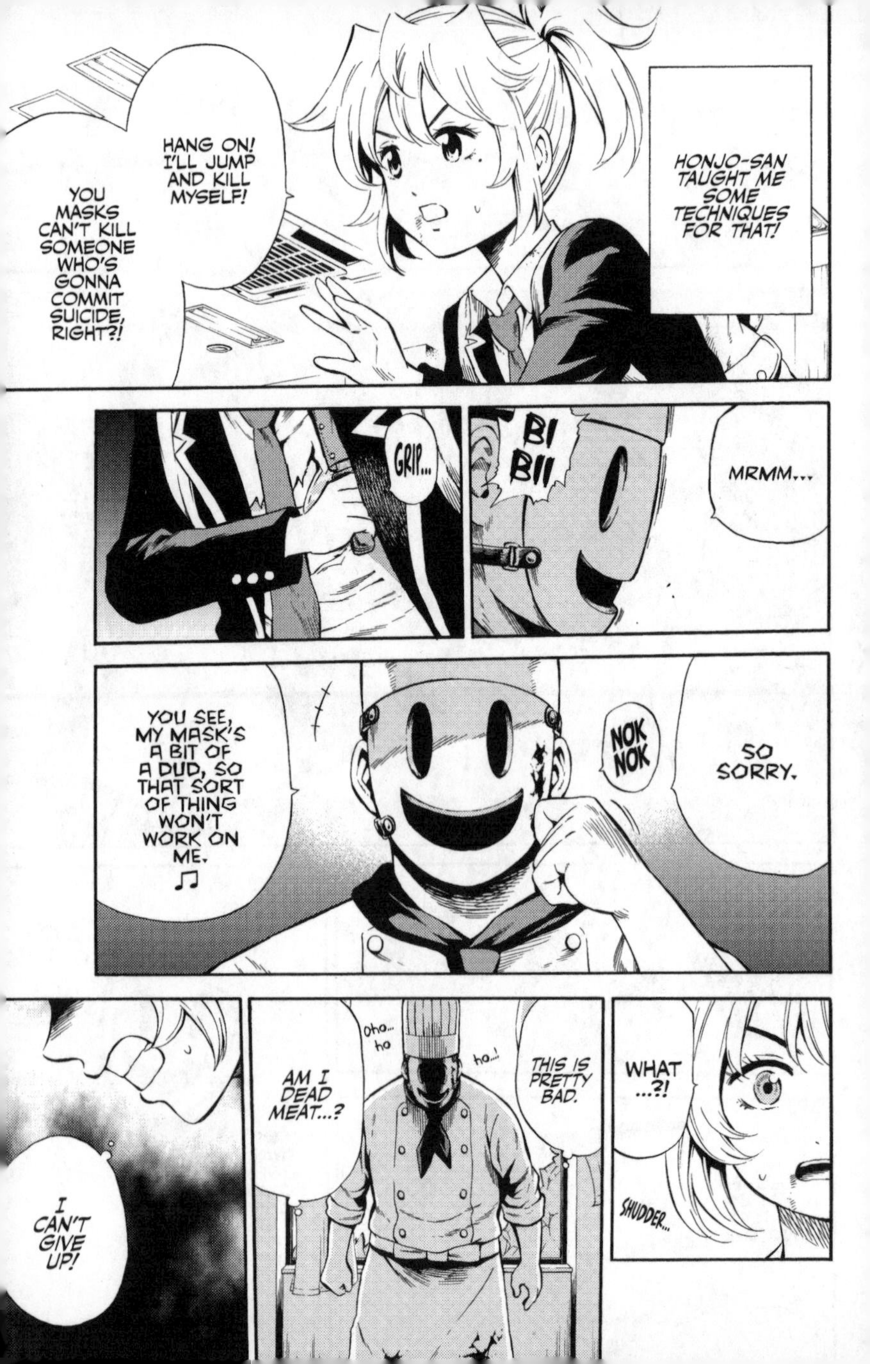
HONJO-SAN TAUGHT ME SOME TECHNIQUES FOR THAT!
HANG ON! I'LL JUMP AND KILL MYSELF!
YOU MASKS CAN'T KILL SOMEONE WHO'S GONNA COMMIT SUICIDE, RIGHT?!
MRMM...
BI BII
GRIP...
SO SORRY.
NOK NOK
YOU SEE, MY MASK'S A BIT OF A DUD, SO THAT SORT OF THING WON'T WORK ON ME. ♫
WHAT ...?!
SHUDDER...
THIS IS PRETTY BAD.
ho...!
oho... ho
AM I DEAD MEAT...?
I CAN'T GIVE UP!

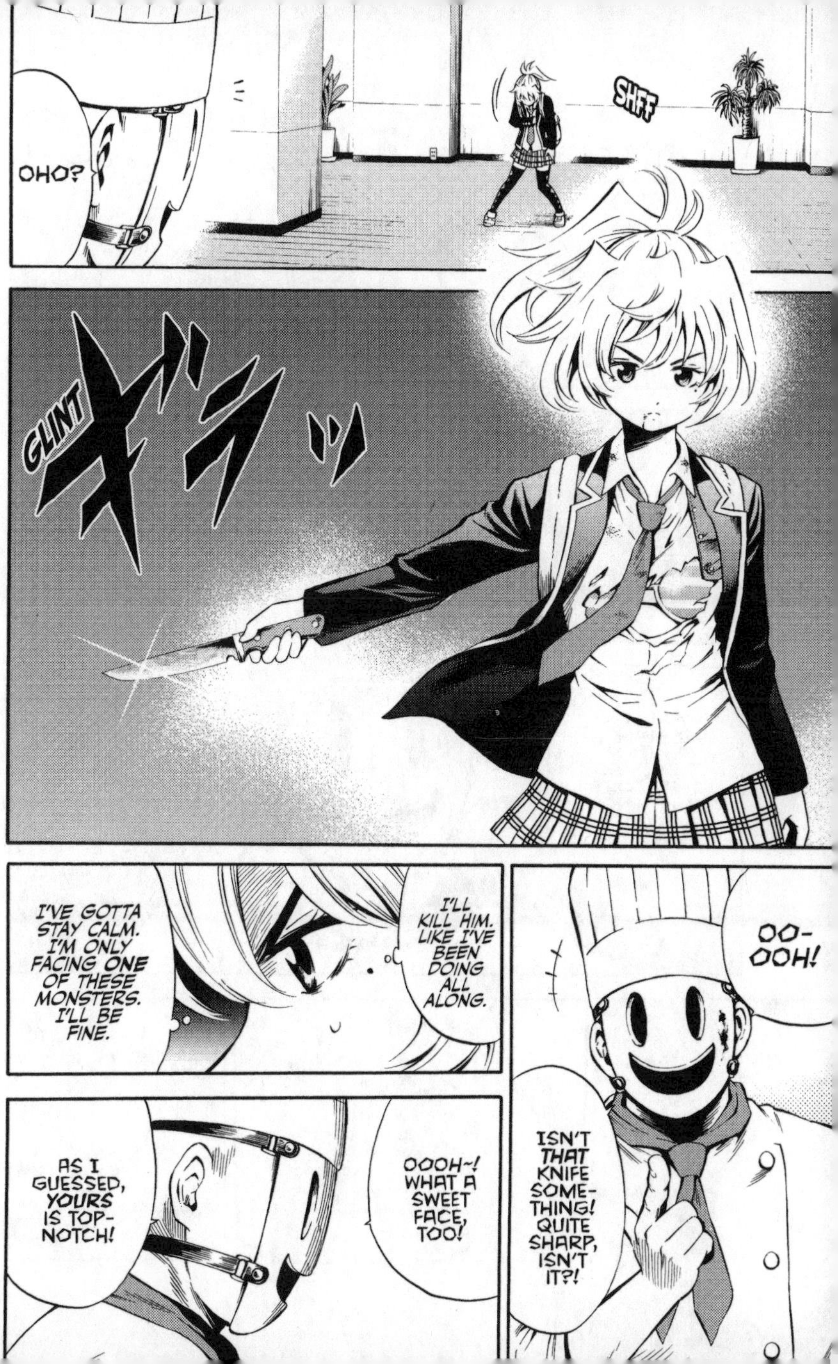
SHFF
OHO?
GLINT
OO-OOH!
ISN'T THAT KNIFE SOMETHING! QUITE SHARP, ISN'T IT?!
I'LL KILL HIM. LIKE I'VE BEEN DOING ALL ALONG.
I'VE GOTTA STAY CALM. I'M ONLY FACING ONE OF THESE MONSTERS. I'LL BE FINE.
OOOH~! WHAT A SWEET FACE, TOO!
AS I GUESSED, YOURS IS TOP-NOTCH!

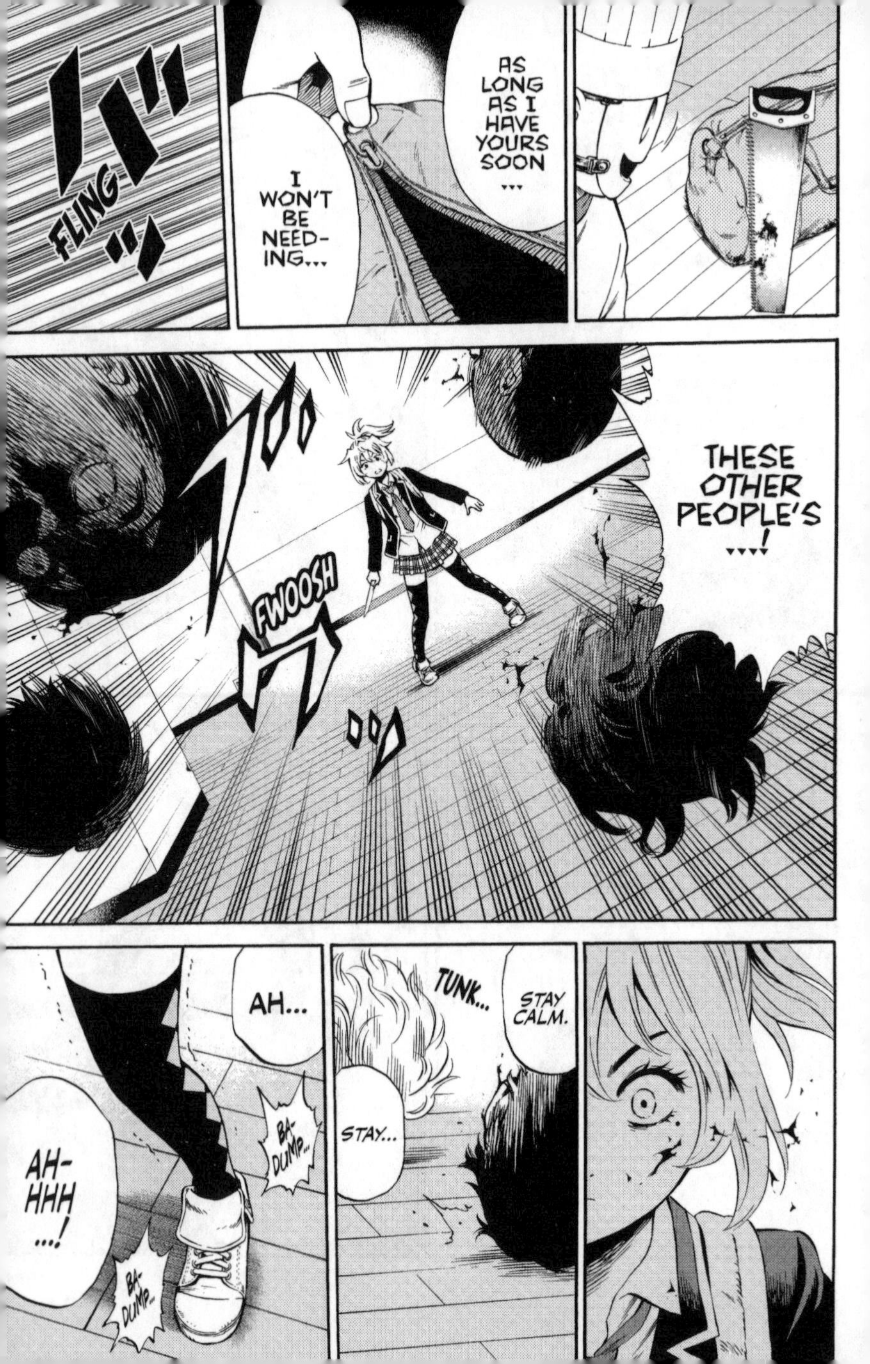
AS LONG AS I HAVE YOURS SOON...
I WON'T BE NEEDING...
FLING
THESE OTHER PEOPLE'S...!
FWOOSH
TUNK...
STAY CALM.
STAY...
BA-DUMP...
AH...
AH-HHH...!
BA-DUMP...

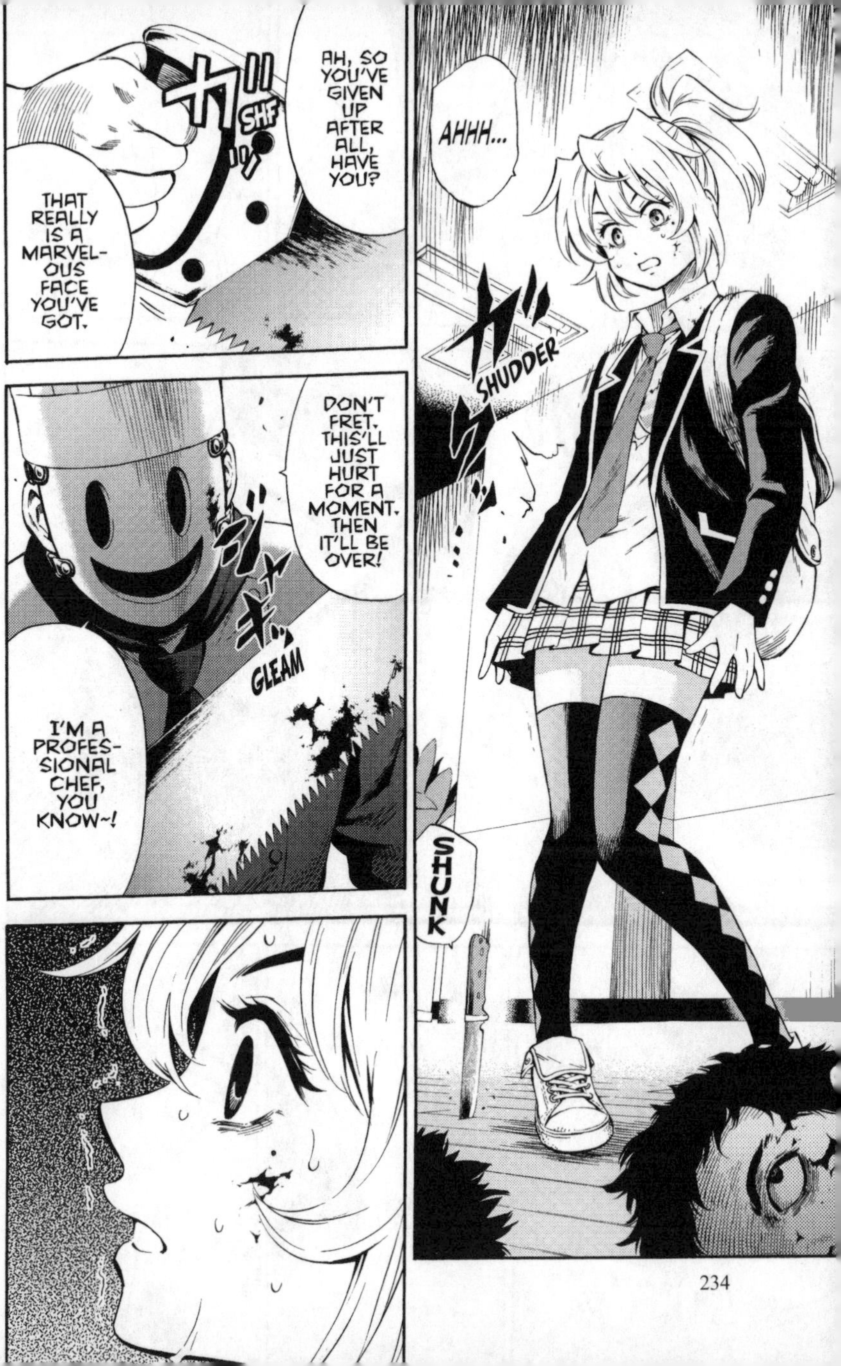
AHHH...
SHUDDER
SHUNK
AH, SO YOU'VE GIVEN UP AFTER ALL, HAVE YOU?
SHF
THAT REALLY IS A MARVELOUS FACE YOU'VE GOT.
DON'T FRET. THIS'LL JUST HURT FOR A MOMENT. THEN IT'LL BE OVER!
GLEAM
I'M A PROFESSIONAL CHEF, YOU KNOW~!

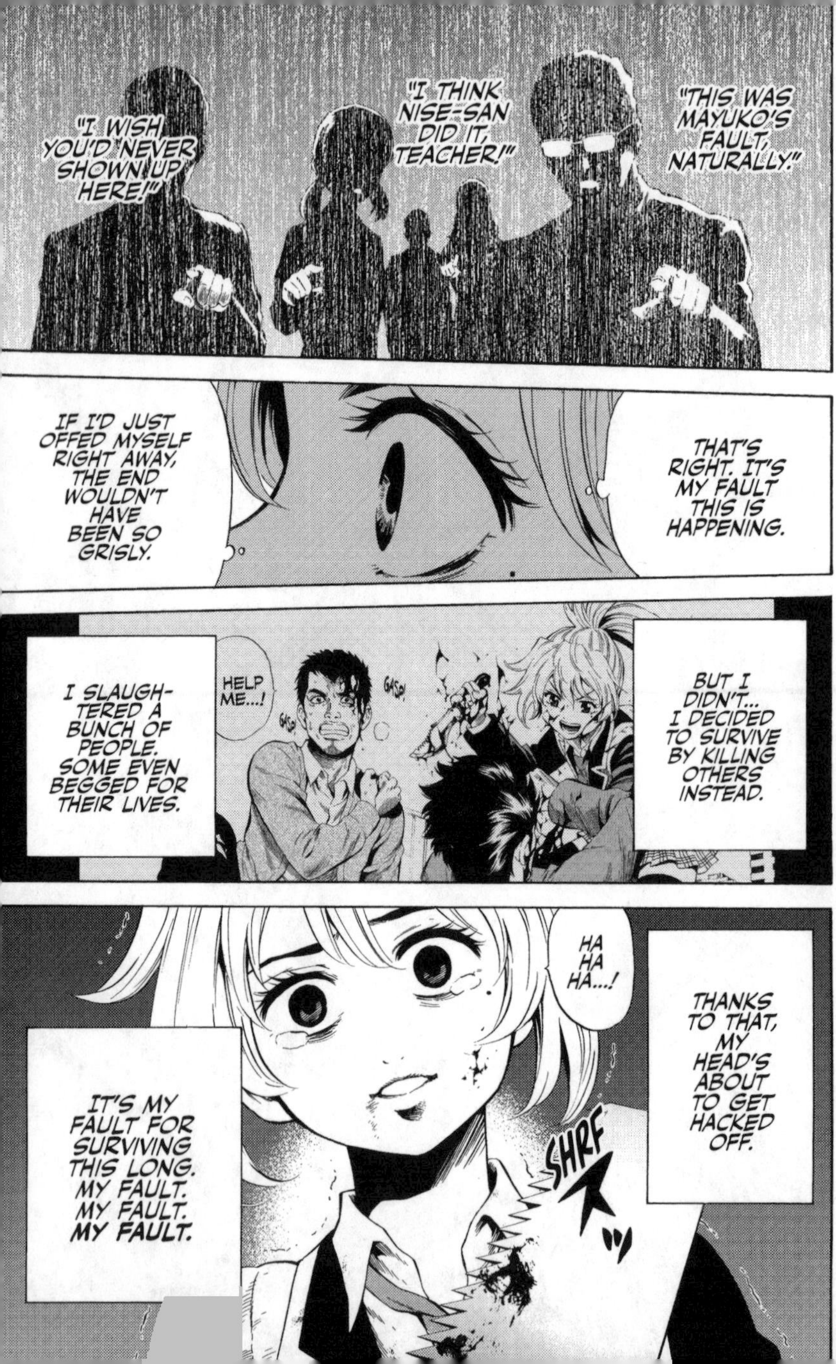
"THIS WAS MAYUKO'S FAULT, NATURALLY."
"I THINK NISE-SAN DID IT, TEACHER!"
"I WISH YOU'D NEVER SHOWN UP HERE!"
THAT'S RIGHT. IT'S MY FAULT THIS IS HAPPENING.
IF I'D JUST OFFED MYSELF RIGHT AWAY, THE END WOULDN'T HAVE BEEN SO GRISLY.
BUT I DIDN'T... I DECIDED TO SURVIVE BY KILLING OTHERS INSTEAD.
GASP
GASP
HELP ME...!
I SLAUGHTERED A BUNCH OF PEOPLE. SOME EVEN BEGGED FOR THEIR LIVES.
THANKS TO THAT, MY HEAD'S ABOUT TO GET HACKED OFF.
HA HA HA...!
SHRF
IT'S MY FAULT FOR SURVIVING THIS LONG. MY FAULT. MY FAULT. MY FAULT.

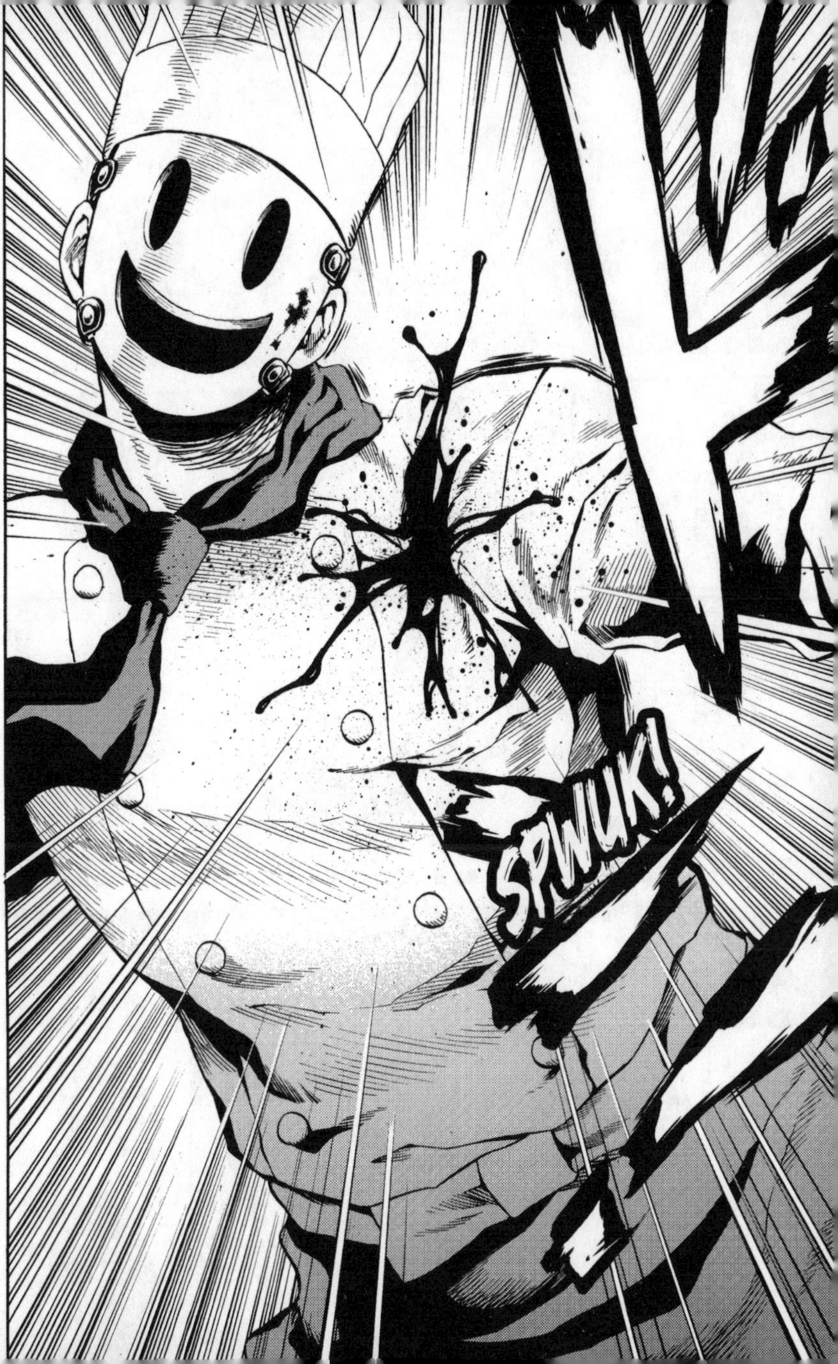
SPWUK!

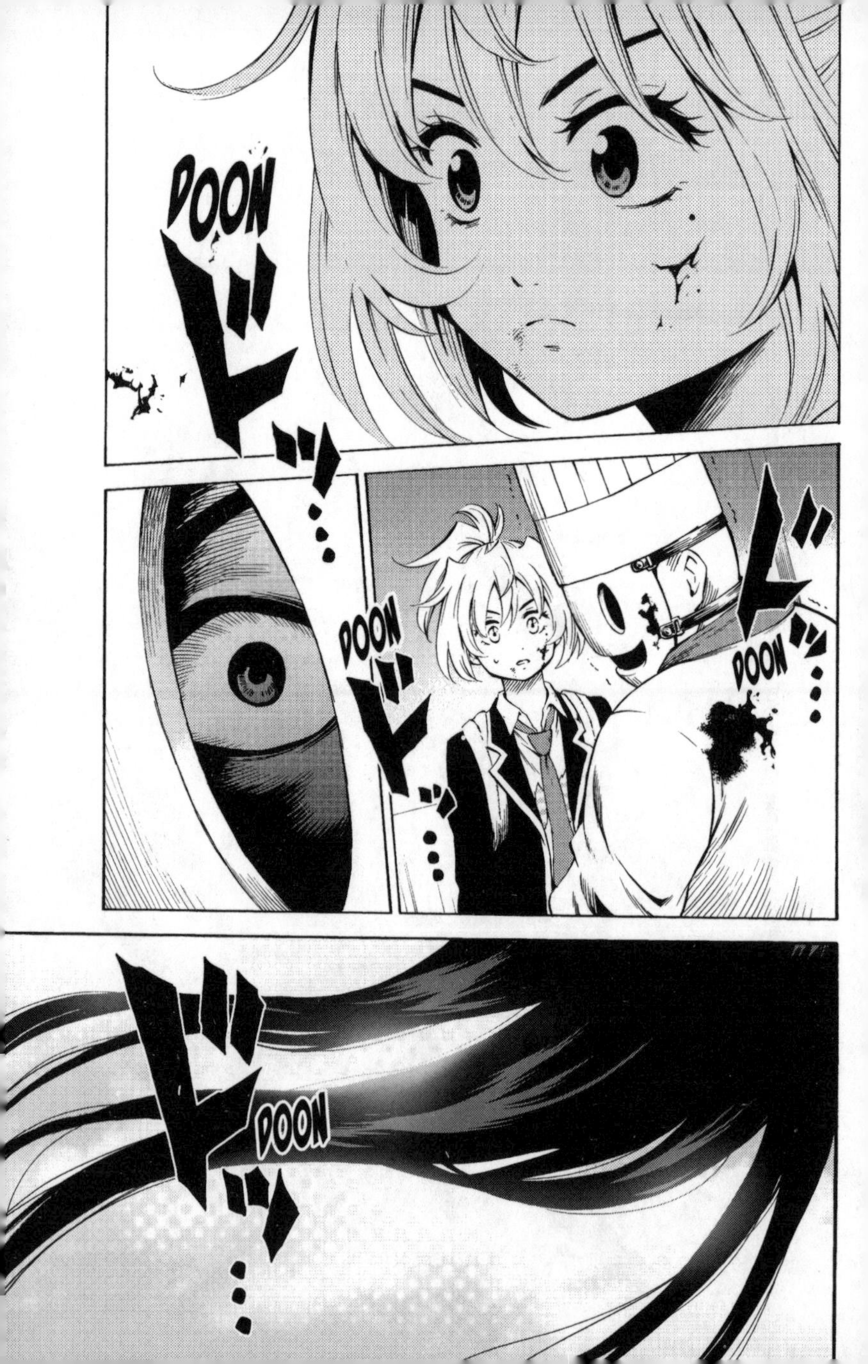
DOON
DOON
DOON
DOON

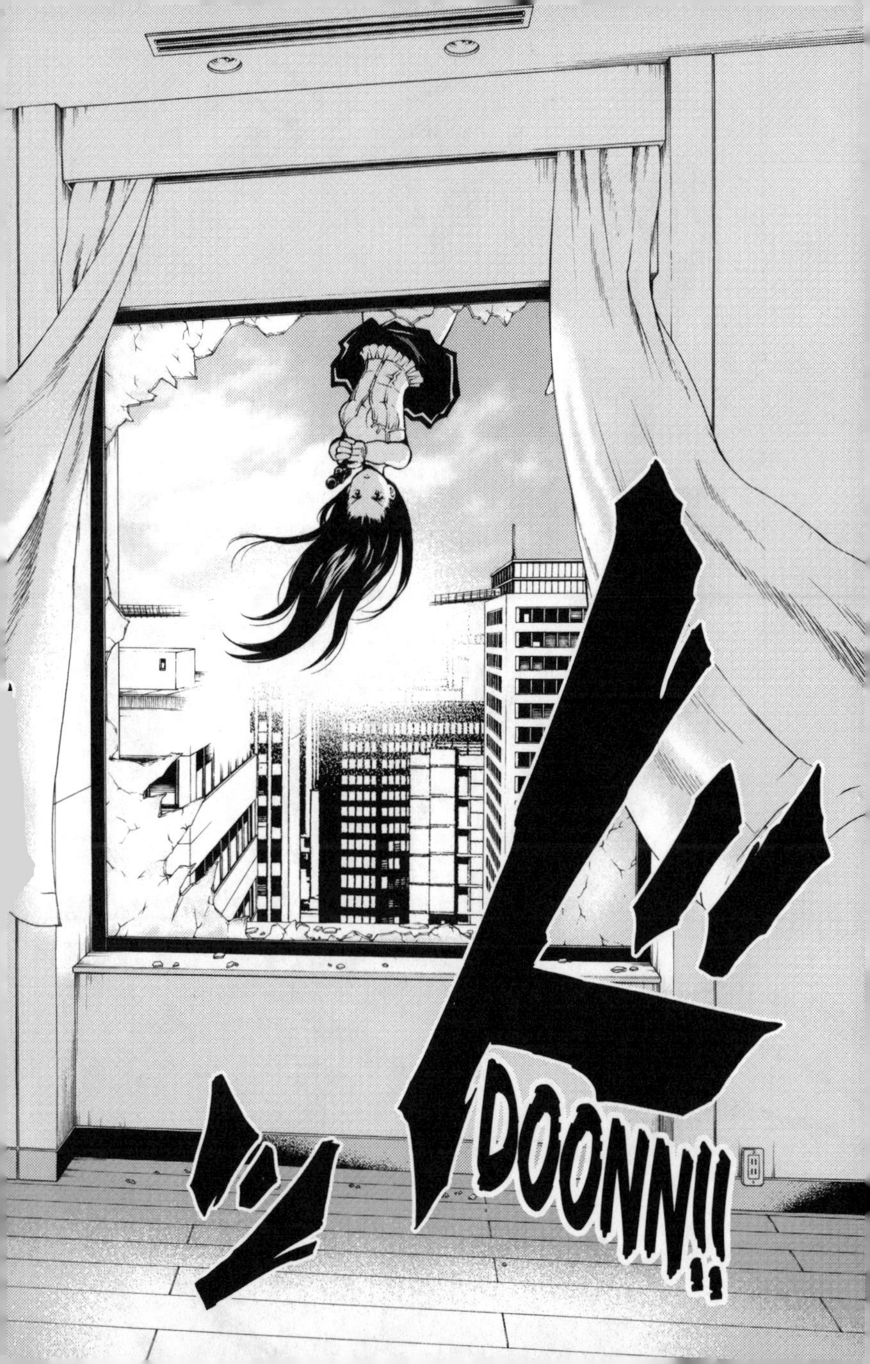
DOONN!!

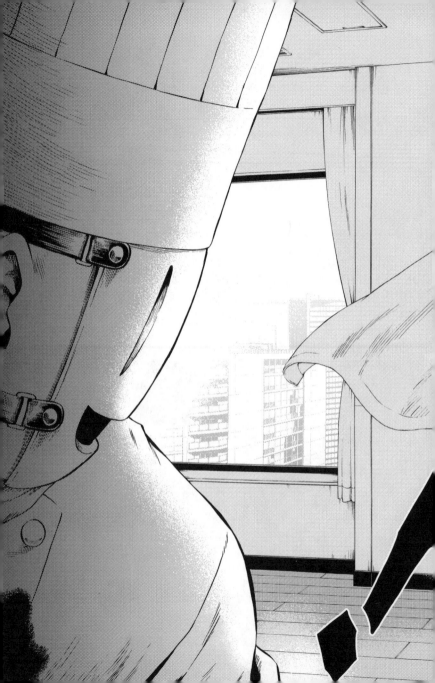

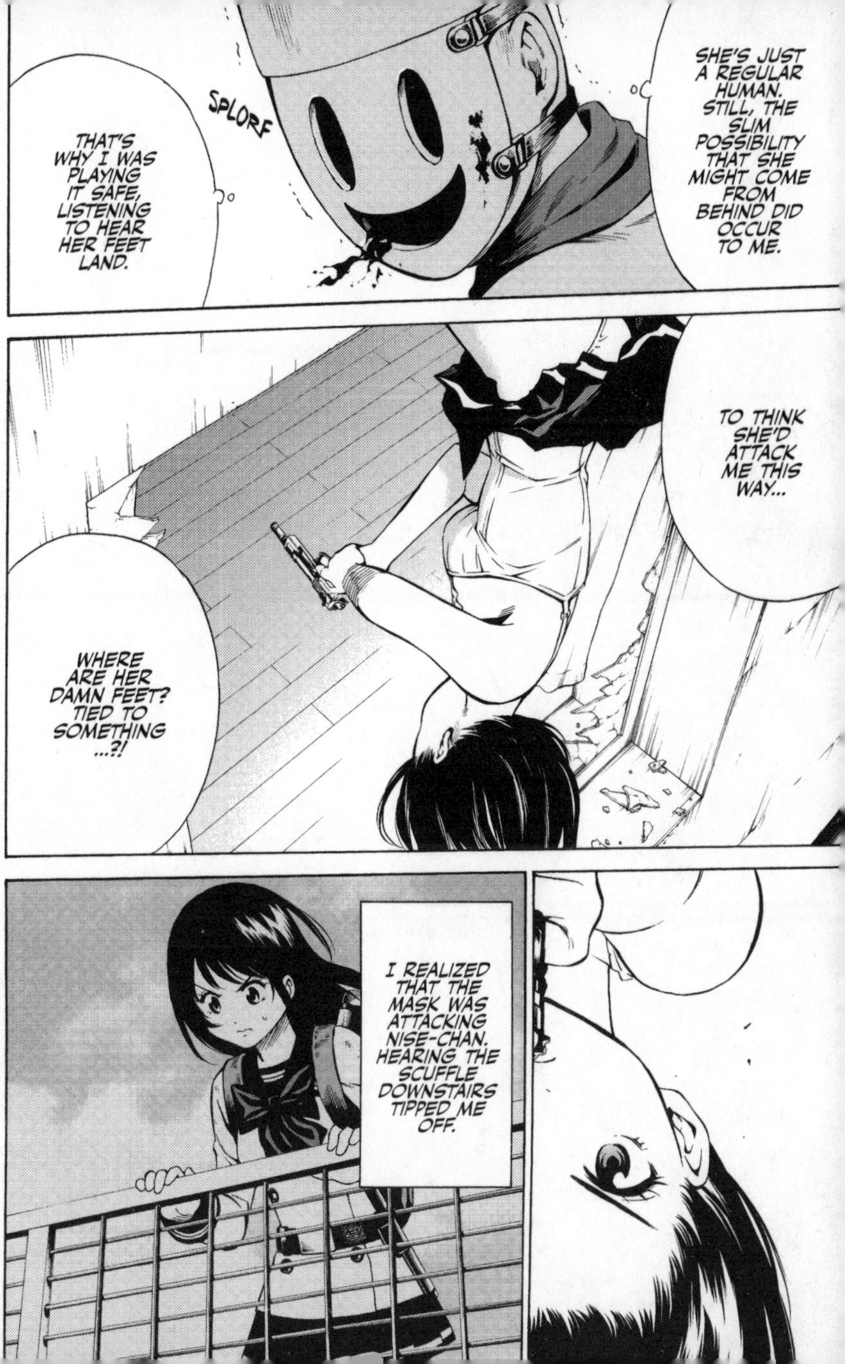
SHE'S JUST A REGULAR HUMAN. STILL, THE SLIM POSSIBILITY THAT SHE MIGHT COME FROM BEHIND DID OCCUR TO ME.
SPLORF
THAT'S WHY I WAS PLAYING IT SAFE, LISTENING TO HEAR HER FEET LAND.
TO THINK SHE'D ATTACK ME THIS WAY...
WHERE ARE HER DAMN FEET? TIED TO SOMETHING ...?!
I REALIZED THAT THE MASK WAS ATTACKING NISE-CHAN. HEARING THE SCUFFLE DOWNSTAIRS TIPPED ME OFF.

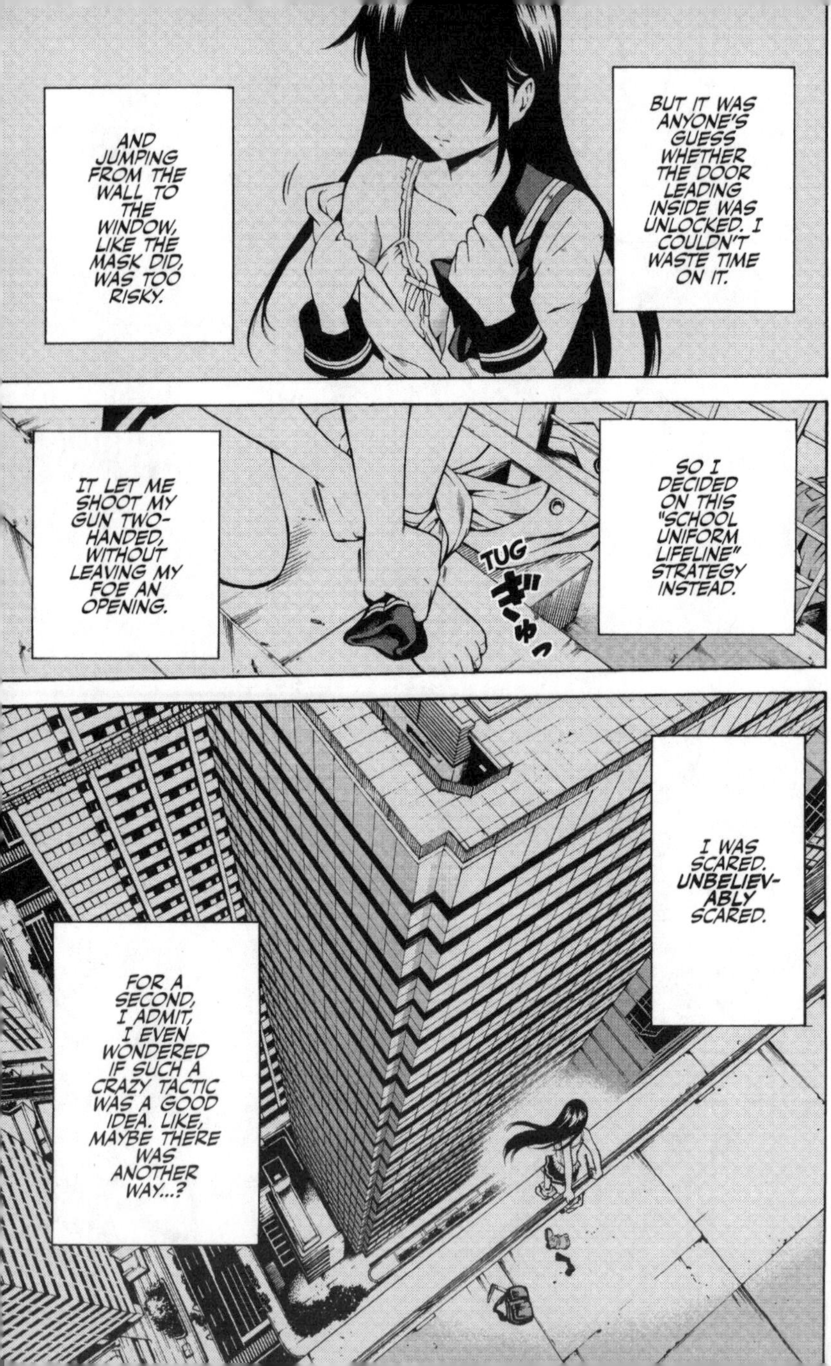
BUT IT WAS ANYONE'S GUESS WHETHER THE DOOR LEADING INSIDE WAS UNLOCKED. I COULDN'T WASTE TIME ON IT.
AND JUMPING FROM THE WALL TO THE WINDOW, LIKE THE MASK DID, WAS TOO RISKY.
SO I DECIDED ON THIS "SCHOOL UNIFORM LIFELINE" STRATEGY INSTEAD.
TUG
ぎゅっ
IT LET ME SHOOT MY GUN TWO-HANDED, WITHOUT LEAVING MY FOE AN OPENING.
I WAS SCARED. UNBELIEVABLY SCARED.
FOR A SECOND, I ADMIT, I EVEN WONDERED IF SUCH A CRAZY TACTIC WAS A GOOD IDEA. LIKE, MAYBE THERE WAS ANOTHER WAY...?

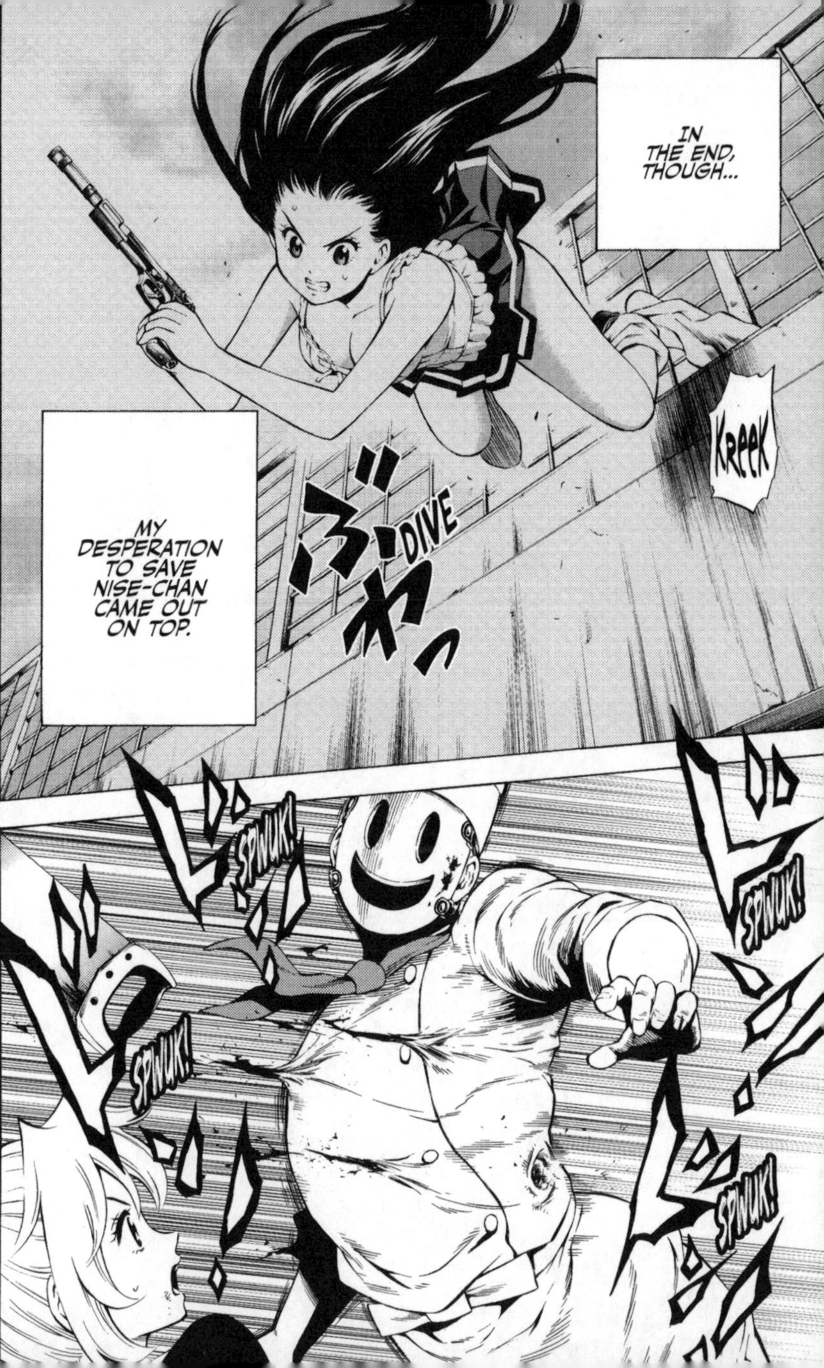
IN THE END, THOUGH...
Kreek
MY DESPERATION TO SAVE NISE-CHAN CAME OUT ON TOP.
ぶわっ
DIVE
SPWUK!
SPWUK!
SPWUK!
SPWUK!

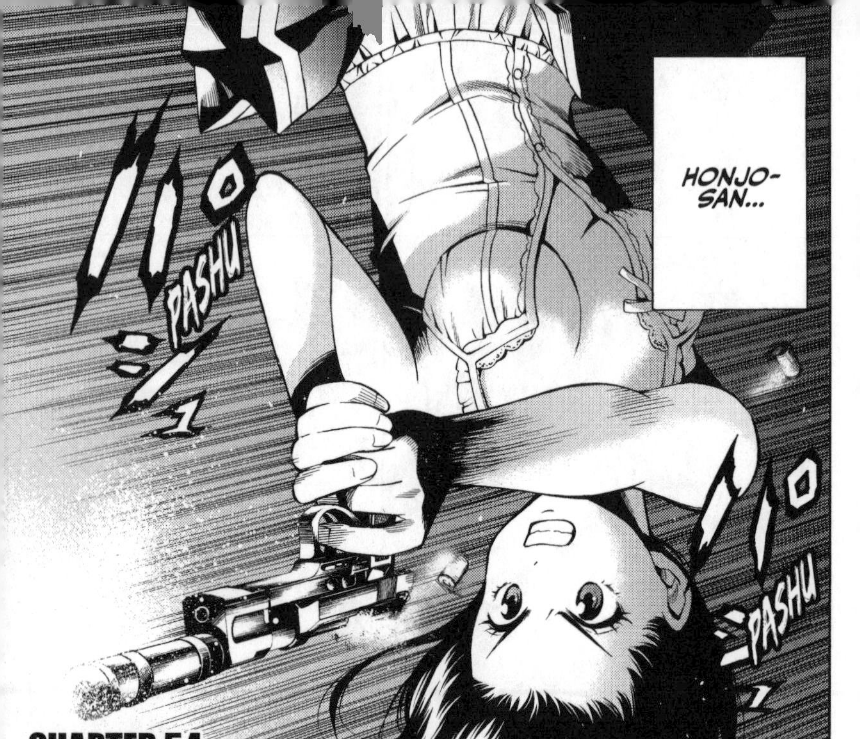
HONJO-SAN...
PASHU
PASHU

CHAPTER 54: The Thing Is...

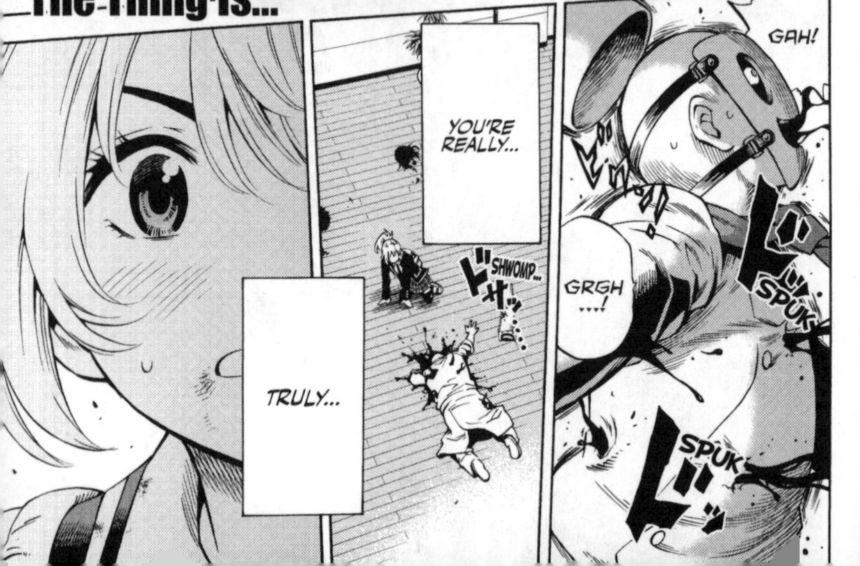
GAH!
SPUK
GRGH ...!
SPUK
YOU'RE REALLY...
SHWOMP...
TRULY...

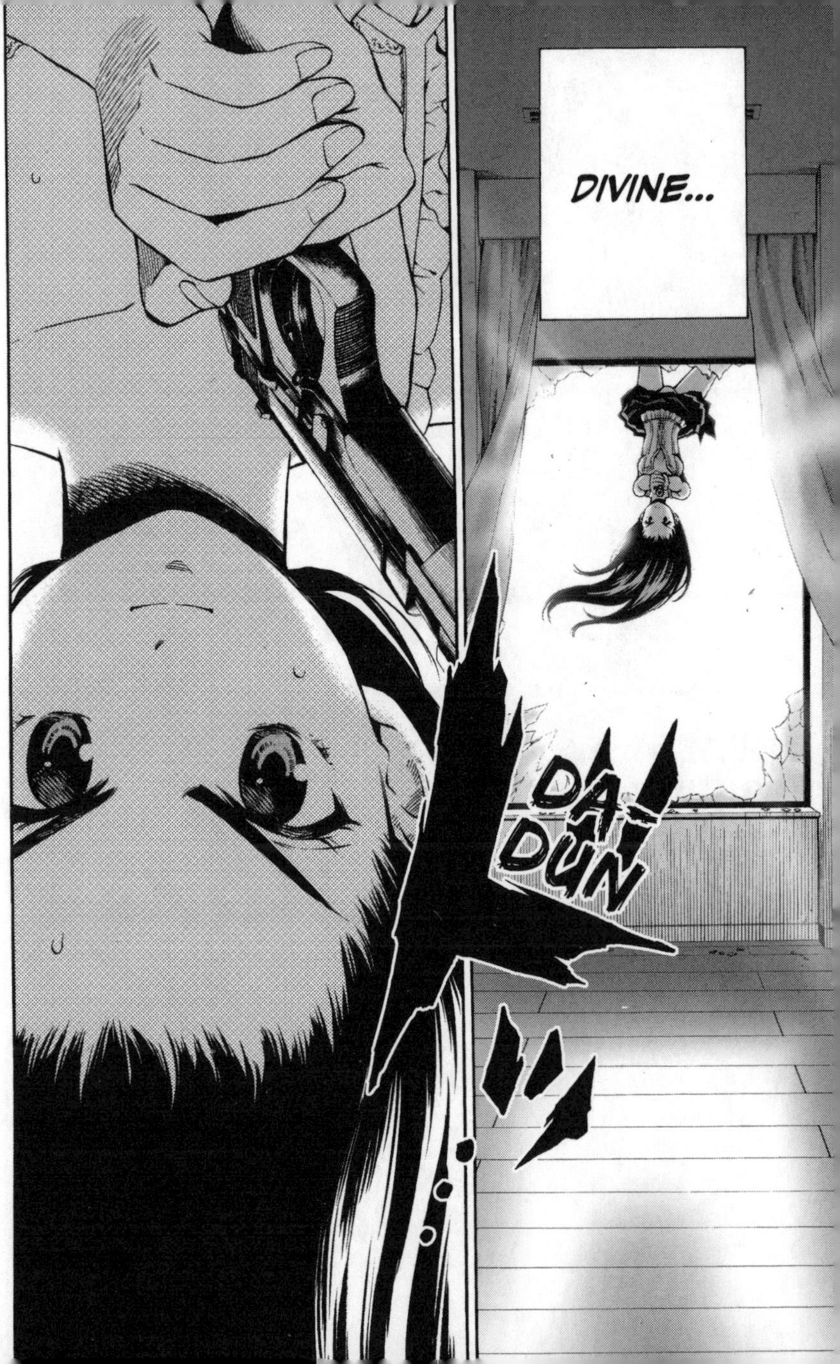
DIVINE...
DA DUN

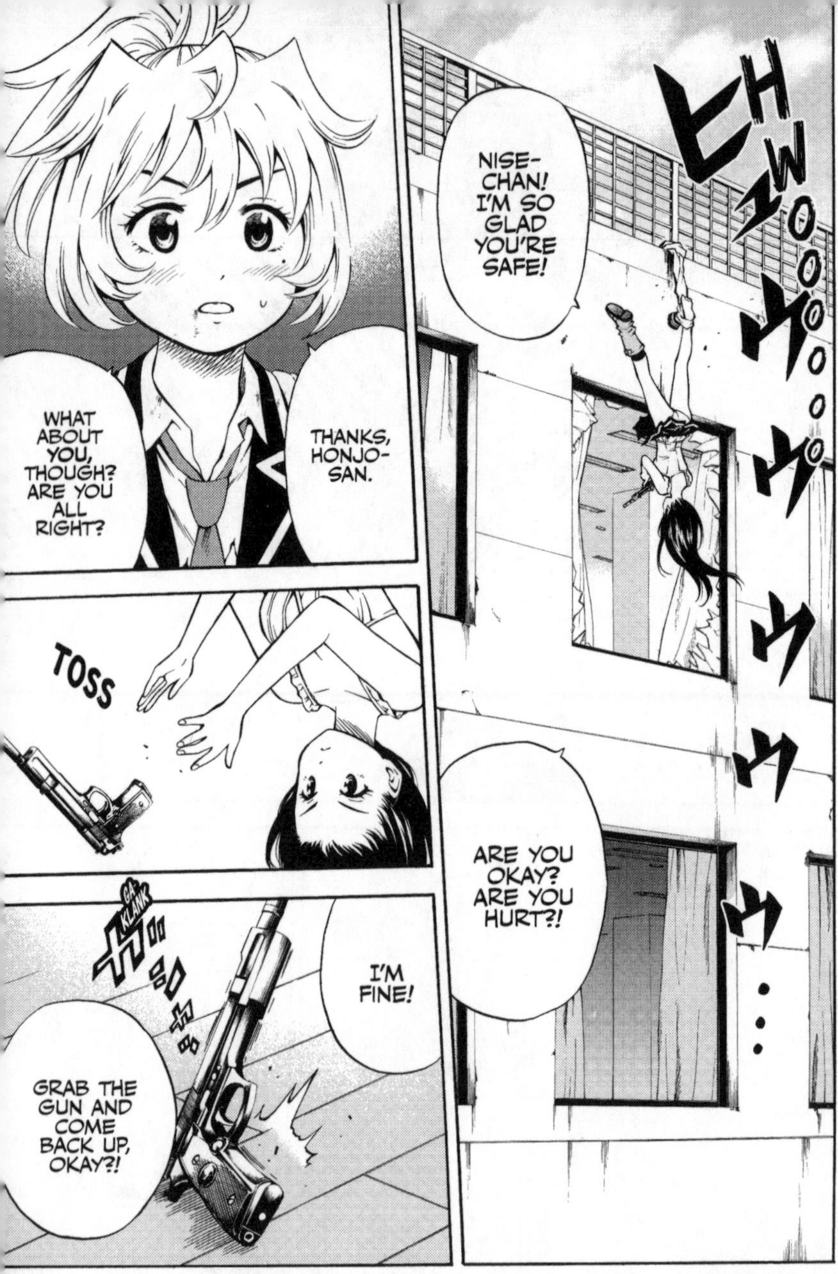
NISE-CHAN! I'M SO GLAD YOU'RE SAFE!
HWOOOOOOO
ARE YOU OKAY? ARE YOU HURT?!
THANKS, HONJO-SAN.
WHAT ABOUT YOU, THOUGH? ARE YOU ALL RIGHT?
TOSS
GA-KLANK
I'M FINE!
GRAB THE GUN AND COME BACK UP, OKAY?!

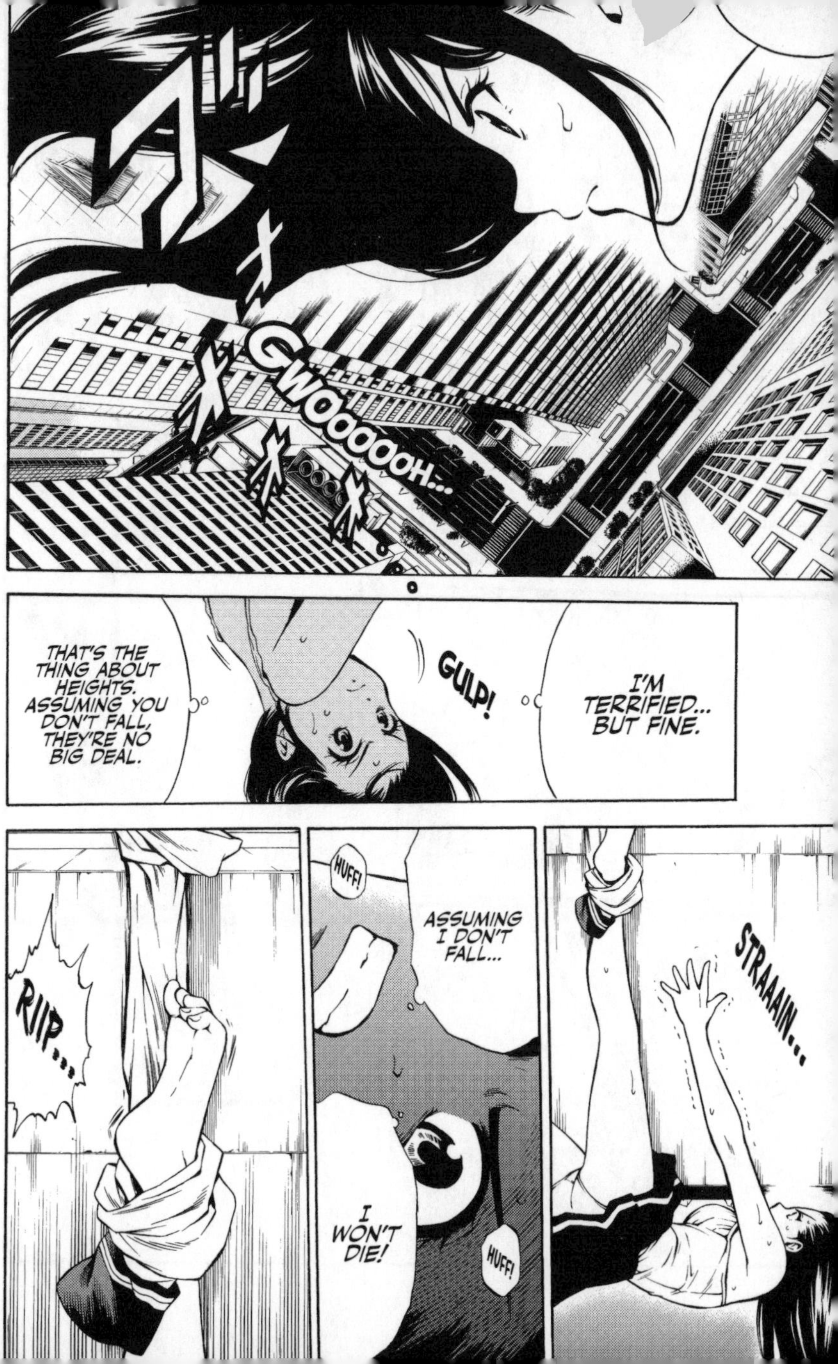
GWOOOOOOH...
I'M TERRIFIED... BUT FINE.
GULP!
THAT'S THE THING ABOUT HEIGHTS. ASSUMING YOU DON'T FALL, THEY'RE NO BIG DEAL.
STRAAAIN...
HUFF!
ASSUMING I DON'T FALL...
I WON'T DIE!
HUFF!
RIIP...

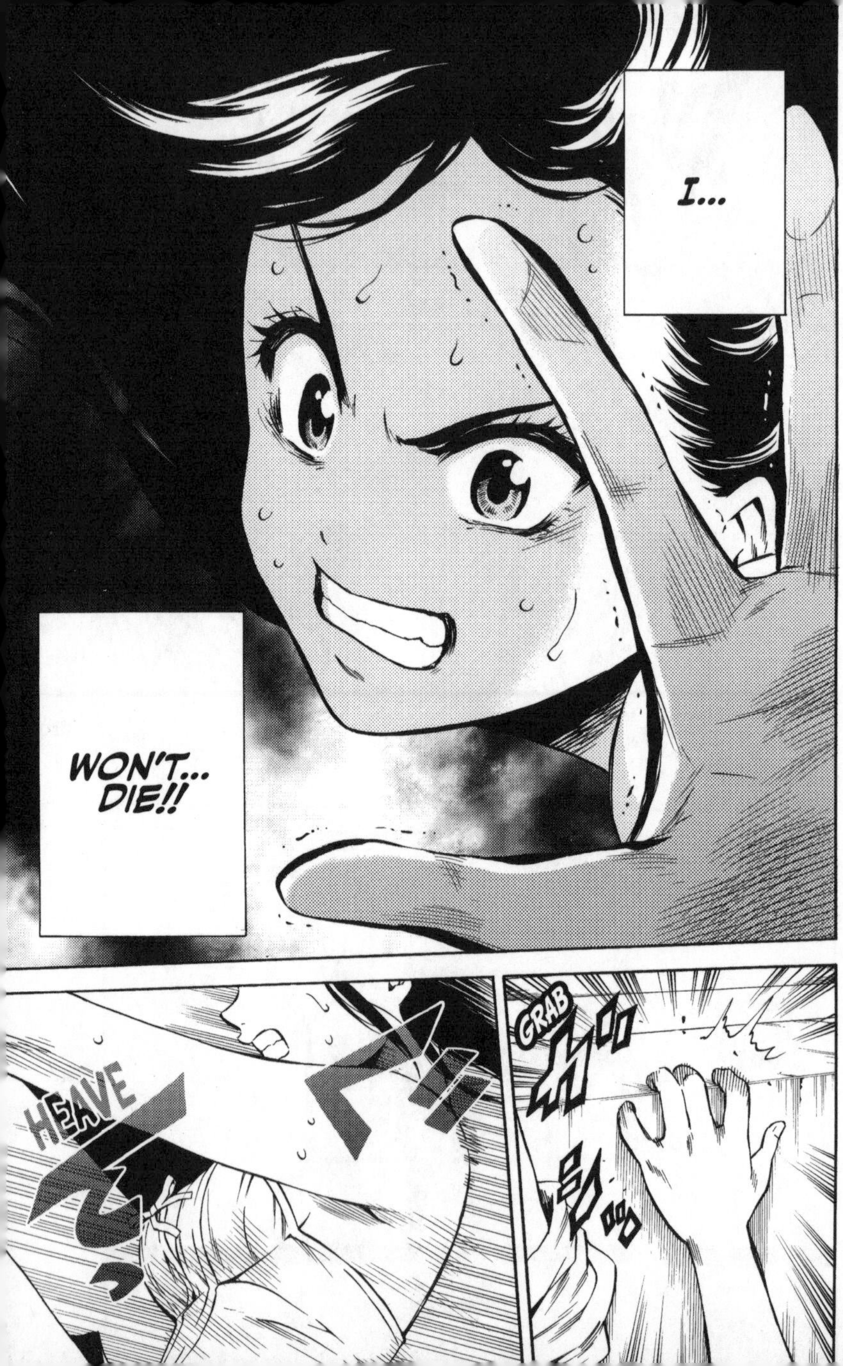
I...
WON'T... DIE!!
GRAB
HEAVE

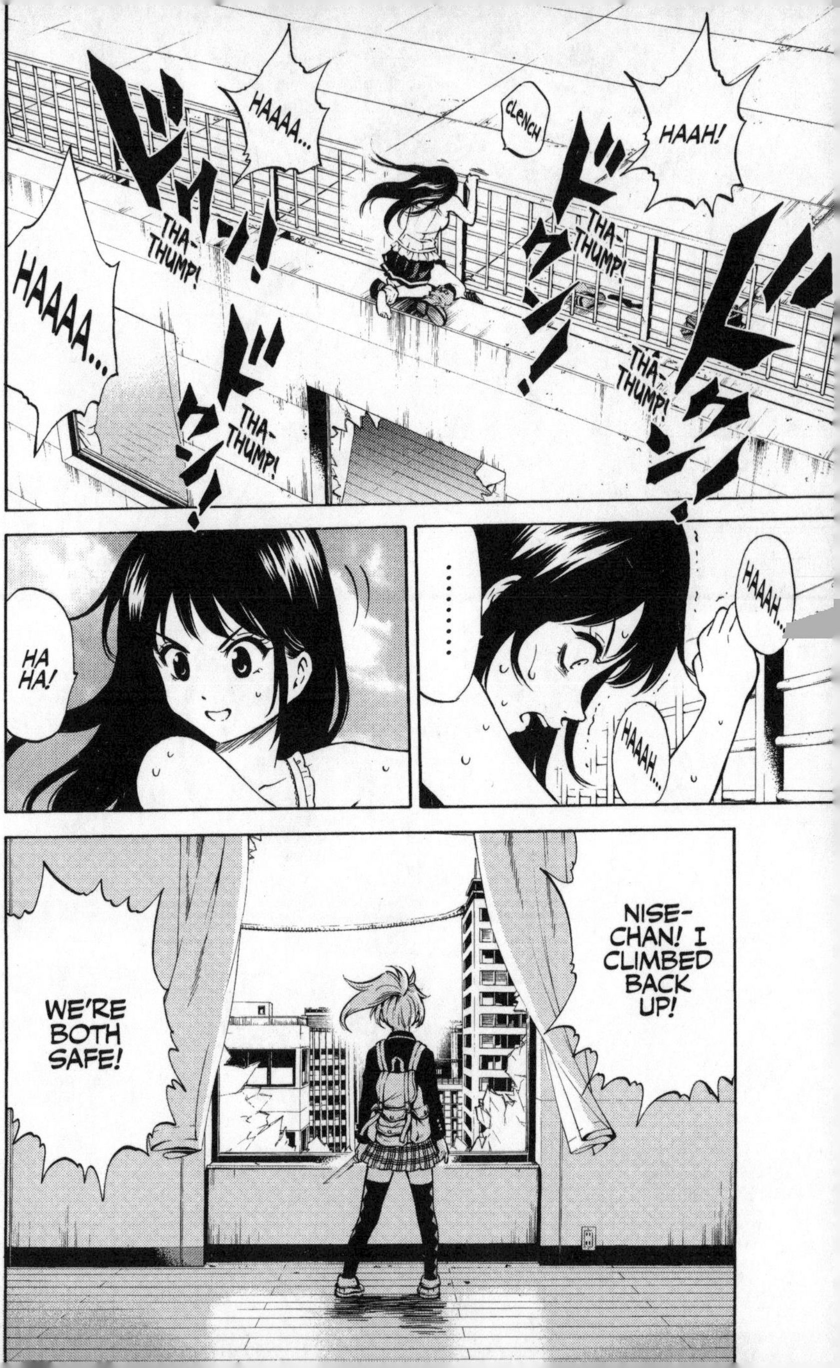
HAAH!
THA-THUMP!
THA-THUMP!
CLENCH
HAAAA...
THA-THUMP!
HAAAA...
THA-THUMP!
HAAAH...
......
HAAAH...
HA HA!
NISE-CHAN! I CLIMBED BACK UP!
WE'RE BOTH SAFE!

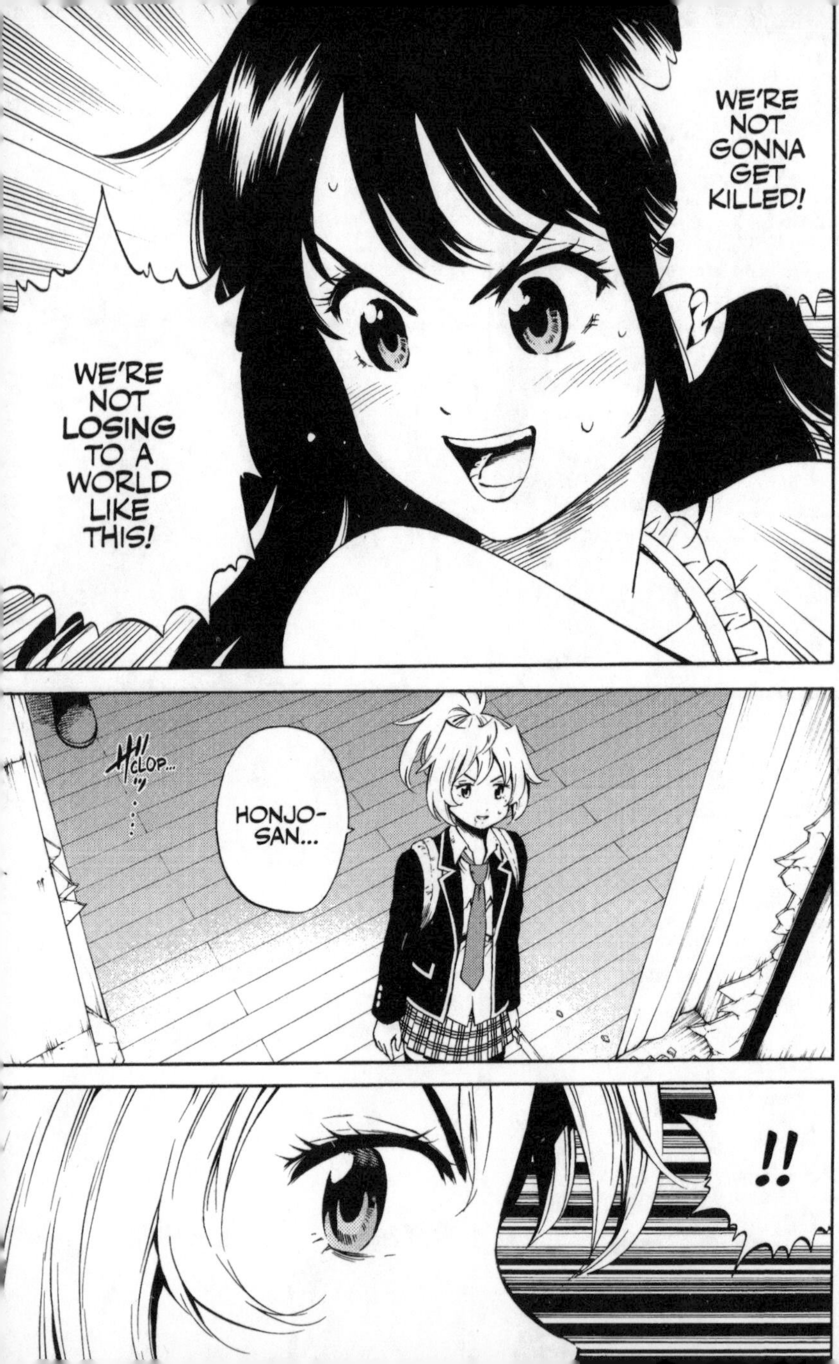
WE'RE NOT GONNA GET KILLED!
WE'RE NOT LOSING TO A WORLD LIKE THIS!
HONJO-SAN...
CLOP...
!!

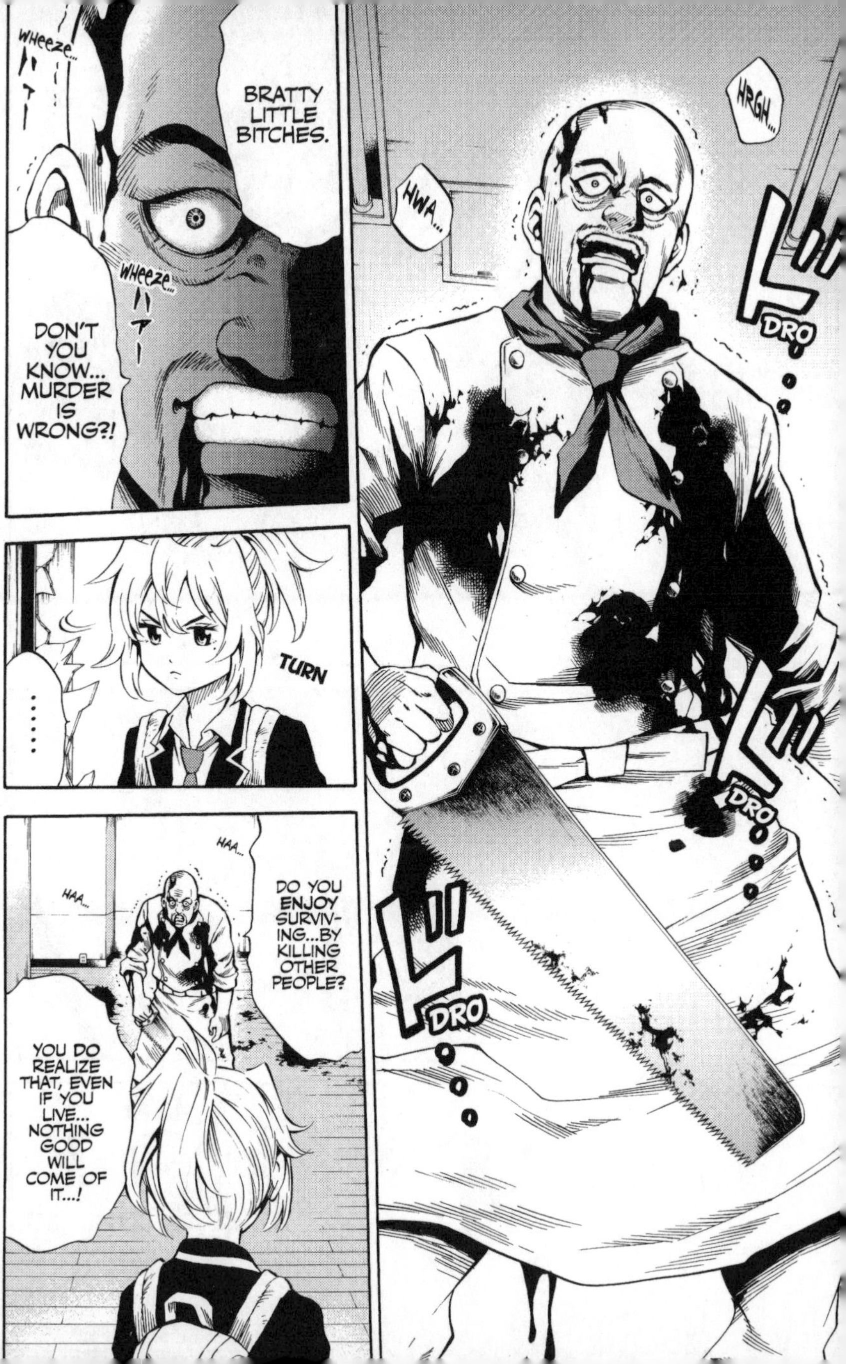
HRGH...
HWA...
DRO
DRO
DRO
wheeze...
BRATTY LITTLE BITCHES.
wheeze...
DON'T YOU KNOW... MURDER IS WRONG?!
TURN
......
HAA...
HAA...
DO YOU ENJOY SURVIVING...BY KILLING OTHER PEOPLE?
YOU DO REALIZE THAT, EVEN IF YOU LIVE... NOTHING GOOD WILL COME OF IT...!

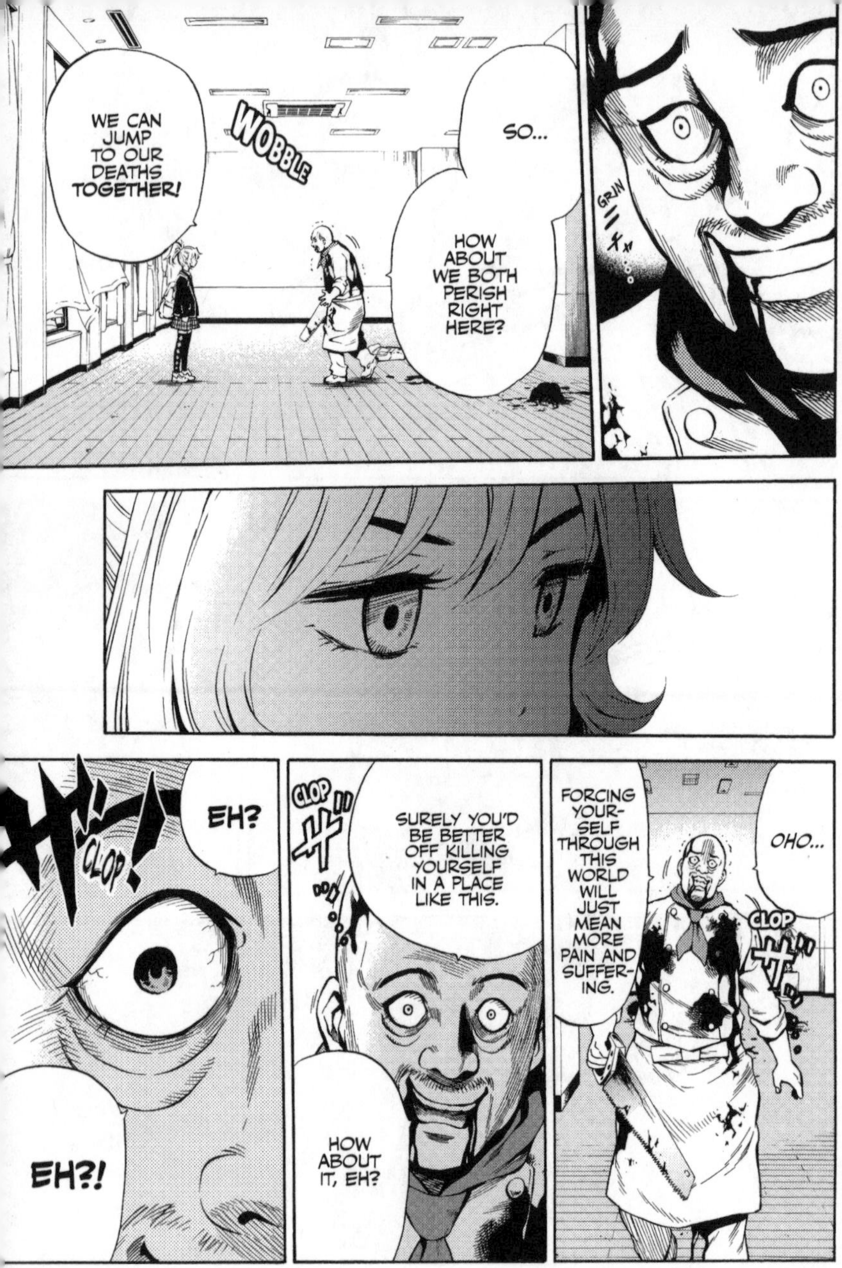
GRIN
SO...
HOW ABOUT WE BOTH PERISH RIGHT HERE?
WOBBLE
WE CAN JUMP TO OUR DEATHS TOGETHER!
OHO...
FORCING YOUR-SELF THROUGH THIS WORLD WILL JUST MEAN MORE PAIN AND SUFFER-ING.
CLOP
SURELY YOU'D BE BETTER OFF KILLING YOURSELF IN A PLACE LIKE THIS.
CLOP
HOW ABOUT IT, EH?
EH?
CLOP!
EH?!

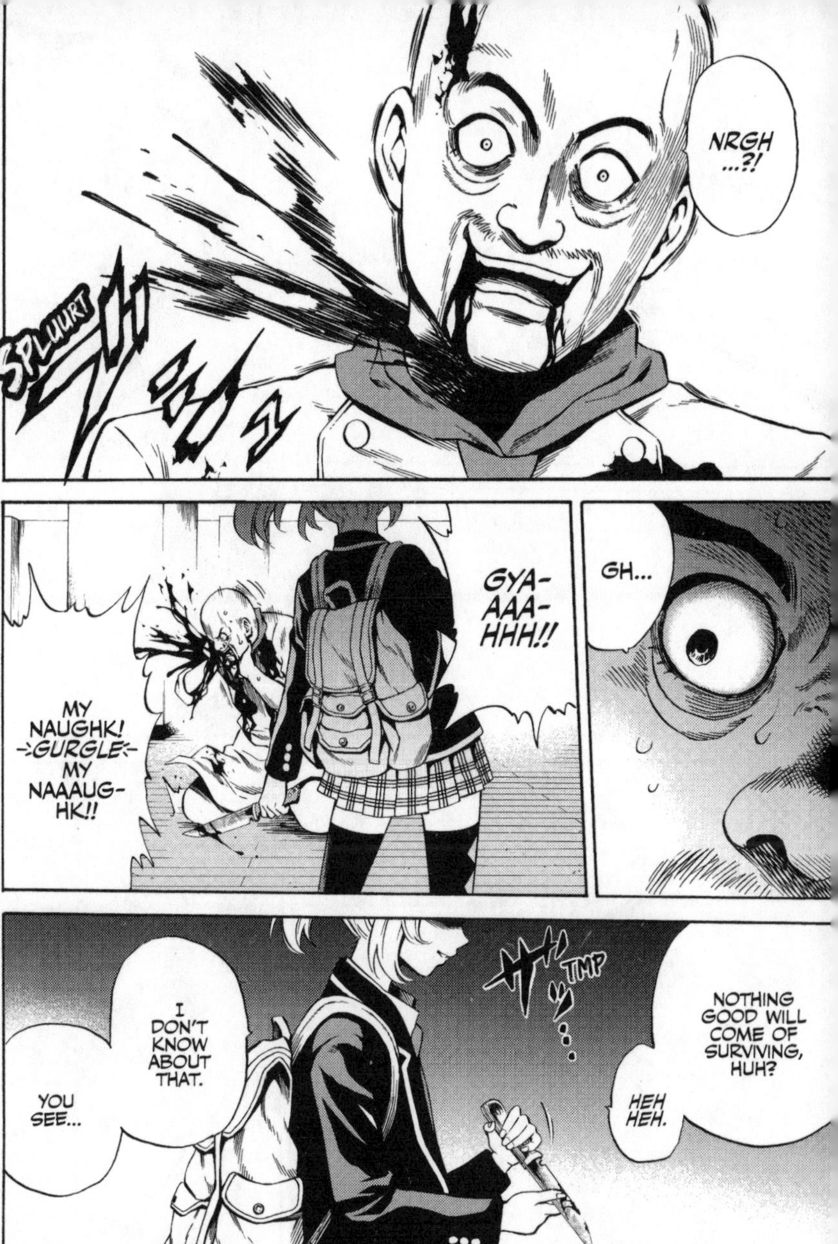
NRGH ...?!
SPLUURT
GH...
GYA-AAA-HHH!!
MY NAUGHK! -GURGLE- MY NAAAUGH-HK!!
NOTHING GOOD WILL COME OF SURVIVING, HUH?
HEH HEH.
TMP
I DON'T KNOW ABOUT THAT.
YOU SEE...

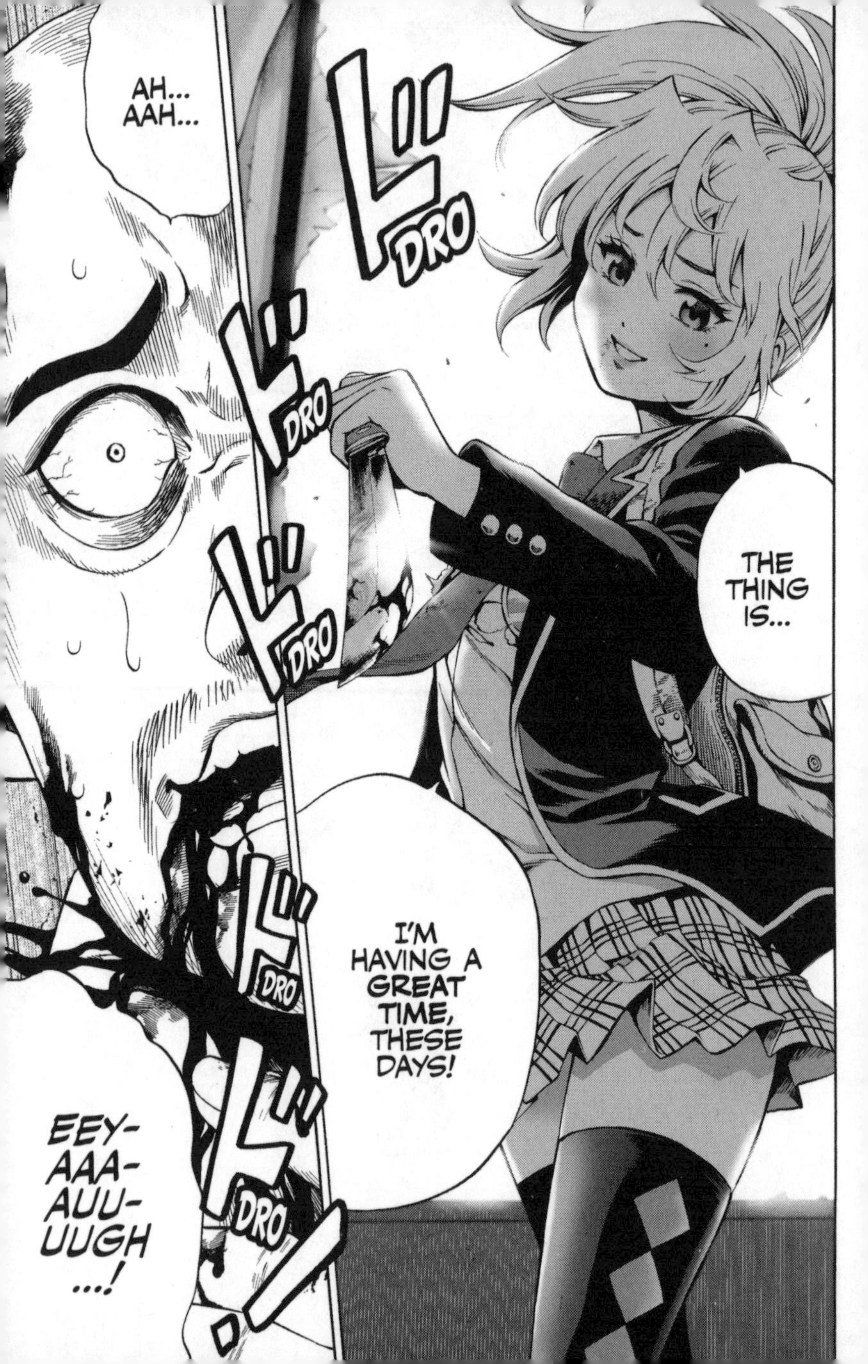
AH... AAH...
DRO
DRO
DRO
THE THING IS...
I'M HAVING A GREAT TIME, THESE DAYS!
DRO
DRO
EEY-AAA-AUU-UUGH...!

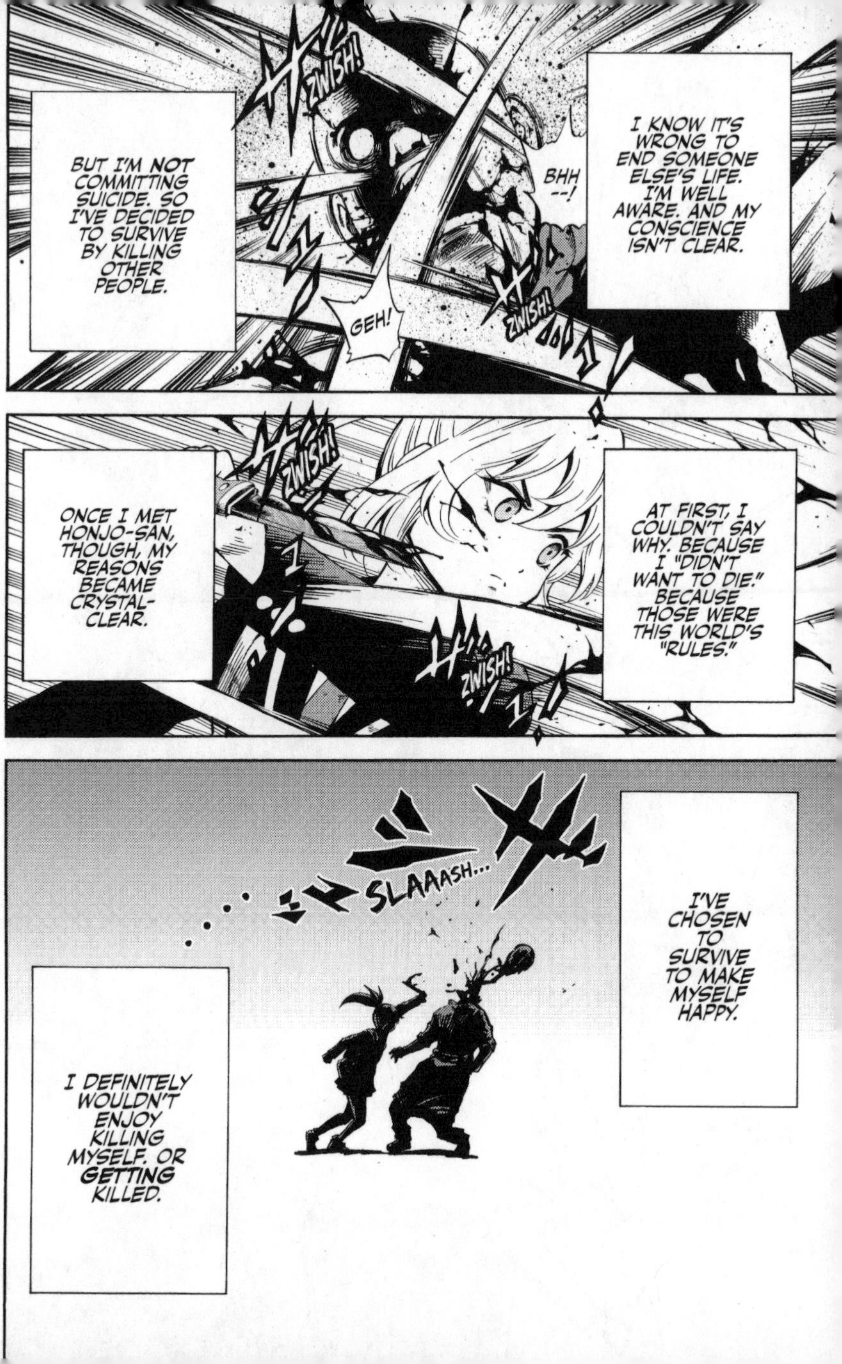
I KNOW IT'S WRONG TO END SOMEONE ELSE'S LIFE. I'M WELL AWARE. AND MY CONSCIENCE ISN'T CLEAR.
ZWISH!
BHH--!
ZWISH!
GEH!
BUT I'M NOT COMMITTING SUICIDE. SO I'VE DECIDED TO SURVIVE BY KILLING OTHER PEOPLE.
AT FIRST, I COULDN'T SAY WHY. BECAUSE I "DIDN'T WANT TO DIE." BECAUSE THOSE WERE THIS WORLD'S "RULES."
ZWISH!
ZWISH!
ONCE I MET HONJO-SAN, THOUGH, MY REASONS BECAME CRYSTAL-CLEAR.
I'VE CHOSEN TO SURVIVE TO MAKE MYSELF HAPPY.
SLAAASH...
I DEFINITELY WOULDN'T ENJOY KILLING MYSELF. OR GETTING KILLED.

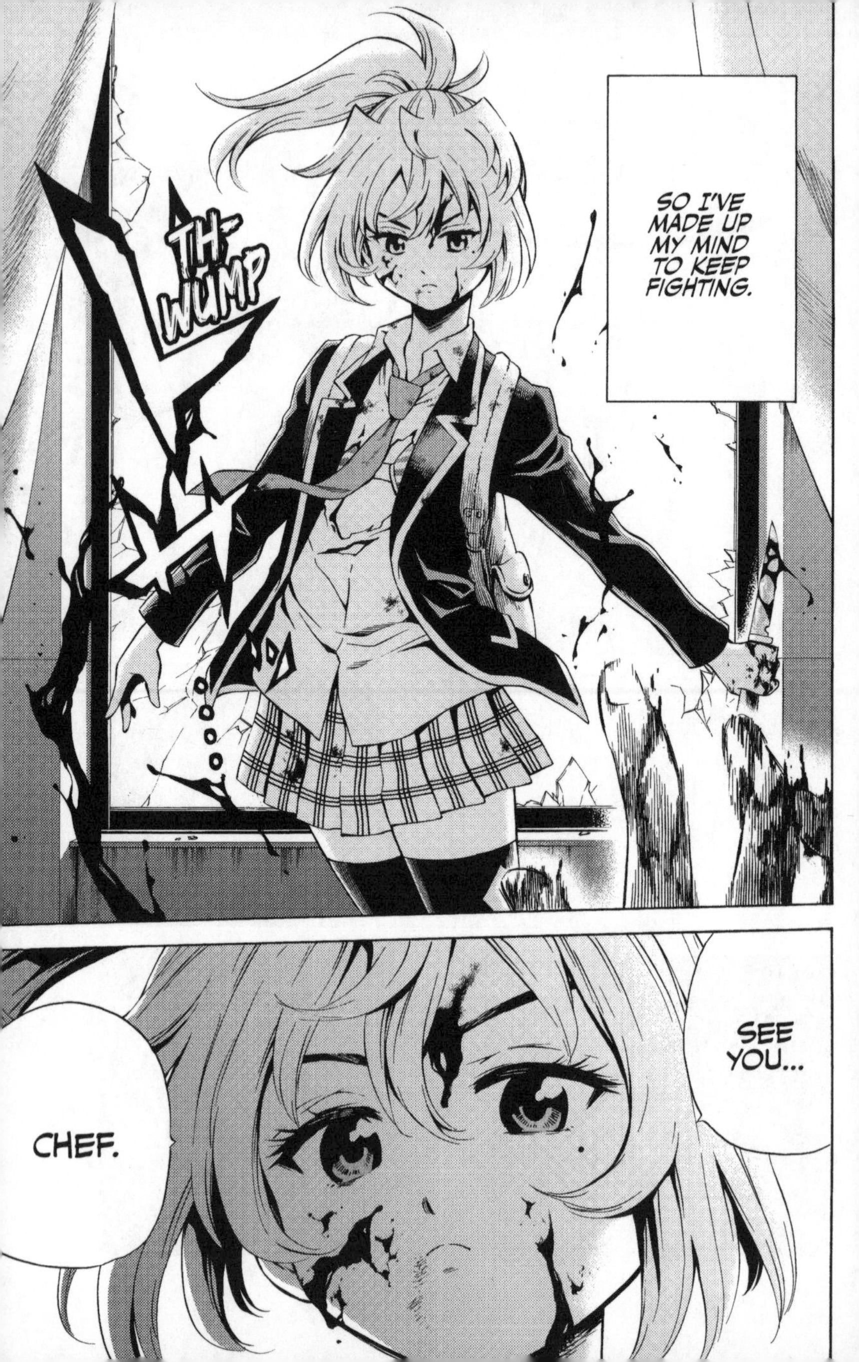
SO I'VE MADE UP MY MIND TO KEEP FIGHTING.
TH-WUMP
SEE YOU...
CHEF.

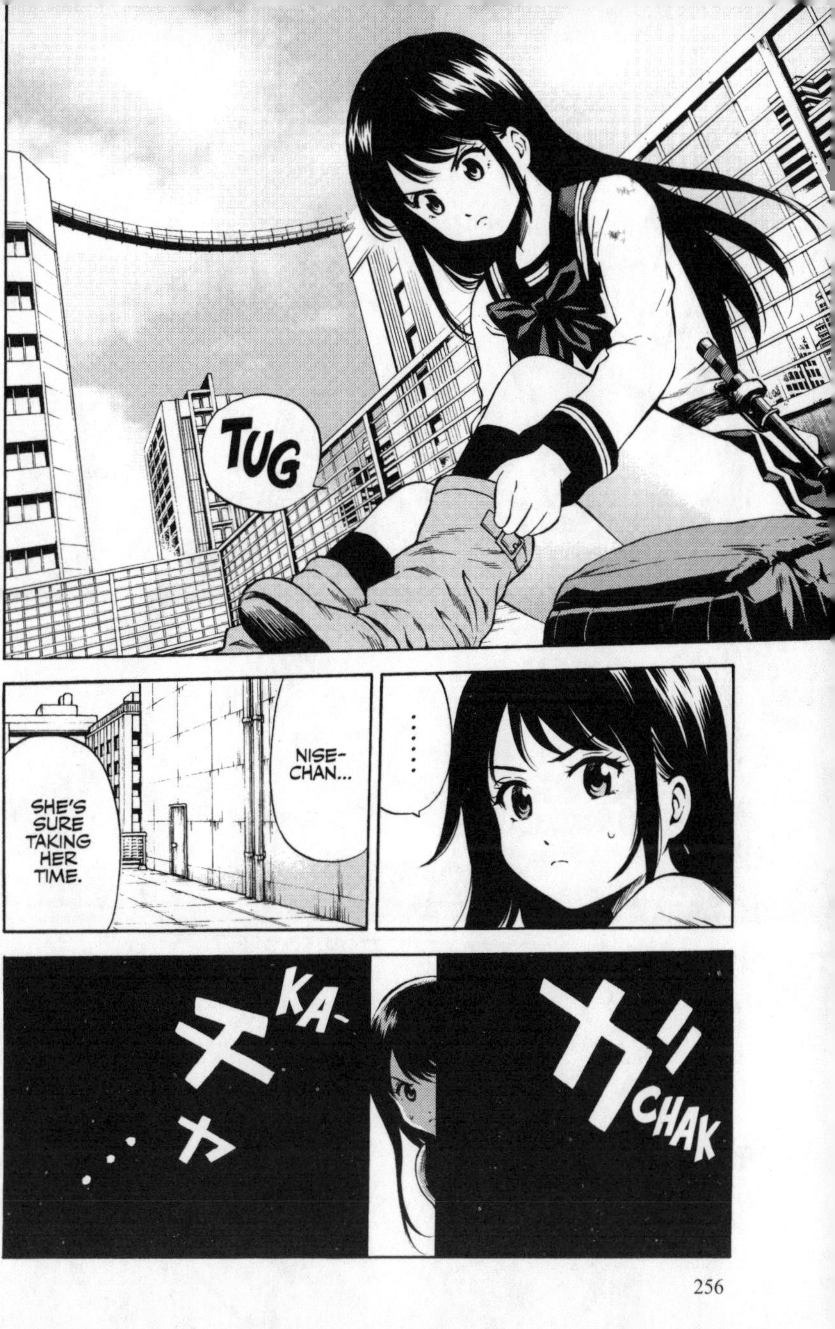
TUG
......
NISE-CHAN...
SHE'S SURE TAKING HER TIME.
KA-
CHAK

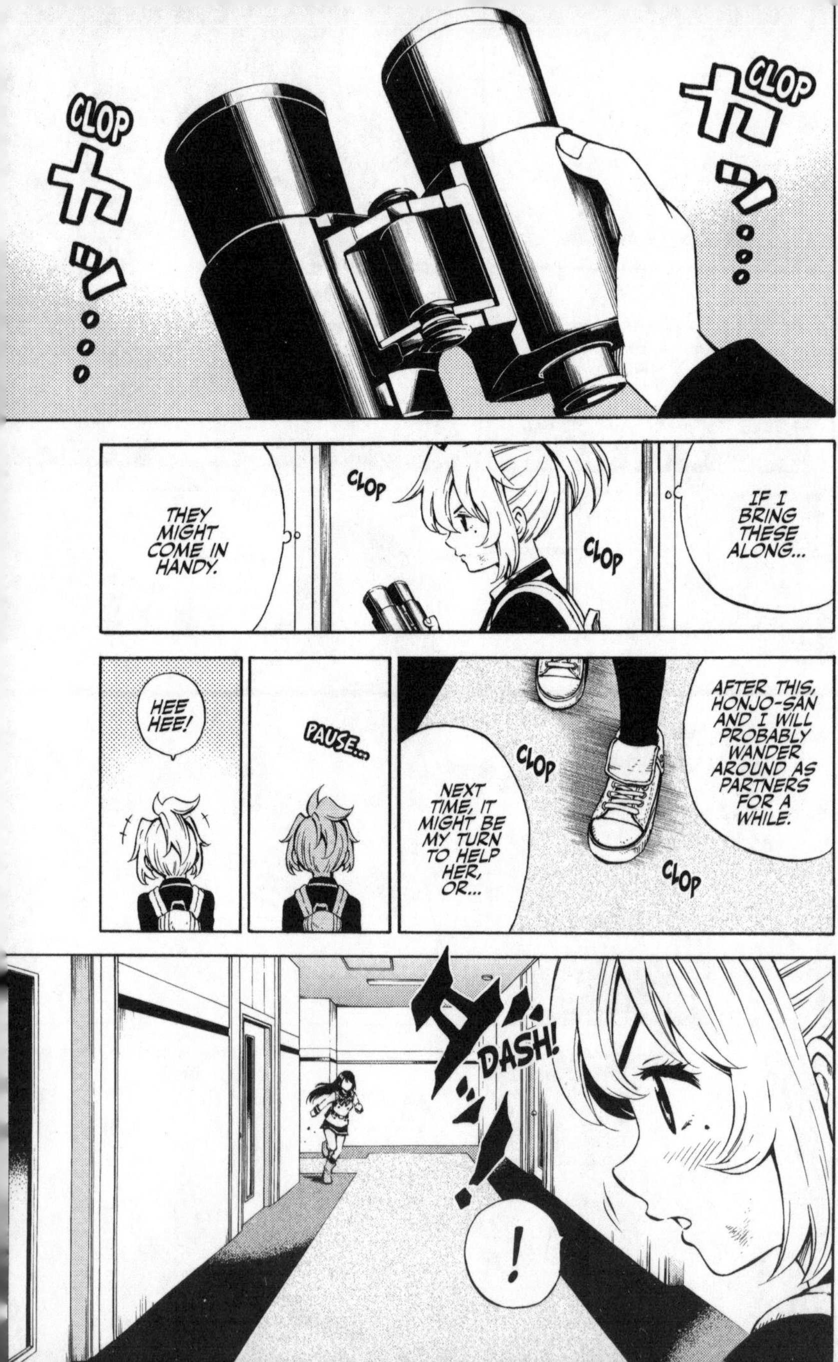
CLOP
カッ…
CLOP
カッ…
IF I BRING THESE ALONG...
CLOP
CLOP
THEY MIGHT COME IN HANDY.
AFTER THIS, HONJO-SAN AND I WILL PROBABLY WANDER AROUND AS PARTNERS FOR A WHILE.
CLOP
CLOP
NEXT TIME, IT MIGHT BE MY TURN TO HELP HER, OR...
PAUSE...
HEE HEE!
DASH!
!

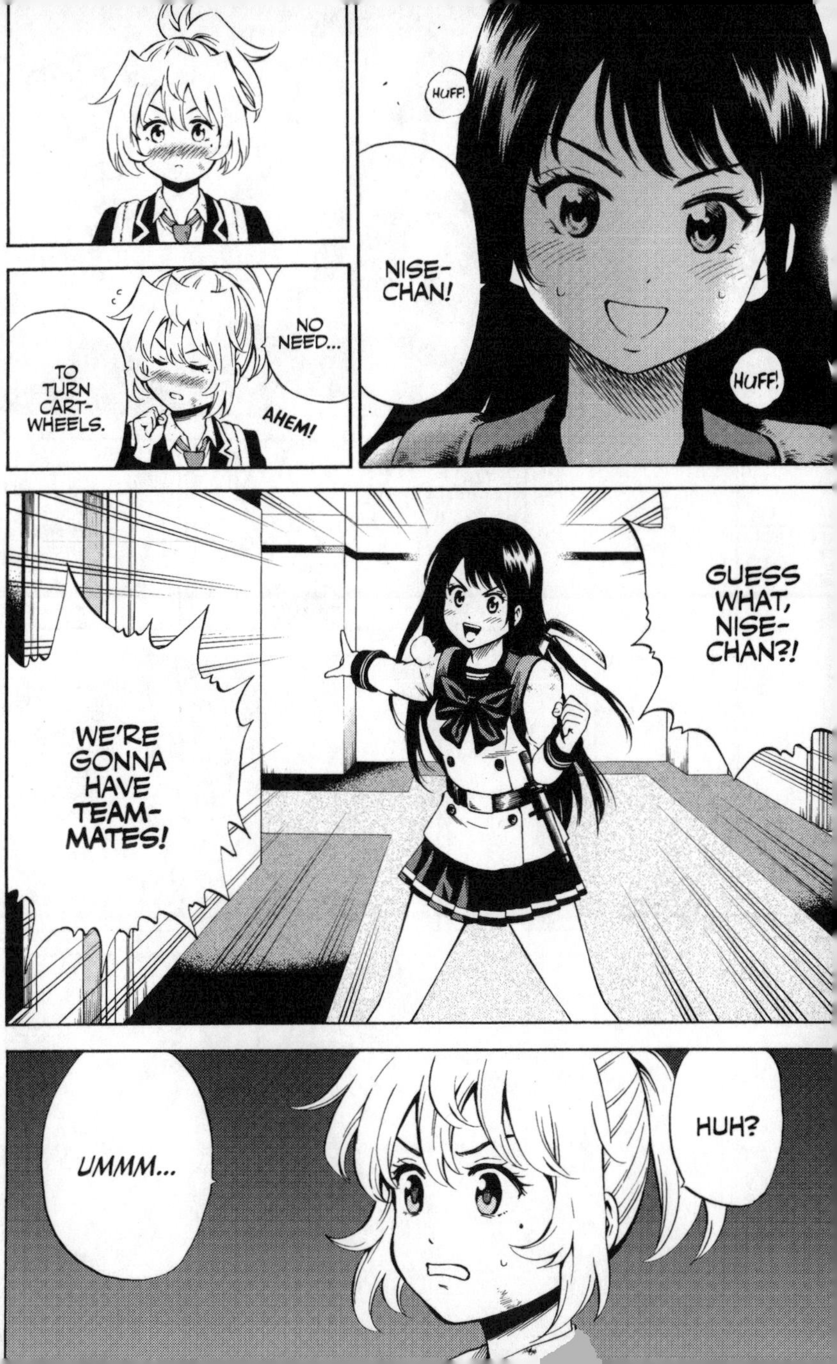
HUFF!
NISE-CHAN!
HUFF!
NO NEED...
TO TURN CART-WHEELS.
AHEM!
GUESS WHAT, NISE-CHAN?!
WE'RE GONNA HAVE TEAM-MATES!
HUH?
UMMM...

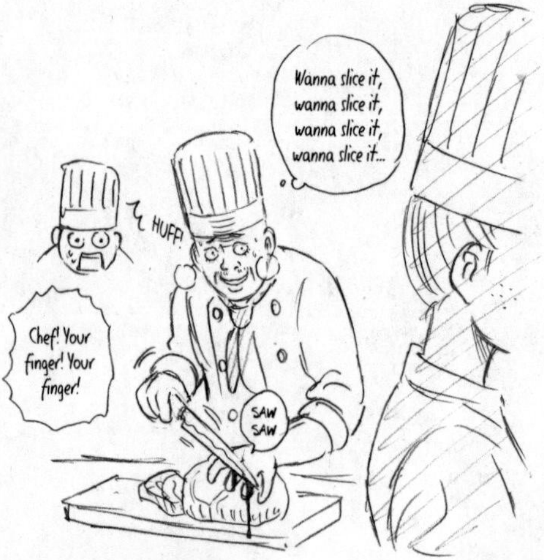
Wanna slice it, wanna slice it, wanna slice it, wanna slice it...
HUFF!
SAW SAW
Chef! Your finger! Your finger!

HIGH-RISE INVASION

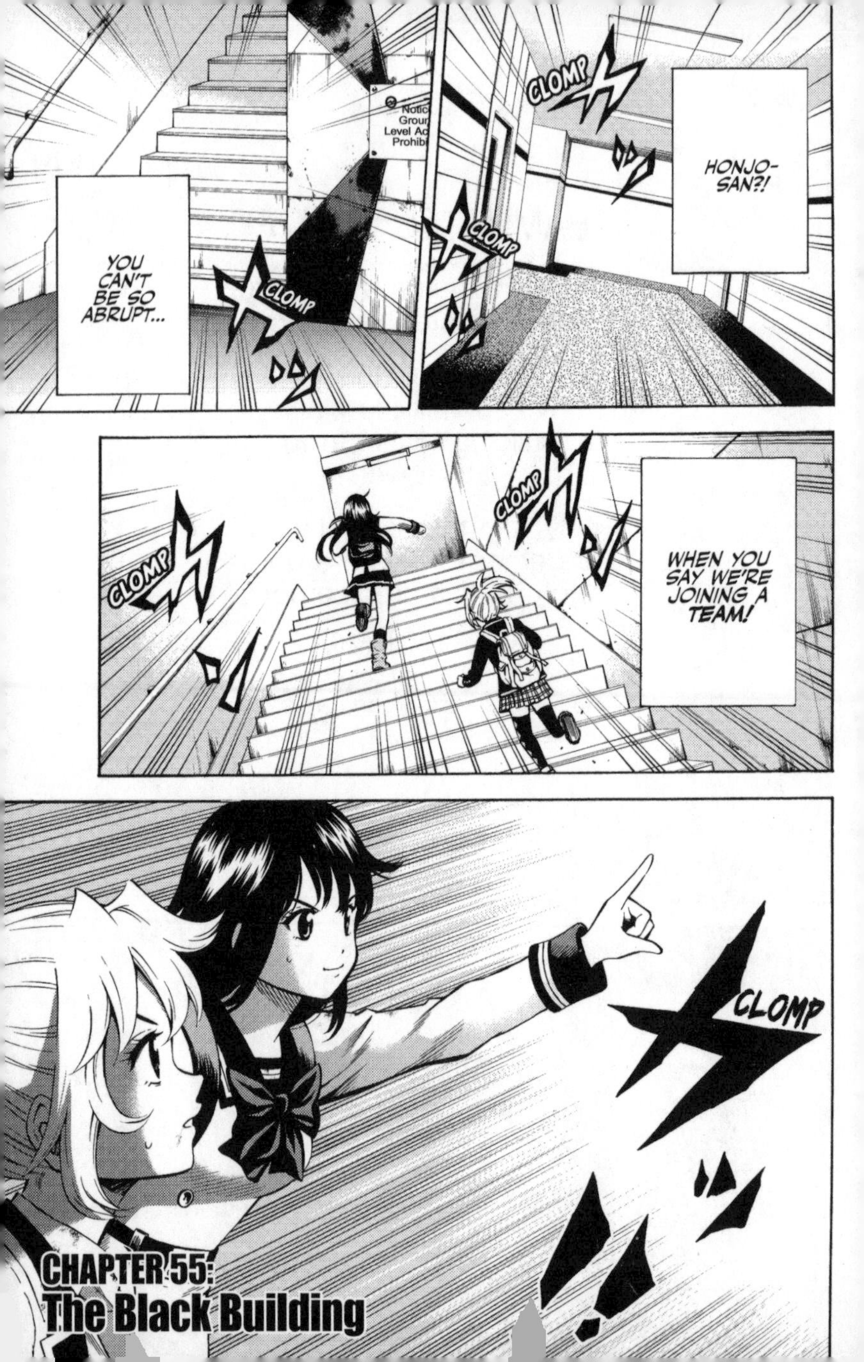
CLOMP
CLOMP
HONJO-SAN?!
CLOMP
YOU CAN'T BE SO ABRUPT...
WHEN YOU SAY WE'RE JOINING A TEAM!
CLOMP
CLOMP
CLOMP
CHAPTER 55:
The Black Building

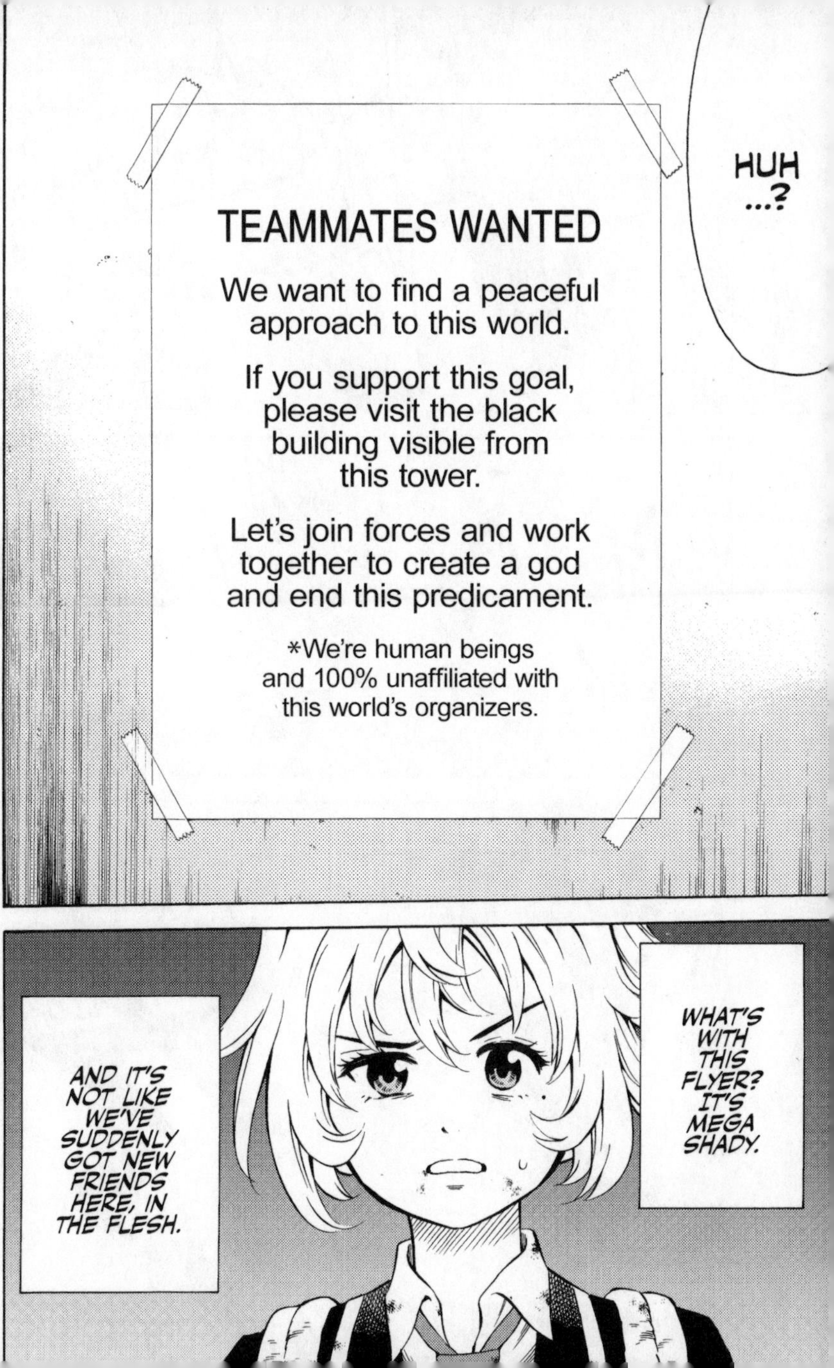
HUH ...?
TEAMMATES WANTED
We want to find a peaceful approach to this world.
If you support this goal, please visit the black building visible from this tower.
Let's join forces and work together to create a god and end this predicament.
*We're human beings and 100% unaffiliated with this world's organizers.
WHAT'S WITH THIS FLYER? IT'S MEGA SHADY.
AND IT'S NOT LIKE WE'VE SUDDENLY GOT NEW FRIENDS HERE, IN THE FLESH.

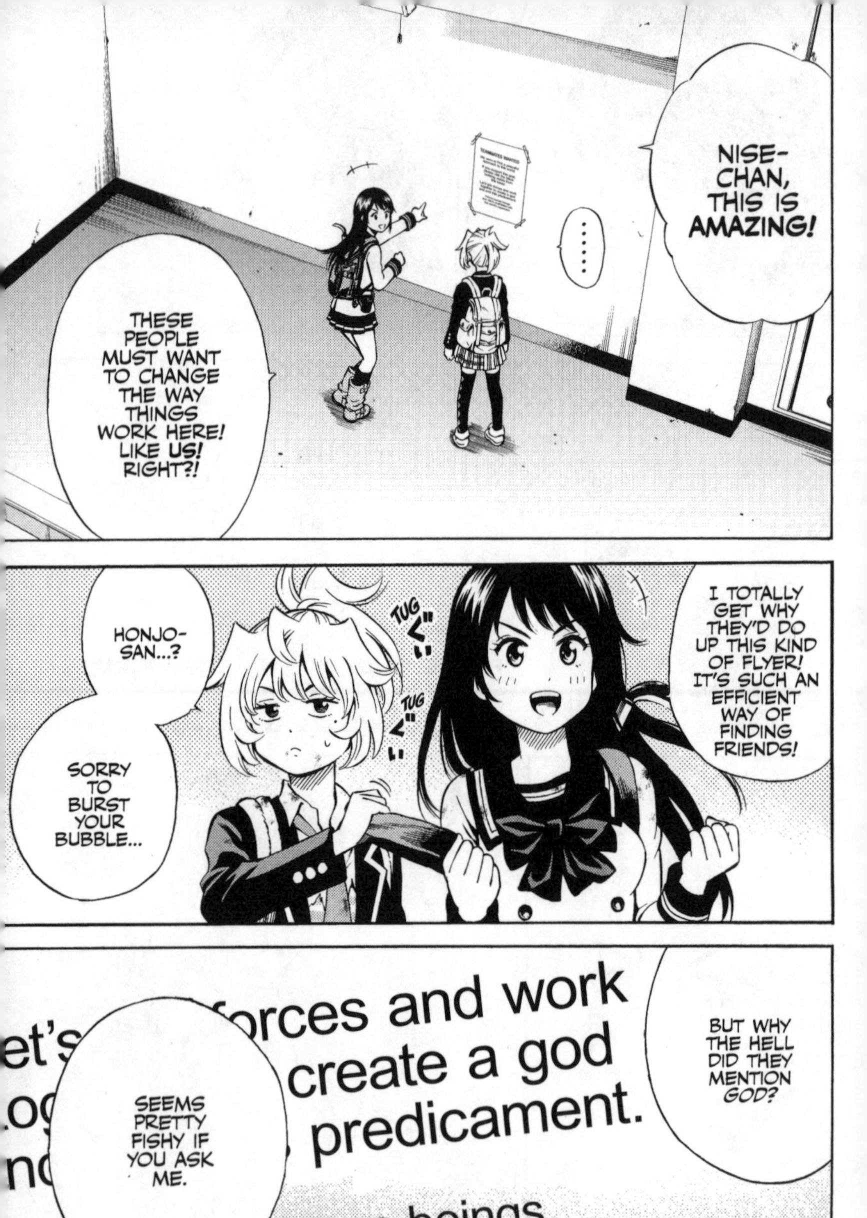
NISE-CHAN, THIS IS AMAZING!
......
THESE PEOPLE MUST WANT TO CHANGE THE WAY THINGS WORK HERE! LIKE US! RIGHT?!
I TOTALLY GET WHY THEY'D DO UP THIS KIND OF FLYER! IT'S SUCH AN EFFICIENT WAY OF FINDING FRIENDS!
TUG
TUG
HONJO-SAN...?
SORRY TO BURST YOUR BUBBLE...
BUT WHY THE HELL DID THEY MENTION *GOD*?
forces and work
create a god
predicament.
human beings
SEEMS PRETTY FISHY IF YOU ASK ME.

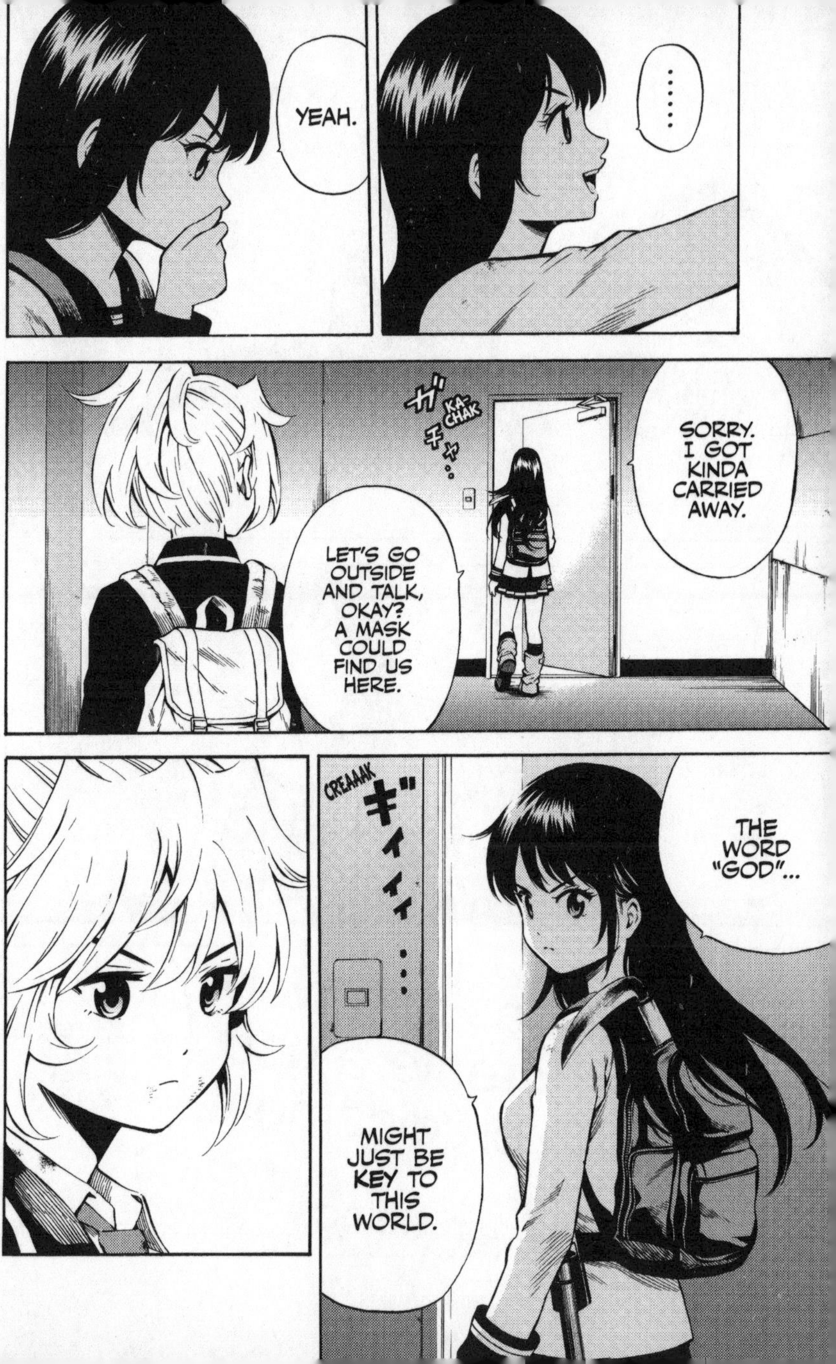
……
YEAH.
SORRY. I GOT KINDA CARRIED AWAY.
ガチャ
KA-CHAK
LET'S GO OUTSIDE AND TALK, OKAY? A MASK COULD FIND US HERE.
THE WORD "GOD"...
CREAAAK
ギィィィ…
MIGHT JUST BE KEY TO THIS WORLD.

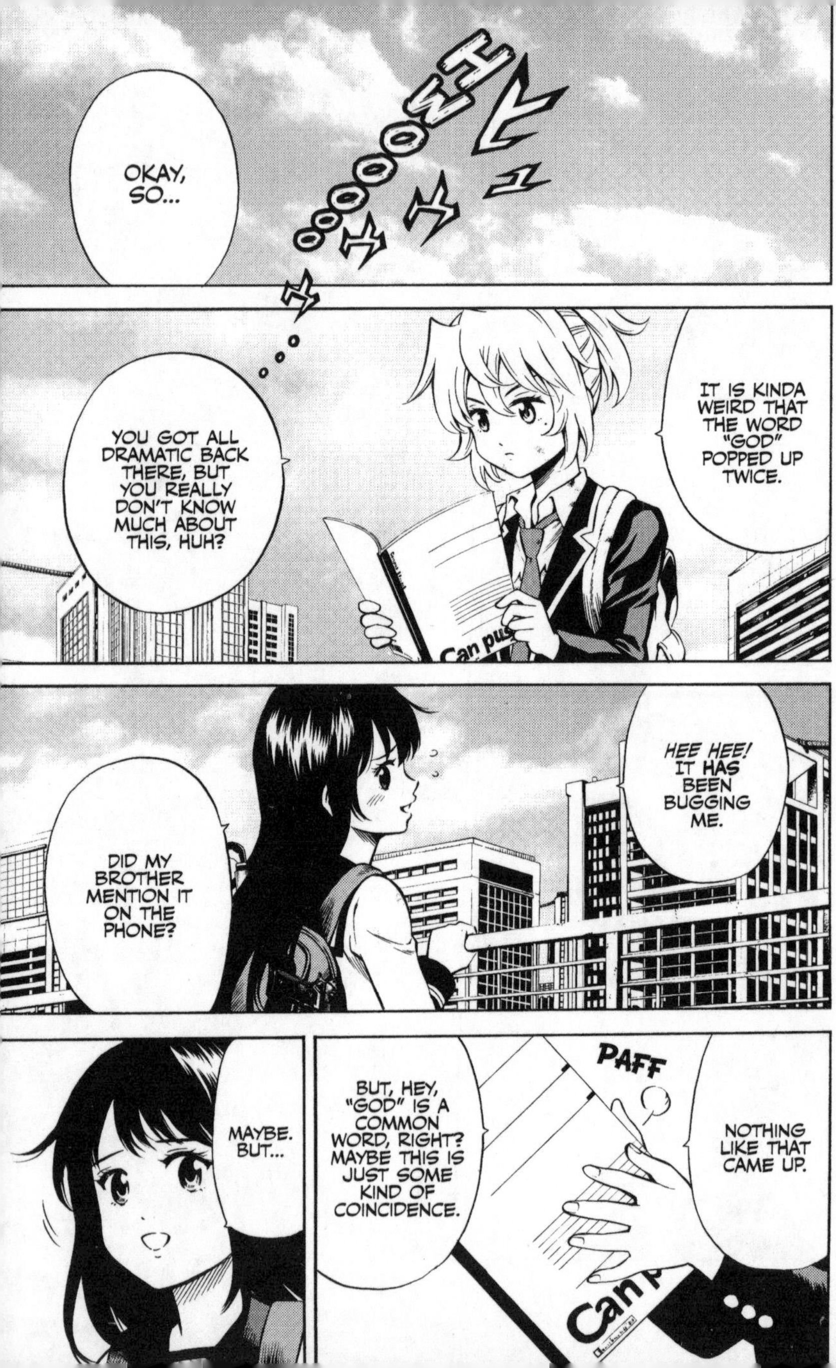
HWOOOOO...
ヒュウウウ
OKAY, SO...
IT IS KINDA WEIRD THAT THE WORD "GOD" POPPED UP TWICE.
YOU GOT ALL DRAMATIC BACK THERE, BUT YOU REALLY DON'T KNOW MUCH ABOUT THIS, HUH?
Can pus
HEE HEE! IT HAS BEEN BUGGING ME.
DID MY BROTHER MENTION IT ON THE PHONE?
NOTHING LIKE THAT CAME UP.
PAFF
BUT, HEY, "GOD" IS A COMMON WORD, RIGHT? MAYBE THIS IS JUST SOME KIND OF COINCIDENCE.
Can p
MAYBE. BUT...

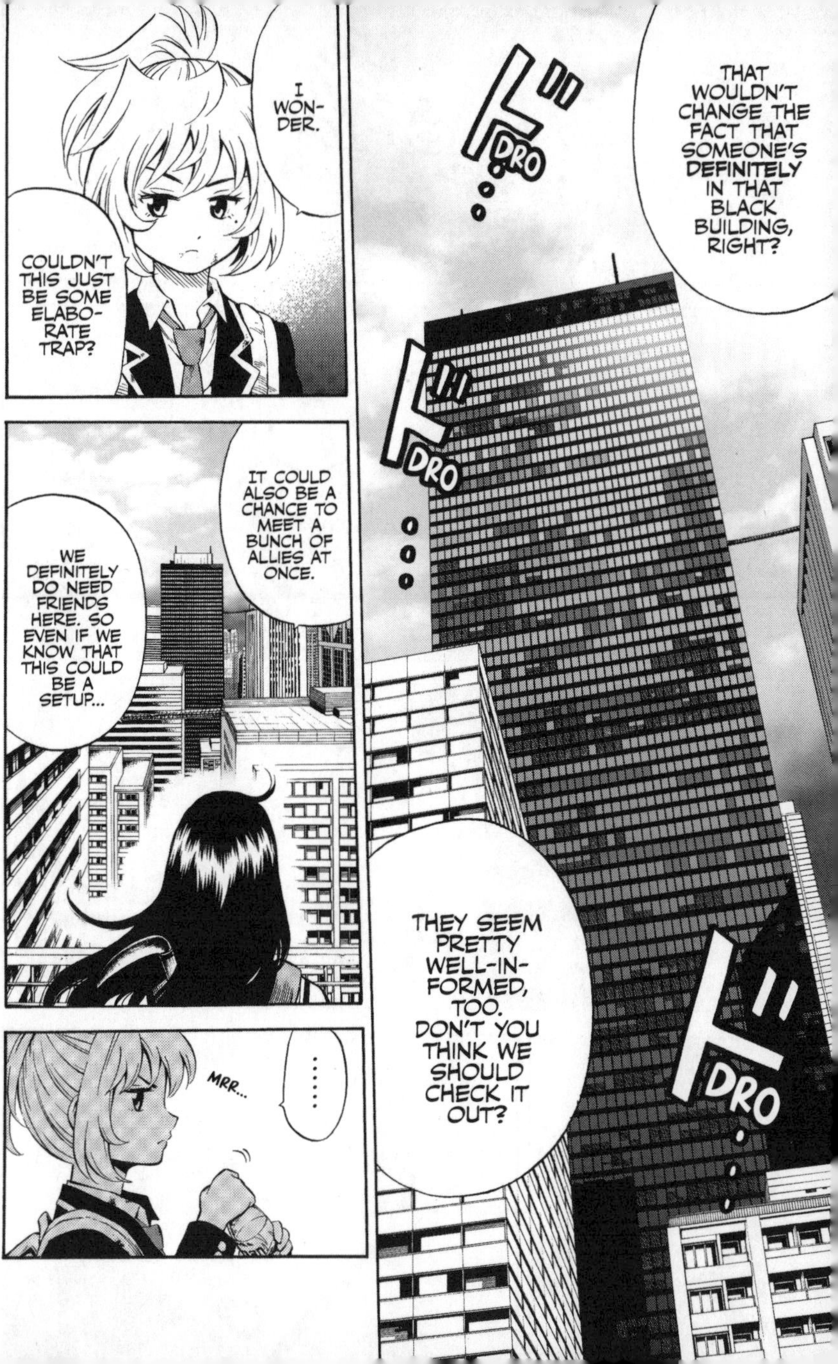
THAT WOULDN'T CHANGE THE FACT THAT SOMEONE'S DEFINITELY IN THAT BLACK BUILDING, RIGHT?
DRO...
DRO...
DRO...
THEY SEEM PRETTY WELL-INFORMED, TOO. DON'T YOU THINK WE SHOULD CHECK IT OUT?
I WONDER.
COULDN'T THIS JUST BE SOME ELABORATE TRAP?
IT COULD ALSO BE A CHANCE TO MEET A BUNCH OF ALLIES AT ONCE.
WE DEFINITELY DO NEED FRIENDS HERE. SO EVEN IF WE KNOW THAT THIS COULD BE A SETUP...
......
MRR...

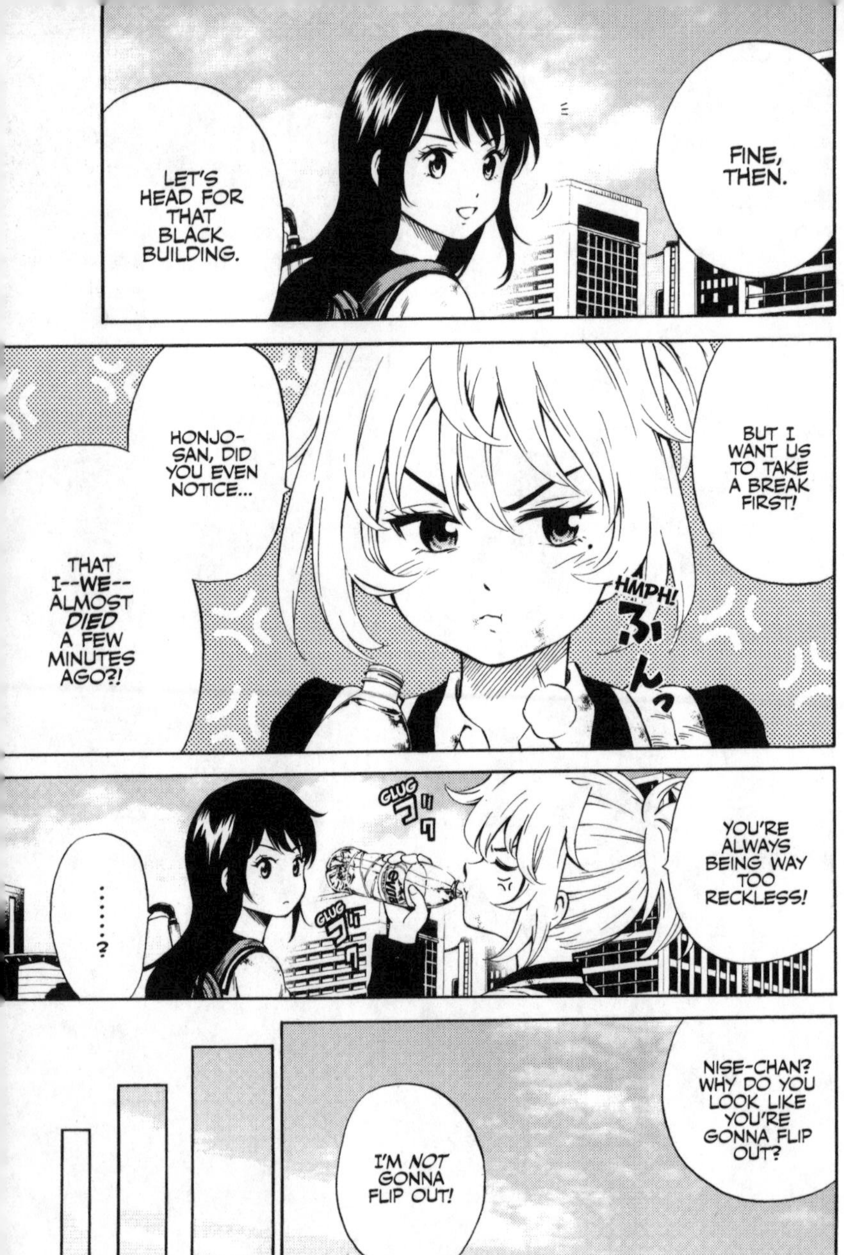
FINE, THEN.
LET'S HEAD FOR THAT BLACK BUILDING.
BUT I WANT US TO TAKE A BREAK FIRST!
HMPH!
ふんっ
HONJO-SAN, DID YOU EVEN NOTICE...
THAT I--WE--ALMOST *DIED* A FEW MINUTES AGO?!
YOU'RE ALWAYS BEING WAY TOO RECKLESS!
GLUG
GLUG
......?
NISE-CHAN? WHY DO YOU LOOK LIKE YOU'RE GONNA FLIP OUT?
I'M *NOT* GONNA FLIP OUT!

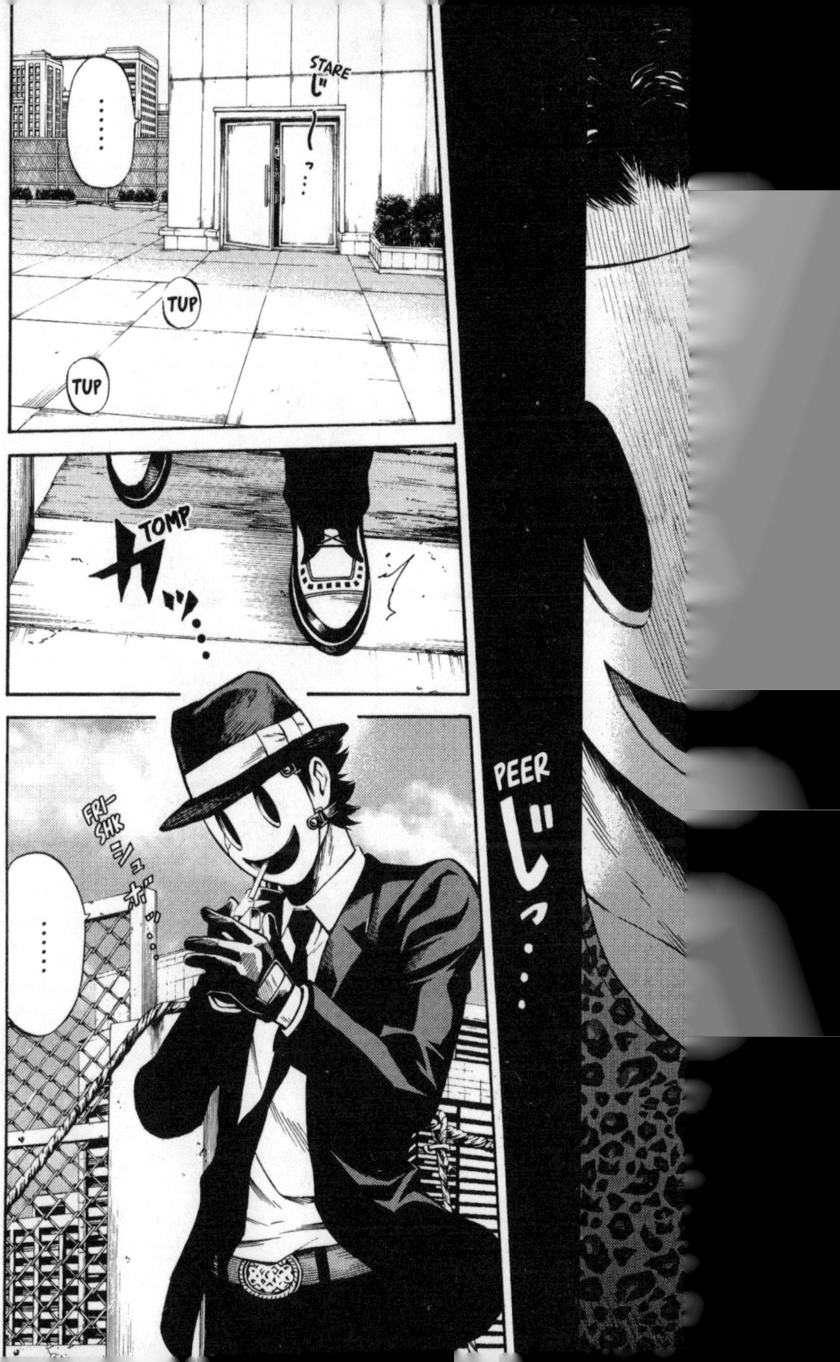
PEER
じっ…
STARE
じーっ…
……
TUP
TUP
TOMP
ガッ…
FRI-SHK
シュボッ
……

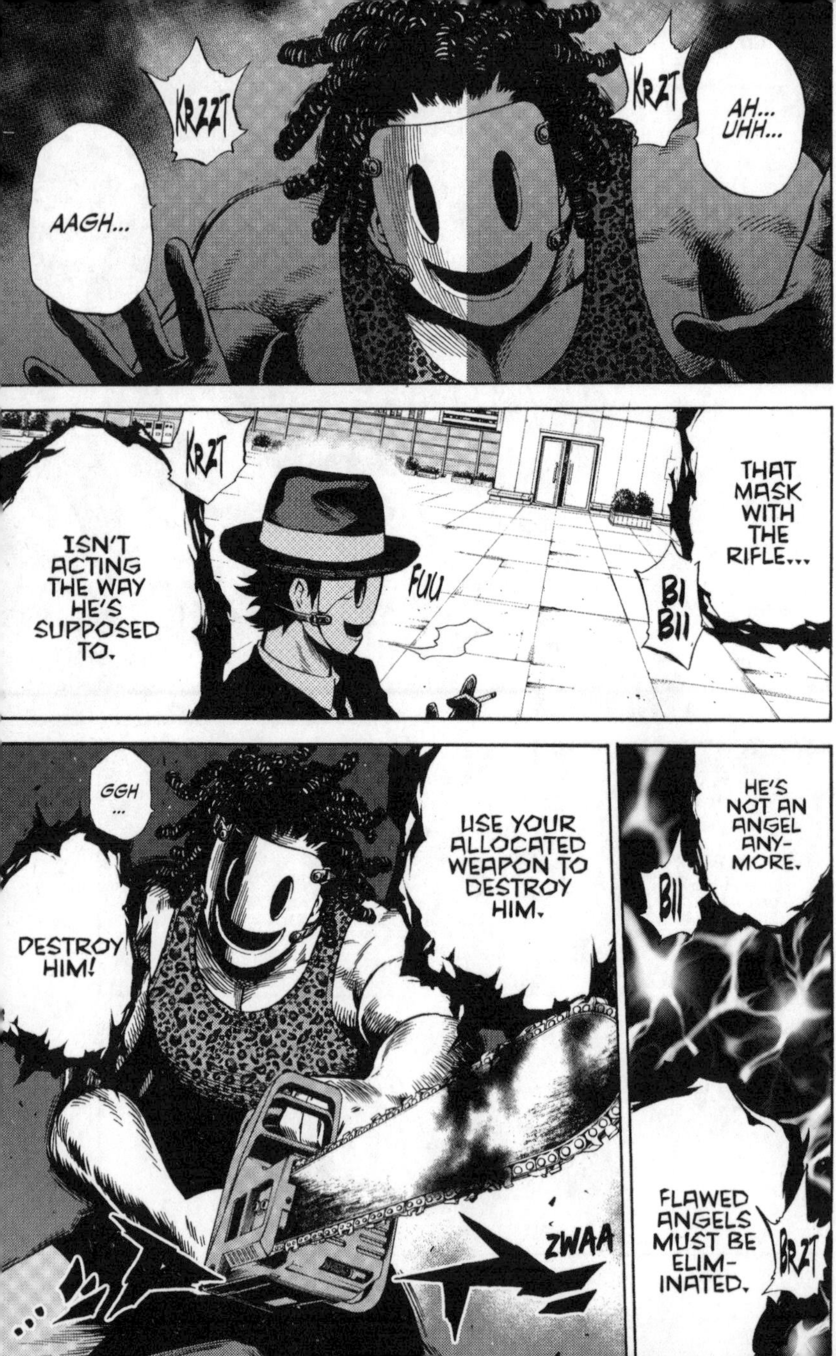
KRZT
AH... UHH...
KRZZT
AAGH...
THAT MASK WITH THE RIFLE...
BI BII
FUU
KRZT
ISN'T ACTING THE WAY HE'S SUPPOSED TO.
HE'S NOT AN ANGEL ANY-MORE.
BII
FLAWED ANGELS MUST BE ELIM-INATED.
BRZT
USE YOUR ALLOCATED WEAPON TO DESTROY HIM.
ZWAA
GGH ...
DESTROY HIM!
...

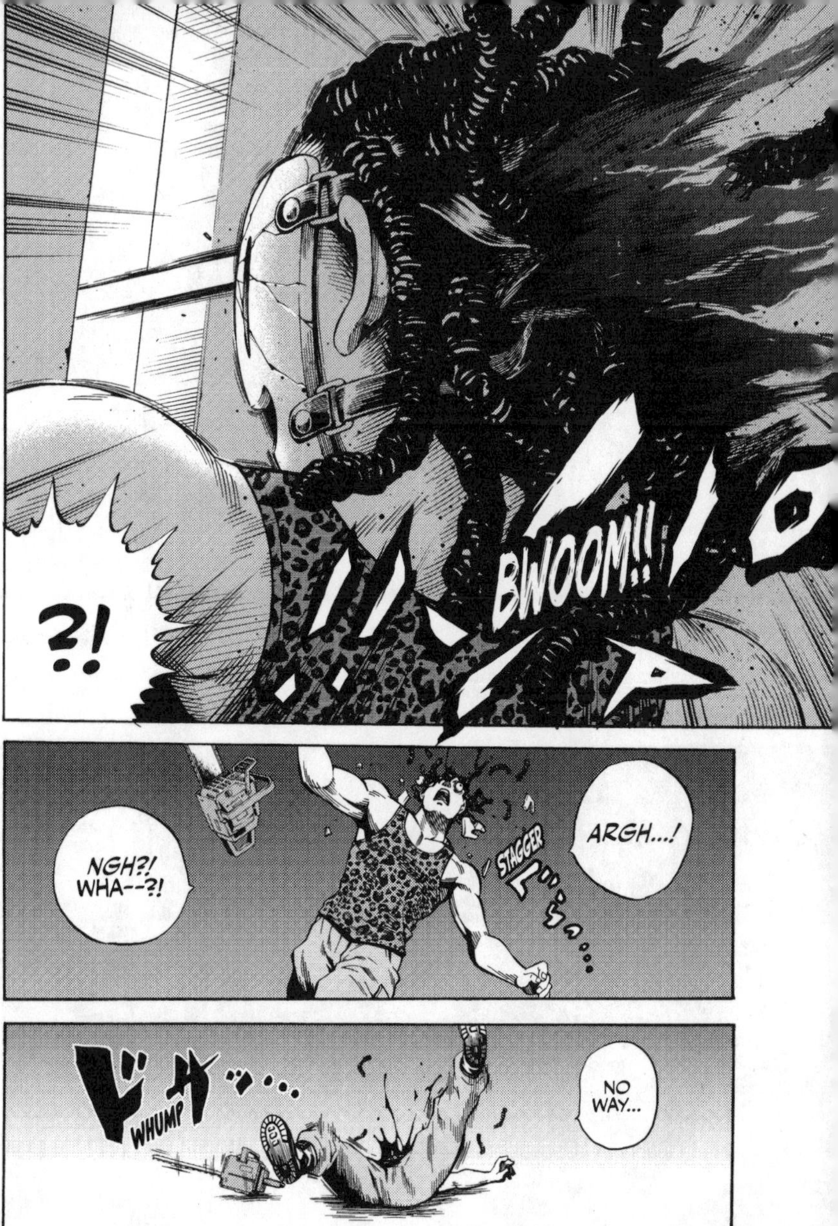
BWOOM!!
?!
ARGH...!
STAGGER
NGH?! WHA--?!
NO WAY...
WHUMP

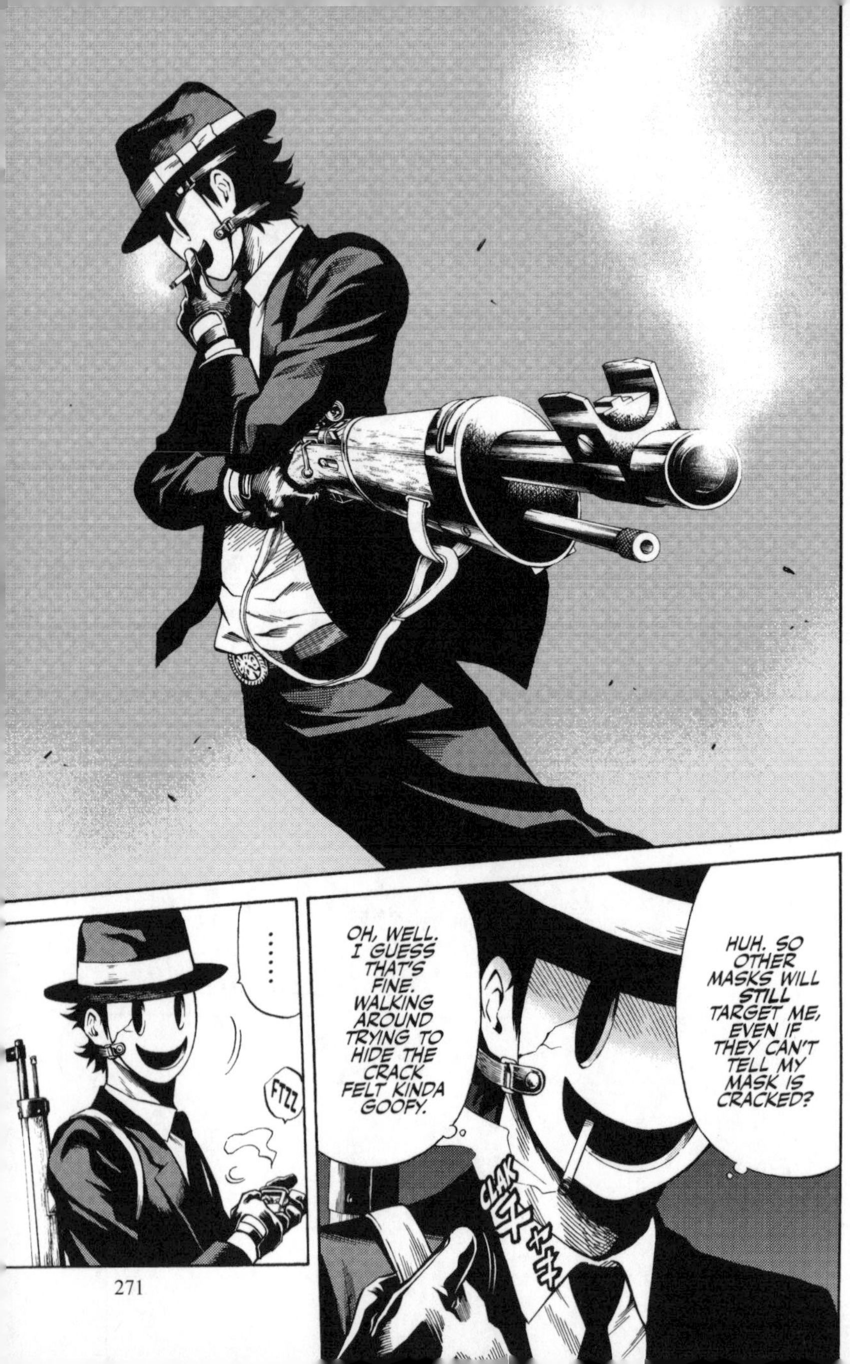
HUH. SO OTHER MASKS WILL STILL TARGET ME, EVEN IF THEY CAN'T TELL MY MASK IS CRACKED?
OH, WELL. I GUESS THAT'S FINE. WALKING AROUND TRYING TO HIDE THE CRACK FELT KINDA GOOFY.
CLAK
......
FTZZ

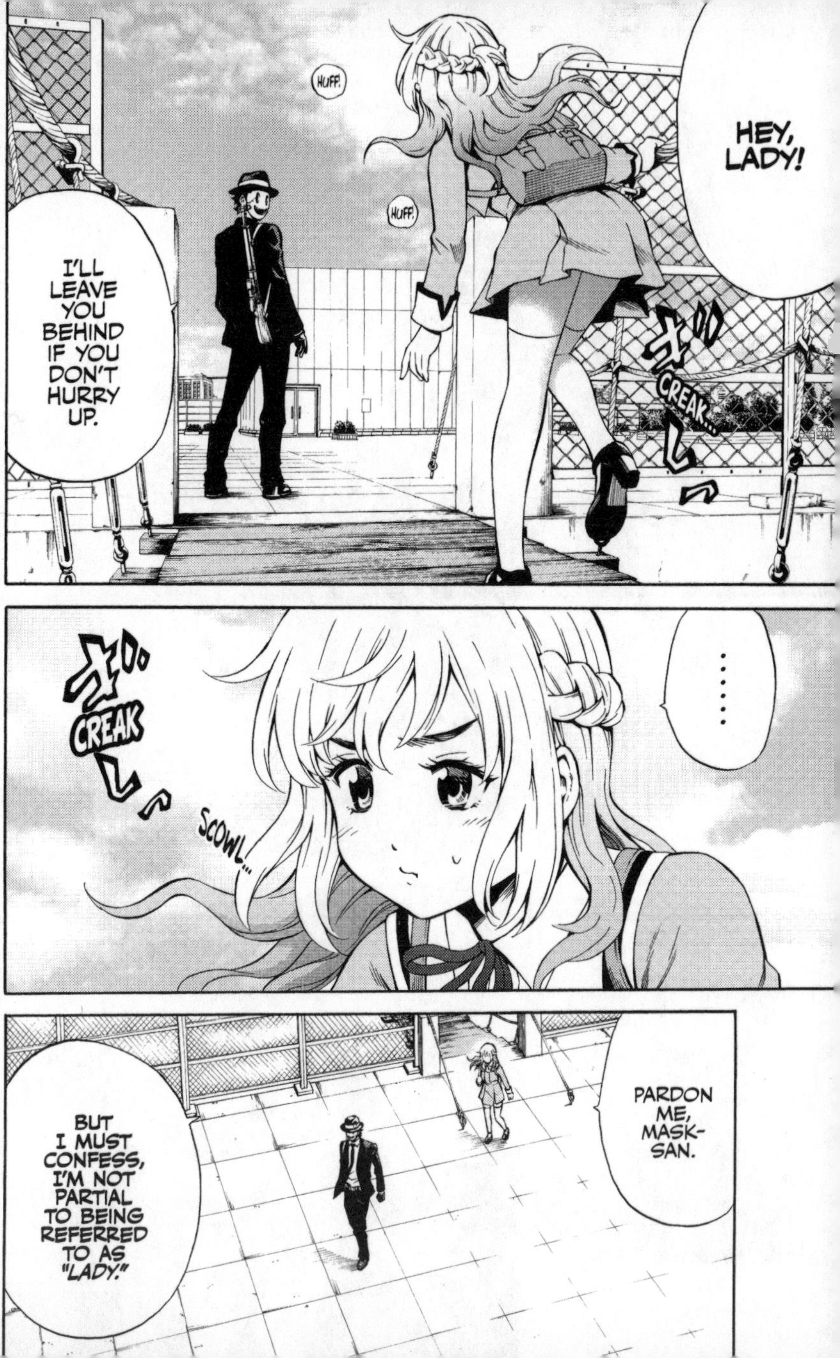
HEY, LADY!
HUFF!
HUFF!
CREAK...
I'LL LEAVE YOU BEHIND IF YOU DON'T HURRY UP.
......
CREAK
SCOWL...
PARDON ME, MASK-SAN.
BUT I MUST CONFESS, I'M NOT PARTIAL TO BEING REFERRED TO AS "LADY."

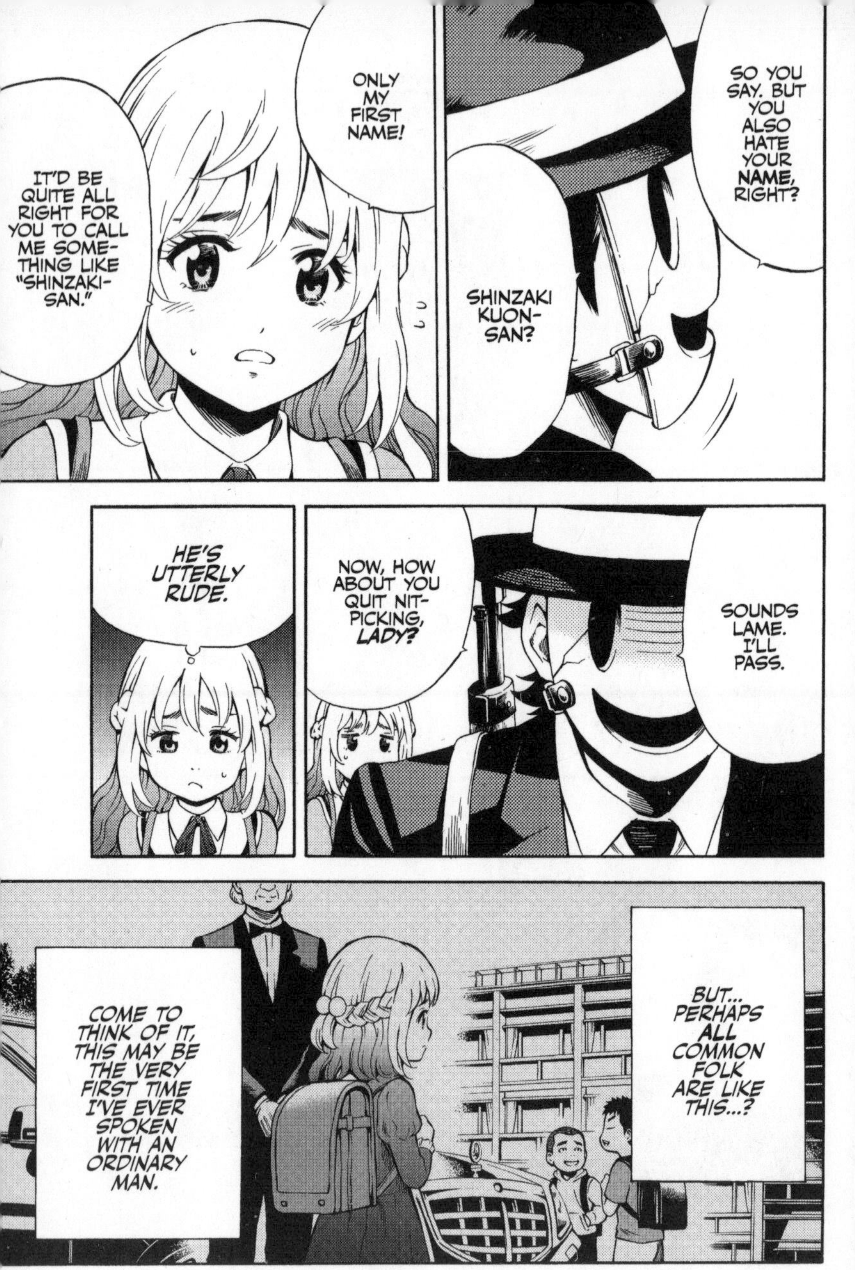
SO YOU SAY. BUT YOU ALSO HATE YOUR NAME, RIGHT?
SHINZAKI KUON-SAN?
ONLY MY FIRST NAME!
IT'D BE QUITE ALL RIGHT FOR YOU TO CALL ME SOME-THING LIKE "SHINZAKI-SAN."
SOUNDS LAME. I'LL PASS.
NOW, HOW ABOUT YOU QUIT NIT-PICKING, LADY?
HE'S UTTERLY RUDE.
BUT... PERHAPS ALL COMMON FOLK ARE LIKE THIS...?
COME TO THINK OF IT, THIS MAY BE THE VERY FIRST TIME I'VE EVER SPOKEN WITH AN ORDINARY MAN.

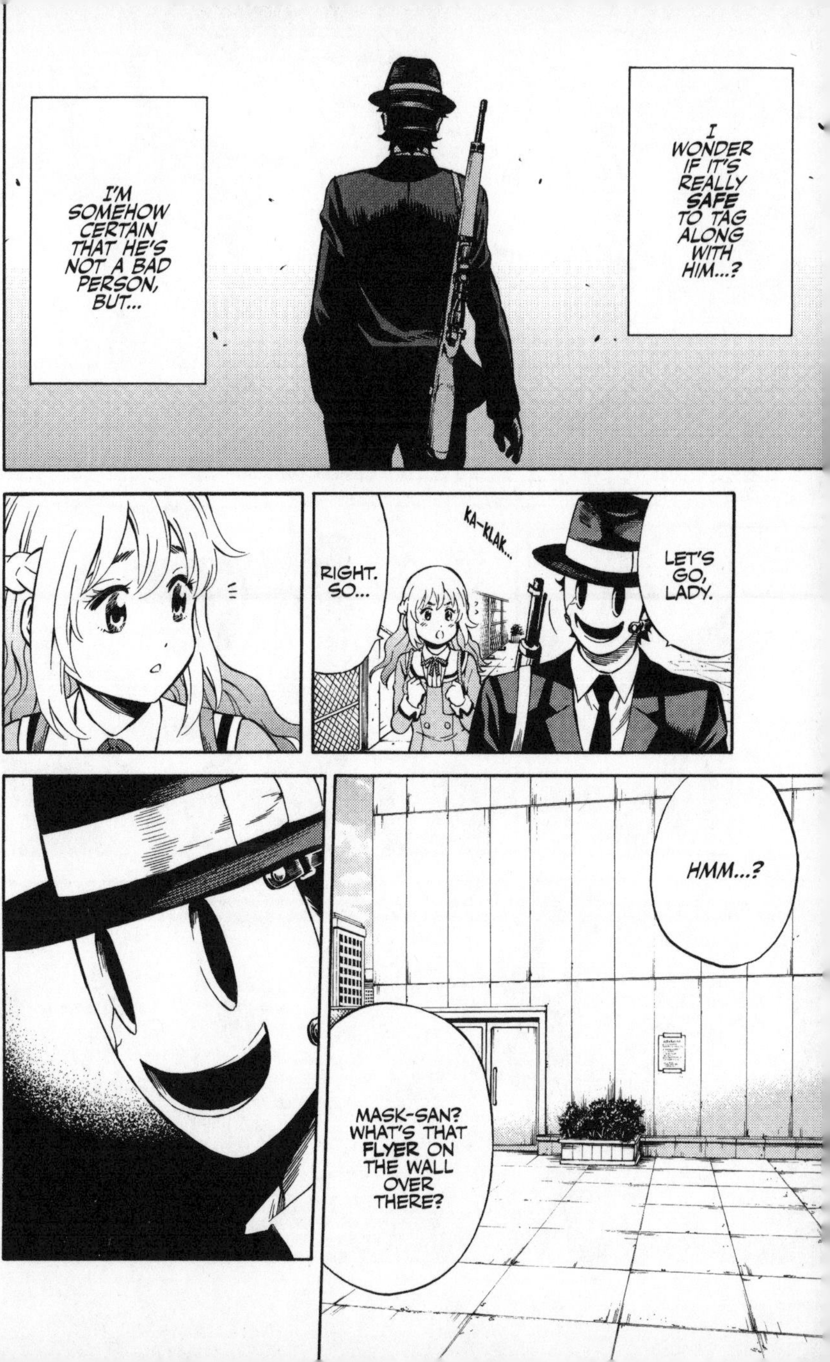
I WONDER IF IT'S REALLY SAFE TO TAG ALONG WITH HIM...?
I'M SOMEHOW CERTAIN THAT HE'S NOT A BAD PERSON, BUT...
LET'S GO, LADY.
KA-KLAK...
RIGHT. SO...
HMM...?
MASK-SAN? WHAT'S THAT FLYER ON THE WALL OVER THERE?

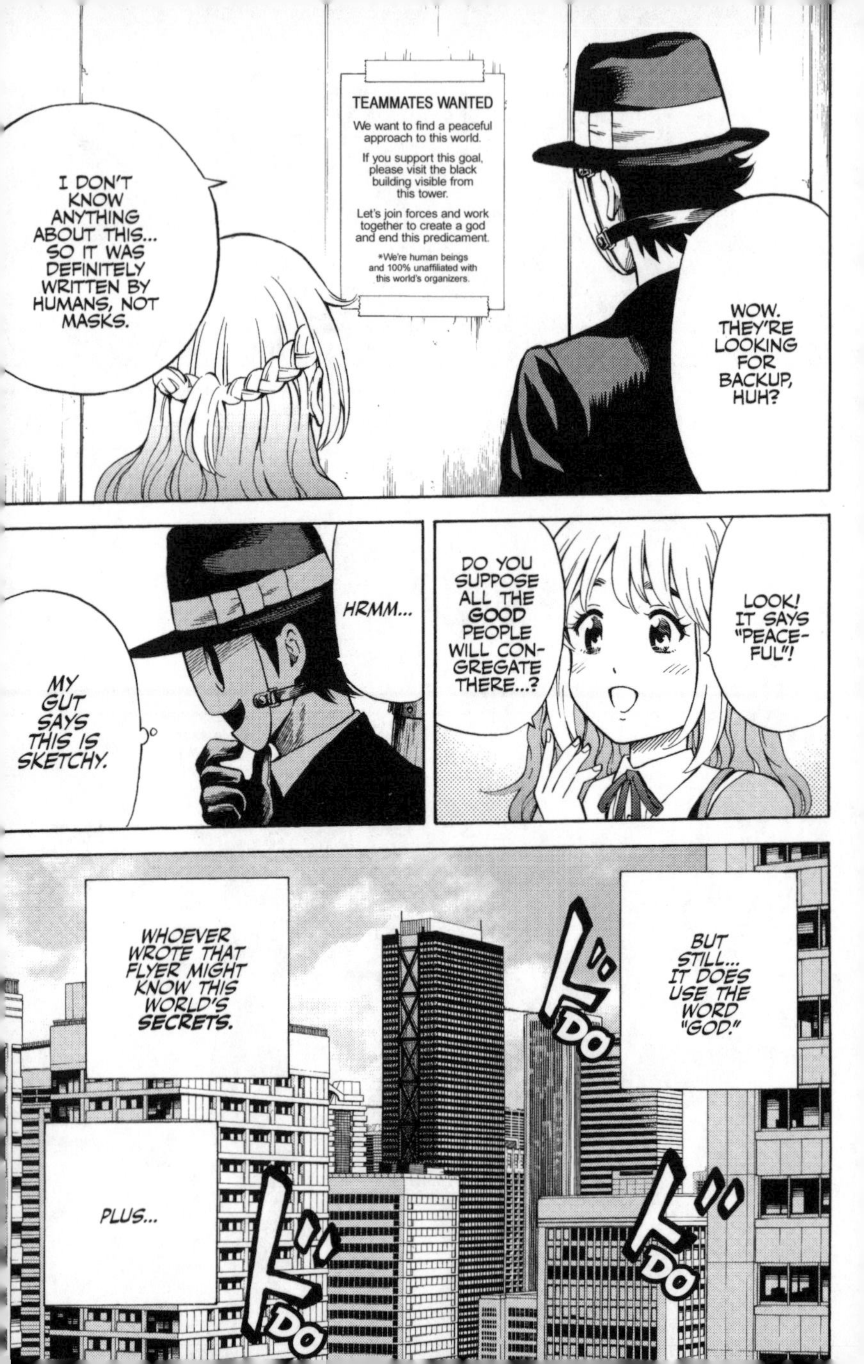
TEAMMATES WANTED
We want to find a peaceful approach to this world.
If you support this goal, please visit the black building visible from this tower.
Let's join forces and work together to create a god and end this predicament.
*We're human beings and 100% unaffiliated with this world's organizers.
WOW. THEY'RE LOOKING FOR BACKUP, HUH?
I DON'T KNOW ANYTHING ABOUT THIS... SO IT WAS DEFINITELY WRITTEN BY HUMANS, NOT MASKS.
LOOK! IT SAYS "PEACE-FUL"!
DO YOU SUPPOSE ALL THE GOOD PEOPLE WILL CON-GREGATE THERE...?
HRMM...
MY GUT SAYS THIS IS SKETCHY.
BUT STILL... IT DOES USE THE WORD "GOD."
DO
WHOEVER WROTE THAT FLYER MIGHT KNOW THIS WORLD'S SECRETS.
DO
PLUS...
DO

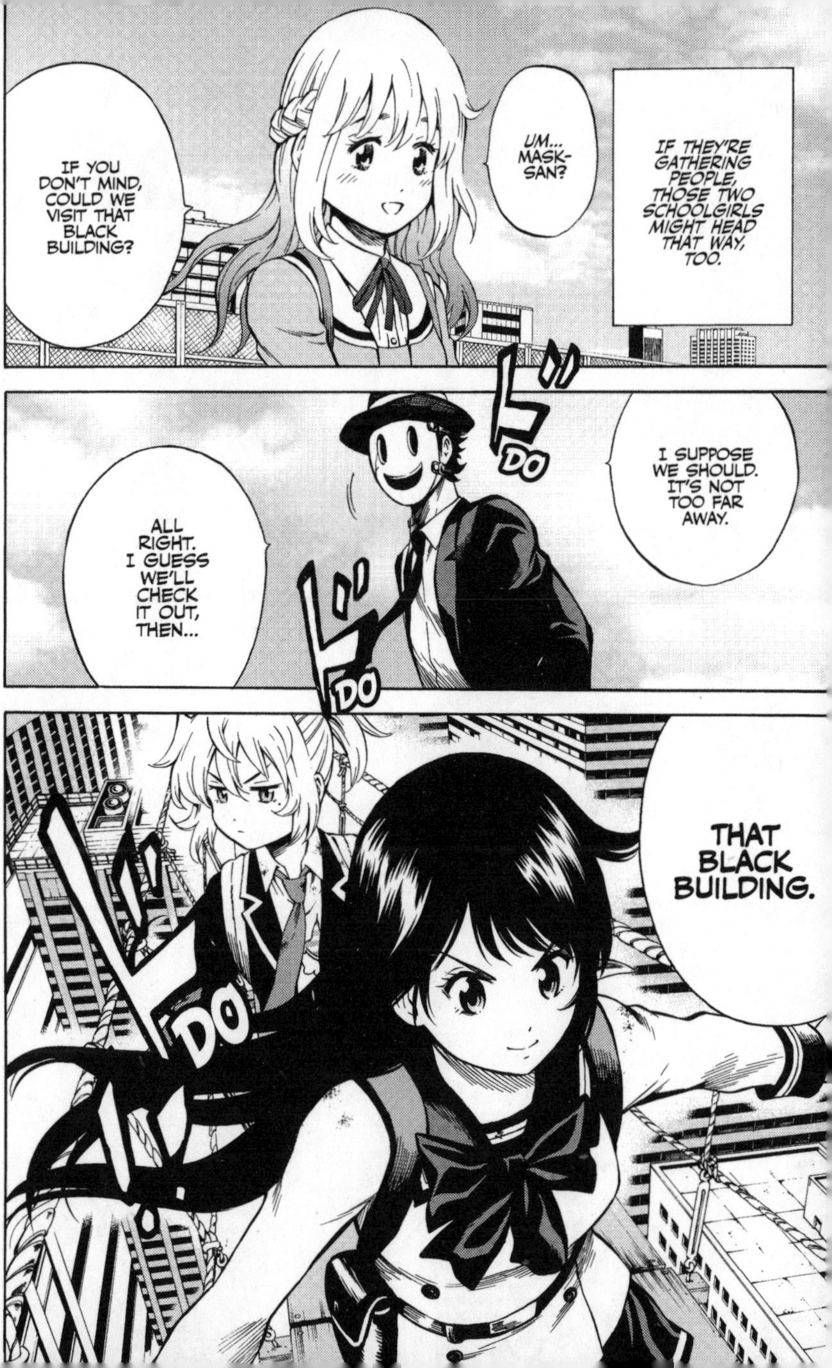
IF THEY'RE GATHERING PEOPLE, THOSE TWO SCHOOLGIRLS MIGHT HEAD THAT WAY, TOO.
UM... MASK-SAN?
IF YOU DON'T MIND, COULD WE VISIT THAT BLACK BUILDING?
I SUPPOSE WE SHOULD. IT'S NOT TOO FAR AWAY.
DO
ALL RIGHT. I GUESS WE'LL CHECK IT OUT, THEN...
DO
THAT BLACK BUILDING.
DO

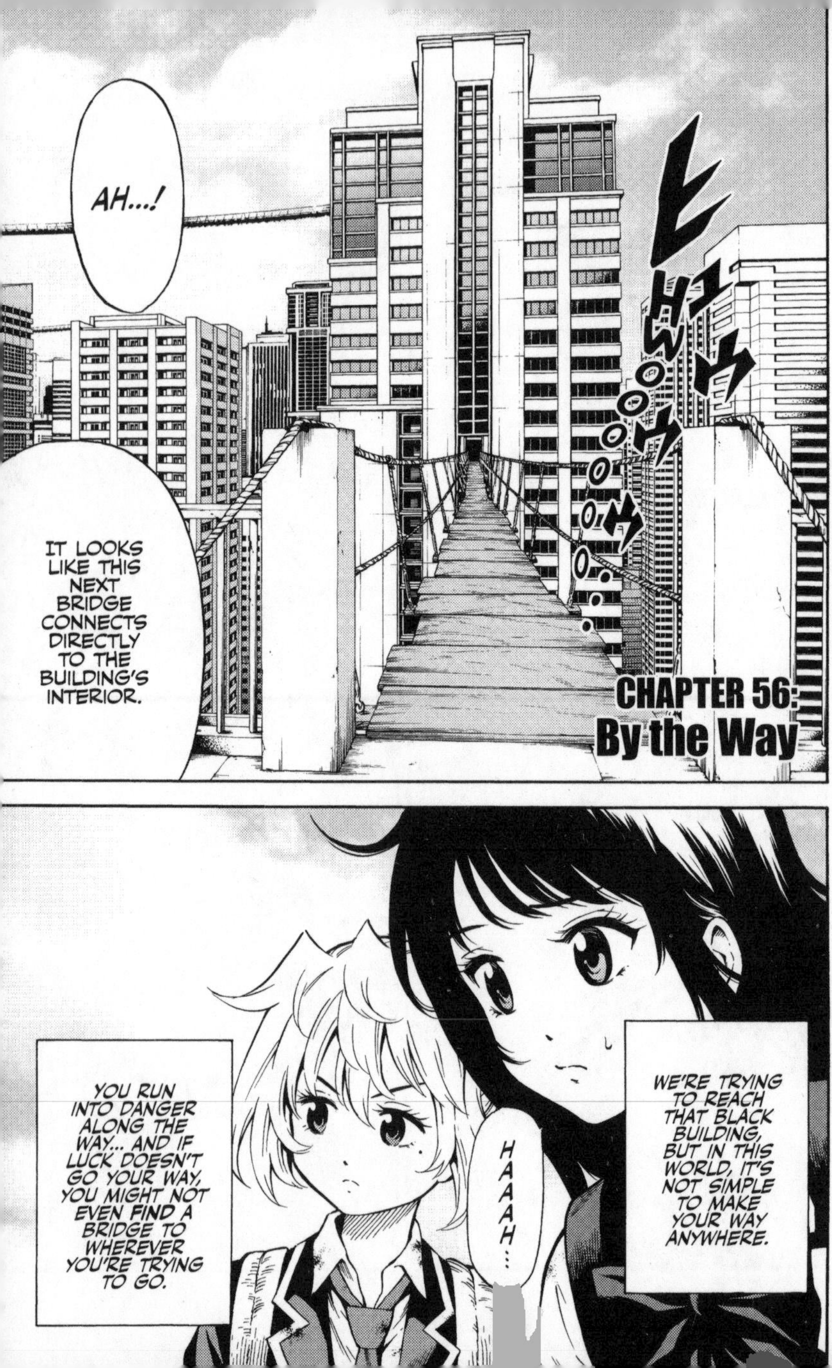
CHAPTER 56:
By the Way
AH...!
IT LOOKS LIKE THIS NEXT BRIDGE CONNECTS DIRECTLY TO THE BUILDING'S INTERIOR.
WE'RE TRYING TO REACH THAT BLACK BUILDING, BUT IN THIS WORLD, IT'S NOT SIMPLE TO MAKE YOUR WAY ANYWHERE.
HAAAAH...
YOU RUN INTO DANGER ALONG THE WAY... AND IF LUCK DOESN'T GO YOUR WAY, YOU MIGHT NOT EVEN FIND A BRIDGE TO WHEREVER YOU'RE TRYING TO GO.

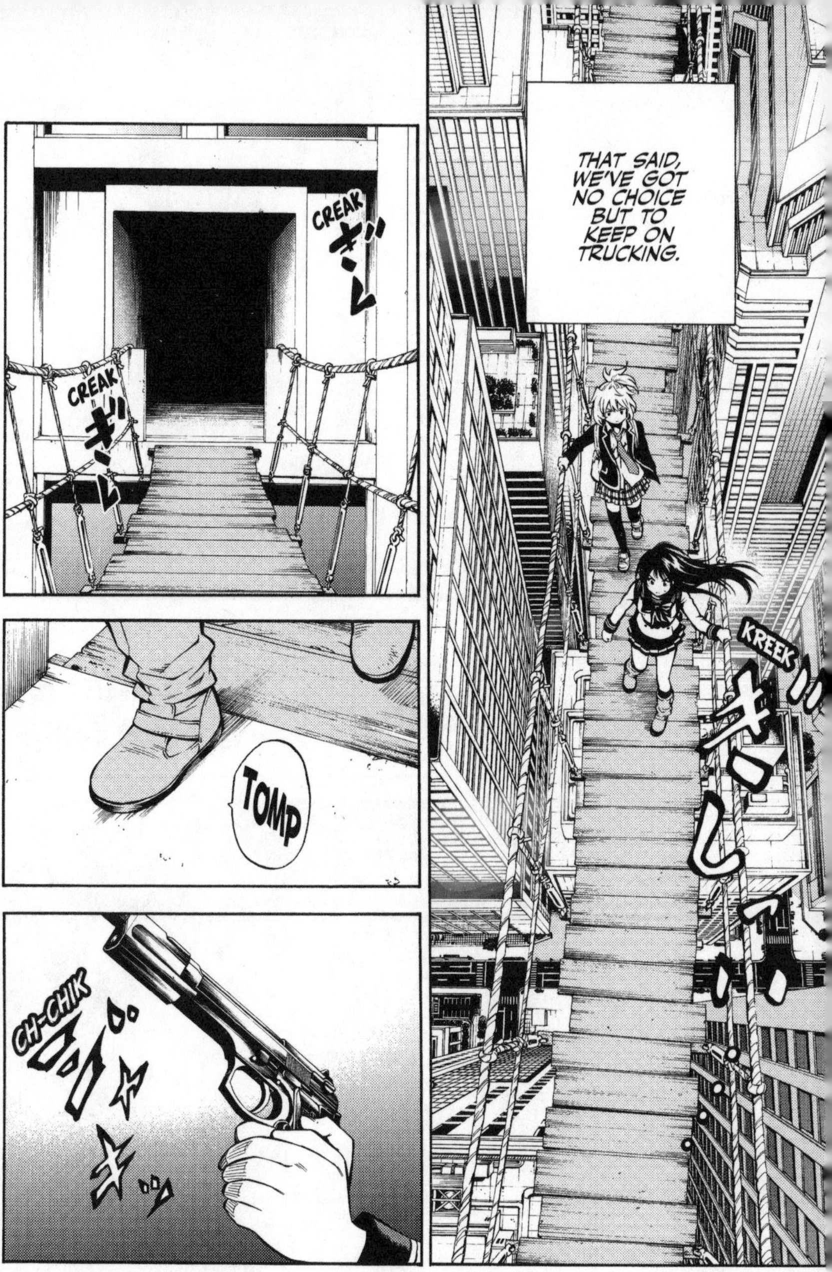
THAT SAID, WE'VE GOT NO CHOICE BUT TO KEEP ON TRUCKING.
KREEK
CREAK
CREAK
TOMP
CH-CHIK

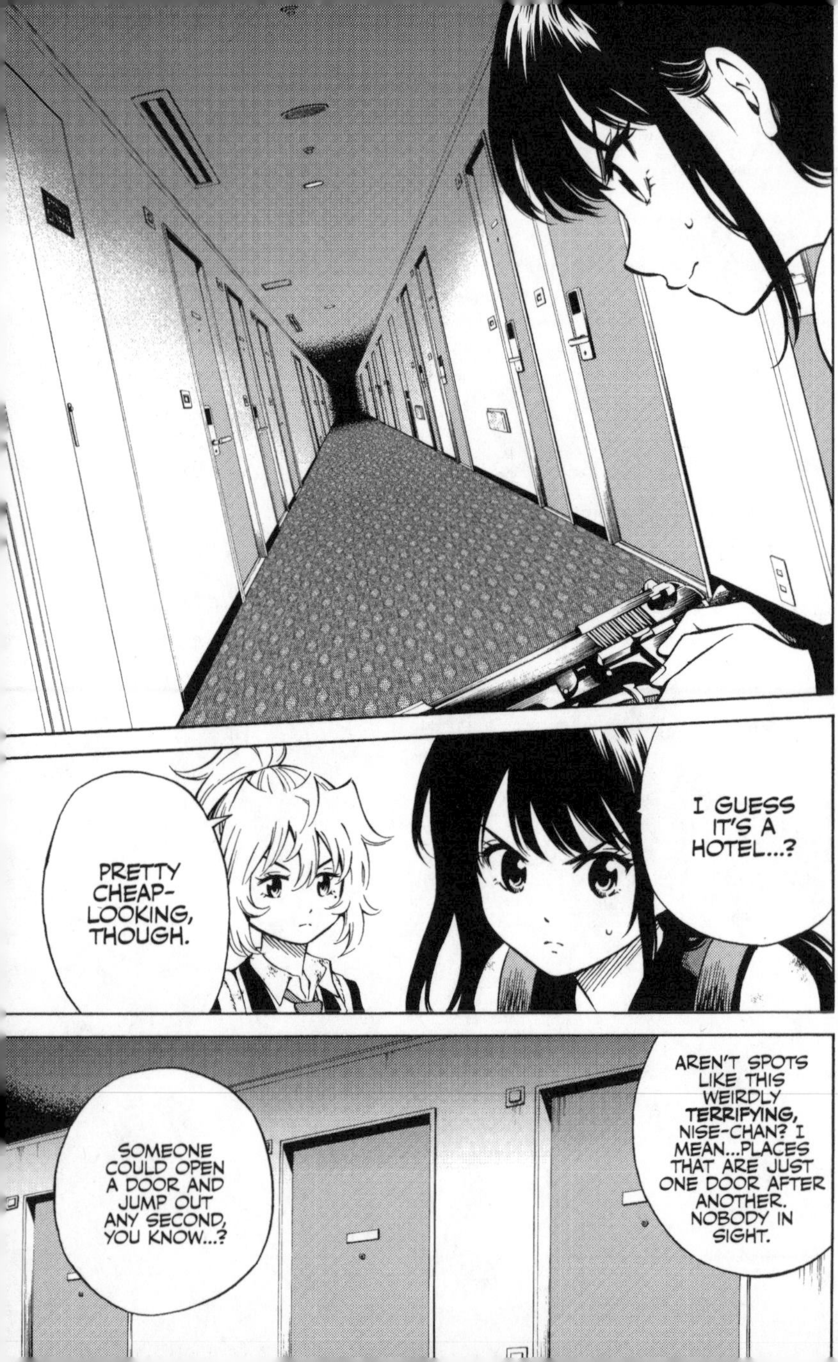
I GUESS IT'S A HOTEL...?
PRETTY CHEAP-LOOKING, THOUGH.
AREN'T SPOTS LIKE THIS WEIRDLY **TERRIFYING,** NISE-CHAN? I MEAN...PLACES THAT ARE JUST ONE DOOR AFTER ANOTHER. NOBODY IN SIGHT.
SOMEONE COULD OPEN A DOOR AND JUMP OUT ANY SECOND, YOU KNOW...?

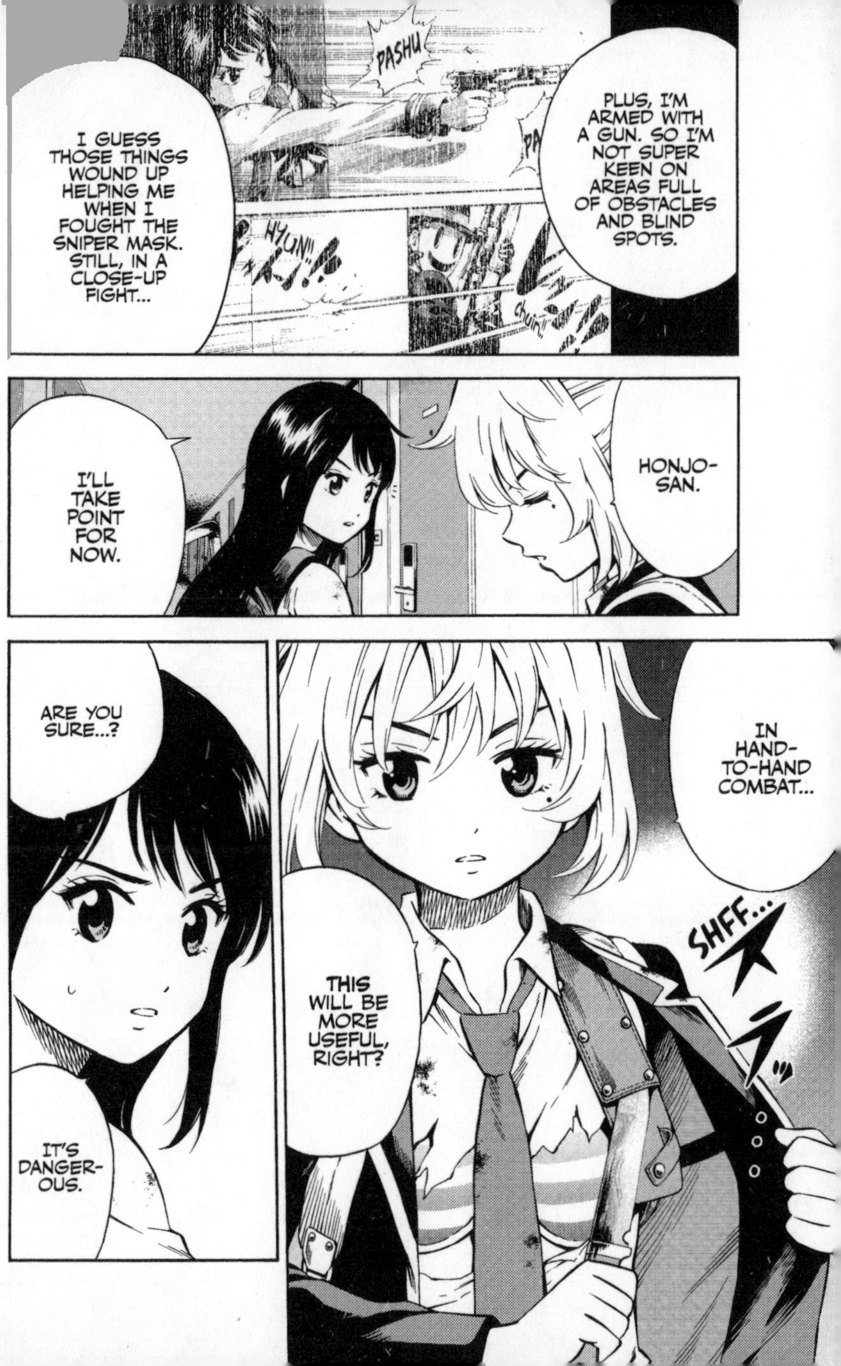
PLUS, I'M ARMED WITH A GUN. SO I'M NOT SUPER KEEN ON AREAS FULL OF OBSTACLES AND BLIND SPOTS.
PASHU
I GUESS THOSE THINGS WOUND UP HELPING ME WHEN I FOUGHT THE SNIPER MASK. STILL, IN A CLOSE-UP FIGHT...
HYUN!!
chuin!!
HONJO-SAN.
I'LL TAKE POINT FOR NOW.
IN HAND-TO-HAND COMBAT...
SHFF...
THIS WILL BE MORE USEFUL, RIGHT?
ARE YOU SURE...?
IT'S DANGER-OUS.

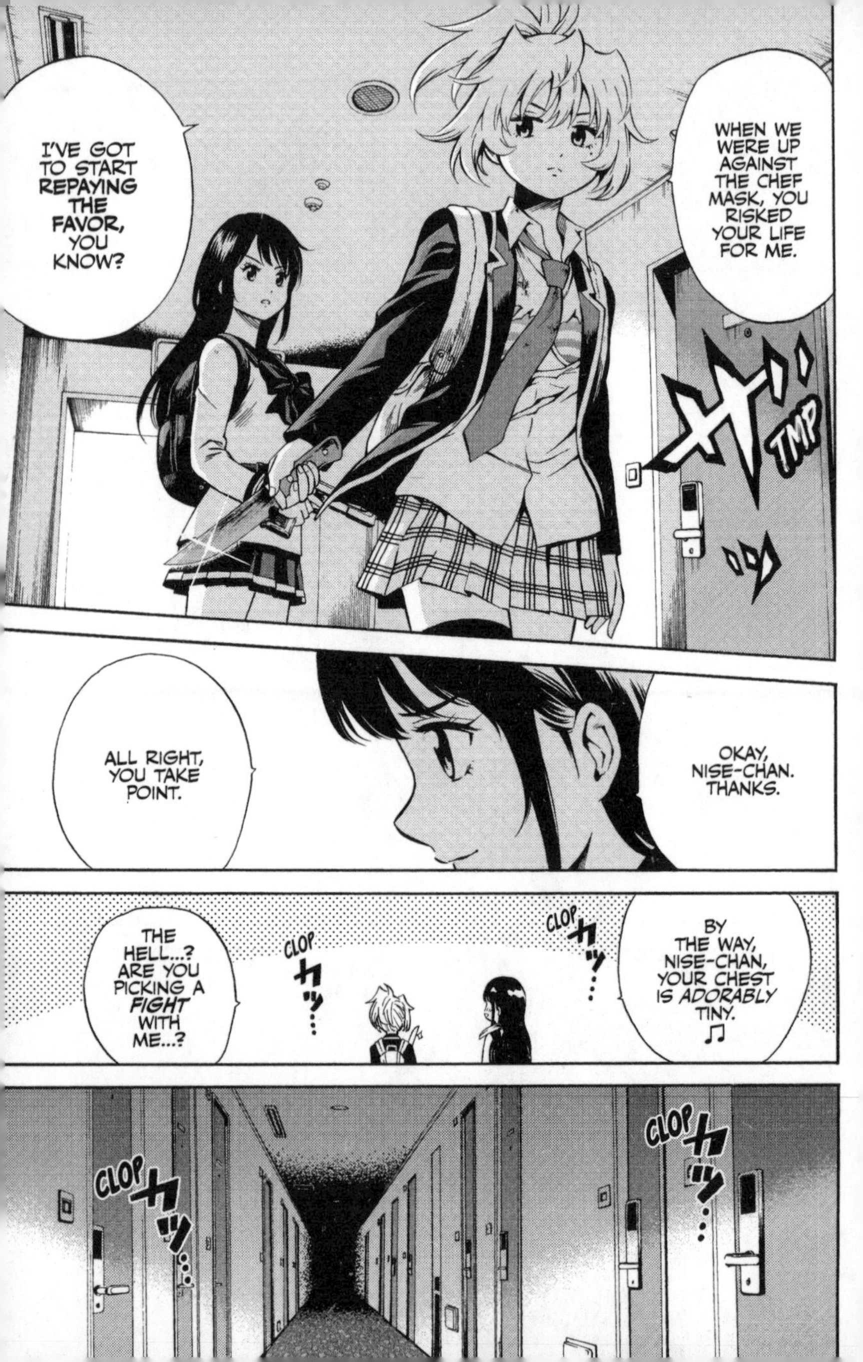
WHEN WE WERE UP AGAINST THE CHEF MASK, YOU RISKED YOUR LIFE FOR ME.
TMP
I'VE GOT TO START REPAYING THE FAVOR, YOU KNOW?
OKAY, NISE-CHAN. THANKS.
ALL RIGHT, YOU TAKE POINT.
BY THE WAY, NISE-CHAN, YOUR CHEST IS *ADORABLY* TINY. ♫
CLOP
CLOP
THE HELL...? ARE YOU PICKING A ***FIGHT*** WITH ME...?
CLOP
CLOP

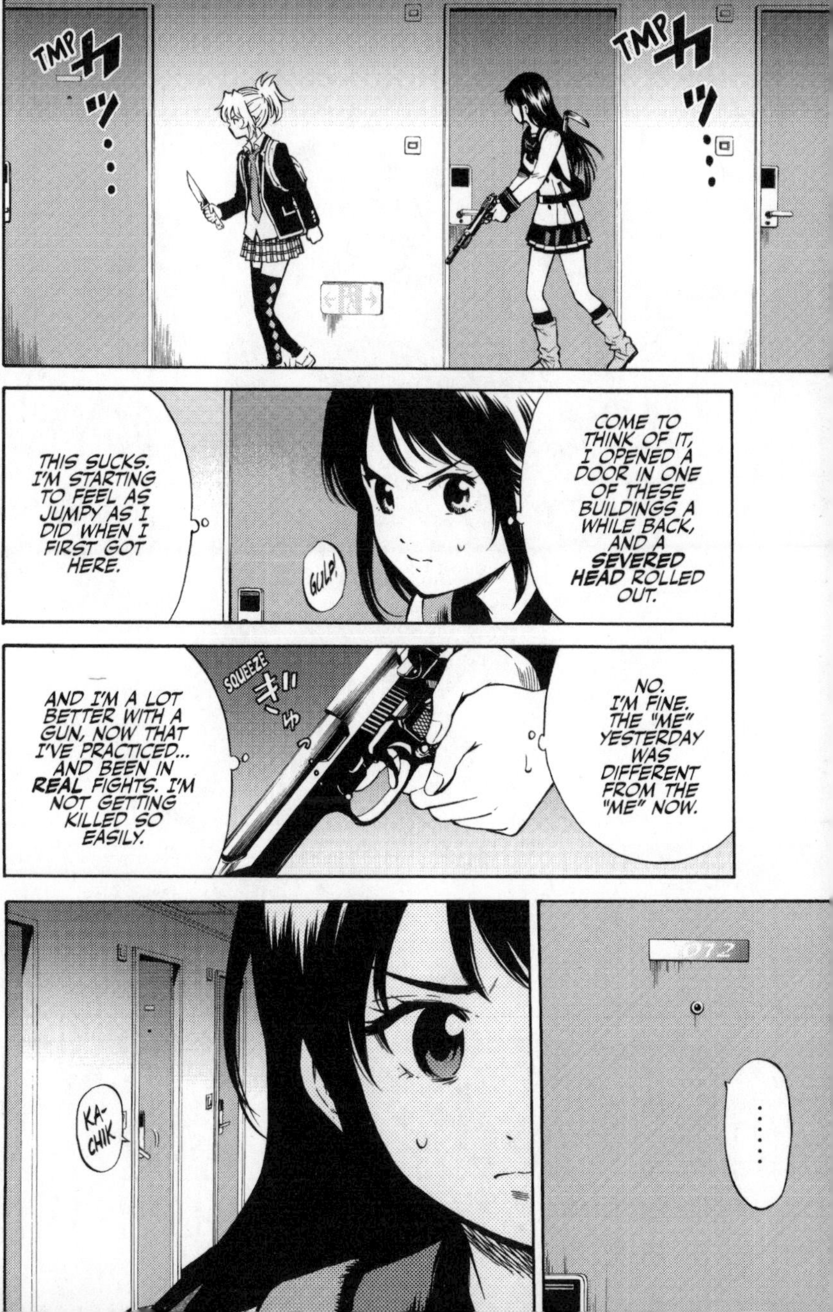
TMP
TMP
COME TO THINK OF IT, I OPENED A DOOR IN ONE OF THESE BUILDINGS A WHILE BACK, AND A **SEVERED HEAD** ROLLED OUT.
GULP!
THIS SUCKS. I'M STARTING TO FEEL AS JUMPY AS I DID WHEN I FIRST GOT HERE.
NO. I'M FINE. THE "ME" YESTERDAY WAS DIFFERENT FROM THE "ME" NOW.
SQUEEZE
AND I'M A LOT BETTER WITH A GUN, NOW THAT I'VE PRACTICED... AND BEEN IN **REAL** FIGHTS. I'M NOT GETTING KILLED SO EASILY.
......
KA-CHIK

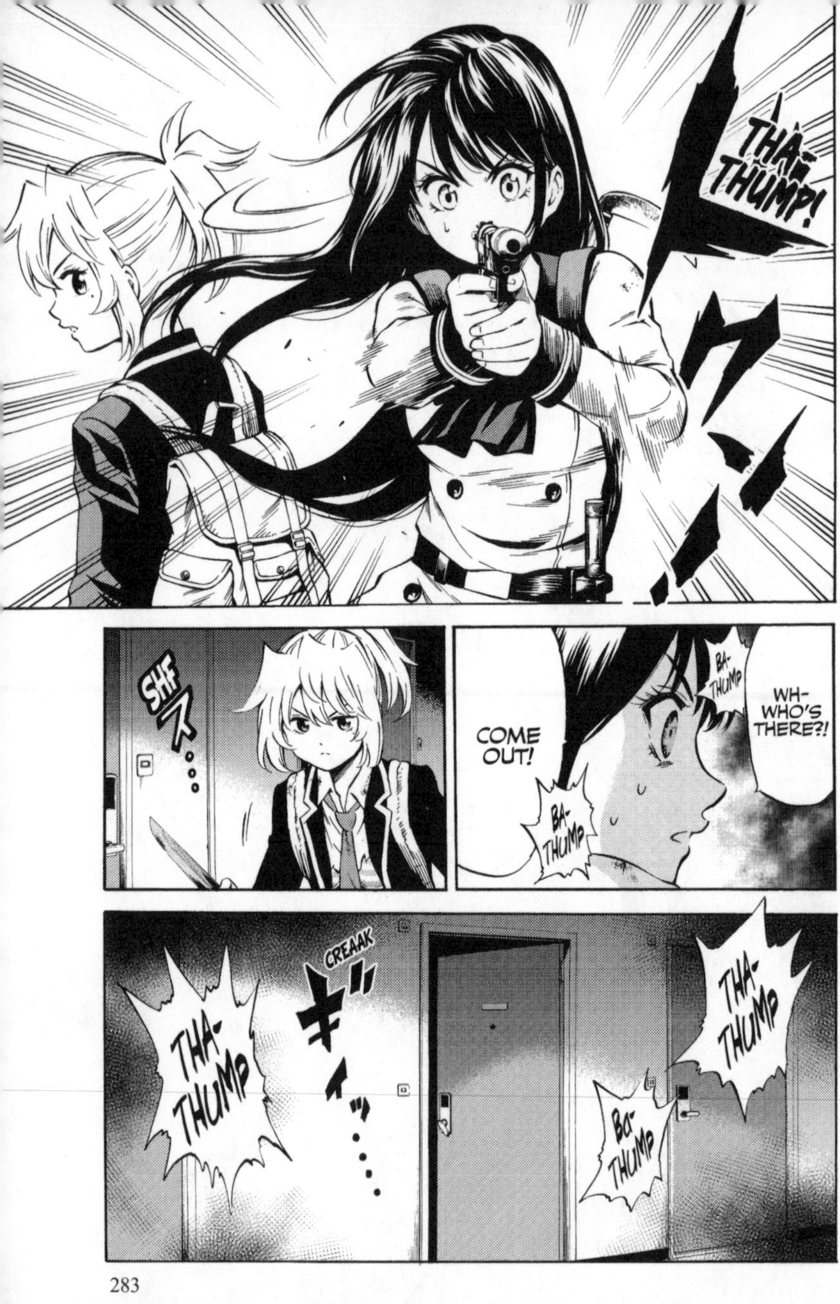
THA-THUMP!
WH-WHO'S THERE?!
BA-THUMP
COME OUT!
BA-THUMP
SHF
THA-THUMP
Ba-THUMP
CREAAK
THA-THUMP

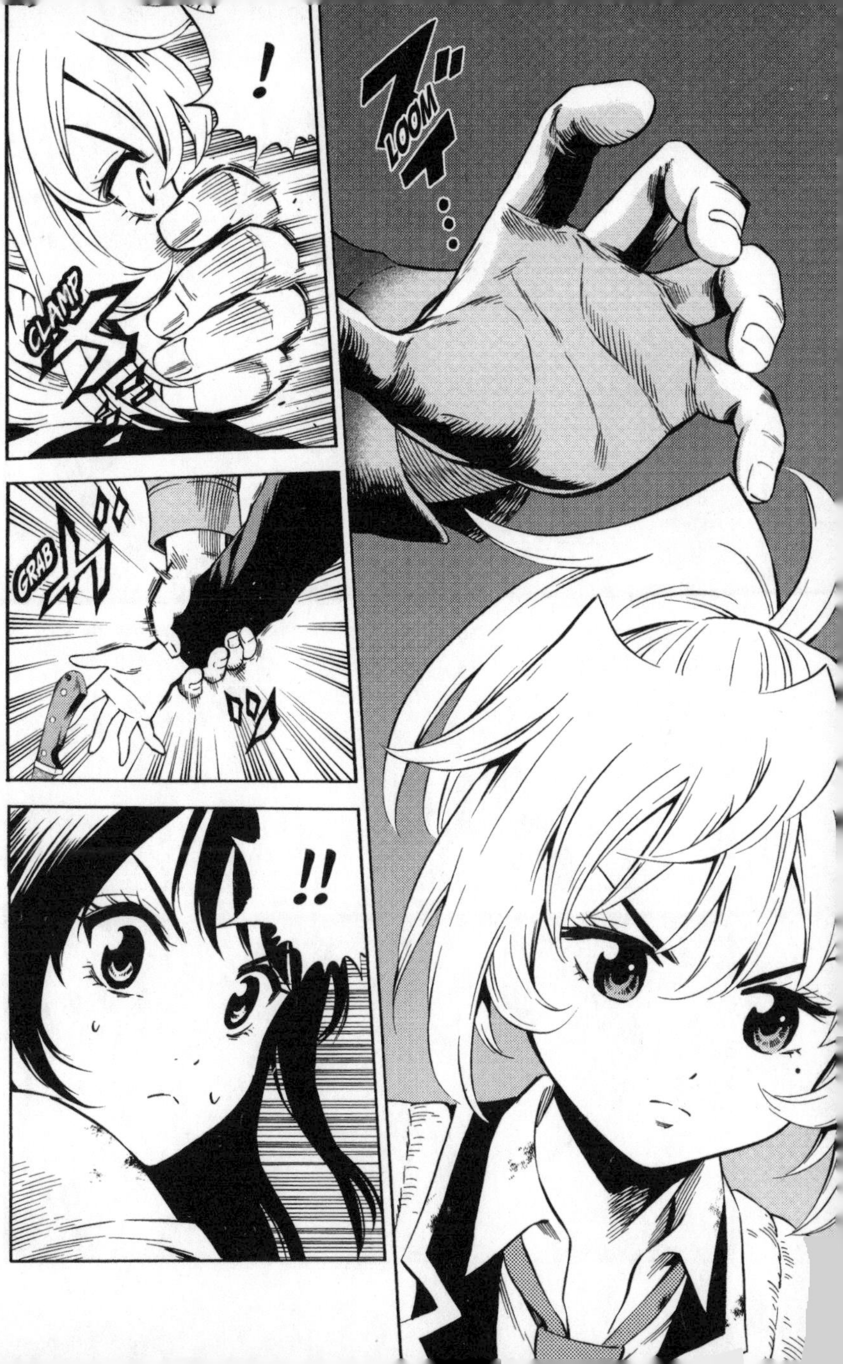
LOOM
...
!
CLAMP
GRAB
!!

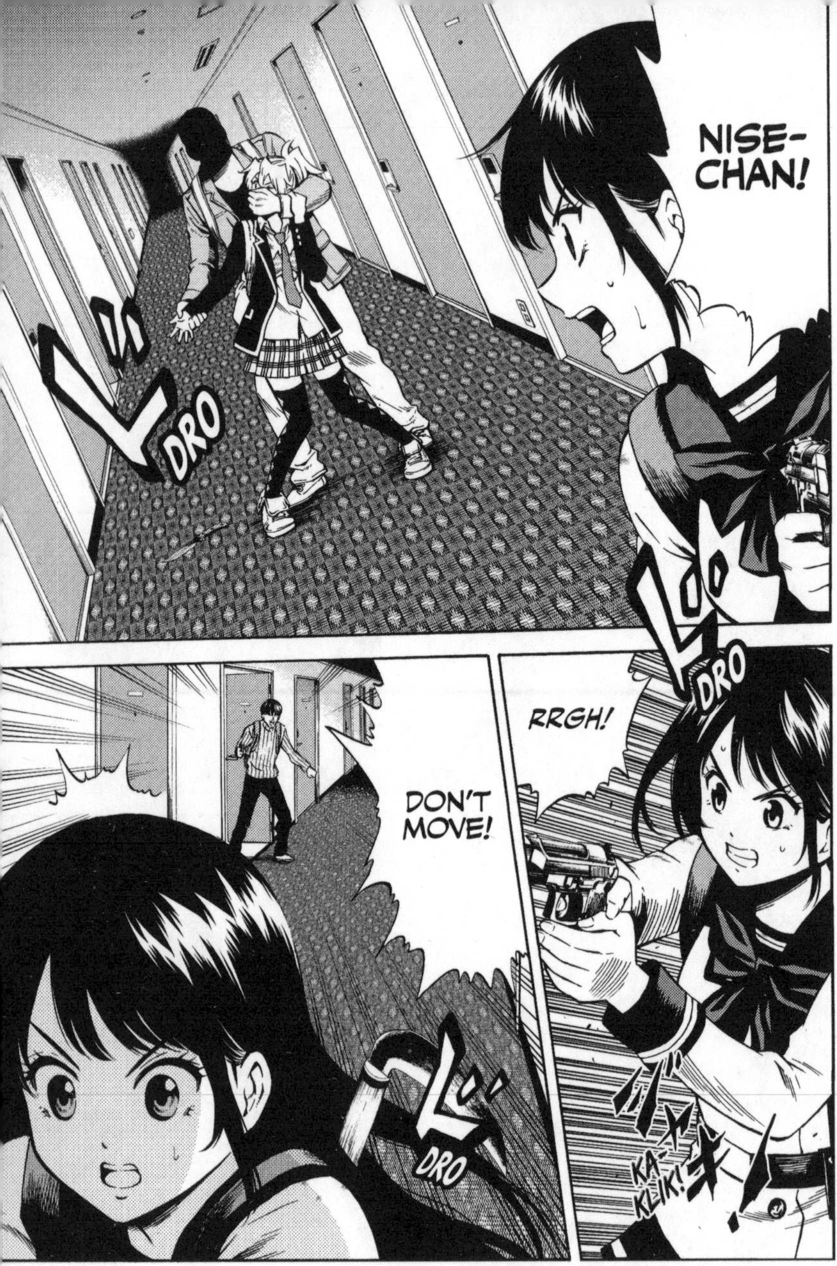
NISE-CHAN!
DRO
DRO
RRGH!
KA-KLIK!
DON'T MOVE!
DRO

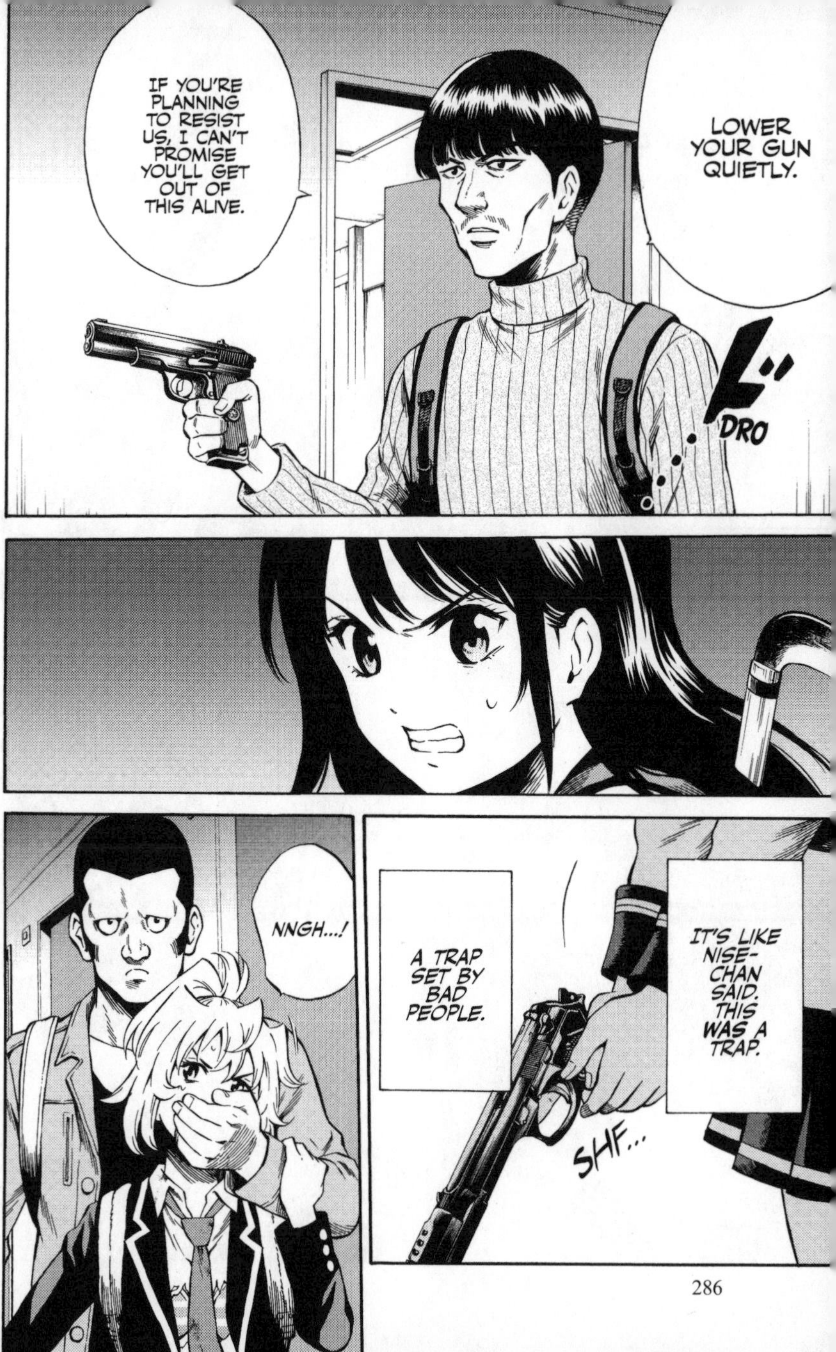
LOWER YOUR GUN QUIETLY.
IF YOU'RE PLANNING TO RESIST US, I CAN'T PROMISE YOU'LL GET OUT OF THIS ALIVE.
DRO
IT'S LIKE NISE-CHAN SAID. THIS WAS A TRAP.
A TRAP SET BY BAD PEOPLE.
SHF...
NNGH...!

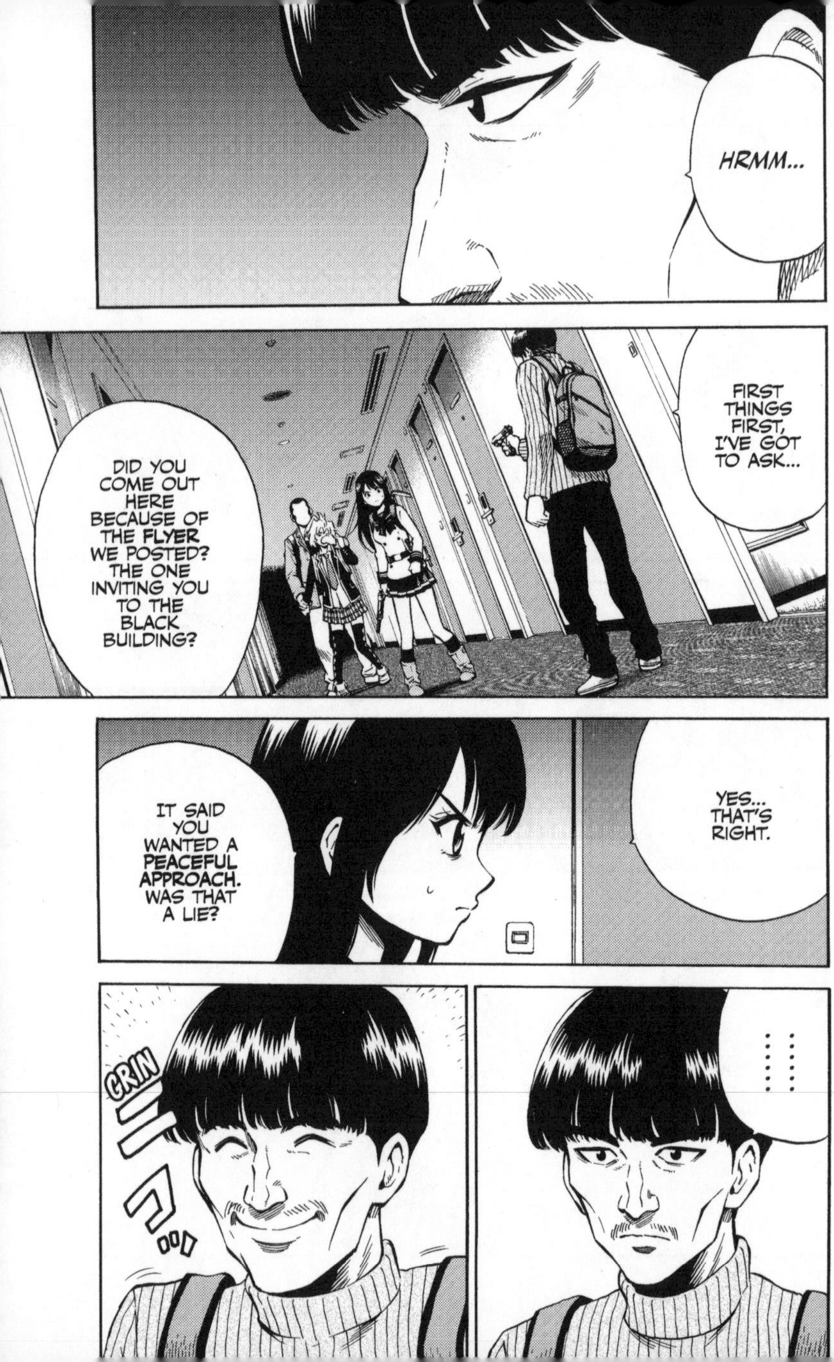
HRMM...
FIRST THINGS FIRST, I'VE GOT TO ASK...
DID YOU COME OUT HERE BECAUSE OF THE FLYER WE POSTED? THE ONE INVITING YOU TO THE BLACK BUILDING?
YES... THAT'S RIGHT.
IT SAID YOU WANTED A PEACEFUL APPROACH. WAS THAT A LIE?
......
GRIN

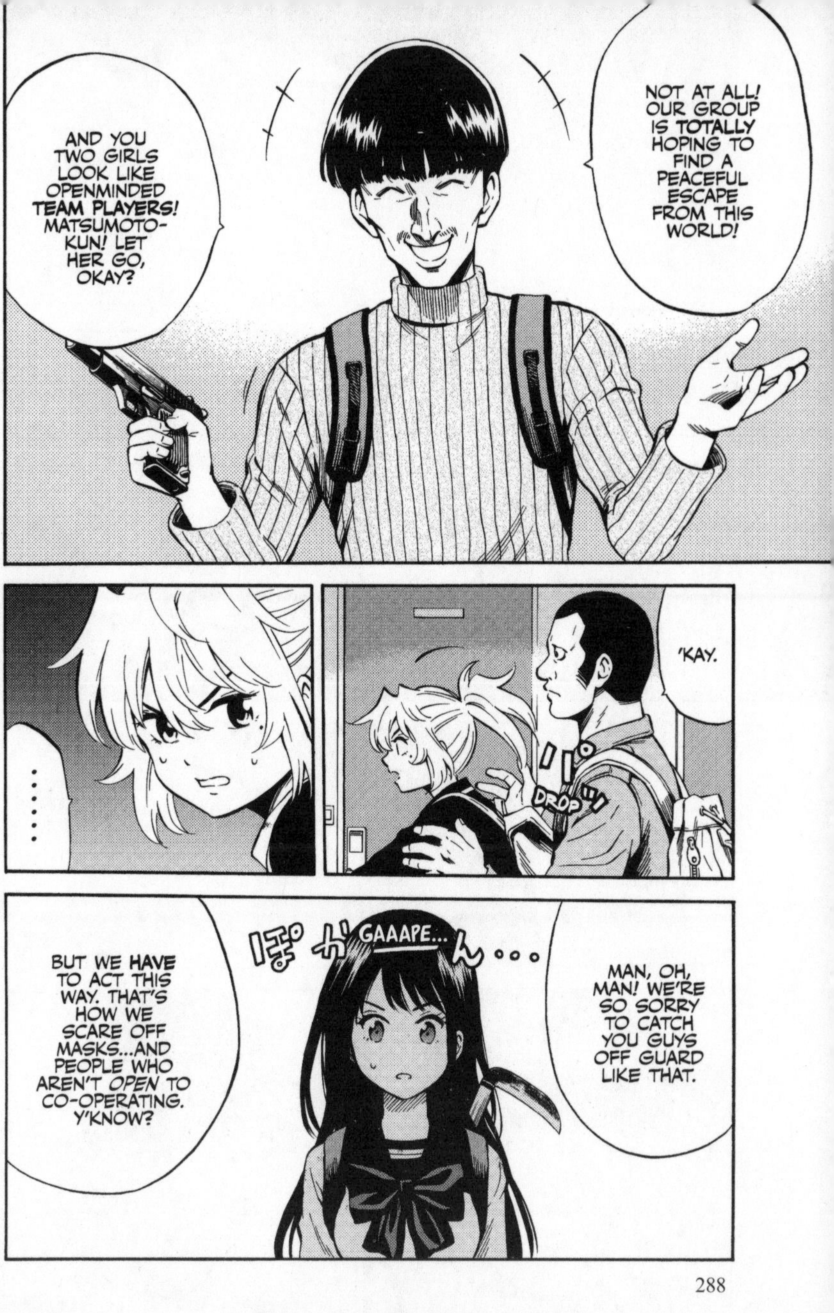
NOT AT ALL! OUR GROUP IS TOTALLY HOPING TO FIND A PEACEFUL ESCAPE FROM THIS WORLD!
AND YOU TWO GIRLS LOOK LIKE OPENMINDED TEAM PLAYERS! MATSUMOTO-KUN! LET HER GO, OKAY?
'KAY.
DROP
......
MAN, OH, MAN! WE'RE SO SORRY TO CATCH YOU GUYS OFF GUARD LIKE THAT.
ぽか ん・・・
GAAAPE...
BUT WE HAVE TO ACT THIS WAY. THAT'S HOW WE SCARE OFF MASKS...AND PEOPLE WHO AREN'T OPEN TO CO-OPERATING. Y'KNOW?

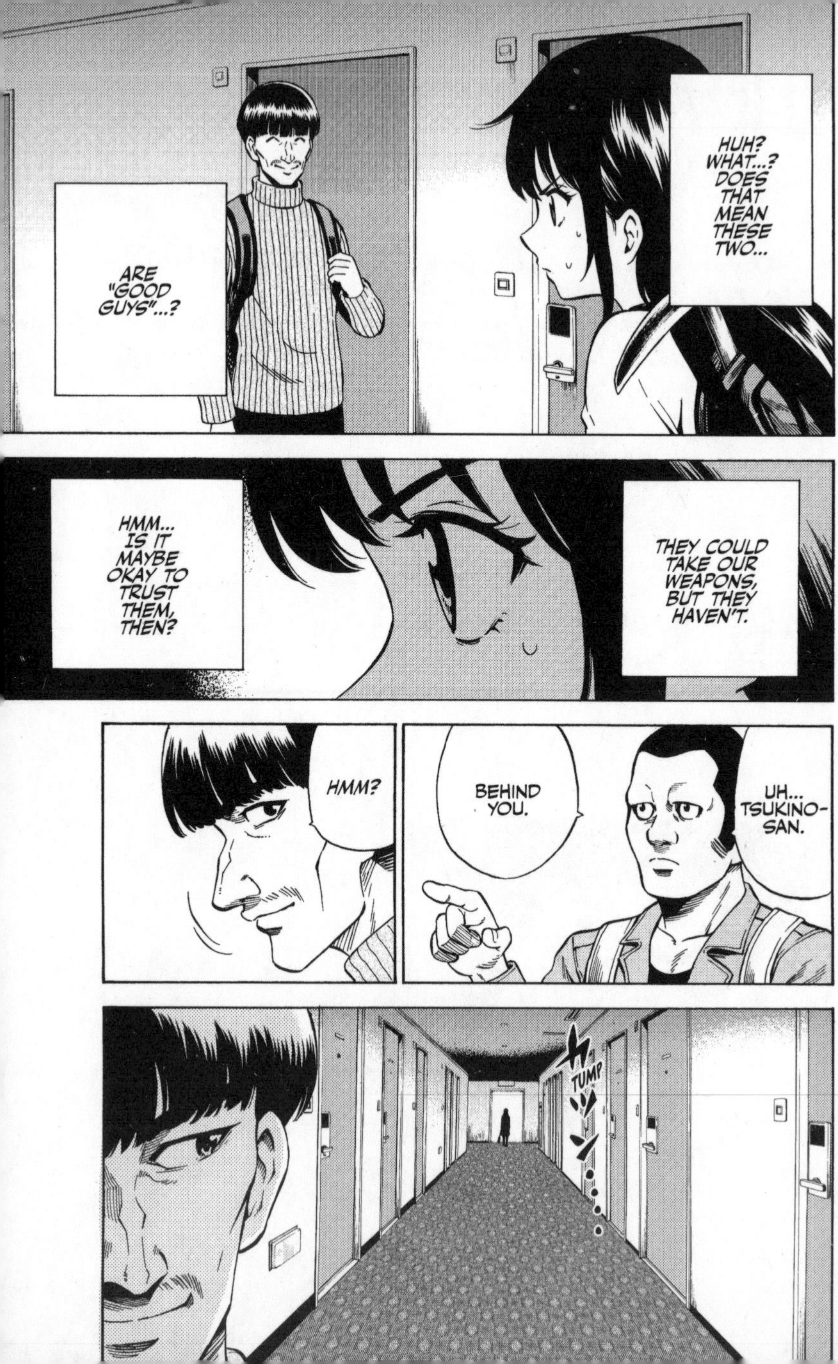
HUH? WHAT...? DOES THAT MEAN THESE TWO...
ARE "GOOD GUYS"...?
THEY COULD TAKE OUR WEAPONS, BUT THEY HAVEN'T.
HMM... IS IT MAYBE OKAY TO TRUST THEM, THEN?
UH... TSUKINO-SAN.
BEHIND YOU.
HMM?
TUMP

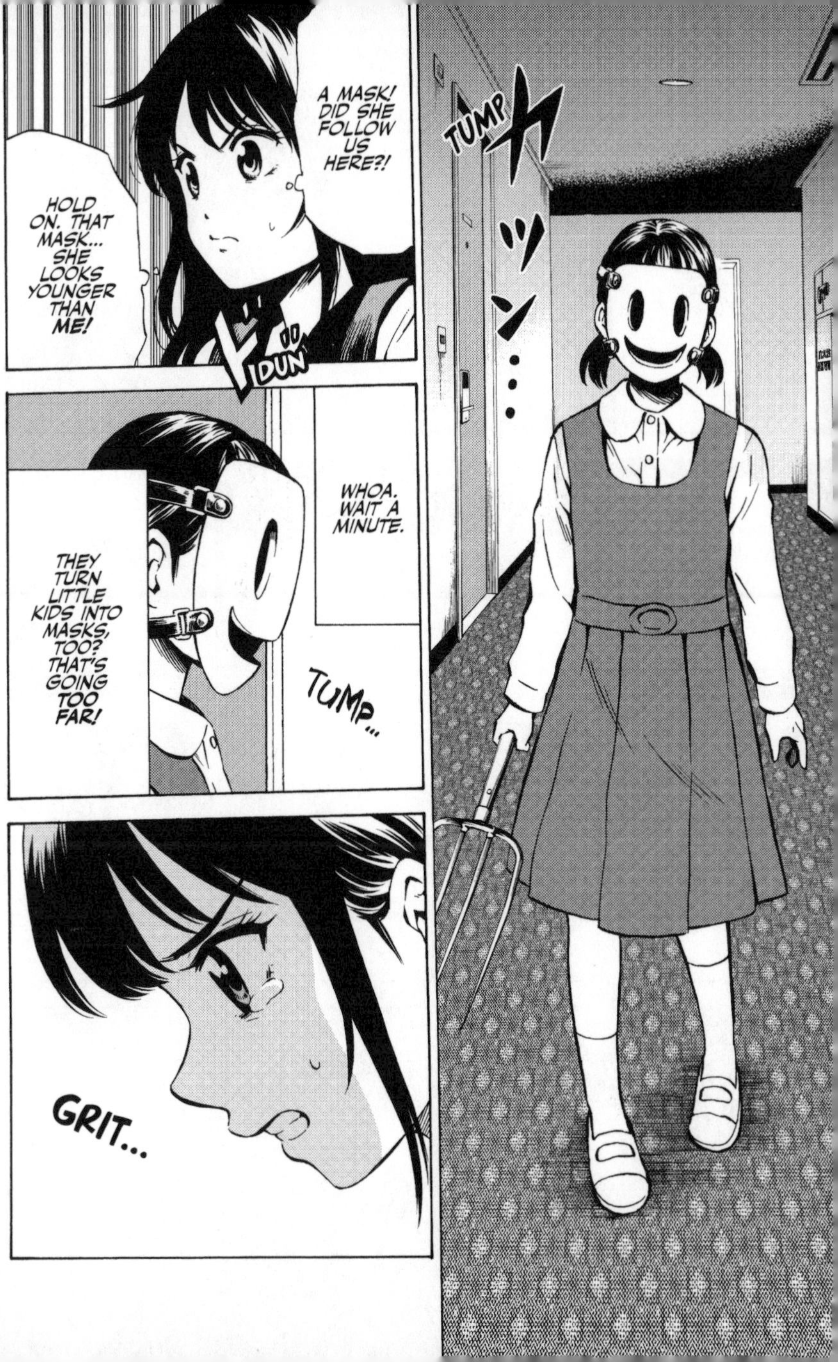
TUMP
カツン…
A MASK! DID SHE FOLLOW US HERE?!
HOLD ON. THAT MASK... SHE LOOKS YOUNGER THAN ME!
DUN
WHOA. WAIT A MINUTE.
THEY TURN LITTLE KIDS INTO MASKS, TOO? THAT'S GOING TOO FAR!
TUMP...
GRIT...

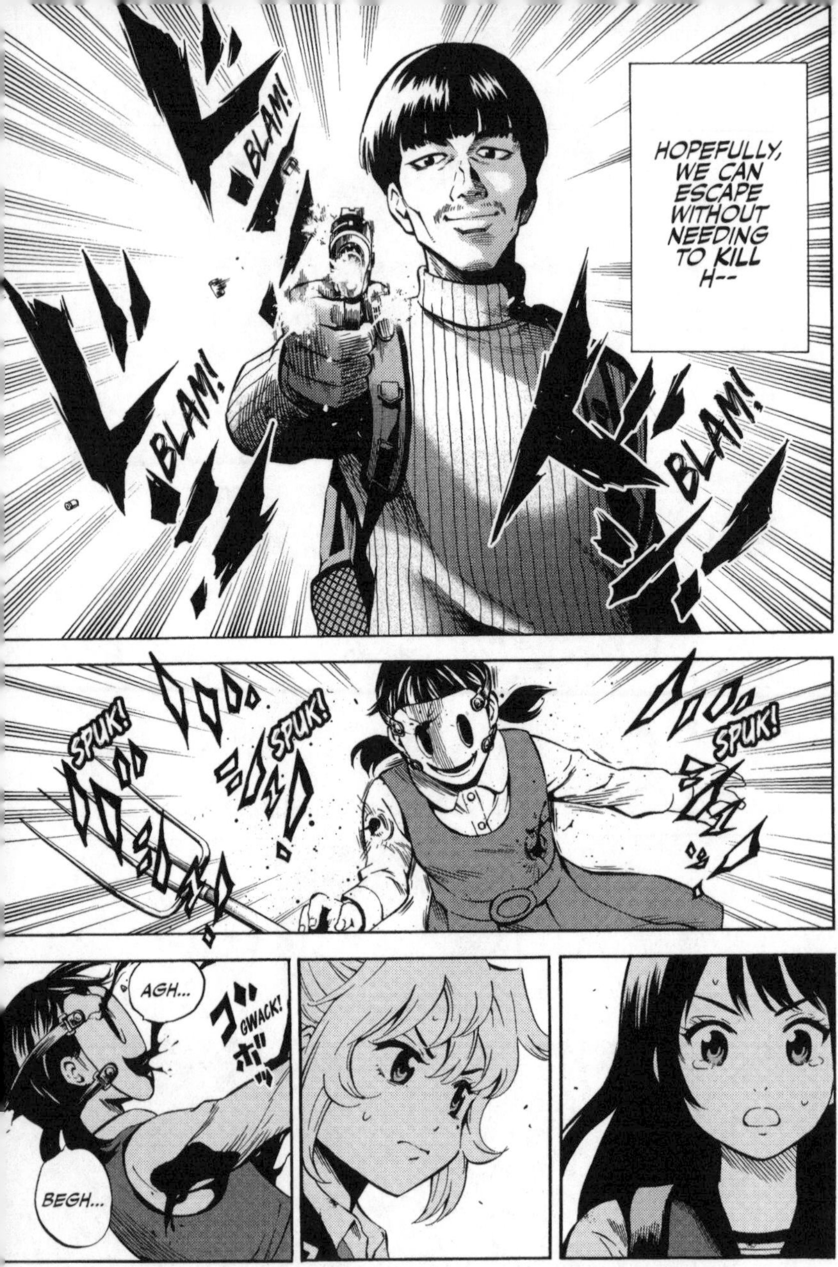
HOPEFULLY, WE CAN ESCAPE WITHOUT NEEDING TO KILL H--
BLAM!
BLAM!
BLAM!
BLAM!
SPUK!
SPUK!
SPUK!
GWACK!
AGH...
BEGH...

I CAN SAFELY ASSUME YOU'RE HAPPY TO WORK WITH US, RIGHT? SINCE OUR FLYER *DID* BRING YOU HERE...?

BY THE WAY...

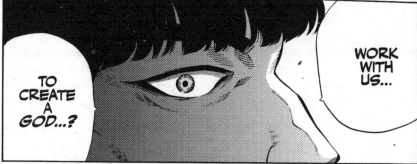

TO CREATE A *GOD*...?

WORK WITH US...

MIGHT BE DANGEROUS AFTER ALL.

THESE GUYS...

BA-DUMP!!

WHAT SHOULD WE DO...?

FROM CHAPTER 59 ONWARD, WEEKLY SHONEN MAGAZINE GAVE US A SPECIAL GUEST RUN FOR TEN WEEKS OR SO. SOME PAGES FROM THIS PERIOD BASICALLY RETELL THE STORY OF THE MANGA'S UNIVERSE, AND THOSE PARTS MIGHT SEEM OUT OF PLACE TO READERS READING VOLUME BY VOLUME. IF YOU'RE SCRATCHING YOUR HEAD, KEEP IN MIND THAT THERE'S A REASON!

HIGH-RISE INVASION

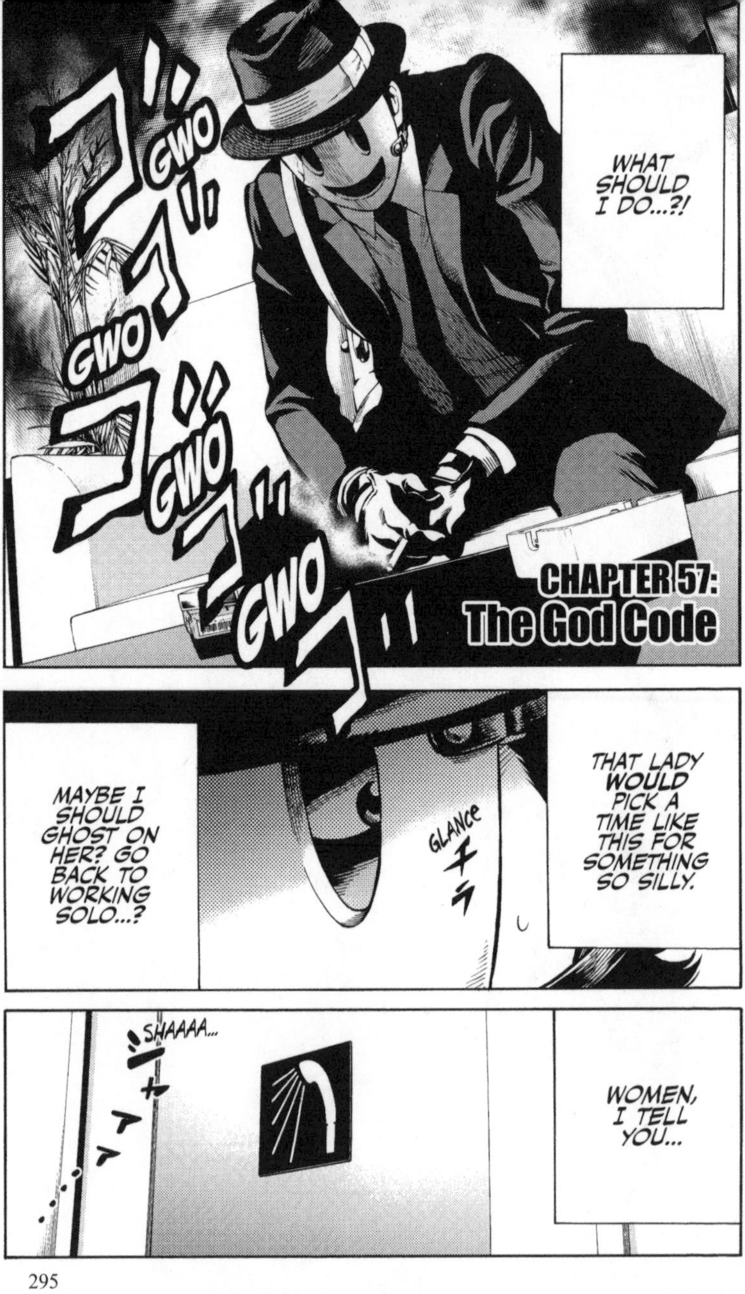
WHAT SHOULD I DO...?!
GWO
GWO
GWO
GWO
CHAPTER 57:
The God Code
THAT LADY WOULD PICK A TIME LIKE THIS FOR SOMETHING SO SILLY.
GLANCE
MAYBE I SHOULD GHOST ON HER? GO BACK TO WORKING SOLO...?
WOMEN, I TELL YOU...
SHAAAA...

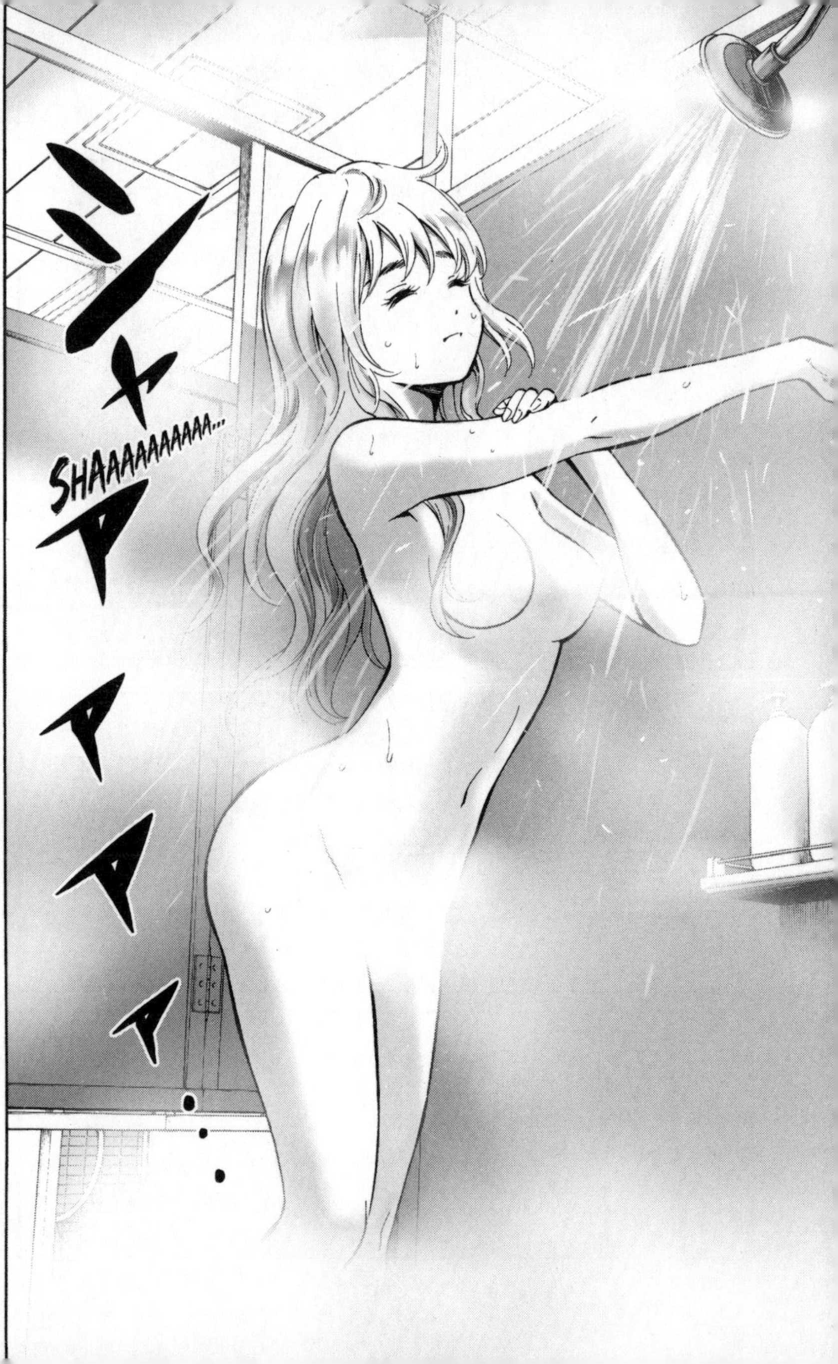
シャアアアア…
SHAAAAAAAAAA...

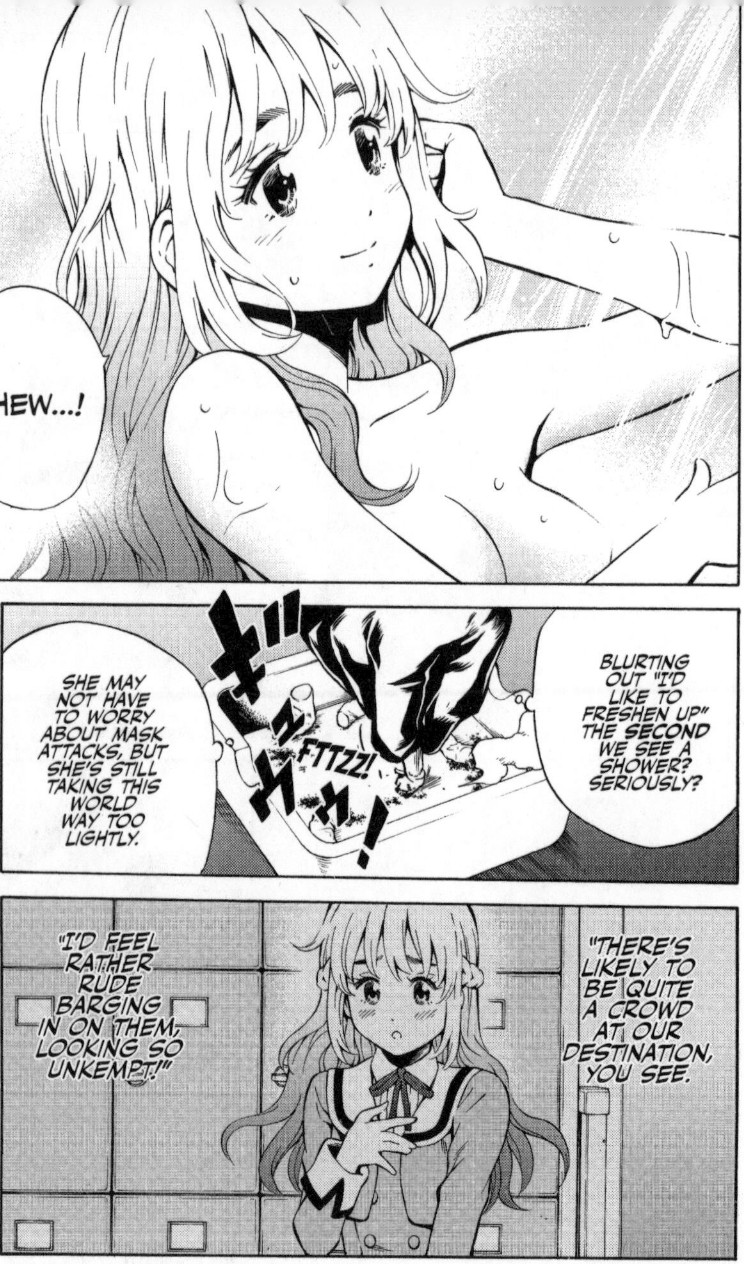
WHEW...!
BLURTING OUT "I'D LIKE TO FRESHEN UP" THE SECOND WE SEE A SHOWER? SERIOUSLY?
FTTZZ!
SHE MAY NOT HAVE TO WORRY ABOUT MASK ATTACKS, BUT SHE'S STILL TAKING THIS WORLD WAY TOO LIGHTLY.
"THERE'S LIKELY TO BE QUITE A CROWD AT OUR DESTINATION, YOU SEE.
"I'D FEEL RATHER RUDE BARGING IN ON THEM, LOOKING SO UNKEMPT!"

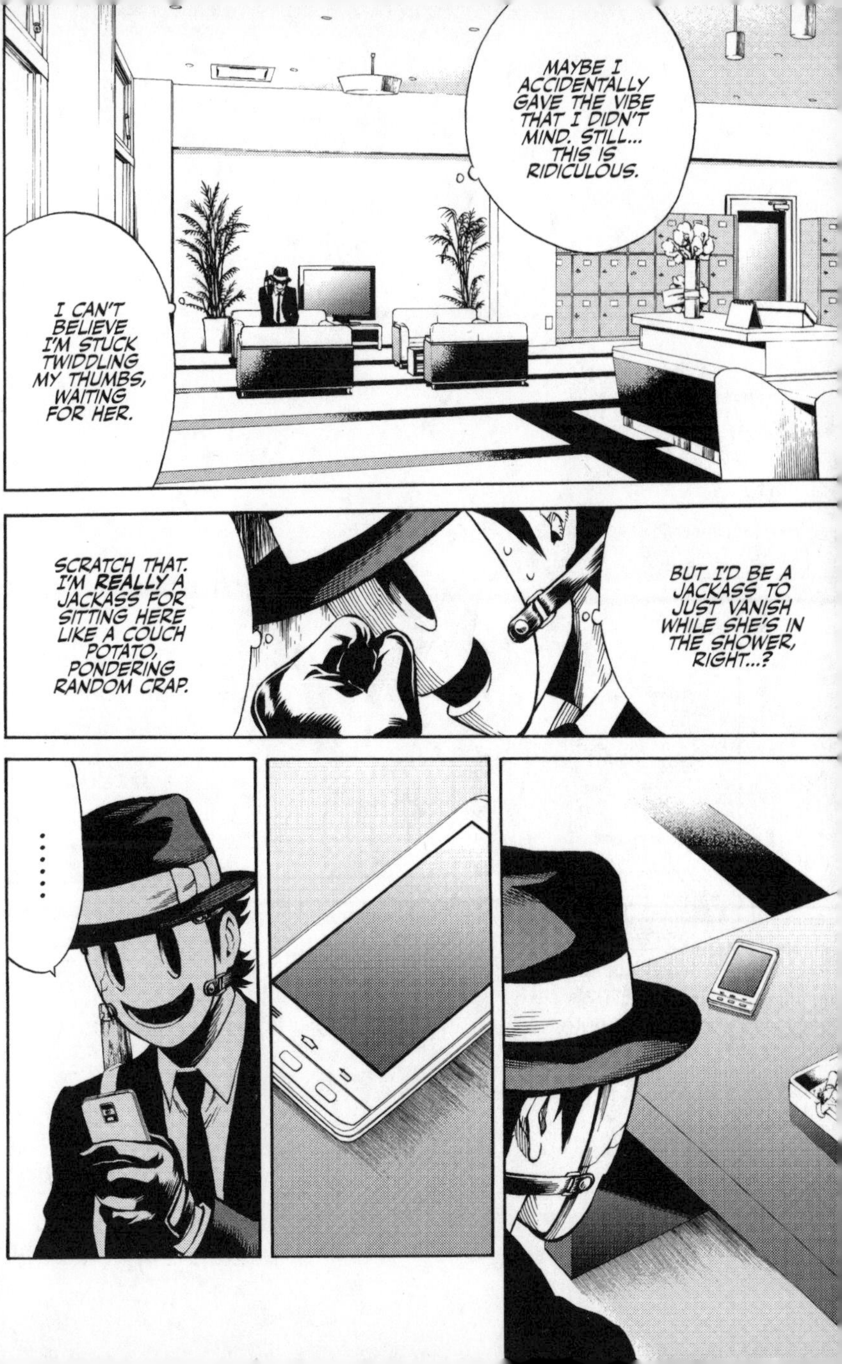
MAYBE I ACCIDENTALLY GAVE THE VIBE THAT I DIDN'T MIND. STILL... THIS IS RIDICULOUS.
I CAN'T BELIEVE I'M STUCK TWIDDLING MY THUMBS, WAITING FOR HER.
BUT I'D BE A JACKASS TO JUST VANISH WHILE SHE'S IN THE SHOWER, RIGHT...?
SCRATCH THAT. I'M **REALLY** A JACKASS FOR SITTING HERE LIKE A COUCH POTATO, PONDERING RANDOM CRAP.
......

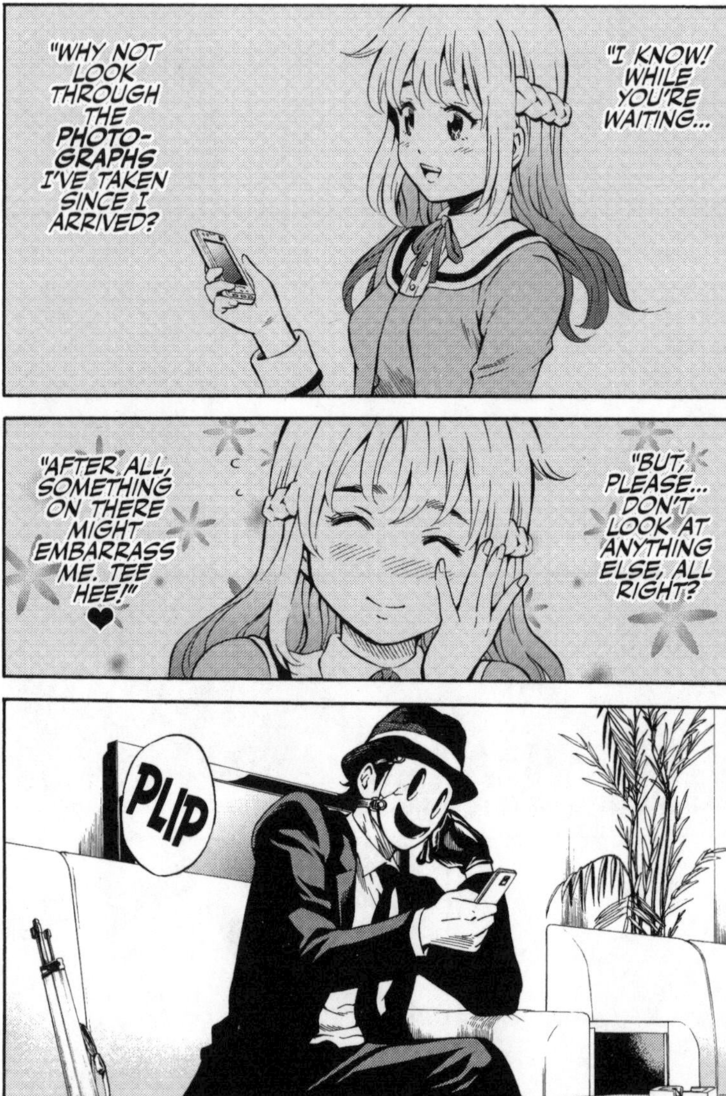
"I KNOW! WHILE YOU'RE WAITING...
"WHY NOT LOOK THROUGH THE PHOTOGRAPHS I'VE TAKEN SINCE I ARRIVED?
"BUT, PLEASE... DON'T LOOK AT ANYTHING ELSE, ALL RIGHT?
"AFTER ALL, SOMETHING ON THERE MIGHT EMBARRASS ME. TEE HEE!" ❤
PLIP

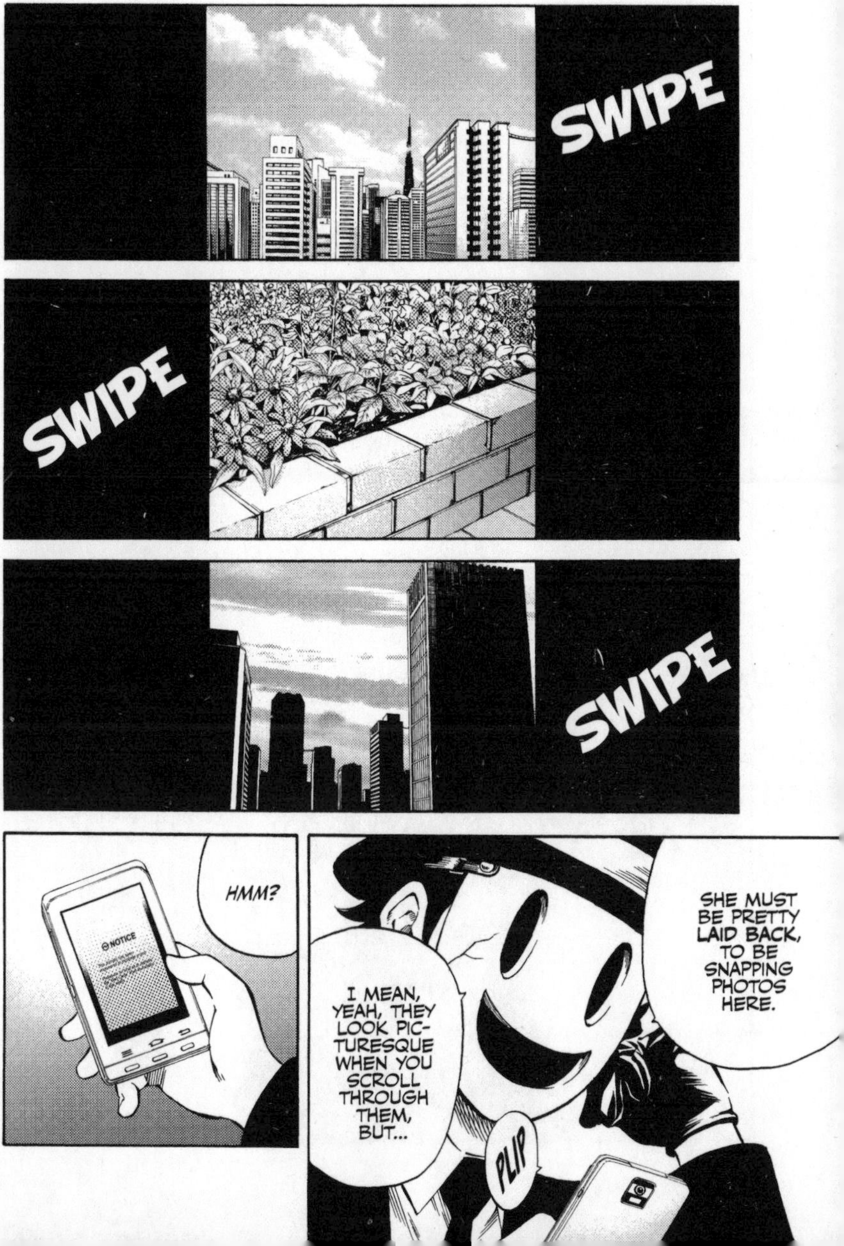
SWIPE
SWIPE
SWIPE
SHE MUST BE PRETTY LAID BACK, TO BE SNAPPING PHOTOS HERE.
I MEAN, YEAH, THEY LOOK PIC-TURESQUE WHEN YOU SCROLL THROUGH THEM, BUT...
PLIP
HMM?

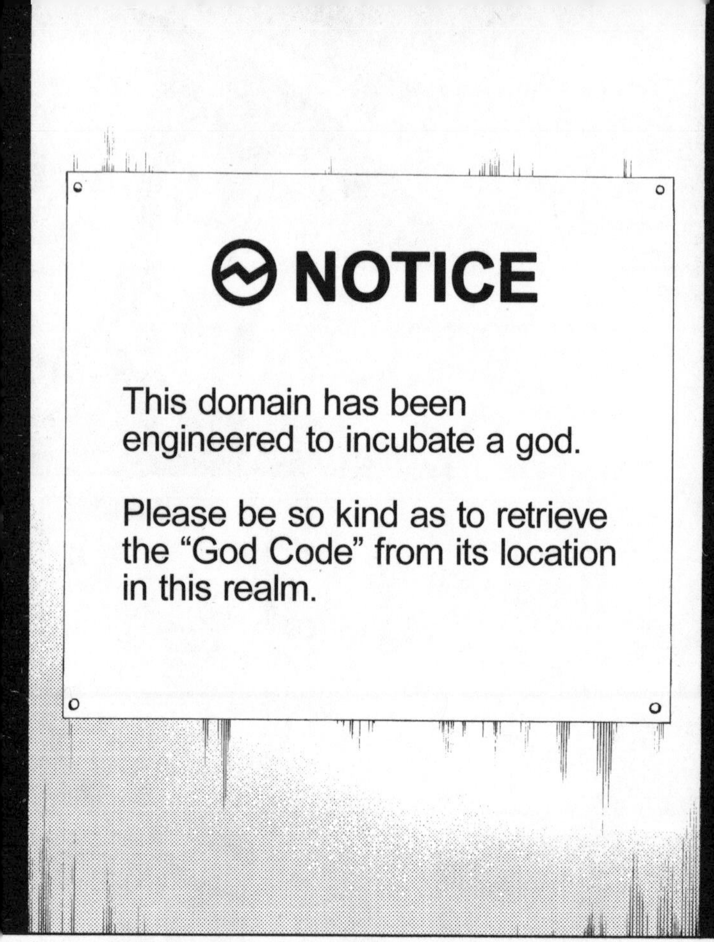
NOTICE
This domain has been engineered to incubate a god.
Please be so kind as to retrieve the "God Code" from its location in this realm.

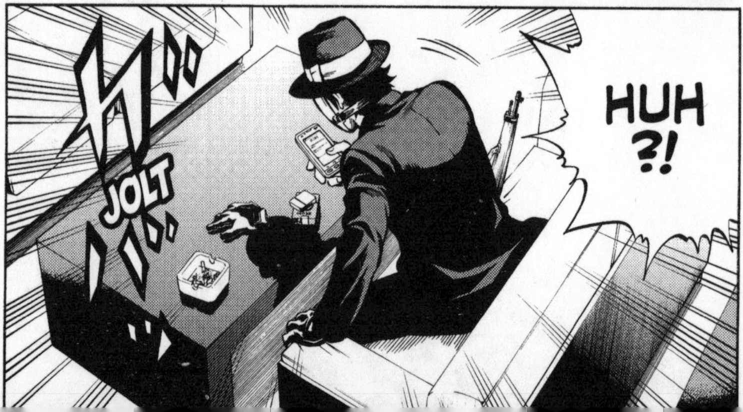
HUH ?!
JOLT

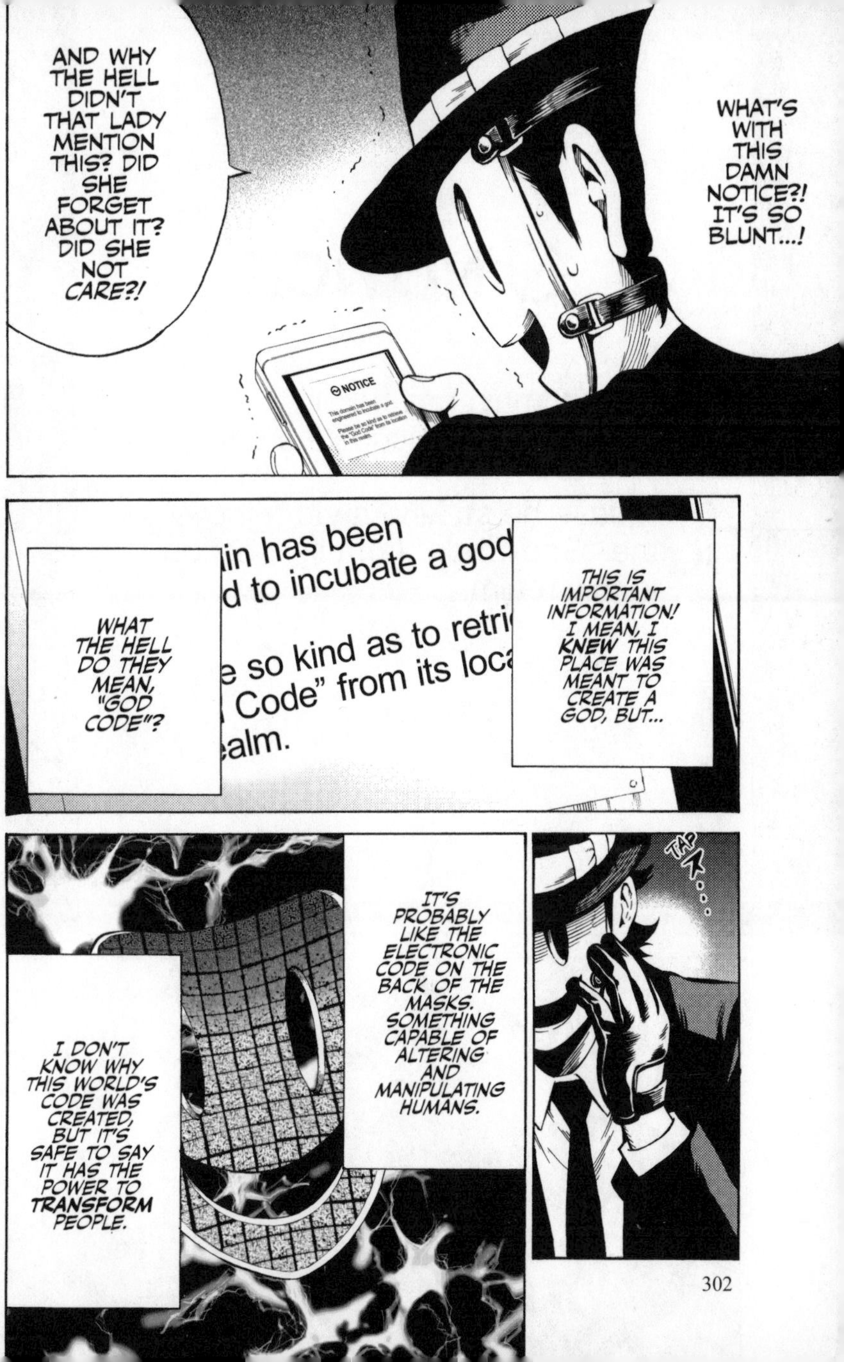
WHAT'S WITH THIS DAMN NOTICE?! IT'S SO BLUNT...!
AND WHY THE HELL DIDN'T THAT LADY MENTION THIS? DID SHE FORGET ABOUT IT? DID SHE NOT *CARE?!*
NOTICE
This domain has been engineered to incubate a god.
Please be so kind as to retrieve the "God Code" from its location in this realm.
THIS IS IMPORTANT INFORMATION! I MEAN, I **KNEW** THIS PLACE WAS MEANT TO CREATE A GOD, BUT...
ain has been
d to incubate a god
e so kind as to retri
Code" from its loc
ealm.
WHAT THE HELL DO THEY MEAN, "GOD CODE"?
TAP...
IT'S PROBABLY LIKE THE ELECTRONIC CODE ON THE BACK OF THE MASKS. SOMETHING CAPABLE OF ALTERING AND MANIPULATING HUMANS.
I DON'T KNOW WHY THIS WORLD'S CODE WAS CREATED, BUT IT'S SAFE TO SAY IT HAS THE POWER TO **TRANSFORM** PEOPLE.

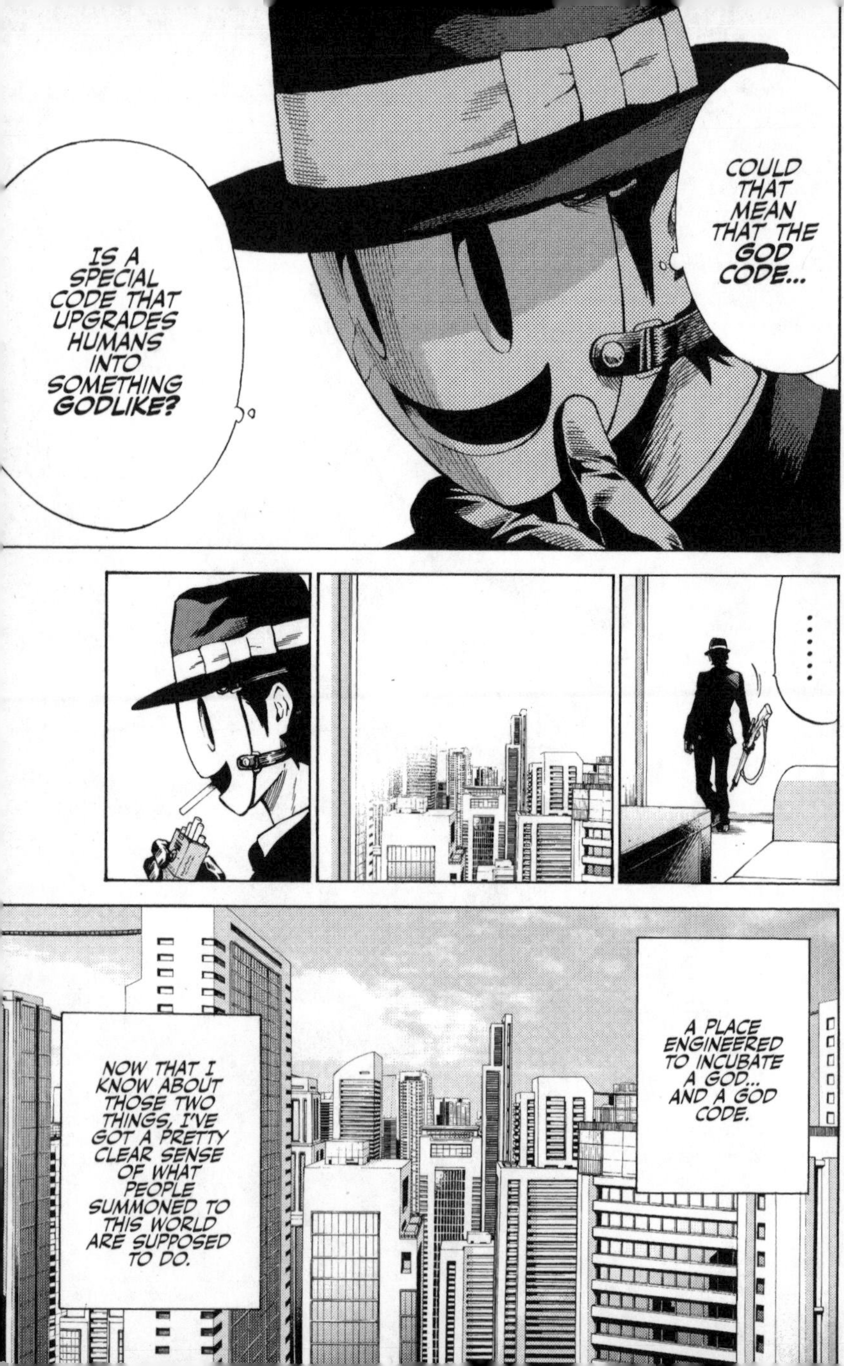
COULD THAT MEAN THAT THE GOD CODE...
IS A SPECIAL CODE THAT UPGRADES HUMANS INTO SOMETHING GODLIKE?
......
A PLACE ENGINEERED TO INCUBATE A GOD... AND A GOD CODE.
NOW THAT I KNOW ABOUT THOSE TWO THINGS, I'VE GOT A PRETTY CLEAR SENSE OF WHAT PEOPLE SUMMONED TO THIS WORLD ARE SUPPOSED TO DO.

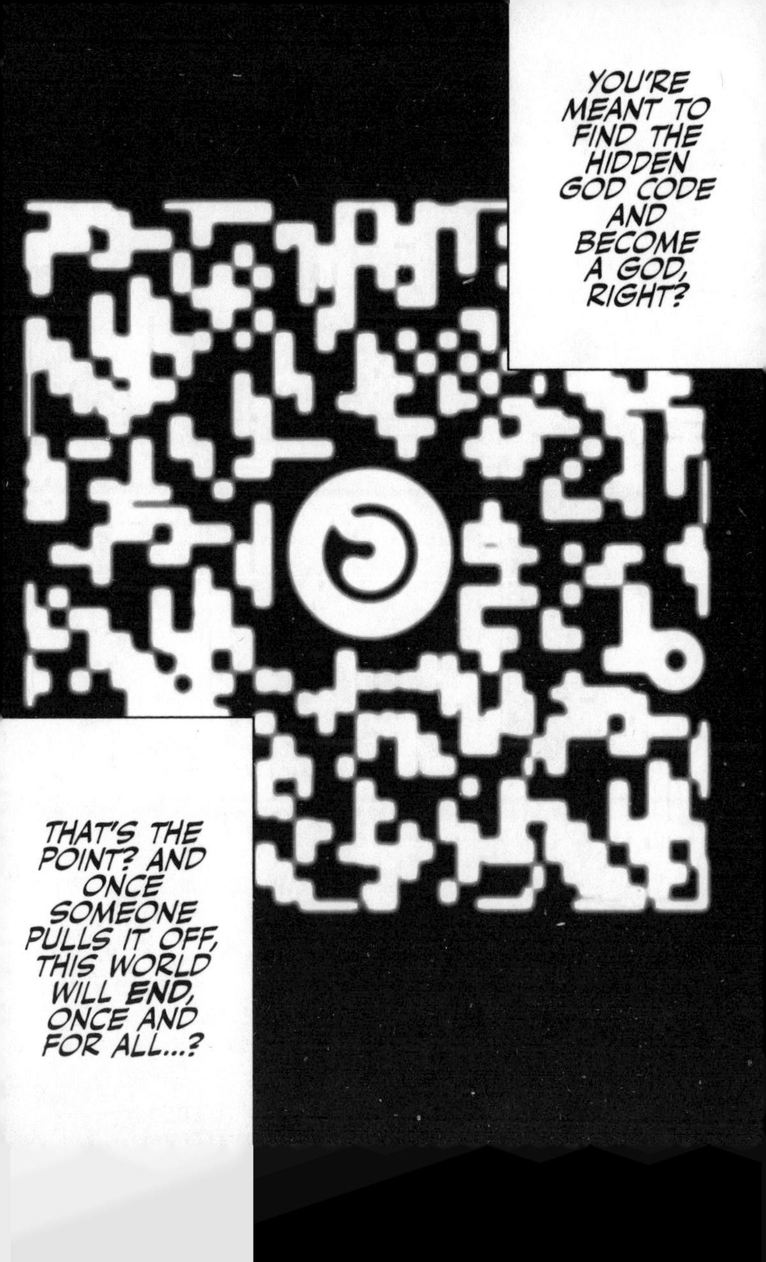
YOU'RE MEANT TO FIND THE HIDDEN GOD CODE AND BECOME A GOD, RIGHT?
THAT'S THE POINT? AND ONCE SOMEONE PULLS IT OFF, THIS WORLD WILL END, ONCE AND FOR ALL...?

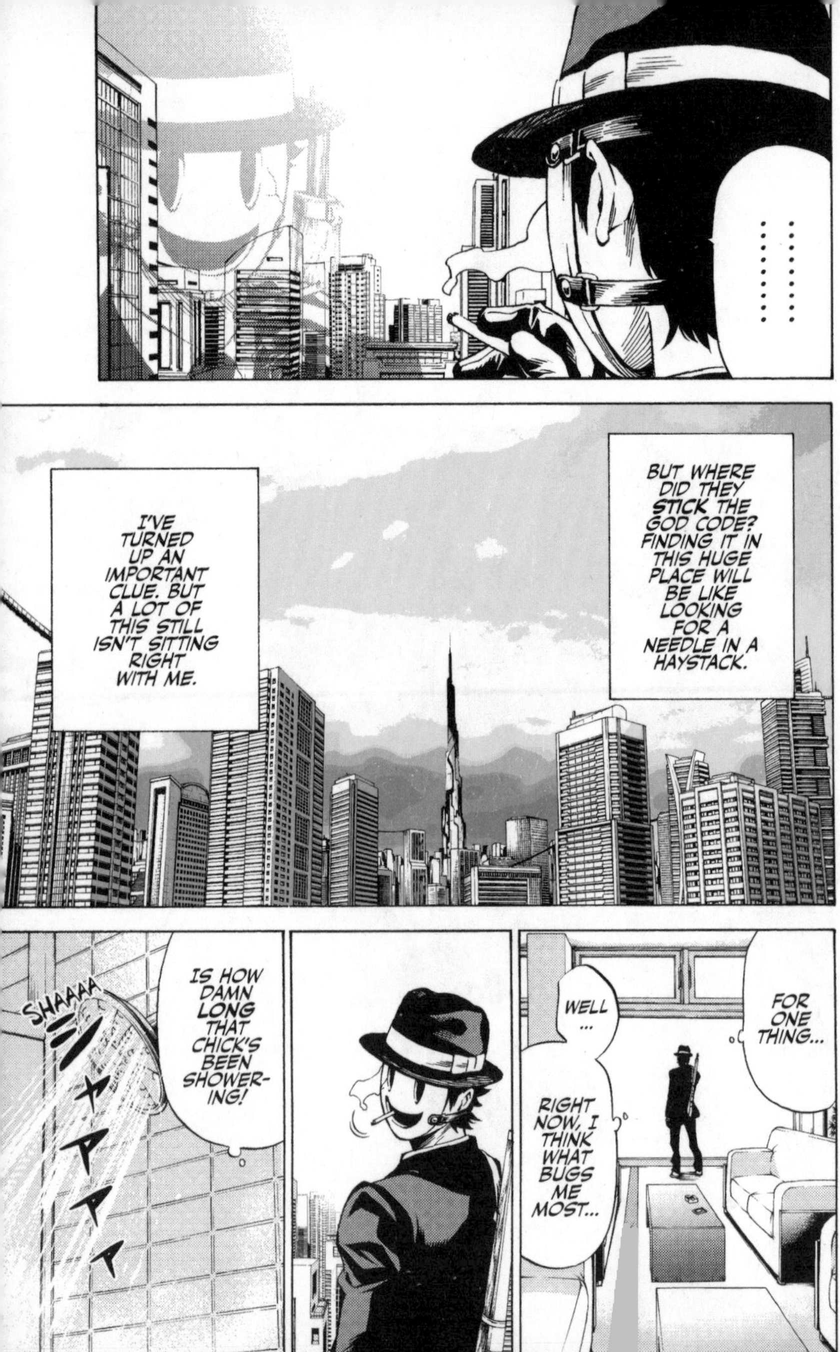
......
BUT WHERE DID THEY STICK THE GOD CODE? FINDING IT IN THIS HUGE PLACE WILL BE LIKE LOOKING FOR A NEEDLE IN A HAYSTACK.
I'VE TURNED UP AN IMPORTANT CLUE. BUT A LOT OF THIS STILL ISN'T SITTING RIGHT WITH ME.
FOR ONE THING...
WELL...
RIGHT NOW, I THINK WHAT BUGS ME MOST...
IS HOW DAMN LONG THAT CHICK'S BEEN SHOWER-ING!
SHAAAA

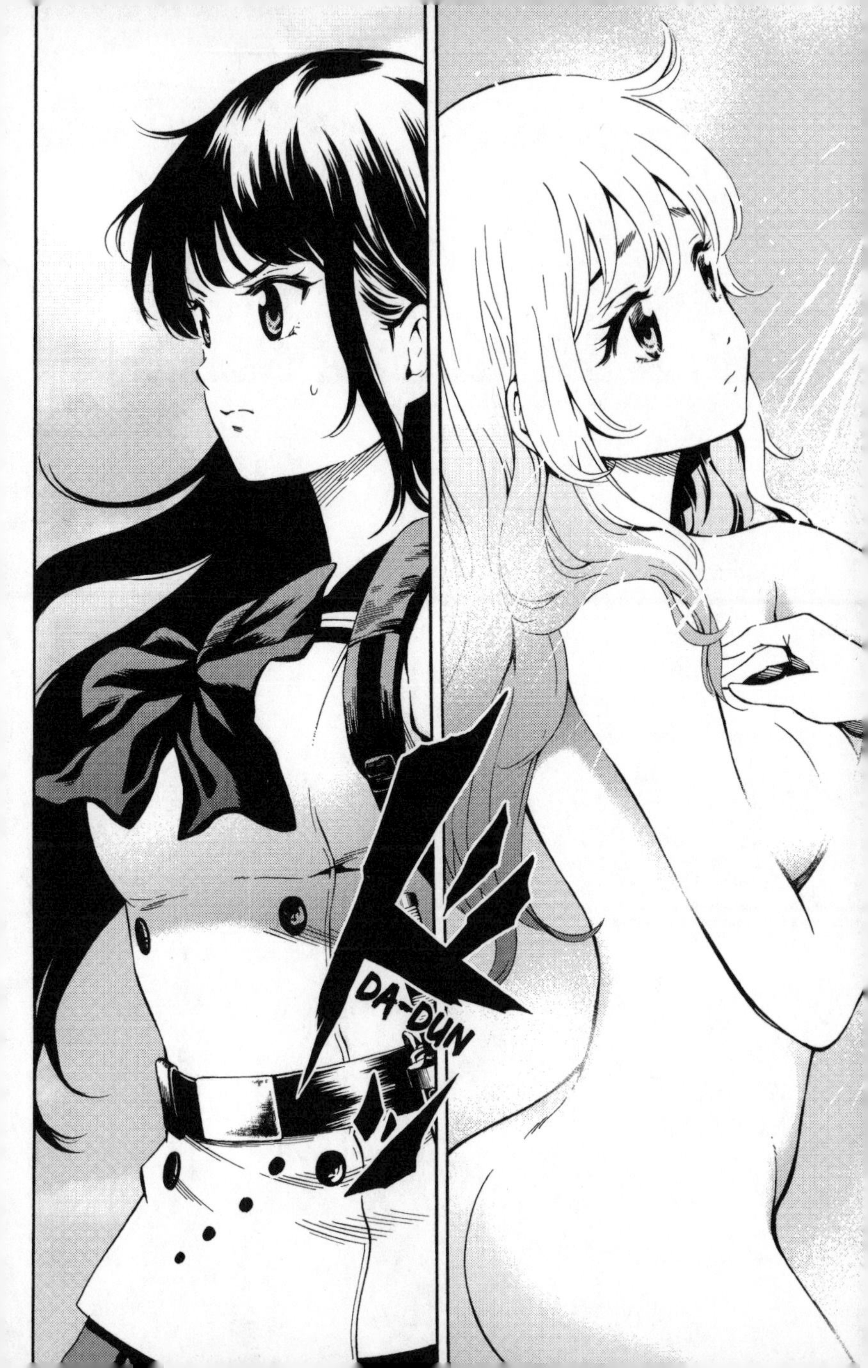
DA-DUN

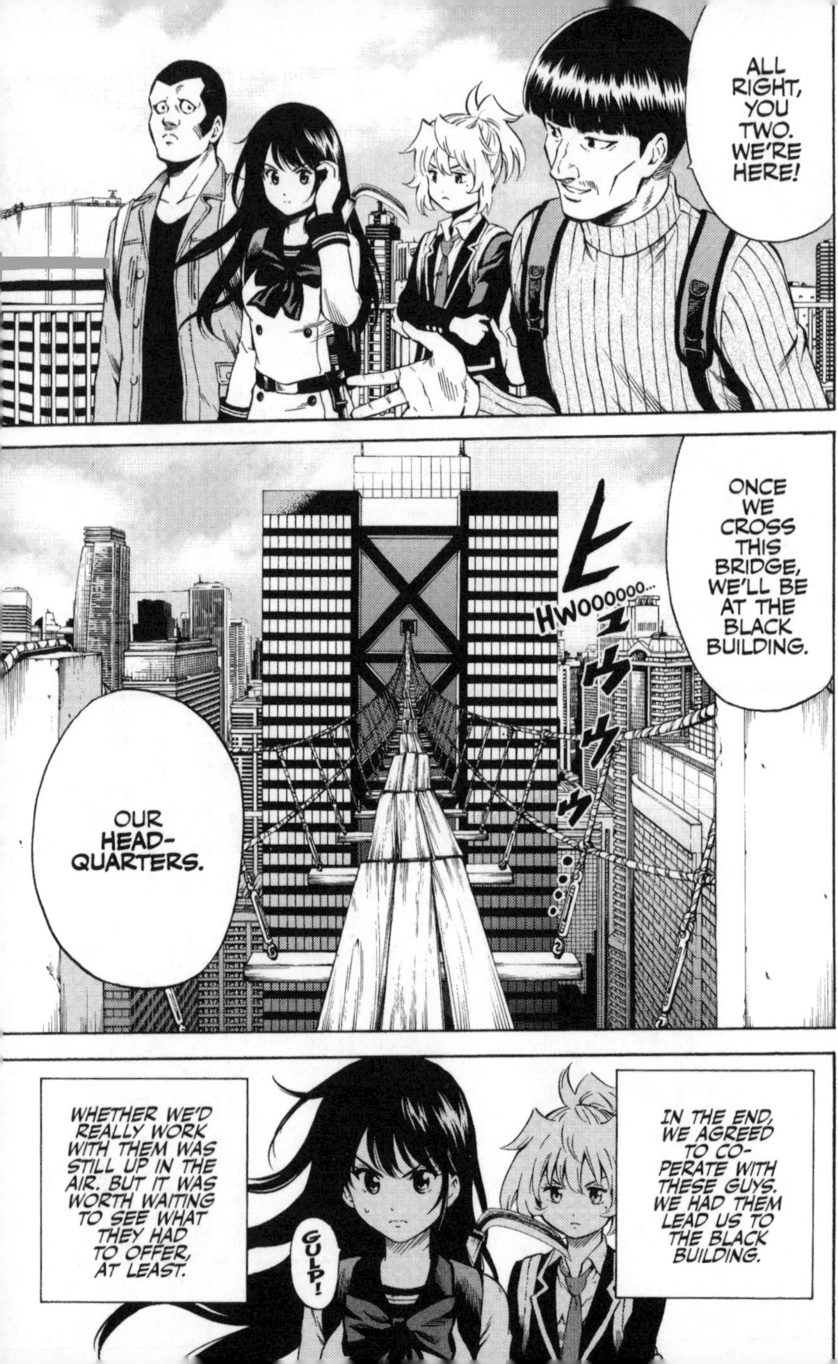
ALL RIGHT, YOU TWO. WE'RE HERE!
ONCE WE CROSS THIS BRIDGE, WE'LL BE AT THE BLACK BUILDING.
HWOOOOOO...
OUR HEAD-QUARTERS.
IN THE END, WE AGREED TO CO-PERATE WITH THESE GUYS. WE HAD THEM LEAD US TO THE BLACK BUILDING.
GULP!
WHETHER WE'D REALLY WORK WITH THEM WAS STILL UP IN THE AIR. BUT IT WAS WORTH WAITING TO SEE WHAT THEY HAD TO OFFER, AT LEAST.

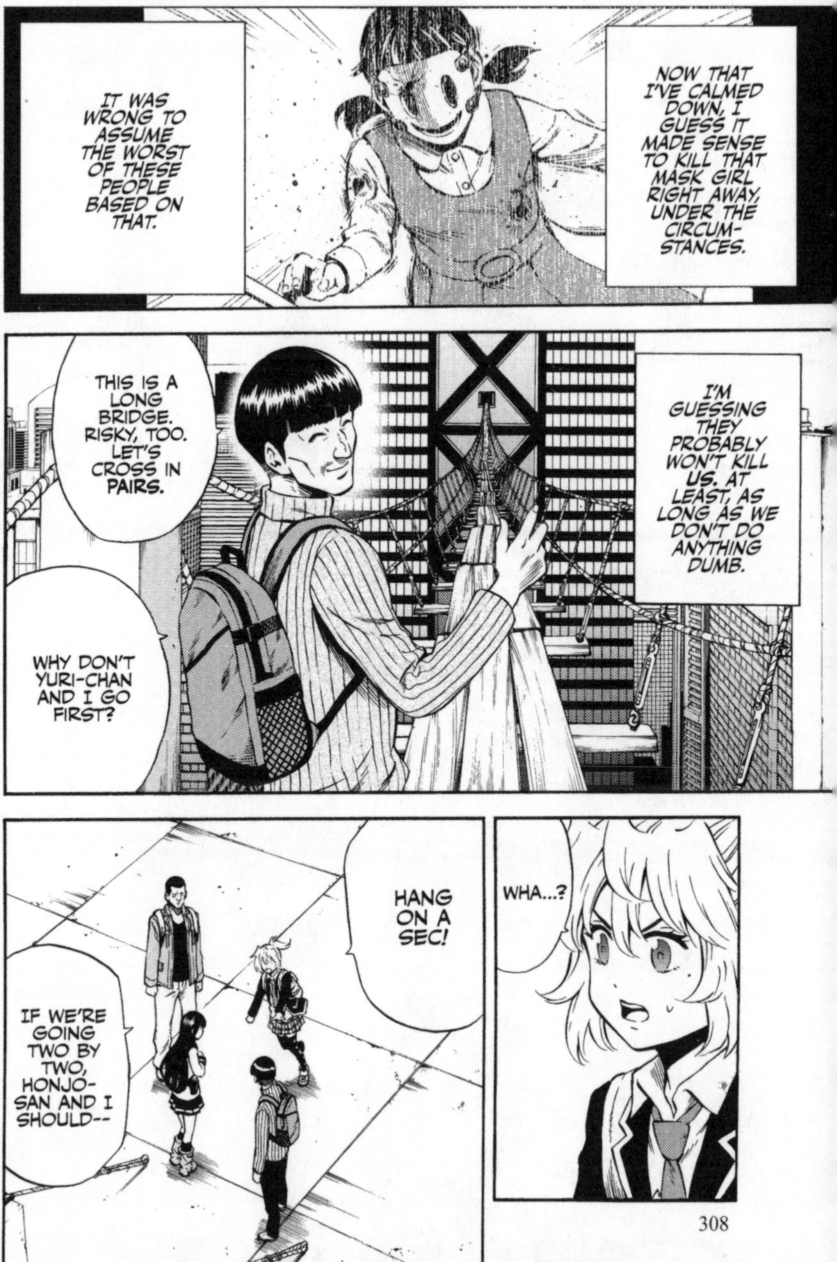
NOW THAT I'VE CALMED DOWN, I GUESS IT MADE SENSE TO KILL THAT MASK GIRL RIGHT AWAY, UNDER THE CIRCUM-STANCES.
IT WAS WRONG TO ASSUME THE WORST OF THESE PEOPLE BASED ON THAT.
I'M GUESSING THEY PROBABLY WON'T KILL US. AT LEAST, AS LONG AS WE DON'T DO ANYTHING DUMB.
THIS IS A LONG BRIDGE. RISKY, TOO. LET'S CROSS IN PAIRS.
WHY DON'T YURI-CHAN AND I GO FIRST?
WHA...?
HANG ON A SEC!
IF WE'RE GOING TWO BY TWO, HONJO-SAN AND I SHOULD--

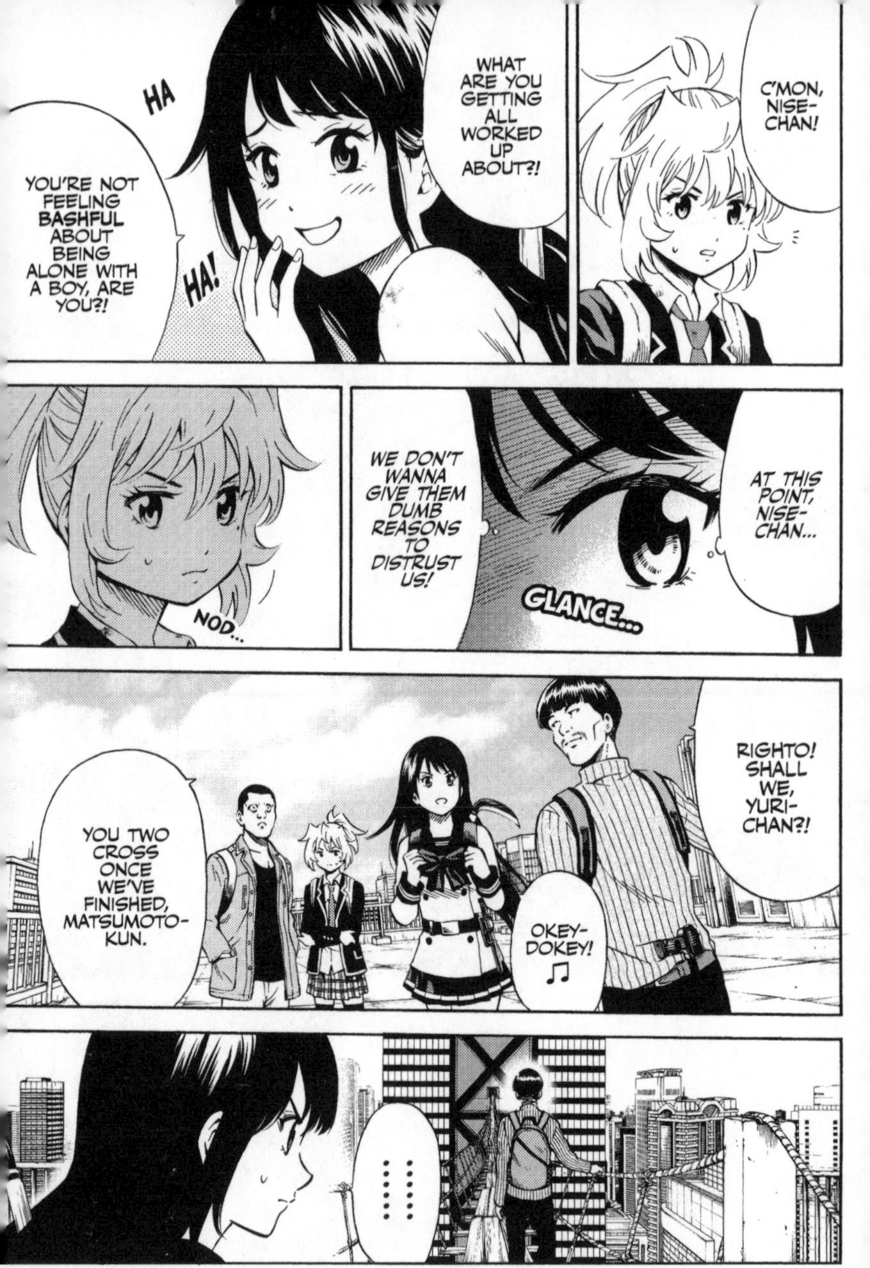
C'MON, NISE-CHAN!
WHAT ARE YOU GETTING ALL WORKED UP ABOUT?!
HA
HA!
YOU'RE NOT FEELING **BASHFUL** ABOUT BEING ALONE WITH A BOY, ARE YOU?!
AT THIS POINT, NISE-CHAN...
GLANCE...
WE DON'T WANNA GIVE THEM DUMB REASONS TO DISTRUST US!
NOD...
RIGHTO! SHALL WE, YURI-CHAN?!
OKEY-DOKEY! ♫
YOU TWO CROSS ONCE WE'VE FINISHED, MATSUMOTO-KUN.
......

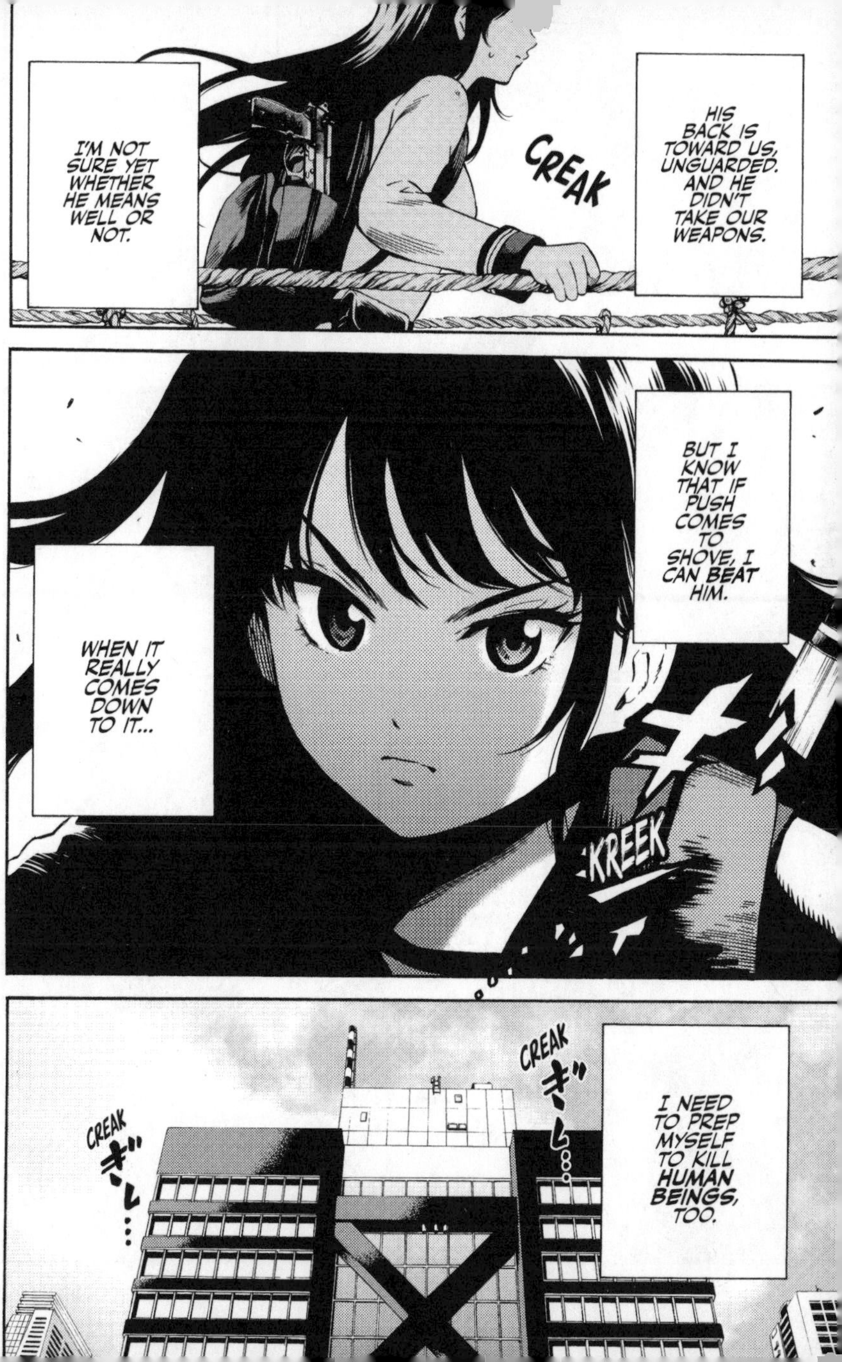
HIS BACK IS TOWARD US, UNGUARDED. AND HE DIDN'T TAKE OUR WEAPONS.
CREAK
I'M NOT SURE YET WHETHER HE MEANS WELL OR NOT.
BUT I KNOW THAT IF PUSH COMES TO SHOVE, I CAN BEAT HIM.
WHEN IT REALLY COMES DOWN TO IT...
KREEK
I NEED TO PREP MYSELF TO KILL HUMAN BEINGS, TOO.
CREAK
CREAK

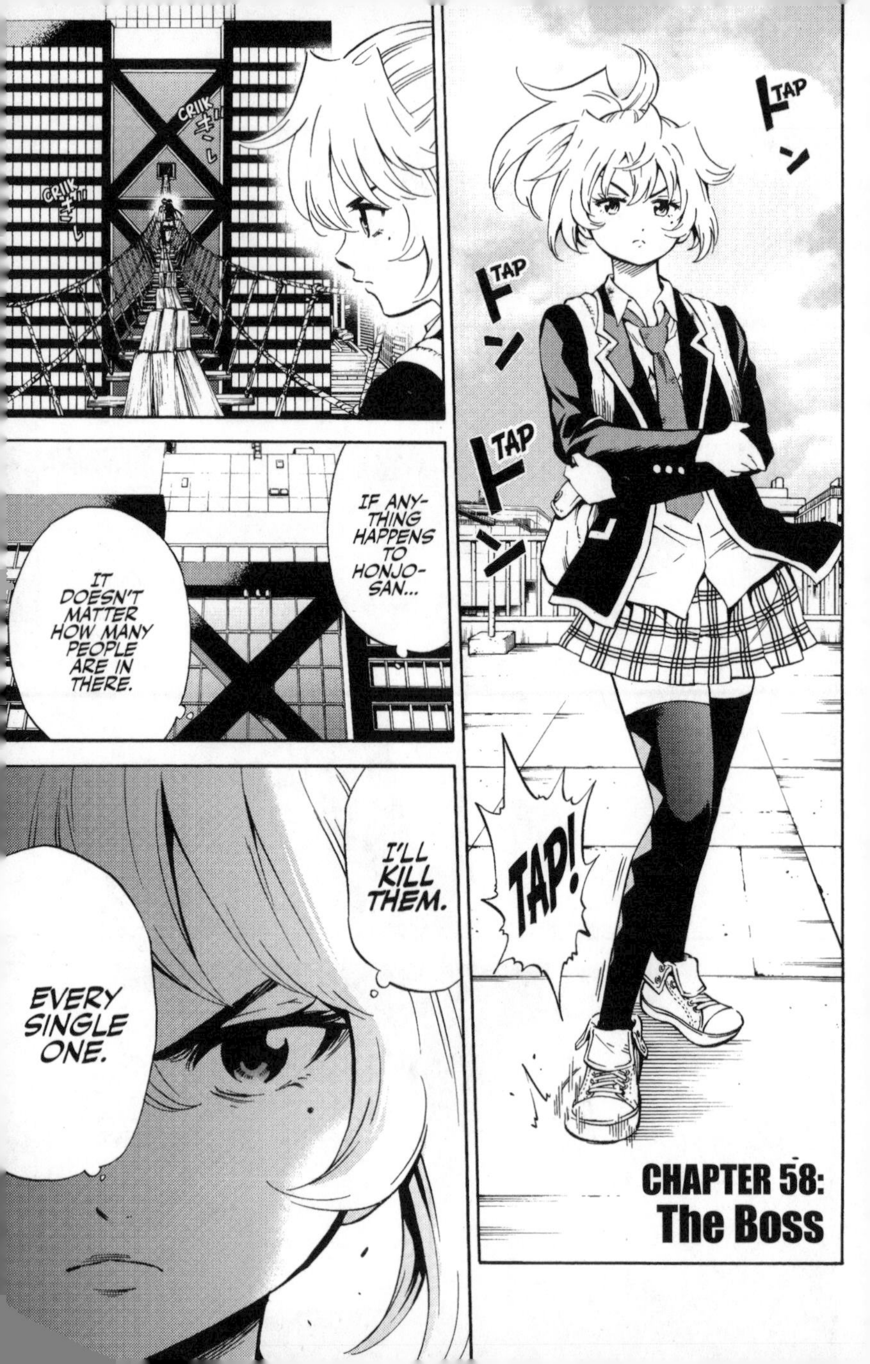
TAP
TAP
TAP
TAP!
CHAPTER 58:
The Boss
CRIIK
CRIIK
IF ANY-THING HAPPENS TO HONJO-SAN...
IT DOESN'T MATTER HOW MANY PEOPLE ARE IN THERE.
I'LL KILL THEM.
EVERY SINGLE ONE.

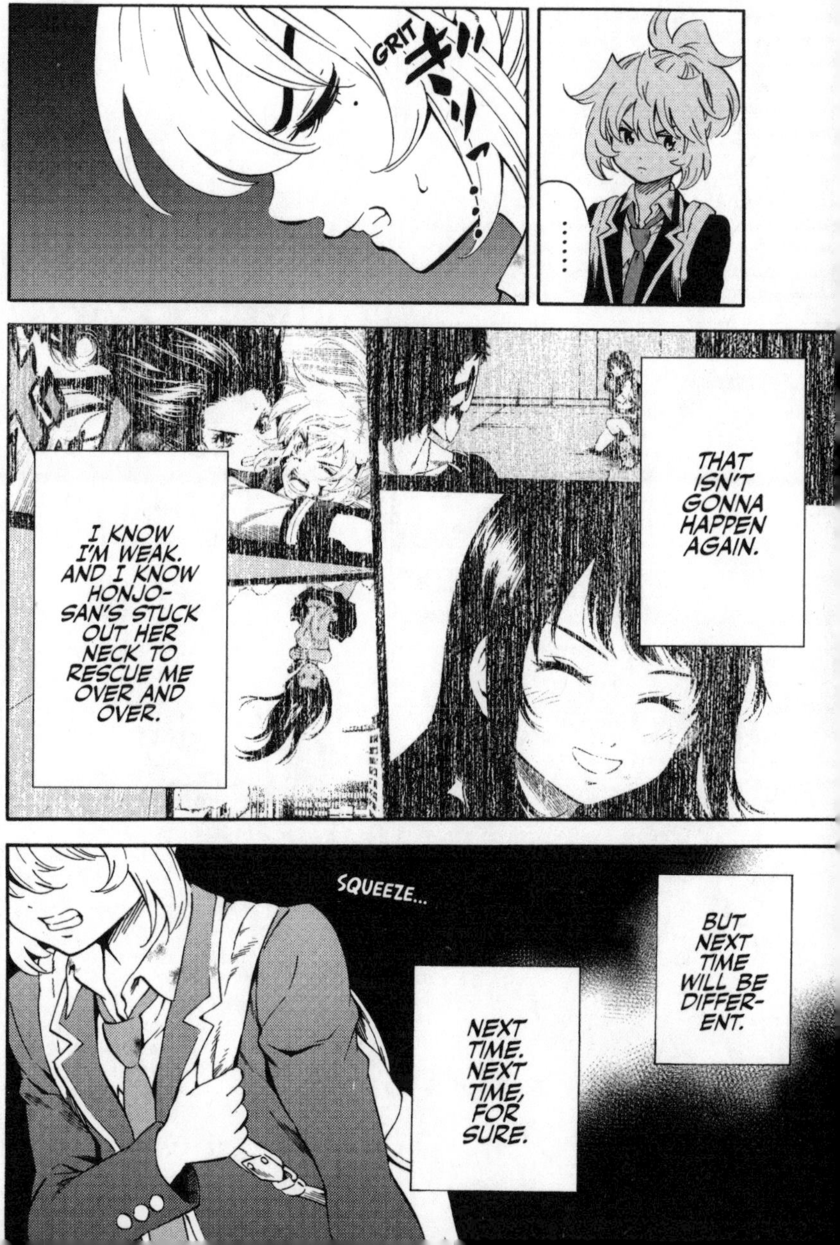
......
GRIT
ギッ
THAT ISN'T GONNA HAPPEN AGAIN.
I KNOW I'M WEAK. AND I KNOW HONJO-SAN'S STUCK OUT HER NECK TO RESCUE ME OVER AND OVER.
BUT NEXT TIME WILL BE DIFFER-ENT.
SQUEEZE...
NEXT TIME. NEXT TIME, FOR SURE.

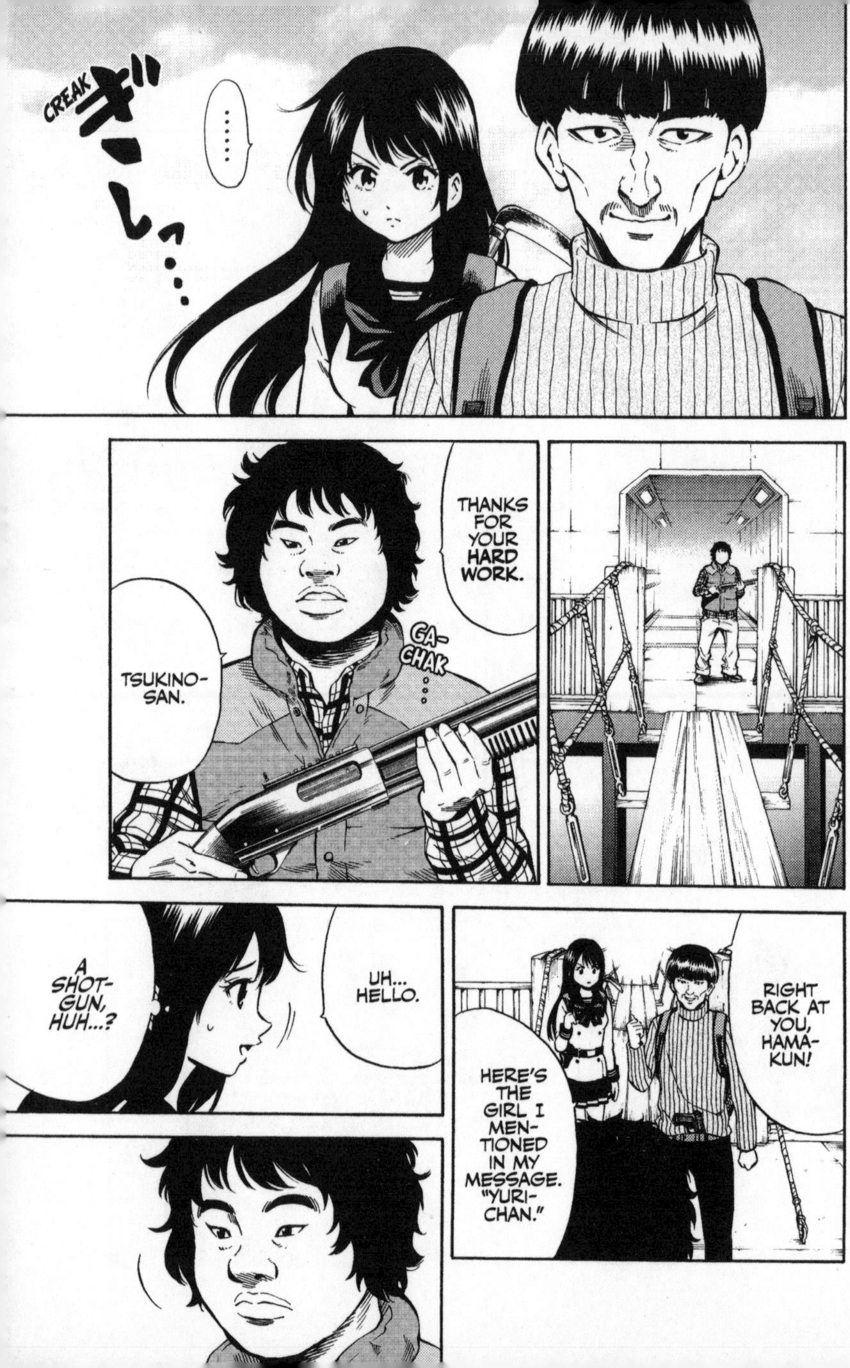
CREAK
ぎしっ…
……
THANKS FOR YOUR HARD WORK.
GA-CHAK
TSUKINO-SAN.
RIGHT BACK AT YOU, HAMA-KUN!
HERE'S THE GIRL I MENTIONED IN MY MESSAGE. "YURI-CHAN."
UH... HELLO.
A SHOTGUN, HUH...?

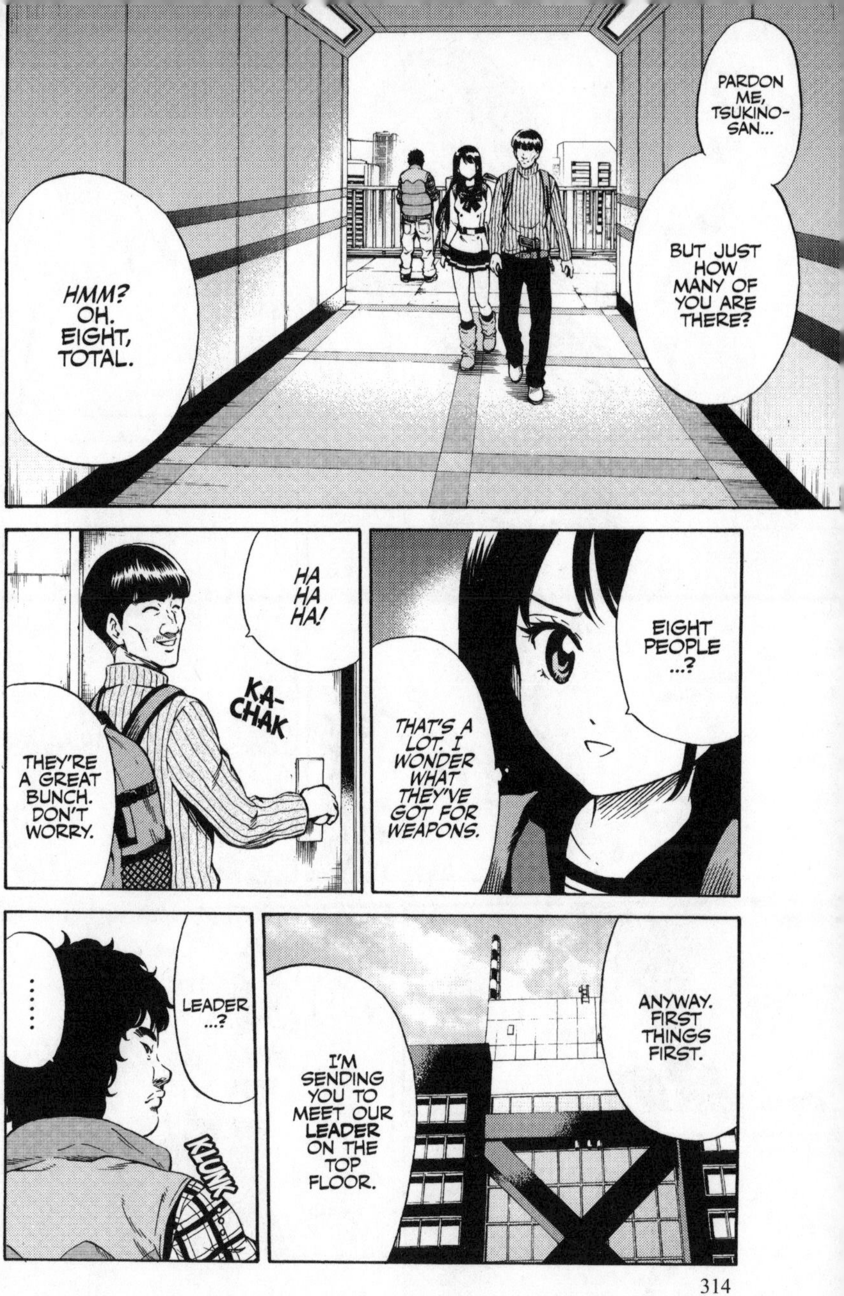
PARDON ME, TSUKINO-SAN...
BUT JUST HOW MANY OF YOU ARE THERE?
HMM? OH. EIGHT, TOTAL.
EIGHT PEOPLE ...?
THAT'S A LOT. I WONDER WHAT THEY'VE GOT FOR WEAPONS.
HA HA HA!
KA-CHAK
THEY'RE A GREAT BUNCH. DON'T WORRY.
ANYWAY. FIRST THINGS FIRST.
I'M SENDING YOU TO MEET OUR LEADER ON THE TOP FLOOR.
LEADER ...?
KLUNK
......

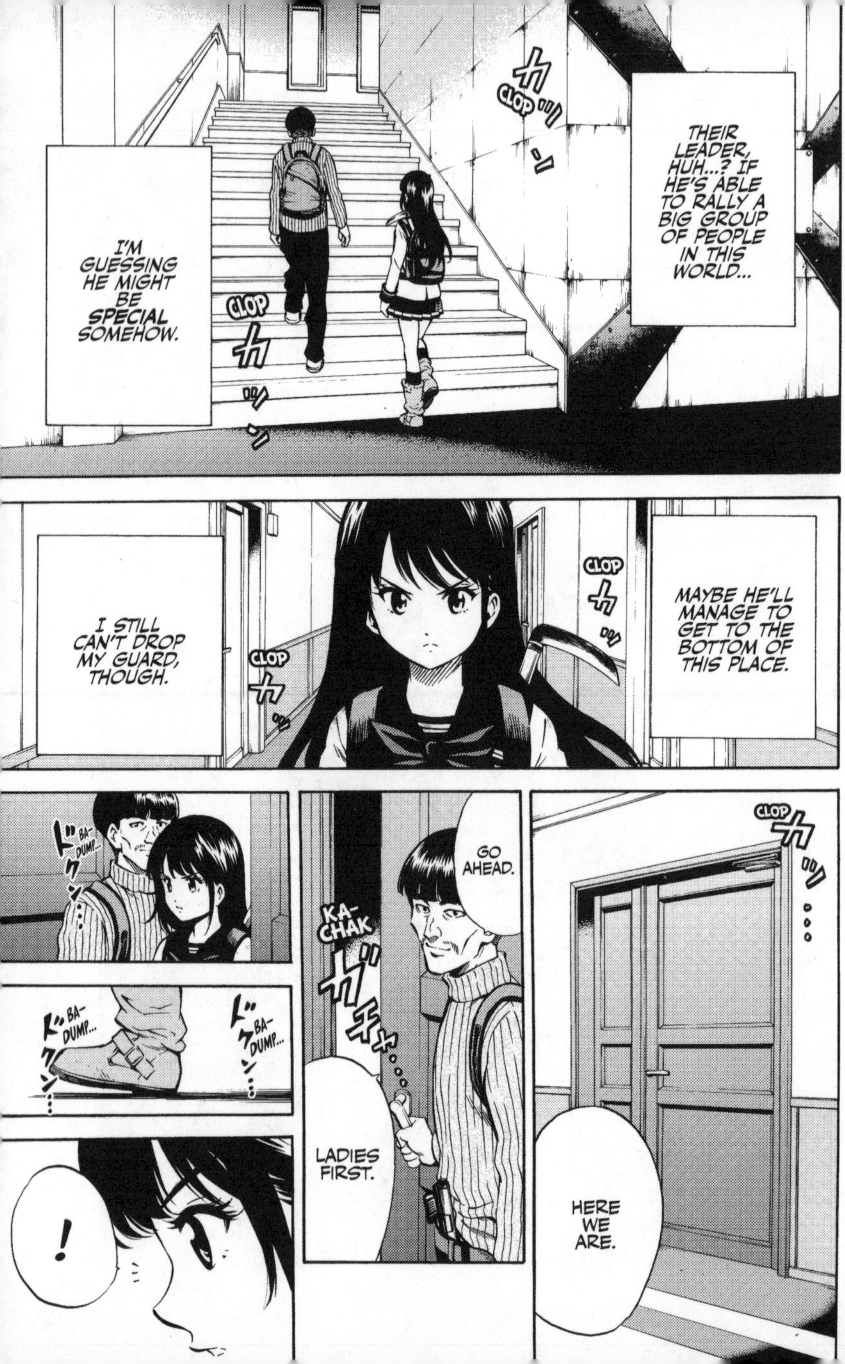
CLOP
THEIR LEADER, HUH...? IF HE'S ABLE TO RALLY A BIG GROUP OF PEOPLE IN THIS WORLD...
CLOP
I'M GUESSING HE MIGHT BE SPECIAL SOMEHOW.
MAYBE HE'LL MANAGE TO GET TO THE BOTTOM OF THIS PLACE.
CLOP
CLOP
I STILL CAN'T DROP MY GUARD, THOUGH.
CLOP
HERE WE ARE.
GO AHEAD.
KA-CHAK
LADIES FIRST.
BA-DUMP...
BA-DUMP...
BA-DUMP...
!

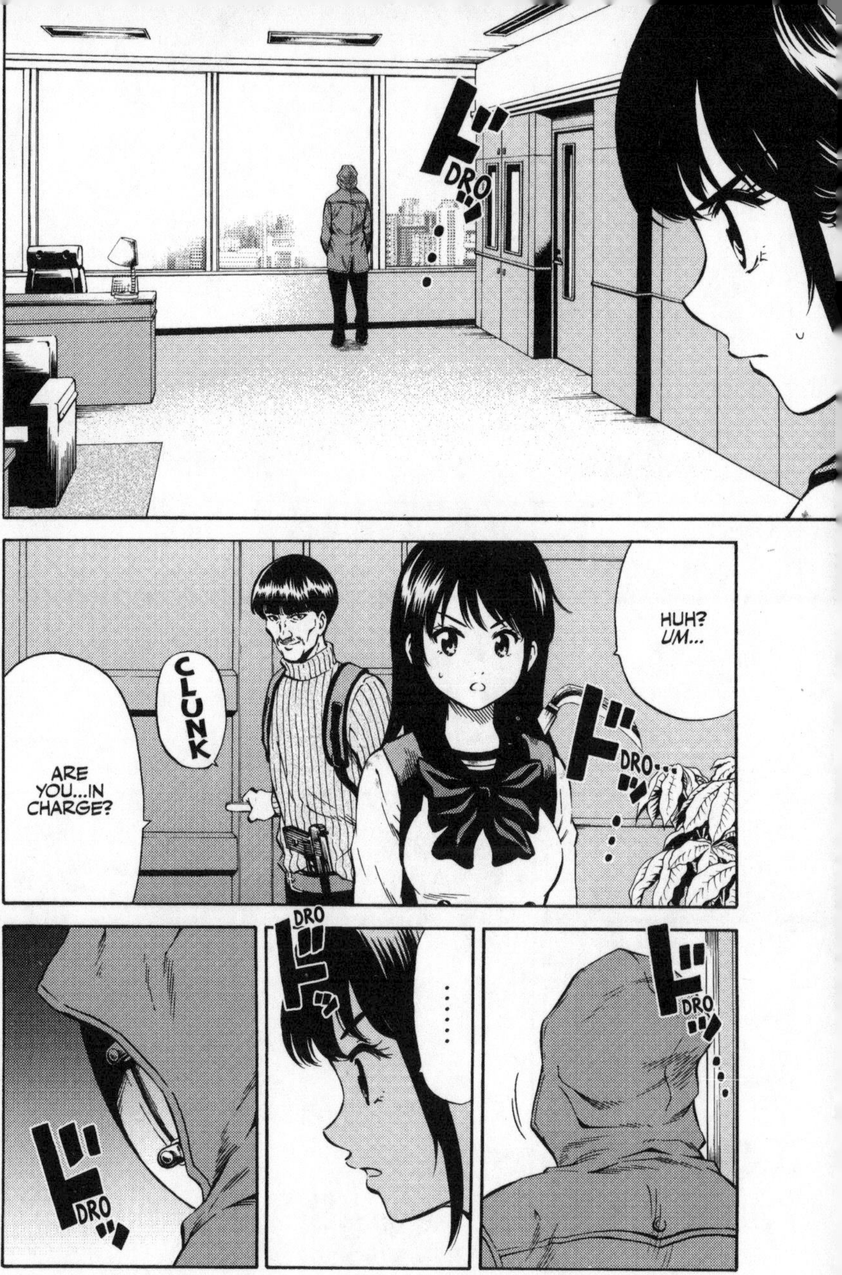
DRO...
HUH? UM...
DRO...
CLUNK
ARE YOU...IN CHARGE?
DRO...
......
DRO
DRO...

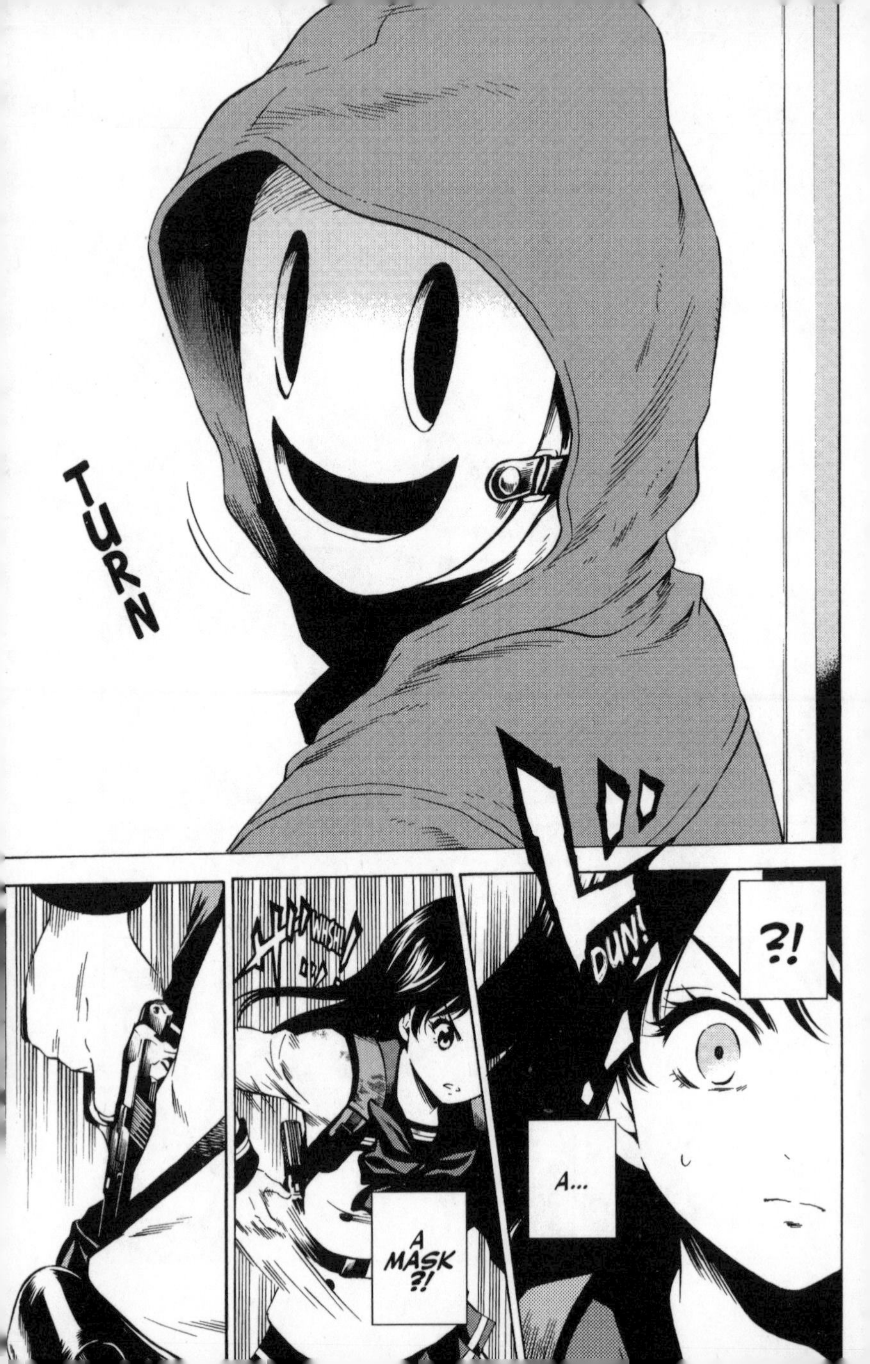
TURN
?!
DUN!
A...
WHSH!
A MASK?!

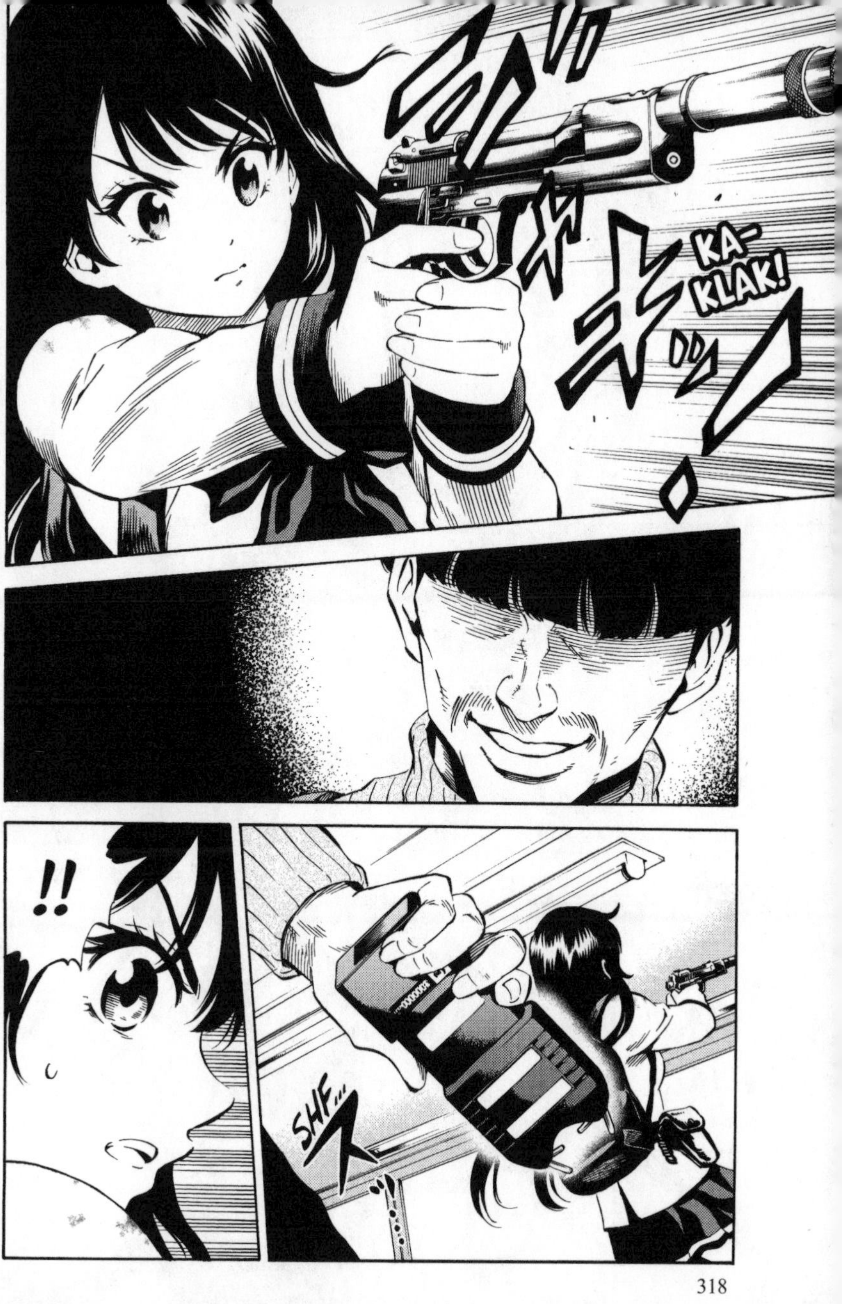
KA-KLAK!
!!
SHF...

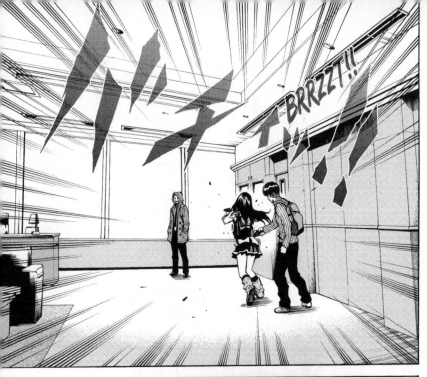

BRRZZT!!

TWITCH

TWITCH

GUN...?!

A...
STUN...

A
TRAP...
AFTER
ALL...

FUMBLE

IT...
WAS...

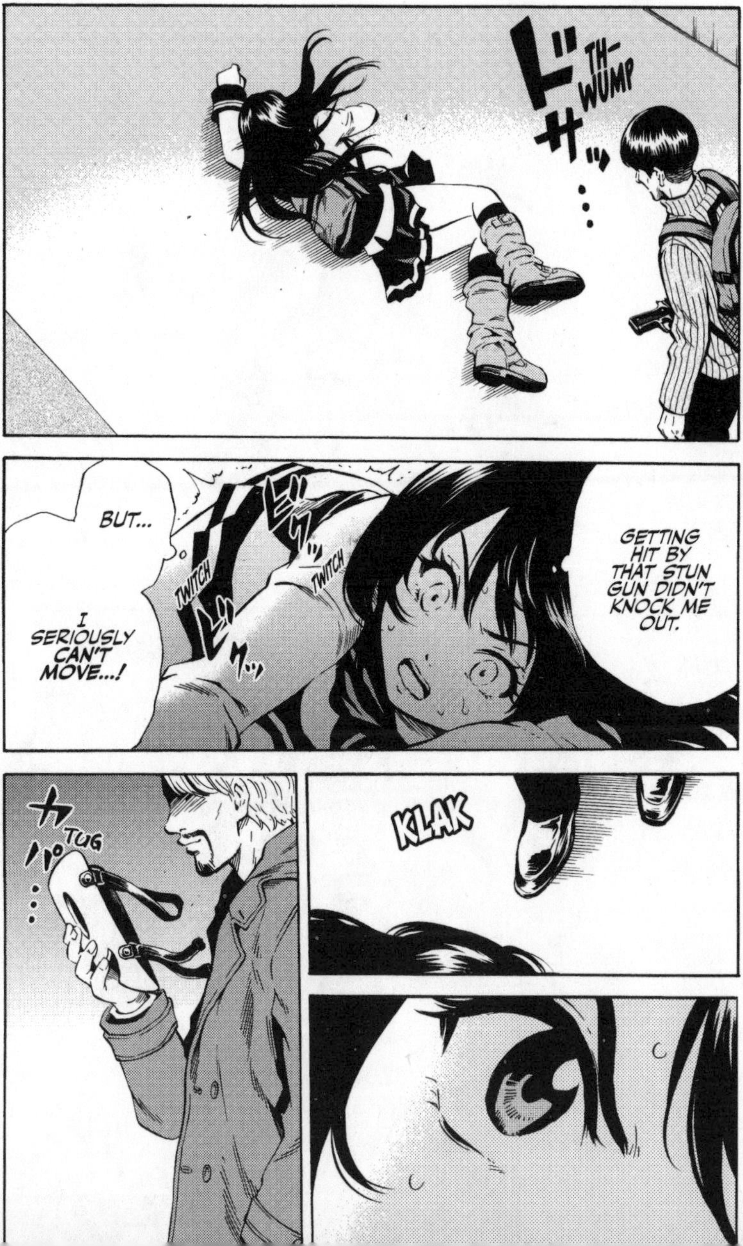
ド
TH-WUMP
サッ
...
GETTING HIT BY THAT STUN GUN DIDN'T KNOCK ME OUT.
BUT...
TWITCH
TWITCH
I SERIOUSLY CAN'T MOVE...!
KLAK
TUG
...

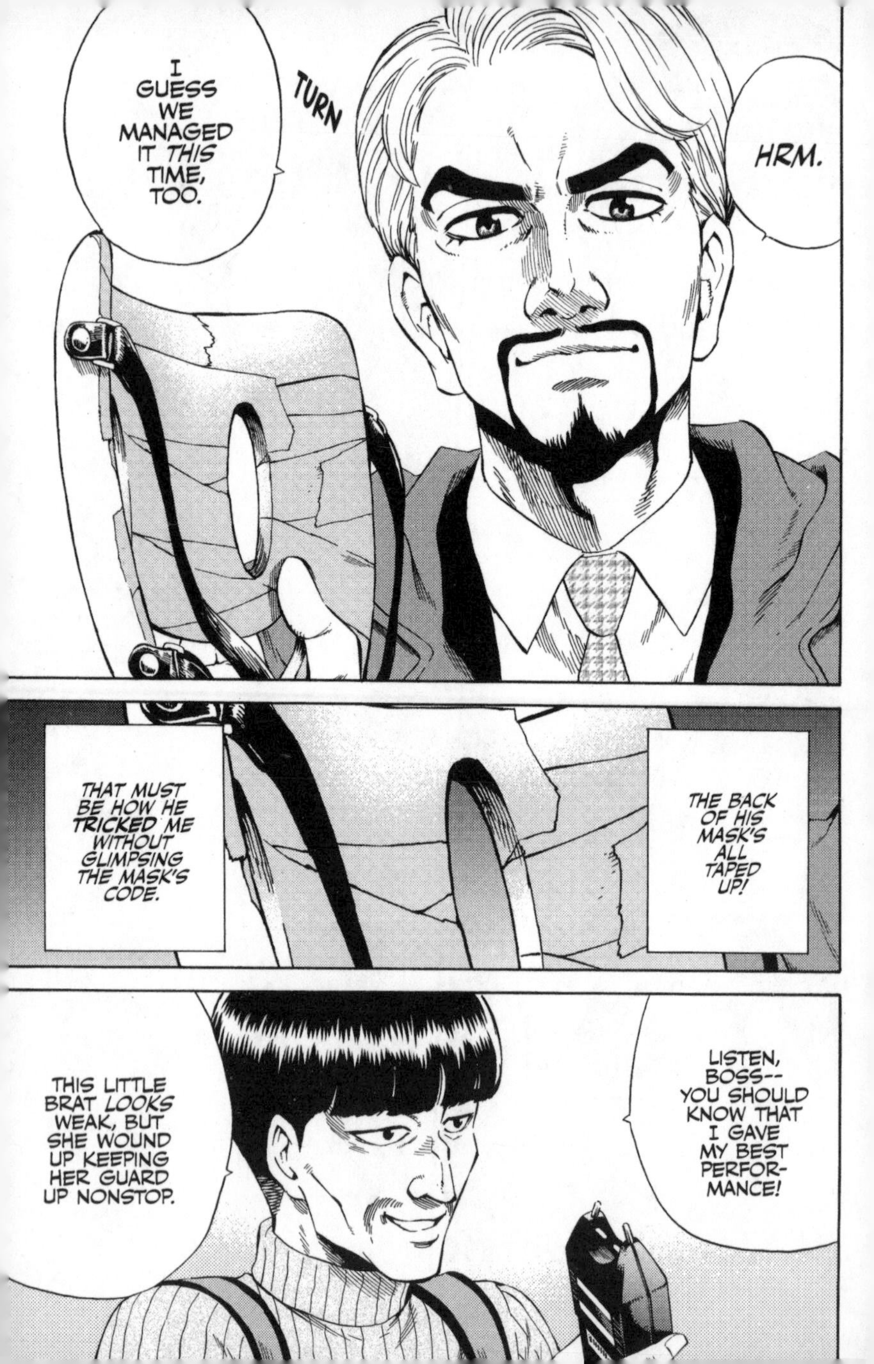
HRM.
TURN
I GUESS WE MANAGED IT *THIS* TIME, TOO.
THE BACK OF HIS MASK'S ALL TAPED UP!
THAT MUST BE HOW HE **TRICKED** ME WITHOUT GLIMPSING THE MASK'S CODE.
LISTEN, BOSS-- YOU SHOULD KNOW THAT I GAVE MY BEST PERFOR-MANCE!
THIS LITTLE BRAT *LOOKS* WEAK, BUT SHE WOUND UP KEEPING HER GUARD UP NONSTOP.

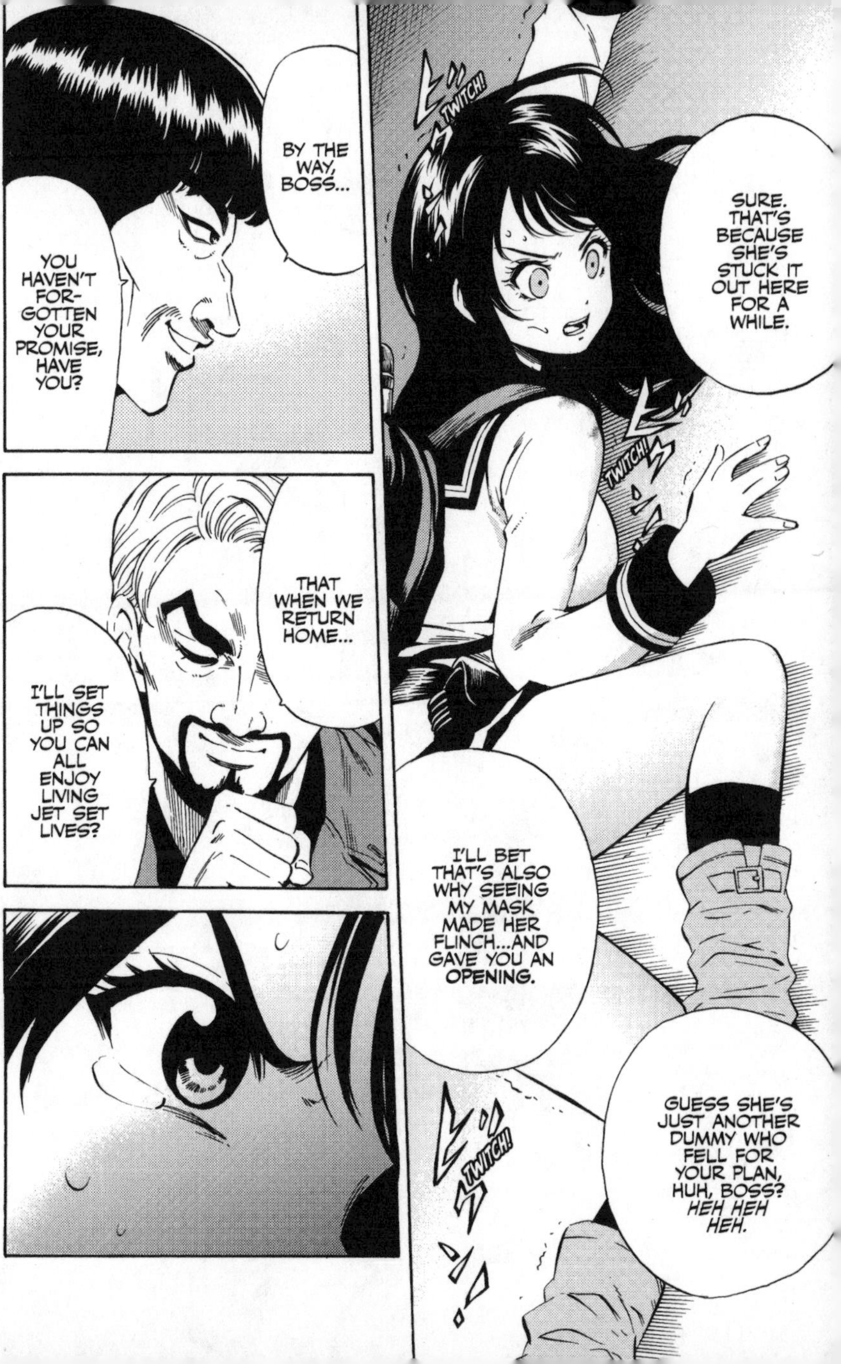TWITCH!
SURE. THAT'S BECAUSE SHE'S STUCK IT OUT HERE FOR A WHILE.
TWITCH!
I'LL BET THAT'S ALSO WHY SEEING MY MASK MADE HER FLINCH...AND GAVE YOU AN OPENING.
GUESS SHE'S JUST ANOTHER DUMMY WHO FELL FOR YOUR PLAN, HUH, BOSS? HEH HEH HEH.
TWITCH!
BY THE WAY, BOSS...
YOU HAVEN'T FOR-GOTTEN YOUR PROMISE, HAVE YOU?
THAT WHEN WE RETURN HOME...
I'LL SET THINGS UP SO YOU CAN ALL ENJOY LIVING JET SET LIVES?

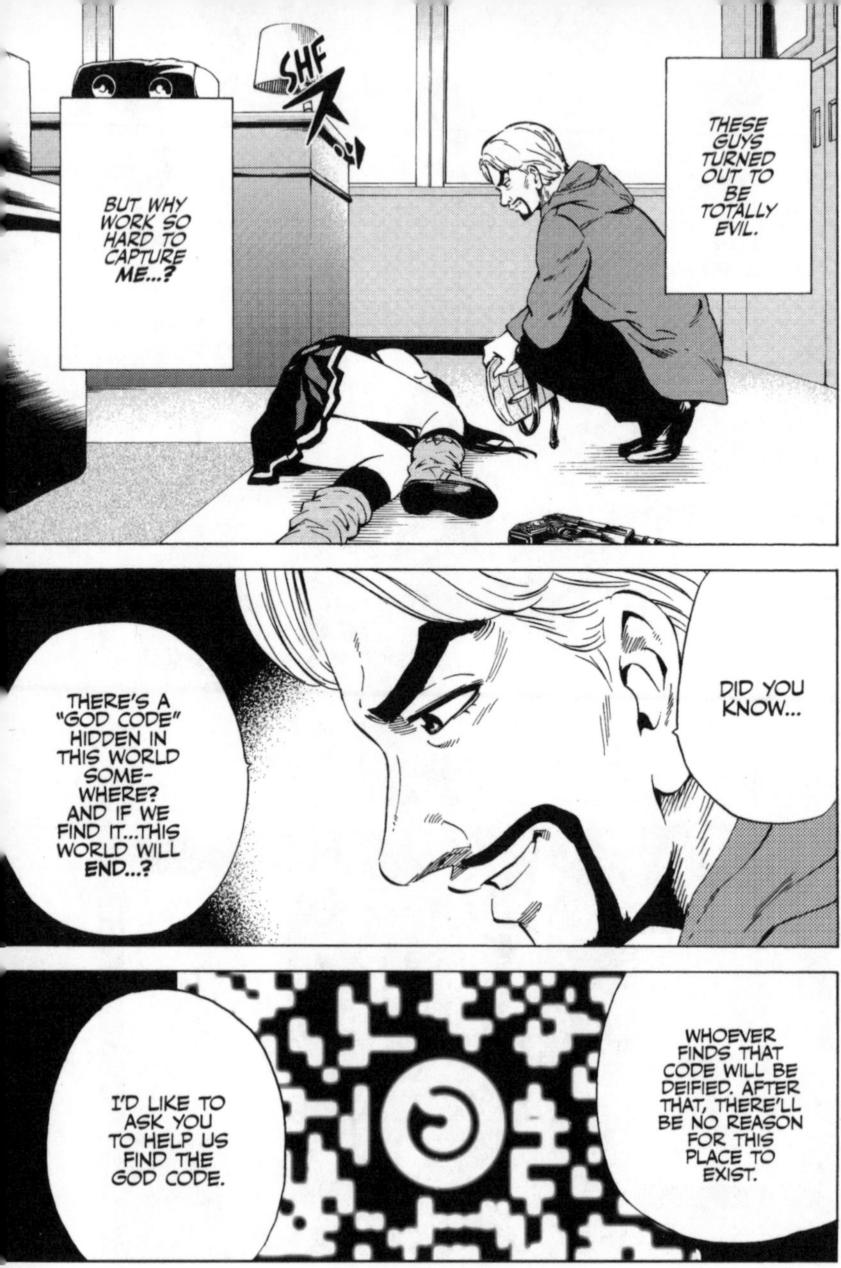
THESE GUYS TURNED OUT TO BE TOTALLY EVIL.
SHF
BUT WHY WORK SO HARD TO CAPTURE ME...?
DID YOU KNOW...
THERE'S A "GOD CODE" HIDDEN IN THIS WORLD SOME-WHERE? AND IF WE FIND IT...THIS WORLD WILL END...?
WHOEVER FINDS THAT CODE WILL BE DEIFIED. AFTER THAT, THERE'LL BE NO REASON FOR THIS PLACE TO EXIST.
I'D LIKE TO ASK YOU TO HELP US FIND THE GOD CODE.

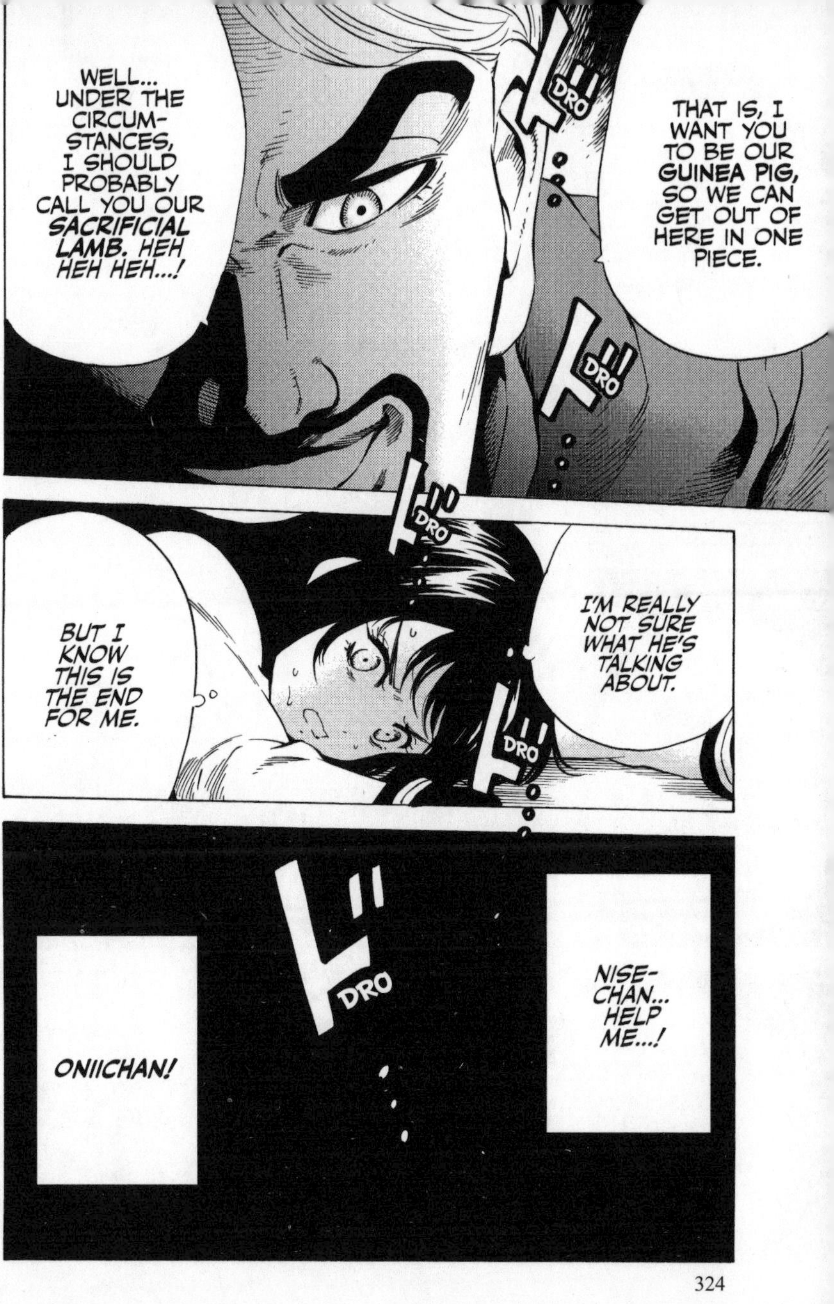
THAT IS, I WANT YOU TO BE OUR GUINEA PIG, SO WE CAN GET OUT OF HERE IN ONE PIECE.
DRO
DRO
WELL... UNDER THE CIRCUM-STANCES, I SHOULD PROBABLY CALL YOU OUR SACRIFICIAL LAMB. HEH HEH HEH...!
DRO
I'M REALLY NOT SURE WHAT HE'S TALKING ABOUT.
DRO
BUT I KNOW THIS IS THE END FOR ME.
NISE-CHAN... HELP ME...!
DRO
ONIICHAN!

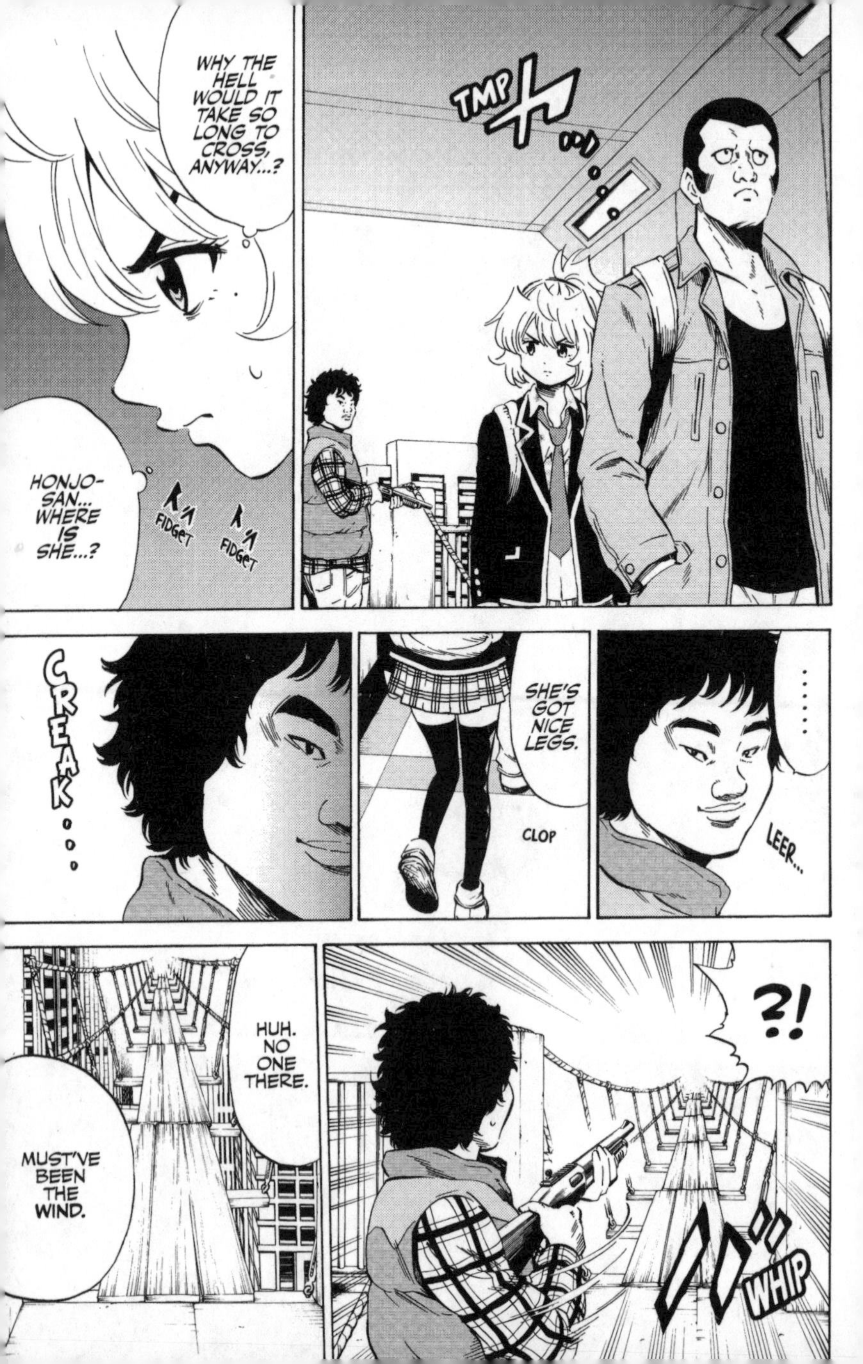
TMP
WHY THE HELL WOULD IT TAKE SO LONG TO CROSS, ANYWAY...?
HONJO-SAN... WHERE IS SHE...?
FIDGET
FIDGET
......
LEER...
SHE'S GOT NICE LEGS.
CLOP
CREAK...
?!
WHIP
HUH. NO ONE THERE.
MUST'VE BEEN THE WIND.

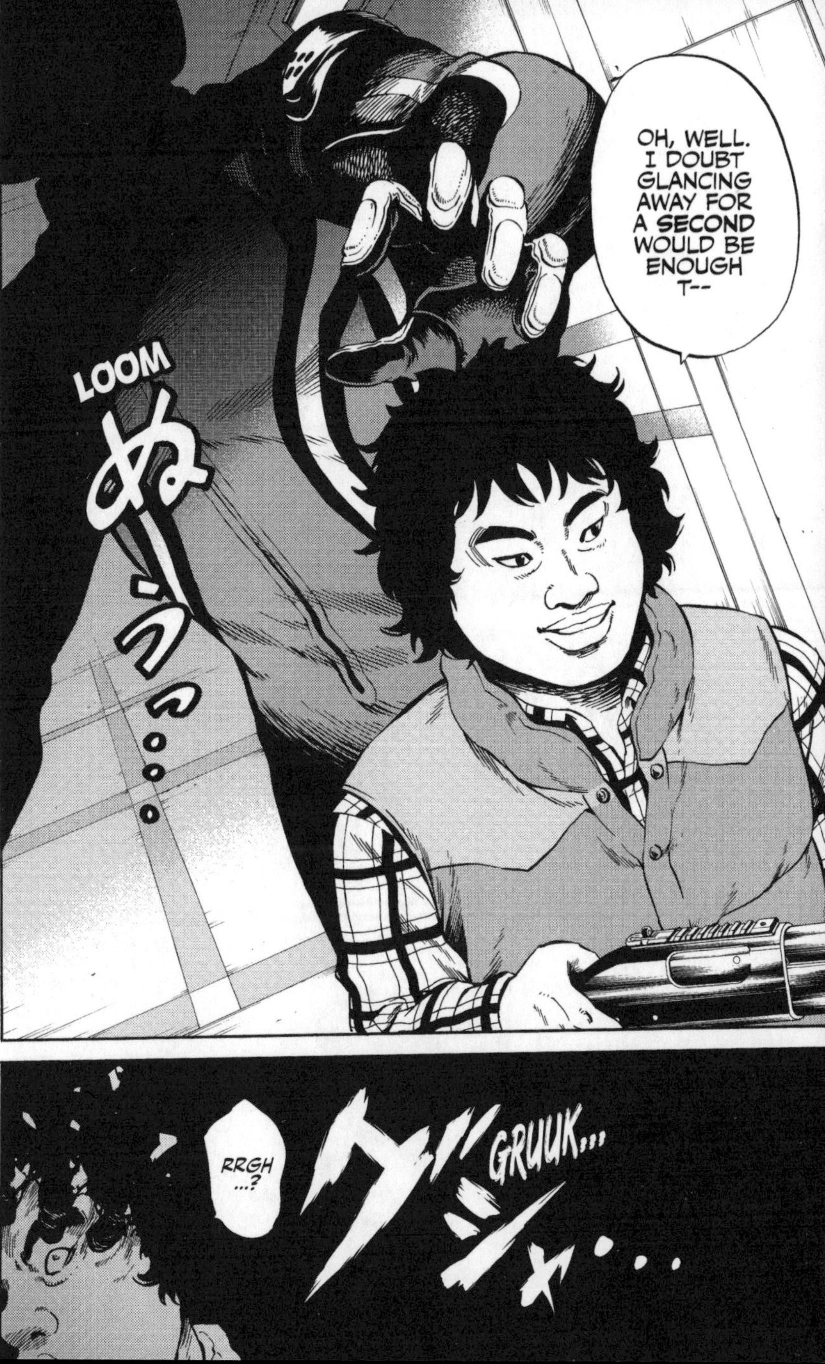
OH, WELL. I DOUBT GLANCING AWAY FOR A SECOND WOULD BE ENOUGH T--
LOOM
ぬうっ…
GRUUK...
RRGH ...?

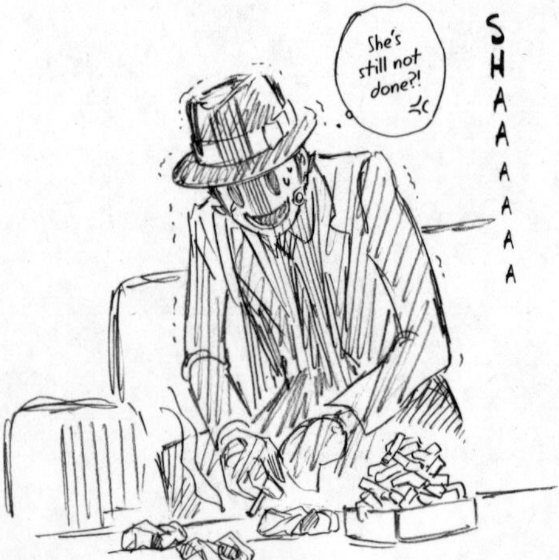
She's still not done?!
SHAAAAAAA

HIGH-RISE INVASION

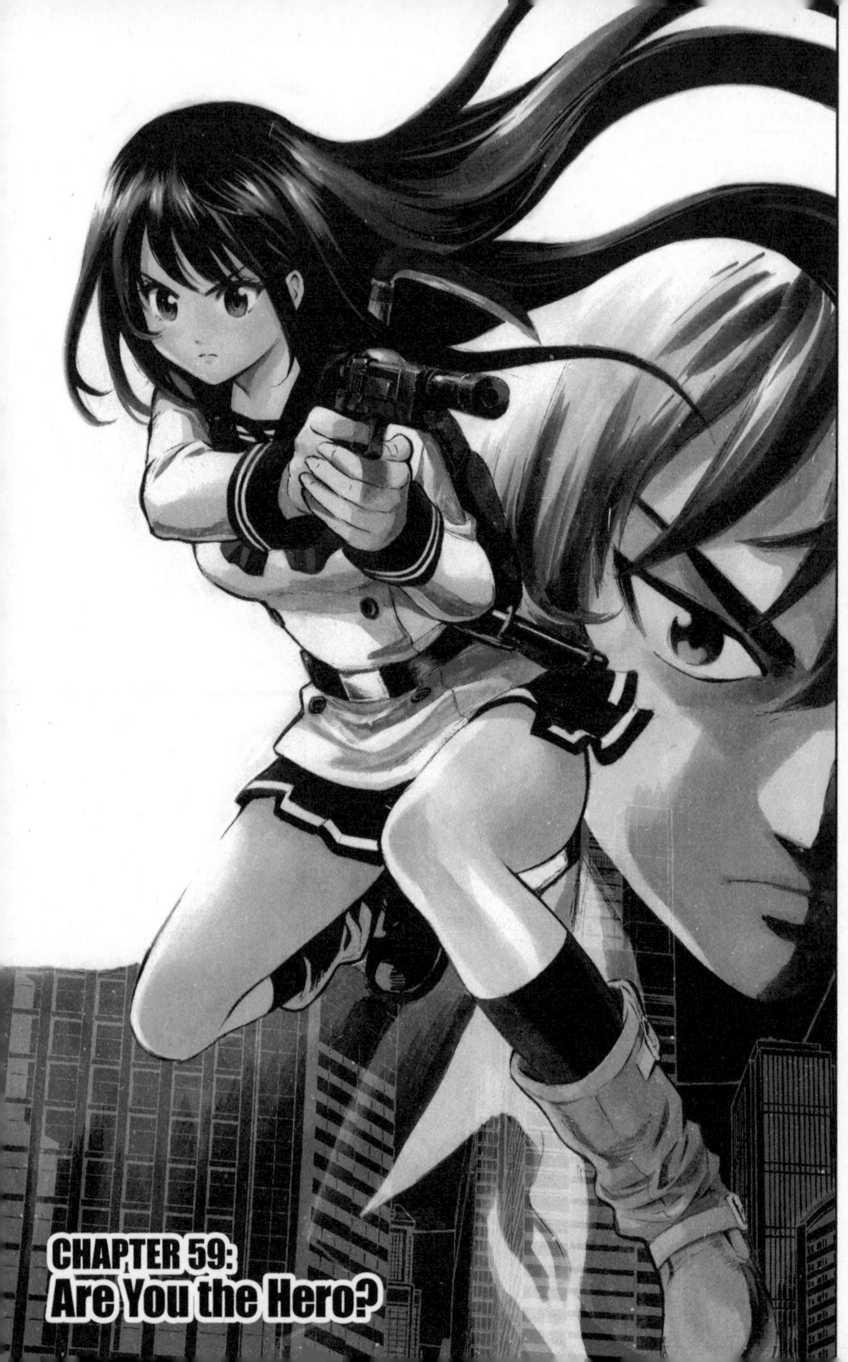

CHAPTER 59:
Are You the Hero?

HIGH-RISE INVASION

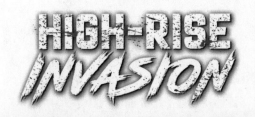

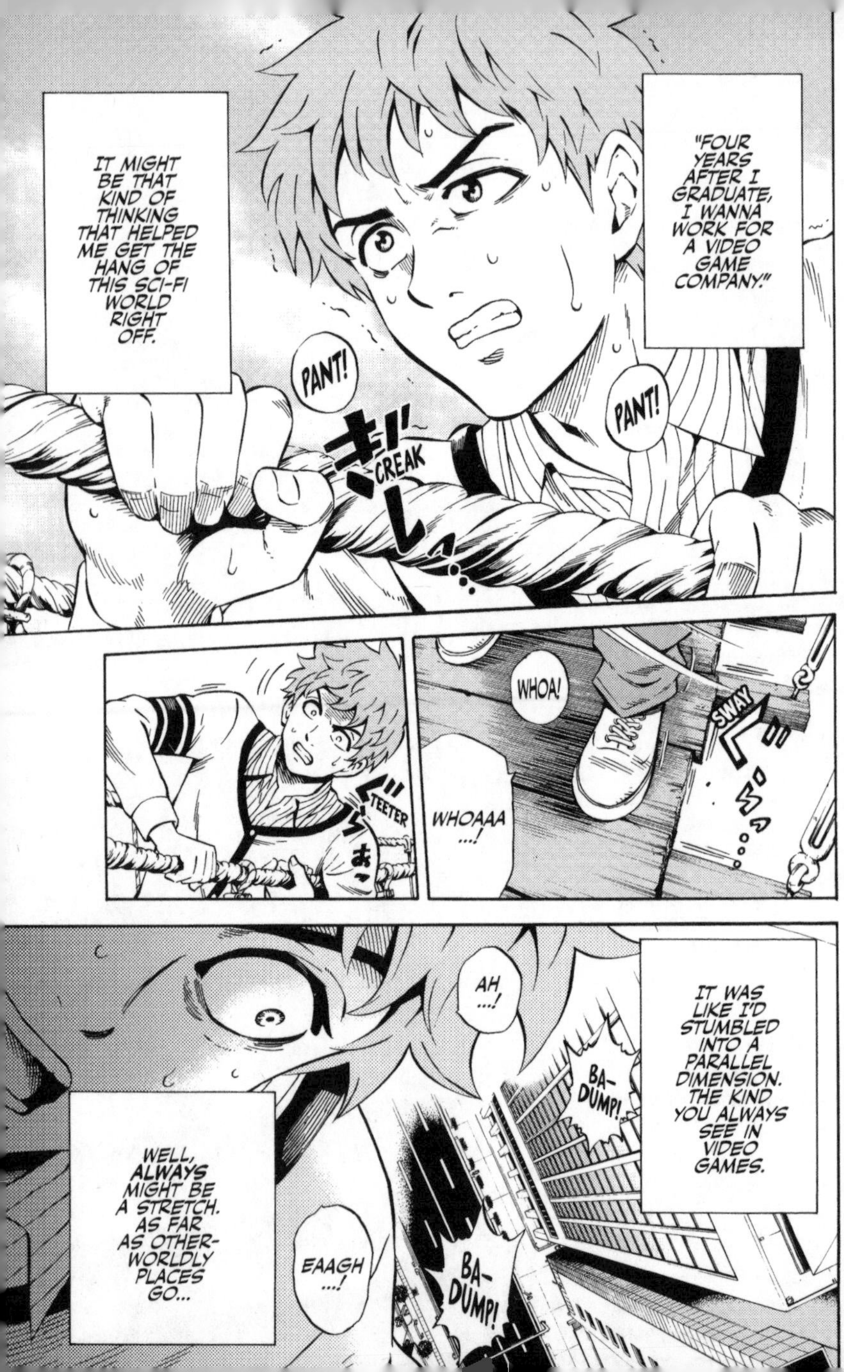
"FOUR YEARS AFTER I GRADUATE, I WANNA WORK FOR A VIDEO GAME COMPANY."
IT MIGHT BE THAT KIND OF THINKING THAT HELPED ME GET THE HANG OF THIS SCI-FI WORLD RIGHT OFF.
PANT!
PANT!
CREAK
WHOA!
SWAY
WHOAAA ...!
TEETER
IT WAS LIKE I'D STUMBLED INTO A PARALLEL DIMENSION. THE KIND YOU ALWAYS SEE IN VIDEO GAMES.
AH ...!
BA-DUMP!
WELL, ALWAYS MIGHT BE A STRETCH. AS FAR AS OTHER-WORLDLY PLACES GO...
BA-DUMP!
EAAGH ...!

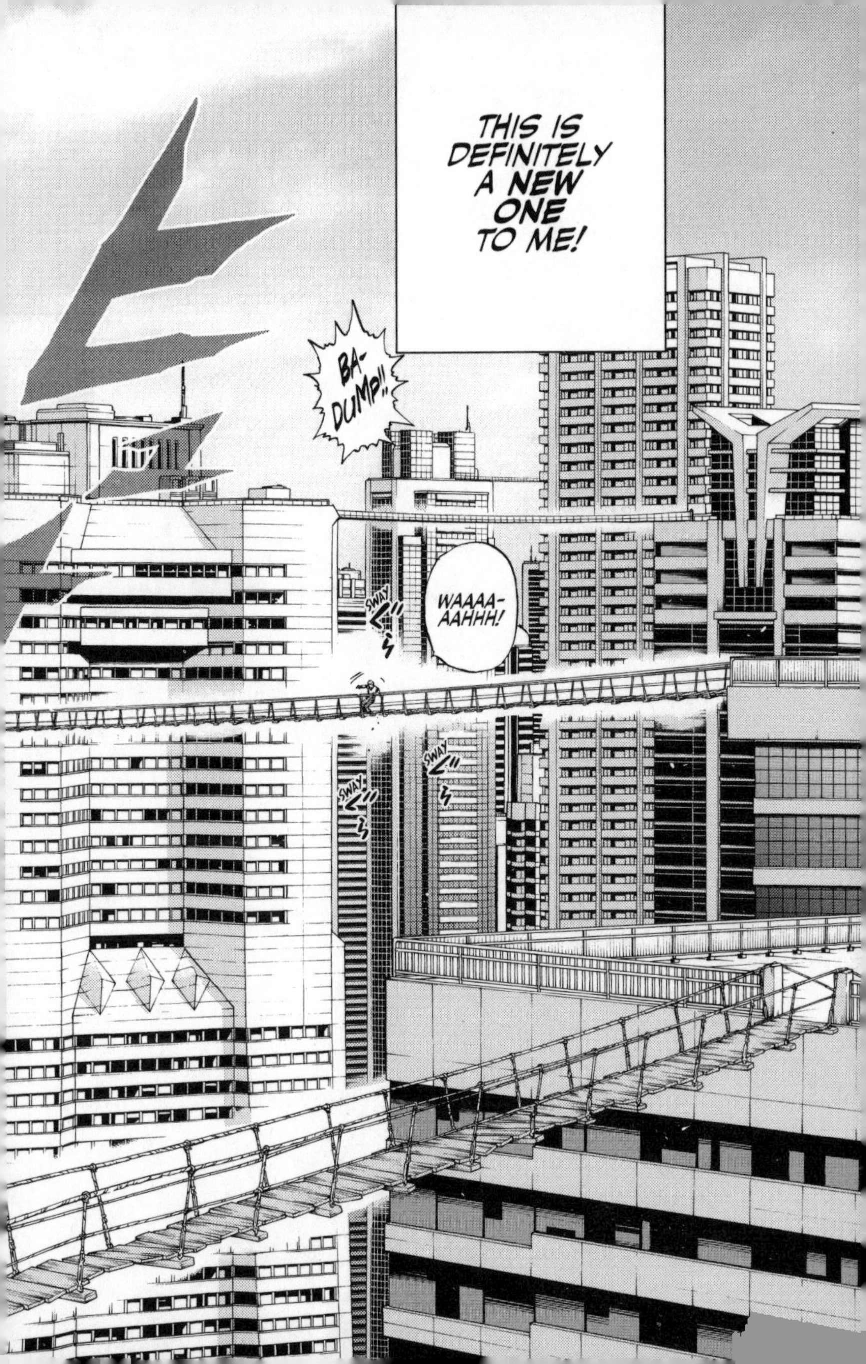
THIS IS DEFINITELY A NEW ONE TO ME!
BA-DUMP!!
WAAAA-AAHHH!
SWAY
SWAY
SWAY

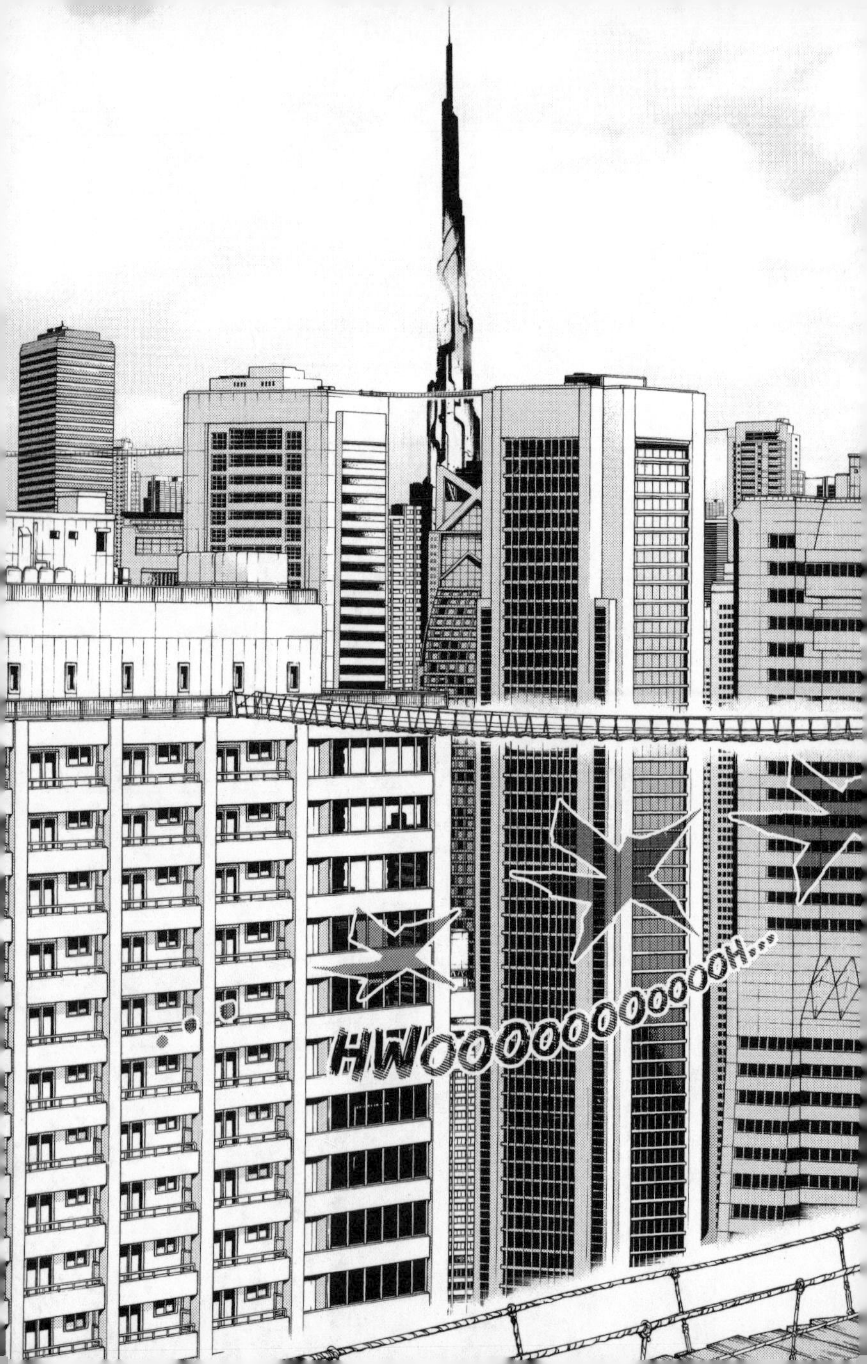
HWOOOOOOOOOOOOOH...

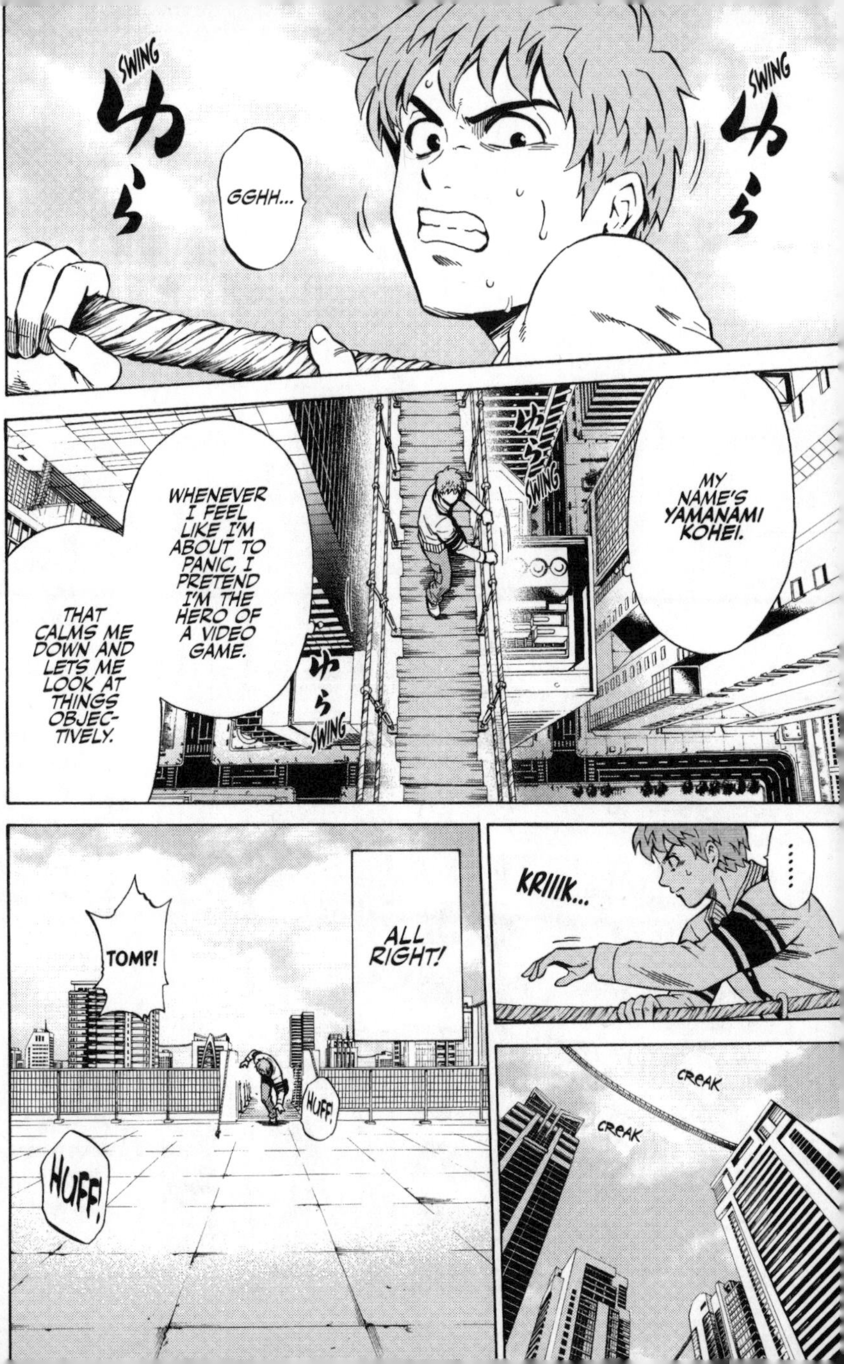
SWING
ゆら
GGHH...
SWING
ゆら
MY NAME'S YAMANAMI KOHEI.
ゆら
SWING
WHENEVER I FEEL LIKE I'M ABOUT TO PANIC, I PRETEND I'M THE HERO OF A VIDEO GAME.
THAT CALMS ME DOWN AND LETS ME LOOK AT THINGS OBJECTIVELY.
ゆら
SWING
......
KRIIIK...
CREAK
CREAK
ALL RIGHT!
TOMP!
HUFF!
HUFF!

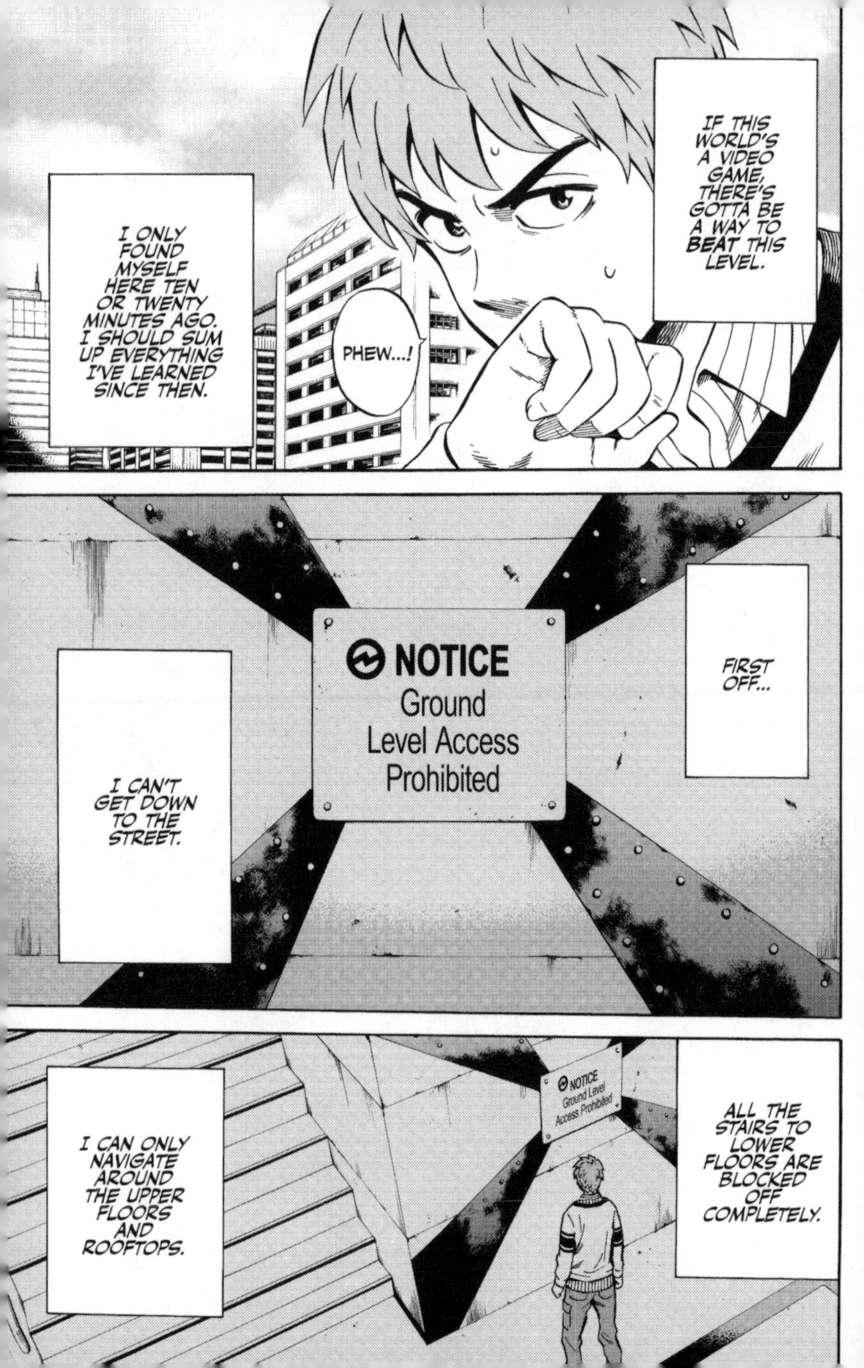
IF THIS WORLD'S A VIDEO GAME, THERE'S GOTTA BE A WAY TO **BEAT** THIS LEVEL.
PHEW...!
I ONLY FOUND MYSELF HERE TEN OR TWENTY MINUTES AGO. I SHOULD SUM UP EVERYTHING I'VE LEARNED SINCE THEN.
FIRST OFF...
NOTICE
Ground Level Access Prohibited
I CAN'T GET DOWN TO THE STREET.
ALL THE STAIRS TO LOWER FLOORS ARE BLOCKED OFF COMPLETELY.
NOTICE
Ground Level Access Prohibited
I CAN ONLY NAVIGATE AROUND THE UPPER FLOORS AND ROOFTOPS.

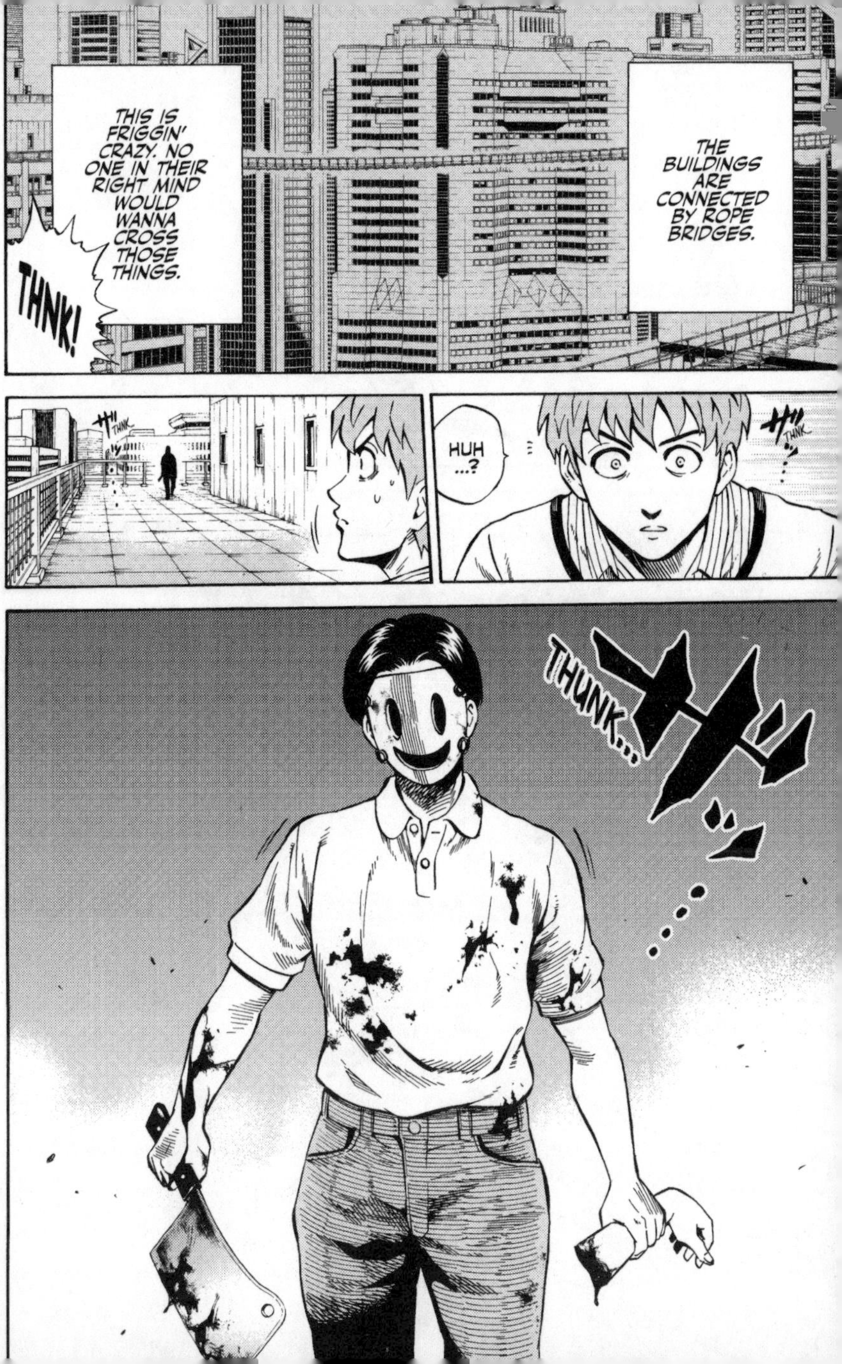
THE BUILDINGS ARE CONNECTED BY ROPE BRIDGES.
THIS IS FRIGGIN' CRAZY. NO ONE IN THEIR RIGHT MIND WOULD WANNA CROSS THOSE THINGS.
THNK!
HUH ...?
THNK...
THNK
THUNK...

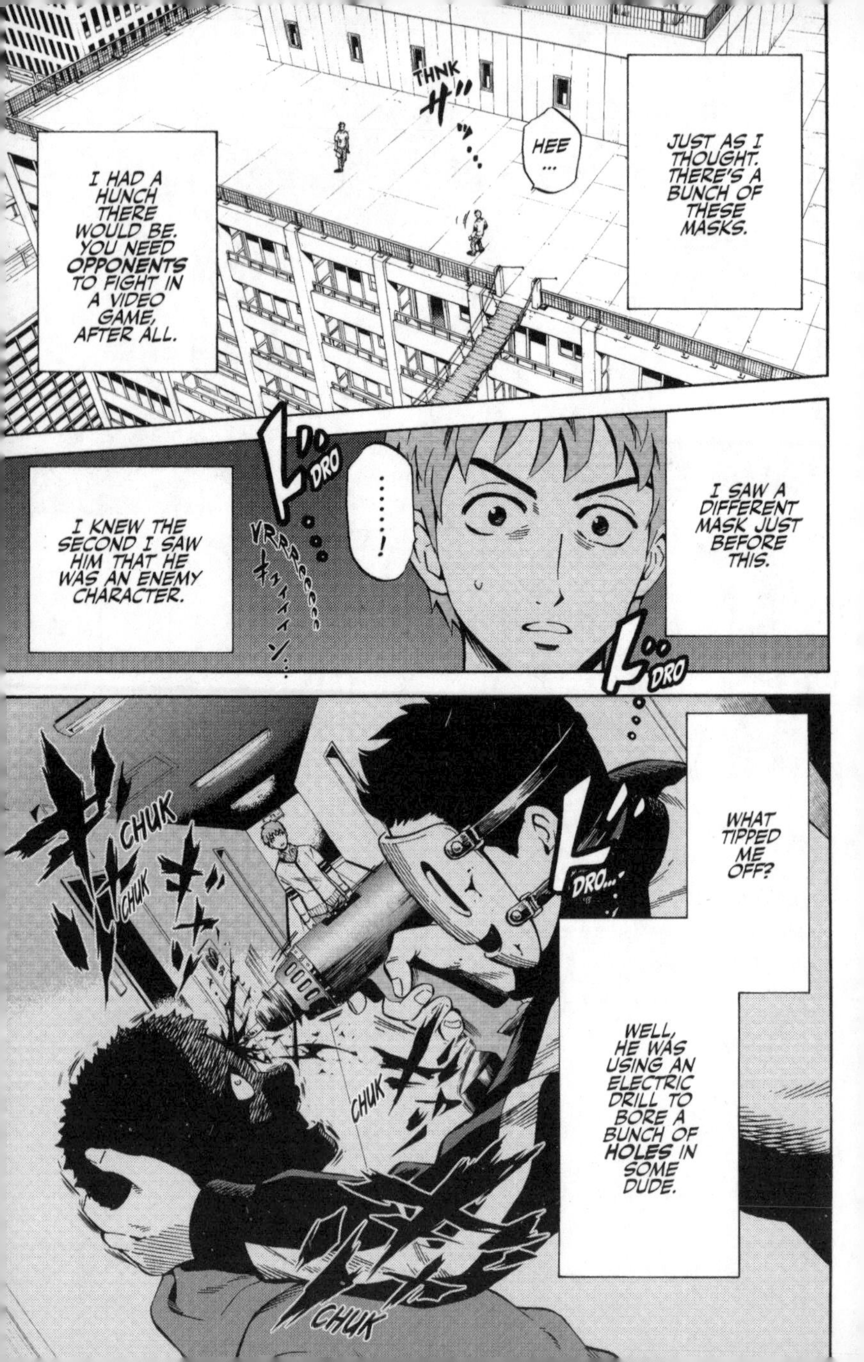
JUST AS I THOUGHT. THERE'S A BUNCH OF THESE MASKS.
HEE ...
THNK
I HAD A HUNCH THERE WOULD BE. YOU NEED OPPONENTS TO FIGHT IN A VIDEO GAME, AFTER ALL.
I SAW A DIFFERENT MASK JUST BEFORE THIS.
DRO
......!
DRO
VRRRReeeee
I KNEW THE SECOND I SAW HIM THAT HE WAS AN ENEMY CHARACTER.
WHAT TIPPED ME OFF?
DRO...
WELL, HE WAS USING AN ELECTRIC DRILL TO BORE A BUNCH OF HOLES IN SOME DUDE.
CHUK
CHUK
CHUK
CHUK

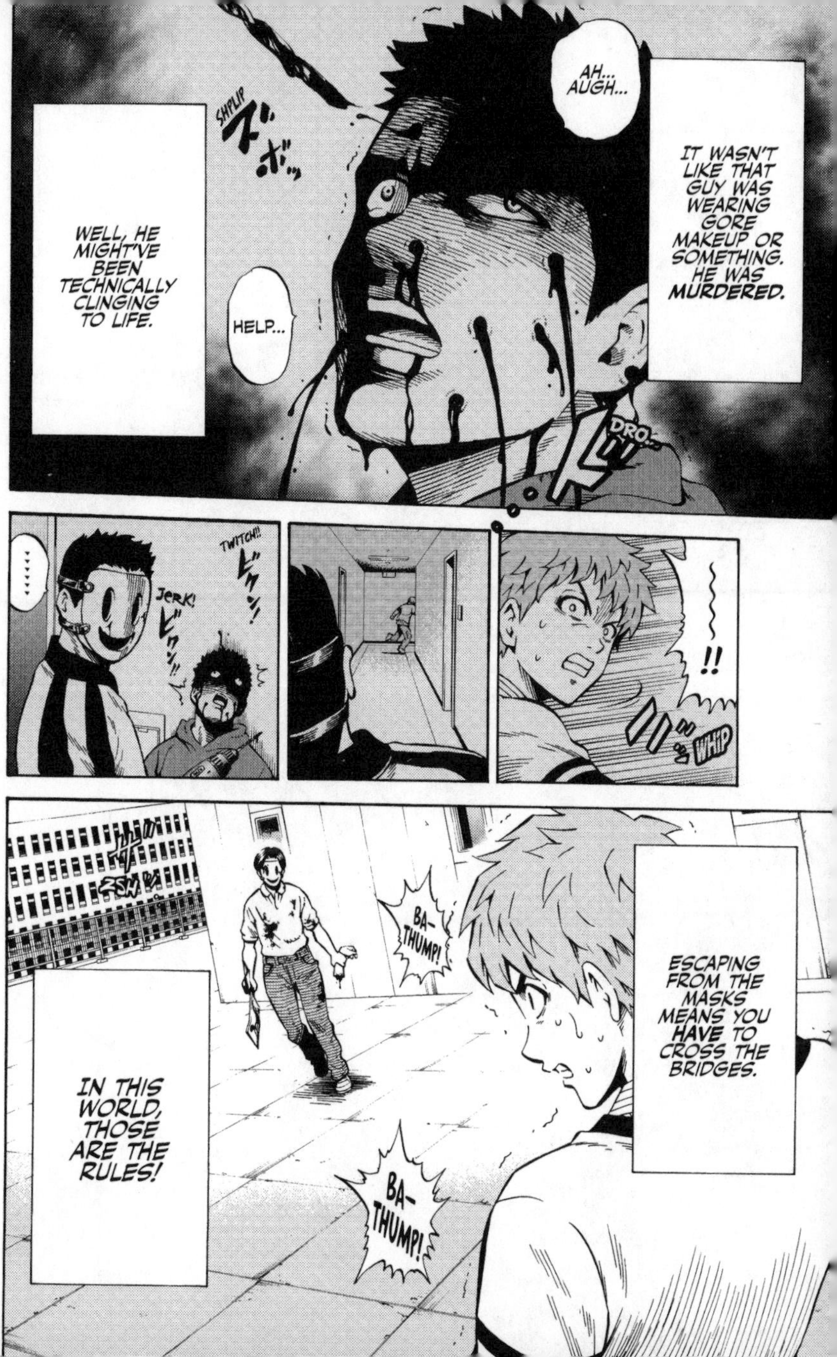
AH... AUGH...
IT WASN'T LIKE THAT GUY WAS WEARING GORE MAKEUP OR SOMETHING. HE WAS **MURDERED.**
SHPLIP
HELP...
WELL, HE MIGHT'VE BEEN TECHNICALLY CLINGING TO LIFE.
DRO...
!!
WHIP
.....
TWITCH!!
JERK!
ESCAPING FROM THE MASKS MEANS YOU **HAVE** TO CROSS THE BRIDGES.
BA-THUMP!
BA-THUMP!
ZSH
IN THIS WORLD, THOSE ARE THE RULES!

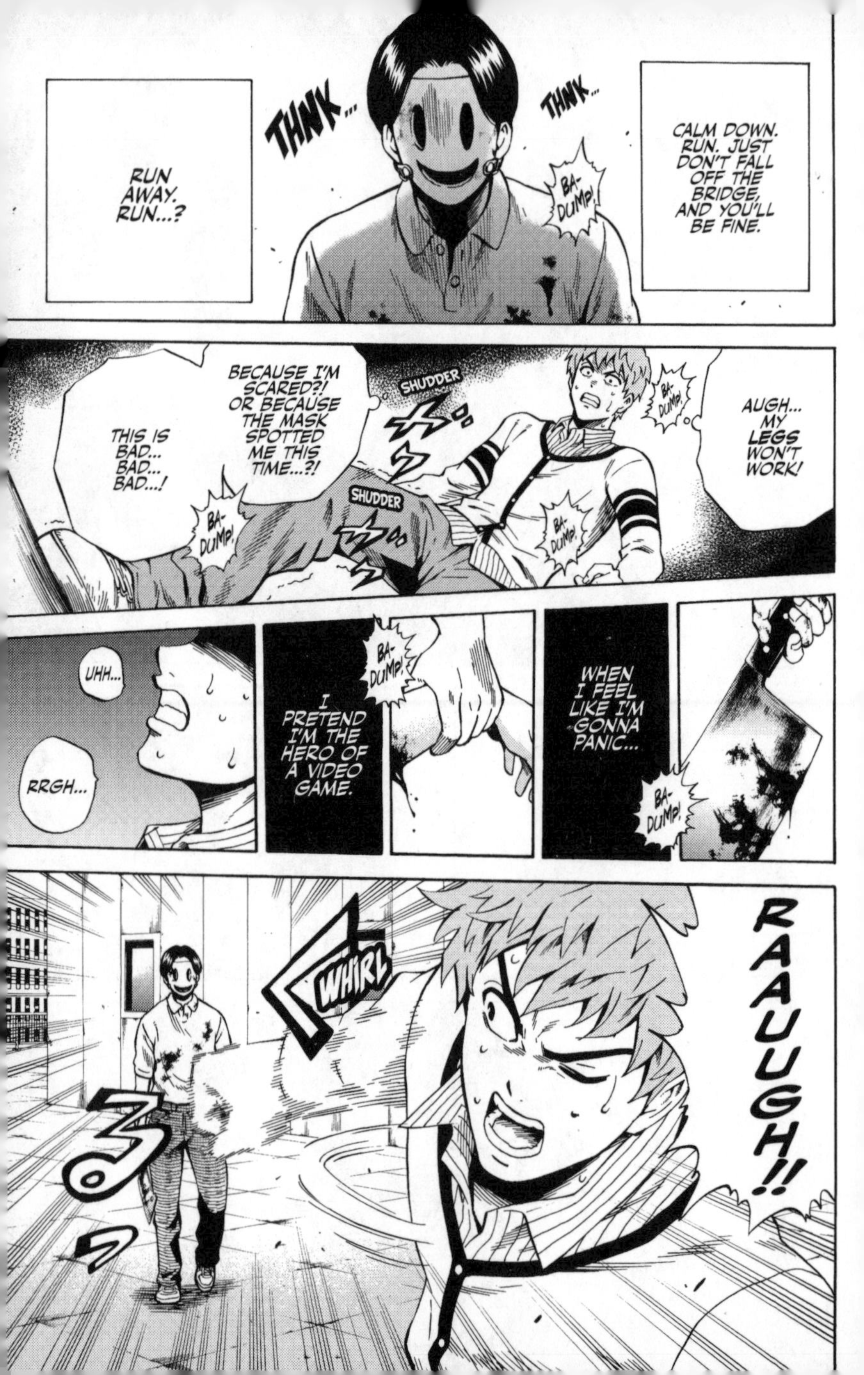

CALM DOWN. RUN. JUST DON'T FALL OFF THE BRIDGE, AND YOU'LL BE FINE.
THNK...
BA-DUMP!
THNK...
RUN AWAY. RUN...?
AUGH... MY LEGS WON'T WORK!
BA-DUMP!
BA-DUMP!
SHUDDER
BECAUSE I'M SCARED?! OR BECAUSE THE MASK SPOTTED ME THIS TIME...?!
SHUDDER
THIS IS BAD... BAD... BAD...!
BA-DUMP!
BA-DUMP!
WHEN I FEEL LIKE I'M GONNA PANIC...
BA-DUMP!
I PRETEND I'M THE HERO OF A VIDEO GAME.
UHH...
RRGH...
RAAUUGH!!
WHIRL

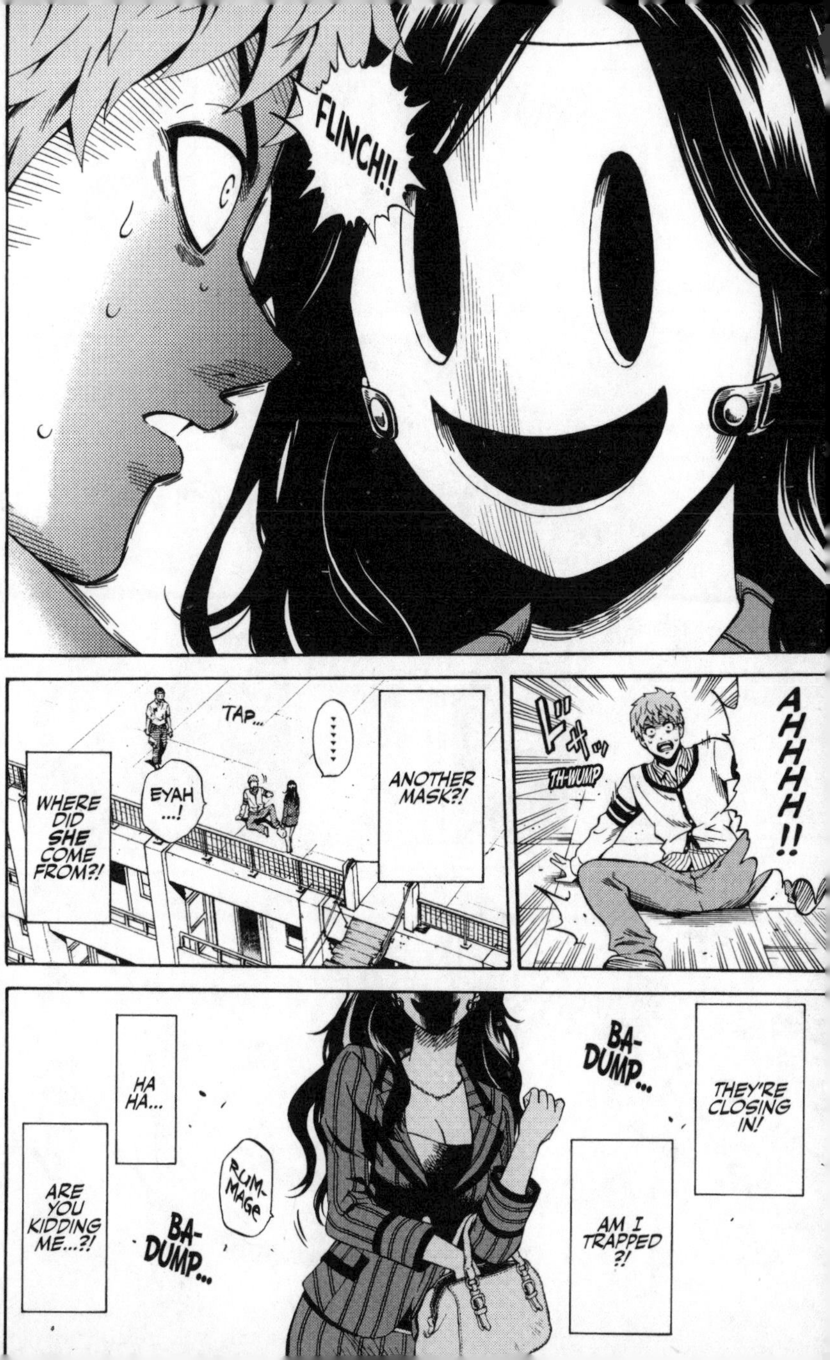
FLINCH!!
TH-WUMP
AHHHH!!
ANOTHER MASK?!
TAP...
EYAH...!
WHERE DID SHE COME FROM?!
THEY'RE CLOSING IN!
BA-DUMP...
AM I TRAPPED?!
HA HA...
RUM-MAGE
BA-DUMP...
ARE YOU KIDDING ME...?!

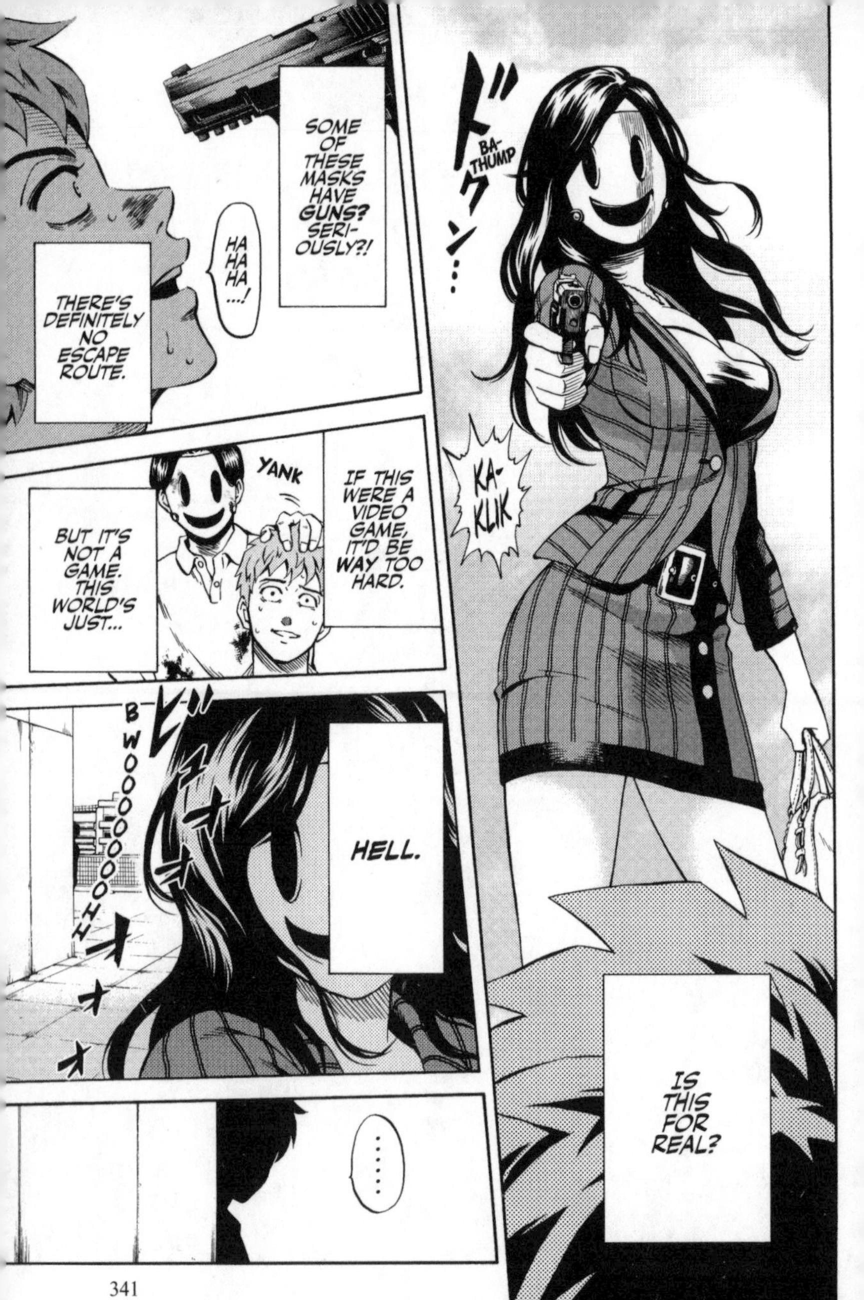
BA-THUMP
KA-KLIK
IS THIS FOR REAL?
SOME OF THESE MASKS HAVE GUNS? SERIOUSLY?!
HA HA HA ...!
THERE'S DEFINITELY NO ESCAPE ROUTE.
IF THIS WERE A VIDEO GAME, IT'D BE WAY TOO HARD.
YANK
BUT IT'S NOT A GAME. THIS WORLD'S JUST...
HELL.
BWOOOOOOOOOOHH
......

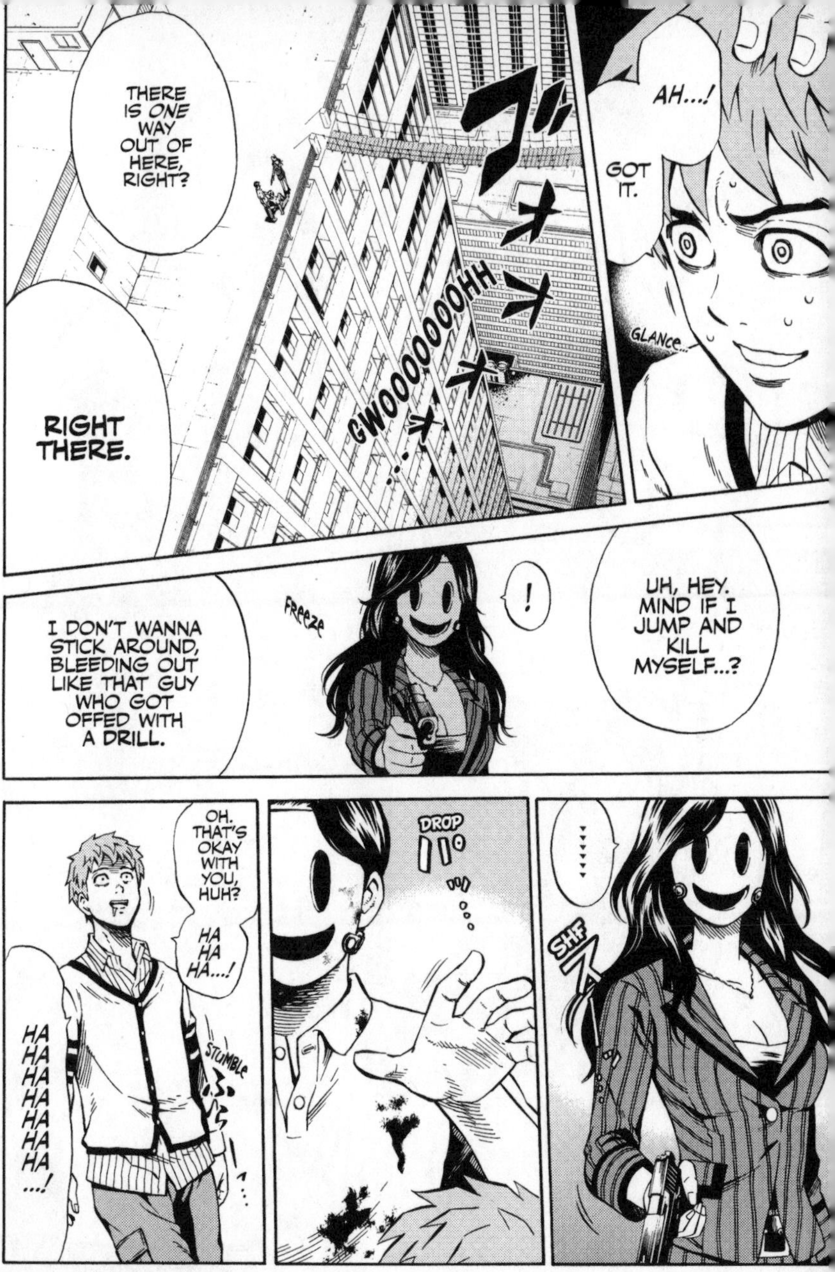
AH...!
GOT IT.
GLANCE...
THERE IS ONE WAY OUT OF HERE, RIGHT?
GWOOOOOOOHH
RIGHT THERE.
UH, HEY. MIND IF I JUMP AND KILL MYSELF...?
!
Freeze
I DON'T WANNA STICK AROUND, BLEEDING OUT LIKE THAT GUY WHO GOT OFFED WITH A DRILL.
......
SHF
DROP
OH. THAT'S OKAY WITH YOU, HUH?
HA HA HA...!
STUMBLE
HA HA HA HA HA HA HA HA ...!

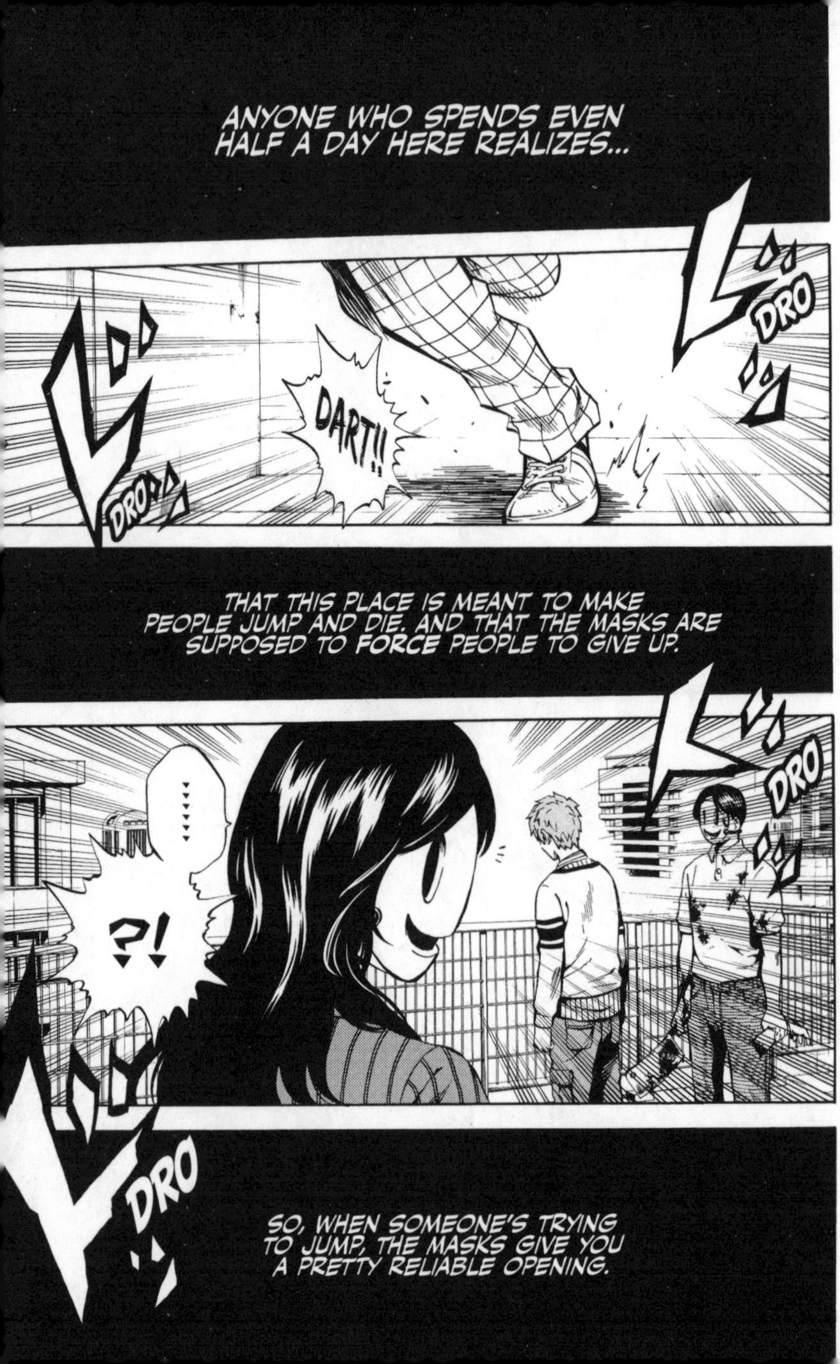
ANYONE WHO SPENDS EVEN HALF A DAY HERE REALIZES...
DRO
DART!!
DRO
THAT THIS PLACE IS MEANT TO MAKE PEOPLE JUMP AND DIE. AND THAT THE MASKS ARE SUPPOSED TO FORCE PEOPLE TO GIVE UP.
DRO
......
?!
DRO
SO, WHEN SOMEONE'S TRYING TO JUMP, THE MASKS GIVE YOU A PRETTY RELIABLE OPENING.

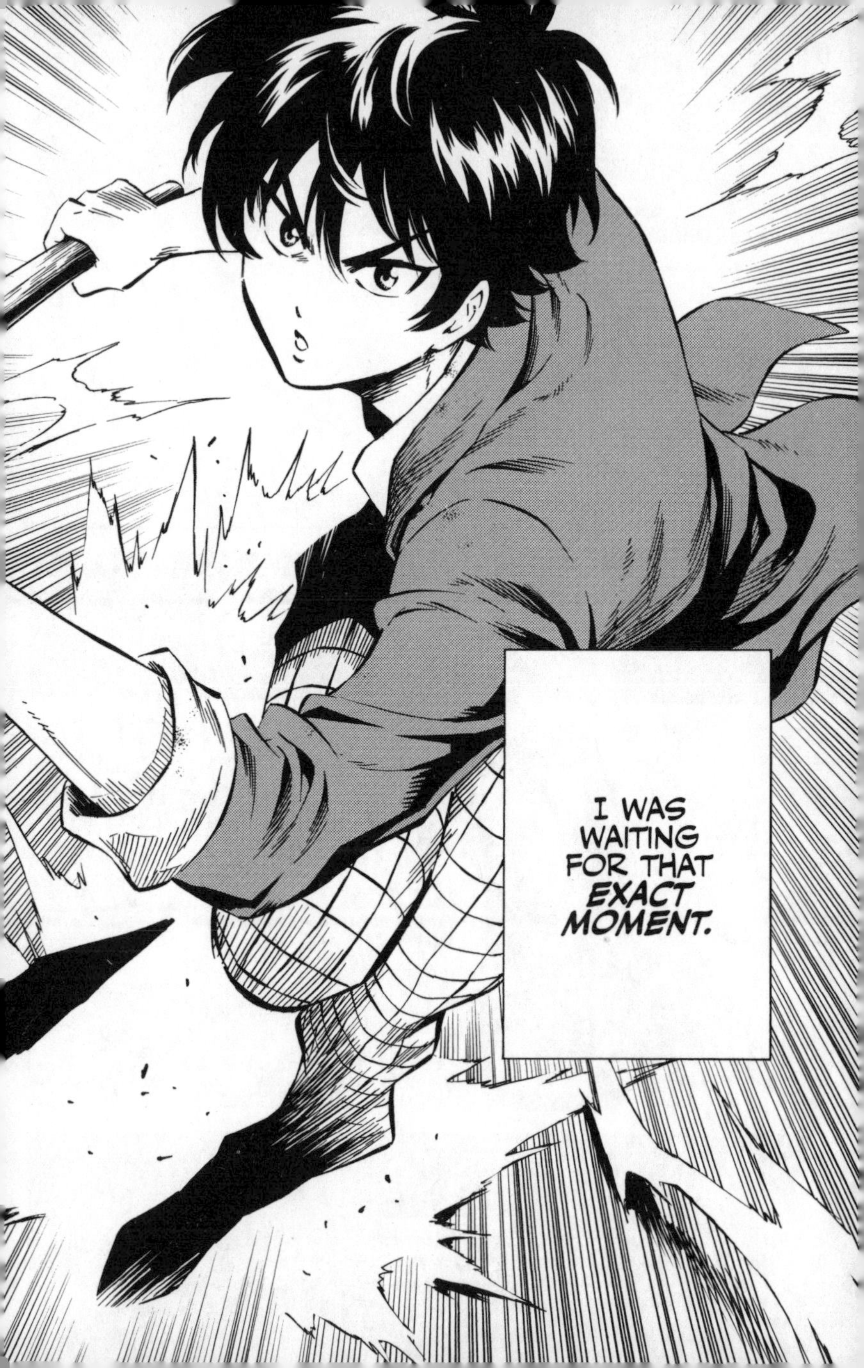
I WAS WAITING FOR THAT *EXACT MOMENT.*

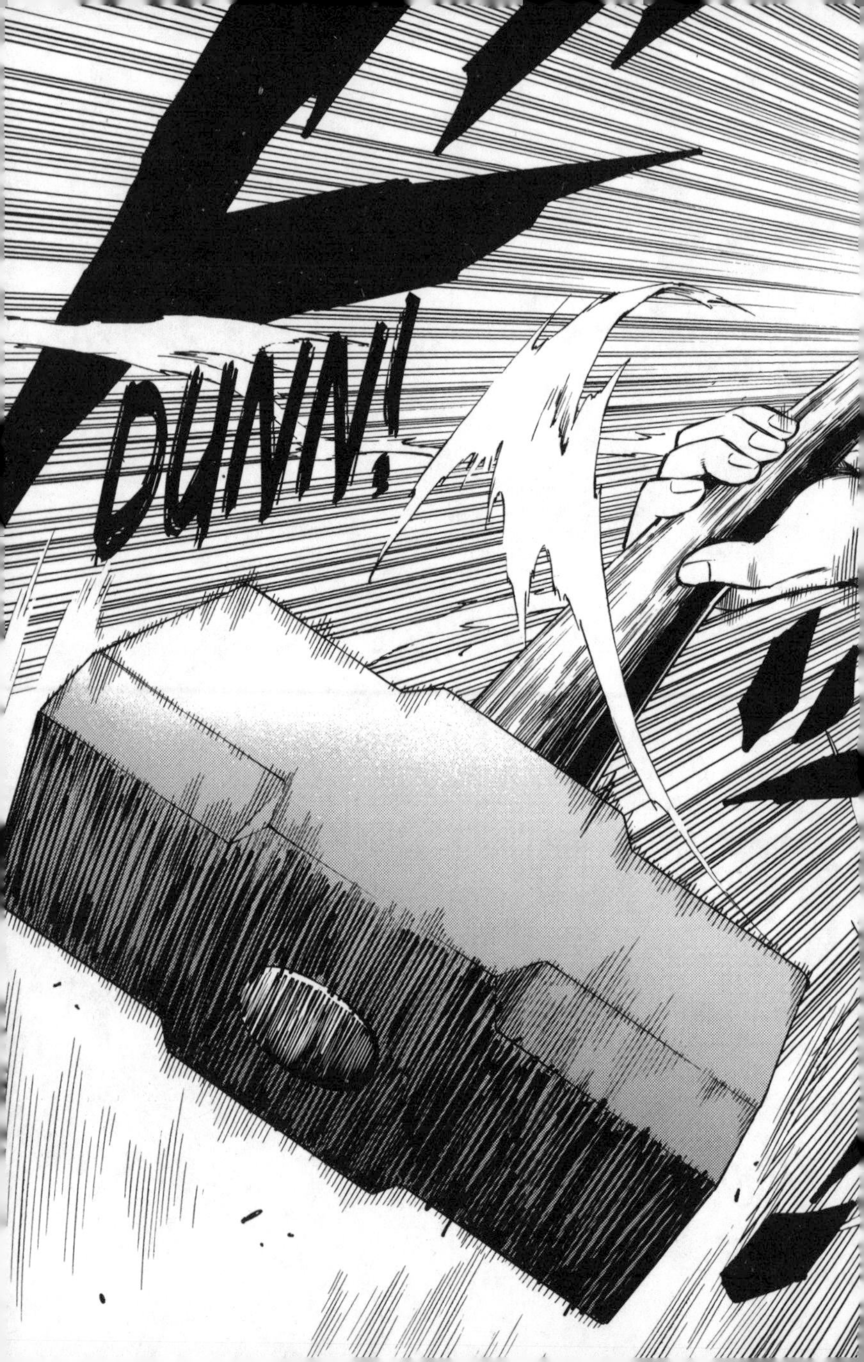
DUNN!

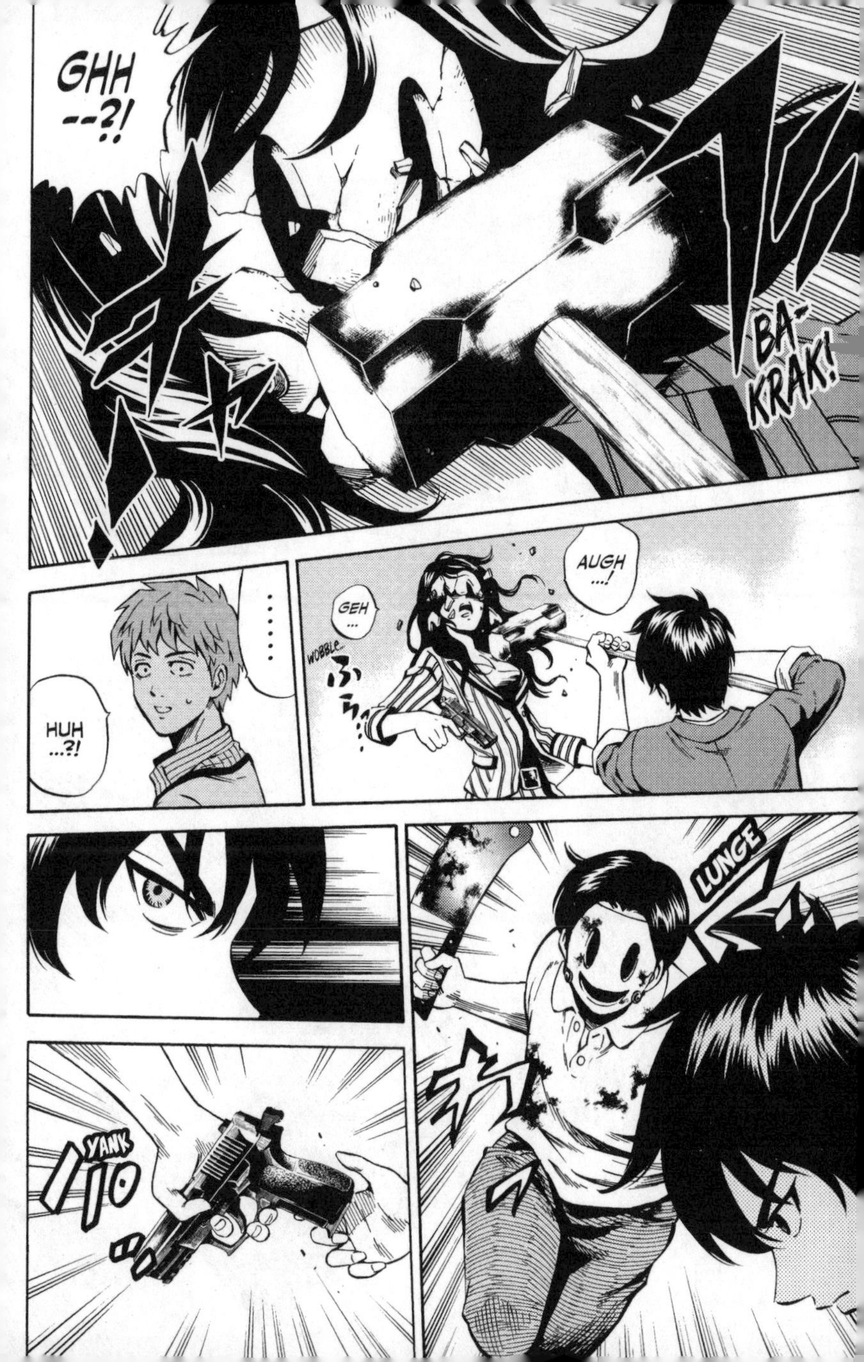
BA-KRAK!
GHH --?!
AUGH ...!
GEH ...
WOBBLE...
......
HUH ...?!
LUNGE
YANK

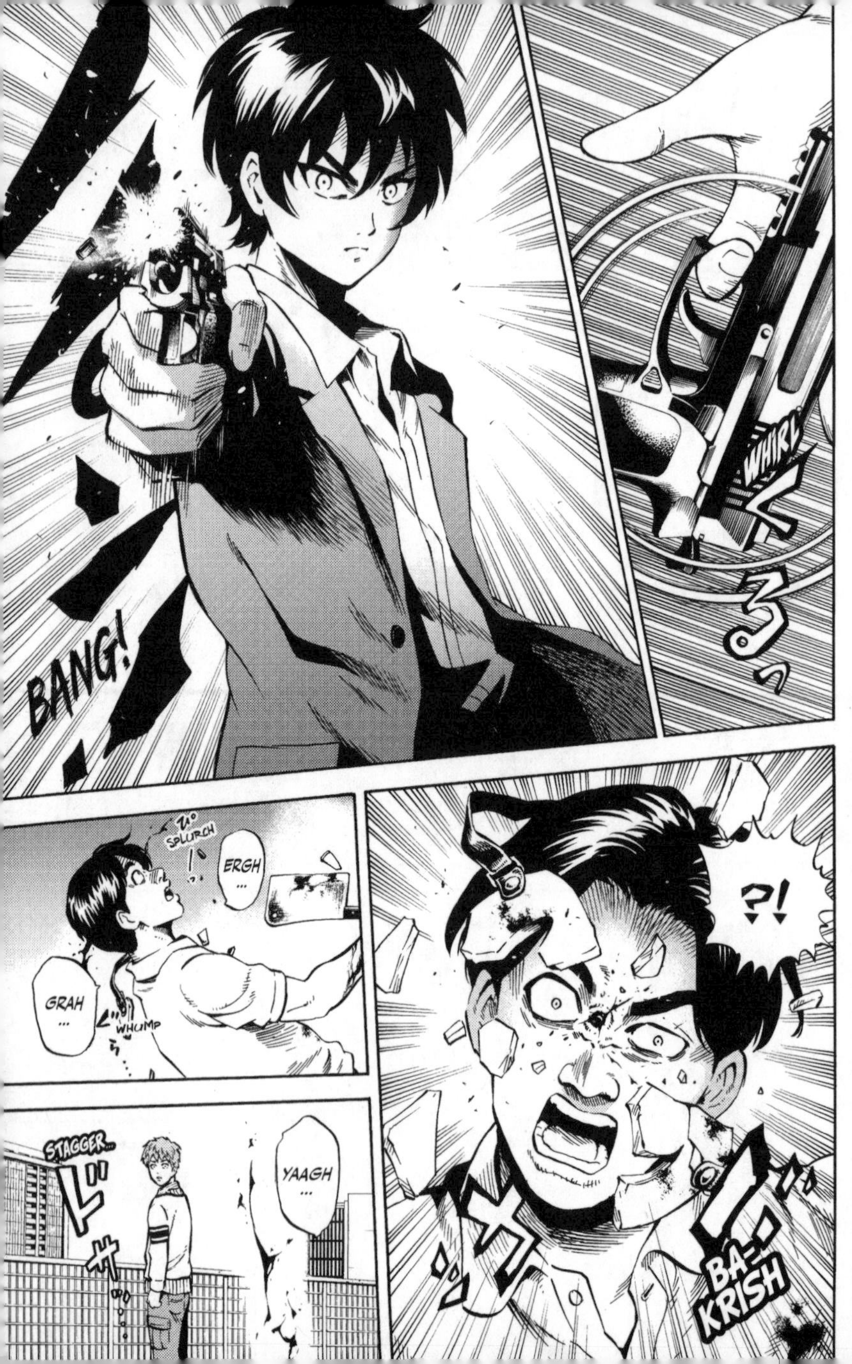
WHIRL
BANG!
?!
BA-KRISH
SPLURCH
ERGH ...
GRAH ...
WHUMP
STAGGER...
YAAGH ...

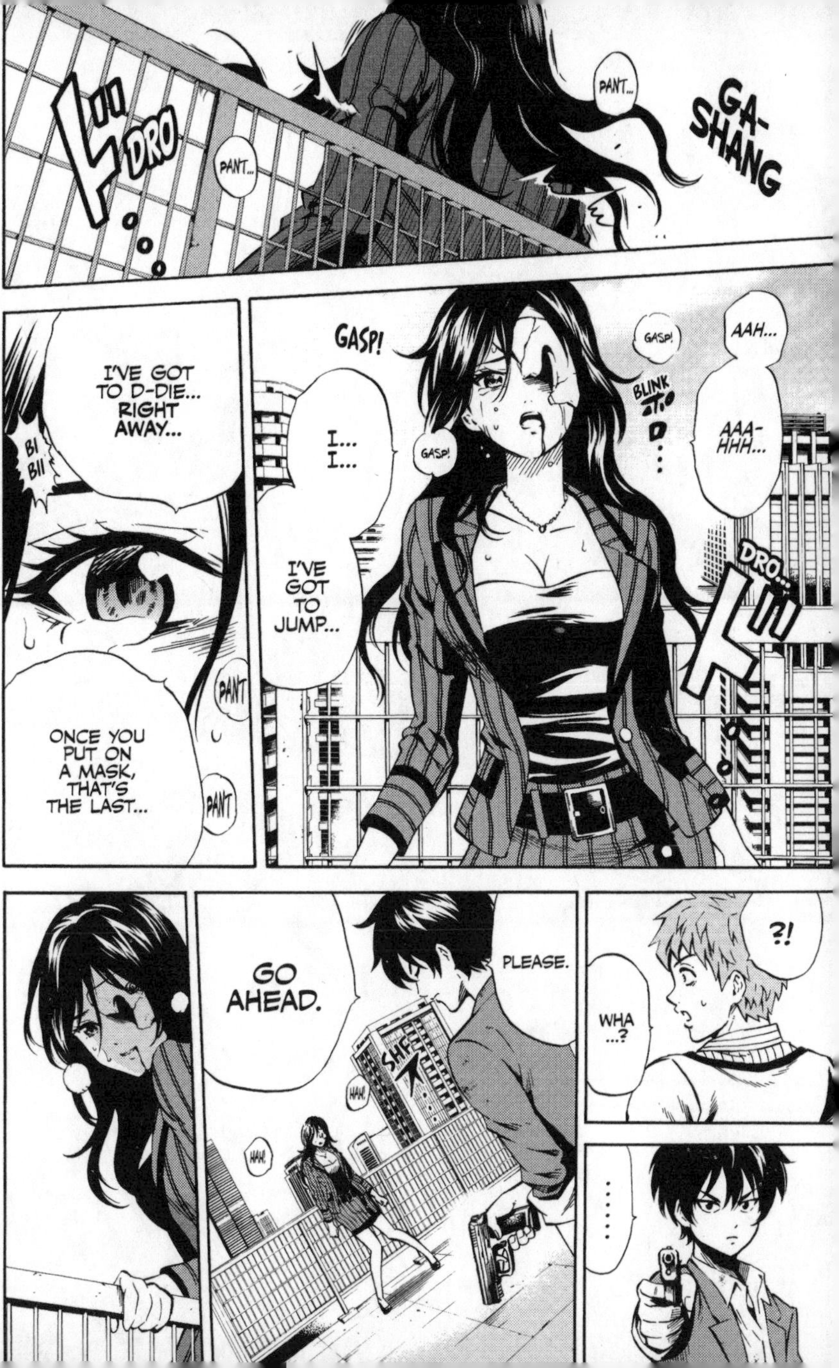
GA-
SHANG
PANT...
PANT...
DRO
AAH...
GASP!
BLINK
D...
AAA-
HHH...
DRO...
GASP!
I...
I...
GASP!
I'VE
GOT
TO
JUMP...
I'VE GOT
TO D-DIE...
RIGHT
AWAY...
BI
BII
PANT
ONCE YOU
PUT ON
A MASK,
THAT'S
THE LAST...
PANT
?!
WHA
...?
......
PLEASE.
GO
AHEAD.
SHF
HAH!
HAH!

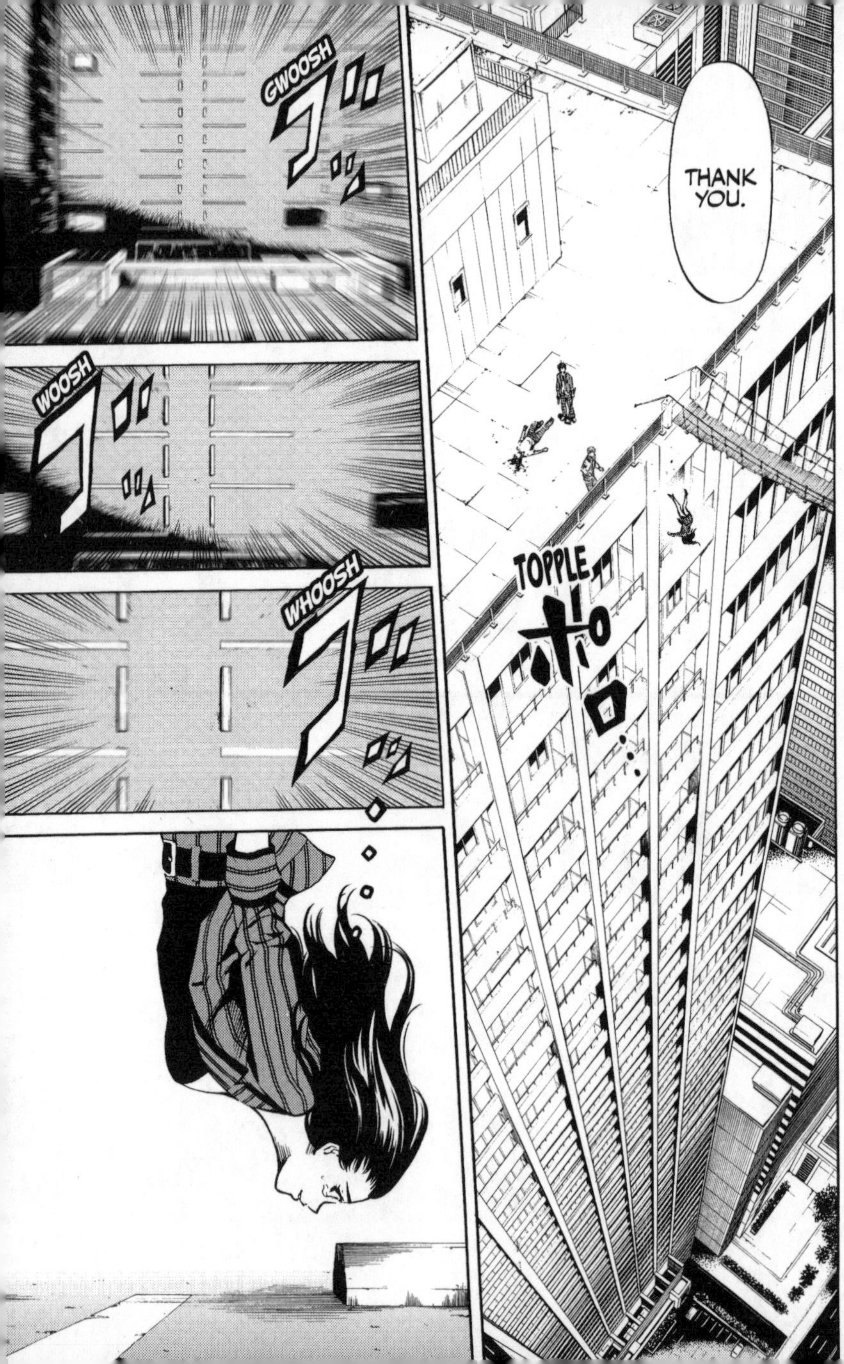
THANK YOU.
TOPPLE
GWOOSH
WOOSH
WHOOSH

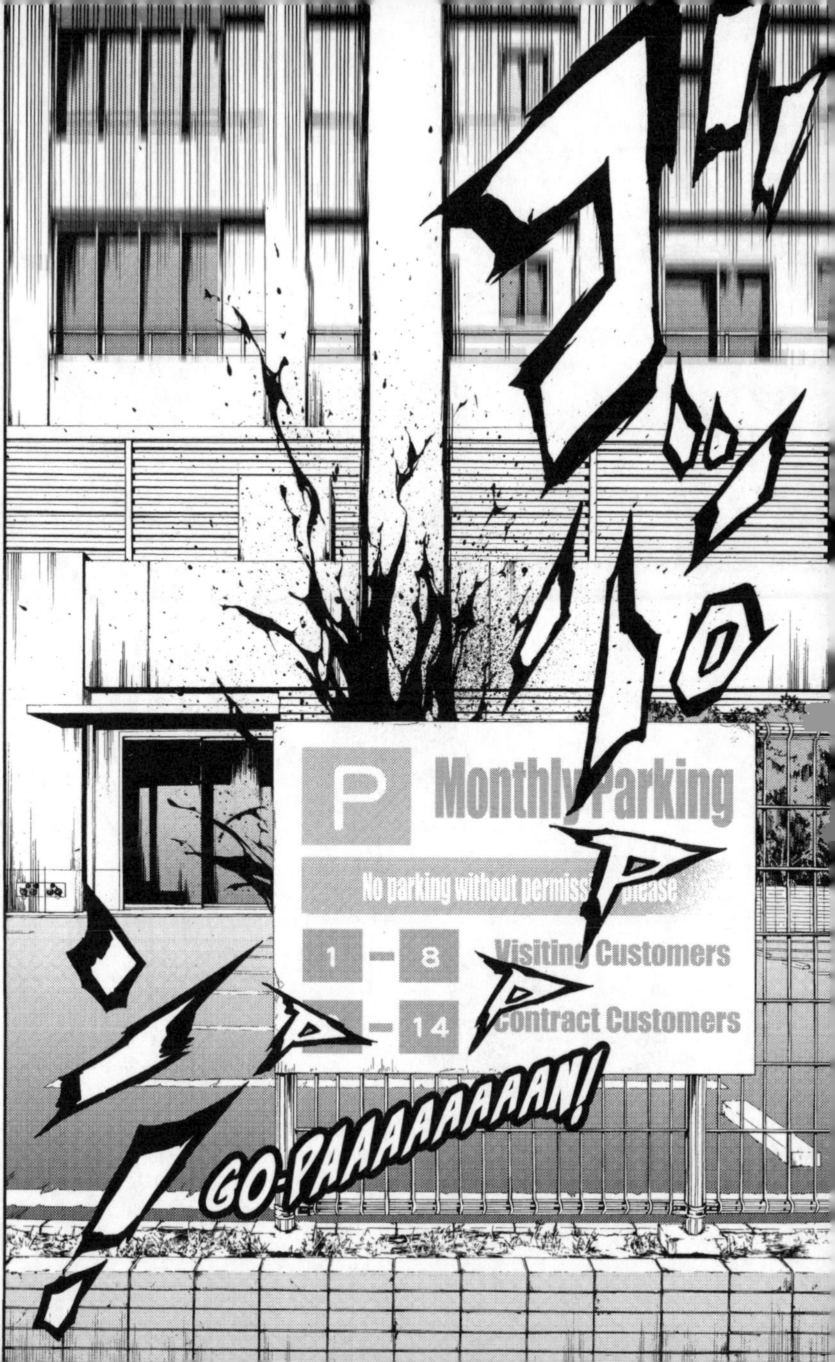
P
Monthly
No parking without permiss
1 – 8
Visiting Customers
– 14
Contract Customers
GO-PAAAAAAAAAN!

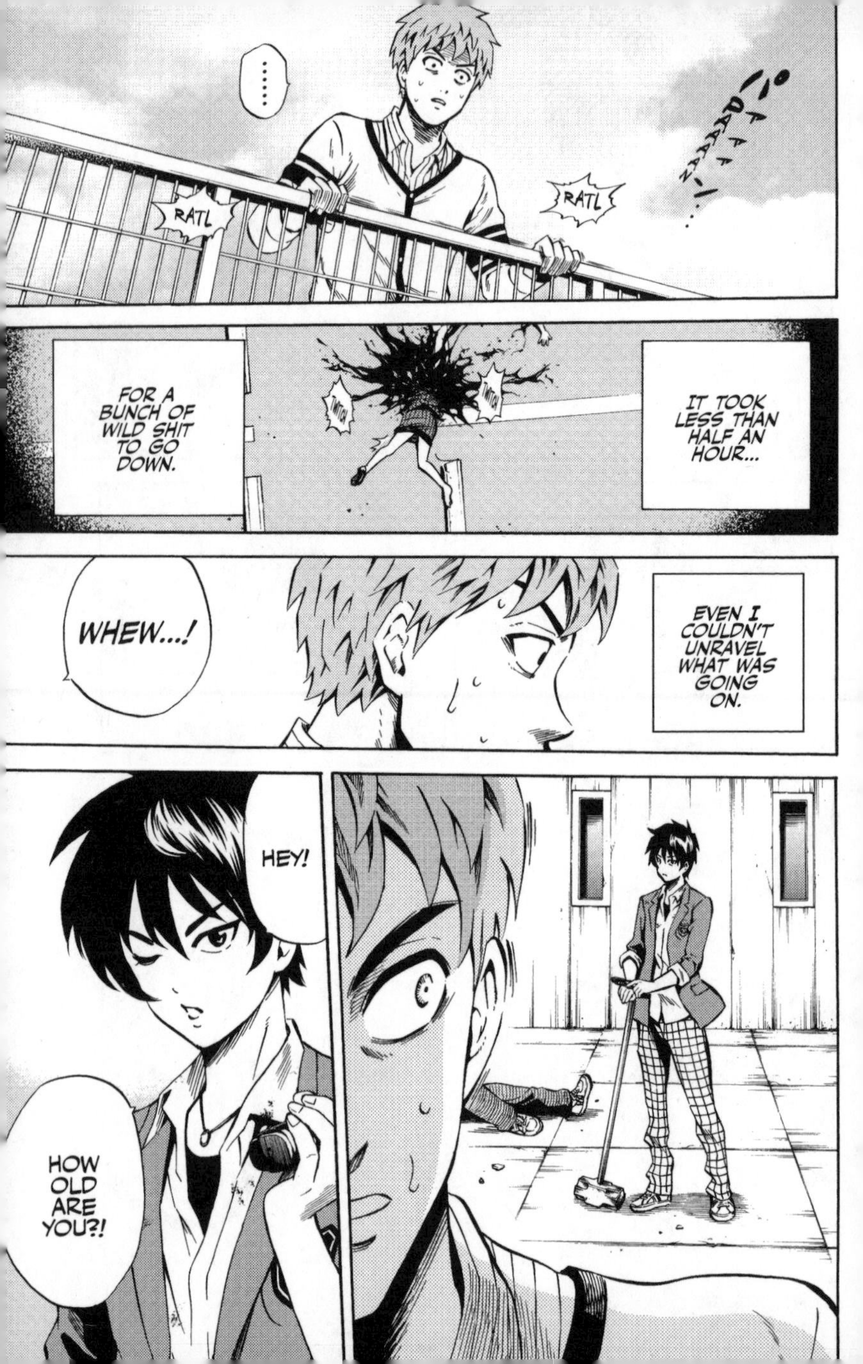
PAAAAN!...
RATL
RATL
......
IT TOOK LESS THAN HALF AN HOUR...
TWITCH
TWITCH
FOR A BUNCH OF WILD SHIT TO GO DOWN.
EVEN I COULDN'T UNRAVEL WHAT WAS GOING ON.
WHEW...!
HEY!
HOW OLD ARE YOU?!

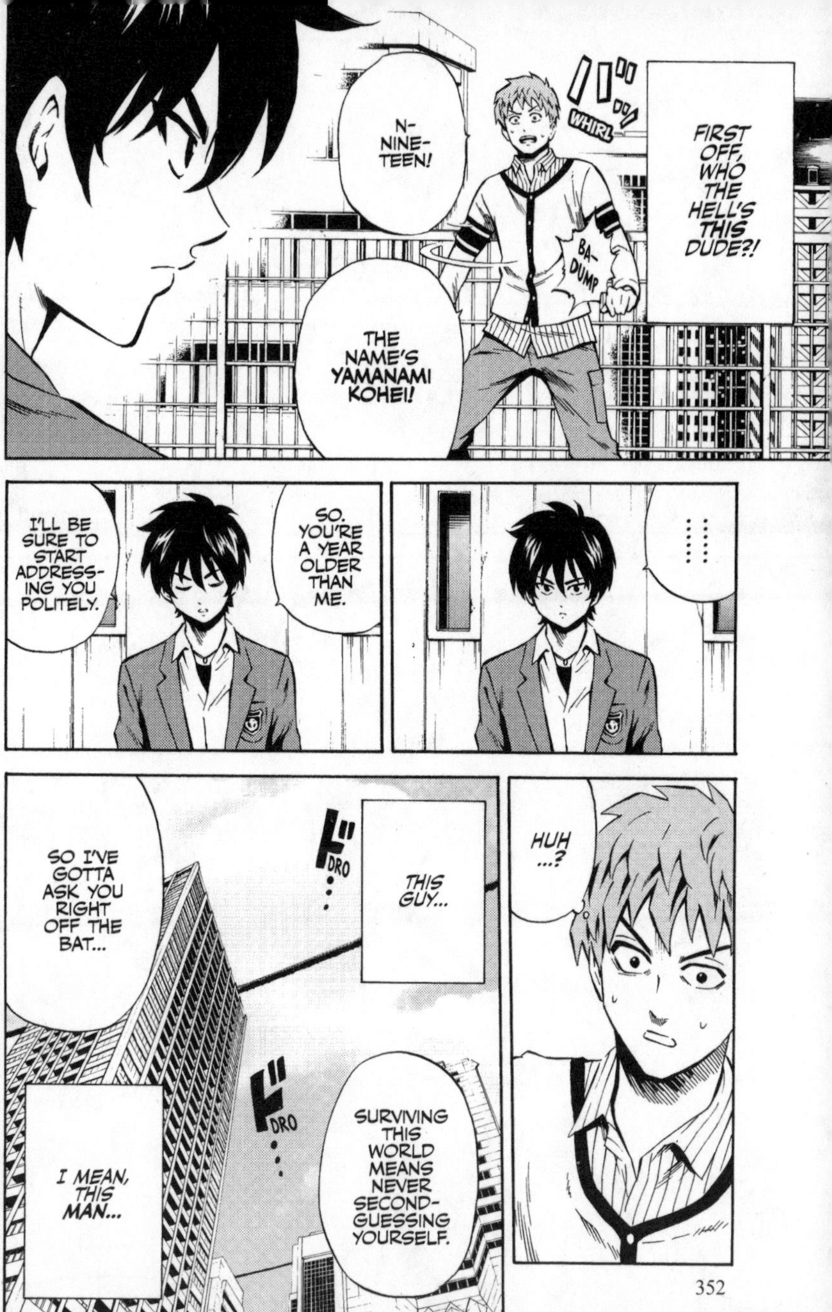
FIRST OFF, WHO THE HELL'S THIS DUDE?!
WHIRL
N-NINETEEN!
BA-DUMP
THE NAME'S YAMANAMI KOHEI!
......
SO. YOU'RE A YEAR OLDER THAN ME.
I'LL BE SURE TO START ADDRESSING YOU POLITELY.
HUH ...?
DRO...
THIS GUY...
SO I'VE GOTTA ASK YOU RIGHT OFF THE BAT...
DRO...
SURVIVING THIS WORLD MEANS NEVER SECOND-GUESSING YOURSELF.
I MEAN, THIS MAN...

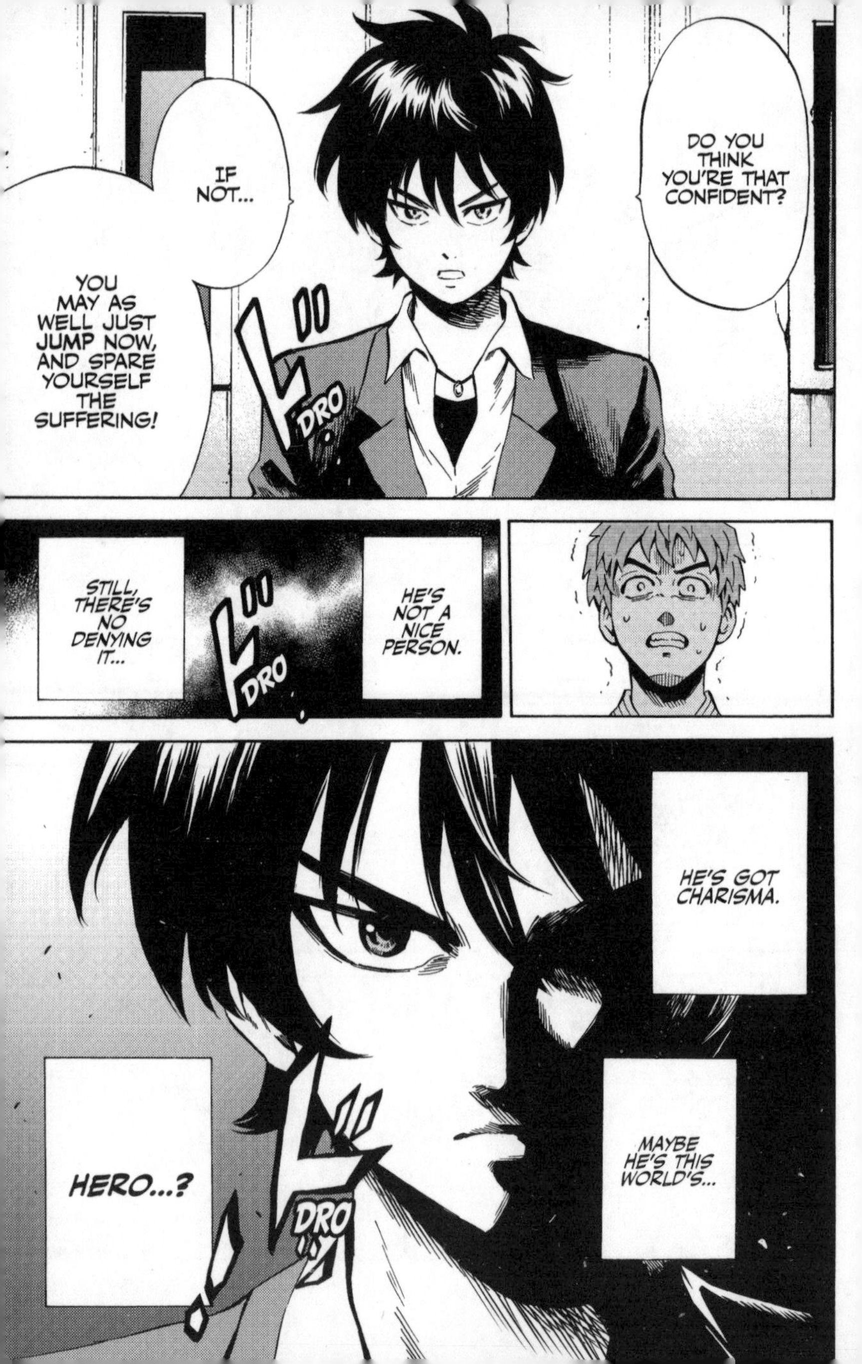
DO YOU THINK YOU'RE THAT CONFIDENT?
IF NOT...
YOU MAY AS WELL JUST JUMP NOW, AND SPARE YOURSELF THE SUFFERING!
DRO
HE'S NOT A NICE PERSON.
DRO
STILL, THERE'S NO DENYING IT...
HE'S GOT CHARISMA.
MAYBE HE'S THIS WORLD'S...
DRO
HERO...?

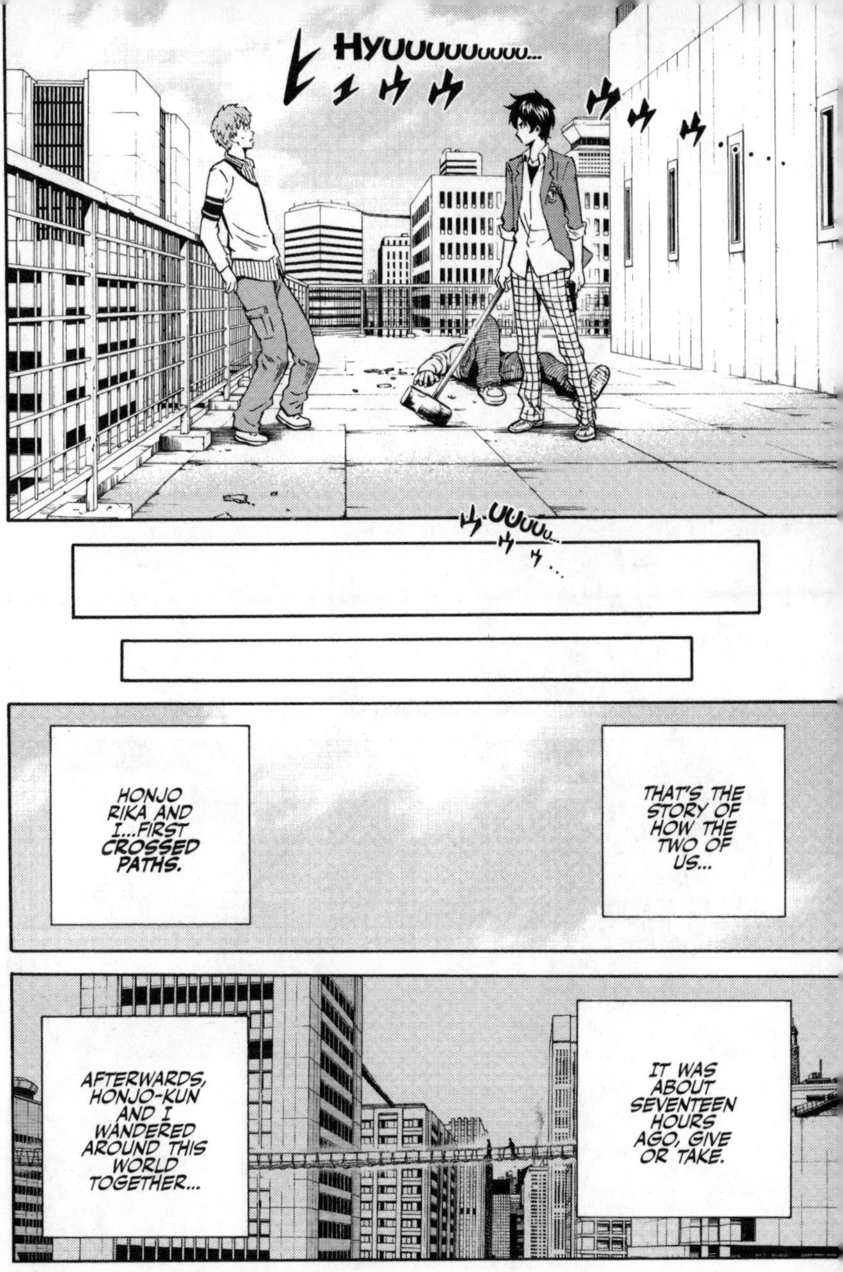
HYUUUUUuuuu...
UUUUu...
THAT'S THE STORY OF HOW THE TWO OF US...
HONJO RIKA AND I...FIRST CROSSED PATHS.
IT WAS ABOUT SEVENTEEN HOURS AGO, GIVE OR TAKE.
AFTERWARDS, HONJO-KUN AND I WANDERED AROUND THIS WORLD TOGETHER...

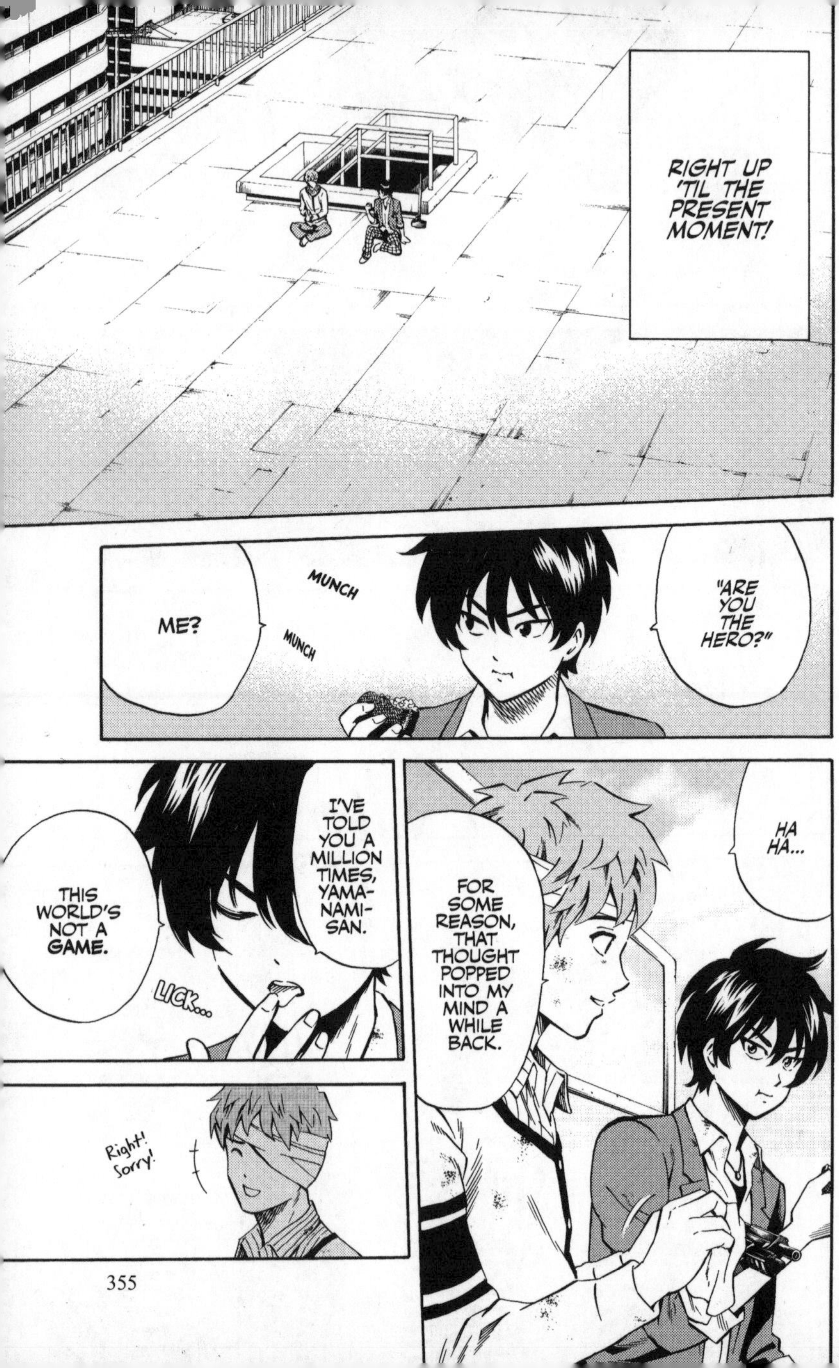
RIGHT UP 'TIL THE PRESENT MOMENT!
"ARE YOU THE HERO?"
MUNCH
MUNCH
ME?
HA HA...
FOR SOME REASON, THAT THOUGHT POPPED INTO MY MIND A WHILE BACK.
I'VE TOLD YOU A MILLION TIMES, YAMA-NAMI-SAN.
THIS WORLD'S NOT A GAME.
LICK...
Right! Sorry!

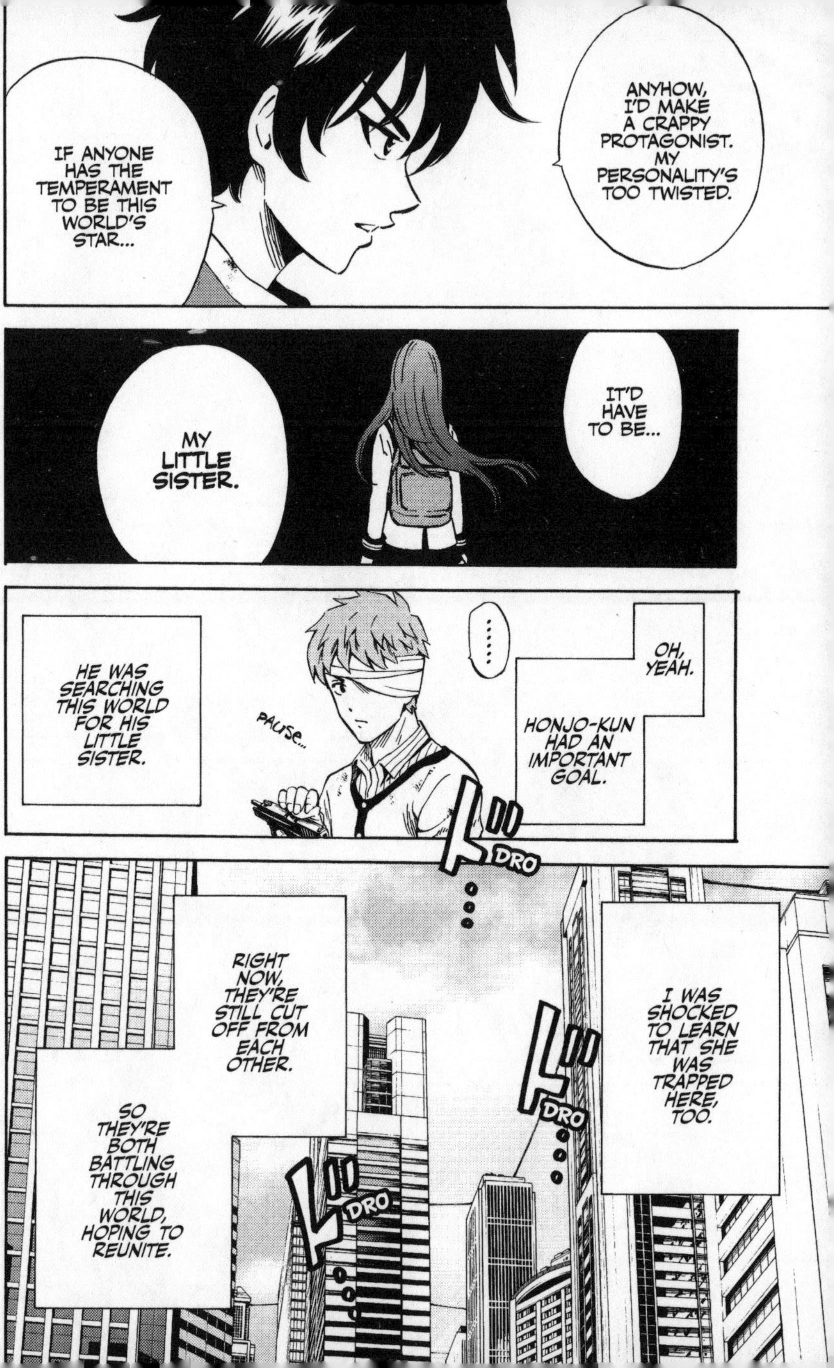
ANYHOW, I'D MAKE A CRAPPY PROTAGONIST. MY PERSONALITY'S TOO TWISTED.
IF ANYONE HAS THE TEMPERAMENT TO BE THIS WORLD'S STAR...
IT'D HAVE TO BE...
MY LITTLE SISTER.
......
OH, YEAH.
HONJO-KUN HAD AN IMPORTANT GOAL.
PAUSE...
HE WAS SEARCHING THIS WORLD FOR HIS LITTLE SISTER.
DRO...
I WAS SHOCKED TO LEARN THAT SHE WAS TRAPPED HERE, TOO.
DRO...
RIGHT NOW, THEY'RE STILL CUT OFF FROM EACH OTHER.
SO THEY'RE BOTH BATTLING THROUGH THIS WORLD, HOPING TO REUNITE.
DRO...

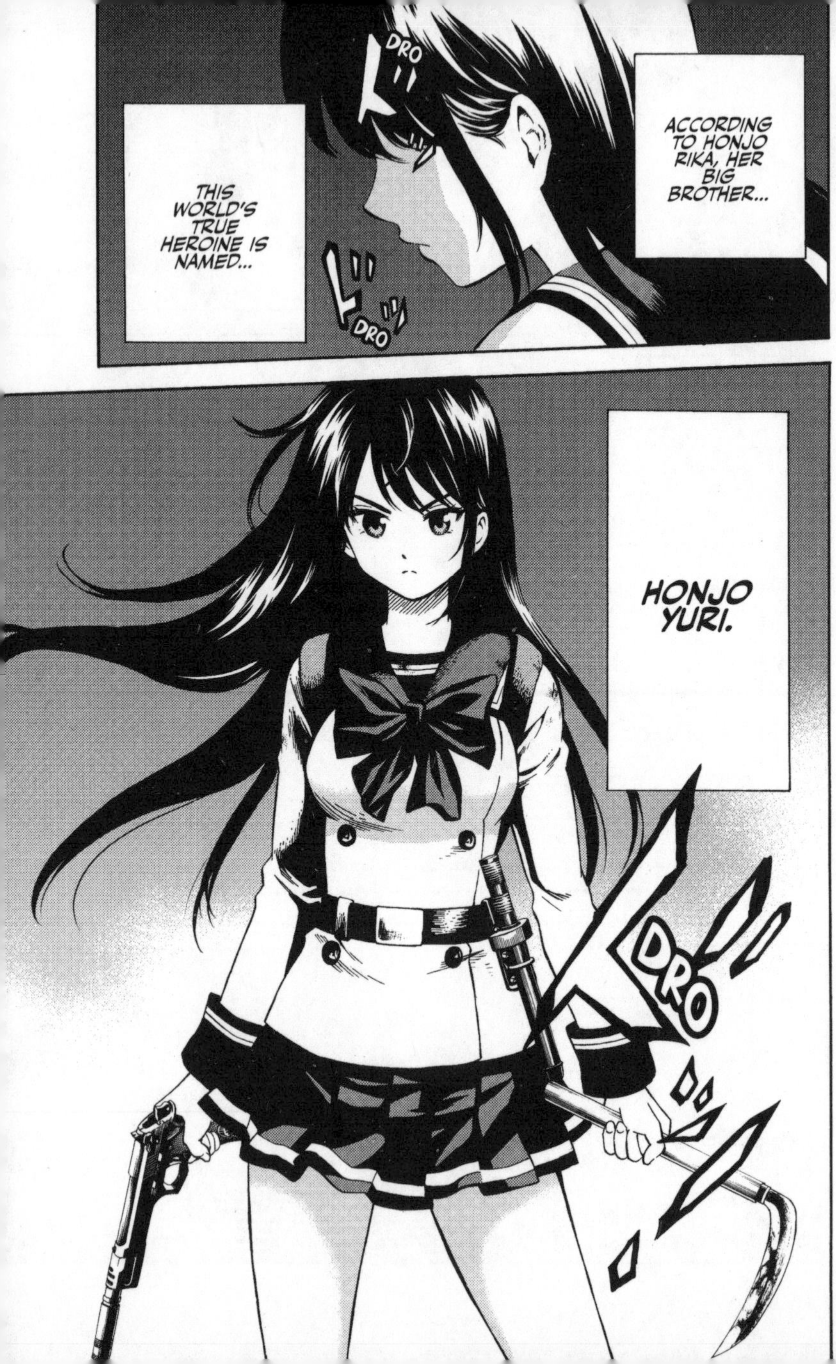
ACCORDING TO HONJO RIKA, HER BIG BROTHER...
DRO
DRO
THIS WORLD'S TRUE HEROINE IS NAMED...
HONJO YURI.
DRO

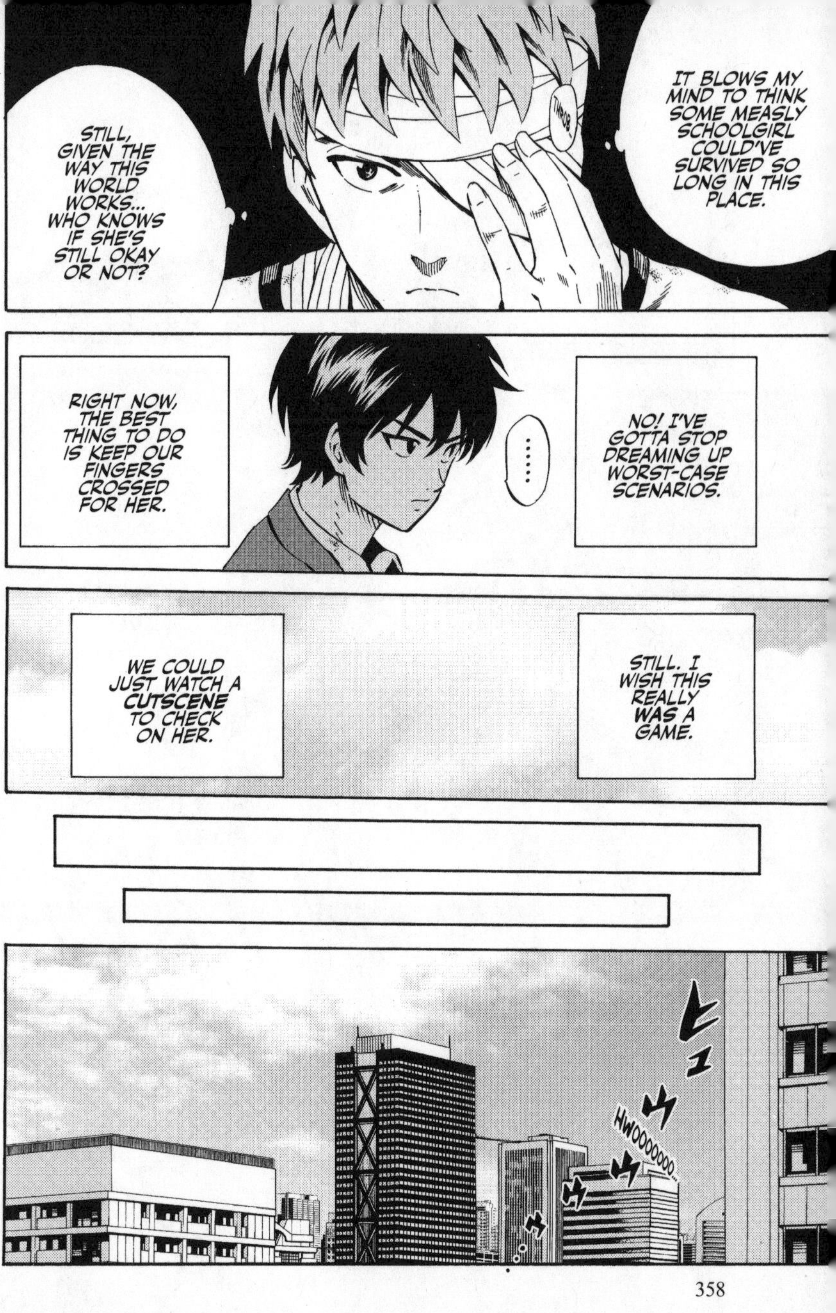
IT BLOWS MY MIND TO THINK SOME MEASLY SCHOOLGIRL COULD'VE SURVIVED SO LONG IN THIS PLACE.
THROB...
STILL, GIVEN THE WAY THIS WORLD WORKS... WHO KNOWS IF SHE'S STILL OKAY OR NOT?
NO! I'VE GOTTA STOP DREAMING UP WORST-CASE SCENARIOS.
......
RIGHT NOW, THE BEST THING TO DO IS KEEP OUR FINGERS CROSSED FOR HER.
STILL. I WISH THIS REALLY WAS A GAME.
WE COULD JUST WATCH A CUTSCENE TO CHECK ON HER.
HWOOOOOOO...

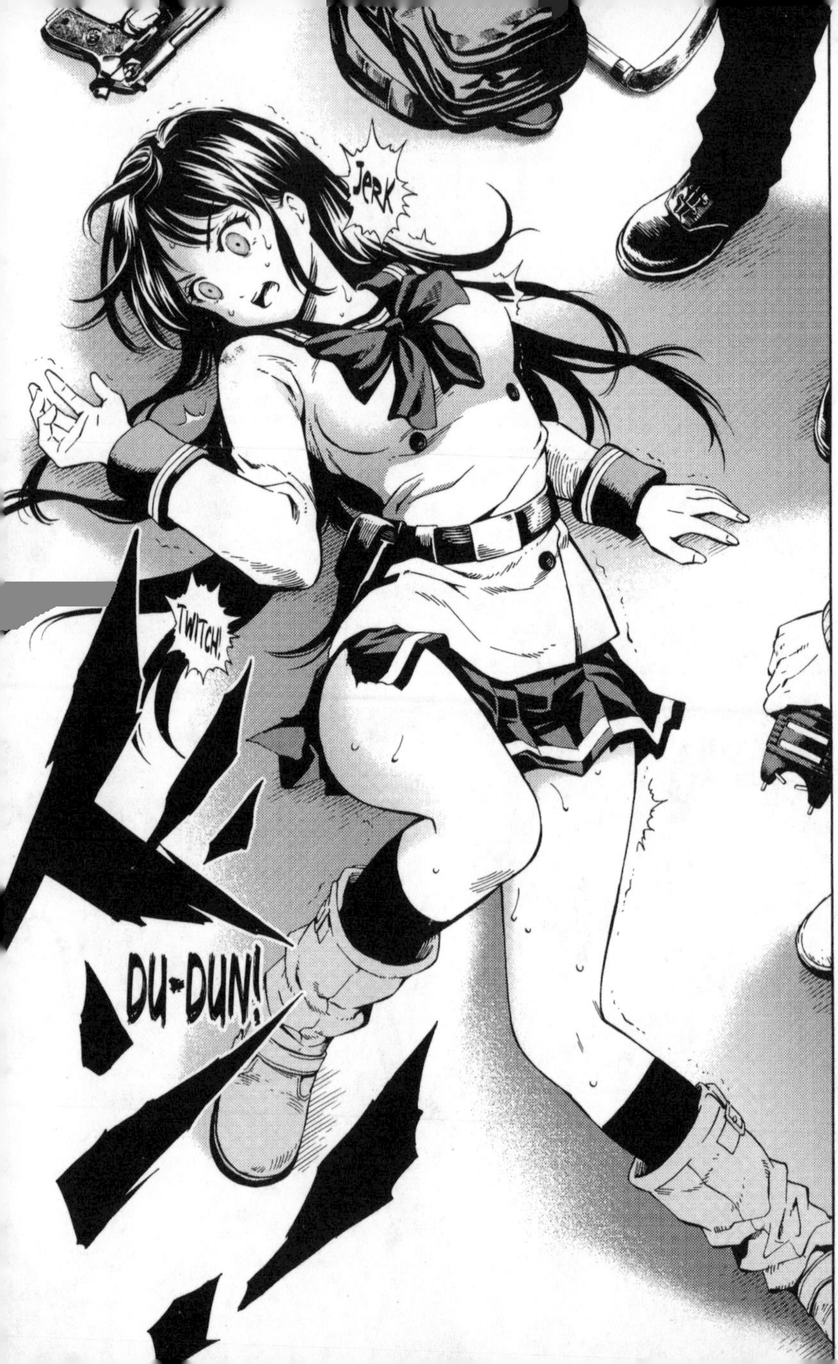
JERK
TWITCH!
DU-DUN!

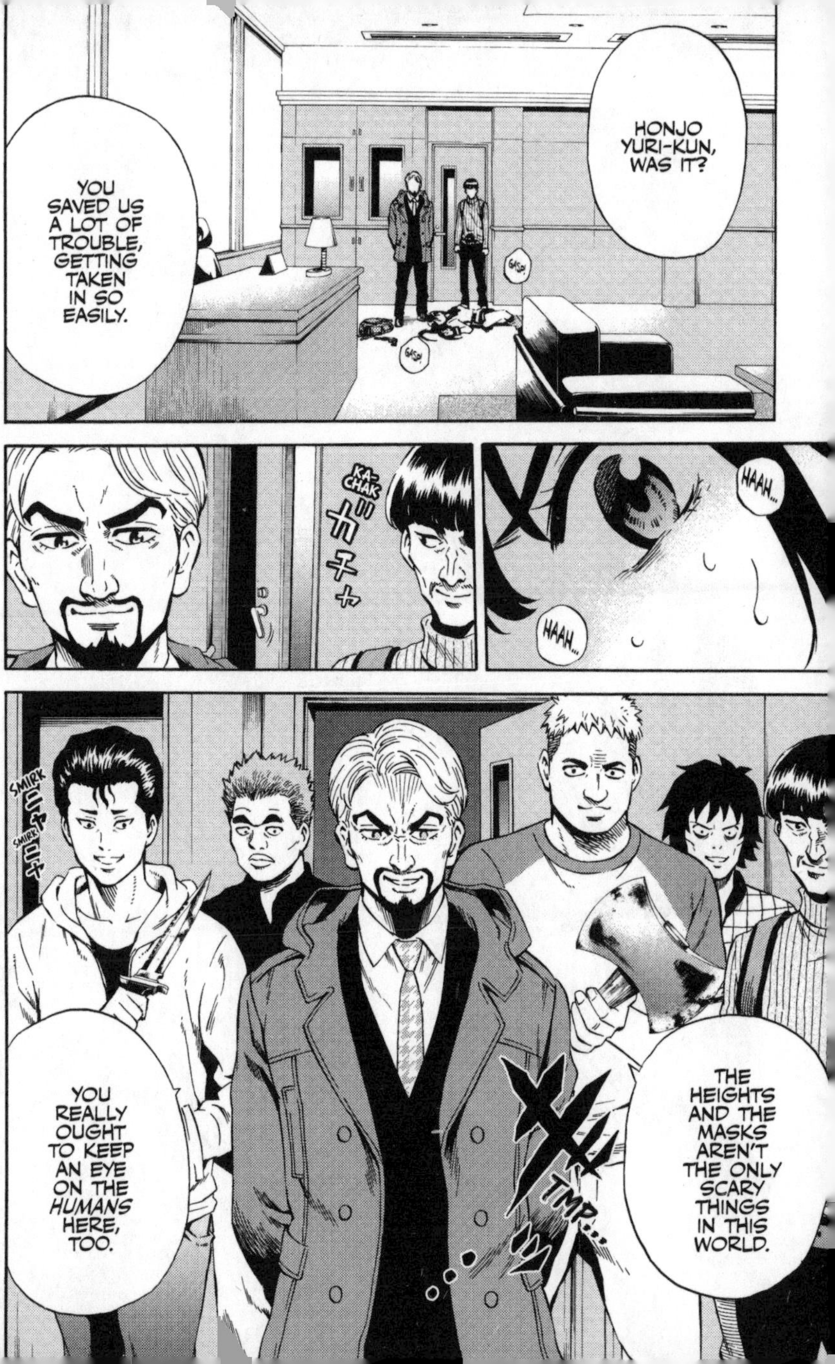
HONJO YURI-KUN, WAS IT?
GASP!
GASP!
YOU SAVED US A LOT OF TROUBLE, GETTING TAKEN IN SO EASILY.
HAAH...
HAAH...
KA-CHAK
THE HEIGHTS AND THE MASKS AREN'T THE ONLY SCARY THINGS IN THIS WORLD.
TMP...
SMIRK
SMIRK
YOU REALLY OUGHT TO KEEP AN EYE ON THE *HUMANS* HERE, TOO.

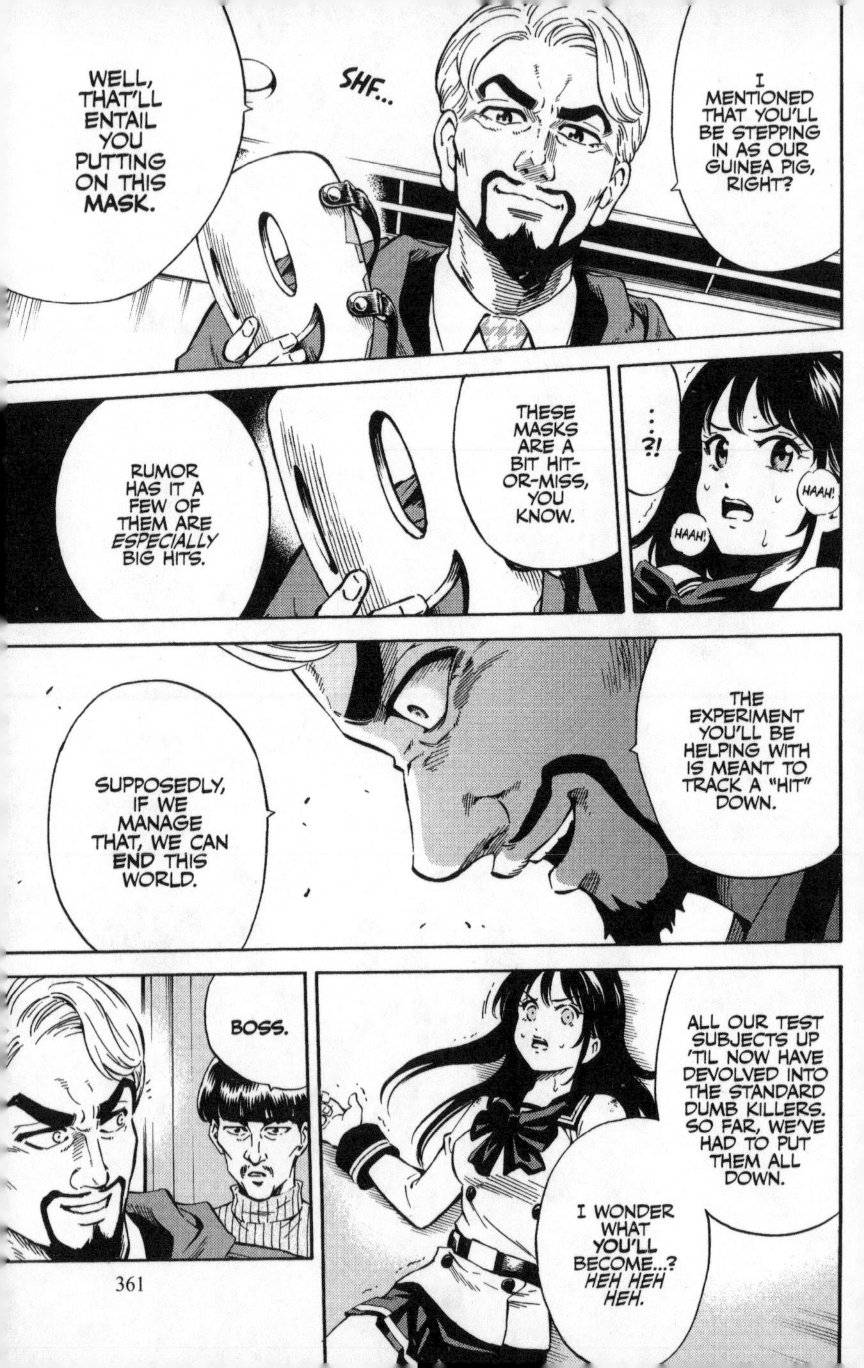
I MENTIONED THAT YOU'LL BE STEPPING IN AS OUR GUINEA PIG, RIGHT?
SHF...
WELL, THAT'LL ENTAIL YOU PUTTING ON THIS MASK.
...?!
HAAH!
HAAH!
THESE MASKS ARE A BIT HIT-OR-MISS, YOU KNOW.
RUMOR HAS IT A FEW OF THEM ARE *ESPECIALLY* BIG HITS.
THE EXPERIMENT YOU'LL BE HELPING WITH IS MEANT TO TRACK A "HIT" DOWN.
SUPPOSEDLY, IF WE MANAGE THAT, WE CAN END THIS WORLD.
ALL OUR TEST SUBJECTS UP 'TIL NOW HAVE DEVOLVED INTO THE STANDARD DUMB KILLERS. SO FAR, WE'VE HAD TO PUT THEM ALL DOWN.
I WONDER WHAT YOU'LL BECOME...? *HEH HEH HEH.*
BOSS.

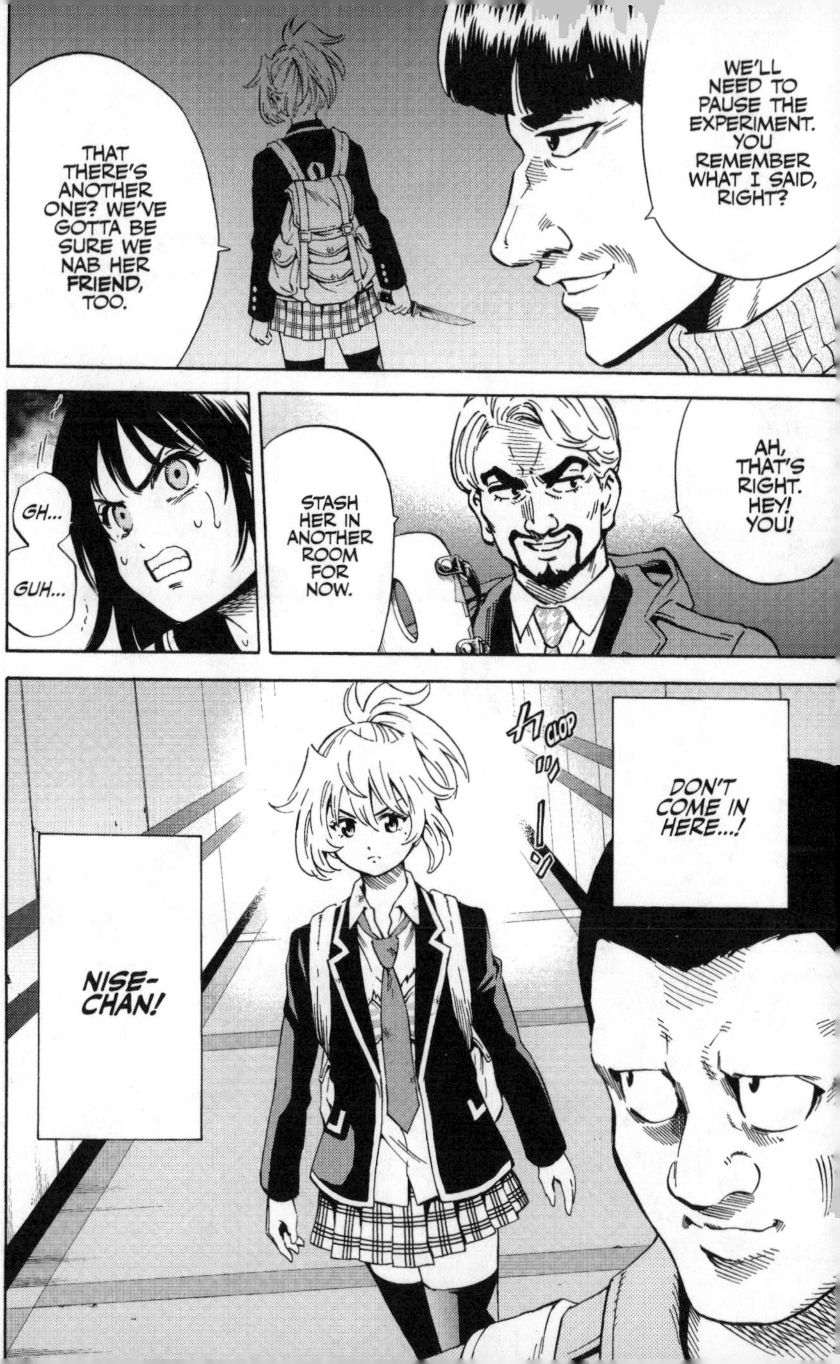
WE'LL NEED TO PAUSE THE EXPERIMENT. YOU REMEMBER WHAT I SAID, RIGHT?
THAT THERE'S ANOTHER ONE? WE'VE GOTTA BE SURE WE NAB HER FRIEND, TOO.
AH, THAT'S RIGHT. HEY! YOU!
STASH HER IN ANOTHER ROOM FOR NOW.
GH...
GUH...
CLOP
DON'T COME IN HERE...!
NISE-CHAN!

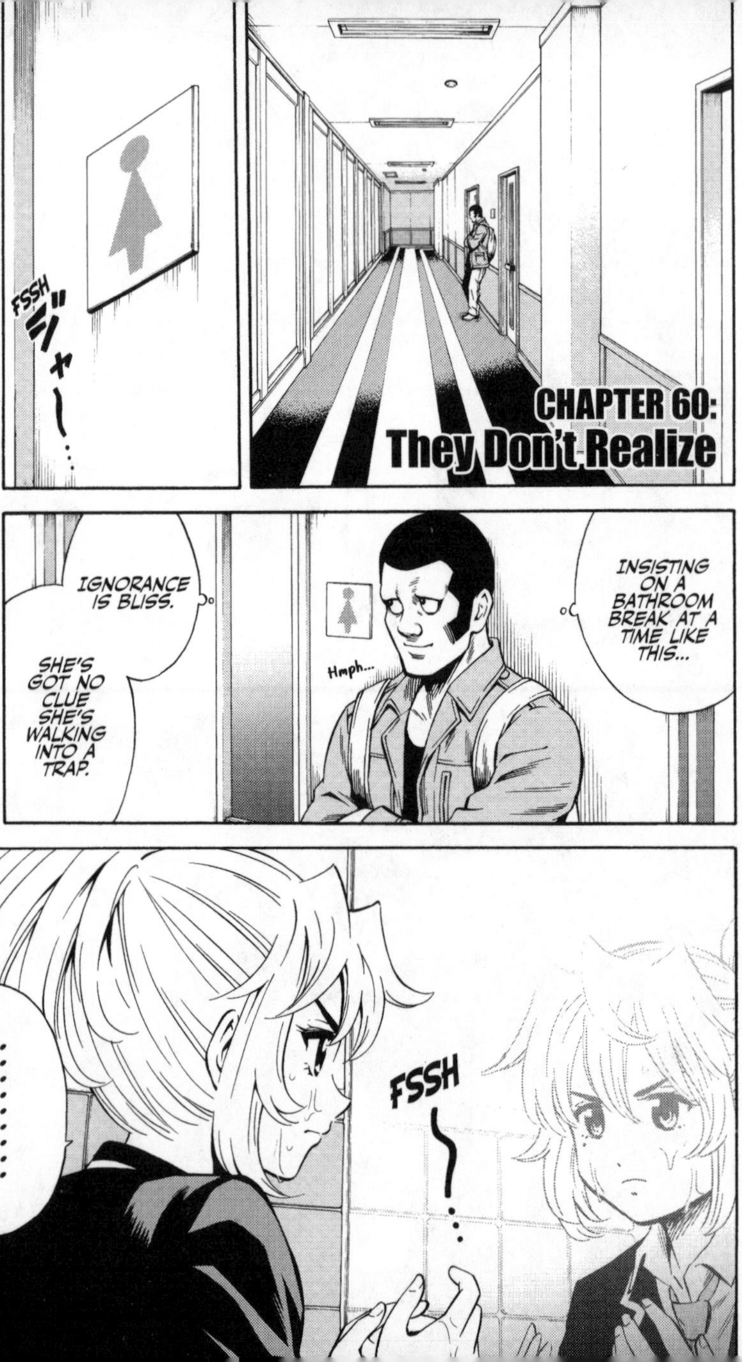
CHAPTER 60:
They Don't Realize
FSSH
ジャー…
INSISTING ON A BATHROOM BREAK AT A TIME LIKE THIS...
Hmph...
IGNORANCE IS BLISS.
SHE'S GOT NO CLUE SHE'S WALKING INTO A TRAP.
FSSH
……
……

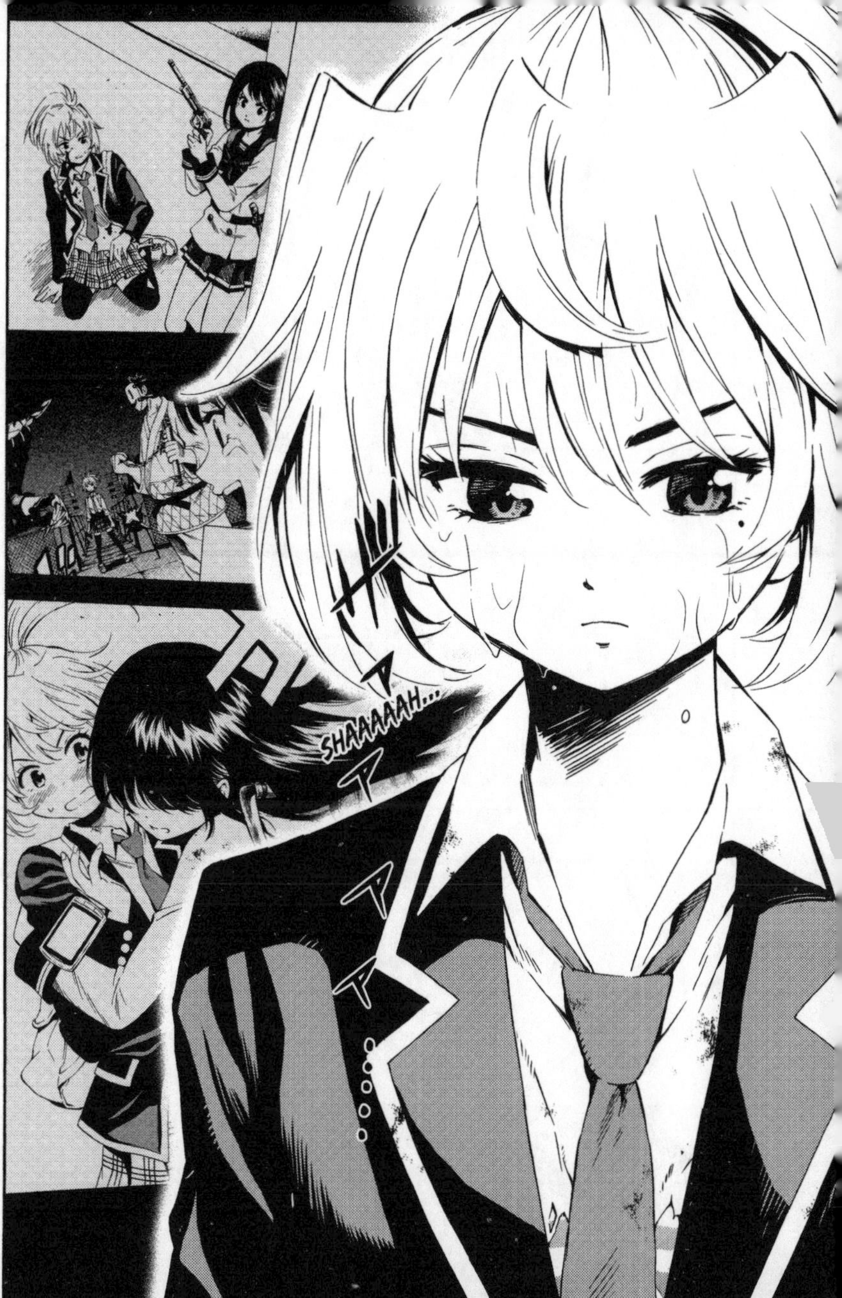
SHAAAAAH...

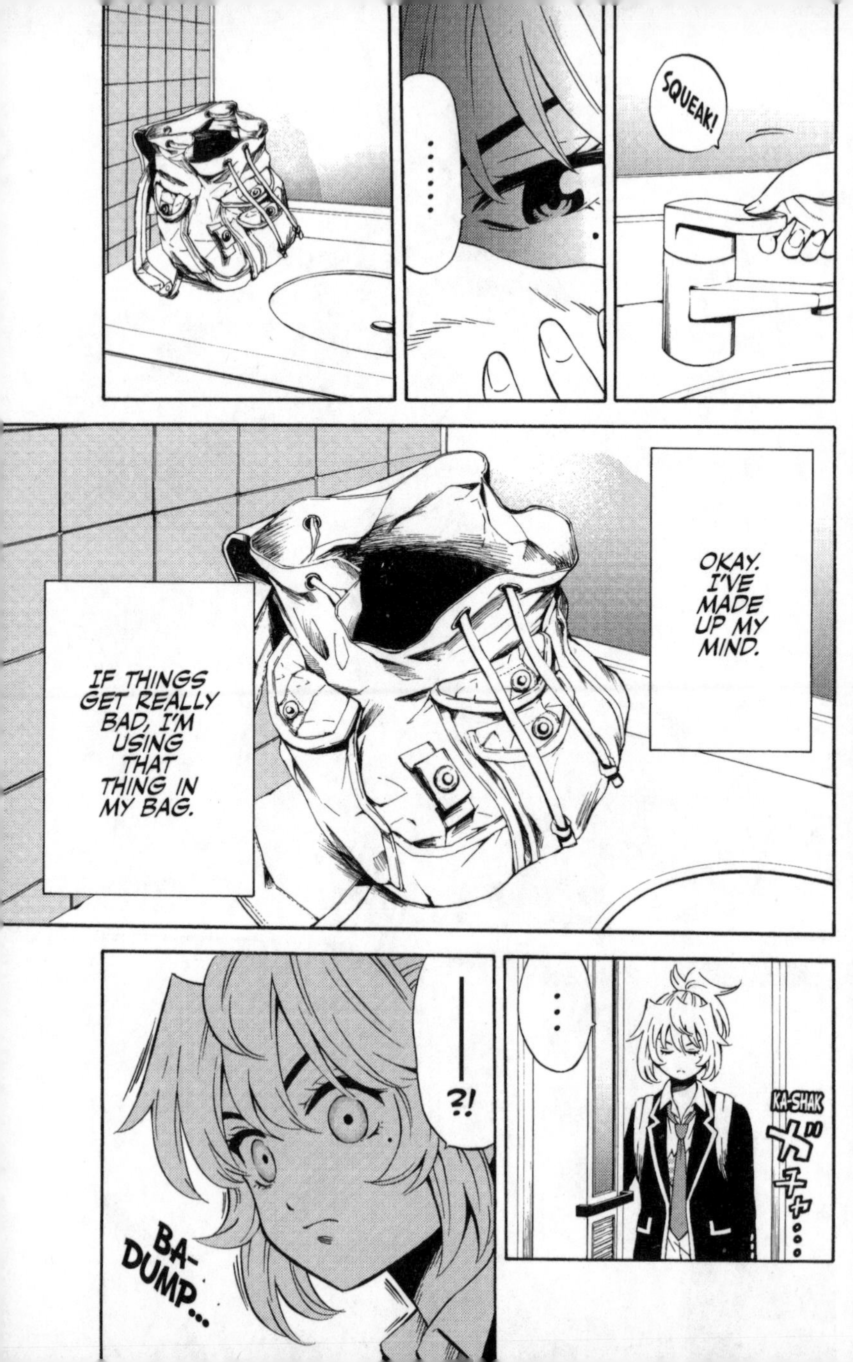
SQUEAK!
......
OKAY. I'VE MADE UP MY MIND.
IF THINGS GET REALLY BAD, I'M USING THAT THING IN MY BAG.
...
KA-SHAK
—?!
BA-DUMP...

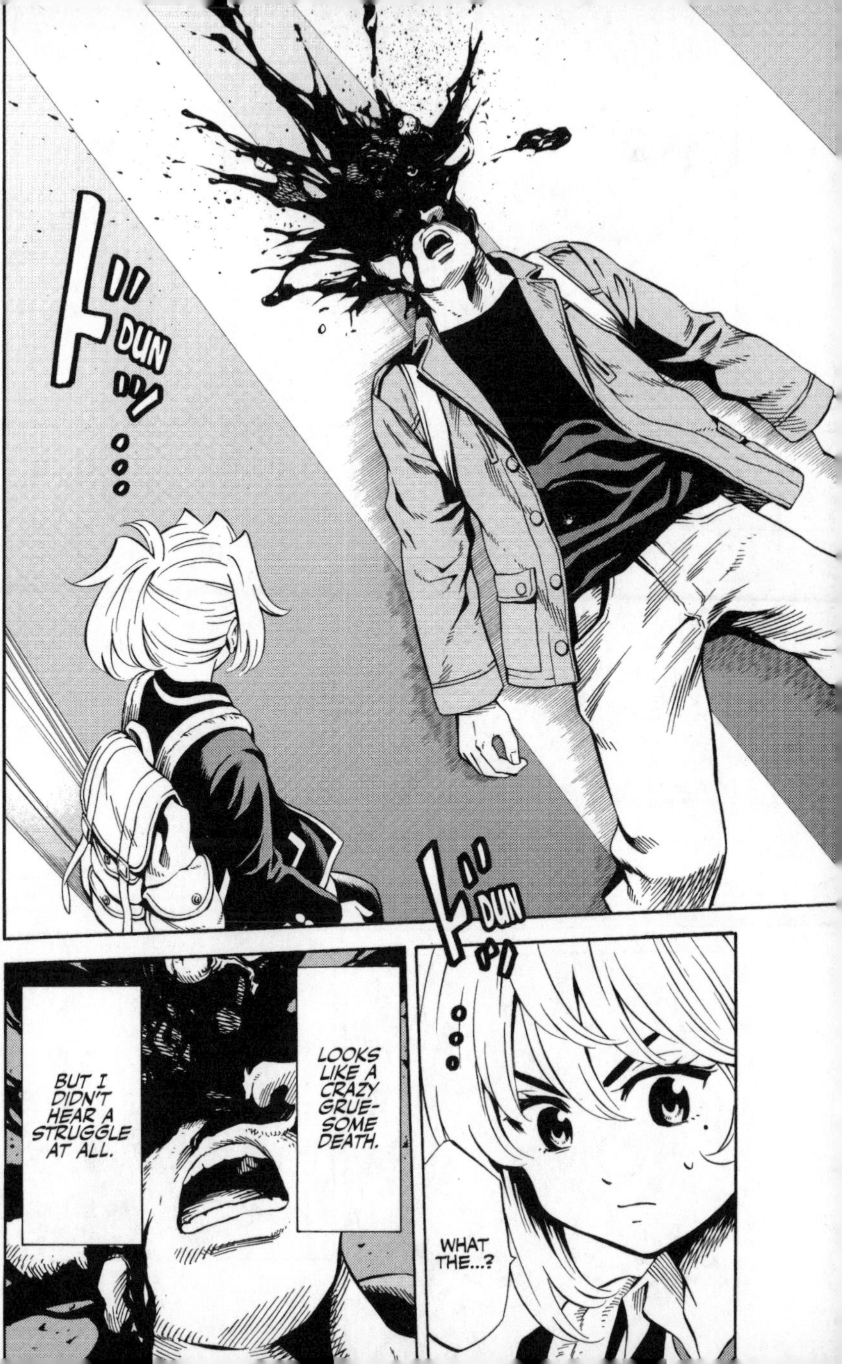
DUN
DUN
WHAT THE...?
LOOKS LIKE A CRAZY GRUE-SOME DEATH.
BUT I DIDN'T HEAR A STRUGGLE AT ALL.

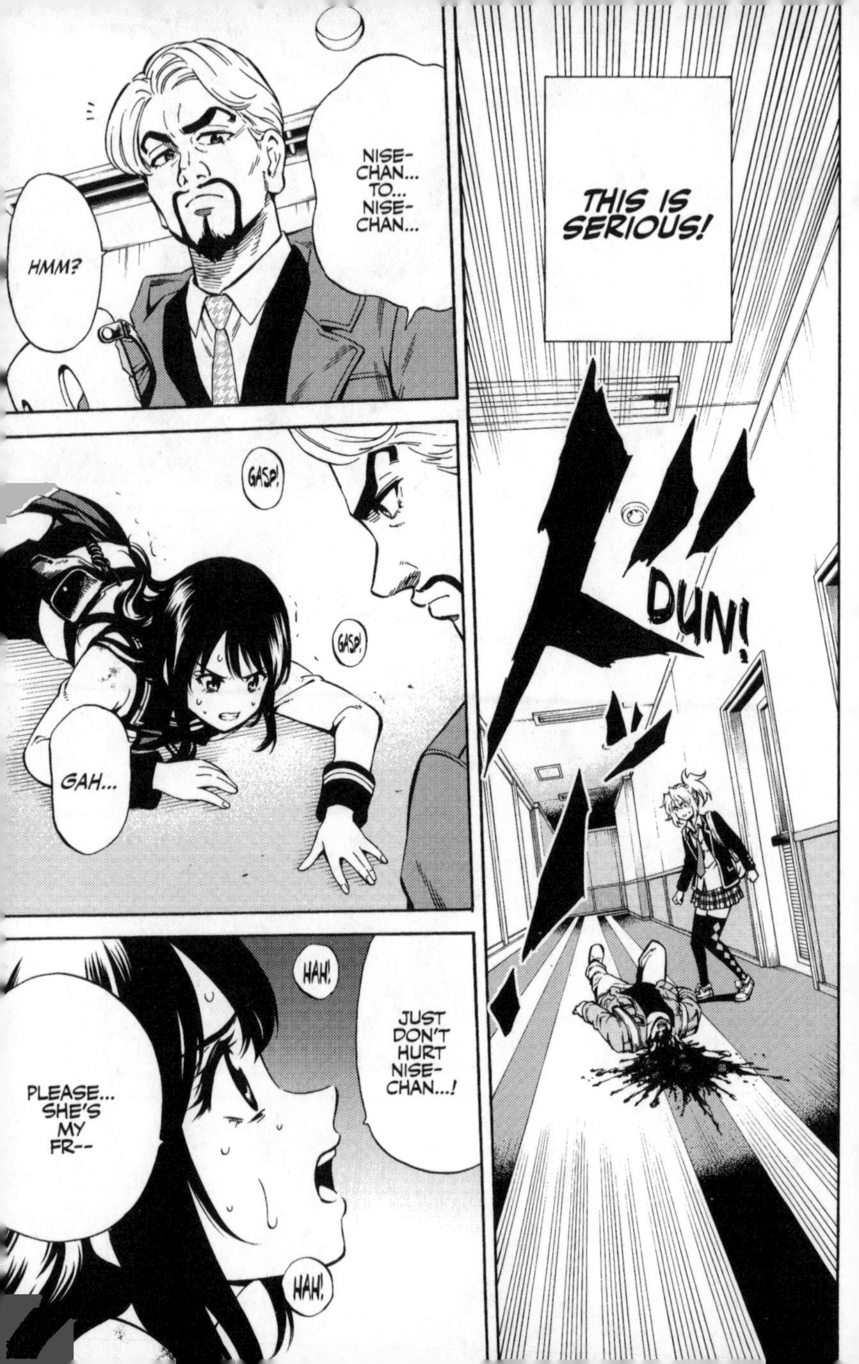
THIS IS SERIOUS!
DUN!
NISE-CHAN... TO... NISE-CHAN...
HMM?
GASP!
GASP!
GAH...
HAH!
JUST DON'T HURT NISE-CHAN...!
PLEASE... SHE'S MY FR--
HAH!

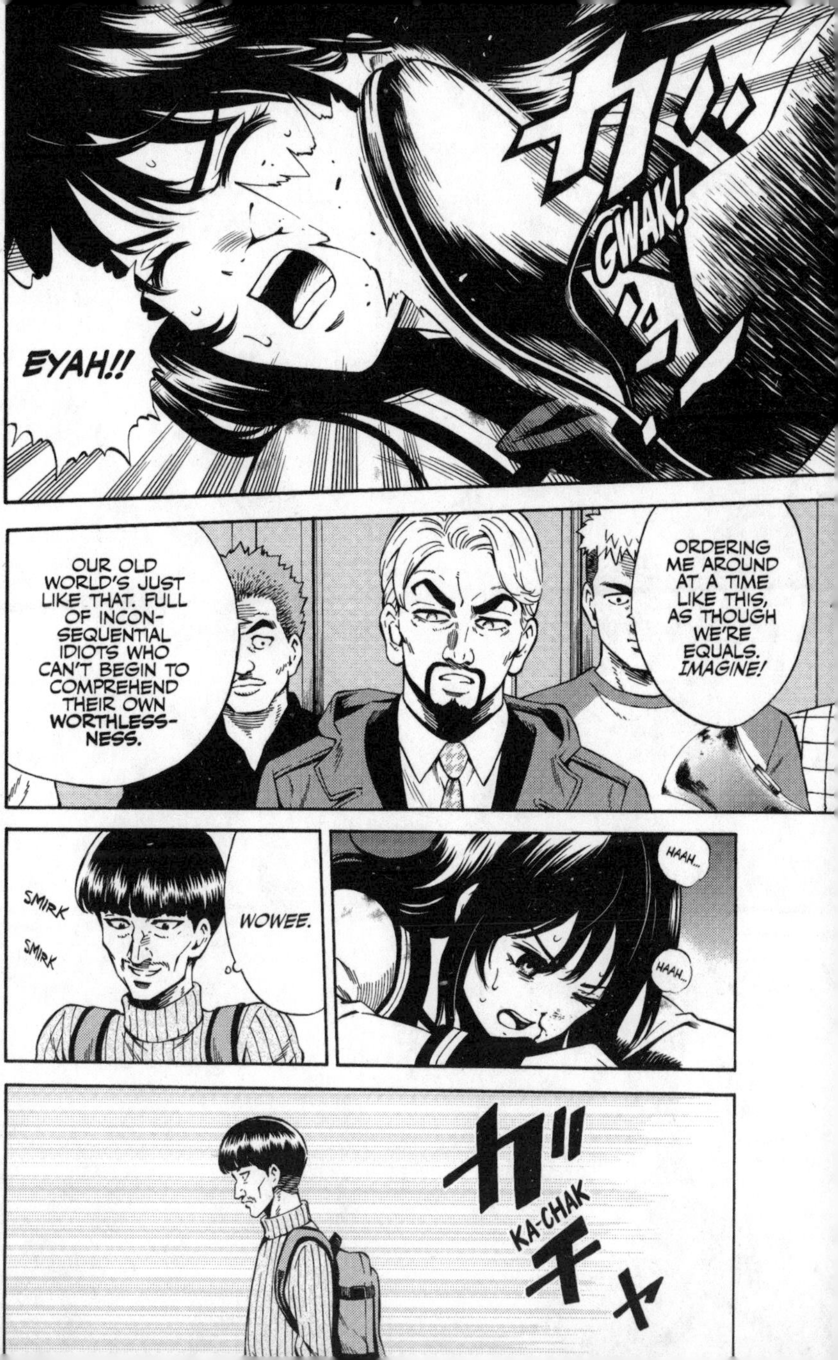
GWAK!
EYAH!!
ORDERING ME AROUND AT A TIME LIKE THIS, AS THOUGH WE'RE EQUALS. IMAGINE!
OUR OLD WORLD'S JUST LIKE THAT. FULL OF INCON-SEQUENTIAL IDIOTS WHO CAN'T BEGIN TO COMPREHEND THEIR OWN WORTHLESS-NESS.
HAAH...
HAAH...
WOWEE.
SMIRK
SMIRK
KA-CHAK

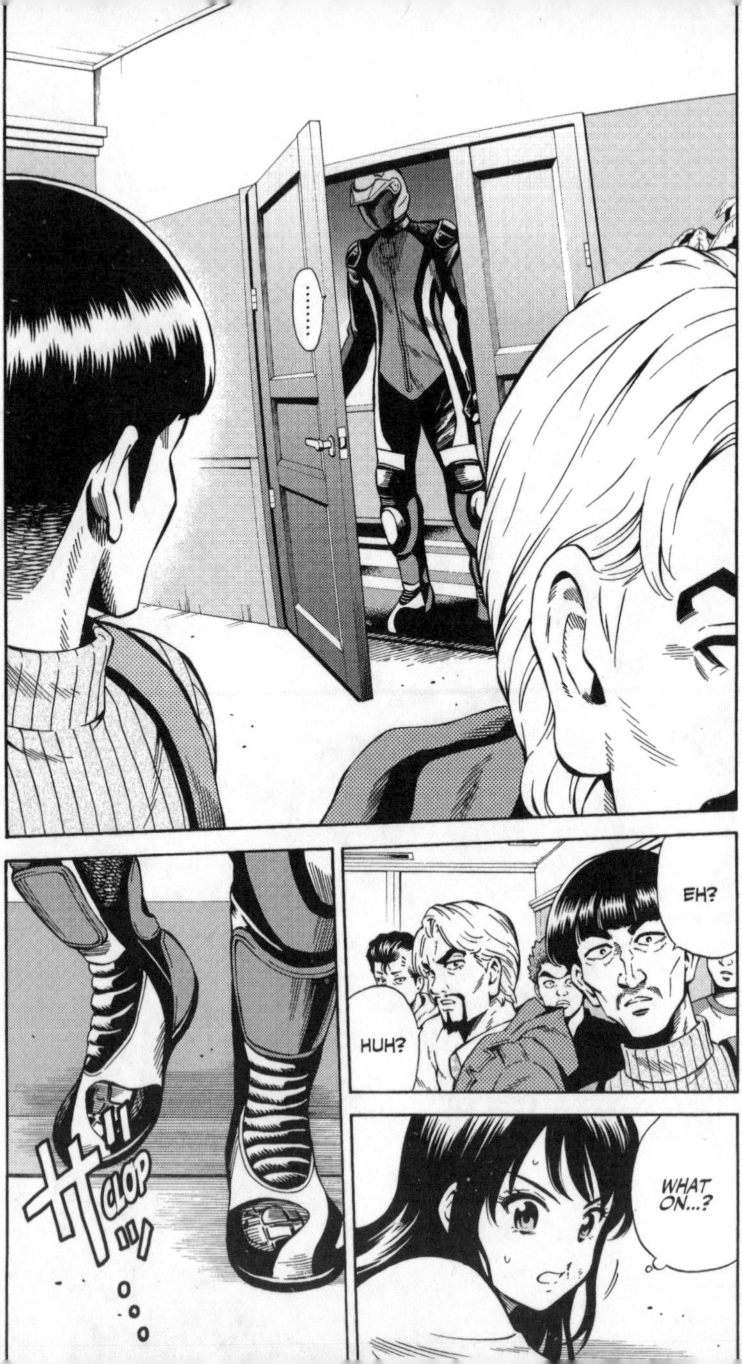
......
EH?
HUH?
WHAT ON...?
CLOP

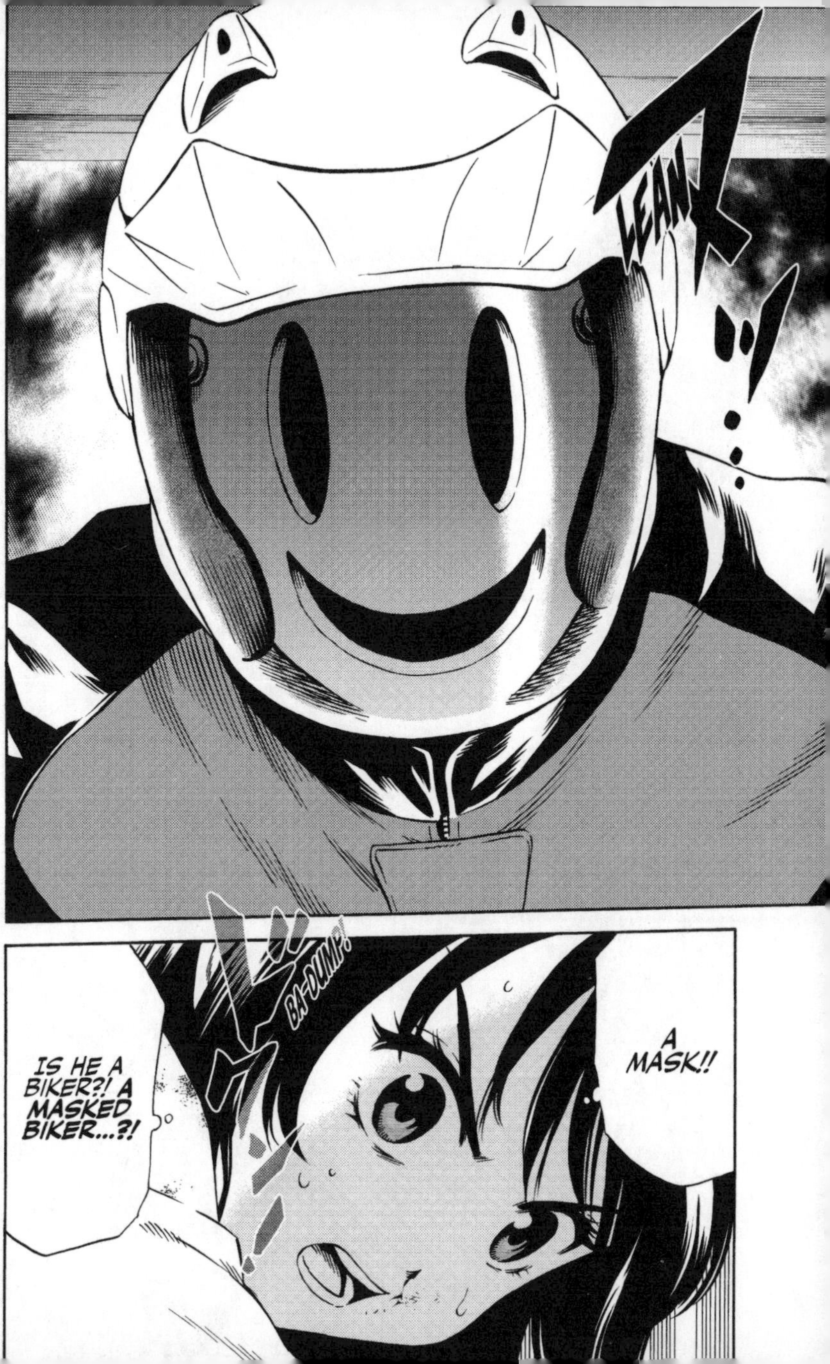
LEAN
..!!
A MASK!!
BA-DUMP!
IS HE A BIKER?! A MASKED BIKER...?!

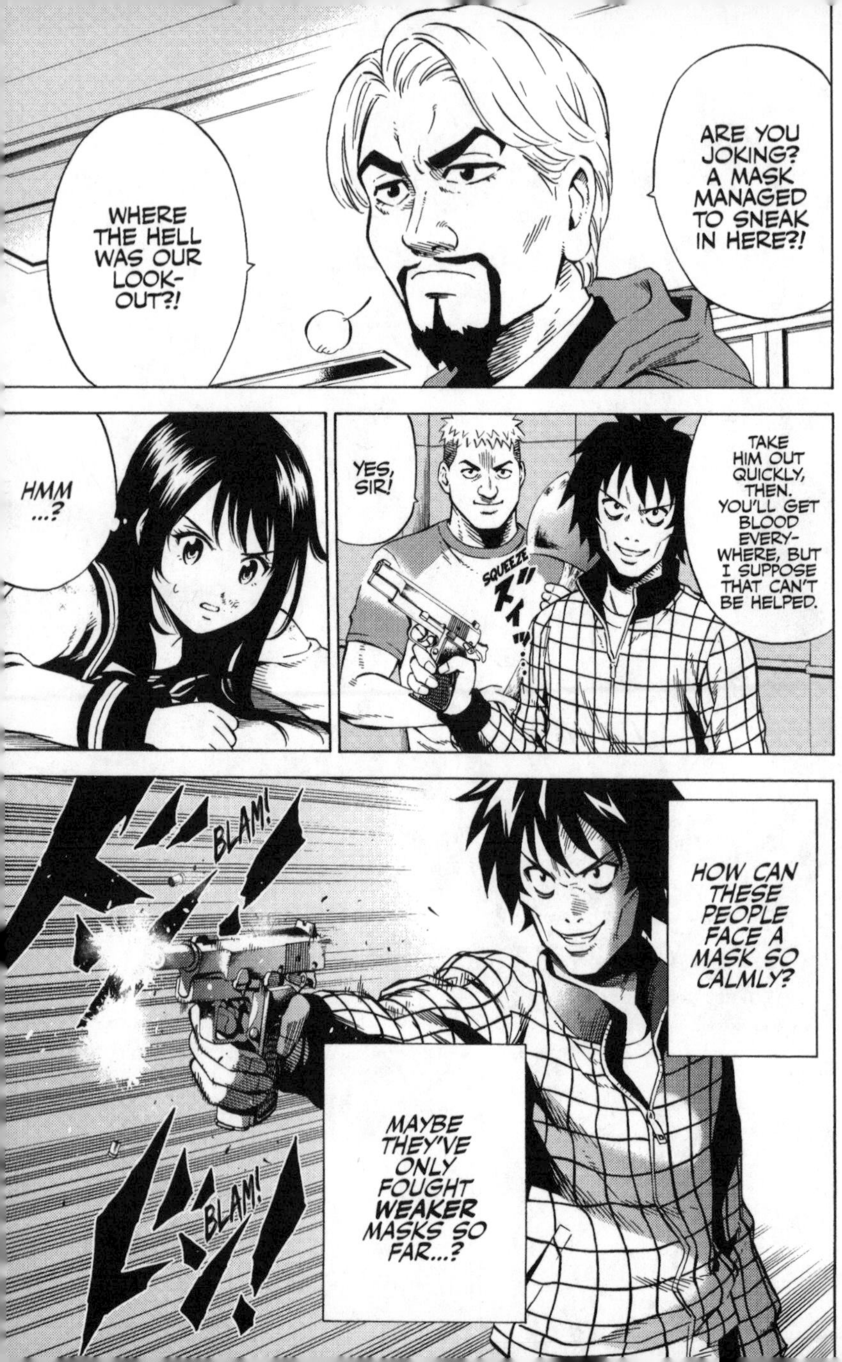
ARE YOU JOKING? A MASK MANAGED TO SNEAK IN HERE?!
WHERE THE HELL WAS OUR LOOK-OUT?!
TAKE HIM OUT QUICKLY, THEN. YOU'LL GET BLOOD EVERYWHERE, BUT I SUPPOSE THAT CAN'T BE HELPED.
YES, SIR!
SQUEEZE
HMM ...?
HOW CAN THESE PEOPLE FACE A MASK SO CALMLY?
BLAM!
MAYBE THEY'VE ONLY FOUGHT WEAKER MASKS SO FAR...?
BLAM!

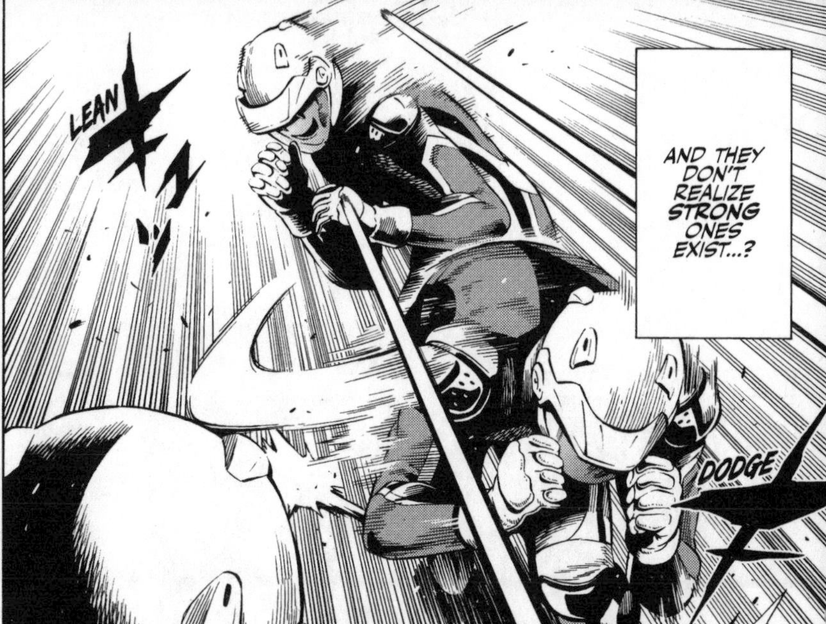
AND THEY DON'T REALIZE STRONG ONES EXIST...?
LEAN
DODGE

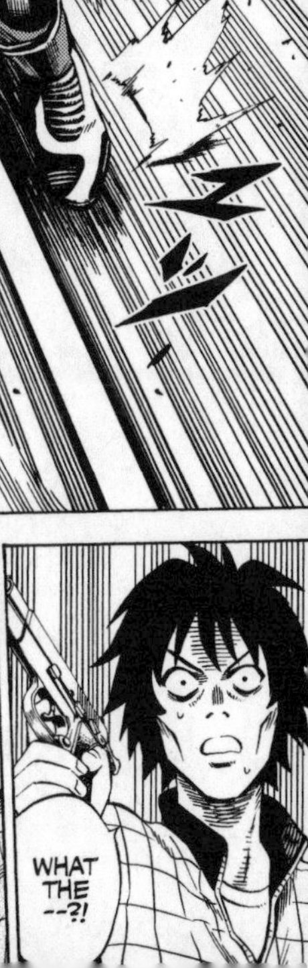
WHAT THE --?!

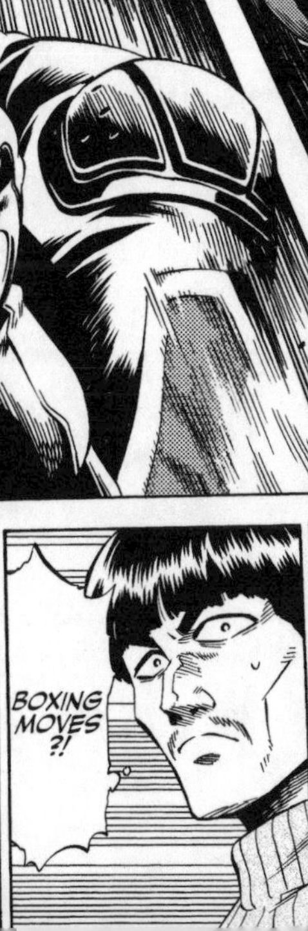
BOXING MOVES ?!

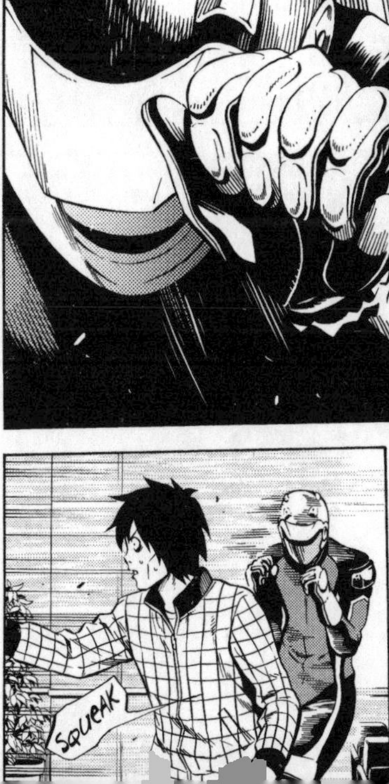
SQUEAK

SPLUTCH

EYAH ...?

WHISH

WHAT THE HELL'S GOING ON?!

THUNK

WHAT ...?!

· · · · ·

CLENCH...

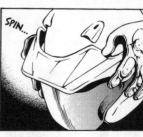

SPIN...

TUNK

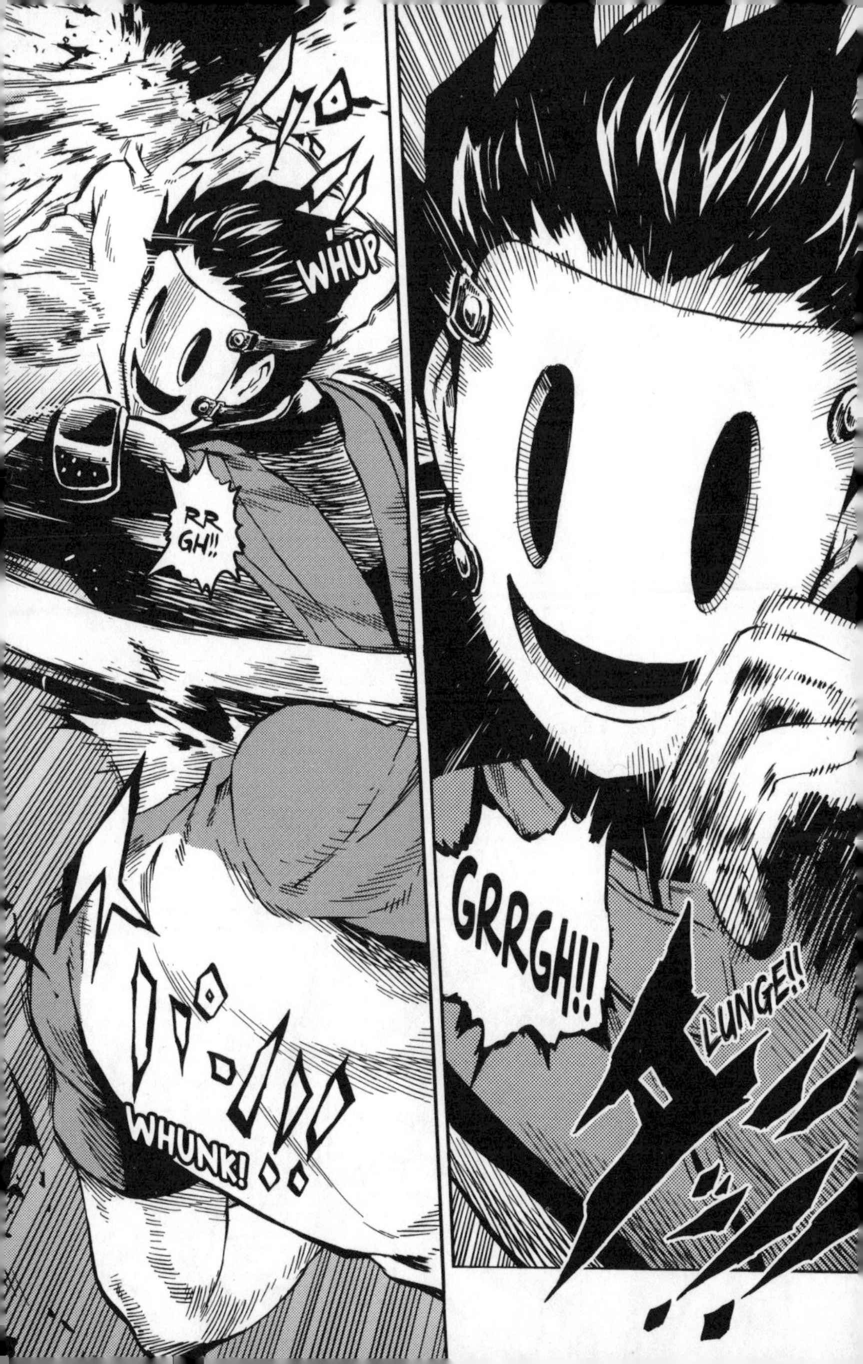
GRRGH!!
LUNGE!!
WHUP
RR GH!!
WHUNK!

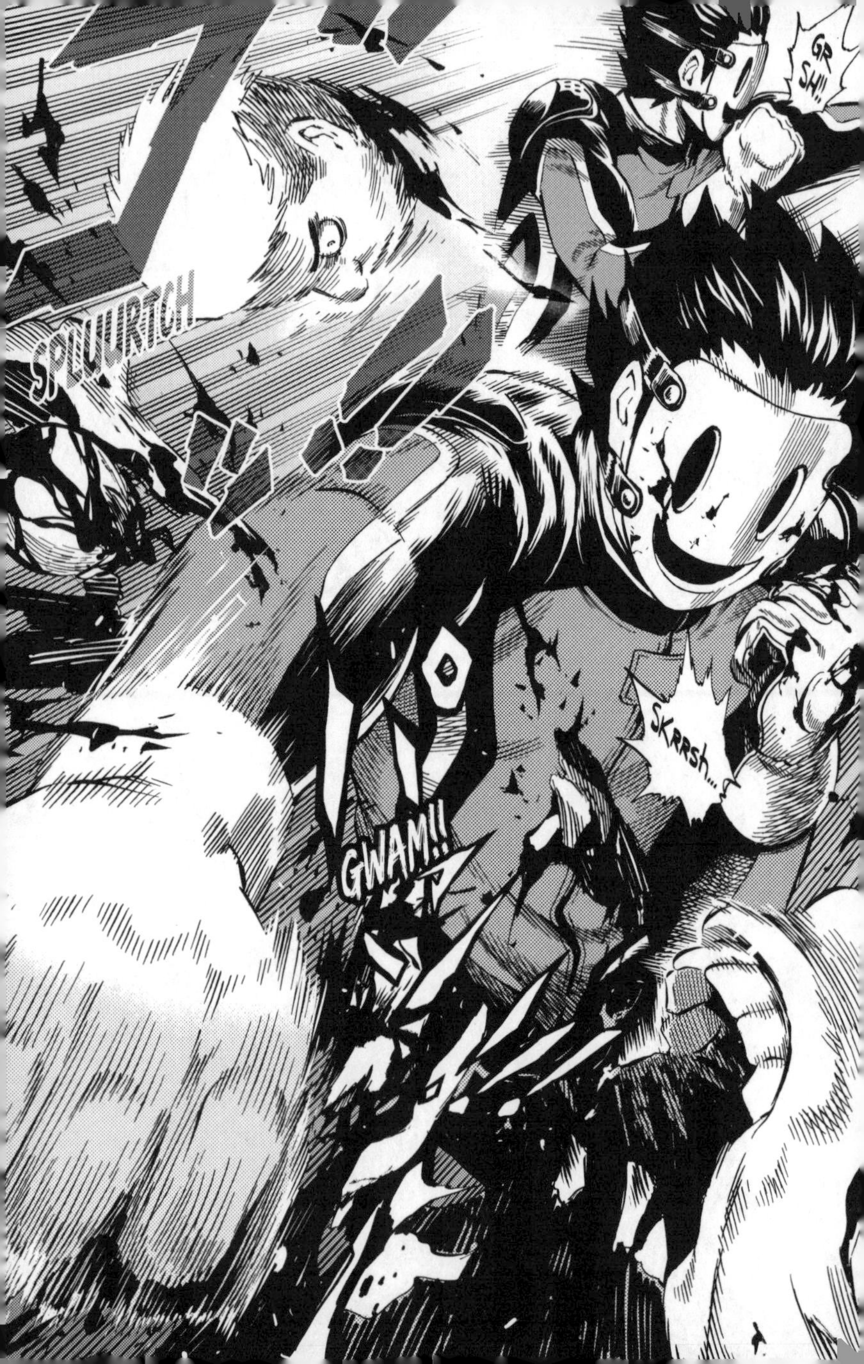
GRSH!!
SPLUURTCH
SKRRSH...
GWAM!!

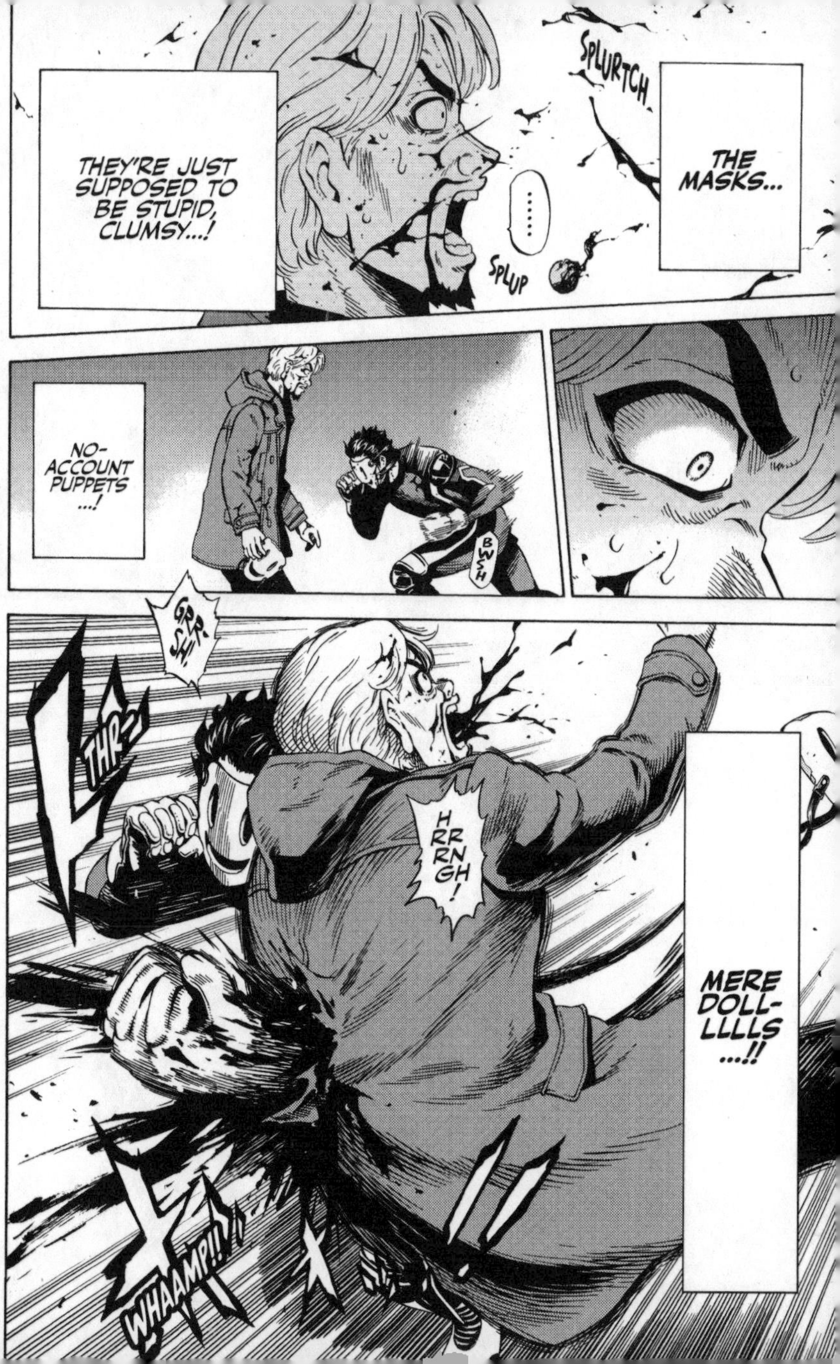
THE MASKS...
SPLURTCH
......
SPLUP
THEY'RE JUST SUPPOSED TO BE STUPID, CLUMSY...!
NO-ACCOUNT PUPPETS ...!
BWSH
MERE DOLL-LLLLS ...!!
GRR-SH!
THR-
HRRRNGH!
WHAAMP!!

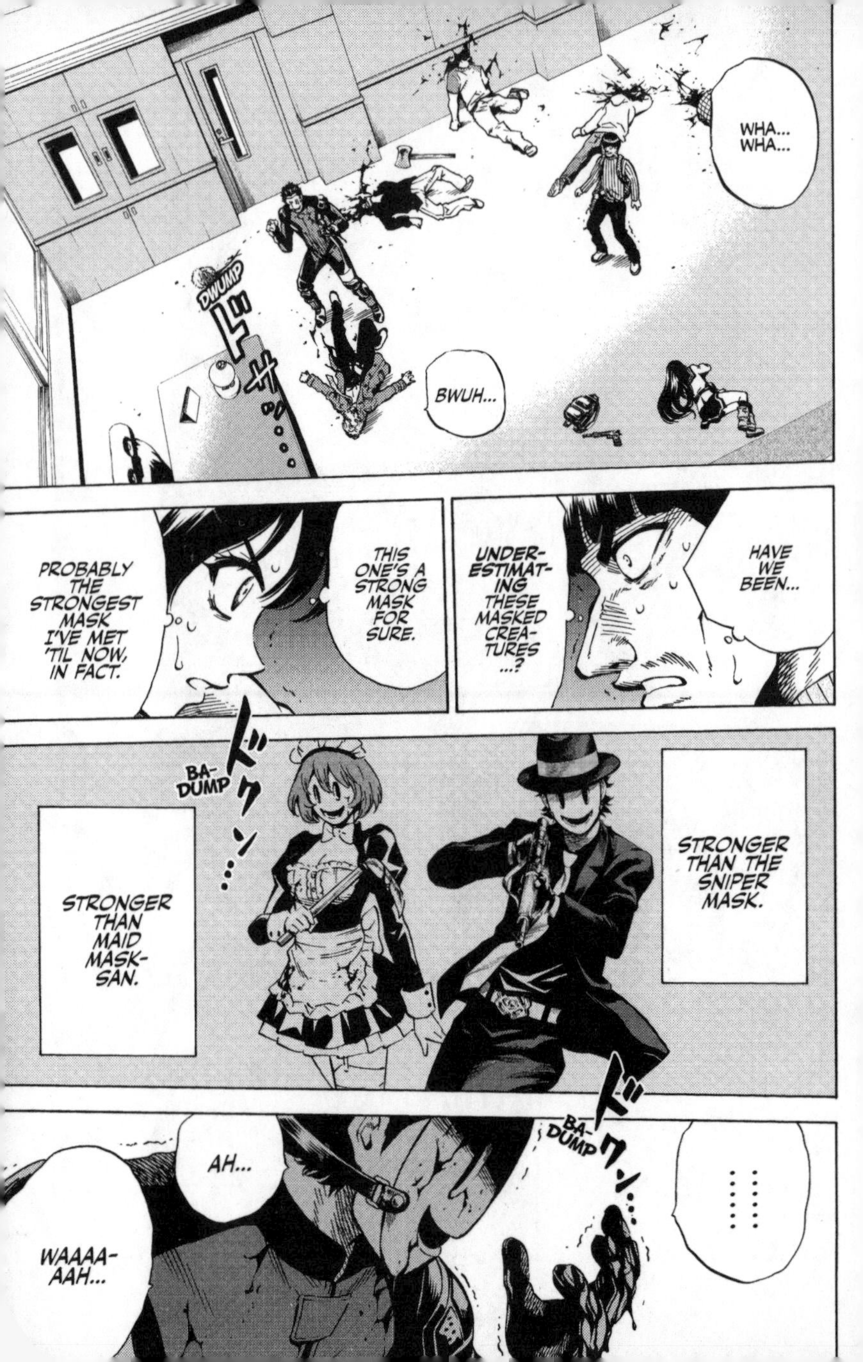
WHA... WHA...
DWUMP
ドサッ
BWUH...
HAVE WE BEEN...
UNDER-ESTIMATING THESE MASKED CREATURES ...?
THIS ONE'S A STRONG MASK FOR SURE.
PROBABLY THE STRONGEST MASK I'VE MET 'TIL NOW, IN FACT.
STRONGER THAN THE SNIPER MASK.
BA-DUMP
ドクン...
STRONGER THAN MAID MASK-SAN.
......
BA-DUMP
ドクン...
AH...
WAAAA-AAH...

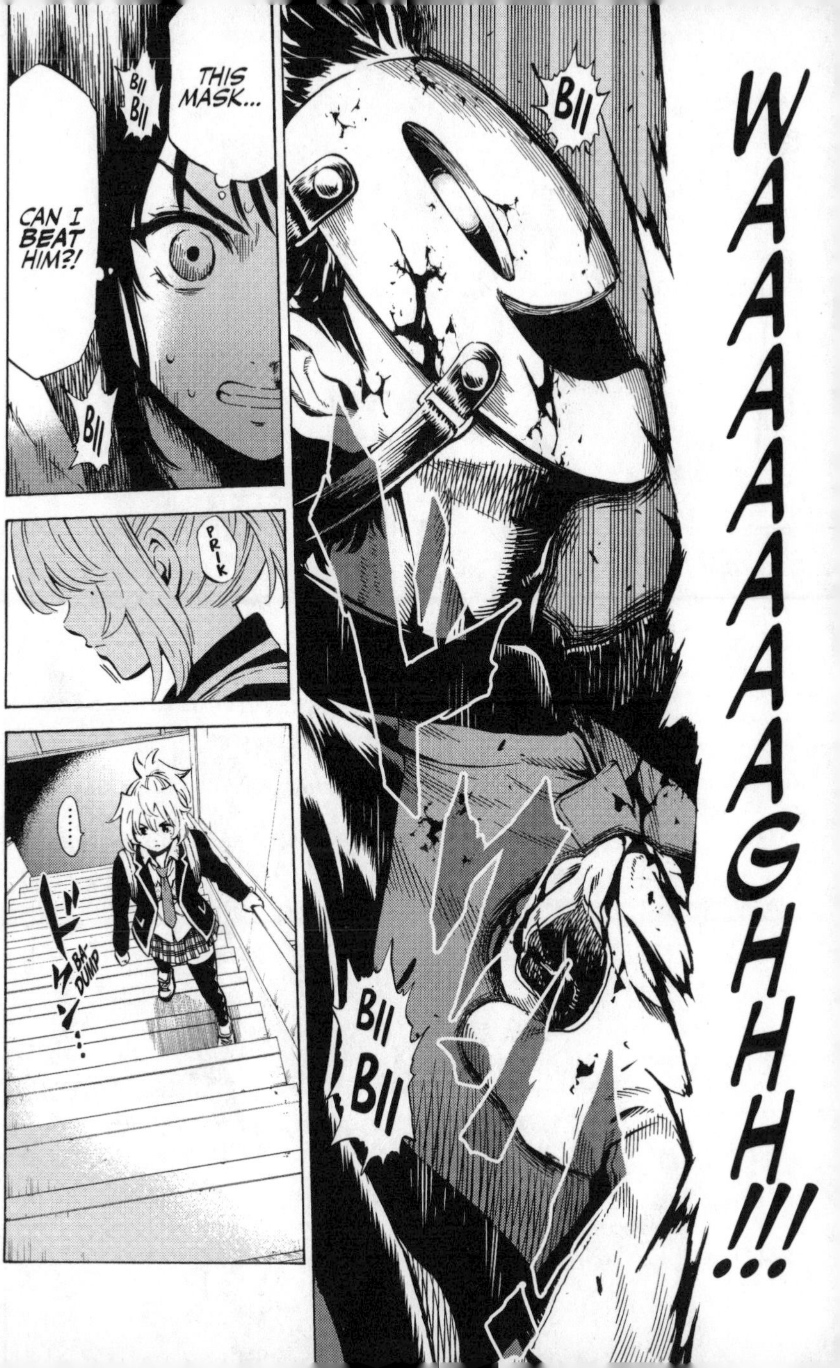
WAAAAAAAAAAGHHH!!!
BII
BII BII
THIS MASK...
BII BII
CAN I BEAT HIM?!
BII
PRIK
...
BA-DUMP

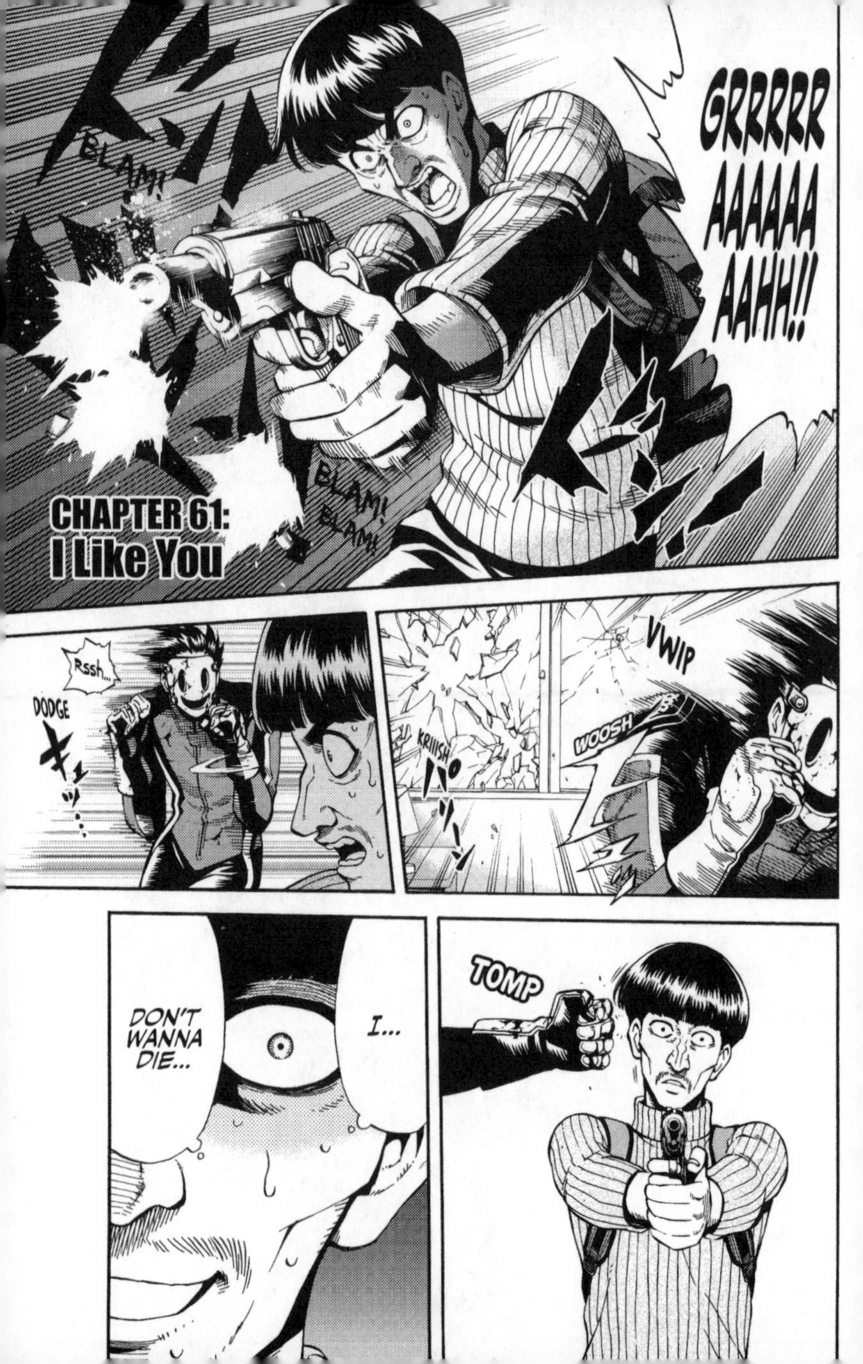

GRRRRR AAAAAA AAHH!!
BLAM!
BLAM! BLAM!
CHAPTER 61: I Like You
VWIP
WOOSH
KRIISH
Rssh...
DODGE
TOMP
I...
DON'T WANNA DIE...

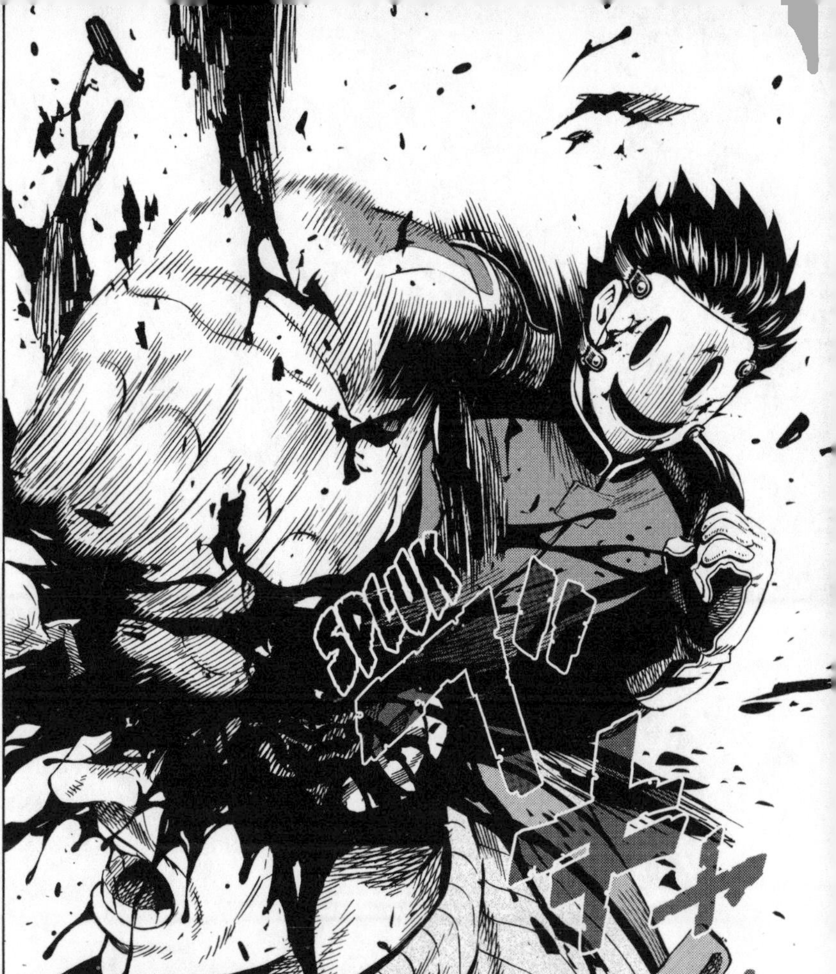
SPLUK

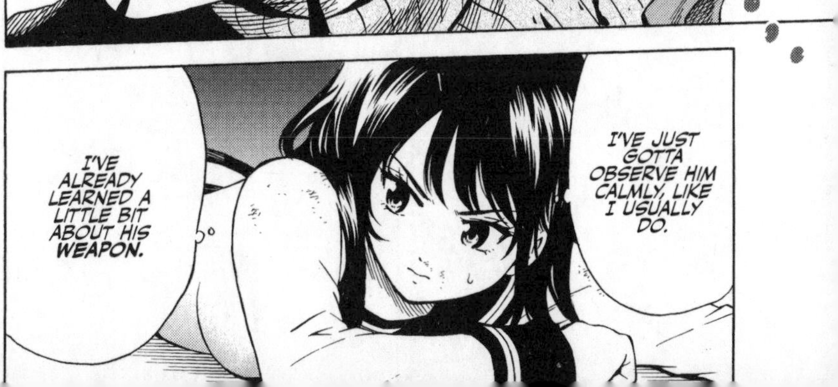
I'VE JUST GOTTA OBSERVE HIM CALMLY, LIKE I USUALLY DO.
I'VE ALREADY LEARNED A LITTLE BIT ABOUT HIS WEAPON.

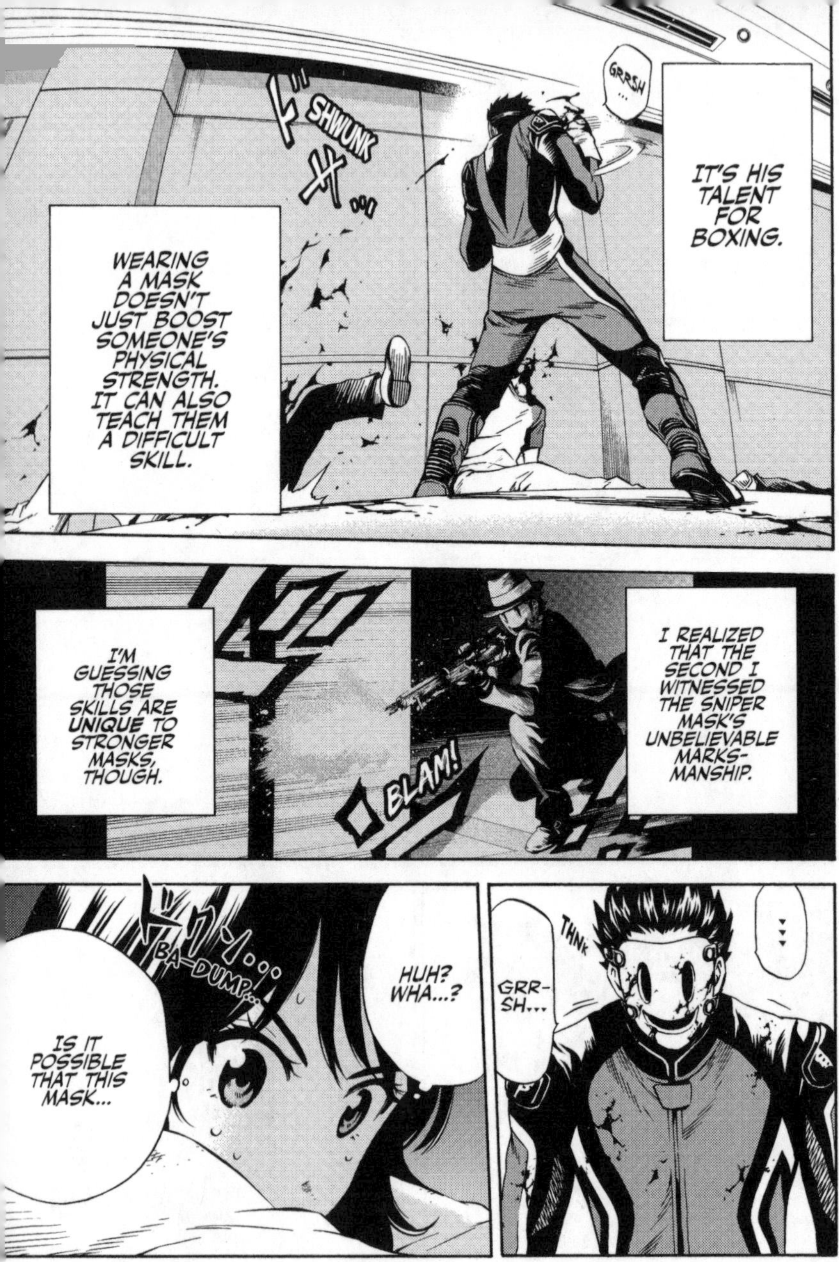
GRRSH...
IT'S HIS TALENT FOR BOXING.
SHWUNK
WEARING A MASK DOESN'T JUST BOOST SOMEONE'S PHYSICAL STRENGTH. IT CAN ALSO TEACH THEM A DIFFICULT SKILL.
I REALIZED THAT THE SECOND I WITNESSED THE SNIPER MASK'S UNBELIEVABLE MARKS-MANSHIP.
BLAM!
I'M GUESSING THOSE SKILLS ARE **UNIQUE** TO STRONGER MASKS, THOUGH.
...
THNK
GRR-SH...
HUH? WHA...?
BA-DUMP...
IS IT POSSIBLE THAT THIS MASK...

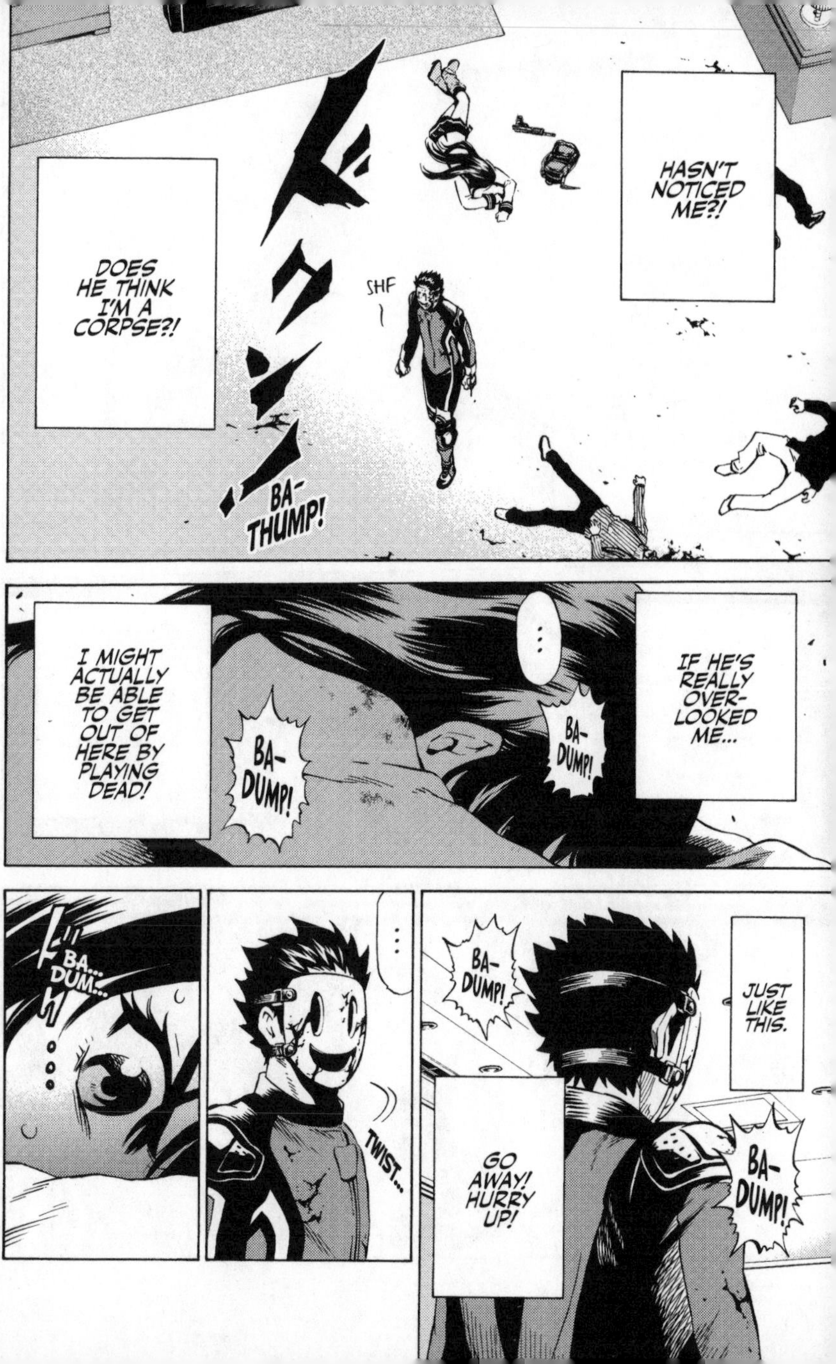

HASN'T NOTICED ME?!
SHF
DOES HE THINK I'M A CORPSE?!
BA-THUMP!
IF HE'S REALLY OVER-LOOKED ME...
...
BA-DUMP!
BA-DUMP!
I MIGHT ACTUALLY BE ABLE TO GET OUT OF HERE BY PLAYING DEAD!
JUST LIKE THIS.
BA-DUMP!
BA-DUMP!
GO AWAY! HURRY UP!
...
TWIST...
BA... DUM...
...

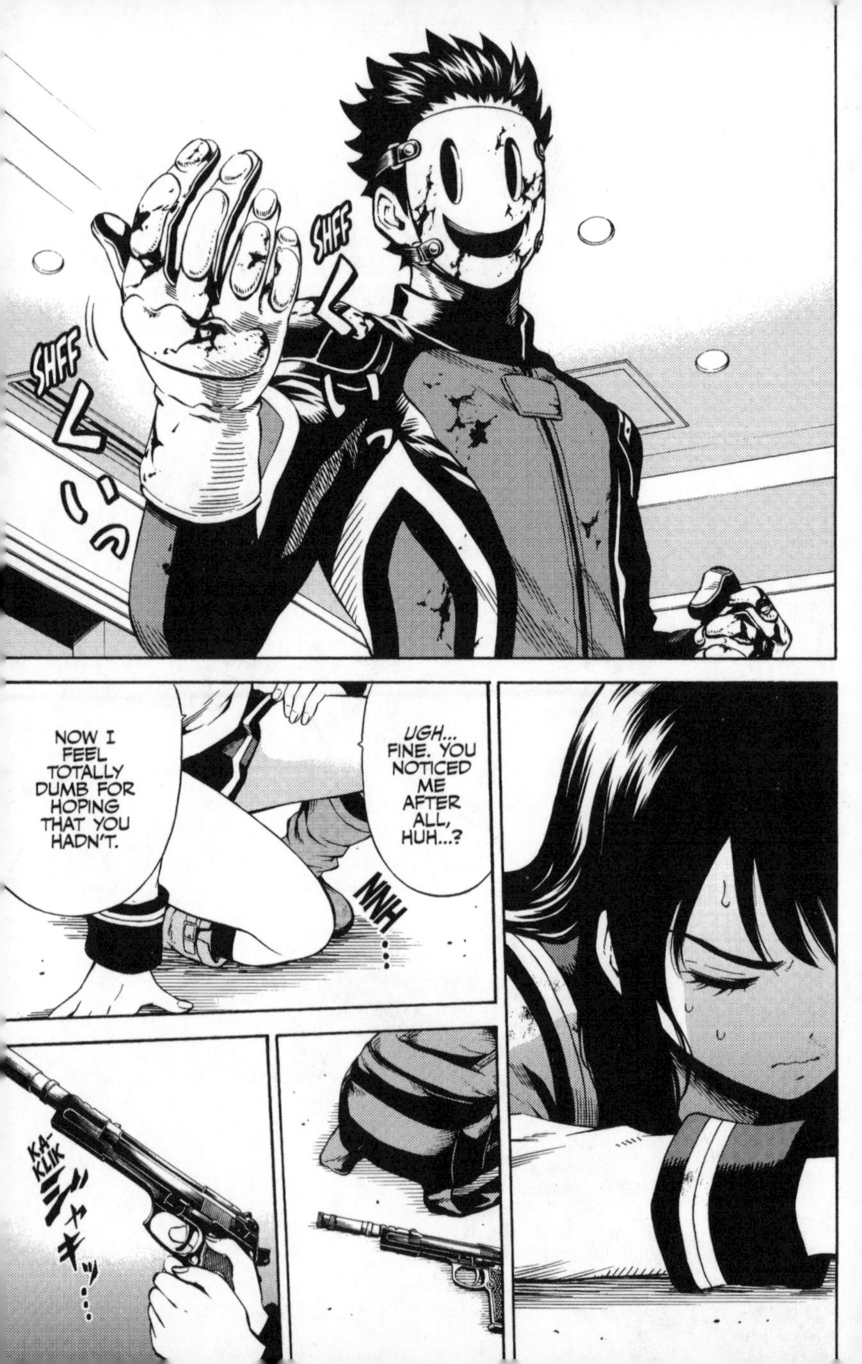
SHFF
SHFF
UGH... FINE. YOU NOTICED ME AFTER ALL, HUH...?
NNH...
NOW I FEEL TOTALLY DUMB FOR HOPING THAT YOU HADN'T.
KA-KLIK
ジャキッ...

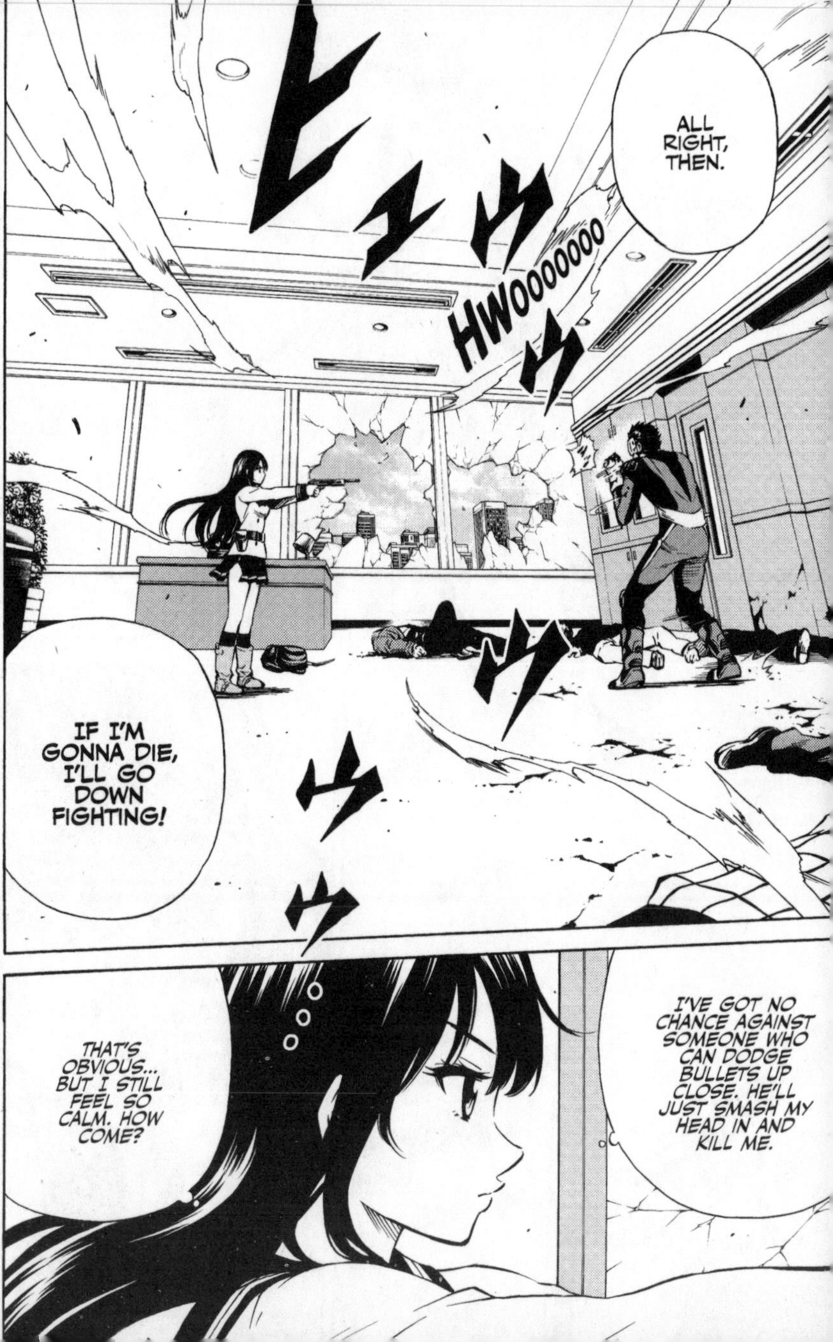
ALL RIGHT, THEN.
HWOOOOOOO
IF I'M GONNA DIE, I'LL GO DOWN FIGHTING!
I'VE GOT NO CHANCE AGAINST SOMEONE WHO CAN DODGE BULLETS UP CLOSE. HE'LL JUST SMASH MY HEAD IN AND KILL ME.
THAT'S OBVIOUS... BUT I STILL FEEL SO CALM. HOW COME?

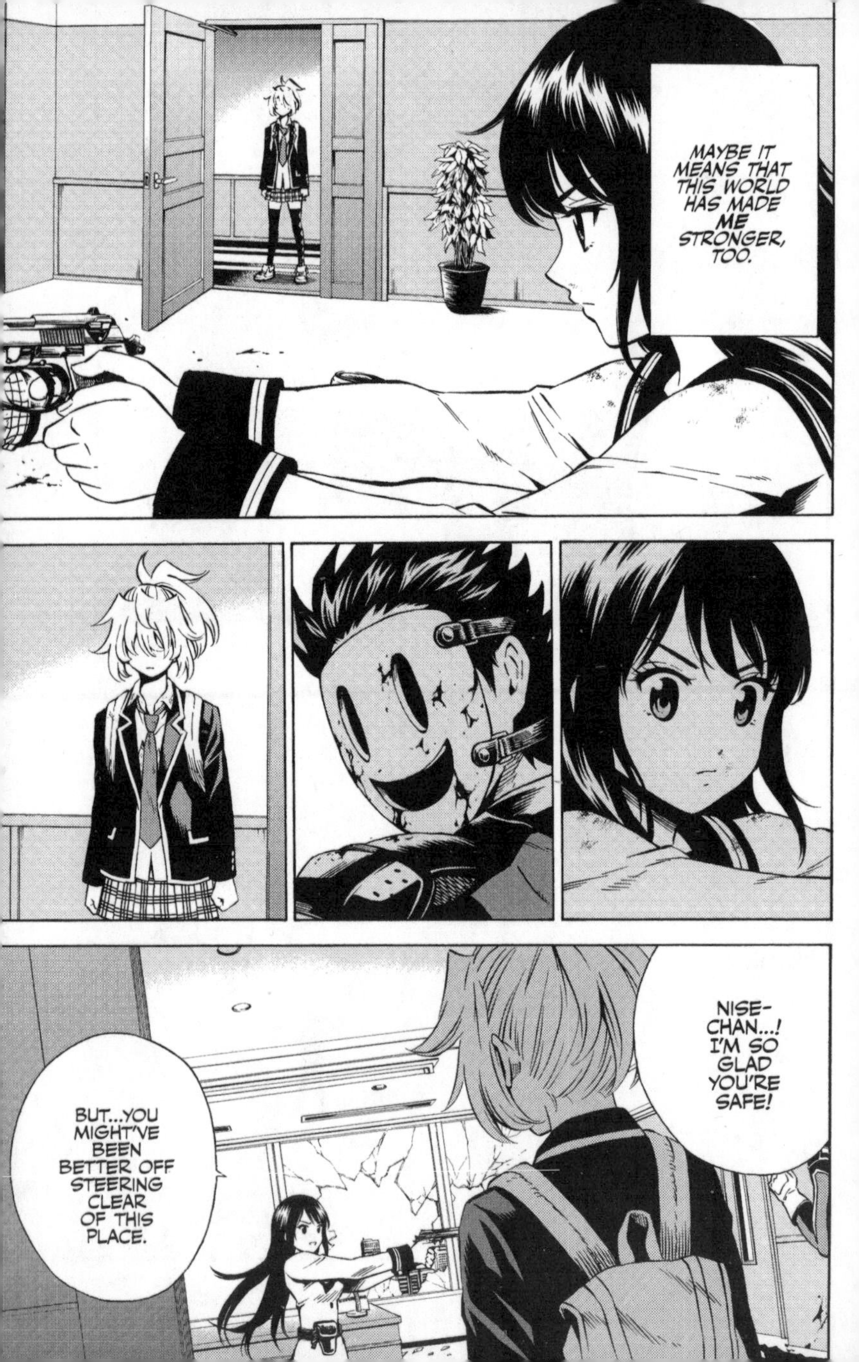
MAYBE IT MEANS THAT THIS WORLD HAS MADE ME STRONGER, TOO.
NISE-CHAN...! I'M SO GLAD YOU'RE SAFE!
BUT...YOU MIGHT'VE BEEN BETTER OFF STEERING CLEAR OF THIS PLACE.

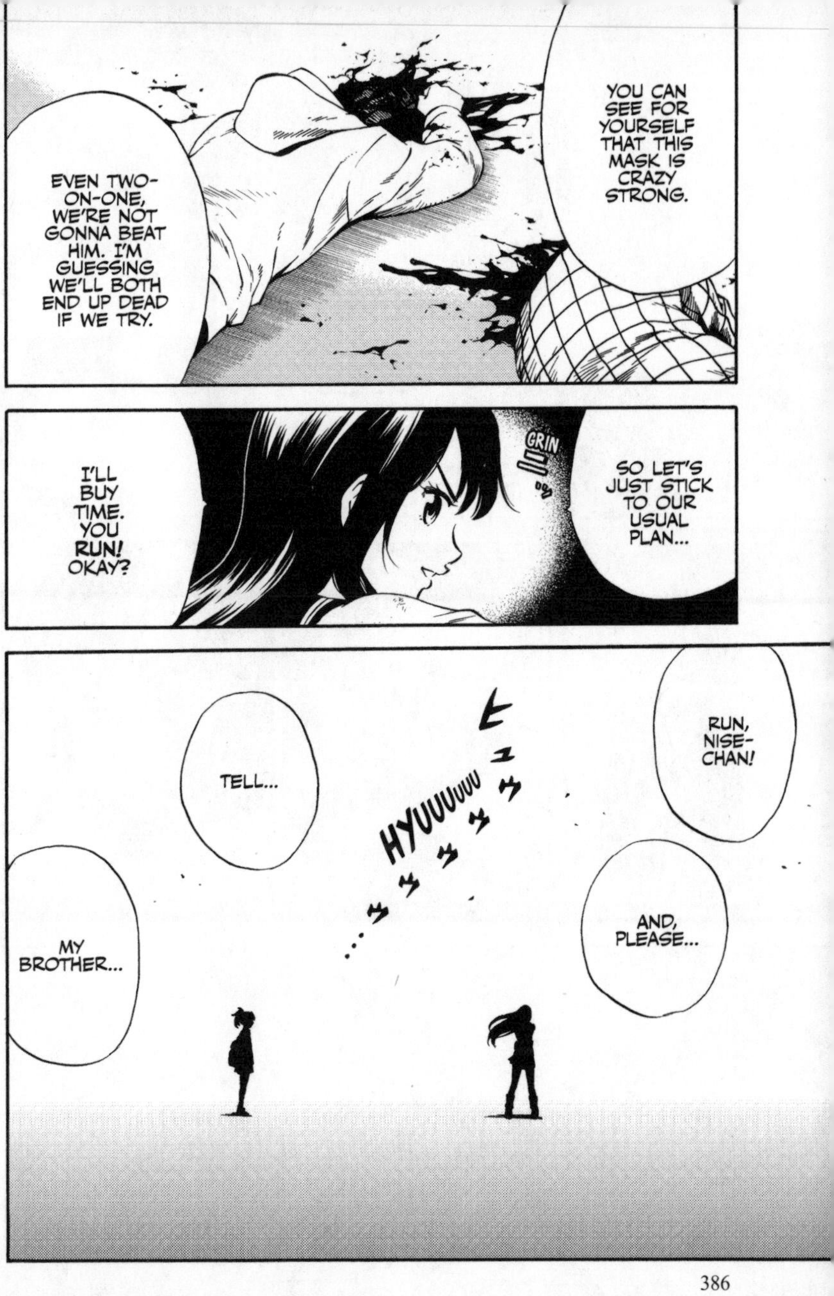
YOU CAN SEE FOR YOURSELF THAT THIS MASK IS CRAZY STRONG.
EVEN TWO-ON-ONE, WE'RE NOT GONNA BEAT HIM. I'M GUESSING WE'LL BOTH END UP DEAD IF WE TRY.
SO LET'S JUST STICK TO OUR USUAL PLAN...
GRIN
I'LL BUY TIME. YOU RUN! OKAY?
RUN, NISE-CHAN!
AND, PLEASE...
HYUUUUUU
TELL...
MY BROTHER...

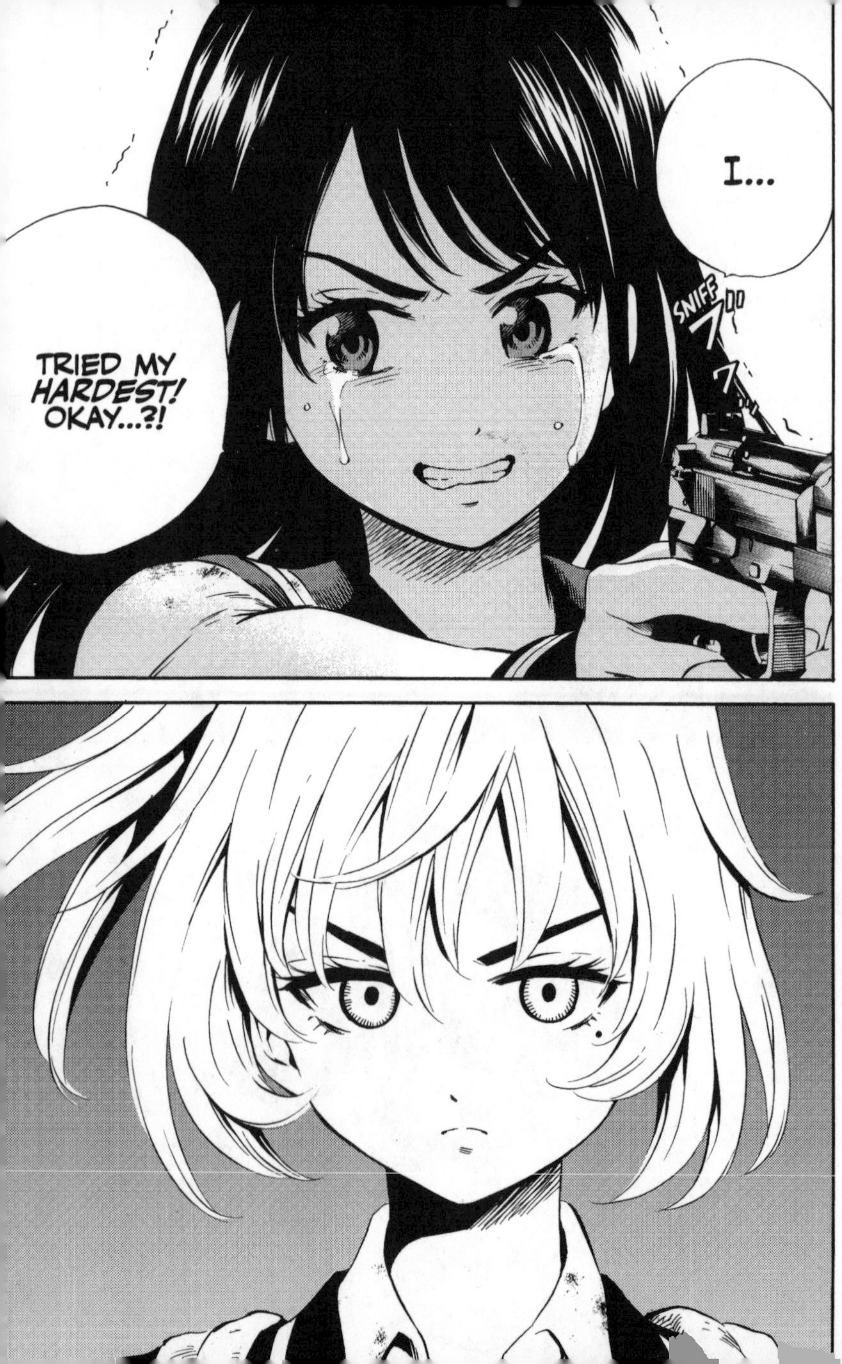
I...
SNIFF
TRIED MY HARDEST! OKAY...?!

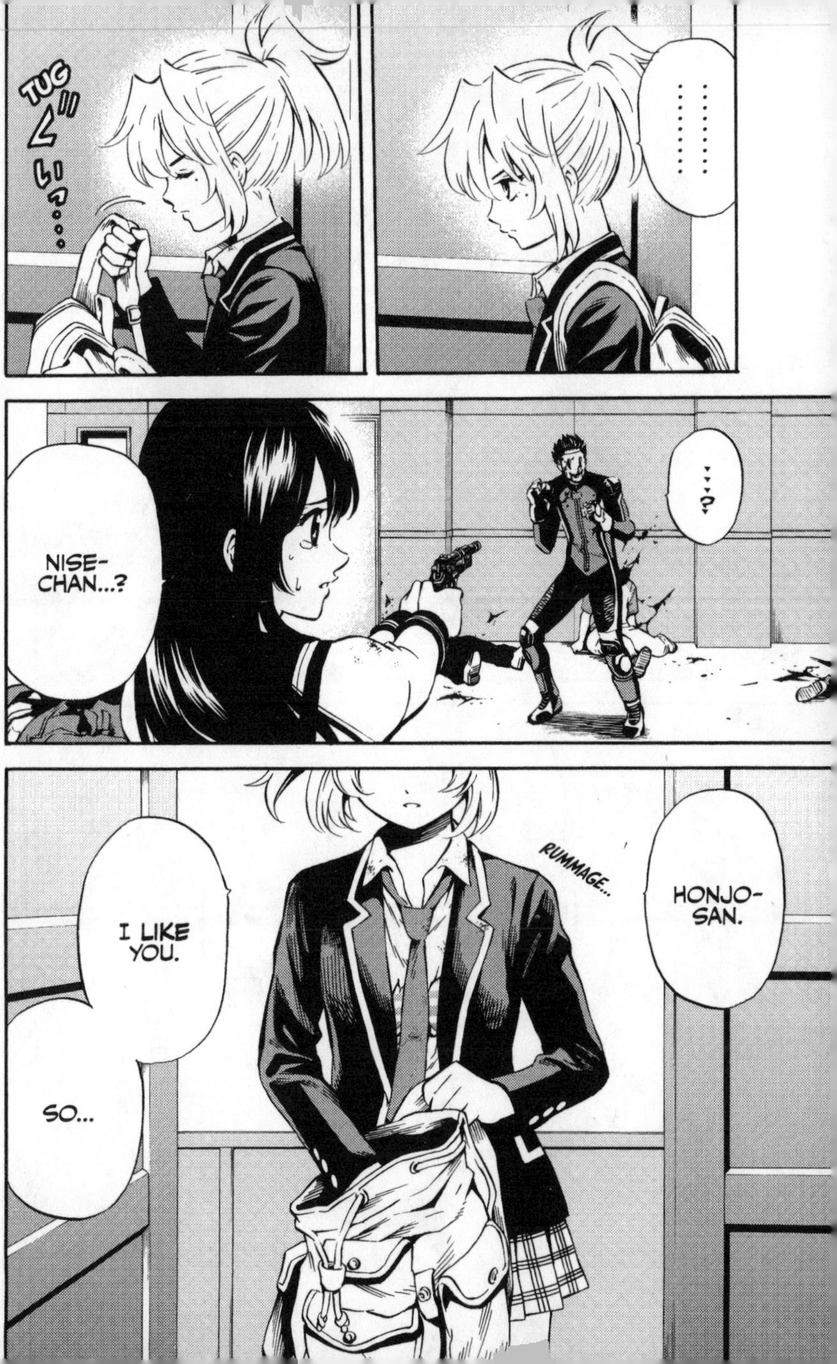
......
TUG
...?
NISE-CHAN...?
HONJO-SAN.
RUMMAGE...
I LIKE YOU.
SO...

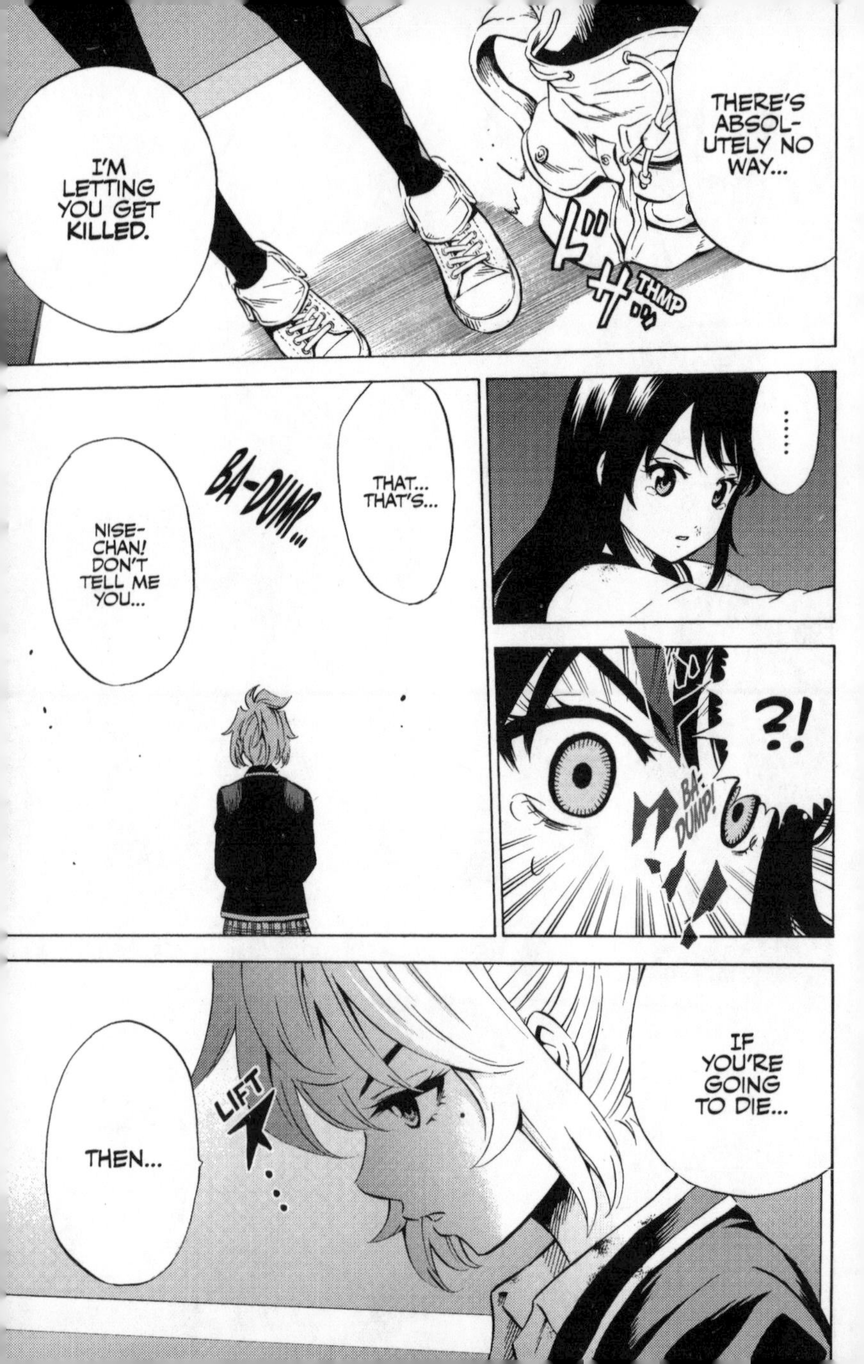
THERE'S ABSOLUTELY NO WAY...
THMP
I'M LETTING YOU GET KILLED.
......
?!
BA-DUMP!
THAT... THAT'S...
BA-DUMP...
NISE-CHAN! DON'T TELL ME YOU...
IF YOU'RE GOING TO DIE...
LIFT
THEN...

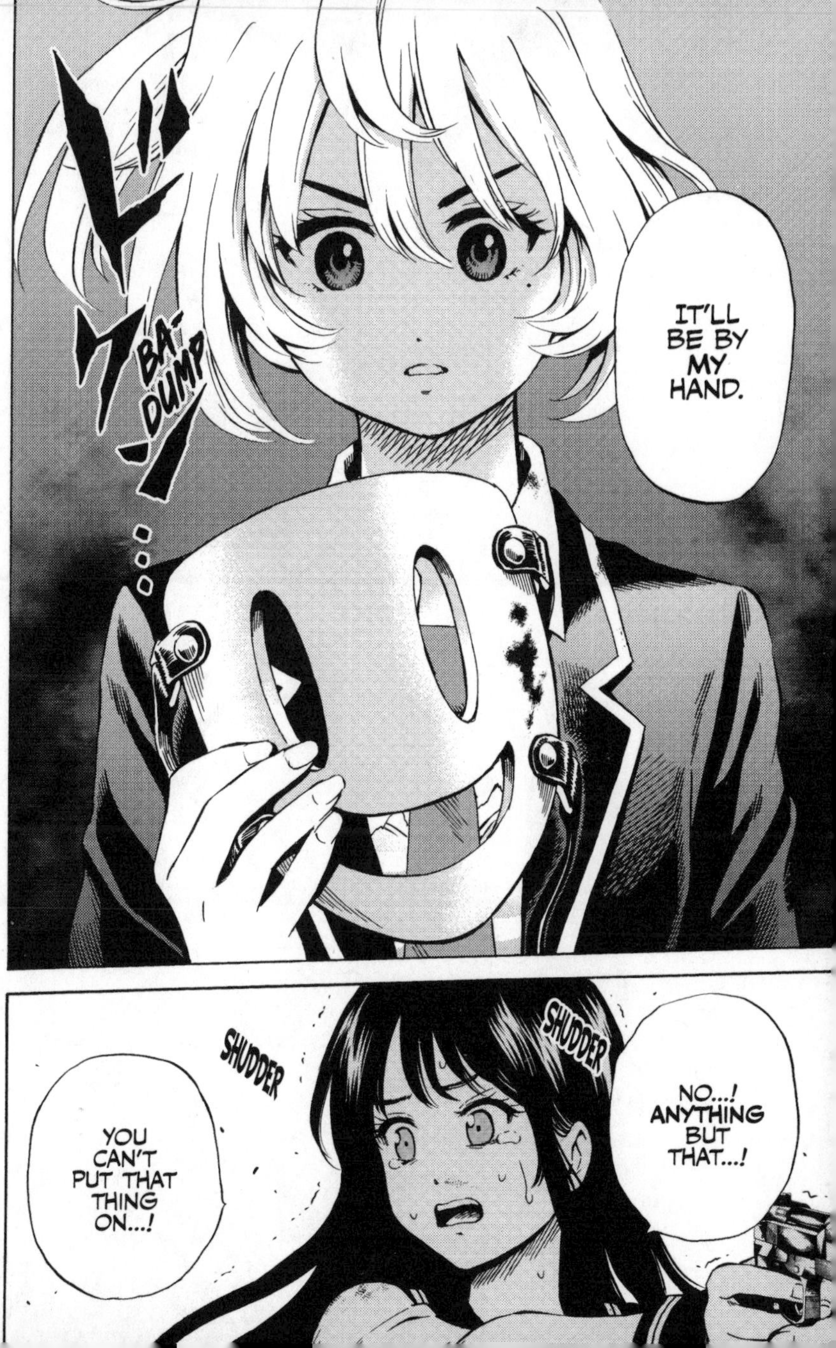
BA-DUMP
IT'LL BE BY MY HAND.
SHUDDER
NO...! ANYTHING BUT THAT...!
SHUDDER
YOU CAN'T PUT THAT THING ON...!

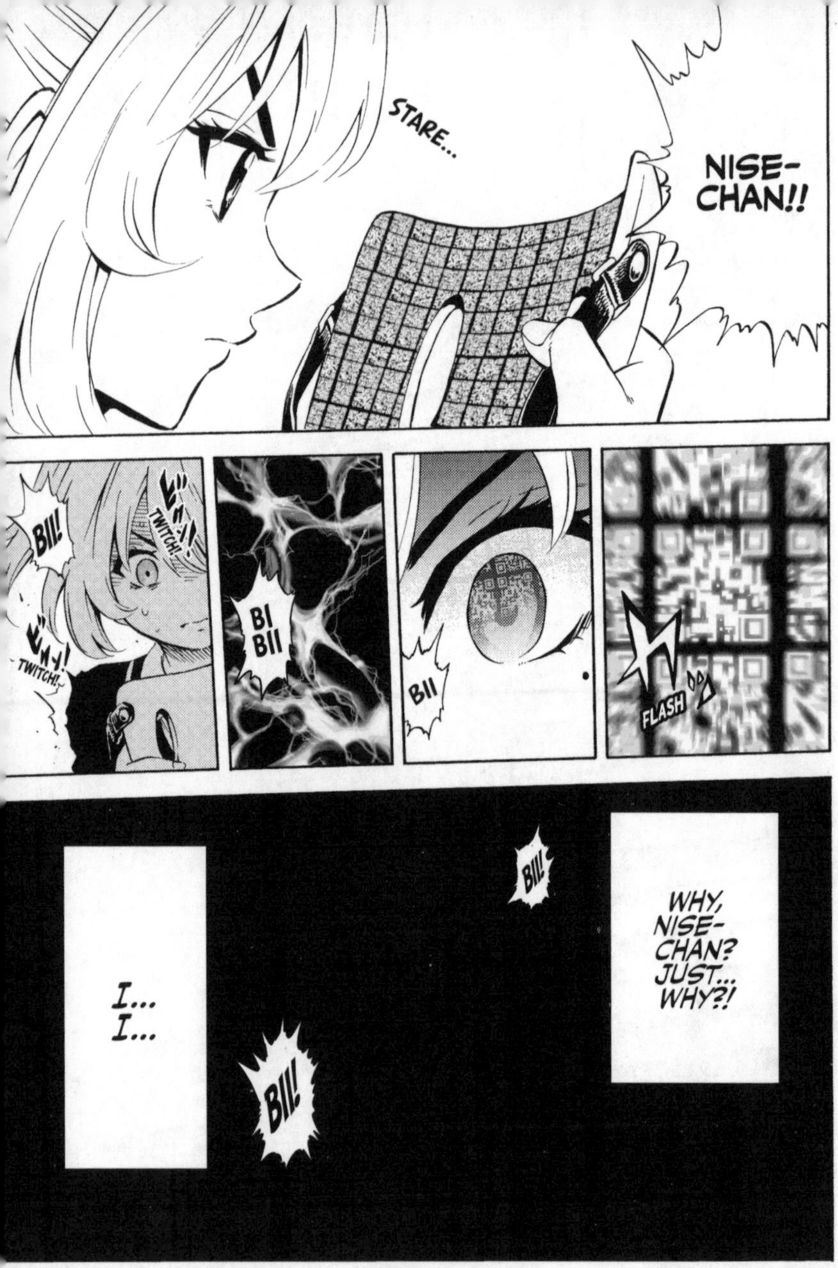

NISE-CHAN!!
STARE...
FLASH
BII
BI BII
ビクッ!!
TWITCH!
BII!
ビクッ!
TWITCH!
WHY, NISE-CHAN? JUST... WHY?!
BII!
BII!
I... I...

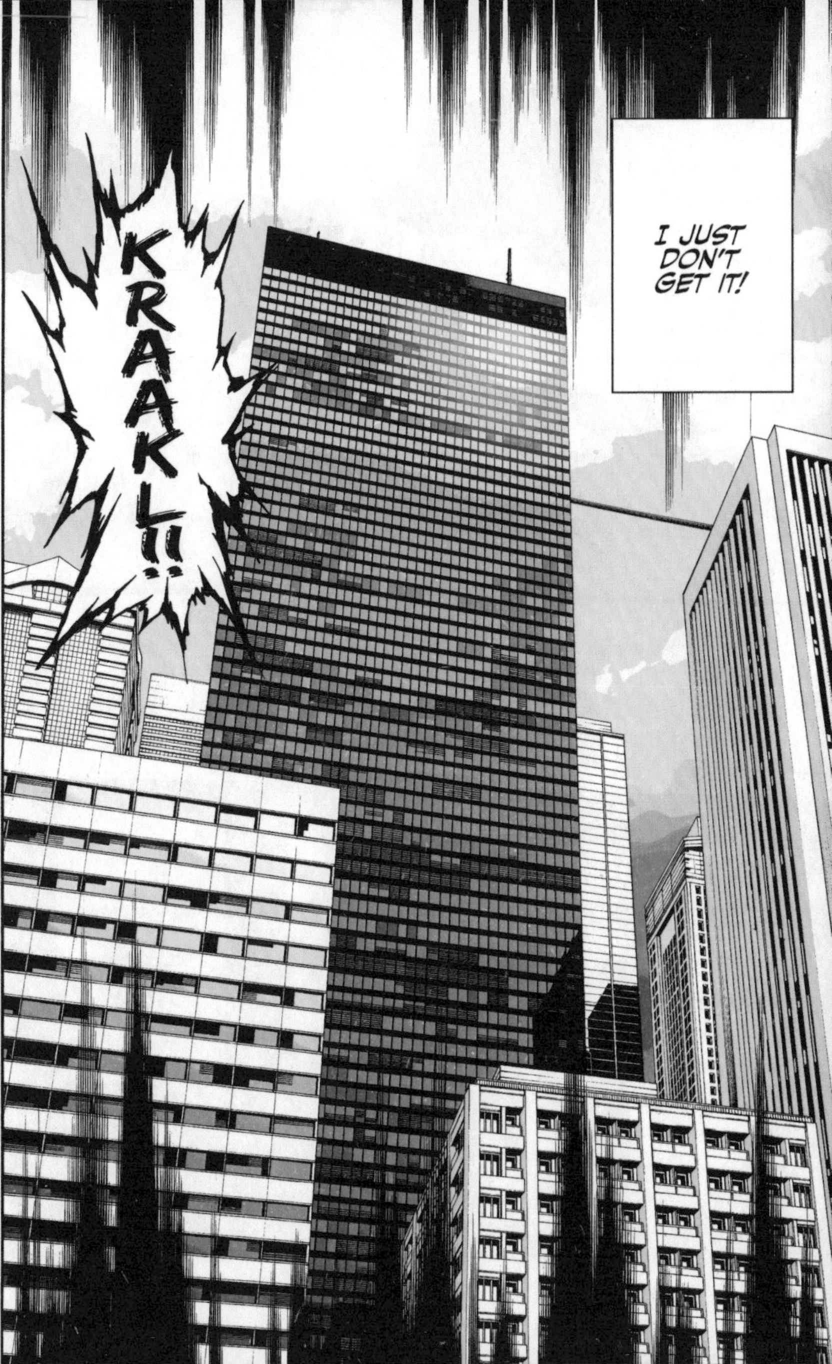
I JUST DON'T GET IT!
KRAAKL!!!

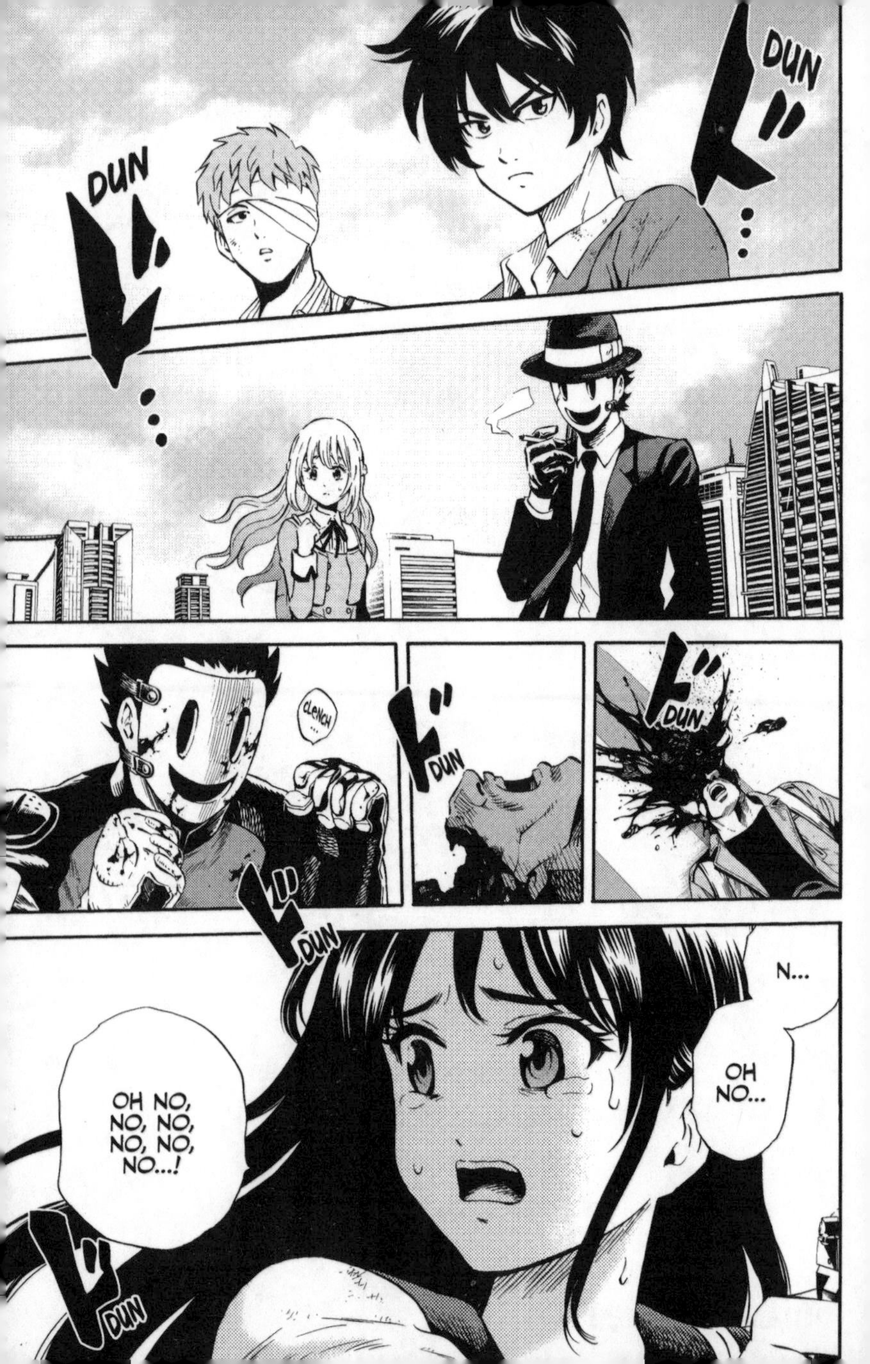
DUN
DUN
DUN
DUN
CLENCH ...
DUN
N...
OH NO...
OH NO, NO, NO, NO, NO, NO...!
DUN

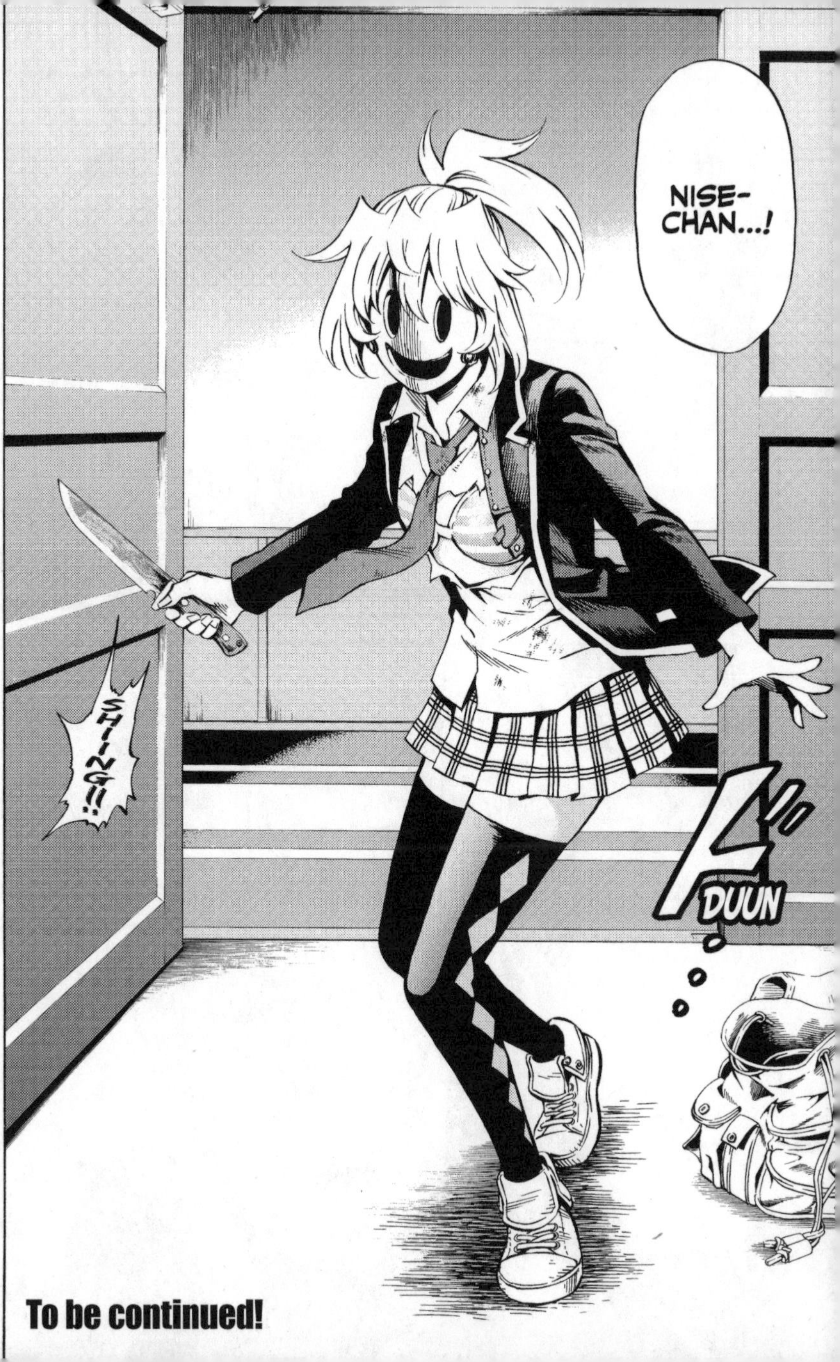
NISE-CHAN...!
DUUN
SHIING!!
To be continued!

HIGH-RISE INVASION

STORY
Tsuina Miura

ART
Takahiro Oba

STAFF
Fukuen Kanako
Saito Yuusaku
Sakurai Hiroshi

EDITOR
Uchida Tomohiro
Nishijima Satoshi

COMICS EDITOR
Nozawa Shinobu

COVER DESIGN
Inadome Ken

The Heartwarming Schoolgirl Comic Begins...

HEY! NISE-CHAN! WANNA TRADE UNIFORMS?
HUH?
HAVEN'T YOU HEARD? IT'S A SUPER-HUGE FAD RIGHT NOW!
YOU TRADE UNIFORMS WITH A FRIEND FROM ANOTHER SCHOOL, THEN PRINT A PHOTO STICKER TOGETHER!
I THINK WE SHOULD TRY IT, TOO! IT SOUNDS CUTE, RIGHT?! ♫
PSHHT! THAT SOUNDS DUMB. LIKE, *REALLY* STUPID.
Eternal Loner
FOR ONE THING, THERE'S *NO WAY* THIS WORLD HAS A PHOTO-BOOTH THAT PRINTS STICKERS.
HM?
BUT I ONLY ASKED YOU BECAUSE I SAW THAT ONE THERE!
Decome
Beauty Mask
FOR REAL ?!
TA-DA!

The Girls Take the Plunge

THEY TRIED IT OUT, SINCE THEY HAD THE CHANCE.
HMM. I GUESS THIS IS KINDA ENTERTAINING.
WHAT THE ...?!
HOW STRANGE.
I CAN'T BUTTON YOUR SHIRT ALL THE WAY UP!
POMP!
OUR SIZES AREN'T ALL *THAT* DIFFERENT!
OH, WELL! I GUESS THIS WORKS. ANYWAY, NISE-CHAN, LET'S TAKE A PIC TO-GETHER!
TWITCH
?!
TWITCH
TWITCH
KA-SNAP! ♫

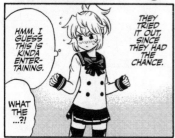

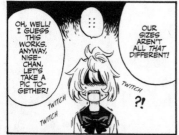

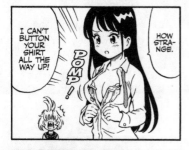

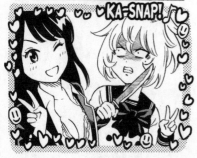

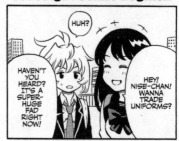

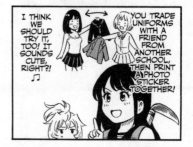

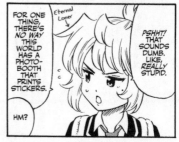

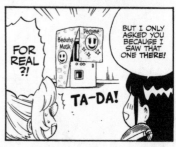

A Schoolgirl Rolling in Dough

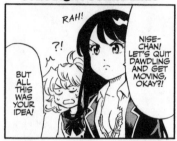

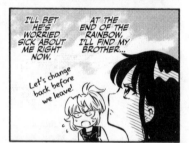

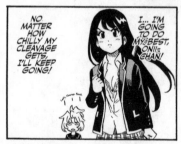

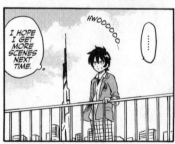

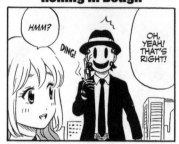

OH, YEAH! THAT'S RIGHT!
DING!
HMM?
SEEING YOUR HAIRDO FROM BEHIND...
IT REALLY REMINDED ME OF SOME-THING, BUT I COULDN'T RECALL WHAT!
I JUST REMEM-BERED...! PICTURE A TYPICAL TAKOYAKI SHOP SIGN.
DA-DUN!
YOUR HAIR LOOKS JUST LIKE THAT TWISTED TOWEL HEAD-BAND THE OCTOPUS WEARS!
HA HA HA!
SORRY... BUT COULD YOU EXPLAIN WHAT "TAKOYAKI" IS?
WHOA... YOUR FAMILY'S THAT RICH, HUH? CRAZY.

The Heartwarming Schoolgirl Comic Ends

NISE-CHAN! LET'S QUIT DAWDLING AND GET MOVING, OKAY?!
RAH!
?!
BUT ALL THIS WAS YOUR IDEA!
AT THE END OF THE RAINBOW, I'LL FIND MY BROTHER...
I'LL BET HE'S WORRIED SICK ABOUT ME RIGHT NOW.
Let's change back before we leave!
I... I'M GOING TO DO MY BEST, ONII-CHAN!
NO MATTER HOW CHILLY MY CLEAVAGE GETS, I'LL KEEP GOING!
......
HWOOOOOOO...
I HOPE I GET MORE SCENES NEXT TIME.

The End

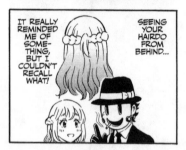

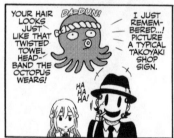

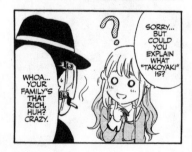

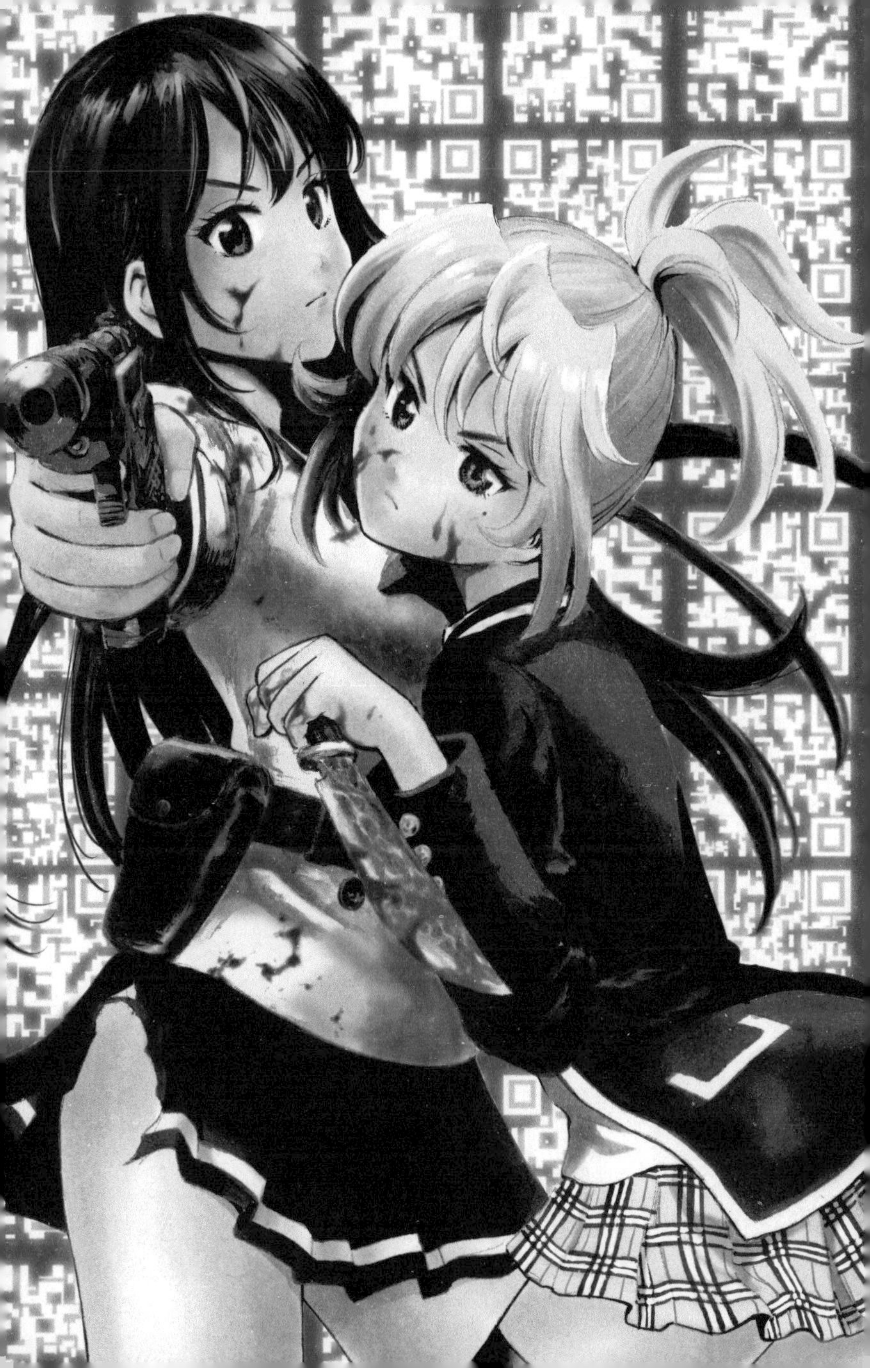

SEVEN SEAS ENTERTAINMENT

W9-AKA-563

HIGH-RISE INVASION Vol. 3-4

story by TSUINA MIURA / art by TAKAHIRO OBA

TRANSLATION
Nan Rymer

ADAPTATION
Rebecca Schneidereit

LETTERING AND RETOUCH
Meaghan Tucker

COVER DESIGN
KC Fabellon

PROOFREADER
Janet Houck
Cae Hawksmoor

EDITOR
J.P. Sullivan

PRODUCTION ASSISTANT
CK Russell

PRODUCTION MANAGER
Lissa Pattillo

EDITOR-IN-CHIEF
Adam Arnold

PUBLISHER
Jason DeAngelis

TENKUU SHINPAN VOLUME 3-4
© Tsuina Miura 2015, © Takahiro Oba 2015
All rights reserved.
First published in Japan in 2015 by Kodansha Ltd., Tokyo.
Publication rights for this English edition arranged through Kodansha Ltd., Tokyo.

Seven Seas books may be purchased in bulk for promotional, educational, or business use. Please contact your local bookseller or the Macmillan Corporate and Premium Sales Department at 1-800-221-7945, extension 5442, or by e-mail at MacmillanSpecialMarkets@macmillan.com.

Seven Seas and the Seven Seas logo are trademarks of Seven Seas Entertainment, LLC. All rights reserved.

ISBN: 978-1-626928-58-9

Printed in Canada

First Printing: August 2018

10 9 8 7 6 5 4 3 2 1

FOLLOW US ONLINE: *www.sevenseasentertainment.com*

READING DIRECTIONS

This book reads from *right to left*, Japanese style. If this is your first time reading manga, you start reading from the top right panel on each page and take it from there. If you get lost, just follow the numbered diagram here. It may seem backwards at first, but you'll get the hang of it! Have fun!!

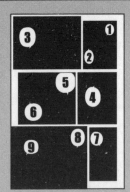